IMPORTANT

HERE IS YOUR REGISTRATION CODE TO ACCESS M PREMIUM CONTENT AND MCGRAW-HILL ONLINE RESOURCES

For key premium online resources you need THIS CODE to gain access. Once the code is entered, you will be able to use the web resources for the length of your course.

Access is provided only if you have purchased a new book.

If the registration code is missing from this book, the registration screen on our website, and within your WebCT or Blackboard course will tell you how to obtain your new code. Your registration code can be used only once to establish access. It is not transferable

To gain access to these online resources

1. **USE** your web browser to go to: **www.mhhe.com/bentley3**
2. **CLICK** on "First Time User"
3. **ENTER** the Registration Code printed on the tear-off bookmark on the right
4. After you have entered your registration code, click on "Register"
5. **FOLLOW** the instructions to setup your personal UserID and Password
6. **WRITE** your UserID and Password down for future reference. Keep it in a safe place.

If your course is using WebCT or Blackboard, you'll be able to use this code to access the McGraw-Hill content within your instructor's online course.

To gain access to the McGraw-Hill content in your instructor's WebCT or Blackboard course simply log into the course with the user ID and Password provided by your instructor. Enter the registration code exactly as it appears to the right when prompted by the system. You will only need to use this code the first time you click on McGraw-Hill content.

These instructions are specifically for student access. Instructors are not required to register via the above instructions.

The McGraw-Hill Companies
McGraw-Hill Higher Education

Thank you, and welcome to your McGraw-Hill Online Resources.

Bentley
Traditions and Encounters, 3/E
0-07-312352-8

2EKK-1TA1-JZFG-ZED8-UKV9

REGISTRATION CODE

REGISTRATION CODE

The McGraw-Hill Companies
McGraw-Hill Higher Education

Traditions & Encounters

TRADITIONS & ENCOUNTERS

A Global Perspective on the Past

VOLUME B: From 1000 to 1800

THIRD EDITION

JERRY H. BENTLEY

University of Hawai`i

HERBERT F. ZIEGLER

University of Hawai`i

Mc Graw Hill

Boston Burr Ridge, IL Dubuque, IA Madison, WI New York San Francisco St. Louis
Bangkok Bogotá Caracas Kuala Lumpur Lisbon London Madrid Mexico City
Milan Montreal New Delhi Santiago Seoul Singapore Sydney Taipei Toronto

The McGraw-Hill Companies

Published by McGraw-Hill, an imprint of The McGraw-Hill Companies, Inc. 1221 Avenue of the Americas, New York, NY, 10020.

This book is printed on acid-free paper.

1 2 3 4 5 6 7 8 9 0 VNH/VNH 0 9 8 7 6 5

ISBN 0-07-299834-2

Editor in Chief: *Emily Barrosse*
Publisher: *Lyn Uhl*
Senior Sponsoring Editor: *Jon-David Hague*
Marketing Manager: *Katherine Bates*
Director of Development: *Lisa Pinto*
Developmental Editors: *Jim Strandberg and Angela Kao*
Managing Editor: *Melissa Williams*
Senior Project Manager: *Christina Gimlin*
Manuscript Editor: *Margaret Moore*
Art Director: *Jeanne Schreiber*
Senior Design Manager: *Kim Menning*
Cover and Interior Design: *Ellen Pettengell*
Art Editor: *Katherine McNab*
Manager, Photo Research: *Brian Pecko*
Supplements Producers: *Louis Swaim and Kate Boylan*
Media Project Manager: *Kate Boylan*
Lead Production Supervisor: *Randy Hurst*

Composition: *10/12 Galliard by Thompson Type*
Printing: *50# Pub Thin, VonHoffmann*

Cover: © Werner Forman/Art Resource, NY

Credits: The credits section for this book begins on page C-1 and is considered an extension of the copyright page.

The following Library of Congress data is for the complete edition of this title.

Library of Congress Cataloging-in-Publication Data

Bentley, Jerry H., 1949–
Traditions & encounters : a global perspective on the past / Jerry H. Bentley, Herbert F. Ziegler.—[3rd ed].
p. cm.
Includes bibliographical references and index.
ISBN 0-07-295754-9 (alk. paper)
1. World history. 2. Intercultural communication—History. I. Title: Traditions and encounters. II. Ziegler, Herbert F., 1949– III. Title.
D20.B42 2005
909.82—dc22

2004063157

www.mhhe.com

Brief Contents

DETAILED CONTENTS

PART IV

AN AGE OF CROSS-CULTURAL INTERACTION, 1000 TO 1500 C.E. 458

PART V

The Origins of Global Interdependence, 1500 to 1800 594

MAPS

Sources from the Past

Contexts & Connections

PREFACE

Since the early 1990s, journalists, politicians, scholars, and others have frequently resorted to the term *globalization* when commenting on the increasingly tight connections linking the world's lands and peoples. By the late twentieth century, global transportation and communication networks had become more intricate than ever before, and they promoted both economic integration and systematic interaction among peoples throughout the world. Trade goods and electronic currency flowed around the world, while manufacturers restlessly sought new sites to produce consumer goods. Globalization brought tremendous wealth to some, and it facilitated both commercial and cultural exchanges that enriched the lives of many peoples. Alongside opportunities, the era of globalization also brought numerous problems: widespread pollution, global warming, cultural challenges, ethnic tensions, political conflicts, and weapons of mass destruction loomed as potential threats to peoples of all world regions.

Yet even though they are more prominent today than ever before, global interactions and global problems are by no means new features of world history. To the contrary, there is a long historical context for contemporary globalization, and only in light of past experience is it possible to understand the contemporary world.

A Global Perspective on the Past

Our purpose in *Traditions & Encounters* is to offer a global perspective on the past—a vision of history that is meaningful and appropriate for the interdependent world of contemporary times. During an era when peoples from all parts of the earth meet, mingle, interact, and do business with one another, a global perspective has become an essential tool for informed and responsible citizenship. Because global interactions profoundly influence the fortunes of peoples in all lands, it is impossible to understand the contemporary world by approaching it exclusively from the viewpoint of western Europe, the United States, Japan, or any other individual society. It is equally impossible to understand the world's history by viewing it exclusively through the lenses of any particular society's historical experience.

A global perspective on the past calls for analysis that respects the historical experiences of all the world's peoples—not just one or a few—and that examines the roles of all in the making of a world inhabited by all. A global perspective calls also for analysis that goes beyond the study of individual societies to examine their larger regional, continental, hemispheric, and global contexts. A global perspective calls further for exploration of the networks and structures that have promoted interactions between peoples of different societies. A global perspective calls finally for attention to the effects of interactions on the lands, peoples, and societies that have participated in large-scale historical processes. By bringing a global perspective to the study of world history, we seek to offer an understanding of the past that places the contemporary world in meaningful historical context.

On the basis of a superficial inspection, *Traditions & Encounters* might look similar to several other textbooks that survey the world's past. Like other books, for example, *Traditions & Encounters* examines the historical development of societies in Asia, Europe, Africa, the Americas, and Oceania. Yet *Traditions & Encounters* differs from other works in two particularly important ways. First, it relies on a pair of prominent themes to bring a global perspective to the study of world history: it traces the historical development of individual societies in all world regions, and it also focuses attention systematically on interactions between peoples of different societies. Second, it organizes the human past into seven eras that represent distinct and coherent periods of global historical development.

THEMES: TRADITION AND ENCOUNTER

How is it possible to make sense of the entire human past? The study of world history is an exhilarating project that offers unparalleled opportunities to understand oneself and one's own society in relation to the larger world. Given the range of human diversity, however, world history also presents a daunting challenge. Human communities have adopted widely varying forms of political, social, and economic organization, and they have elaborated even more diverse cultural, religious, and philosophical legacies. Given the manifold diversity of human societies, it might seem that masses of unrelated detail threaten to swamp any effort to deal with all the world's history.

In this book we concentrate on two main themes—tradition and encounter—that help to bring order to world history. These two themes bring focus to some of the most important features of human experience on the earth. In combination, they account for much of the historical development of human societies.

The theme of tradition draws attention to the formation, maintenance, and sometimes collapse of individual societies. From their earliest days on earth, human groups have generated distinctive political, social, economic, and cultural traditions that have guided affairs in their own societies. Some of these traditions arose and disappeared relatively quickly, while others influenced human affairs over the centuries and millennia, sometimes down to the present day. Thus one of our principal concerns in this book is to examine the development of the diverse political, social, economic, and cultural traditions that have shaped the lives and experiences of the world's various peoples. Individual chapters explore the traditions that different peoples have relied on to organize and sustain societies in Asia, Europe, Africa, the Americas, and Oceania. Emphasis falls especially on the large, densely populated, complex, city-based societies that have most deeply influenced world affairs for the past six thousand years, but smaller and less powerful societies also receive their share of attention. This third edition of *Traditions & Encounters* draws on recent scholarship to offer updated and enhanced understanding of the world's individual societies.

While elaborating distinctive political, social, economic, and cultural traditions to organize their affairs, the world's peoples have also interacted regularly with one another since the earliest days of human history. The theme of encounter directs attention to communications, interactions, networks, and exchanges that have linked individual societies to their neighbors and others in the larger world. By systematically examining encounters among peoples of different societies, we draw attention to processes of cross-cultural interaction that have been some of the most effective agents of change in all of world history. In the form of mass migrations, campaigns of imperial expansion, long-distance trade, diffusions of food crops, the spread of infectious and contagious diseases, transfers of technological skills, and the spread of religious and cultural traditions, these interactions have profoundly influenced the experiences of individual societies and the development of the world as a whole. Thus, while presenting a wide-ranging discussion of individual societies and their traditions, this book also devotes considerable attention to the many and varied forms of interaction that have linked the fortunes of peoples from different societies. Many of the book's chapters also examine the large-scale structures of transportation, communication, and exchange that supported interactions among the world's peoples. Just as it updates treatments of individual societies, this third edition of *Traditions & Encounters* also draws on recent scholarship to enhance discussions of encounters and focus attention more clearly than before on processes of cross-cultural interaction.

Organization: Seven Eras of Global History

While relying on the themes of tradition and encounter to bring the diversity of world history into focus, we also seek to bring about improved understanding of the world's development through time by organizing it into seven eras of global history. These eras, treated successively in the seven parts of this book, represent coherent epochs that form the larger architecture of world history as we see it. The seven eras do not reflect the particular experience of any single society so much as the common experiences of all societies participating in processes of cross-cultural interaction. Thus our seven eras of global history owe their coherence particularly to patterns in the networks of transportation, communication, and exchange that have linked peoples of different societies at different times in the past. Even in ancient times these networks supported interactions that shaped the experiences of peoples from different lands, and with the development of increasingly effective technologies of transportation and communication, interactions have grown more frequent, systematic, and intense over time. By studying the world's peoples in the framework of the seven eras of global history, we seek to offer meaningful comparisons between different societies and also to highlight the role of cross-cultural interactions in shaping the experiences of individual societies and influencing the development of the world as a whole.

Thus from the beginning to the end of this book we focus on the twin themes of tradition and encounter, which in combination go a long way toward accounting for the historical development of the human species on planet earth, and we situate the experiences of individual societies in their larger regional, continental, hemispheric, and global contexts. By bringing a global perspective to the study of humanity's common historical experience, we seek to offer a vision of the past that is both meaningful and appropriate for the interdependent world of contemporary times. We hope that *Traditions & Encounters* will enable readers to understand the development of human societies through time and also to place the contemporary world in its proper historical context.

Changes for the Third Edition

In preparing this third edition of *Traditions & Encounters,* we have paid close attention to recent scholarship that has transformed historians' understanding of the global past—sometimes dramatically so. This effort has resulted in revised, updated, and expanded treatments of societies in all world regions. In addition to reflecting the best recent scholarship, we have also sought to enhance the book's global perspective by emphasizing historical comparisons and by bringing clearer focus to historical processes that have linked the world's peoples and societies. Thus we have reorganized the treatment of the early modern era (Part V) so as to integrate Russian experience more clearly into both European history and world history. Similarly, we have reorganized the treatment of the twentieth century (Part VII) so as to explain more clearly the roles of developing societies in the modern world. This effort has led us to include a new chapter discussing nationalism and political identities in Asian, African, and Latin American lands (Chapter 36).

Two additional features that are new to this third edition of *Traditions & Encounters* also merit mention. First, we have added questions for reflection at the end of all the excerpts from primary sources in the "Sources from the Past" boxes. Second, we have included a new series of brief essays in "Contexts & Connections" boxes. These essays take a specific issue from an individual chapter as a point of departure, then venture widely through time and space in seeking to understand the larger contexts of particular historical experiences. We hope that both "Sources from the Past" boxes and "Contexts & Connections" essays will promote improved understanding of the world and its development through time.

Tools for the Student

McGraw-Hill's *Primary Source Investigator* (PSI) CD-ROM is bound into each copy of *Traditions & Encounters* text and provides students with instant access to hundreds of world history documents, images, artifacts, audio recordings, and videos. PSI helps students practice the art of "doing history" on a real archive of historical sources. Students follow the three basic steps of *Ask, Research,* and *Argue* to examine sources, take notes on them, and then save or print copies of the sources as evidence for their papers or presentations. After researching a particular theme, individual, or time period, students can use PSI's writing guide to walk them through the steps of developing a thesis, organizing their evidence, and supporting their conclusion.

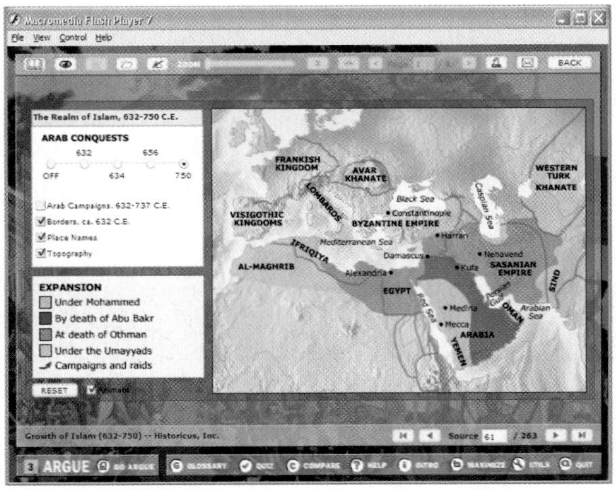

More than just a history or writing tool, the PSI is also a student study tool that contains 43 interactive maps, quiz questions, and an interactive glossary with audio pronunciation guide. The maps and glossary may also be found on the student website www.mhhe.com/bentley3 with additional supporting materials such as part timelines, chapter summaries, and multiple choice quizzes.

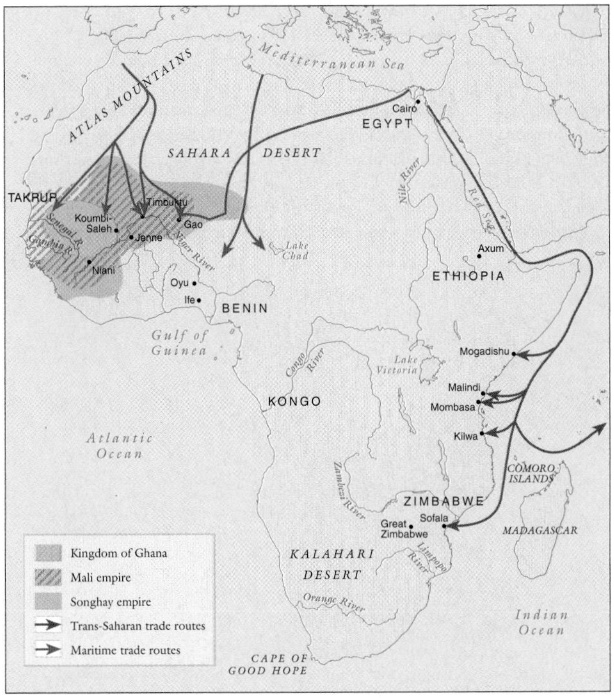

As we strengthened the substantive content of *Traditions & Encounters*, we also worked to produce a book more accessible and useful for readers. The entire map program has been revised for clarity, greater detail, and more topographical information. Any map with a global Online Learning Center (OLC) icon also has an interactive counterpart on the book's website and on the PSI CD.

The interactive maps offer a variety of learning functions. Students can use the maps to view topography, territories, borders, developing trends, and other topics. Visit the site at www.mhhe.com/bentley3.

New to this edition are *Contexts & Connections* essays which appear in about half of the chapters. Each essay highlights historical subjects with interesting links across different geographic regions and eras. Many of these essays utilize objects of material culture as clues to discerning the past or to examining historical issues in detail with a view toward present-day relevance. They were written to capture the imagination, to bring the past closer to the present, and to provide a basis for classroom discussion.

Contexts & Connections

The World's First Coins

When relating the story of Cyrus's victory over King Croesus of Lydia, the Greek historian Herodotus offered a description of Croesus's kingdom. He characterized the Lydians as an exceptionally prosperous people. "So far as we have any knowledge," he reported, "they were the first nation to introduce the use of gold and silver coin, and the first who sold goods by retail." The king himself had a reputation as the wealthiest person in the world—a view reflected in the popular expression that particularly wealthy individuals are "as rich as Croesus." The wealth of the Lydian kingdom arose partly from use of the coins that Herodotus mentioned.

Mesopotamian and Egyptian peoples had long used silver and gold fashioned into rings, rods, and ingots as currency to facilitate exchanges of goods. It was much simpler to purchase goods for a certain quantity of silver than to barter goods directly for one another. Yet silver and gold currencies had their own problems. Careful merchants had to weigh tokens in their scales to make sure they came to the right amount. Even then it was possible for unscrupulous individuals to dilute the silver or gold content of a token by alloying it with some cheaper metal.

Beginning about 640 B.C.E. the kings of Lydia issued the first coins of precisely measured metal bearing guarantees of their value. They minted their early coins from electrum, a rare but naturally occurring alloy of gold and silver found in local rivers. Croesus later minted coins of pure gold and silver. These coins immediately caught the attention of Lydia's trading partners, and officially sponsored coins were soon in use throughout the eastern Mediterranean region. (Chinese rulers independently issued bronze coins about the same time.)

The availability of officially minted coins with guaranteed values provided a tremendous boost to trade. The earliest beneficiary was the kingdom of Lydia itself, which drew crowds of foreign merchants to vast markets in the capital at Sardis. There Lydians traded merchandise that they obtained from Mesopotamia, Egypt, and the eastern Mediterranean region, as well as the highly prized perfumes that were the most famous products of Lydian manufacturers. This bustling trade in large, officially sponsored marketplaces is what Herodotus had in mind when he said the Lydians were "the first who sold goods by retail." In later centuries, Greeks, Romans, and others made use of their own minted coins as they built commercial empires throughout the Mediterranean basin.

Coins did not entirely displace other currencies: in various world regions, cattle, cowry shells, cacao beans, and other items functioned as mediums of exchange long after the invention of coins. Even in regions where they were in common use, coins have not always dominated economic exchange: after the invention of printed paper money, and especially after the more recent development of electronic currency, coins increasingly became impractical except for small-scale transactions. Meanwhile, however, for two millennia and more, officially minted coins lubricated trade and facilitated economic transactions throughout much of the world.

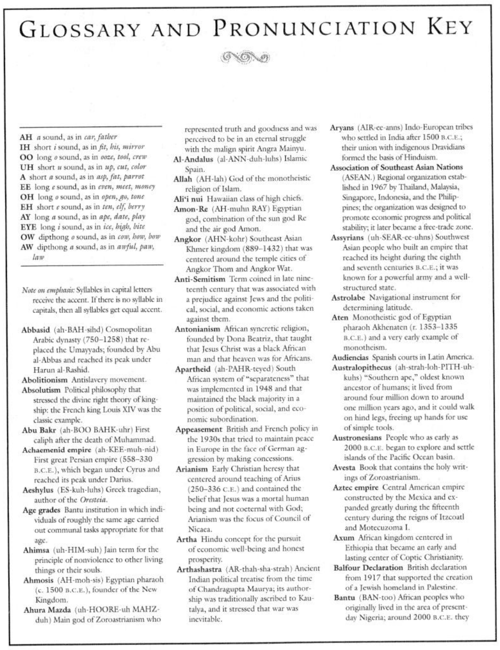

GLOSSARY AND PRONUNCIATION KEY

AH *a* sound, as in *car, father*
IH short *i* sound, as in *fit, his, mirror*
OO long *o* sound, as in *ooze, tool, crew*
UH short *u* sound, as in *up, cut, color*
A short *a* sound, as in *asp, fat, parrot*
EE long *e* sound, as in *even, meet, money*
OH long *o* sound, as in *open, go, tone*
EH short *e* sound, as in *ten, elf, berry*
AY long *a* sound, as in *ape, date, play*
EYE long *i* sound, as in *ice, high, bite*
OW dipthong *o* sound, as in *cow, how, bow*
AW dipthong *a* sound, as in *awful, paw, law*

Note on emphasis: Syllables in capital letters receive the accent. If there is no syllable in capitals, then all syllables get equal accent.

Abbasid (ah-BAH-sihd) Cosmopolitan Arabic dynasty (750–1258) that replaced the Umayyads; founded by Abu al-Abbas and reached its peak under Harun al-Rashid.
Abolitionism Antislavery movement.
Absolutism Political philosophy that stressed the divine right theory of kingship: the French king Louis XIV was the classic example.
Abu Bakr (ah-BOO BAHK-uhr) First caliph after the death of Muhammad.
Achaemenid empire (ah-KEE-muh-nid) First great Persian empire (558–330 B.C.E.), which began under Cyrus and reached its peak under Darius.
Aeshylus (ES-kuh-luhs) Greek tragedian, author of the *Oresteia*.
Age grades Bantu institution in which individuals of roughly the same age carried out communal tasks appropriate for that age.
Ahimsa (uh-HIM-suh) Jain term for the principle of nonviolence to other living things or their souls.
Ahmosis (AH-moh-sis) Egyptian pharaoh (c. 1500 B.C.E.), founder of the New Kingdom.
Ahura Mazda (uh-HOORE-uh MAHZ-duh) Main god of Zoroastrianism who represented truth and goodness and was perceived to be in an eternal struggle with the malign spirit Angra Mainyu.
Al-Andalus (al-ANN-duh-luhs) Islamic Spain.
Allah (AH-lah) God of the monotheistic religion of Islam.
Ali'i nui Hawaiian class of high chiefs.
Amon-Re (AH-muhn RAY) Egyptian god, combination of the sun god Re and the air god Amon.
Angkor (AHN-kohr) Southeast Asian Khmer kingdom (889–1432) that was centered around the temple cities of Angkor Thom and Angkor Wat.
Anti-Semitism Term coined in late nineteenth century that was associated with a prejudice against Jews and the political, social, and economic actions taken against them.
Antonianism African syncretic religion, founded by Dona Beatriz, that taught that Jesus Christ was a black African man and that heaven was for Africans.
Apartheid (ah-PAHR-teyed) South African system of "separateness" that was implemented in 1948 and that maintained the black majority in a position of political, social, and economic subordination.
Appeasement British and French policy in the 1930s that tried to maintain peace in Europe in the face of German aggression by making concessions.
Arianism Early Christian heresy that centered around teaching of Arius (250–336 C.E.) and contained the belief that Jesus was a mortal human being and not coeternal with God; Arianism was the focus of Council of Nicaea.
Artha Hindu concept for the pursuit of economic well-being and honest prosperity.
Arthashastra (AR-thah-sha-strah) Ancient Indian political treatise from the time of Chandragupta Maurya; its authorship was traditionally ascribed to Kautalya, and it stressed that war was inevitable.
Aryans (AIR-ee-anns) Indo-European tribes who settled in India after 1500 B.C.E.; their union with indigenous Dravidians formed the basis of Hinduism.
Association of Southeast Asian Nations (ASEAN.) Regional organization established in 1967 by Thailand, Malaysia, Singapore, Indonesia, and the Philippines; the organization was designed to promote economic progress and political stability; it later became a free-trade zone.
Assyrians (uh-SEAR-ee-uhns) Southwest Asian people who built an empire that reached its height during the eighth and seventh centuries B.C.E.; it was known for a powerful army and a well-structured state.
Astrolabe Navigational instrument for determining latitude.
Aten Monotheistic god of Egyptian pharaoh Akhenaten (r. 1353–1335 B.C.E.) and a very early example of monotheism.
Audiencias Spanish courts in Latin America.
Australopithecus (ah-strah-loh-PITH-uh-kuhs) "Southern ape," oldest known ancestor of humans; it lived from around four million down to around one million years ago, and it could walk on hind legs, freeing up hands for use of simple tools.
Austronesians People who as early as 2000 B.C.E. began to explore and settle islands of the Pacific Ocean basin.
Avesta Book that contains the holy writings of Zoroastrianism.
Aztec empire Central American empire constructed by the Mexica and expanded greatly during the fifteenth century during the reigns of Itzcoatl and Motecuzoma I.
Axum African kingdom centered in Ethiopia that became an early and lasting center of Coptic Christianity.
Balfour Declaration British declaration from 1917 that supported the creation of a Jewish homeland in Palestine.
Bantu (BAN-too) African peoples who originally lived in the area of present-day Nigeria; around 2000 B.C.E. they

We have taken the book's glossary and pronunciation guide one step further by rendering it interactive. A multimedia version of this glossary is available on the book's website www.mhhe.com/bentley3 and on the *Primary Source Investigator* CD-ROM packaged with the book. Students and teachers can now listen to hard-to-pronounce words, and students can switch to the flashcard feature to quiz themselves on important terms. For reminders of these study tools, new PSI and OLC icons appear at the end of each chapter.

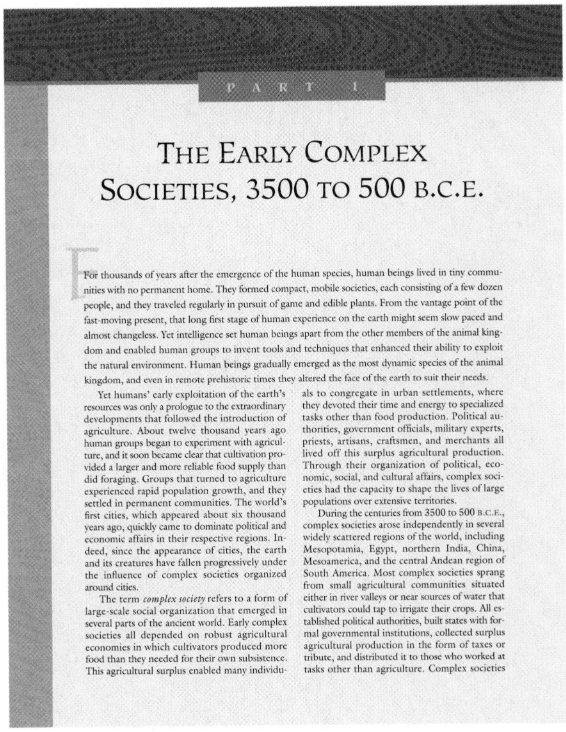

PART I

THE EARLY COMPLEX SOCIETIES, 3500 TO 500 B.C.E.

For thousands of years after the emergence of the human species, human beings lived in tiny communities with no permanent home. They formed compact, mobile societies, each consisting of a few dozen people, and they traveled regularly in pursuit of game and edible plants. From the vantage point of the fast-moving present, that long first stage of human experience on the earth might seem slow paced and almost changeless. Yet intelligence set human beings apart from the other members of the animal kingdom and enabled human groups to invent tools and techniques that enhanced their ability to exploit the natural environment. Human beings gradually emerged as the most dynamic species of the animal kingdom, and even in remote prehistoric times they altered the face of the earth to suit their needs.

Yet humans' early exploitation of the earth's resources was only a prologue to the extraordinary developments that followed the introduction of agriculture. About twelve thousand years ago human groups began to experiment with agriculture, and it soon became clear that cultivation provided a larger and more reliable food supply than did foraging. Groups that turned to agriculture experienced rapid population growth, and they settled in permanent communities. The world's first cities, which appeared about six thousand years ago, quickly came to dominate political and economic affairs in their respective regions. Indeed, since the appearance of cities, the earth and its creatures have fallen progressively under the influence of complex societies organized around cities.

The term *complex society* refers to a form of large-scale social organization that emerged in several parts of the ancient world. Early complex societies all depended on robust agricultural economies in which cultivators produced more food than they needed for their own subsistence. This agricultural surplus enabled many individuals to congregate in urban settlements, where they devoted their time and energy to specialized tasks other than food production. Political authorities, government officials, military experts, priests, artisans, craftsmen, and merchants all lived off this surplus agricultural production. Through their organization of political, economic, social, and cultural affairs, complex societies had the capacity to shape the lives of large populations over extensive territories.

During the centuries from 3500 to 500 B.C.E., complex societies arose independently in several widely scattered regions of the world, including Mesopotamia, Egypt, northern India, China, Mesoamerica, and the central Andean region of South America. Most complex societies sprang from small agricultural communities situated either in river valleys or near sources of water that cultivators could tap to irrigate their crops. All established political authorities, built states with formal governmental institutions, collected surplus agricultural production in the form of taxes or tribute, and distributed it to those who worked at tasks other than agriculture. Complex societies

Effective pedagogical features from the first edition have been retained. Each of the book's seven parts opens with an introduction that outlines the themes running through all the chapters in that part. This information creates a strong framework for understanding the details of individual chapters.

ASIA	100,000	8,000	3,500	2,000
SOUTHWEST ASIA	Neandertal appearance (100,000) Cro-Magnon appearance (40,000) Beginnings of agriculture (10,000) Neolithic age	Jericho (8000) Çatal Hüyük (7250) Pottery (7000) Copper metallurgy; textile production (6000) Rise of cities (4000)	Cuneiform Bronze metallurgy Migration of Hittites into Anatolia (3000) Phoenicians dominate Mediterranean trade (2500) Mesopotamian unification under Sargon of Akkad (2334) Collapse of Sargon's empire (2100)	Hebrew patriarch Abraham migrates out of Mesopotamia (1800) Early monotheism Hammurabi (1792–1750) Code of Hammurabi Phoenician creation of first alphabet (1500) Rise of Hittites (1400) Iron metallurgy Moses and Ten Commandments (1300)
EAST AND CENTRAL ASIA	Arrival of *Homo erectus* (1.5 million) Arrival of *Homo sapiens* (200,000)	Domestication of rice (7000) Neolithic villages in Yellow River (Huang He) valley (5000) Yangshao culture (5000–3000) Banpo	Xia dynasty (2200–1766) Erlitou Dikes, dams, flood control projects Metallurgy	Shang dynasty (1766–1122) Ao and Yin Written language Bronze metallurgy Oracle bones Zhou dynasty (1122–256) Mandate of Heaven
SOUTH AND SOUTHEAST ASIA	Arrival of *Homo erectus* (1.5 million) Arrival of *Homo sapiens* (200,000)	Beginnings of agriculture (7000) Cultivation of cotton (5000)	Neolithic villages (3500) Rise of cities (3000) Trade with Mesopotamia (3000–1750) Harappan society Harappa and Mohenjo-Daro Written language Sophisticated water and sewage system	Decline of Harappan society (2000) Deforestation of Indus valley Mohenjo-Daro and Harappa cease to exist (1700) Collapse of Harappan society (1500) Migration of Aryans (Indo-Europeans) Sanskrit language Caste system Vedas (1300)

Bronze ritual vessel of an elephant buried with departed kin Cultural Relics Publishing House, Beijing

Part opening timelines have been revised and are now available with each book as a mini-poster.

CHAPTER 2

EARLY SOCIETIES IN SOUTHWEST ASIA AND THE INDO-EUROPEAN MIGRATIONS

THE QUEST FOR ORDER
Mesopotamia: "The Land between the Rivers"
The Course of Empire
The Later Mesopotamian Empires

THE FORMATION OF A COMPLEX SOCIETY AND SOPHISTICATED CULTURAL TRADITIONS
Economic Specialization and Trade
The Emergence of a Stratified Patriarchal Society
The Development of Written Cultural Traditions

THE BROADER INFLUENCE OF MESOPOTAMIAN SOCIETY
Hebrews, Israelites, and Jews
The Phoenicians

THE INDO-EUROPEAN MIGRATIONS
Indo-European Origins
Indo-European Expansion and Its Effects

By far the best-known individual of ancient Mesopotamian society was a man named Gilgamesh. According to historical sources, Gilgamesh was the fifth king of the city of Uruk. He ruled about 2750 B.C.E.—for a period of 126 years, according to one semilegendary source—and he led his community in its conflicts with Kish, a nearby city that was the principal rival of Uruk. Historical sources record very little additional detail about Gilgamesh's life and deeds.

But Gilgamesh was a figure of Mesopotamian mythology and folklore as well as history. He was the subject of numerous poems and legends, and Mesopotamian bards made him the central figure in a cycle of stories known collectively as the *Epic of Gilgamesh*. As a figure of legend, Gilgamesh became the greatest hero figure of ancient Mesopotamia. According to the stories, the gods granted Gilgamesh a perfect body and endowed him with superhuman strength and courage. He was "the man to whom all things were known," a supremely wise individual who "saw mysteries and knew secret things." The legends declare that he constructed the massive city walls of Uruk as well as several of the city's magnificent temples to Mesopotamian deities.

The stories that make up the *Epic of Gilgamesh* recount the adventures of this hero and his cherished friend Enkidu as they sought fame. They killed an evil monster, rescued Uruk from a ravaging bull, and matched wits with the gods. In spite of their heroic deeds, Enkidu offended the gods and fell under a sentence of death. His loss profoundly affected Gilgamesh, who sought for some means to cheat death and gain eternal life. He eventually found a magical plant that had the power to confer immortality, but a serpent stole the plant and carried it away, forcing Gilgamesh to recognize that death is the ultimate fate of all human beings. Thus, while focusing on the activities of Gilgamesh and Enkidu, the stories explored themes of friendship, loyalty, ambition, fear of death, and longing for immortality. In doing so they reflected the interests and concerns of the complex, urban-based society that had recently emerged in Mesopotamia.

Productive agricultural economies supported the development of the world's first complex societies, in which sizable numbers of people lived in cities and extended their political, social, economic, and cultural influence over large regions. The earliest urban societies so far known emerged during the early fourth millennium B.C.E. in southwest Asia, particularly in Mesopotamia.

As people congregated in cities, they needed to find ways to resolve disputes—sometimes between residents within individual settlements, other times between

31

Each chapter opens with a story of individual experiences that draw students into the chapter and illustrate its main themes.

Sources from the Past

The Wealth and Commerce of Constantinople

The Spanish rabbi Benjamin of Tudela traveled throughout Europe, north Africa, and southwest Asia between 1165 and 1173 C.E. He may have ventured as far as India, and he mentioned both India and China in his travel account. His main purpose was to record the conditions of Jewish communities, but he also described the many lands and about three hundred cities that he visited. His travels took place during an era of political decline for the Byzantine empire, yet he still found Constantinople a flourishing and prosperous city.

The circumference of the city of Constantinople is eighteen miles; half of it is surrounded by the sea, and half by land, and it is situated upon two arms of the sea, one coming from the sea of Russia [the Black Sea], and one from the sea of Sepharad [the Mediterranean].

All sorts of merchants come here from the land of Babylon, from the land of Shinar [Mesopotamia], from Persia, Media [western Iran], and all the sovereignty of the land of Egypt, from the land of Canaan [Palestine], and the empire of Russia, from Hungary, Patzinakia [Ukraine], Khazaria [southern Russia], and the land of Lombardy [northern Italy] and Sepharad [Spain].

Constantinople is a busy city, and merchants come to it from every country by sea or land, and there is none like it in the world except Baghdad, the great city of Islam. In Constantinople is the church of Hagia Sophia, and the seat of the pope of the Greeks, since Greeks do not obey the pope of Rome. There are also as many churches as there are days of the year. . . . And in this church [Hagia Sophia] there are pillars of gold and silver, and lamps of silver and gold more than a man can count.

Close to the walls of the palace is also a place of amusement belonging to the emperor, which is called the Hippodrome, and every year on the anniversary of the birth of Jesus the emperor gives a great entertainment there. And in that place men from all the races of the world come before the emperor and empress with jugglery and without jugglery, and they introduce lions, leopards, bears, and wild asses, and they engage them in combat with one another; and the same thing is done with birds. No entertainment like this is to be found in any other land. . . .

From every part of the Byzantine empire tribute is brought here every year, and they fill strongholds with garments of silk, purple, and gold. Like unto these storehouses and this wealth there is nothing in the whole world to be found. It is said that the tribute of the city amounts every year to 20,000 gold pieces, derived both from the rents of shops and markets and from the tribute of merchants who enter by sea or land.

The Greek inhabitants are very rich in gold and precious stones, and they go clothed in garments of silk and gold embroidery, and they ride horses and look like princes. Indeed, the land is very rich in all cloth stuffs and in bread, meat, and wine.

Wealth like that of Constantinople is not to be found in the whole world. Here also are men learned in all the books of the Greeks, and they eat and drink, every man under his vine and his fig-tree.

SOURCE: Benjamin of Tudela. *The Itinerary of Benjamin of Tudela.* Trans. by M. N. Adler. London: H. Frowde, 1907. (Translation slightly modified.)

How is it possible to account for the prosperity that Benjamin of Tudela found in Constantinople?

The Sources from the Past boxes bring the past to life, spotlighting significant primary source documents relevant to the chapter, such as poems, journal accounts, religious writings, and letters. Introductions place the documents in context and explain their significance; new thought provoking questions prompt readers to contextualize and think critically about key issues raised in the document.

348 PART III | THE POSTCLASSICAL ERA, 500 TO 1000 C.E.

Muhammad's time. Although he was not deeply knowledgeable about Judaism or Christianity, Muhammad had a basic understanding of both faiths. He may even have traveled by caravan to Syria, where he would certainly have dealt with Jewish and Christian merchants.

Muhammad's Spiritual Transformation

About 610 C.E., as he approached age forty, Muhammad underwent a profound spiritual experience that transformed his life and left a deep mark on world history. His experience left him with the convictions that in all the world there was only one true deity, Allah ("God"), that he ruled the universe, that idolatry and the recognition of other gods amounted to wickedness, and that Allah would soon bring his judgment on the world, rewarding the righteous and punishing the wicked. Muhammad experienced visions, which he understood as messages or revelations from Allah, delivered through the archangel Gabriel (also recognized by Jews and Christians as a special messenger of God), instructing him to explain his faith to others. He did not set out to construct a new religion by combining elements of Arab, Jewish, and Christian beliefs. In light of his cultural context, however, it is not surprising that he shared numerous specific beliefs with Jews and Christians—and indeed also with Zoroastrians, whose views had profoundly influenced the development of both Judaism and Christianity. In any case, in accordance with instructions transmitted to him by Gabriel, Muhammad began to expound his faith to his family and close friends. Gradually, others showed interest in his message, and by about 620 C.E. a zealous and expanding minority of Mecca's citizenry had joined his circle.

The Quran

Muhammad originally presented oral recitations of the revelations he received during his visions. As the Islamic community grew, his followers prepared written texts of his teachings. During the early 650s devout Muslims compiled these written versions of Muhammad's revelations and issued them as the Quran ("recitation"), the holy book of Islam. A work of magnificent poetry, the Quran communicates in powerful and moving terms Muhammad's understanding of Allah and his relation to the world, and it serves as the definitive authority for Islamic religious doctrine and social organization.

Apart from the Quran, several other sources have provided moral and religious guidance for the Islamic community. Most important after the Quran itself are traditions known as *hadith,* which include sayings attributed to Muhammad and accounts of the prophet's deeds. Several collections of *hadith* appeared between the ninth and eleventh century C.E., and Muslim scholars have often taken them as guides for interpretation of the Quran. Regarded as less authoritative than the Quran and the *hadith,* but still important as inspirations for Islamic thought, were early works describing social and legal customs, biographies of Muhammad, and pious commentaries on the Quran.

Muhammad's Migration to Medina

Conflict at Mecca

The growing popularity of Muhammad's preaching brought him into conflict with the ruling elites at Mecca. Conflict centered on religious issues. Muhammad's insistence that Allah was the only divine power in the universe struck many polytheistic Arabs as offensive and dangerous as well, since it disparaged long-recognized deities and spirits thought to wield influence over human affairs. The tensions also had a personal dimension. Mecca's ruling elites, who were also the city's wealthiest merchants, took it as a personal affront and a threat to their position when Muhammad denounced greed as moral wickedness that Allah would punish.

Muhammad's attack on idolatry also represented an economic threat to those who owned and profited from the many shrines to deities that attracted merchants

Marginal notes highlight key terms, events, and concepts as they appear within the narrative.

A concise chronological table summarizes the critical events covered in the chapter.

CHRONOLOGY	
589–618	Sui dynasty (China)
602–664	Life of Xuanzang
604–618	Reign of Sui Yangdi
618–907	Tang dynasty (China)
627–649	Reign of Tang Taizong
669–935	Silla dynasty (Korea)
710–794	Nara period (Japan)
755–757	An Lushan's rebellion
794–1185	Heian period (Japan)
875–884	Huang Chao's rebellion
960–1279	Song dynasty (China)
960–976	Reign of Song Taizu
1024	First issuance of government-sponsored paper money
1130–1200	Life of Zhu Xi
1185–1333	Kamakura period (Japan)
1336–1573	Muromachi period (Japan)

A paragraph summary at the end of each chapter reinforces the chapter's key points, making student review easier.

The revival of centralized imperial rule in China had profound implications for all of east Asia and indeed for most of the eastern hemisphere. When the Sui and Tang dynasties imposed their authority throughout China, they established a powerful state that guided political affairs throughout east Asia. Tang armies extended Chinese influence to Korea, Vietnam, and central Asia. They did not invade Japan, but the impressive political organization of China prompted the islands' rulers to imitate Tang examples. Moreover, the Sui and Tang dynasties laid a strong political foundation for rapid economic development. Chinese society prospered throughout the postclassical era, partly because of technological and industrial innovation. Tang and Song prosperity touched all of China's neighbors, since it encouraged surging commerce in east Asia. Chinese silk, porcelain, and lacquerware were prized commodities among trading peoples from southeast Asia to east Africa. Chinese inventions such as paper, printing, gunpowder, and the magnetic compass found a place in societies throughout the eastern hemisphere as they diffused across the silk roads and sea lanes. The postclassical era was an age of religious as well as commercial and technological exchanges: Nestorian Christians, Zoroastrians, Manichaeans, and Muslims all maintained communities in Tang China, and Buddhism became the most popular religious faith in all of east Asia. During the postclassical era, Chinese social organization and economic dynamism helped to sustain interactions between the peoples of the eastern hemisphere on an unprecedented scale.

Each chapter concludes with a For Further Reading section that contains a list and brief description of the most important books available about topics discussed in the chapter. This list can help students get started with research projects or follow up on subjects that they find especially interesting.

FOR FURTHER READING

Kenneth Ch'en. *Buddhism in China: A Historical Survey.* Princeton, 1964. A clear and detailed account by an eminent scholar.

Hugh R. Clark. *Community, Trade, and Networks: Southern Fujian Province from the Third to the Thirteenth Century.* Cambridge, 1991. Excellent scholarly study exploring the transformation of a region by trade and market forces.

Peter Duus. *Feudalism in Japan.* 2nd ed. New York, 1976. A brief survey of early Japanese political history, concentrating on the Kamakura and Muromachi periods.

Patricia Buckley Ebrey. *Chinese Civilization: A Sourcebook.* 2nd ed. New York, 1993. A splendid collection of documents in translation.

Patricia Buckley Ebrey and Peter N. Gregory, eds. *Religion and Society in T'ang and Sung China.* Honolulu, 1993. Important collection of scholarly essays dealing with the early entry of Buddhism in China.

Mark Elvin. *The Pattern of the Chinese Past.* Stanford, 1973. A brilliant analysis of Chinese history, concentrating particularly on economic, social, and technological themes.

Jacques Gernet. *Buddhism in Chinese Society: An Economic History from the Fifth to the Tenth Century.* Trans. by F. Verellen. New York, 1995. An important study emphasizing the economic and social significance of Buddhist monasteries in the Chinese countryside.

———. *Daily Life in China on the Eve of the Mongol Invasion, 1250–1276.* Trans. by H. M. Wright. New York, 1962. Rich portrait of Southern Song China, emphasizing social history.

Ivan Morris. *The World of the Shining Prince: Court Life in Ancient Japan.* Harmondsworth, 1964. Vividly reconstructs the court life of Heian Japan.

Joseph Needham. *Science in Traditional China.* Cambridge, Mass., 1981. Essays on the history of Chinese science and technology.

Edward H. Schafer. *The Golden Peaches of Samarkand: A Study of T'ang Exotics.* Berkeley, 1963. Deals with relations between China and central Asian lands during the Tang dynasty.

———. *The Vermilion Bird: T'ang Images of the South.* Berkeley, 1967. Evocative study of relations between China and Vietnam during the Tang dynasty.

SUPPLEMENTS

The supplements listed here may accompany *Traditions & Encounters: A Global Perspective on the Past.* Please contact your local McGraw-Hill representative for details concerning policies, prices, and availability, as some restrictions may apply.

For the Instructor

- **The Instructor's Resource CD-ROM (or IRCD)** contains several instructor tools in one location. For lecture preparation, teachers will find an Instructor's Manual and PowerPoint samples by chapter with over 100 images, maps, graphs, and tables. For quizzes and tests, the IRCD also contains a Test Bank and Computerized Test Bank.
- **The Instructor's Manual and Test Bank** have both been heavily revised for clarity and consistency. The Instructor's Manual was prepared by Rose Mary Sheldon and Timothy Dowling at the Virginia Military Institute. The Test Bank was prepared by Eric Osborne and Douglas Harmon at the Virginia Military Institute.
- **A Computerized Test Bank** is available on the Instructor's Resource CD-ROM in Brownstone Diploma for Windows and Macintosh. This version of the Test Bank allows instructors to customize each test to suit any course syllabus.
- **A Set of Overhead Transparencies** is available to adopters of the book. It contains over 120 maps, charts, and illustrations, organized by chapter.
- **The Online Learning Center for Instructors** at www.mhhe.com/bentley3. At the homepage for the text-specific website, instructors will find a series of online tools to meet a wide range of classroom needs. The Instructor's Manual, PowerPoint presentations, and blank maps can be downloaded by instructors, but are password-protected to prevent tampering. Instructors can create web-based homework assignments or classroom activities by linking to the student's side of the Online Learning Center. Instructors can also create an interactive course syllabus using McGraw-Hill's PageOut (www.mhhe.com/pageout).
- **PageOut** at www.mhhe.com/pageout. On the PageOut website, instructors can create their own course websites. PageOut requires no prior knowledge of HTML, no long hours of coding, and no design skills on the instructor's part. Simply plug the course information into a template and click on one of sixteen designs. The process takes no time at all and leaves instructors with a professionally designed website. Powerful features include an interactive course syllabus that lets instructors post content and links, an online gradebook, lecture notes, bookmarks, and even a discussion board where instructors and students can discuss course-related topics.
- **Videos** on topics in world history is available through the Films for the Humanities and Sciences collection. Contact your local McGraw-Hill sales representative for further information.
- **Readers.** McGraw-Hill offers a number of readers that complement this text. Visit our online catalogue at www.mhhe.com.
- **Advanced Placement Instructor's Manual.** Written by Ane Lintvedt, Bard Keeler, and Joan Arno, the Instructor's Manual for Advanced Placement teachers contains lecture topics, teaching strategies, group activities, world history skills, and habits of mind specifically tailored around the six themes. Visit the book website at www.mhhe.com/bentley3 for more information.
- **Classroom Performance System (CPS).** The Classroom Performance System brings ultimate interactivity to *Traditions & Encounters.* CPS is a wireless response

system that gives you immediate feedback from every student in the class. With CPS you can ask subjective and objective questions during your lecture, prompting every student to respond with their individual, wireless response pad, and providing you with instant results. A complete CPS Tutorial is at www.einstruction.com.

For the Student

- **The Online Learning Center for Students** at www.mhhe.com/bentley3 provides students with a wide range of tools for students to use in testing their knowledge of the book. It includes chapter overviews, more new interactive maps, multiple choice and essay quizzes, matching and identification games, as well as primary source indexes for further research. This new edition also contains a new feature based on the book's "Contexts & Connections" box, an interactive timeline, and an interactive glossary with an audio pronunciation guide.
- Each chapter of the **Student Study Guide with Map Exercises** includes a synopsis of the chapter, an outline, student quizzes, map identification exercises, primary source documents, and other resources to help students master the material covered in the text. New to this edition of the study guide are matching and sequencing exercises and group activities.
- **Map Workbooks** test students' knowledge of the geography relevant to each chapter. Exercises require students to fill in important items on a blank map or to answer questions by interpreting a completed map.
- ***History and the Internet: A Guide*** is a brief guide that explores the many ways that the World Wide Web facilitates the study of history. It also includes a history of the Internet, instructions for searching and navigating the Web, a glossary of Web jargon, and lists of significant websites in history.
- **PowerWeb: World History,** an online supplement, is a collection of readings delivered electronically, along with other tools for conducting research in history. In addition, student study tools, web research tips and exercises, and free access to the global content provider Factiva are included. A card with a password for accessing PowerWeb has been packaged free with the textbook.
- Two **After the Fact Interactive** units are available for use with *Traditions & Encounters:* "After the Fact Interactive: Tracing the Silk Roads" for volume 1, and "After the Fact Interactive: Envisioning the Atlantic World" for volume 2. These rich, visually appealing modules on CD-ROM allow students to be apprentice historians, examining a variety of multimedia primary source materials and constructing arguments based on their research.

A Brief Note on Usage

This book qualifies dates as B.C.E. ("Before the Common Era") or C.E. ("Common Era"). In practice, B.C.E. refers to the same epoch as B.C. ("Before Christ"), and C.E. refers to the same epoch as A.D. (*Anno Domini*, a Latin term meaning "in the year of the Lord"). As historical study becomes a global, multicultural enterprise, however, scholars increasingly prefer terminology that does not apply the standards of one society to all the others. Thus reference in this book to B.C.E. and C.E. reflects emerging scholarly convention concerning the qualification of historical dates.

Measurements of length and distance appear here according to the metric system, followed by their English-system equivalents in parentheses.

The book transliterates Chinese names and terms into English according to the *pinyin* system, which has largely displaced the more cumbersome Wade-Giles system. Transliteration of names and terms from other languages follows contemporary scholarly conventions.

About the Authors

Jerry H. Bentley is professor of history at the University of Hawai`i and editor of the *Journal of World History.* He has written extensively on the cultural history of early modern Europe and on cross-cultural interactions in world history. His research on the religious, moral, and political writings of the Renaissance led to the publication of *Humanists and Holy Writ: New Testament Scholarship in the Renaissance* (1983) and *Politics and Culture in Renaissance Naples* (1987). His more recent research has concentrated on global history and particularly on processes of cross-cultural interaction. His book *Old World Encounters: Cross-Cultural Contacts and Exchanges in Pre-Modern Times* (1993) studies processes of cultural exchange and religious conversion before modern times, and his pamphlet *Shapes of World History in Twentieth-Century Scholarship* (1996) discusses the historiography of world history. His current interests include processes of cross-cultural interaction and cultural exchange in modern times.

Herbert F. Ziegler is an associate professor of history at the University of Hawai`i. He has taught world history since 1980 and currently serves as director of the world history program at the University of Hawai`i. He also serves as book review editor of the *Journal of World History.* His interest in twentieth-century European social and political history led to the publication of *Nazi Germany's New Aristocracy* (1990). He is at present working on a study that explores from a global point of view the demographic trends of the past ten thousand years, along with their concomitant technological, economic, and social developments. His other current research project focuses on the application of complexity theory to a comparative study of societies and their internal dynamics.

ACKNOWLEDGMENTS

Many individuals have contributed to this book, and the authors take pleasure in recording deep thanks for all the comments, criticism, advice, and suggestions that helped to improve the work. The editorial team at McGraw-Hill did an outstanding job of keeping the authors focused on the project. Special thanks go to Lyn Uhl, Jon-David Hague, Katherine Bates, Jim Strandberg, Angela Kao, and Christina Gimlin, who provided crucial support by helping the authors work through difficult issues and solve the innumerable problems of content, style and organization that arise in any project to produce a history of the world. Many colleagues at the University of Hawai`i and elsewhere aided and advised the authors on matters of organization and composition. Mimi Henriksen was especially generous with her time and advice. Finally, we would like to express our appreciation for the advice of the following individuals who read and commented on the original manuscript and previous editions of this text:

Henry Abramson
Florida Atlantic University

Roger Adelson
Arizona State University

William Alexander
Norfolk State University

Alfred Andrea
University of Vermont

Ed Anson
University of Arkansas at Little Rock

Henry Antkiewicz
East Tennessee State University

Maria Arbelaez
University of Nebraska at Omaha

Peter Arnade
University of California—San Marcos

Karl Bahm
University of Wisconsin, Superior

Vaughan Baker
University of Louisiana at Lafayette

Ian Barrow
Middlebury College

Dixee Bartholomew-Feis
Buena Vista University

Guy Beckwith
Auburn University

Lynda Bell
University of California—Riverside

Norman Bennett
Boston University

Houri Berberian
California State University, Long Beach

Robert Blackey
California State University—San Bernardino

Wayne Bodle
Indiana University of Pennsylvania

Michael Brescia
State University of New York, Fredonia

Samuel Brunk
University of Texas, El Paso

Deborah Buffton
University of Wisconsin, La Crosse

Maureen Burgess
Colorado State University

Rainer Buschmann
Hawaii Pacific University

Sharon L. Bush
LeMoyne-Owen College

Antonio Calabria
University of Texas, San Antonio

Lewis Call
California Polytechnic State University, San Luis Obispo

Thomas Callahan, Jr.
Rider University

Alice-Catherine Carls
University of Tennessee at Martin

Kay Carr
Southern Illinois University

James Carroll
Iona College

Tom Carty
Springfield College

Bruce Castleman
San Diego State University

Douglas Catterall
Cameron University

Douglas Chambers
University of Southern Mississippi Hattiesburg

Choi Chatterjee
California State University, Los Angeles

Orazio Ciccarelli
University of Southern Mississippi

Andrew Clark
University of North Carolina at Wilmington

Hugh R. Clark
Usrinus College

Tim Coates
College of Charleston

Joan Coffey
Sam Houston State University

Daniel Connerton
North Adams State

Bruce Cruikshank
Hastings College

Graciella Cruz-Tara
Florida Atlantic University

Richard Cusimano
University of Louisiana at Lafayette
Ken Czech
St. Cloud State University
Touraj Daryaee
California State University, Fullerton
Jon Davidann
Hawaii Pacific University
Allen Davidson
Georgia Southern University
Brian Davies
University of Texas, San Antonio
John Davis
Radford University
Thomas Davis
Virginia Military Institute
Elisa Denlinger
University of Wisconsin, LaCrosse
Stewart Dippel
University of the Ozarks
Ross Doughty
Ursinus College
Cathi Dunkle
Mid-Michigan Community College
Ross Dunn
San Diego State University
Lane Earns
University of Wisconsin, Oshkosh
Christopher Ehret
University of California, Los Angeles
Laura Endicott
Southwestern Oklahoma State
Nancy Erickson
Erskine College
James Evans
Southeastern Community College
David Fahey
Miami University
Edward Farmer
University of Minnesota
James David Farthing
Oklahoma Baptist University
Lanny Fields
California State University—San Bernardino
Robert Frankle
University of Memphis
Bonnie Frederick
Washington State University
Karl Friday
University of Georgia
Amy Froide
University of Tennessee, Chattanooga
James Fuller
University of Indianapolis
Robert Gomez
San Antonio College
Paul Goodwin
University of Connecticut, Storrs
Matthew Gordon
Miami University of Ohio
Steve Gosch
University of Wisconsin, Eau Claire
Joseph Gowaskie
Rider University
John Haag
University of Georgia
Jeffrey Hamilton
Baylor University
Michael Hamm
Centre College
Travis Hanes III
University of North Carolina—Wilmington
Preston Hardy, Jr.
University of Tennessee, Martin
Russell Hart
Hawaii Pacific University
John Hayden
Southwestern Oklahoma State
Randolph Head
University of California, Riverside
Mary Hedberg
Saginaw Valley State University
Gerald Herman
Northeastern University
David Hertzel
Southwestern Oklahoma State
Udo Heyn
California State University—Los Angeles
Kathryn Hodgkinson
The Hockaday School
Peter Hoffenberg
University of Hawaii, Manoa
Blair Holmes
Brigham Young University
Mary Hovanec
Cuyahoga Community College
Scott Howlett
Saddleback Community College
Kailai Huang
Massachusetts College of Liberal Arts
J. Sanders Huguenin
University of Science and Arts of Oklahoma
Richard Hume
Washington State University
Carol Sue Humphrey
Oklahoma Baptist University
Alfred Hunt
State University of New York
Raymond Hylton
J. Sergeant Reynolds Community College
Phyllis Jestice
University of Southern Mississippi, Hattiesburg
Cheryl Johnson-Odim
Loyola University
Kimberley Jones-de Oliveira
Long Island University
Jonathan Judaken
University of Memphis
Alan Karras
University of California, Berkeley
Thomas Kay
Wheaton College
Charles Keller
Pittsburgh State University
Winston Kinsey
Appalachian State University
Cengiz Kirli
Purdue University
Paul Knoll
University of Southern California
Keith Knuuti
University of Hawaii, Hilo
Kenneth Koons
Virginia Military Institute
Cheryl Koos
California State University, Los Angeles
Cynthia Kosso
Northern Arizona University
Zoltan Kramer
Central Washington University
James Krokar
DePaul University
Glenn Lamar
University of Louisiana at Lafayette
Lisa Lane
Miracosta College
George Lankevich
Bronx Community College
Dennis Laumann
University of Memphis
Donald Layton
Indiana State University
Loyd Lee
SUNY-New Paltz
Jess LeVine
Brookdale Community College
Richard Lewis
St. Cloud State University

Yi Li
Tacoma Community College
Tony Litherland
Oklahoma Baptist University
James Long
Colorado State University
David Longfellow
Baylor University
Ben Lowe
Florida Atlantic University
Jared Ludlow
Brigham Young University, Hawaii
Herbert Luft
Pepperdine Univeristy
Lu Lui
University of Tennessee—Knoxville
Paul Madden
Hardin-Simmons University
Farid Mahdavi
San Diego State University
Dorothea A. L. Martin
Appalachian State University
Tracey Martin
Benedictine University
Ken Mason
Santa Monica College
Robert Mathews
Northshore Community College
William Maynard
Arkansas State University
Robert McCormick
University of South Carolina—Spartanburg
Jeff McEwen
Chattanooga State Technical College
Randall McGowen
University of Oregon
Adam McKeown
Columbia University
John McNeill
Georgetown University
James McSwain
Tuskegee University
Pamela McVay
Ursuline College
John Mears
Southern Methodist University
Daniel Miller
Calvin College
Monserrat Miller
Marshall University
Laura Mitchell
University of Texas, San Antonio
David Montgomery
Brigham Young University
Garth Montgomery
Radford University
George Moore
San Jose State University
Gloria Morrow
Morgan State University
David Mungello
Baylor University
Jeffrey Myers
Avila College
Peter Nayenga
Saint Cloud State University
Ruth Necheles-Jansyn
Long Island University
Marian Nelson
University of Nebraska
Janise Nuckols
Windward Community College
Deanne Nuwer
University of Southern Mississippi, Hattiesburg
Greg O'Brien
University of Southern Mississippi, Hattiesburg
Veena Talwar Oldenburg
Baruch College
Brian O'Neil
University of Southern Mississippi
Patricia O'Niell
Central Oregon Community College
Samuel Oppenheim
California State University, Stanislaus
John Oriji
California Polytechnic State University, San Luis Obispo
Anne Osborne
Rider University
James Overfield
University of Vermont
Keith Pacholl
State University of West Georgia
Melvin Page
East Tennessee State University
Loretta Pang
Kapiolani Community College
Jean Paquette
Lander University
Jotham Parsons
University of Delaware
Denis Paz
University of North Texas
Patrick Peebles
University of Missouri—Kansas City
Peter W. Petschauer
Appalachian State University
Phyllis Pobst
Arkansas State University
Jon Porter
Franklin College
Clifton Potter
Lynchburg College
David Price
Santa Fe Community College
Alfonso Quiroz
Bernard M. Baruch College, CUNY
Stephen Rapp
Georgia State University
Vera Reber
Shippensburg University
John Reid
Georgia Southern University
Thomas Renna
Saginaw Valley State University
Diana Reynolds
Point Loma Nazarene University
Douglas Reynolds
Georgia State University
Ira Rice
Ball State University
Cheryl Riggs
California State University—San Bernardino
John Ritter
Chemeketa Community College
Bill Rodner
Tidewater Community College, Virginia Beach
Dan Russell
Springfield College
Eric Rust
Baylor University
John Ryan
Kansas City Kansas Community College
William Schell
Murray State University
Daryl Schuster
University of Central Florida
Jane Scimeca
Brookdale Community College
Gary Scudder
Georgia Perimiter College
Kimberly Sebold
University of Maine, Presque Isle
Tara Sethia
California State University, Pomona
Howard Shealy
Kennesaw State College
Nancy Shoemaker
University of Connecticut, Storrs

MaryAnn Sison
University of Southern Mississippi, Hattiesburg
Jonathan Skaff
Shippensburg University
David Smith
California State Polytechnic University, Pomona
Michael Smith
Purdue University
Roland Spickerman
University of Detroit—Mercy
Wendy St. Jean
Springfield College
Michelle Staley
East Mississippi Community College
Tracy Steele
Sam Houston State University
Richard Steigmann-Gall
Kent State University, Kent
John Steinberg
Georgia Southern University
Heather Streets
Washington State University
Laichen Sun
California State University, Fullerton
Roshanna Sylvester
California State University, Fullerton
John Thornton
Millersville University
Robert Tignor
Princeton University
James Tueller
Brigham Young University, Hawaii
Kirk Tyvela
Ohio University
Sandra Wagner-Wright
University of Hawaii, Hilo
Jeff Wasserstrom
Indiana University—Bloomington
Watrous-Schlesinger
Washington State University, Pullman
Theodore Weeks
Southern Illinois University
Robert Wenke
University of Washington
Sally West
Truman State University
Sherri West
Brookdale Community College
Scott Wheeler
West Point
Joe Whitehorne
Lord Fairfax Community College
S. Jonathan Wiesen
Southern Illinois University, Carbondale
Anne Will
Skagit Valley Community College
Richard Williams
Washington State University
Allen Wittenborn
San Diego State University
David Wittner
Utica College
William Wood
Point Loma Nazarene University
John Woods
University of Chicago
John Voll
Georgetown University
Anand Yang
University of Utah
Ping Yao
California State University, Los Angeles
C. K. Yoon
James Madison University
Herb Zettl
Springfield College

PART III

THE POSTCLASSICAL ERA, 500 TO 1000 C.E.

The postclassical era was a period of major readjustment for societies throughout the eastern hemisphere. The early centuries C.E. brought turbulence and instability to classical societies in China, India, southwest Asia, and the Mediterranean basin. Most of the classical empires collapsed under the strain of internal power struggles, external invasions, or a combination of the two. During the postclassical era the settled societies of the eastern hemisphere underwent political, social, economic, and cultural change that would shape their experiences over the long term. Indeed, the influence of the postclassical era continues to the present day.

The first task that settled societies faced in the postclassical era was the need to restore political and social order. They went about this task in very different ways. In the eastern Mediterranean the eastern half of the Roman empire survived as the Byzantine empire—the only empire that outlasted the difficulties of the late classical era—but underwent political and social reorganization in order to deal with external pressures. In southwest Asia, Arab conquerors inspired by the recently founded Islamic faith overcame the Sasanid empire of Persia. In China the Sui and Tang dynasties restored centralized imperial authority after almost four centuries of rule by competing regional kingdoms and nomadic conquerors. In India, by contrast, centralized imperial rule did not return: authority devolved instead to a series of regional kingdoms, some of them quite large. In western Europe centralized imperial rule returned only for a brief moment during the eighth and ninth centuries under the Carolingian empire. Economic difficulties and new rounds of invasions, however, brought down the empire and encouraged devolution of authority to local rulers: the result was the development of a decentralized political order in western Europe. In different ways, then, all the settled societies of the eastern hemisphere embarked upon a quest for political and social order during the centuries after the collapse of the classical empires.

The reestablishment of political and social order enabled postclassical societies to revive networks of long-distance trade and participate more actively in processes of cross-cultural communication and exchange. As a result, the postclassical era was a time of rapid economic growth in most of the eastern hemisphere. The volume of long-distance trade increased dramatically, and manufacturers began to produce goods explicitly for export rather than local consumption. Meanwhile, increased trade facilitated biological and technological as well as commercial exchanges: agricultural crops migrated far beyond the lands of their origin, and improved techniques of irrigation and cultivation spread through much of Eurasia. New crops and improved agricultural techniques led to enlarged harvests and enriched diets particularly in China, India, and southwest Asia.

As agricultural production increased, so did human population. Growing numbers of people devoted their efforts to trade and manufacturing rather than cultivation. China, India, and the eastern Mediterranean region were especially prominent sites for the production of textiles, ceramics, and metal goods. Increased trade and manufacturing activity encouraged a remarkable round of technological invention and innovation. The magnetic compass, printing technologies, and gunpowder, for example, first appeared in postclassical China and then diffused to other lands. These inventions and others of the era have profoundly influenced the course of human history since their first appearance.

The postclassical era was also crucially important for the formation and development of cultural and religious traditions. Islam first appeared during the postclassical era, and it soon became the cultural and religious foundation of an expansive empire stretching from north Africa to northern India. Buddhism expanded beyond the Indian subcontinent and central Asia, attracting converts in China, Korea, Japan, and southeast Asia. Christianity was the official faith of the Byzantine empire, where the Eastern Orthodox church emerged and gave shape to a distinctive form of Christianity. Orthodox missionaries also spread their faith to formerly pagan lands throughout much of eastern Europe and Russia. Farther west, Christianity spread from the Mediterranean basin to western and northern Europe, where papal leadership guided the emergence of the Roman Catholic church. For a millennium and more, Roman Catholic Christianity served as the foundation for cultural unity in the politically disunited world of western and northern Europe. Meanwhile, quite apart from the expansion of religious faiths, the postclassical era also witnessed the spread of literacy and formal education throughout much of the eastern hemisphere.

The empires and regional states of the postclassical era disappeared long ago, but the social, economic, and cultural legacies of the age are noticeable even today. Long-distance trade surged in postclassical times and helped to structure economic and social development throughout much of the eastern hemisphere. Even more notable, perhaps, religious and cultural traditions continue to flourish in lands where they first attracted converts in postclassical times. In some ways, then, the postclassical age survives even in the modern world.

A sixth-century icon depicting an enthroned Virgin Mary and infant Jesus attended by angels and saints.

CHAPTER 13

THE COMMONWEALTH OF BYZANTIUM

According to the Byzantine historian Procopius, two Christian monks from Persia set out on a momentous journey about the middle of the sixth century C.E. The result of their travels was the introduction of high-quality silk production to the eastern Mediterranean. Although local crafts workers had long produced coarse fabrics from the cocoons of wild silkworms, fine silks had come to the Mediterranean only from China, where manufacturers closely guarded both their carefully bred strains of silkworms and the complex technology that yielded high-quality textiles. Mediterranean consumers did not obtain silk directly from Chinese producers but, rather, through intermediaries subject to the Sasanid empire of Persia.

According to Procopius's account, the two Christian monks observed the techniques of silk production during the course of a mission to China. Upon departure they hollowed out their walking staffs and filled them with silkworm eggs, which they smuggled out of China, through their native land of Persia, and into the Byzantine empire.

The monks' motives are unknown. Perhaps they resented Sasanid religious policies favoring Zoroastrians and sought to aid Christians in the Byzantine empire. Perhaps they hoped to receive a handsome reward for their efforts. Whatever their motives may have been, though, it is certain that the monks by themselves could not have introduced a full-blown silk industry to Byzantium. The production of fine, Chinese-style silks required more than a few silkworm eggs. It called also for understanding of sophisticated technologies and elaborate procedures that must have reached the Byzantine empire by several different routes. Thus it seems that Procopius simplified a complex story by focusing attention on the monks.

In any case, Byzantine crafts workers soon learned how to breed silkworms, feed them mulberry leaves, unravel their cocoons, and produce high-quality silk fabrics. By the late sixth century, Byzantine silks matched the quality of Chinese products. Mediterranean consumers no longer relied on Chinese producers and Persian intermediaries, and local production of high-quality silk greatly strengthened the Byzantine economy. Thus Procopius's anonymous monks participated in a momentous transfer of technology between distant lands. Their efforts contributed to the vibrance of Byzantine society, and their story highlights the significance of cross-cultural interactions during the postclassical era.

During the centuries after 200 C.E., most of the classical societies faced a series of problems—epidemic disease, declining population, economic contraction, political turmoil, social unrest, and military threats from outside—that brought about their collapse. Only in the eastern Mediterranean did a classical empire survive. The eastern half of the Roman empire, known as the Byzantine empire, withstood the various problems that brought down other classical societies and survived for almost a millennium after the collapse of the western Roman empire in the fifth century C.E.

The Byzantine empire did not reconstitute the larger Mediterranean society of classical times. The Roman empire had dominated an integrated Mediterranean basin; the Byzantine empire mostly faced a politically and culturally fragmented Mediterranean region. After the seventh century C.E., Islamic states controlled lands to the east and south of the Mediterranean, Slavic peoples dominated lands to the north, and western Europeans organized increasingly powerful states in lands to the west.

Although it was more compact than the Roman empire, the Byzantine empire was a political and economic powerhouse of the postclassical era. Until the twelfth century, Byzantine authority dominated the wealthy and productive eastern Mediterranean region. Manufactured goods from the Byzantine empire enjoyed a reputation for high quality in markets from the Mediterranean basin to India. The Byzantine empire also deeply influenced the historical development of the Slavic peoples of eastern Europe and Russia. Byzantine missionaries and diplomats introduced writing, Christianity, codified law, and sophisticated political organization into lands settled by Slavic peoples. Because Byzantine political, economic, and cultural influence stretched so far, historians often refer to it as the "Byzantine commonwealth." Just as Greek and Roman initiative brought Mediterranean lands into a larger integrated society during classical times, Byzantine policies led to the formation of a large, multicultural zone of trade, communication, interaction, and exchange in eastern Europe and the eastern Mediterranean basin during the postclassical era.

THE EARLY BYZANTINE EMPIRE

The Byzantine empire takes its name from Byzantion—latinized as Byzantium—a modest market town and fishing village that occupied a site of enormous strategic significance. Situated on a defensible peninsula and blessed with a magnificent natural harbor known as the Golden Horn, Byzantion had the potential to control the Bosporus, the strait of water leading from the Black Sea to the Sea of Marmara and beyond to the Dardanelles, the Aegean Sea, and the Mediterranean. Apart from its maritime significance, Byzantion also offered convenient access to the rich lands of Anatolia, southwestern Asia, and southeastern Europe. Trade routes linked Byzantion to ports throughout the Mediterranean basin.

Because of its strategic value, the Roman emperor Constantine designated Byzantion as the site of a new imperial capital, which he named Constantinople ("city of Constantine"). He built the new capital partly because the eastern Mediterranean was the wealthier and more productive part of the Roman empire and partly because relocation enabled the imperial court to maintain close watch over both the Sasanid empire in Persia and the Germanic peoples who lived along the lower stretches of the Danube River. The imperial government moved to Constantinople in 340 C.E., and the new capital rapidly reached metropolitan dimensions. By the late fourth century, it was the most important political and military center of the eastern Roman empire, and it soon became the dominant economic and commercial center in the eastern Mediterranean basin. The city kept the name Constantinople until 1453 C.E., when it fell to the Ottoman Turks, who renamed it Istanbul. By convention, however, historians refer to the realm governed from Constantinople between the fifth and fifteenth centuries C.E. as the Byzantine empire, or simply as Byzantium, in honor of the original settlement.

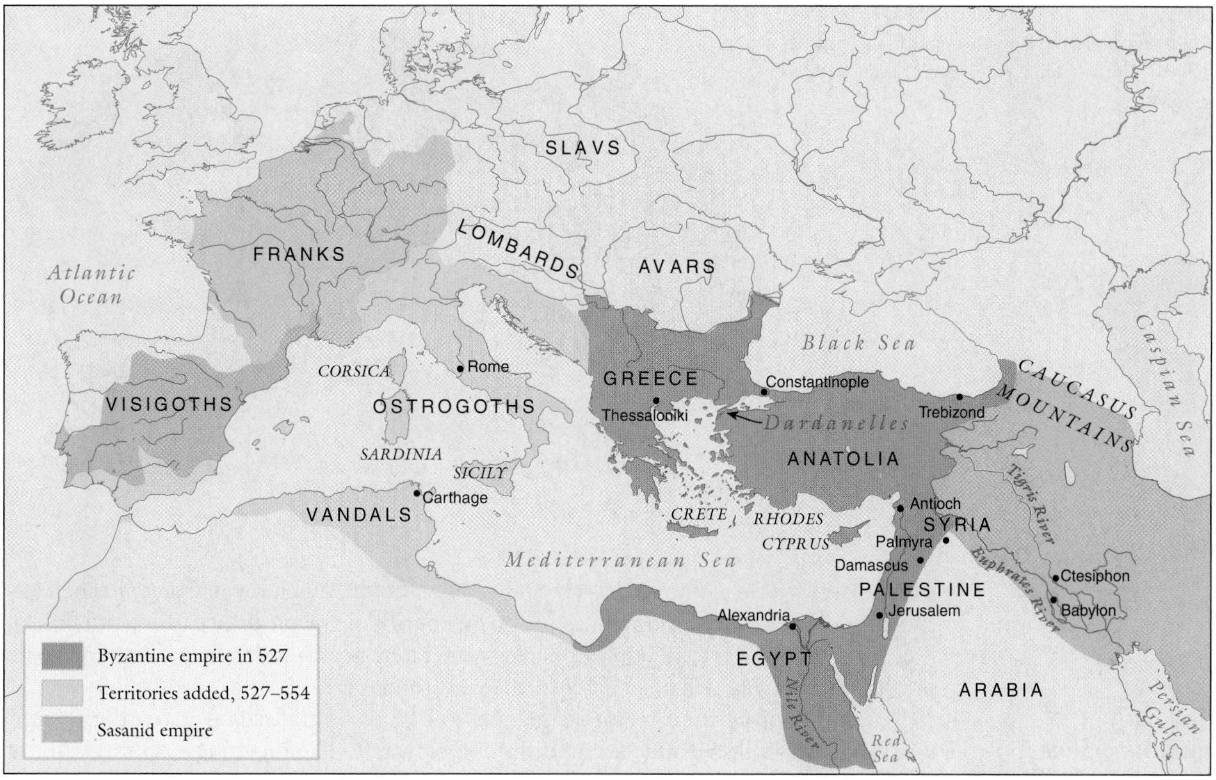

MAP [13.1]
The Byzantine empire and its neighbors, 527–554 C.E.

The Later Roman Empire and Byzantium

The Byzantine empire originated as the eastern half of the classical Roman empire, which survived the collapse of the western Roman empire in the fifth century C.E. In its early days the Byzantine empire embraced Greece, the Balkan region, Anatolia, Syria, Palestine, Egypt, and northeast Africa. Byzantine rulers occasionally expanded their boundaries, and neighboring peoples sometimes seized portions of the Byzantine empire for themselves. During the seventh and eighth centuries C.E., for example, the southern regions of the empire fell into the hands of Arab Muslim conquerors. Generally speaking, however, Byzantium figured as a major power of the eastern Mediterranean basin until the thirteenth century C.E.

The Later Roman Empire

As the western Roman empire crumbled in the fifth century C.E., the eastern half of the empire remained intact, complete with roads, communications, lines of authority, and a set of functioning imperial institutions, all inherited from Roman predecessors. Yet the early Byzantine emperors faced challenges different from those of their predecessors, and they built a state significantly different from the classical Roman empire.

The principal challenges that confronted the late Roman and early Byzantine empires were the consolidation of the dynamic Sasanid dynasty (226–641 C.E.) in Persia and the invasions of migratory peoples from the north and east. The Sasanid emperors sought to rebuild the Achaemenid empire of classical Persia, a goal that brought them into conflict with Roman forces in Mesopotamia and Syria. By the late third century, Roman armies had largely stabilized their eastern borders, but until their fall in the seventh century, the Sasanids remained the principal foreign threat to the eastern Roman empire. Germanic invasions also menaced the late Roman empire. Because they did

In 260 C.E. the Sasanid emperor Shapur I (right) captured the Roman emperor Valerian, as depicted in this cameo medallion of the fourth century.

not have adequate resources to respond strongly to the threat on all fronts, Roman authorities concentrated on maintaining the integrity of the wealthy eastern portion of the empire. As a result, migratory peoples were rarely a serious threat to Constantinople or the other heavily defended cities of the eastern empire.

The Early Byzantine State

Having secured their realm against Sasanids and migratory invaders, the Byzantine emperors built a distinctive tradition of statecraft. The most important feature of the Byzantine state was tightly centralized rule that concentrated power in the hands of a highly exalted emperor. This characteristic was noticeable already in the time of Constantine, who built his new capital to lavish standards. He filled it with libraries, museums, and artistic treasures, and he constructed magnificent marble palaces, churches, baths, and public buildings—all in an effort to create a new Rome fit for the ruler of a mighty empire.

Caesaropapism

Constantine also set a precedent by hedging his rule with an aura of divinity. As protector of the Christians and a baptized Christian himself, Constantine could not claim the divine status that some of his imperial predecessors had sought to appropriate. As the first Christian emperor, however, Constantine claimed divine favor and sanction for his rule. He intervened in theological disputes and used his political position to support views that he considered orthodox and condemn those that he regarded as heretical. Constantine initiated a policy that historians call "caesaropapism," whereby the emperor not only ruled as secular lord but also played an active and prominent role in ecclesiastical affairs.

Particularly after the sixth century, Byzantine emperors became exalted, absolute rulers. According to Roman law, emperors stood above the law: theoretically, they wielded absolute authority in political, military, judicial, financial, and religious matters. They also enjoyed the services of a large and complex bureaucracy. Indeed, its intricacy gave rise to the adjective *byzantine,* which suggests unnecessary complexity and convolution. In combination, law and bureaucracy produced an exceptionally centralized state.

The Byzantine Court

Even dress and court etiquette drew attention to the lofty status of Byzantine rulers. The emperors wore heavily bejeweled crowns and dressed in magnificent silk robes dyed a dark, rich purple—a color reserved for imperial use and strictly forbidden to those not associated with the ruling house. High officials presented themselves to the emperor as slaves, not subjects. When approaching him, they prostrated themselves three times and then ceremoniously kissed the imperial hands and feet before taking up matters of business. By the tenth century, engineers had contrived a series of mechanical devices that worked dazzling effects and impressed foreign envoys at the Byzantine court: imitation birds sang as ambassadors approached the emperor while mechanical lions roared and swished their tails. During an audience the imperial throne itself sometimes moved up and down to emphasize the awesome splendor of the emperor.

Justinian and His Legacy

Justinian and Theodora

The most important of the early Byzantine emperors was Justinian (527–565 C.E.), an energetic and tireless worker known to his subjects as "the sleepless emperor," who profoundly influenced the development of the Byzantine empire with the aid of his ambitious wife Theodora. The imperial couple came from obscure origins: Justinian was born into a Macedonian peasant family, and Theodora, the daughter of a bear keeper in the circus, worked as a striptease artist before meeting the future emperor. Yet both Justinian and Theodora were intelligent, strong willed, and disciplined. Thanks to these qualities, Justinian received an excellent education, found a position in the imperial bureaucracy, and soon mastered the intricacies of Byzantine finance. Theodora proved to be a sagacious advisor: she offered Justinian advice on sensitive political, diplomatic, and theological issues, and she contributed to the formation of a grand imperial court.

Like Constantine, Justinian lavished resources on the imperial capital. During the early years of his rule, riots against high taxes had destroyed much of Constantinople. After Theodora persuaded him to deploy the imperial army and quash the disturbances, Justinian embarked on an ambitious construction program that thoroughly remade the city. The most notable building erected during this campaign was the church of Hagia Sophia, a magnificent domed structure that later became a mosque and a museum and that ranks as one of the world's most important examples of Christian architecture. Visitors marveled at the church's enormous dome, which they likened to the heavens encircling the earth, and they expressed awe at the gold, silver, gems, precious stones, and thousands of lamps that decorated and illuminated Hagia Sophia. Over time, the church even acquired a reputation for working miraculous cures: its columns and doors reportedly healed the illnesses of people who stood beside them or rubbed against them.

Justinian's Code

Justinian's most significant political contribution was his codification of Roman law. The origins of Roman law go back to the time of the kings of Rome, and legal scholars worked to systematize Roman law during the Roman republic and the early empire. Almost immediately upon taking the throne, Justinian ordered a systematic review of Roman law that was more thorough than any that had taken place before. On the basis of this work, he issued the *Corpus iuris civilis (Body of the Civil Law)*, which immediately won recognition as the definitive codification of Roman law. Later emperors updated Roman law by adding new provisions, but Justinian's code continued to serve as a source of legal inspiration. Through Justinian's code, for example, Roman law influenced civil law codes throughout much of western Europe.

Belisarius and Byzantine Conquests

Justinian's most ambitious venture was his effort to reconquer the western Roman empire from Germanic peoples and reestablish Roman authority throughout the Mediterranean basin. Beginning in 533 he sent his brilliant general Belisarius on military campaigns that returned Italy, Sicily, northwestern Africa, and southern Spain to imperial hands. By the end of his reign in 565, Justinian had reconstituted a good portion of the classical Roman empire.

Justinian's accomplishment, however, did not long survive his own rule. Byzantium simply did not possess the resources to sustain Belisarius's conquests. Reconstitution of

Justinian wears imperial purple robes in this mosaic from the church of San Vitale in Ravenna, which depicts him in the company of ecclesiastical, military, and court officials.

the Roman empire would have required a long-term occupation of reconquered regions and a costly reassertion of imperial authority. Yet Byzantine forces were unable to hold Rome itself for very long, and the city of Ravenna on Italy's Adriatic coast became the headquarters of Byzantine authority in the western Mediterranean. As a result, Ravenna possesses magnificent Byzantine art and architecture. But Justinian's dream of restoring Roman authority throughout the Mediterranean basin soon faded.

Indeed, Justinian's efforts clearly showed that the classical Roman empire was beyond recovery. While Justinian devoted his attention to the western Mediterranean, the Sasanids threatened Byzantium from the east and Slavic peoples approached from the north. Justinian's successors had no choice but to withdraw their resources from the western Mediterranean and redeploy them in the east. Even though Belisarius's reconquest of the western Roman empire was a spectacular military accomplishment, it was also something of an anachronism, since the lands of the eastern and western Mediterranean had already begun to follow different historical trajectories.

Islamic Conquests and Byzantine Revival

After the seventh century C.E., the emergence of Islam and the development of a powerful and expansive Islamic state (topics discussed in chapter 14) posed a serious challenge to Byzantium. Inspired by their Islamic faith, Arab peoples conquered the Sasanid empire and overran large portions of the Byzantine empire as well. By the mid-seventh century, Byzantine Syria, Palestine, Egypt, and north Africa had fallen

The interior of the church of Hagia Sophia ("Holy Wisdom"), built by Justinian and transformed into a mosque in the fifteenth century. The dome rises almost 60 meters (197 feet) above the floor, and its windows allow abundant light to enter the massive structure.

under Islamic rule. During the late seventh and early eighth centuries, Islamic forces threatened the heart of the empire and subjected Constantinople itself to prolonged siege (in 674–678 and again in 717–718). Byzantium resisted this northern thrust of Islam partly because of military technology. Byzantine forces used a weapon known as "Greek fire"—a devastating incendiary weapon compounded of sulphur, lime, and petroleum—which they launched at both the fleets and the ground forces of the invaders. Greek fire burned even when floating on water and thus created a serious hazard when deployed around wooden ships. On land it caused panic among enemy forces, since it was very difficult to extinguish and often burned troops to death. As a result of this defensive effort, the Byzantine empire retained its hold on Anatolia, Greece, and the Balkan region.

Imperial Organization

Though much reduced by the Islamic conquests, the Byzantine empire was more compact and manageable after the eighth century than was the far-flung realm of Justinian. Byzantine rulers responded to the challenge of Islam with political and social adjustments that strengthened the empire that remained in their hands. The most important innovation was the reorganization of Byzantine society under the *theme* system, which Byzantine rulers had tentatively experimented with during earlier periods of hostility with Sasanid Persia. The *theme* system placed an imperial province *(theme)* under the jurisdiction of a general, who assumed responsibility for both its

Illustration in a manuscript depicts Byzantine naval forces turning Greek fire on their Arab enemies.

military defense and its civil administration. Generals received their appointments from the imperial government, which closely supervised their activities to prevent decentralization of power and authority. Generals recruited armies from the ranks of free peasants, who received allotments of land in exchange for military service. The armies proved to be effective military forces, and the system as a whole strengthened the class of free peasants, which in turn solidified Byzantium's agricultural economy. The *theme* system enabled Byzantine forces to mobilize quickly and resist further Islamic advances and also undergirded the political order and social organization of the empire from the eighth through the twelfth century.

Indeed, strengthened by the *theme* system, Byzantium vastly expanded its influence between the late ninth and the late eleventh century. During the tenth century Byzantine forces shored up defenses in Anatolia and reconquered Syria from Arab Muslims. During the reign of Basil II (976–1025 C.E.), known as "Basil the Bulgar-Slayer," Byzantine armies turned west and crushed the neighboring Bulgars, who had built a large and expansive kingdom in the Balkans. After his victory at the battle of Kleidion in 1014 C.E., Basil reportedly commanded his forces to blind fourteen thousand Bulgarian survivors, though he spared one eye in a few who then guided the others home. By the mid-eleventh century the Byzantine empire embraced lands from Syria and Armenia in the east to southern Italy in the west, from the Danube River in the north to Cyprus and Crete in the south. Byzantine expansion brought in so much wealth that Basil was able to waive the collection of taxes for two years. Once again, Byzantium dominated the eastern Mediterranean.

Byzantium and Western Europe

Tensions between Byzantium and Western European States

While they went to war with their Arab Muslim and pagan Slavic neighbors, Byzantines also experienced tense ecclesiastical and political relations with their Christian counterparts in the western Mediterranean. The Christian church of Constantinople conducted its affairs in Greek and bowed to the will of the caesaropapist emperors, whereas the Christian church of Rome conducted its affairs in Latin and rejected imperial claims to oversee ecclesiastical matters. Ecclesiastical authorities in Byzantium regarded Roman Christians as poorly educated and uncouth. Church leaders in Rome considered their Byzantine counterparts subtle and learned but insincere and insufficiently wary of heresy.

Political grievances also strained relations between Byzantium and western European lands. During the fifth and sixth centuries, imperial authorities could do little more than watch as Germanic peoples established successor states to the western Roman empire. Visigoths, Vandals, Franks, and others imposed their rule on lands that Byzantine emperors regarded as their rightful inheritance. Worse yet, some of the upstart powers claimed imperial authority for themselves. In 800, for example, the Frankish ruler Charlemagne received an imperial crown from the pope in Rome, thereby directly challenging Byzantine claims to imperial authority over western lands. Charlemagne's empire soon dissolved, but in 962 Otto of Saxony lodged his own claim to rule as emperor over the western lands of the former Roman empire. Adding injury to insult, Otto then attacked lands in southern Italy that had been in Byzantine possession since the days of Justinian.

Liudprand of Cremona

The tenor of relations between Byzantium and western European lands emerges clearly from the report of an ambassador named Liudprand of Cremona, whom Otto sent on a diplomatic mission to Constantinople in 968. Liudprand described the Byzantine emperor as "a monstrosity of a man, a dwarf, fat-headed and with tiny mole's eyes; disfigured by a short, broad, thick beard half going gray; disgraced by a neck scarcely an inch long; piglike by reason of the big close bristles on his head." Liudprand despised Byzantine food, drink, dress, and shelter, and he denounced his diplomatic counterparts as slippery, scheming liars. He described Constantinople itself as a formerly prosperous and illustrious city that had become shabby, sleazy, and pretentious. In light of these attitudes, it is hardly surprising that Byzantium and western European lands experienced almost continuously strained relations until the fall of the Byzantine empire.

Byzantine Economy and Society

Byzantium dominated the political and military affairs of the eastern Mediterranean largely because of its strong economy. Ever since classical times, the territories embraced by the Byzantine empire had produced abundant agricultural surpluses, supported large numbers of crafts workers, and participated in trade with lands throughout the Mediterranean. The economic and social assets of the eastern Mediterranean did not disappear with the classical Roman empire. Instead, they continued to provide a solid material foundation for Byzantium, and they helped to make the Byzantine empire an economic powerhouse of the postclassical era.

Rural Economy and Society

Until its conquest by Arab forces, Egypt was the major source of grain for Byzantium. Afterward, Anatolia and the lower Danube region served as the imperial breadbasket. All these lands produced abundant harvests of wheat, which supported large populations in Constantinople, Thessaloniki, Antioch, Trebizond, and other major cities. Throughout most of Byzantium's existence, Constantinople was the largest city in Europe: between the fifth and the early thirteenth century, its population approached or exceeded one million people. Only on the basis of a reliable and productive agricultural economy was it possible for a city of this size to survive and flourish.

The Peasantry

Byzantine economy and society were strongest when the empire supported a large class of free peasants who owned small plots of land. Besides serving as the backbone of the Byzantine military system, free peasants cultivated their land intensively in hopes of improving their families' fortunes. As in other societies, however, wealthy individuals

Peasants—probably sharecroppers—receive seeds and tend to vineyards in this painting from a Byzantine manuscript.

and families sought to accumulate land, the principal source of wealth in Byzantium as elsewhere. Especially in the early centuries of the Byzantine empire, wealthy cultivators ran large estates and supervised the peasantry as a dependent class. Peasants did not become slaves, but neither did they remain entirely free. Sometimes they were bound to the land, forbidden to depart without permission of their lords. Other times they worked under sharecropping arrangements, whereby landlords contracted landless peasants to cultivate their lands in exchange for a large portion of the yield. Rarely did sharecroppers accumulate enough wealth to gain their independence: often they worked the same holdings for years—or for life—on terms set by the landlords.

The invasions of the sixth and seventh centuries broke up many large estates and afforded peasants an opportunity to rebuild small holdings. The *theme* system strengthened the free peasantry by making land available to those who performed military service. The imperial government also made periodic efforts to support free peasants and prevent wealthy landowners from gaining control over their lands. During the sixth, eighth, and tenth centuries in particular, Byzantine authorities limited the accumulation of land by wealthy classes and thereby strengthened the peasantry. Over the long term, however, wealthy landowners built ever larger estates. From the eleventh century onward, they transformed the peasants into an increasingly dependent class, and by the thirteenth century free peasants accounted for only a small portion of the rural population.

Decline of the Free Peasantry

Quite apart from its social effects, the accumulation of landholdings had important implications for financial and military affairs. Large estates did not contribute to imperial tax coffers at the rate of small peasants' holdings, since wealthy landowners had the influence to obtain concessions and exemptions. Moreover, the decline of the free peasantry diminished the pool of recruits available for service in military forces organized under the *theme* system. Large landowners raised forces from their estates, but they often deployed them to advance their own interests rather than those of the imperial government. Concentration of land and rural resources worked against the financial interests of the central government, and it caused political, military, and economic difficulties for the Byzantine state during the last three centuries of its existence.

Industry and Trade

In spite of social and economic problems, Byzantium remained a wealthy land. Byzantine prosperity derived both from the empire's productive capacity and from the importance of Constantinople as a center of trade.

Manufacturing Enterprises

Constantinople was already a major site of crafts and industry in classical times, and it became even more important as capital of the Byzantine empire. The city was home to many artisans and crafts workers, not to mention thousands of imperial officials and bureaucrats. Byzantine crafts workers enjoyed a reputation especially for their glassware, linen and woolen textiles, gems, jewelry, and fine work in gold and silver.

By the late sixth century, after the arrival of silkworms in monks' walking staffs and no doubt by other routes as well, crafts workers had added high-quality silk textiles to the list of products manufactured in the Byzantine empire. Silk was a most

A manuscript illustration depicts one Byzantine woman weaving cloth (left), while another spins thread (right). Both women veil their hair for modesty. Women workers were prominent in Byzantine textile production.

important addition to the economy, and Byzantium became the principal supplier of this fashionable fabric to lands in the Mediterranean basin. The silk industry was so important to the Byzantine economy that the government closely supervised every step in its production and sale. Regulations allowed individuals to participate in only one activity—such as weaving, dyeing, or sales—to prevent the creation of a monopoly in the industry by a few wealthy or powerful entrepreneurs.

Trade

Trade also helped to sustain the Byzantine economy. Situated astride routes going east and west as well as north and south, Constantinople served as the main clearinghouse for trade in the western part of Eurasia. The merchants of Constantinople maintained direct commercial links with manufacturers and merchants in central Asia, Russia, Scandinavia, northern Europe, and the lands of the Black Sea and the Mediterranean basin. Even after the early Islamic conquests, Byzantine merchants dealt regularly with their Muslim counterparts in Persia, Syria, Palestine, and Egypt except during periods of outright war between Byzantium and Islamic states. Byzantium dominated trade to such an extent that trading peoples recognized the Byzantine gold coin, the *bezant,* as the standard currency of the Mediterranean basin for more than half a millennium, from the sixth through the twelfth centuries.

Byzantium drew enormous wealth simply from the control of trade and the levying of customs duties on merchandise that passed through its lands. More important, Byzantium served as the western anchor of a Eurasian trading network that revived the silk roads of classical times. Silk and porcelain came to Constantinople from China, spices from India and southeast Asia. Carpets arrived from Persia, woolen textiles from western Europe, and timber, furs, honey, amber, and slaves came from Russia and Scandinavia. Byzantine subjects consumed some commodities from distant lands, but they redistributed most merchandise, often after adding to its value by further processing—by fashioning jewelry out of gems imported from India, for example, or by dyeing raw woolen cloth imported from western Europe.

The Organization of Trade

Banks and business partnerships helped to fuel Byzantine trade. Banks advanced loans to individuals seeking to launch business ventures and thus made trade possible even when merchants did not personally possess large supplies of liquid wealth. Byzantine merchants often formed partnerships, which allowed them to pool their resources and limit their risks. Neither banking nor partnership was an altogether new technique: both had origins in classical Mediterranean business practices. Yet Byzantine businessmen made much more extensive use than their predecessors had of banking and cooperative partnerships, which provided both support and stimulus for a dynamic commercial economy.

Urban Life

Constantinople had no rival among Byzantine cities. Subjects of the Byzantine empire referred to it simply as "the City." The heart of the City was the imperial palace, which

A manuscript illustration from the ninth century depicts Byzantine shipbuilders at work.

Sources from the Past

The Wealth and Commerce of Constantinople

The Spanish rabbi Benjamin of Tudela traveled throughout Europe, north Africa, and southwest Asia between 1165 and 1173 C.E. He may have ventured as far as India, and he mentioned both India and China in his travel account. His main purpose was to record the conditions of Jewish communities, but he also described the many lands and about three hundred cities that he visited. His travels took place during an era of political decline for the Byzantine empire, yet he still found Constantinople a flourishing and prosperous city.

The circumference of the city of Constantinople is eighteen miles; half of it is surrounded by the sea, and half by land, and it is situated upon two arms of the sea, one coming from the sea of Russia [the Black Sea], and one from the sea of Sepharad [the Mediterranean].

All sorts of merchants come here from the land of Babylon, from the land of Shinar [Mesopotamia], from Persia, Media [western Iran], and all the sovereignty of the land of Egypt, from the land of Canaan [Palestine], and the empire of Russia, from Hungary, Patzinakia [Ukraine], Khazaria [southern Russia], and the land of Lombardy [northern Italy] and Sepharad [Spain].

Constantinople is a busy city, and merchants come to it from every country by sea or land, and there is none like it in the world except Baghdad, the great city of Islam. In Constantinople is the church of Hagia Sophia, and the seat of the pope of the Greeks, since Greeks do not obey the pope of Rome. There are also as many churches as there are days of the year. . . . And in this church [Hagia Sophia] there are pillars of gold and silver, and lamps of silver and gold more than a man can count.

Close to the walls of the palace is also a place of amusement belonging to the emperor, which is called the Hippodrome, and every year on the anniversary of the birth of Jesus the emperor gives a great entertainment there. And in that place men from all the races of the world come before the emperor and empress with jugglery and without jugglery, and they introduce lions, leopards, bears, and wild asses, and they engage them in combat with one another; and the same thing is done with birds. No entertainment like this is to be found in any other land. . . .

From every part of the Byzantine empire tribute is brought here every year, and they fill strongholds with garments of silk, purple, and gold. Like unto these storehouses and this wealth there is nothing in the whole world to be found. It is said that the tribute of the city amounts every year to 20,000 gold pieces, derived both from the rents of shops and markets and from the tribute of merchants who enter by sea or land.

The Greek inhabitants are very rich in gold and precious stones, and they go clothed in garments of silk and gold embroidery, and they ride horses and look like princes. Indeed, the land is very rich in all cloth stuffs and in bread, meat, and wine.

Wealth like that of Constantinople is not to be found in the whole world. Here also are men learned in all the books of the Greeks, and they eat and drink, every man under his vine and his fig-tree.

SOURCE: Benjamin of Tudela. *The Itinerary of Benjamin of Tudela.* Trans. by M. N. Adler. London: H. Frowde, 1907. (Translation slightly modified.)

How is it possible to account for the prosperity that Benjamin of Tudela found in Constantinople?

employed twenty thousand workers as palace staff. Peacocks strutted through gardens filled with sculptures and fountains. Most famous was a gold fountain in the shape of a pineapple that spouted wine for imperial guests.

Housing in Constantinople

Aristocrats maintained enormous palaces that included courtyards, reception halls, libraries, chapels, and quarters for members of the extended family as well as servants and slaves. Women lived in separate apartments and did not receive male visitors from outside the household. Indeed, women often did not participate in banquets and parties, especially when wine flowed freely or when the affairs were likely to become so festive that they could compromise a woman's honor.

The less privileged classes of Constantinople occupied less splendid dwellings. Artisans and crafts workers usually lived in rooms above their shops, while clerks and government officials lived in multistory apartment buildings. Workers and the poor occupied dangerous and rickety tenements, sharing kitchens and sanitary facilities with their neighbors.

Attractions of Constantinople

Even for the poor, though, the City had its attractions. As the heir to Rome, Constantinople was a city of baths, which were sites of relaxation and exercise as well as hygienic bathing. Taverns and restaurants offered settings for social gatherings—checkers, chess, and dice games were especially popular activities at taverns—and theaters provided entertainment in the form of song, dance, and striptease. Mass entertainment took place in the Hippodrome, a large stadium adjacent to the imperial palace. There Byzantine subjects watched athletic matches, contests between wild animals, and circuses featuring clowns, jugglers, acrobats, and dwarfs.

Greens and Blues

Most popular of the City's pastimes were the chariot races that took place in the Hippodrome. Spectators' passions for chariot teams ran high, and until the seventh century they often contributed to public disturbances. Racing fans formed two factions—the Greens and the Blues—that pursued their rivalry well beyond the Hippodrome. Greens and Blues frequently fought in the streets and constantly sought to influence imperial officials to favor one group over the other. On one occasion, Greens and Blues united and mounted a serious popular uprising against the high taxes imposed by Justinian. In 532 they seized the Hippodrome and proclaimed a new emperor. Belisarius's army quelled the disturbance, but only after killing thousands of rioters. The rebellion left Constantinople in shambles, and Justinian took the opportunity to rebuild the city on a lavish scale. By the late seventh century, the rivalry between Greens and Blues had faded. The parties remained, but they increasingly took on the character of civic societies, and leaders of the two groups became respected officials at the imperial court.

CLASSICAL HERITAGE AND ORTHODOX CHRISTIANITY

The first Christian emperor of the Roman empire gave both his name and his faith to Constantinople. Like the Byzantine state, however, Byzantine Christianity developed along distinctive lines, and it became a faith different from the early Christianity of the Roman empire. The philosophy and literature of classical Greece had a much deeper influence in Byzantium than in western Europe, and the classical legacy helped to shape Byzantine education and cultural development as well as Orthodox Christianity. Byzantine church leaders disagreed with their western counterparts on matters of doctrine, ritual, and church authority. By the mid-eleventh century, differences between the eastern and western churches had become so great that their leaders formally divided Mediterranean Christianity into the Eastern Orthodox and Roman Catholic churches.

The Legacy of Classical Greece

Although local inhabitants spoke Greek, the official language of early Constantinople was Latin, the language of Rome. The connection between Byzantium and Rome was apparent in Justinian's code of laws, which appeared in Latin. After the sixth century, however, Greek replaced Latin as the language of government in the Byzantine empire. Byzantine scholars often did not learn to read Latin, and they drew intellectual inspiration from the New Testament (originally composed in Greek) and the philosophy and literature of classical Greece rather than classical Rome.

Byzantine Education

The legacy of classical Greece was especially noticeable in Byzantine education. An educational system was necessary because of the large bureaucracy that administered the empire: government machinery called for large numbers of literate and intelligent individuals. Byzantine aristocrats often hired tutors to provide private instruction for their children, girls as well as boys. But the bureaucratic workforce emerged mostly from a state-organized school system that offered a primary education in reading, writing, and grammar, followed by studies of classical Greek literature, philosophy, and science.

Although most peasants and many urban workers had no formal education, basic literacy was widespread in Byzantine society. Alongside the bureaucrats, Byzantine merchants, manufacturers, clergy, and military personnel usually had at least a primary education. At the pinnacle of the state educational system was a school of higher learning in Constantinople that offered advanced instruction in law, medicine, and philosophy. This school functioned almost continuously from its founding in 425 C.E. until the end of the Byzantine empire more than one thousand years later in 1453.

Byzantine Scholarship

Like the educational system, Byzantine scholarship also reflected the cultural legacy of classical Greece. Byzantine scholars concentrated on the humanities—literature, history, and philosophy—rather than on the natural sciences or medicine. They produced commentaries on Homer, Plato, Aristotle, and other prominent figures, and their works served as textbooks studied in schools alongside writings from classical times. Byzantines with a literary education considered themselves the direct heirs of classical Greece, and they went to great lengths to preserve and transmit the classical legacy. Indeed, almost all literary and philosophical works of classical Greece that survive have come down to the present in copies made between the tenth and twelfth centuries in the Byzantine empire.

The Byzantine Church

Church and State

The most distinctive feature of Byzantine Christianity was its close relationship with the imperial government. From the time of Constantine on, caesaropapist emperors participated actively in religious and theological matters. Constantine himself intervened in theological debates, even when the issues at stake had little or no direct political implication. In 325 C.E., for example, Constantine organized the Council of Nicaea, which brought together bishops, spokesmen, and leaders from all the important Christian churches in order to consider the views of the Arians. Followers of a priest from Alexandria named Arius (250–336 C.E.), the Arians taught that Jesus had been a mortal human being and that he was a creation of God rather than a divine being coeternal with God. Yet many Christian theologians held to the contrary: that in a unique and mysterious way Jesus was both a mortal human being and a manifestation of God himself, that Jesus simultaneously possessed fully human and fully divine natures. Although he originally favored Arian views, Constantine came to accept the alternative and personally attended sessions of the Council of Nicaea in order to support it. His presence encouraged the council to endorse his preferred view as orthodox and to condemn Arianism as heresy.

Throughout Byzantine history the emperors treated the church as a department of state. They appointed individuals to serve as patriarch of Constantinople—the highest ecclesiastical official in the Byzantine church, counterpart of the pope in

Rome—and they instructed patriarchs, bishops, and priests to deliver sermons that supported imperial policy and encouraged obedience to imperial authorities. This caesaropapism was a source of constant conflict between imperial and ecclesiastical authorities, and it also had the potential to generate large-scale dissent and protest when imperial views clashed with those of the larger society.

Iconoclasm

The most divisive ecclesiastical policy implemented by Byzantine emperors was iconoclasm, inaugurated by Emperor Leo III (reigned 717–741 C.E.). By the time of Leo's rule, Byzantium had a long tradition of producing icons—paintings of Jesus, saints, and other figures of religious significance—many of which were splendid works of art. For most theologians these icons served a useful purpose in that they inspired the popular imagination and encouraged reverence for holy personages. Leo, however, became convinced that the veneration of religious images was sinful, tantamount to the worship of physical idols. In 726 C.E. he embarked on the policy of iconoclasm (which literally means "the breaking of icons"), destroying religious images and prohibiting their use in churches. The policy immediately sparked protests and riots throughout the empire, since icons were extremely popular among the laity. Debates about iconoclasm raged in Byzantium for more than a century. Only in 843 did the iconoclasts abandon their efforts. Meanwhile, the controversy demonstrated once again the willingness of Byzantine emperors to involve themselves directly in religious and theological matters.

In its theology, Byzantine Christianity reflected the continuing influence of classical Greek philosophy. Christianity had originally emerged from Jewish sources. As it attracted adherents in the Roman empire, theologians sought ways to harmonize

This illustration from a psalter prepared about 900 C.E. depicts an iconoclast whitewashing an image of Jesus painted on a wall.

Christianity with other, long-established cultural traditions, notably Greek philosophy. A faith embracing both Christian revelation and Greek reason, they recognized, would have a powerful appeal.

Greek Philosophy and Byzantine Theology

The influence of Greek philosophy in Christian theology was especially prominent in Greek-speaking Byzantium. Theologians invested a great deal of time and intellectual energy in the examination of religious questions from a philosophical point of view. They looked to classical philosophy, for example, when seeking to understand the nature of Jesus and the extent to which he possessed both human and divine characteristics. Although these debates often became extremely technical, they illustrate the continuing influence of classical Greek philosophy. Debates about Jesus' nature represented an effort to understand Christian doctrine in light of the terms and concepts that classical philosophers had employed in their analysis of the world. A school maintained by the patriarch of Constantinople provided instruction for clergy and church officials in advanced theology of this sort. Though it differed in many ways from Mediterranean society of classical times, Byzantium built its own cultural and religious traditions on a solid classical foundation.

Monasticism and Popular Piety

Caesaropapist emperors, powerful patriarchs, and other high church officials concerned themselves with theological and ritual matters and rarely dealt directly with the lay population of the Byzantine church. For their part the Byzantine laity had little interest in fine points of theology or high-level church administration, and they positively resented policies like iconoclasm that infringed on cherished patterns of worship. For religious inspiration, the laity looked less to the church hierarchy than to the local monasteries.

Asceticism

Byzantine monasticism grew out of the efforts of devout individuals to lead especially holy lives. Drawing inspiration from early Christian ascetics in Egypt, Mesopotamia, and Persia, these individuals observed regimes of extreme asceticism and self-denial. Some abandoned society altogether and went to live in the desert or in caves as hermits. Others dedicated themselves to celibacy, fasting, and prayer. During the fifth century a few men and at least two women demonstrated their ascetic commitments by perching for years at a time atop tall pillars. St. Simeon Stylite, the first and most famous of these "pillar saints," attracted the attention of admirers from as far away as Gaul.

Byzantine Monasticism and St. Basil

Because of the extreme dedication of hermits and ascetics, disciples often gathered around them and established communities of men and women determined to follow their example. These communities became the earliest monasteries of the Byzantine church. They had few rules until St. Basil of Caesarea (329–379 C.E.), the patriarch of Constantinople during the mid-fourth century, urged them to adopt reforms that enhanced their effectiveness. In Basilian monasteries, monks and nuns gave up their personal possessions and lived communally. They obeyed the rule of elected superiors, and all community members devoted themselves to work and prayer. After the fourth century, Basilian monasticism spread rapidly throughout the Byzantine empire.

Mt. Athos

Unlike their counterparts in western Europe and other lands, Byzantine monasteries for the most part did not become centers of education, study, learning, and scholarship. Yet monasteries under the rule of St. Basil had a reputation for piety and devotion that endeared them to the Byzantine laity. Basilian monks went to great lengths in search of mystical union with God through meditation and prayer. Some employed special techniques such as controlled breathing and intensely focused gazing to bring divine illumination. Others retired to remote destinations to lead a strict

Sources from the Past

Anna Comnena on the Suppression of Bogomil Heretics

Anna Comnena (1083–1148), daughter of the Byzantine emperor Alexius I (reigned 1081–1118), wrote the Alexiad, *a laudatory history of her father's reign. In the following selection, she discusses his prosecution in 1110 of Bogomil heretics, who revived the dualist teachings of the Manichaeans. Her account makes it clear that the caesaropapist Byzantine emperors took seriously their commitment to the Orthodox church and their obligation to protect its interests.*

Later . . . there arose an extraordinary "cloud of heretics," a new hostile group, hitherto unknown to the Church . . . Apparently it was in existence before my father's time, but was unperceived (for the Bogomils' sect is most adept at feigning virtue). No worldly hairstyles are to be seen among Bogomils: their wickedness is hidden beneath cloak and cowl. Your Bogomil wears a somber look; muffled up to the nose, he walks with a stoop, quietly muttering to himself—but inside he's a ravening wolf. This unpleasant race, like a serpent lurking in its hole, was brought to the light and lured out by my father with magical incantations. . . .

The fame of the Bogomils had by now spread to all parts, for the impious sect was controlled with great cunning by a certain monk called Basil. He had twelve followers whom he called "apostles" and also dragged along with him certain female disciples, women of bad character, utterly depraved. In all quarters he made his wicked influence felt and when the evil, like some consuming fire, devoured many souls, the emperor could no longer bear it. He instituted a thorough inquiry into the heresy. . . .

. . . Alexius condemned the heretics out of hand: chorus and chorus-leader alike were to suffer death by burning. When the Bogomils had been hunted down and brought together in one place, some clung to the heresy, but others denied the charges completely, protesting strongly against their accusers and rejecting the Bogomilian heresy with scorn. . . .

The emperor glared at them and said, "Two pyres will have to be lit today. By one a cross will be planted firmly in the ground. Then a choice will be offered to all: those who are prepared to die for their Christian faith will separate themselves from the rest and take up position by the pyre with the cross; the Bogomilian adherents will be thrown on the other. Surely it is better that even Christians should die than live to be hounded down as Bogomils and offend the conscience of the majority. Go away, then, all of you, to whichever pyre you choose". . . .

A huge crowd gathered and stood all about them. Fires were then lit, burning seven times more fiercely than usual. . . . The flames leapt to the heavens. By one pyre stood the cross. Each of the condemned was given his choice, for all were to be burnt. Now that escape was clearly impossible, the orthodox to a man moved over to the pyre with the cross, truly prepared to suffer martyrdom; the godless adherents of the abominable heresy went off to the other. Just as they were about to be thrown on the flames, all the bystanders broke into mourning for the Christians; they were filled with indignation against the emperor (they did not know of his plan). But an order came from him just in time to stop the executioners. Alexius had in this way obtained firm evidence of those who were really Bogomils. The Christians, who were victims of calumny, he released after giving them much advice; the rest [i.e., the Bogomils] were committed once again to prison, but the [Bogomil] "apostles" were kept apart. Later he sent for some of these men every day and personally taught them, with frequent exhortations to abandon their abominable cult. . . . And some did change for the better and were freed from prison, but others died in their heresy, still incarcerated, although they were supplied with plentiful food and clothing.

SOURCE: Anna Comnena. *The Alexiad of Anna Comnena.* Trans. by E. R. A. Sewter. Harmondsworth: Penguin, 1969, pp. 496–505. (Translation slightly modified.)

Why did Byzantine rulers go to such lengths to suppress heresy?

existence. Most famous of the austere monasteries are those of Mt. Athos, a cold and windswept peninsula in northern Greece that has been the site of monasteries since the ninth century C.E. Since the eleventh century, monastic authorities have made Mt. Athos off-limits for all females, both human and animal, out of concern that they might inspire carnal thoughts among the monks. The strict devotion of the monks of Mt. Athos and other Basilian monasteries inspired piety among the Byzantine laity because the monks represented a religious faith more immediate and meaningful than that of the theologians and ecclesiastical bureaucrats of Constantinople.

Monks and nuns also provided social services to their communities. They provided spiritual counsel to local laity, and they organized relief efforts by bringing food and medical attention to communities struck by disasters. They won the support of the Byzantine populace, too, when they vigorously opposed the policy of iconoclasm and fought to restore icons to churches and monasteries. Tensions sometimes arose between clergy and laity because monasteries often owned extensive tracts of land, and the monks had different economic interests from the peasants who worked the land. Nevertheless, by setting examples of devotion and by tending to the needs and interests of the laity, monks helped to maintain support for their faith in the Byzantine empire.

Tensions between Eastern and Western Christianity

Byzantine Christianity developed in tension particularly with the Christian faith of western Europe. During the centuries following Constantine's legalization of Christianity, church leaders in Jerusalem, Alexandria, Antioch, Constantinople, and Rome exercised great influence in the larger Christian community. After Arab peoples conquered most of southwest Asia and introduced Islam there in the seventh century, the influence of the patriarchs in Jerusalem, Alexandria, and Antioch declined, leaving only Constantinople and Rome as the principal centers of Christian authority.

Constantinople and Rome

The tensions that developed between Constantinople and Rome mirrored political strains between Byzantine and western European societies. The specific issues that divided the two Christian communities, however, were religious and theological. One of them was the iconoclastic movement of the eighth and ninth centuries. Western theologians regarded religious images as perfectly appropriate aids to devotion and resented Byzantine claims to the contrary, whereas the iconoclasts took offense at the efforts of their Roman counterparts to have images restored in Byzantium.

In later centuries, Christian churches based in Constantinople and Rome disagreed on many other points. Some ritual and doctrinal differences concerned forms of worship and the precise wording of theological teachings—relatively minor issues that by themselves need not have caused deep division in the larger Christian community. Byzantine theologians objected, for example, to the fact that western priests shaved their beards and used unleavened instead of leavened bread when saying Mass. Other differences concerned substantive theological matters such as the precise relationship between God, Jesus, and the Holy Spirit—all regarded as manifestations of God by most Christian theologians.

Schism

Alongside these ritual and doctrinal differences, the Byzantine patriarchs and Roman popes disputed their respective rights and powers. Patriarchs argued for the autonomy of all major Christian jurisdictions, including that of Constantinople, while popes asserted the primacy of Rome as the sole seat of authority for all Christendom. Ultimately, relations became so strained that the eastern and western churches went separate ways. In 1054 C.E. the patriarch and pope mutually excommunicated each other, each refusing to recognize the other's church as properly Christian. Despite efforts at reconciliation, the resulting schism between eastern and western churches persists to the present day. In recognition of the split, historians refer to the eastern Christian church after 1054 as the Eastern Orthodox church and its western counterpart as the Roman Catholic church.

The Influence of Byzantium in Eastern Europe

Byzantines called themselves *Romaioi* ("Romans"), and aristocrats sometimes traced their lineage to ancestors who went to Constantinople with Constantine himself. Yet by about 1000 C.E., Byzantium differed profoundly from Mediterranean society of classical times. Under Roman rule the Mediterranean basin had formed a coherent political and economic unit, as trade and cultural exchanges linked all lands and peoples of the region. By the second millennium C.E., however, a dynamic society founded on the Islamic faith had seized control of the lands on the Mediterranean's southern and eastern rims, and Byzantines and western Europeans contested the northern rim. Hemmed in and increasingly pressured by Islamic and western European societies, Byzantium entered a period of decline beginning about the late eleventh century.

As its Mediterranean influence waned, however, Byzantium turned its attention to eastern Europe and Russia. Through political, commercial, and cultural relations, Byzantium decisively influenced the history of Slavic peoples. The Byzantine state itself came to an end in the fifteenth century C.E. But because of the Byzantine commonwealth—the larger collection of societies in eastern Europe and the eastern Mediterranean basin that developed under Byzantine political, economic, and cultural influence during the postclassical era—the legacy of Byzantium survives and continues to shape the lives of millions of people in Russia and eastern Europe.

Domestic Problems and Foreign Pressures

When Basil II, "the Bulgar-Slayer," died in 1025 C.E., the Byzantine empire was a political, military, and economic dynamo. Within fifty years, however, the empire was suffering from serious internal weaknesses and had endured a series of military reverses. In fact, it had entered a long period of gradual but sustained decline from which it never fully recovered. Both domestic and foreign problems help to explain this decline.

Social Problems

Domestic problems arose, ironically, from the success of the *theme* system. Generals who governed the *themes* were natural allies of local aristocrats who held large tracts of land. Generals and their offspring intermarried with the local aristocracies, creating an elite class with tremendous military, political, social, and economic power. Some of these powerful families resisted the policies of the imperial government and even mounted rebellions against central authorities. The rebels never managed to defeat the imperial forces, but their revolts seriously disrupted local economies. Moreover, the elite class accumulated vast estates that placed the free peasantry under increasing pressure. Formerly the backbone of Byzantium's military system and its agricultural economy, by the mid-eleventh century the free peasantry was declining both in numbers and in prosperity. As a result, Byzantine military forces had fewer recruits available for service, and declining tax receipts from free peasants caused fiscal problems for the imperial government.

Challenges from the West

As domestic problems mounted, Byzantium also faced fresh foreign challenges. From the west came representatives of a dynamic and expanding western European so-

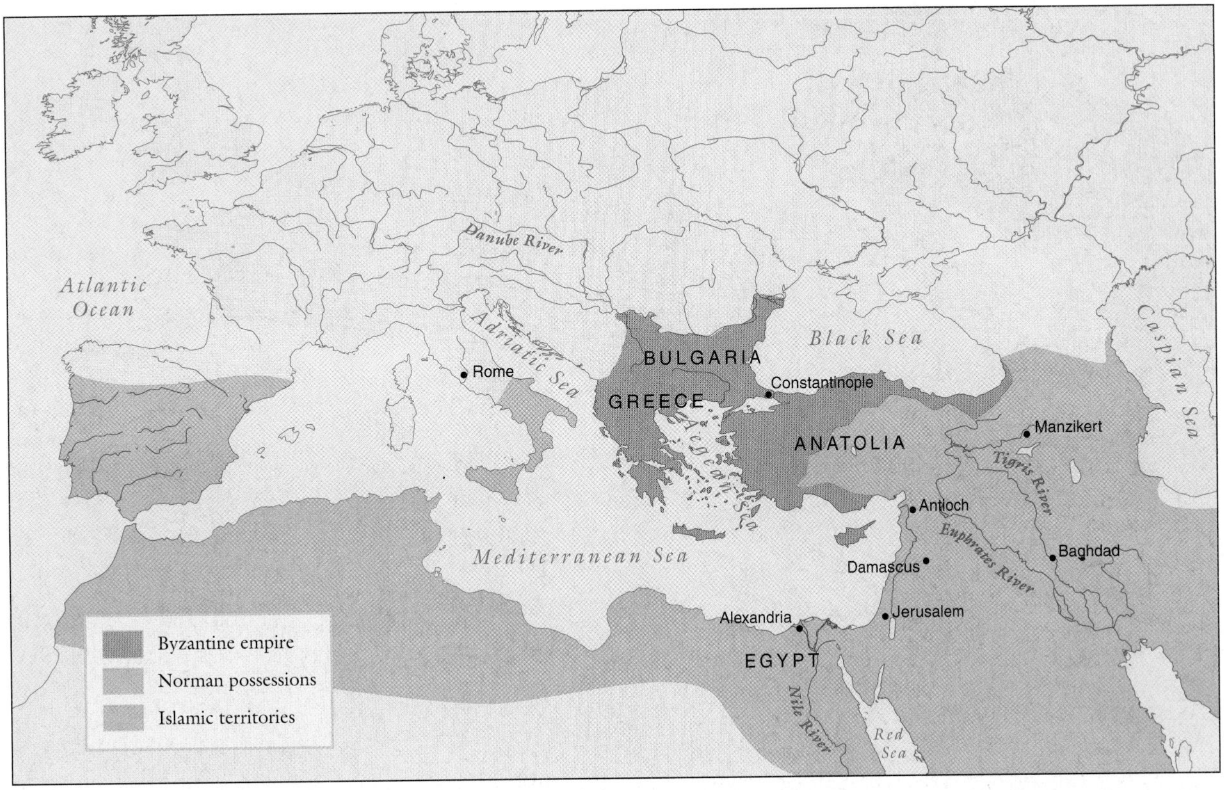

MAP [13.2]
The Byzantine empire and its neighbors, about 1100 C.E.

For an interactive version of this map, go to www.mhhe.com/bentley3ch13maps.

ciety. Beginning in the eleventh century, vigorous economic development in western Europe supported a remarkable round of military and political expansion. During the early eleventh century, the Normans—a Scandinavian people who had seized Normandy (in northern France) and settled there—established themselves as an independent power in southern Italy. By midcentury Norman adventurers led by Robert Guiscard had taken control of southern Italy and expelled Byzantine authorities there.

During the twelfth and thirteenth centuries, the Normans and other western European peoples mounted a series of crusades—vast military campaigns intended to recapture Jerusalem and other sites holy to Christians from Muslims—and took the opportunity to carve out states in the heart of the Byzantine empire. Venetian merchants even managed to divert the fourth crusade (1202–1204) from its original mission in the eastern Mediterranean to Constantinople. Venetians had become prominent in the commercial life of the eastern Mediterranean, and they viewed the fourth crusade as an opportunity to strengthen their position against Byzantine competition. As it happened, the expedition never got beyond Constantinople, which crusaders conquered and sacked in 1204. Byzantine forces recaptured the capital in 1261, but the destruction of Constantinople dealt the Byzantine empire a blow from which it never completely recovered.

Challenges from the East

As Europeans expanded into Byzantine territory from the west, nomadic Turkish peoples invaded from the east. Most important among them were the Muslim Saljuqs, who beginning in the eleventh century sent waves of invaders into Anatolia. Given the military and financial problems of the Byzantine empire, the Saljuqs found Anatolia ripe for plunder. In 1071 they subjected the Byzantine army to a demoralizing defeat at the battle of Manzikert. Byzantine factions then turned on each other

During the sack of Constantinople in 1204, crusading forces seized and carted away Byzantine treasures of all sorts—including the great bronze horses that now stand over the entrance to St. Mark's basilica in Venice.

in civil war, allowing the Saljuqs almost free rein in Anatolia. By the late twelfth century, the Saljuqs had seized much of Anatolia, and crusaders from western Europe held most of the remainder.

The loss of Anatolia—the principal source of Byzantine grain, wealth, and military forces—sealed the fate of the Byzantine empire. A territorially truncated Byzantium survived until the mid-fifteenth century, but the late Byzantine empire enjoyed little autonomy and continually faced fresh challenges from Italian merchants, western European adventurers, and Turkish nomads. In 1453, after a long era of decline, the Byzantine empire came to an end when Ottoman Turks captured Constantinople and absorbed its territories into their own expanding realm.

Early Relations between Byzantium and Slavic Peoples

By the time Constantinople fell, Byzantine traditions had deeply influenced the political and cultural development of Slavic peoples in eastern Europe and Russia. Close relations between Byzantium and Slavic peoples date from the sixth century. When Justinian deployed Byzantium's military resources in the western Mediterranean, Slavic peoples from the north took advantage of the opportunity to move into Byzantine territory. Serbs and Croats moved into the Balkan peninsula, and Bulgars established a powerful kingdom in the lower Danube region.

Relations between Byzantium and Bulgaria were especially tense. By the eighth century, however, as a result of its wealth and sophisticated diplomacy, Byzantium had begun to influence Bulgarian politics and society. Byzantine emperors recognized Bulgarian rulers, enhancing their status as legitimate sovereigns. Byzantium and Bulgaria entered into political, commercial, and cultural relations. Members of Bulgarian ruling families often went to Constantinople for a formal education in Greek language and literature and followed Byzantine examples in organizing their court and capital.

This illustration from a twelfth-century manuscript depicts ninth-century incursions of Bulgarians into Byzantine territory, culminating in a lecture by the Bulgarian king to the Byzantine emperor, shown here with bound hands.

Cyril and Methodius

Byzantium also sent missionaries to Balkan lands, and Bulgars and other Slavic peoples began to convert to Orthodox Christianity. The most famous of the missionaries to the Slavs were Saints Cyril and Methodius, two brothers from Thessaloniki in Greece. During the mid-ninth century Cyril and Methodius conducted missions in Bulgaria and Moravia (which included much of the modern Czech, Slovakian, and Hungarian territories). While there, they devised an alphabet, known as the Cyrillic alphabet, for the previously illiterate Slavic peoples. Though adapted from written Greek, the Cyrillic alphabet represented the sounds of Slavic languages more precisely than did the Greek, and it remained in use in much of eastern Europe until supplanted by the Roman alphabet in the twentieth century. In Russia and most other parts of the former Soviet Union, the Cyrillic alphabet survives to the present day.

Missions to the Slavs

The creation of a written Slavic language enabled Slavic peoples to organize complex political structures and develop sophisticated traditions of thought and literature. More immediately, the Cyrillic alphabet stimulated conversion to Orthodox Christianity. Missionaries translated the Christian scriptures and church rituals into Slavonic, and Cyrillic writing helped them explain Christian values and ideas in Slavic terms. Meanwhile, schools organized by missionaries ensured that Slavs would receive religious instruction alongside their introduction to basic literacy. As a result, Orthodox Christianity deeply influenced the cultural traditions of many Slavic peoples.

Byzantium and Russia

North of Bulgaria another Slavic people began to organize large states: the Russians. About the mid-ninth century Russians created several principalities governed from thriving trading centers, notably Kiev. Strategically situated on the Dnieper River along the main trade route linking Scandinavia and Byzantium, Kiev became a wealthy and powerful center, and it dominated much of the territory between the Volga and the Dnieper from the tenth to the thirteenth century. Russian merchants visited Constantinople in large numbers and became well acquainted with Byzantine society. Russian princes sought alliances with Byzantine rulers and began to express an interest in Orthodox Christianity.

The Conversion of Prince Vladimir

About 989 Prince Vladimir of Kiev converted to Orthodox Christianity and ordered his subjects to follow his example. Vladimir was no paragon of virtue: he lauded drunkenness and reportedly maintained a harem of eight hundred girls. After his conversion, however, Byzantine influences flowed rapidly into Russia. Cyrillic writing, literacy, and Orthodox missions all spread quickly throughout Russia. Byzantine teachers traveled north to establish schools, and Byzantine priests conducted services for Russian converts. For two centuries Kiev served as a conduit for the spread of Byzantine cultural and religious influence in Russia.

Byzantine art and architecture dominated Kiev and other Russian cities. Icons in the Byzantine style encouraged popular piety, and religious images became a principal form of Russian artistic expression. The onion domes that are a distinctive feature of early Russian churches were the result of architects' efforts to imitate the domed structures of Constantinople using wood as their principal building material.

The Growth of Kiev

The princes of Kiev established firm, caesaropapist control over the Russian Orthodox church—so called to distinguish it from the Eastern Orthodox church of the Byzantine empire. They also drew inspiration from Byzantine legal tradition and compiled a written law code for their lands. By controlling trade with Byzantium and other lands, they gained financial resources to build a flourishing society. In the eleventh century Kiev reportedly had four hundred churches and eight large marketplaces. By the early twelfth century its population approached thirty thousand, and a fire in 1124 consumed six hundred churches.

Eventually, Russians even claimed to inherit the imperial mantle of Byzantium. According to a popular theory of the sixteenth century, Moscow was the world's third Rome: the first Rome had fallen to Germanic invaders in the fifth century, whereas the second Rome, Constantinople, had fallen to the Turks a thousand years later. Moscow survived as the third Rome, the cultural and religious beacon that would guide the world to Orthodox Christian righteousness. Inspired by this theory, missionaries took their Russian Orthodox faith to distant lands. During the sixteenth and later centuries, they brought Siberia into the fold of the Orthodox church, crossed the Bering Strait, and dispatched missions to Alaska and even northern California. Thus, long after the collapse of the eastern Roman empire, the Byzantine legacy continued to work its influence through the outward reach of the Russian Orthodox church.

The Byzantine empire originated as a survivor of the classical era. Byzantium inherited a hardy economy, a set of governing institutions, an imperial bureaucracy, an official religion, an established church, and a rich cultural tradition from classical Mediterranean society and the Roman empire. Byzantine leaders drew heavily on this legacy as they dealt with new challenges. Throughout Byzantine history, classical inspiration was especially noticeable in the imperial office, the bureaucracy, the church, and the educational system. Yet in many ways Byzantium changed profoundly over the course of its thousand-year history. After the seventh century the Byzantine empire shrank dramatically in size, and after the eleventh century it faced relentless foreign pressure from western Europeans and nomadic Turkish peoples. Changing times also brought transformations in Byzantine social and economic organization. Yet from the fifth to the twelfth century and beyond, Byzantium brought political stability and economic prosperity to the eastern Mediterranean basin, and Byzantine society served as a principal anchor supporting commercial and cultural exchanges in the postclassical world. Through its political, economic, and cultural influence, Byzantium also helped shape the development of the larger Byzantine commonwealth in eastern Europe and the eastern Mediterranean basin.

CHRONOLOGY

313–337	Reign of Constantine
325	Council of Nicaea
329–379	Life of St. Basil of Caesarea
340	Transfer of Roman government to Constantinople
527–565	Reign of Justinian
717–741	Reign of Leo III
726–843	Iconoclastic controversy
ninth century	Missions of St. Cyril and St. Methodius to the Slavs
976–1025	Reign of Basil II, "the Bulgar-Slayer"
989	Conversion of Prince Vladimir of Kiev to Orthodox Christianity
1054	Beginning of the schism between the eastern and western Christian churches
1071	Battle of Manzikert
1202–1204	Fourth crusade
1453	Fall of Constantinople

FOR FURTHER READING

Peter Arnott. *The Byzantines and Their World.* New York, 1973. A lively, popular, personal vision of Byzantine history.

Louis Bréhier. *The Life and Death of Byzantium.* Trans. by M. Vaughan. Amsterdam, 1977. A detailed political history of the Byzantine empire.

Averil Cameron. *The Mediterranean World in Late Antiquity,* A.D. *395–600.* London, 1993. A thoughtful synthesis that places Byzantium in the context of the late Roman empire.

Francis Dvornik. *Byzantine Missions among the Slavs: SS. Constantine-Cyril and Methodius.* New Brunswick, 1970. Deals with the spread of Orthodox Christianity to eastern Europe.

John V. A. Fine Jr. *The Early Medieval Balkans: A Critical Survey from the Sixth to the Late Twelfth Century.* Ann Arbor, 1983. An excellent introduction to Balkan history in the postclassical era.

Garth Fowden. *Empire to Commonwealth: Consequences of Monotheism in Late Antiquity.* Princeton, 1993. A provocative volume that interprets Byzantine political and cultural development as a monotheist Christian society.

Deno John Geanakoplos. *Byzantium: Church, Society, and Civilization Seen through Contemporary Eyes.* Chicago, 1984. Rich collection of translated documents that throw light on all aspects of Byzantine society.

J. M. Hussey. *The Byzantine World.* London, 1982. A brief and reliable survey.

Liudprand of Cremona. *The Works of Liudprand of Cremona.* Trans. by F. A. Wright. London, 1930. Translations that include accounts of tenth-century Byzantium and of Liudprand's diplomatic mission to Constantinople.

Dimitri Obolensky. *The Byzantine Commonwealth: Eastern Europe, 500–1453.* New York, 1971. A well-informed overview of early Slavic history and relations between Byzantine and Slavic peoples.

George Ostrogorsky. *History of the Byzantine State.* Rev. ed. Trans. by J. Hussey. New Brunswick, 1969. Comprehensive and detailed survey emphasizing political developments.

Procopius. *History of the Wars, Secret History, and Buildings.* Trans. by A. Cameron. New York, 1967. Translations of writings by the most important historian in the time of Justinian.

Michael Psellus. *Fourteen Byzantine Rulers.* Trans. by E. R. A. Sewter. Harmondsworth, 1966. Memoirs of eleventh-century Byzantium by a highly placed advisor to several emperors.

Steven Runciman. *Byzantine Civilization.* Cleveland, 1965. An authoritative overview concentrating on Byzantine institutions by a distinguished scholar.

———. *The Byzantine Theocracy.* Cambridge, 1977. Set of engaging lectures on the Orthodox church.

Speros Vryonis Jr. *Byzantium and Europe.* London, 1967. Well-illustrated and well-written perusal of Byzantine history and Byzantine relations with western Europe.

———. *The Decline of Medieval Hellenism in Asia Minor and the Process of Islamization from the Eleventh through the Fifteenth Century.* Berkeley, 1971. Authoritative analysis of the Turkish conquest of the Byzantine empire.

Mark Whittow. *The Making of Byzantium, 600–1025.* Berkeley, 1996. Concentrates on Byzantine military and political relations with neighboring societies.

Serge A. Zenkovsky, ed. *Medieval Russia's Epics, Chronicles, and Tales.* New York, 1963. A rich collection of literary and historical sources in English translation.

See our **Online Learning Center at www.mhhe.com/bentley3** for additional readings, practice maps, quizzes, and internet activities.

Unfamiliar words? Check out the **Primary Source Investigator CD-ROM** for an interactive glossary, interactive maps, more images, and primary sources.

A fifteenth-century Persian manuscript depicts pilgrims praying at Mecca in the mosque surrounding the Ka'ba.

CHAPTER 14

The Expansive Realm of Islam

In 632 C.E. the prophet Muhammad visited his native city of Mecca from his home in exile at Medina, and in doing so he set an example that devout Muslims have sought to emulate ever since. The *hajj*—the holy pilgrimage to Mecca—draws Muslims by the hundreds of thousands from all parts of the world to Saudi Arabia. Each year Muslims travel to Mecca by land, sea, and air to make the pilgrimage and visit the holy sites of Islam.

In centuries past the numbers of pilgrims were smaller, but their observance of the hajj was no less conscientious. By the ninth century, pilgrimage had become so popular that Muslim rulers went to some lengths to meet the needs of travelers passing through their lands. With the approach of the pilgrimage season—the last month of the Islamic lunar calendar—crowds gathered at major trading centers like Baghdad, Damascus, and Cairo. There they lived in tent cities, surviving on food and water provided by government officials, until they could join caravans bound for Mecca. Muslim rulers invested considerable sums in the maintenance of roads, wells, cisterns, and lodgings that accommodated pilgrims—as well as castles and police forces that protected travelers—on their journeys to Mecca and back.

The hajj was not only solemn observance but also an occasion for joy and celebration. Muslim rulers and wealthy pilgrims often made lavish gifts to caravan companions and others they met en route to Mecca. During her famous hajj of 976–977, for example, the Mesopotamian princess Jamila bint Nasir al-Dawla provided food and fresh green vegetables for her fellow pilgrims and furnished five hundred camels for handicapped travelers. She also purchased freedom for five hundred slaves and distributed fifty thousand fine robes among the common people of Mecca.

Most pilgrims did not have the resources to match Jamila's generosity, but for common travelers, too, the hajj became a special occasion. Merchants and craftsmen made acquaintances and arranged business deals with pilgrims from other lands. Students and scholars exchanged ideas during their weeks of traveling together. For all pilgrims, participation in ritual activities lent new meaning and significance to their faith.

The word *Islam* means "submission," signifying obedience to the rule and will of Allah, the only deity recognized in the strictly monotheistic Islamic religion. An individual who accepts the Islamic faith is a *Muslim,* meaning "one who has submitted." Though it began as one man's expression of unqualified faith in Allah, Islam quickly attracted followers and took on political and social as well as religious significance. During the first century of the new faith's existence, Islam reached far beyond its Arabian homeland, bringing Sasanid Persia and parts of the Byzantine empire into its orbit. By the eighth century the realm of Islam stood alongside the Byzantine empire as a political and economic anchor of the postclassical world.

Islamic society originally reflected the nomadic and mercantile Arabian society from which Islam arose. Yet over time, Muslims drew deep inspiration from other societies as well. After toppling the Sasanid dynasty, Muslim conquerors adopted Persian techniques of government and finance to administer their lands. Persian literature, science, and religious values also found a place in Islamic society. During later centuries Muslims drew inspiration from Greek and Indian traditions as well. Thus Muslims did not invent a new Islamic society but, rather, fashioned it by blending elements from Arab, Persian, Greek, and Indian societies.

While drawing influence from other societies, however, the Islamic faith thoroughly transformed the cultural traditions that it absorbed. The expansive realm of Islam eventually provided a political framework for trade and diplomacy over a vast portion of the eastern hemisphere, from west Africa to the islands of southeast Asia. Many lands of varied cultural background thus became part of a larger society often called the *dar al-Islam*—an Arabic term that means the "house of Islam" and that refers to lands under Islamic rule.

A Prophet and His World

Islam arose in the Arabian peninsula, and the new religion faithfully reflected the social and cultural conditions of its homeland. Desert covers most of the peninsula, and agriculture is possible only in the well-watered area of Yemen in the south and in a few other places, such as the city of Medina, where oases provide water. Yet human communities have occupied Arabia for millennia. Nomadic peoples known as bedouin kept herds of sheep, goats, and camels, migrating through the deserts to find grass and water for their animals. The bedouin organized themselves in family and clan groups. Individuals and their immediate families depended heavily on their larger kinship networks for support in times of need. In an environment as harsh and unforgiving as the Arabian desert, cooperation with kin often made the difference between death and survival. Bedouin peoples developed a strong sense of loyalty to their clans and guarded their common interests with determination. Clan identities and loyalties survived for centuries after the appearance of Islam.

Arabia also figured prominently in the long-distance trade networks of the postclassical era. Commodities arrived at ports on the Persian Gulf (near modern Bahrain), the Arabian Sea (near modern Aden), and the Red Sea (near Mecca), and then traveled overland by camel caravan to Palmyra or Damascus, which offered access to the Mediterranean basin. After the third century C.E., Arabia became an increasingly important link in trade between China and India in the east and Persia and Byzantium in the west. With the weakening of classical empires, trade routes across central Asia had become insecure. Merchants abandoned the overland routes in favor of sea lanes connecting with land routes in the Arabian peninsula. Trade passing across the peninsula was especially important for the city of Mecca, which became an important site of fairs and a stopping point for caravan traffic.

Muhammad and His Message

Muhammad's Early Life

The prophet Muhammad came into this world of nomadic bedouin herders and merchants. Born about 570 C.E. into a reputable family of merchants in Mecca, Muhammad ibn Abdullah lost both of his parents by the time he was six years old. His

Some northern Arabs went to great lengths to demonstrate their devotion to Christianity. This structure, carved out of sheer rock along the wall of a ravine at Petra in modern-day Jordan, served as a monastery.

grandfather and uncle cared for him and provided him with an education, but Muhammad's early life was difficult. As a young man, he worked for a woman named Khadija, a wealthy widow whom he married about the year 595. Through this marriage he gained a position of some prominence in Meccan society, although he did not by any means enter the ranks of the elite.

By age thirty Muhammad had established himself as a merchant. He made a comfortable life for himself in Arabian society, where peoples of different religious and cultural traditions regularly dealt with one another. Most Arabs recognized many gods, goddesses, demons, and nature spirits whose favor they sought through prayers and sacrifices. Large communities of Jewish merchants also worked throughout Arabia, and especially in the north, many Arabs had converted to Christianity by

Muhammad's time. Although he was not deeply knowledgeable about Judaism or Christianity, Muhammad had a basic understanding of both faiths. He may even have traveled by caravan to Syria, where he would certainly have dealt with Jewish and Christian merchants.

Muhammad's Spiritual Transformation

About 610 C.E., as he approached age forty, Muhammad underwent a profound spiritual experience that transformed his life and left a deep mark on world history. His experience left him with the convictions that in all the world there was only one true deity, Allah ("God"), that he ruled the universe, that idolatry and the recognition of other gods amounted to wickedness, and that Allah would soon bring his judgment on the world, rewarding the righteous and punishing the wicked. Muhammad experienced visions, which he understood as messages or revelations from Allah, delivered through the archangel Gabriel (also recognized by Jews and Christians as a special messenger of God), instructing him to explain his faith to others. He did not set out to construct a new religion by combining elements of Arab, Jewish, and Christian beliefs. In light of his cultural context, however, it is not surprising that he shared numerous specific beliefs with Jews and Christians—and indeed also with Zoroastrians, whose views had profoundly influenced the development of both Judaism and Christianity. In any case, in accordance with instructions transmitted to him by Gabriel, Muhammad began to expound his faith to his family and close friends. Gradually, others showed interest in his message, and by about 620 C.E. a zealous and expanding minority of Mecca's citizenry had joined his circle.

The Quran

Muhammad originally presented oral recitations of the revelations he received during his visions. As the Islamic community grew, his followers prepared written texts of his teachings. During the early 650s devout Muslims compiled these written versions of Muhammad's revelations and issued them as the Quran ("recitation"), the holy book of Islam. A work of magnificent poetry, the Quran communicates in powerful and moving terms Muhammad's understanding of Allah and his relation to the world, and it serves as the definitive authority for Islamic religious doctrine and social organization.

Apart from the Quran, several other sources have provided moral and religious guidance for the Islamic community. Most important after the Quran itself are traditions known as *hadith,* which include sayings attributed to Muhammad and accounts of the prophet's deeds. Several collections of *hadith* appeared between the ninth and eleventh century C.E., and Muslim scholars have often taken them as guides for interpretation of the Quran. Regarded as less authoritative than the Quran and the *hadith,* but still important as inspirations for Islamic thought, were early works describing social and legal customs, biographies of Muhammad, and pious commentaries on the Quran.

Muhammad's Migration to Medina

Conflict at Mecca

The growing popularity of Muhammad's preaching brought him into conflict with the ruling elites at Mecca. Conflict centered on religious issues. Muhammad's insistence that Allah was the only divine power in the universe struck many polytheistic Arabs as offensive and dangerous as well, since it disparaged long-recognized deities and spirits thought to wield influence over human affairs. The tensions also had a personal dimension. Mecca's ruling elites, who were also the city's wealthiest merchants, took it as a personal affront and a threat to their position when Muhammad denounced greed as moral wickedness that Allah would punish.

Muhammad's attack on idolatry also represented an economic threat to those who owned and profited from the many shrines to deities that attracted merchants

Current Islamic doctrine forbids artistic representations of Muhammad and Allah to prevent the worship of their images as idols. Although artists of previous centuries occasionally produced paintings of Muhammad, Islamic art has emphasized geometric design and calligraphy. This handsome page from a Quran written on vellum dates from the ninth or early tenth century.

and pilgrims to Mecca. The best known of these shrines was a large black rock long considered to be the dwelling of a powerful deity. Housed in a cube-shaped building known as the Ka'ba, it drew worshipers from all over Arabia and brought considerable wealth to Mecca. As Muhammad relentlessly condemned the idolatry officially promoted at the Ka'ba and other shrines, the ruling elites of Mecca began to persecute the prophet and his followers.

The Hijra

The pressure became so great that some of Muhammad's followers fled to Abyssinia (modern Ethiopia). Muhammad himself remained in Mecca until 622 C.E., when he too fled and joined a group of his followers in Yathrib, a rival trading city 345 kilometers (214 miles) north of Mecca. Muslims called their new home Medina ("the city," meaning "the city of the prophet"). Known as the *hijra* ("migration"), Muhammad's move to Medina serves as the starting point of the official Islamic calendar.

The Umma

In Mecca Muhammad had lived within the established political framework and concentrated on the moral and religious dimensions of his faith. In Medina he found himself at the head of a small but growing society in exile that needed guidance in practical as well as spiritual affairs. He organized his followers into a cohesive community called the *umma* ("community of the faithful") and provided it with a comprehensive legal and social code. He led this community both in daily prayers to Allah and in battle with enemies at Medina, Mecca, and other places. He looked after the economic welfare of the *umma*—sometimes by organizing commercial ventures and sometimes by launching raids against caravans from Mecca. Remembering the difficult days of his own youth, he provided relief for widows, orphans, and the poor, and he made almsgiving a prime moral virtue.

The "Seal of the Prophets"

Muhammad's understanding of his religious mission expanded during his years at Medina. He began to refer to himself as a prophet, indeed as the "seal of the prophets"—the final prophet through whom Allah would reveal his message to humankind. Muhammad accepted the authority of earlier Jewish and Christian prophets,

Sources from the Past

The Quran on Allah and His Expectations of Humankind

The foundation of the Islamic faith is the understanding of Allah, his nature, and his plan for the world as outlined in the Quran. Through his visions Muhammad came to understand Allah as the one and only god, the creator and sustainer of the world in the manner of the Jews' Yahweh and the Christians' God. Those who rejected Allah and his message would suffer eternal punishment, while those who recognized and obeyed him would receive his mercy and secure his blessings.

In the name of Allah, most benevolent, ever-merciful.
All praise be to Allah,
Lord of all the worlds,
Most beneficent, ever-merciful,
King of the Day of Judgement.
You alone we worship, and to You
alone turn for help.
Guide us (O Lord) to the path that is straight,
The path of those You have blessed,
Not of those who have earned Your anger,
nor those who have gone astray. . . .

Verily men and women who have come to submission,
men and women who are believers,
men and women who are devout,
truthful men and women,
men and women with endurance,
men and women who are modest,
men and women who give alms,
men and women who observe fasting,
men and women who guard their private parts,
and those men and women who remember God a great deal,
for them God has forgiveness and a great reward.
No believing men and women have any choice in a matter
after God and His Apostle [i.e., Muhammad] have decided it.
Whoever disobeys God and His Apostle
has clearly lost the way and gone astray. . . .

O you who believe, remember God a great deal,
And sing His praises morning and evening.
It is He who sends His blessings on you,
as (do) His angels, that He may lead you out of darkness into light,
for He is benevolent to the believers. . . .

I call to witness
the early hours of the morning,
And the night when dark and still,
Your Lord has neither left you,
nor despises you.
What is to come is better for you
than what has gone before;
For your Lord will certainly give you,
and you will be content.
Did He not find you an orphan
and take care of you?
Did He not find you poor
and enrich you?
So do not oppress the orphan,
And do not drive
the beggar away,
And keep recounting the favours of your Lord. . . .

Say: "He is God
the one the most unique,
God the immanently indispensable.
He has begotten no one,
and is begotten of none.
There is no one comparable to Him."

SOURCE: *Al-Qur'an: A Contemporary Translation.* Trans. by Ahmed Ali. Princeton: Princeton University Press, 1984, pp.11, 358, 359, 540, 559.

Compare the Quran's teachings on the relationship between Allah and human beings with the views of Zoroastrians, Jews, and Christians discussed in earlier chapters.

including Abraham, Moses, and Jesus, and he held the Hebrew scriptures and the Christian New Testament in high esteem. He also accepted his predecessors' monotheism: Allah was the same omnipotent, omniscient, omnipresent, and exclusive deity as the Jews' Yahweh and the Christians' God. Muhammad taught, however, that the message entrusted to him offered a more complete revelation of Allah and his will than Jewish and Christian faiths had made available. Thus, while at Medina, Muhammad came to see himself consciously as Allah's final prophet: not simply as a devout man who explained his spiritual insights to a small circle of family and friends, but as the messenger who communicated Allah's wishes and his plan for the world to all humankind.

The Establishment of Islam in Arabia

Muhammad's Return to Mecca

Throughout their sojourn at Medina, Muhammad and his followers planned ultimately to return to Mecca, which was both their home and the leading city of Arabia. In 629 C.E. they arranged with the authorities to participate in the annual pilgrimage to the Ka'ba, but they were not content with a short visit. In 630 they attacked Mecca and conquered the city. They forced the elites to adopt Muhammad's faith, and they imposed a government dedicated to Allah. They also destroyed the pagan shrines and replaced them with mosques, buildings that sought to instill a sense of sacredness and community where Muslims gathered for prayers. Only the Ka'ba escaped their efforts to cleanse Mecca of pagan monuments.

Muhammad and his followers denied that the Ka'ba was the home of a deity, but they preserved the black rock and its housing as a symbol of Mecca's greatness. They allowed only the faithful to approach the shrine, and in 632 Muhammad himself led the first Islamic pilgrimage to the Ka'ba, thus establishing the hajj as an example for all devout Muslims. Building on the conquest of Mecca, Muhammad and his followers launched campaigns against other towns and bedouin clans, and by the time of the prophet's death in 632, shortly after his hajj, they had brought most of Arabia under their control.

The Five Pillars of Islam

Muhammad's faith and his personal leadership decisively shaped the values and the development of the Islamic community. The foundation of the Islamic faith as elaborated by Muhammad consists of obligations known as the Five Pillars of Islam: (1) Muslims must acknowledge Allah as the only god and Muhammad as his prophet. (2) They must pray to Allah daily while facing Mecca. (3) They must observe a fast during the daylight hours of the month of Ramadan. (4) They must contribute alms for the relief of the weak and poor. (5) Finally, in honor of Muhammad's visits to Mecca in 629 and 632, those who are physically and financially able must undertake the hajj and make at least one pilgrimage to Mecca. During the centuries since its appearance, Islam has generated many schools and sects, each with its own particular legal, social, and doctrinal features. The Five Pillars of Islam, however, constitute a simple but powerful framework that has bound the *umma* as a whole into a cohesive community of faith.

Jihad

Some Muslims, though by no means all, have taken *jihad* as an additional obligation for the faithful. The term *jihad* literally means "struggle," and Muslims have understood its imperatives in various ways. In one sense, *jihad* imposes spiritual and moral obligations on Muslims by requiring them to combat vice and evil. In another sense, *jihad* calls on Muslims to struggle against ignorance and unbelief by spreading the word of Islam and seeking converts to the faith. In some circumstances, *jihad* also involves physical struggle, obliging Muslims to take up the sword and wage war against unbelievers who threaten Islam.

Context & Connections

The Hajj, Past and Present

Modern-day pilgrims circle the Ka'ba in hajj observations.

"Announce the Pilgrimage to the people," proclaimed the Islamic scriptures. "They will come to you on foot and riding along distant roads on lean and slender beasts" (Quran 22:27). Over the centuries, Muslims obeying the Quran's teachings have turned the hajj into the world's largest public gathering. It is impossible to know how many pilgrims made the hajj in premodern times, but it is clear that within two or three centuries of Muhammad's death, thousands of Muslims traveled each year to Mecca.

In the earliest days, pilgrims approached Mecca by one of the camel caravans that organized travelers into groups departing from Cairo, Damascus, and Baghdad, as well as from various points within the Arabian peninsula itself. As Islam became popular in India, southeast Asia, and east Africa, pilgrims increasingly arrived aboard ships sailing through the Indian Ocean and the Red Sea. In the late nineteenth and twentieth centuries, steamships and railroads enabled larger and larger numbers of pilgrims to visit

Islamic Law: The Sharia

Beyond the general obligations prescribed by the Five Pillars, Islamic holy law, known as the *sharia,* emerged during the centuries after Muhammad and offered detailed guidance on proper behavior in almost every aspect of life. Elaborated by jurists and legal scholars, the *sharia* drew its inspiration especially from the Quran and the early historical accounts of Muhammad's life and teachings. It offered precise guidance on matters as diverse as marriage and family life, inheritance, slavery, business and commercial relationships, political authority in the *dar al-Islam,* and crime. Through the *sharia,* Islam became more than a religious doctrine: it developed into a way of life complete with social and ethical values derived from Islamic religious principles.

The Expansion of Islam

After Muhammad's death the Islamic community might well have unraveled and disappeared. Muhammad had made no provision for a successor, and there was serious

Mecca: in 1965 participants numbered 294,000. Since the introduction of jumbo jets in the 1970s, pilgrim numbers have reached a new order of magnitude: in recent years, more than two million pilgrims have traveled annually to Mecca.

While methods of travel and numbers of participants have changed dramatically over the years, hajj rituals themselves have remained remarkably stable since the time of Muhammad. Since Muhammad's conquest of Mecca (630 C.E.), the hajj has been open only to Muslims, although from time to time a very few non-Muslims have managed to sneak into the observances. To prepare for hajj rituals, pilgrims enter a state of consecration by removing their usual attire and donning simple white garments that symbolize the equality of all Muslims. The ceremonies of the hajj itself take place in a five-day period during the last month of the Islamic lunar calendar. Pilgrims first undertake a circular procession around the Ka'ba, then visit several sites near Mecca, where they perform a precisely defined set of rituals that symbolize the most important tenets of Islam and commemorate the experiences of the patriarch Abraham. Hajj observances conclude with another circular procession around the Ka'ba. Some pilgrims then depart from Mecca, while others visit Medina and other sites sacred to Islam.

The hajj places formidable logistical demands on the Saudi Arabian government, which has hosted the annual pilgrimage since its conquest of the Hijaz (the western region of the Arabian peninsula, including the cities of Mecca and Medina) in 1926. Thousands of volunteers work to provide food, water, lodging, sanitation facilities, health care, transportation, and guide services for the masses of pilgrims who inundate Mecca. Servicing the hajj and the needs of pilgrims constitutes one of the world's most challenging exercises in public administration.

For devout Muslims the significance of the hajj lies not in logistical proficiency but, rather, in the intensification of their Islamic faith. According to tradition, Muhammad taught that as a reward for their efforts, those who performed the hajj properly would emerge from the experience as newly born babies free of sin.

division within the *umma* concerning the selection of a new leader. Many of the towns and bedouin clans that had recently accepted Islam took the opportunity of Muhammad's death to renounce the faith, reassert their independence, and break free from Mecca's control. Within a short time, however, the Islamic community had embarked on a stunningly successful round of military expansion that extended its political and cultural influence far beyond the boundaries of Arabia. These conquests laid the foundation for the rapid growth of Islamic society.

The Early Caliphs and the Umayyad Dynasty

The Caliph

Because Muhammad was the "seal of the prophets," it was inconceivable that another prophet should succeed him. Shortly after Muhammad's death his advisors selected Abu Bakr, a genial man who was one of the prophet's closest friends and most devoted disciples, to serve as *caliph* ("deputy"). Thus Abu Bakr and later caliphs led the *umma* not as prophets, but as lieutenants or substitutes for Muhammad. Abu Bakr became head of state for the Islamic community as well as chief judge, religious

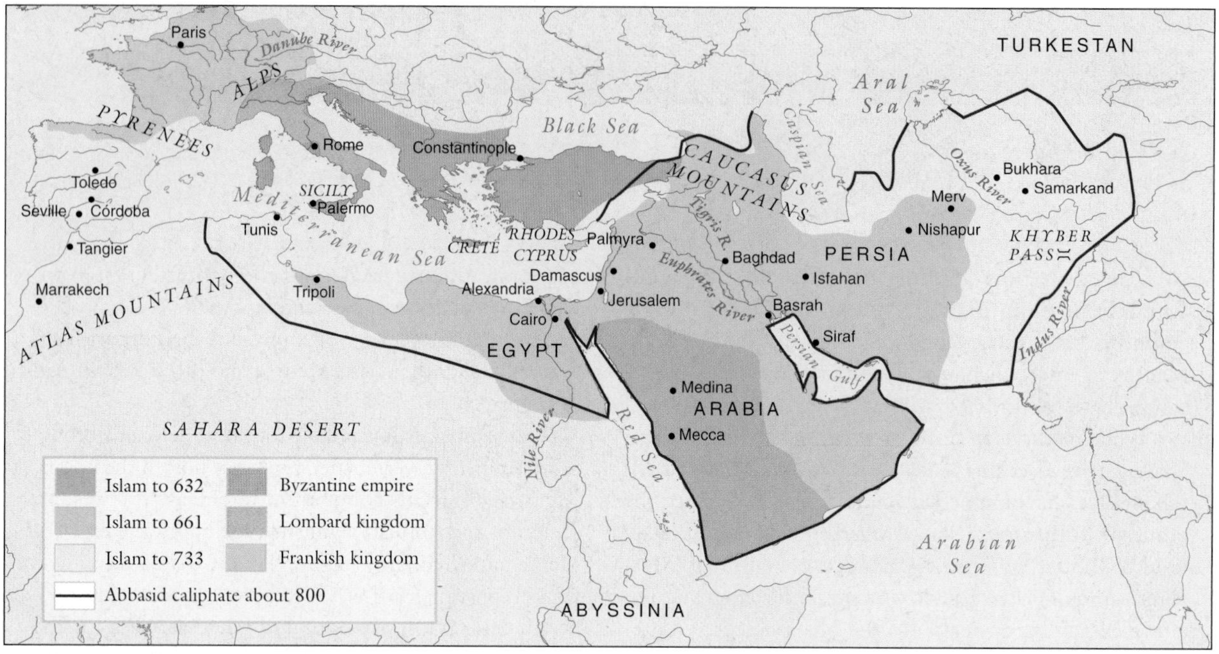

MAP [14.1]
The expansion of Islam, 632–733 C.E.

leader, and military commander. Under the new caliph's leadership, the *umma* went on the offensive against the towns and bedouin clans that had renounced Islam after Muhammad's death, and within a year it had compelled them to recognize the faith of Islam and the rule of the caliph.

The Expansion of Islam

Indeed, during the century after Muhammad's death, Islamic armies ranged well beyond the boundaries of Arabia, carrying their religion and their authority to Byzantine and Sasanid territories and beyond. Although much less powerful than either the Byzantine empire or the Sasanid empire, early Islamic warriors fought with the zeal of new converts. Moreover, they attacked at a moment when the larger empires—both of them already exhausted because of perennial conflicts with each other—also faced internal uprisings by overtaxed peasants and oppressed ethnic or religious minorities. Between 633 and 637 C.E., taking advantage of these difficulties, Muslim forces seized Byzantine Syria and Palestine and took most of Mesopotamia from the Sasanids. During the 640s they conquered Byzantine Egypt and north Africa. In 651 they toppled the Sasanid dynasty and incorporated Persia into their expanding empire. In 711 they conquered the Hindu kingdom of Sind in northwestern India. Between 711 and 718 they extended their authority to northwest Africa and crossed the Strait of Gibraltar, conquering most of the Iberian peninsula and threatening the Frankish kingdom in Gaul. By the mid-eighth century an immense Islamic empire ruled lands from India and the central Asian steppe lands in the east to northwest Africa and Iberia in the west.

During this rapid expansion the empire's rulers encountered difficult problems of governance and administration. One problem had to do with the selection of caliphs. During the early decades after Muhammad's death, leaders of the most powerful Arab clans negotiated among themselves and appointed the first four caliphs. Political ambitions, personal differences, and clan loyalties complicated their deliberations, however, and disputes soon led to the rise of factions and parties within the Islamic community.

The Shia

Disagreements over succession led to the emergence of the Shia sect, the most important and enduring of all the alternatives to the faith observed by the majority of Muslims, known as Sunni Islam. The Shia sect originated as a party supporting the appointment of Ali and his descendants as caliphs. A cousin and son-in-law of Muhammad, Ali was a candidate for caliph when the prophet died, but support for Abu Bakr was stronger. Ali served briefly as the fourth caliph (656–661 C.E.), but his enemies assassinated him, killed many of his relatives, and imposed their own candidate as caliph. Partisans of Ali then organized the Shia ("party"), furiously resisted the victorious faction, and struggled to return the caliphate to the line of Ali. Although persecuted, the Shia survived and strengthened its identity by adopting doctrines and rituals distinct from those of the Sunnis ("traditionalists"), who accepted the legitimacy of the early caliphs. Shia partisans, for example, observed holy days in honor of their leaders and martyrs to their cause, and they taught that descendants of Ali were infallible, sinless, and divinely appointed to rule the Islamic community. Shia Muslims also advanced interpretations of the Quran that support the party's views, and the Shia itself has often served as a source of support for those who oppose the policies of Sunni leaders.

The Umayyad Dynasty

After the assassination of Ali, the establishment of the Umayyad dynasty (661–750 C.E.) solved the problem of succession, at least temporarily. The Umayyads ranked among the most prominent of the Meccan merchant clans, and their reputation and network of alliances helped them bring stability to the Islamic community. Despite their association with Mecca, the Umayyads established their capital at Damascus, a thriving commercial city in Syria, whose central location enabled them to maintain better communication with the vast and still-expanding Islamic empire.

Although the Umayyads' dynasty solved the problem of succession, their tightly centralized rule and the favor they showed to their fellow Arabs generated an administrative problem. The Umayyads ruled the *dar al-Islam* as conquerors, and their policies reflected the interests of the Arab military

The early expansion of Islam was a bloody affair. This illustration from an Arabic manuscript of the thirteenth century depicts a battle between Muhammad's cousin Ali and his adversaries.

aristocracy. The Umayyads appointed members of this elite as governors and administrators of conquered lands, and they distributed the wealth that they extracted among this privileged class.

Policy toward Conquered Peoples

This policy contributed to high morale among Arab conquerors, but it caused severe discontent among the scores of ethnic and religious groups embraced by the Umayyad empire. Apart from Muslims the empire included Christians, Jews, Zoroastrians, and Buddhists. Apart from Arabs and bedouin, it included Indians, Persians, Mesopotamians, Greeks, Egyptians, and nomadic Berbers in north Africa. The Arabs mostly allowed conquered peoples to observe their own religions—particularly Christians and Jews—but they levied a special head tax, called the *jizya,* on those who did not convert to Islam. Even those who converted did not enjoy access to wealth and positions of authority, which the Umayyads reserved almost exclusively for members of the Arab military aristocracy. These policies caused deep resentment among conquered peoples and led to restiveness against Umayyad rule.

Umayyad Decline

Beginning in the early eighth century, the Umayyad caliphs became alienated even from other Arabs. They devoted themselves increasingly to luxurious living rather than to zealous leadership of the *umma,* and they scandalized devout Muslims by their casual attitudes toward Islamic doctrine and morality. By midcentury the Umayyad caliphs faced not only the resistance of the Shia faction, whose members continued to promote descendants of Ali for caliph, but also the discontent of conquered peoples throughout their empire and even the disillusionment of Muslim Arab military leaders.

The Abbasid Dynasty

Abu al-Abbas

Rebellion in Persia brought the Umayyad dynasty to an end. The chief leader of the rebellion was Abu al-Abbas, a descendant of Muhammad's uncle. Although he was a Sunni Arab, Abu al-Abbas allied readily with Shias and with Muslims who were not Arabs, such as converts to Islam from southwest Asia. Particularly prominent among his supporters were Persian converts who resented the preference shown by the Umayyads to Arab Muslims. During the 740s Abu al-Abbas's party rejected Umayyad authority and seized control of Persia and Mesopotamia. In 750 his army shattered Umayyad forces in a massive battle. Afterward Abu al-Abbas invited the remaining members of the Umayyad clan to a banquet under the pretext of reconciling their differences. During the festivities his troops arrested the Umayyads and slaughtered them, effectively annihilating the clan. Abu al-Abbas then founded the Abbasid dynasty, which was the principal source of authority in the *dar al-Islam* until the Mongols toppled it in 1258 C.E.

The Abbasid Dynasty

The Abbasid dynasty differed considerably from the Umayyad. For one thing the Abbasid state was far more cosmopolitan than its predecessor. Even though they sprang from the ranks of conquering Arabs, Abbasid rulers did not show special favor to the Arab military aristocracy. Arabs continued to play a large role in government, but Persians, Egyptians, Mesopotamians, and others also rose to positions of wealth and power.

The Abbasid dynasty differed from the Umayyad also in that it was not a conquering dynasty. The Abbasids sparred intermittently with the Byzantine empire, they clashed frequently with nomadic peoples from central Asia, and in 751 they defeated a Chinese army at Talas River near Samarkand. The battle of Talas River was exceptionally important: it ended the expansion of China's Tang dynasty into central Asia (discussed in chapter 15), and it opened the door for the spread of Islam among

Turkish peoples. Only marginally, however, did the Abbasids expand their empire by conquest. The *dar al-Islam* as a whole continued to grow during the Abbasid era, but the caliphs had little to do with the expansion. During the ninth and early tenth centuries, for example, largely autonomous Islamic forces from distant Tunisia mounted naval expeditions throughout the Mediterranean, conquering Crete, Sicily, and the Balearic Islands while seizing territories also in Cyprus, Rhodes, Sardinia, Corsica, southern Italy, and southern France.

Abbasid Administration

Instead of conquering new lands, the Abbasids largely contented themselves with administering the empire they inherited. Fashioning a government that could administer a sprawling realm with scores of linguistic, ethnic, and cultural groups was a considerable challenge. In designing their administration, the Abbasids relied heavily on Persian techniques of statecraft. Central authority came from the court at Baghdad (capital of modern Iraq), the magnificent new city that the early Abbasid caliphs built near the Sasanid capital of Ctesiphon. Baghdad was a round city protected by three round walls. At the heart of the city was the caliph's green-domed palace from which instructions flowed to the distant reaches of the Abbasid realm. In the provinces, governors represented the caliph and implemented his political and financial policies.

Learned officials known as *ulama* ("people with religious knowledge") and *qadis* ("judges") set moral standards in local communities and resolved disputes. *Ulama* and *qadis* were not priests—Islam does not recognize priests as a distinct class of religious specialists—but they had a formal education that emphasized study of the Quran and the *sharia*. *Ulama* were pious scholars who sought to develop public policy in accordance with the Quran and *sharia*. *Qadis* heard cases at law and rendered decisions based on the Quran and *sharia*. Because of their moral authority, *ulama* and *qadis* became extremely influential officials who helped to ensure widespread observance of Islamic values. Apart from provincial governors, *ulama*, and *qadis*, the Abbasid caliphs kept a standing army, and they established bureaucratic ministries in charge of taxation, finance, coinage, and postal services. They also maintained the magnificent network of roads that the Islamic empire inherited from the Sasanids.

Harun al-Rashid

The high point of the Abbasid dynasty came during the reign of the caliph Harun al-Rashid (786–809 C.E.). By the late eighth century, Abbasid authority had lost some of its force in provinces distant from Baghdad, but it remained strong enough to bring reliable tax revenues from most parts of the empire. Flush with wealth, Baghdad became a center of banking, commerce, crafts, and industrial production, a metropolis with a population of several hundred thousand people. According to stories from his own time, Harun al-Rashid provided liberal support for artists and writers, bestowed lavish and luxurious gifts on his favorites, and distributed money to the poor and the common classes by tossing coins into the streets of Baghdad. Once he sent an elephant and a collection of rich presents as gifts to his contemporary Charlemagne, who ruled the Carolingian empire of western Europe.

Abbasid Decline

Soon after Harun al-Rashid's reign, the Abbasid empire entered a period of decline. Civil war between Harun's sons seriously damaged Abbasid authority, and disputes over succession rights became a recurring problem for the dynasty. Provincial governors took advantage of disorder in the ruling house by acting independently of the caliphs: instead of implementing imperial policies and delivering taxes to Baghdad, they built up local bases of power and in some cases actually seceded from the Abbasid state. Meanwhile, popular uprisings and peasant rebellions, which often enjoyed the support of dissenting sects and heretical movements, further weakened the empire.

Sources from the Past

Benjamin of Tudela on the Caliph's Court at Baghdad

Like Constantinople, Baghdad was in a period of decline when the Spanish rabbi Benjamin of Tudela visited in the later twelfth century. Nevertheless, again like the Byzantine capital, Baghdad remained an immensely prosperous city. Benjamin's report on Baghdad concentrated largely on the court and palace of the Abbasid caliph.

The caliph is the head of the Muslim religion, and all the kings of Islam obey him; he occupies a similar position to that held by the pope over the Christians. He has a palace in Baghdad three miles in extent, wherein there is a great park with all varieties of trees, fruit-bearing and otherwise, and all manner of animals. The whole is surrounded by a wall, and in the park there is a lake whose waters are fed by the river Hiddekel. Whenever the king desires to indulge in recreation and to rejoice and feast, his servants catch all manner of birds, game, and fish, and he goes to his palace with his counsellors and princes. . . .

Each of his brothers and the members of his family has an abode in his palace, but they are all fettered in chains of iron, and guards are placed over each of their houses so that they may not rise against the great caliph. For once it happened to a predecessor that his brothers rose up against him and proclaimed one of themselves as caliph; then it was decreed that all the members of his family should be bound, that they might not rise up against the ruling caliph. Each one of them resides in his palace in great splendor, and they own villages and towns, and their stewards bring them the tribute thereof, and they eat and drink and rejoice all the days of their life.

Within the domains of the palace of the caliph there are great buildings of marble and columns of silver and gold, and carvings upon rare stones are fixed in the walls. In the caliph's palace are great riches and towers filled with gold, silken garments, and all precious stones. . . .

The caliph is a benevolent man. On the other side of the river, on the banks of an arm of the Euphrates which there borders the city, he built a hospital consisting of blocks of houses and hospices for the sick poor who come to be healed. Here there are about sixty physicians' stores which are provided from the caliph's house with drugs and whatever else may be required. Every sick man who comes is maintained at the caliph's expense and is medically treated. Here is a building which is called Dar-al-Maristan, where they keep charge of the demented people who have become insane in the towns through the great heat in the summer, and they chain each of them in iron chains until their reason becomes restored to them in the winter. While they abide there, they are provided with food from the house of the caliph, and when their reason is restored they are dismissed and each one of them goes to his house and his home. Money is given to those that have stayed in the hospices on their return to their homes. Every month the officers of the caliph inquire and investigate whether they have regained their reason, in which case they are discharged. All this the caliph does out of charity to those that come to the city of Baghdad, whether they be sick or insane. The caliph is a righteous man, and all his actions are for good. . . .

The city of Baghdad is twenty miles in circumference, situated in a land of palms, gardens, and plantations, the like of which is not to be found in the whole land of Mesopotamia. People come thither with merchandise from all lands. Wise men live there, philosophers who know all manner of wisdom, and magicians expert in all manner of witchcraft.

SOURCE: Benjamin of Tudela. *The Itinerary of Benjamin of Tudela.* Trans. by M. N. Adler. London: H. Frowde, 1907, pp.35–42. (Translation slightly modified.)

Compare Baghdad and Constantinople on the basis of descriptions provided by Benjamin of Tudela.

As a result of these difficulties, the Abbasid caliphs became mere figureheads long before the Mongols extinguished the dynasty in 1258. In 945 members of a Persian noble family seized control of Baghdad and established their clan as the power behind the Abbasid throne. Later, imperial authorities in Baghdad fell under the control of the Saljuq Turks, a nomadic people from central Asia who also invaded the Byzantine empire. In response to rebellions mounted by peasants and provincial governors, authorities in Baghdad allied with the Saljuqs, who began to enter the Abbasid realm and convert to Islam about the mid-tenth century. By the mid-eleventh century the Saljuqs effectively controlled the Abbasid empire. During the 1050s they took possession of Baghdad, and during the following decades they extended their authority to Syria, Palestine, and Anatolia. They retained Abbasid caliphs as nominal sovereigns, but for two centuries, until the arrival of the Mongols, the Saljuq *sultan* ("ruler") was the true source of power in the Abbasid empire.

Economy and Society of the Early Islamic World

In the *dar al-Islam,* as in other agricultural societies, peasants tilled the land as their ancestors had done for centuries before them while manufacturers and merchants supported a thriving urban economy. Here, as in other lands, the creation of large empires had dramatic economic implications. The Umayyad and Abbasid empires created a zone of trade, exchange, and communication stretching from India to Iberia. Commerce throughout this zone served as a vigorous economic stimulus for both the countryside and the cities of the early Islamic world.

New Crops, Agricultural Experimentation, and Urban Growth

The Spread of Food and Industrial Crops

As soldiers, administrators, diplomats, and merchants traveled throughout the *dar al-Islam,* they encountered plants, animals, and agricultural techniques peculiar to the empire's various regions. They often introduced particularly useful crops to new regions. The most important of the transplants traveled west from India to Persia, southwest Asia, Arabia, Egypt, north Africa, Spain, and the Mediterranean islands of Cyprus, Crete, Sicily, and Sardinia. They included staple crops such as sugarcane, rice, and new varieties of sorghum and wheat; vegetables such as spinach, artichokes, and eggplants; fruits such as oranges, lemons, limes, bananas, coconuts, watermelons, and mangoes; and industrial crops such as cotton, indigo, and henna.

Effects of New Crops

The introduction of these crops into the western regions of the Islamic world had wide-ranging effects. New food crops led to a richer and more varied diet. They also increased quantities of food available because they enabled cultivators to extend the growing season. In much of the Islamic world, summers are so hot and dry that cultivators traditionally left their fields fallow during that season. Most of the transplanted crops grew well in high heat, however, so cultivators in southwest Asia, north Africa, and other hot zones could till their lands year-round. The result was a dramatic increase in food supplies.

Some new crops had industrial uses. The most important of these was cotton, which became the basis for a thriving textile industry throughout much of the Islamic world. Indigo and henna yielded dyes that textile manufacturers used in large quantities.

Agricultural Experimentation

Travel and communication in the *dar al-Islam* also encouraged experimentation with agricultural methods. Cultivators paid close attention to methods of irrigation, fertilization, crop rotation, and the like, and they outlined their findings in hundreds of

In a thirteenth-century manuscript illustration, a fictional Muslim traveler passes a lively agricultural village. On the left a woman spins cotton thread. Sheep, goats, chickens, and date palms figure prominently in the local economy.

agricultural manuals. Copies of these works survive in numerous manuscripts that circulated widely throughout the Islamic world. The combined effect of new crops and improved techniques was a far more productive agricultural economy, which in turn supported vigorous economic growth throughout the *dar al-Islam.*

Urban Growth

Increased agricultural production contributed to the rapid growth of cities in all parts of the Islamic world from India to Spain. Delhi, Samarkand, Bukhara, Merv, Nishapur, Isfahan, Basra, Baghdad, Damascus, Jerusalem, Cairo, Alexandria, Palermo, Tunis, Tangier, Córdoba, and Toledo were all bustling cities, some with populations of several hundred thousand people. All these cities had flourishing markets supporting thousands of artisans, craftsmen, and merchants. Most of them were also important centers of industrial production, particularly of textiles, pottery, glassware, leather, iron, and steel.

One new industry appeared in Islamic cities during the Abbasid era: paper manufacture. Chinese craftsmen had made paper since the first century C.E., but their technology did not spread far beyond China until Arab forces defeated a Chinese army at the battle of Talas River in 751 and took prisoners skilled in paper production. Paper was cheaper and easier to use than writing materials such as vellum sheets made from calfskin, and it soon became popular throughout the Islamic world. Paper facilitated the keeping of administrative and commercial records, and it made possible the dissemination of books and treatises in larger quantities than ever before. By the tenth century, mills produced paper in Persia, Mesopotamia, Arabia, Egypt, and Spain, and the industry soon spread to western Europe.

The Formation of a Hemispheric Trading Zone

From its earliest days Islamic society drew much of its prosperity from commerce. Muhammad himself was a merchant, and he held merchants in high esteem. According to early accounts of his life, Muhammad once said that honest merchants would stand alongside martyrs to the faith on the day of judgment. By the time of the

Abbasid caliphate, elaborate trade networks linked all the regions of the Islamic world and joined it to a larger, hemispheric economy.

Overland Trade

When they overran the Sasanid empire, Muslim conquerors brought the prosperous trading cities of central Asia under control of the expanding *dar al-Islam.* Merv, Nishapur, Bukhara, and Samarkand were long-established commercial centers, and they made it possible for Muslim merchants to trade over a revived silk roads network extending from China in the east to the Mediterranean in the west. Thus Muslim merchants were able to take advantage of the extensive road networks originally built during the classical era by imperial authorities in India, Persia, and the Mediterranean basin. Umayyad and Abbasid rulers maintained the roads that they inherited because they provided splendid routes for military forces and administrative officials traveling through the *dar al-Islam.* But these same roads also made excellent highways for merchants as well as missionaries and pilgrims. Travel along these roads could be remarkably speedy and efficient. After the tenth century, for example, the Muslim rulers of Egypt regularly imported ice from the mountains of Syria to their palace in Cairo. Even during the summer months, they received five camel loads of ice weekly to cool their food and drink.

Caravanserais offered splendid facilities for caravan merchants, but they sometimes harbored dangers. In this illustration from a thirteenth-century manuscript, drugged merchants sleep soundly while burglars relieve them of their valuables.

Camels and Caravans

Overland trade traveled mostly by camel caravan. Although they are unpleasant and often uncooperative beasts, camels endure the rigors of desert travel much better than horses or donkeys. Moreover, when fitted with a well-designed saddle, camels can carry heavy loads. During the early centuries C.E., the manufacture of camel saddles spread throughout Arabia, north Africa, southwest Asia, and central Asia, and camels became the favored beasts of burden in deserts and other dry regions. As camel transport became more common, the major cities of the Islamic world and central Asia built and maintained caravanserais—inns offering lodging for caravan merchants as well as food, water, and care for their animals.

Maritime Trade

Meanwhile, innovations in nautical technology contributed to a steadily increasing volume of maritime trade in the Red Sea, Persian Gulf, Arabian Sea, and Indian Ocean. Arab and Persian mariners borrowed the compass from its Chinese inventors and used it to guide them on the high seas. From southeast Asian and Indian mariners, they

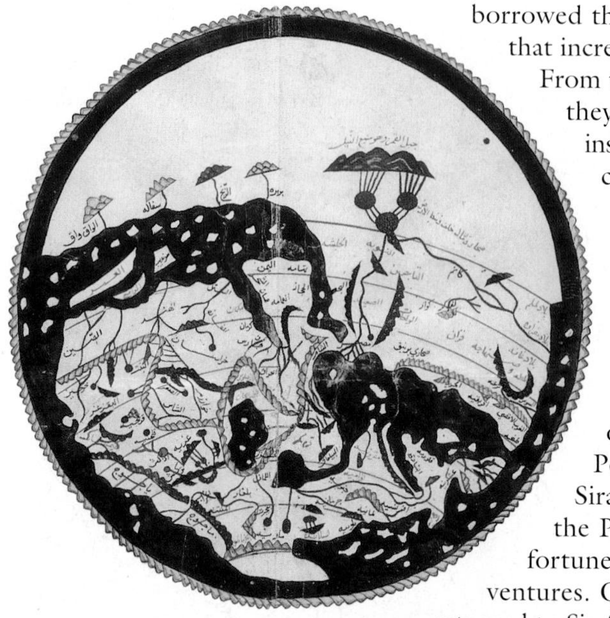

A map produced in the eleventh century by the Arab geographer al-Idrisi shows the lands known and reported by Muslim merchants and travelers. Note that, in accordance with Muslim cartographic convention, this map places south at the top and north at the bottom.

borrowed the lateen sail, a triangular sail that increased a ship's maneuverability. From the Hellenistic Mediterranean they borrowed the astrolabe, an instrument that enabled them to calculate latitude.

Thus equipped, Arab and Persian mariners ventured throughout the Indian Ocean basin, calling at ports from southern China to southeast Asia, Ceylon, India, Persia, Arabia, and the eastern coast of Africa. The twelfth-century Persian merchant Ramisht of Siraf (a flourishing port city on the Persian Gulf) amassed a huge fortune from long-distance trading ventures. One of Ramisht's clerks once returned to Siraf from a commercial voyage to China with a cargo worth half a million dinars—gold coins that were the standard currency in the Islamic world. Ramisht himself was one of the wealthiest men of his age, and he spent much of his fortune on pious causes. He outfitted the Ka'ba with a Chinese silk cover that reportedly cost him eighteen thousand dinars, and he also founded a hospital and a religious sanctuary in Mecca.

Banks

Banking also stimulated the commercial economy of the Islamic world. Banks had operated since classical antiquity, but Islamic banks of the Abbasid period conducted business on a much larger scale and provided a more extensive range of services than did their predecessors. They not only lent money to entrepreneurs but also served as brokers for investments and exchanged different currencies. They established multiple branches that honored letters of credit known as *sakk*—the root of the modern word for "check"—drawn on the parent bank. Thus merchants could draw letters of credit in one city and cash them in another, and they could settle accounts with distant business partners without having to deal in cash.

The Organization of Trade

Trade benefited also from techniques of business organization. Like banking, these techniques had precedents in classical Mediterranean society, but increasing volumes of trade enabled entrepreneurs to refine their methods of organization. Furthermore, Islamic law provided security for entrepreneurs by explicitly recognizing certain forms of business organization. Usually Islamic businessmen preferred not to embark on solo ventures, since an individual could face financial ruin if an entire cargo of commodities fell prey to pirates or went down with a ship that sank in a storm. Instead, like their counterparts in other postclassical societies, Abbasid entrepreneurs often pooled their resources in group investments. If several individuals invested in several cargoes, they could distribute their risks and more easily absorb losses. Furthermore, if several groups of investors rented cargo space on several different ships, they spread their risks even more. Entrepreneurs entered into a variety of legally recognized joint endeavors during the Abbasid caliphate. Some involved simply the investment of money in an enterprise, whereas others called for some or all of the partners to play active roles in their business ventures.

As a result of improved transportation, expanded banking services, and refined techniques of business organization, long-distance trade surged in the early Islamic

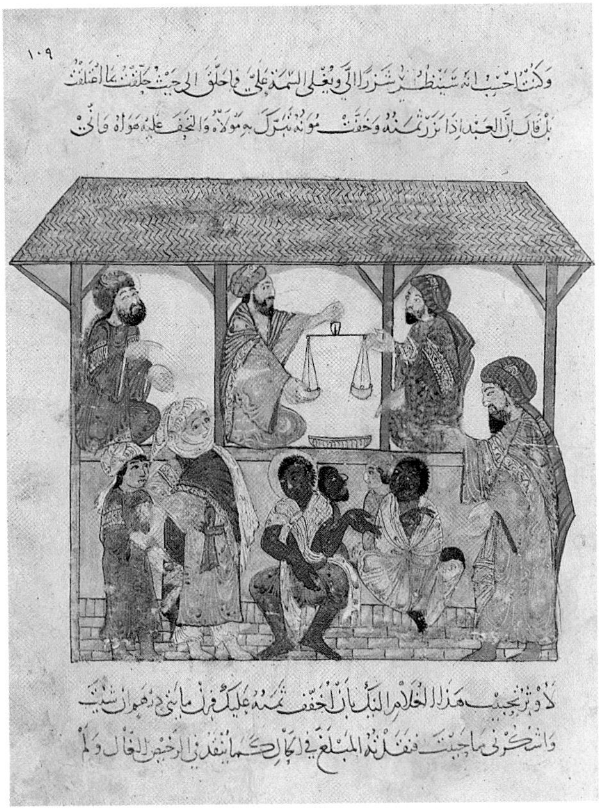

In this thirteenth-century manuscript illustration, merchants at a slave market in southern Arabia deal in black slaves captured in sub-Saharan Africa. Slaves traded in Islamic markets also came from Russia and eastern Europe.

world. Muslim merchants dealt in silk and ceramics from China, spices and aromatics from India and southeast Asia, and jewelry and fine textiles from the Byzantine empire. Merchants also ventured beyond settled societies in China, India, and the Mediterranean basin to distant lands that previously had not engaged systematically in long-distance trade. They crossed the Sahara desert by camel caravan to trade salt, steel, copper, and glass for gold and slaves from the kingdoms of west Africa. They visited the coastal regions of east Africa, where they obtained slaves and exotic local commodities such as animal skins. They engaged in trade with Russia and Scandinavia by way of the Dnieper and Volga rivers and obtained high-value commodities such as animal skins, furs, honey, amber, and slaves as well as bulk goods such as timber and livestock. The vigorous economy of the Abbasid empire thus helped to establish networks of communication and exchange throughout much of the eastern hemisphere.

Al-Andalus

The prosperity of Islamic Spain, known as al-Andalus, illustrates the far-reaching effects of long-distance trade during the Abbasid era. Most of the Iberian peninsula had fallen into the hands of Muslim Berber conquerors from north Africa during the early eighth century. As allies of the Umayyads, the governors of al-Andalus refused to recognize the Abbasid dynasty, and beginning in the tenth century they styled themselves caliphs in their own right rather than governors subject to Abbasid authority. Despite political and diplomatic tensions, al-Andalus participated actively in the commercial life of the larger Islamic world. The merchant-scholar al-Marwani of Córdoba, for example, made his hajj in 908 and then traveled to Iraq and India on commercial ventures. His profits amounted to thirty thousand dinars—all of which

Interior of the mosque at Córdoba, originally built in the late eighth century and enlarged during the ninth and tenth centuries. One of the largest structures in the *dar al-Islam,* the mosque rests on 850 columns and features nineteen aisles.

he lost in a shipwreck during his return home.

Imported crops increased the supply of food and enriched the diet of al-Andalus, enabling merchants and manufacturers to conduct thriving businesses in cities like Córdoba, Toledo, and Seville. Ceramics, painted tiles, lead crystal, and gold jewelry from al-Andalus enjoyed a reputation for excellence and helped pay for imported goods and the building of a magnificent capital city at Córdoba. During the tenth century Córdoba had more than 16 kilometers (10 miles) of publicly lighted roads as well as free Islamic schools, a gargantuan mosque, and a splendid library with four hundred thousand volumes.

The Changing Status of Women

A patriarchal society had emerged in Arabia long before Muhammad's time, but Arab women enjoyed rights not accorded to women in many other lands. They could legally inherit property, divorce husbands on their own initiative, and engage in business ventures. Khadija, the first of Muhammad's four wives, managed a successful commercial business.

The Quran and Women

In some respects the Quran enhanced the security of women in Arabian society. It outlawed female infanticide, and it provided that dowries went directly to brides rather than to their husbands and male guardians. It portrayed women not as the property of their menfolk, but as honorable individuals, equal to men before Allah, with their own rights and needs. Muhammad's own kindness and generosity toward his wives, as related in early accounts of the prophet's life, also served as an example that may have improved the lives of Muslim women.

For the most part, however, the Quran—and later the *sharia* as well—reinforced male dominance. The Quran and Islamic holy law recognized descent through the male line, and to guarantee proper inheritance, they placed a high premium on genealogical purity. To ensure the legitimacy of heirs, they subjected the social and sexual lives of women to the strict control of male guardians—fathers, brothers, and husbands. While teaching that men should treat women with sensitivity and respect, the Quran and the *sharia* permitted men to follow Muhammad's example and take up to four wives, whereas women could have only one husband. The Quran and the *sharia* thus provided a religious and legal foundation for a decisively patriarchal society.

Veiling of Women

When Islam expanded into the Byzantine and Sasanid empires, it encountered strong patriarchal traditions, and Muslims readily adopted long-standing customs such as the veiling of women. Social and family pressures had induced upper-class urban women to veil themselves in Mesopotamia as early as the thirteenth century B.C.E., and long before Muhammad the practice of veiling had spread to Persia and the eastern Mediterranean. As a sign of modesty, upper-class urban women covered their faces and ventured outside their homes only in the company of servants or chaperones so as to discourage the attention of men from other families. When Muslim Arabs conquered Mesopotamia, Persia, and eastern Mediterranean lands, they adopted the practice. A conspicuous symbol of male authority thus found a prominent place in the early Islamic community.

The Quran served as the preeminent source of authority in the world of Islam, and it provided specific rights for Muslim women. Over the centuries, however, jurists and legal scholars interpreted the Quran in ways that progressively limited those rights and placed women increasingly under the control of male guardians. To a large extent the increased emphasis on male authority in Islamic law reflected the influence of the strongly hierarchical and patriarchal societies of Mesopotamia, Persia, and eastern Mediterranean lands as Islam developed from a local faith to a large-scale complex society.

Islamic Values and Cultural Exchanges

Since the seventh century C.E., the Quran has served as the cornerstone of Islamic society. Arising from a rich tradition of bedouin poetry and song, the Quran established Arabic as a flexible and powerful medium of communication. Even today Muslims regard the Arabic text of the Quran as the only definitive and reliable scripture: translations do not possess the power and authority of the original. When carrying their faith to new lands during the era of Islamic expansion, Muslim missionaries spread the message of Allah and provided instruction in the Quran's teachings, although usually they also permitted continued observance of pre-Islamic traditions. Muslim intellectuals drew freely from the long-established cultural traditions of Persia, India, and Greece, which they became acquainted with during the Umayyad and Abbasid eras.

The Formation of an Islamic Cultural Tradition

Muslim theologians and jurists looked to the Quran, stories about Muhammad's life, and other sources of Islamic doctrine in their efforts to formulate moral guidelines appropriate for their society. The body of civil and criminal law embodied in the *sharia* provided a measure of cultural unity for the vastly different lands of the Islamic world. Islamic law did not by any means erase the differences, but it established a common cultural foundation that facilitated dealings between peoples of various Islamic lands and that lent substance to the concept of the *dar al-Islam.*

Promotion of Islamic Values

On a more popular level, *ulama, qadis,* and missionaries helped to bridge differences in cultural traditions and to spread Islamic values throughout the *dar al-Islam. Ulama* and *qadis* held positions at all Islamic courts, and they were prominent in the

In this manuscript illustration a Muslim teacher (the figure with the open book) instructs students in the fine points of Islamic law in a library near Baghdad.

public life of all cities in the Islamic world. By resolving disputes according to Islamic law and ordering public observance of Islamic social and moral standards, they helped to bring the values of the Quran and the *sharia* into the lives of peoples living far from the birthplace of Islam.

Formal educational institutions also helped promote Islamic values. Many mosques maintained schools that provided an elementary education and religious instruction, and wealthy Muslims sometimes established schools and provided endowments for their support. By the tenth century institutions of higher education known as *madrasas* had begun to appear, and by the twelfth century they had become established in the major cities of the Islamic world. Muslim rulers often supported the *madrasas* in the interests of recruiting literate and learned students with an advanced education in Islamic theology and law for administrative positions. Inexpensive paper enhanced scholars' ability to instruct students and disseminate their views.

Sufis

Among the most effective Islamic missionaries were mystics known as Sufis. The term *Sufi* probably came from the patched woolen garments favored by the mystics. Sufis did not deny Islamic doctrine, and indeed many of them had an advanced education in Islamic theology and law. But they also did not find formal religious teachings to be especially meaningful. Thus, instead of concerning themselves with fine points of doctrine, Sufis worked to deepen their spiritual awareness. Most Sufis led pious and ascetic lives. Some devoted themselves to helping the poor. A few gave up their possessions and lived as mendicant beggars. Many sought a mystical, ecstatic union with Allah, relying on rousing sermons, passionate singing, or spirited dancing to bring them to a state of high emotion. Muslim theologians sometimes mistrusted Sufis, fearing that in their lack of concern for doctrine they would adopt erroneous beliefs. Nevertheless, after the ninth century Sufis became increasingly popular in Muslim societies because of their piety, devotion, and eagerness to minister to the needs of their fellow human beings.

Al-Ghazali

Most important of the early Sufis was the Persian theologian al-Ghazali (1058–1111), who argued that human reason was too frail to understand the nature of Allah and hence could not explain the mysteries of the world. Only through devotion and guidance from

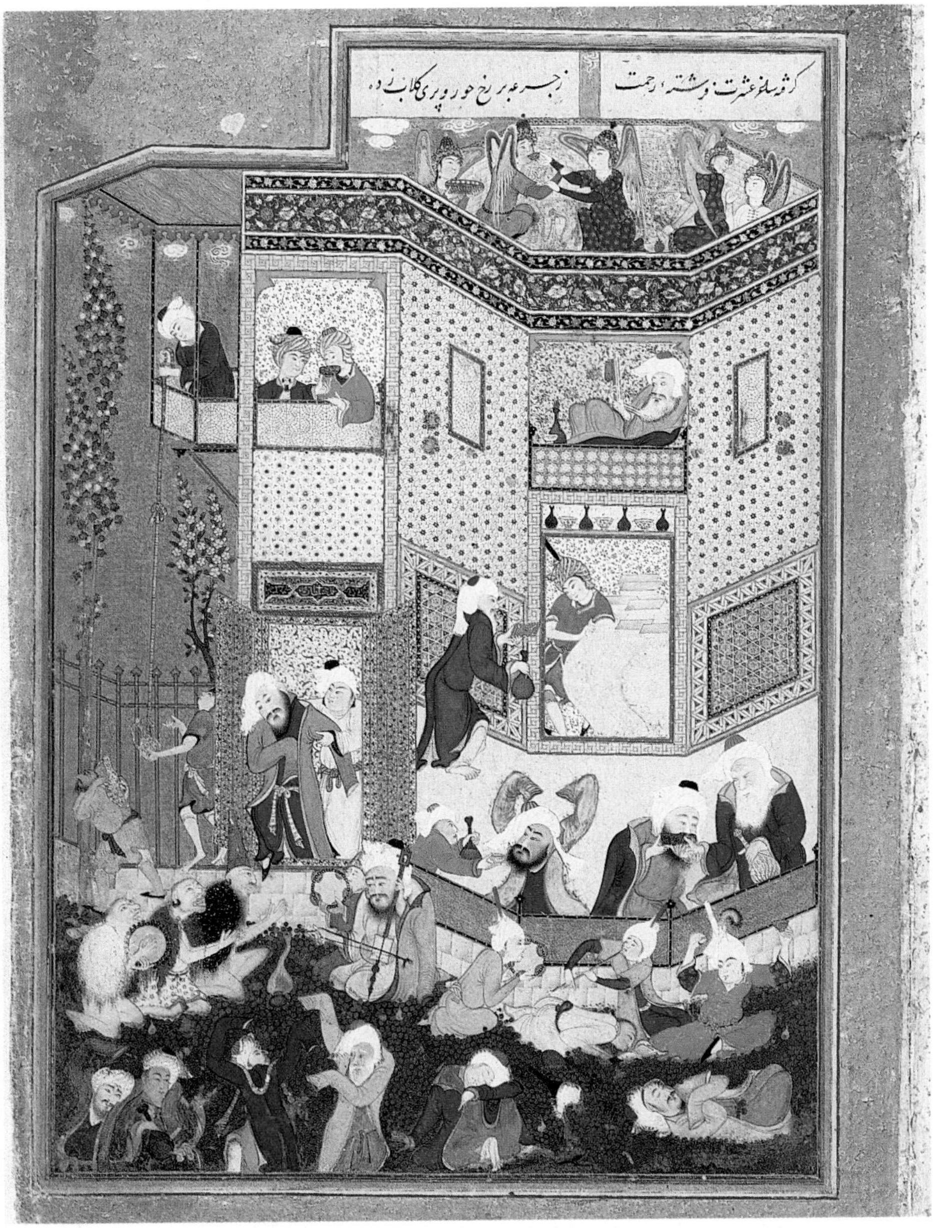

Through song, dance, and ecstatic experiences, sometimes enhanced by wine, Persian Sufis expressed their devotion to Allah, as in this sixteenth-century painting.

the Quran could human beings begin to appreciate the uniqueness and power of Allah. Indeed, al-Ghazali held that philosophy and human reasoning were vain pursuits that would inevitably lead to confusion rather than understanding.

Sufi Missionaries

Sufis were especially effective as missionaries because they emphasized devotion to Allah above mastery of doctrine. They sometimes encouraged individuals to revere Allah in their own ways, even if their methods did not have a basis in the Quran. They tolerated the continued observance of pre-Islamic customs, for example, as well as the association of Allah with deities recognized and revered in other faiths. The Sufis themselves led ascetic and holy lives, which won them the respect of the peoples to whom they preached. Because of their kindness, holiness, tolerance, and charismatic appeal, Sufis attracted numerous converts particularly in lands like Persia and India, where long-established religious faiths such as Zoroastrianism, Christianity, Buddhism, and Hinduism had enjoyed a mass following for centuries.

Hajj

The symbol of Islamic cultural unity was the Ka'ba at Mecca, which from an early date attracted pilgrims from all parts of the Islamic world. The Abbasid caliphs especially encouraged observance of the hajj: they saw themselves as supreme leaders of a cohesive Islamic community, and as a matter of policy they sought to enhance the cultural unity of their realm. They built inns along the main roads to Mecca for the convenience of travelers, policed the routes to ensure the safety of pilgrims, and made lavish gifts to shrines and sites of pilgrimage. Individuals from far-flung regions of the Abbasid empire made their way to Mecca, visited the holy sites, and learned first hand the traditions of Islam. Over the centuries these pilgrims helped to spread Islamic beliefs and values to all parts of the Islamic world, and alongside the work of *ulama, qadis,* and Sufi missionaries, their efforts helped to make the *dar al-Islam* not just a name, but a reality.

Islam and the Cultural Traditions of Persia, India, and Greece

As the Islamic community expanded, Muslims of Arab ancestry interacted regularly with peoples from other cultural traditions, especially those of Persia, India, and Greece. In some cases, particularly in lands ruled by the Umayyad and Abbasid dynasties, large numbers of conquered peoples converted to Islam, and they brought elements of their inherited cultural traditions into Islamic society. In other cases, particularly in lands beyond the authority of Islamic rulers, Muslims became acquainted with the literary, artistic, philosophical, and scientific traditions of peoples who chose not to convert. Nevertheless, their traditions often held considerable interest for Muslims, who adapted them for their own purposes.

Persian Influences on Islam

Persian traditions quickly found a place in Islamic society, since the culturally rich land of Persia fell under Islamic rule at an early date. Especially after the establishment of the Abbasid dynasty and the founding of its capital at Baghdad, Persian traditions deeply influenced Islamic political and cultural leaders. Persian administrative techniques, which Muslim conquerors borrowed from the Sasanid empire, were crucial for the organization of the imperial structure through which Umayyad and Abbasid rulers governed their vast empire. Meanwhile, Persian ideas of kingship profoundly influenced Islamic political thought. Muslim caliphs and regional governors drew readily on Persian views of kings as wise and benevolent but nonetheless absolute rulers.

Persian influence was also noticeable in literary works from the Abbasid dynasty. While Arabic served as the language of religion, theology, philosophy, and law, Persian was the principal language of literature, poetry, history, and political reflection. The verses of Omar Khayyam entitled the *Rubaiyat* ("quatrains") are widely known, thanks to a popular English translation by the Victorian poet Edward Fitzgerald, but many other writers composed works that in Persian display even greater literary elegance and originality. The marvelous collection of stories known as *The Arabian Nights* or *The Thousand and One Nights,* for example, presented popular tales of adventure and romance set in the Abbasid empire and the court of Harun al-Rashid.

Indian Influences on Islam

Indian mathematics, science, and medicine captured the attention of Arab and Persian Muslims who established Islamic states in northern India. The sophisticated mathematical tradition of Gupta India was attractive to Muslims both as a field of scholarship and for the practical purposes of reckoning and keeping accounts. Muslims readily adopted what they called "Hindi" numerals, which European peoples later called "Arabic" numerals, since they learned about them through Arab Muslims. Hindi numerals enabled Muslim scholars to develop an impressive tradition of advanced mathematics, concentrating on algebra (an Arabic word) as well as trigonometry and geometry. From a more practical point of view, Indian numerals vastly simplified bookkeeping for Muslim merchants working in the lively commercial economy of the Abbasid dynasty.

Muslims also found much to appreciate in the scientific and medical thought they encountered in India. With the aid of their powerful and flexible mathematics, Indian scholars were able to carry out precise astronomical calculations, which helped inspire the development of Muslim astronomy. Similarly, Indian medicine appealed to Muslims because of its treatments for specific ailments and its use of antidotes for poisons. Muslim visitors often railed against Indian religious beliefs—both Hindu and Buddhist—but they uniformly praised Indian mathematical, scientific, and medical thought, which they avidly adopted for their own uses and purposes.

Greek Influences on Islam

Muslims also admired the philosophical, scientific, and medical writings of classical Greece. They became especially interested in Plato and Aristotle, whose works they translated and interpreted in commentaries. During the tenth and eleventh centuries, some Muslim philosophers sought to synthesize Greek and Muslim thought by harmonizing Plato with the teachings of Islam. They encountered resistance among conservative theologians like the Sufi al-Ghazali, who considered Greek philosophy a completely unreliable guide to ultimate truth, since it relied on frail human reason rather than the revelation of the Quran.

Partly in response to al-Ghazali's attacks, twelfth-century Muslim philosophers turned their attention more to Aristotle than Plato. The most notable figure in this development was Ibn Rushd (1126–1198), *qadi* of Seville in the caliphate of Córdoba, who followed Aristotle in seeking to articulate a purely rational understanding of the world. Ibn Rushd's work not only helped to shape Islamic philosophy but also found its way to the schools and universities of western Europe, where Christian scholars knew Ibn Rushd as Averroes. During the thirteenth century his work profoundly influenced the development of scholasticism, the effort of medieval European philosophers to harmonize Christianity with Aristotelian thought.

Ibn Rushd's reliance on natural reason went too far for many Muslims, who placed more value on the revelations of the Quran than on the fruits of human logic. After the thirteenth century, Muslim philosophers and theologians who dominated the *madrasas* drew inspiration more from Islamic sources than from Greek philosophy. Platonic and Aristotelian influences did not disappear, but they lost favor in official seats of learning and fell increasingly under the shadow of teachings from the Quran and Sufi mystics. As they did with political and cultural traditions from Persia and India, Muslim thinkers absorbed Greek philosophy, reconsidered it, and used it to advance the interests of their own society.

Quite apart from philosophy, Greek mathematics, science, and medicine also appealed strongly to Muslims. Like their Indian counterparts, scholars in classical Greek and Hellenistic societies had developed elaborate traditions of scientific thought. Greek mathematics did not make use of Indian numerals, but it offered a solid body of powerful reasoning, particularly when dealing with calculations in algebra and geometry. Greek mathematics supported the development of astronomical and geographical scholarship, while studies of anatomy and physiology served as foundations for medical thought. Muslim scholars quickly absorbed these Greek traditions, combined them with influences from India, and used them all as points of departure for their own studies. The result was a brilliant flowering of mathematical, scientific, and medical scholarship that provided Muslim societies with powerful tools for understanding the natural world.

The prophet Muhammad did not intend to found a new religion. Instead, his intention was to express his faith in Allah and perfect the teachings of earlier Jewish and Christian prophets by announcing a revelation more comprehensive than those Allah had entrusted to his predecessors. His message soon attracted a circle of devout and committed disciples, and by the time of his death most of Arabia had accepted Islam, the faith founded on the individual's submission to Allah and his will. During the two centuries following the prophet's death, Arab conquerors spread Islam throughout southwest Asia and north Africa and introduced their faith to central Asia, India, the Mediterranean islands, and Iberia. This rapid expansion of Islam encouraged the development of a massive trade and communication network: merchants, diplomats, and other travelers moved easily throughout the Islamic world exchanging goods and introducing agricultural crops to new lands. Rapid expansion also led to encounters between Islam and long-established religious and cultural traditions such as Hinduism, Judaism, Zoroastrianism, Christianity, Persian literature and political thought, and classical Greek philosophy and science. Muslim rulers built a society that made a place for those of different faiths, and Muslim thinkers readily adapted earlier traditions to their own needs. As a result of its expansion, its extensive trade and communication networks, and its engagement with other religious and cultural traditions, the *dar al-Islam* became one of the most prosperous and cosmopolitan societies of the postclassical world.

CHRONOLOGY

570–632	Life of Muhammad
622	The *hijra*
632	Muhammad's *hajj*
650s	Compilation of the Quran
661–750	Umayyad dynasty
750–1258	Abbasid dynasty
786–809	Reign of Harun al-Rashid
1050s	Establishment of Saljuq control over the Abbasid dynasty
1058–1111	Life of al-Ghazali
1126–1198	Life of Ibn Rushd

FOR FURTHER READING

Muhammad Manazir Ahsan. *Social Life under the Abbasids.* New York, 1979. Draws on a wide range of sources in discussing dress, food, drink, housing, and daily life during the Abbasid era.

Richard W. Bulliet. *The Camel and the Wheel.* New York, 1990. Fascinating study of the domestication of camels and transportation technologies based on camels.

Richard C. Foltz. *Spirituality in the Land of the Noble: How Iran Shaped the World's Religions.* Oxford, 2004. Includes an accessible discussion of Persian influences on the Islamic faith.

Abu Hamid Muhammad al-Ghazzali. *The Alchemy of Happiness.* Trans. by Claude Field. Rev. by Elton L. Daniel. New York, 1991. Translation of one of the classic works of early Islamic religious and moral thought.

H. A. R. Gibb. *Mohammedanism.* 2nd ed. London, 1953. A short, analytical overview of the Islamic faith and its history by a prominent scholar.

Ahmad Y. al-Hassan and Donald R. Hill. *Islamic Technology: An Illustrated History.* Cambridge, 1986. Thorough survey of Islamic science and technology, with attention both to original inventions and to elements borrowed by Muslims from other societies.

Mahmood Ibrahim. *Merchant Capital and Islam.* Austin, 1990. Examines the role of trade in Arabia during Muhammad's time and in early Islamic society.

Salma Khadra Jayyusi, ed. *The Legacy of Muslim Spain.* Leiden, 1992. Important collection of scholarly essays on Muslim influences at the western end of the Islamic world.

Ira M. Lapidus. *A History of Islamic Societies.* Cambridge, 1988. Authoritative survey of Islamic history, concentrating on social and cultural issues.

Ilse Lichtenstadter. *Introduction to Classical Arabic Literature.* New York, 1974. A brief overview, accompanied by an extensive selection of texts in English translation.

M. Lombard. *The Golden Age of Islam.* Princeton, 2004. Concentrates on the social and economic history of the Abbasid period.

William H. McNeill and Marilyn R. Waldman, eds. *The Islamic World.* New York, 1973. An excellent collection of primary sources in translation.

F. E. Peters. *The Hajj: The Muslim Pilgrimage to Mecca and the Holy Places.* Princeton, 1994. Draws on scores of travelers' reports in studying the Muslim practice through the ages of making a pilgrimage to Mecca.

———. *Muhammad and the Origins of Islam.* Albany, 1994. Excellent introduction to Muhammad's life and thought and the early days of his movement.

Al Qur'an: A Contemporary Translation. Trans. by Ahmed Ali. Princeton, 1984. A sensitive translation of the holy book of Islam.

Francis Robinson, ed. *The Cambridge Illustrated History of the Islamic World.* Cambridge, 1996. An excellent and lavishly illustrated introduction to Islam and the Muslim world.

Maxime Rodinson. *Islam and Capitalism.* Trans. by B. Pearce. New York, 1973. An influential volume that examines Islamic teachings on economic matters as well as economic practice in the Muslim world.

———. *Mohammed.* Trans. by Anne Carter. New York, 1971. Places Muhammad in his social and economic context.

Andrew M. Watson. *Agricultural Innovation in the Early Islamic World: The Diffusion of Crops and Farming Techniques, 700–1100.* Cambridge, 1983. Important scholarly study of the diffusion of food and industrial crops throughout the early Islamic world.

Frances Wood. *The Silk Road: Two Thousand Years in the Heart of Asia.* Berkeley, 2002. A brilliantly illustrated volume discussing the history of the silk roads from antiquity to the twentieth century.

OLC

See our **Online Learning Center at www.mhhe.com/bentley3** for additional readings, practice maps, quizzes, and internet activities.

PSI

Unfamiliar words? Check out the **Primary Source Investigator CD-ROM** for an interactive glossary, interactive maps, more images, and primary sources.

The features of the emperor Tang Taizong reflect his Turkish and Chinese ancestry.

CHAPTER 15

The Resurgence of Empire in East Asia

The Restoration of Centralized Imperial Rule in China
The Sui Dynasty
The Tang Dynasty
The Song Dynasty

The Economic Development of Tang and Song China
Agricultural Development
Technological and Industrial Development
The Emergence of a Market Economy

Cultural Change in Tang and Song China
The Establishment of Buddhism
Neo-Confucianism

Chinese Influence in East Asia
Korea and Vietnam
Early Japan
Medieval Japan

Early in the seventh century C.E., the emperor of China issued an order forbidding his subjects to travel beyond Chinese borders into central Asia. In 629, however, in defiance of the emperor, a young Buddhist monk slipped past imperial watchtowers under cover of darkness and made his way west. His name was Xuanzang, and his destination was India, homeland of Buddhism. Although educated in Confucian texts as a youth, Xuanzang had followed his older brother into a monastery where he became devoted to Buddhism. While studying the Sanskrit language, Xuanzang noticed that Chinese writings on Buddhism contained many teachings that were confusing or even contradictory to those of Indian Buddhist texts. He decided to travel to India, visit the holy sites of Buddhism, and study with the most knowledgeable Buddhist teachers and sages to learn about his faith from the purest sources.

Xuanzang could not have imagined the difficulties he would face. Immediately after his departure from China, his guide abandoned him in the Gobi desert. After losing his water bag and collapsing in the heat, Xuanzang made his way to the oasis town of Turpan on the silk roads. The Buddhist ruler of Turpan provided the devout pilgrim with travel supplies and rich gifts to support his mission. Among the presents were twenty-four letters of introduction to rulers of lands on the way to India, each one attached to a bolt of silk, five hundred additional bolts of silk and two carts of fruit for the most important ruler, thirty horses, twenty-five laborers, and five hundred bolts of silk along with gold, silver, and silk clothes for Xuanzang to use as travel funds. After departing from Turpan, Xuanzang crossed three of the world's highest mountain ranges—the Tian Shan, Hindu Kush, and Pamir ranges—and lost one-third of his party to exposure and starvation in the Tian Shan. He crossed yawning gorges thousands of meters deep on footbridges fashioned from rope or chains, and he faced numerous attacks by bandits as well as confrontations with demons, dragons, and evil spirits.

Yet Xuanzang persisted and arrived in India in 630. He lived there for more than twelve years, visiting the holy sites of Buddhism and devoting himself to the study of languages and Buddhist doctrine, especially at Nalanda, the center of advanced Buddhist education in India. He also amassed a huge collection of relics and images as well as some 657 books, all of which he packed into 527 crates and transported back to China in order to advance the understanding of Buddhism in his native land.

By the time of his return in 645, Xuanzang had logged more than 16,000 kilometers (10,000 miles) on the road. News of the holy monk's efforts had reached the imperial court, and even though Xuanzang had violated the ban on travel, he received a hero's welcome and an audience with the emperor. Until his death in 664, Xuanzang spent his remaining years translating Buddhist treatises into Chinese and promoting his faith. His efforts helped to popularize Buddhism and bring about nearly universal adoption of the faith throughout China.

Xuanzang undertook his journey at a propitious time. For more than 350 years after the fall of the Han dynasty, war, invasion, conquest, and foreign rule disrupted Chinese society. Toward the end of the sixth century, however, centralized imperial rule returned to China. The Sui and Tang dynasties restored order and presided over an era of rapid economic growth in China. Agricultural yields rose dramatically, and technological innovations boosted the production of manufactured goods. China stood alongside the Byzantine and Abbasid empires as a political and economic anchor of the postclassical world.

For China the postclassical era was an age of intense interaction with other peoples. Chinese merchants participated in trade networks that linked most regions of the eastern hemisphere. Buddhism spread beyond its homeland of India, attracted a large popular following in China, and even influenced the thought of Confucian scholars. A resurgent China made its influence felt throughout east Asia: diplomats and armed forces introduced Chinese ways into Korea and Vietnam, and rulers of the Japanese islands looked to China for guidance in matters of political organization. Korea, Vietnam, and Japan retained their distinctiveness, but all three lands drew deep inspiration from China and participated in a larger east Asian society centered on China.

The Restoration of Centralized Imperial Rule in China

During the centuries following the Han dynasty, several regional kingdoms made bids to assert their authority over all of China, but none possessed the resources to dominate its rivals over the long term. In the late sixth century, however, Yang Jian, an ambitious ruler in northern China, embarked on a series of military campaigns that brought all of China once again under centralized imperial rule. Yang Jian's Sui dynasty survived less than thirty years, but the tradition of centralized rule outlived his house. The Tang dynasty replaced the Sui, and the Song succeeded the Tang. The Tang and Song dynasties organized Chinese society so efficiently that China became a center of exceptional agricultural and industrial production. Indeed, much of the eastern hemisphere felt the effects of the powerful Chinese economy of the Tang and Song dynasties.

The Sui Dynasty

Establishment of the Dynasty

Like Qin Shihuangdi some eight centuries years earlier, Yang Jian imposed tight political discipline on his own state and then extended his rule to the rest of China. Yang Jian began his rise to power when a Turkish ruler appointed him duke of Sui in northern China. In 580 Yang Jian's patron died, leaving a seven-year-old son as his heir. Yang Jian installed the boy as ruler but forced his abdication one year later, claiming the throne and the Mandate of Heaven for himself. During the next decade Yang Jian sent military expeditions into central Asia and southern China. By 589 the house of Sui ruled all of China.

Like the rulers of the Qin dynasty, the emperors of the Sui dynasty (589–618 C.E.) placed enormous demands on their subjects in the course of building a strong, centralized government. The Sui emperors ordered the construction of palaces and granaries,

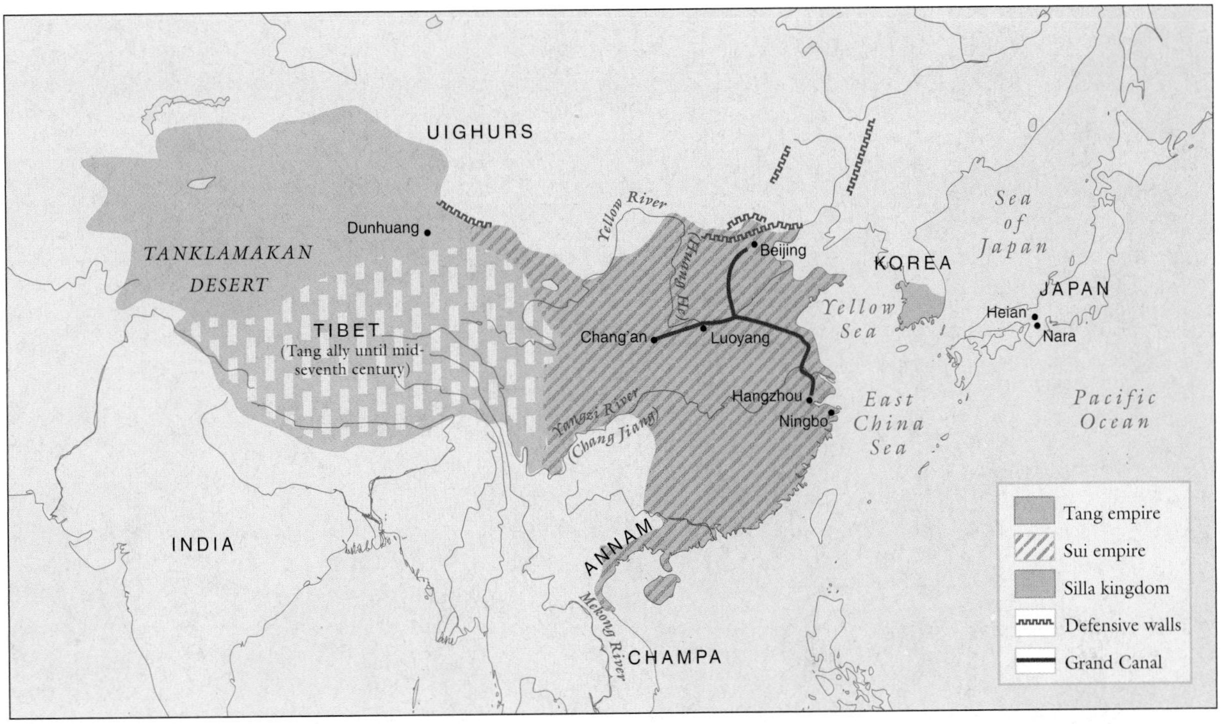

MAP [15.1]
The Sui and Tang dynasties, 589–907 C.E.

carried out extensive repairs on defensive walls, dispatched military forces to central Asia and Korea, levied high taxes, and demanded compulsory labor services.

The Grand Canal

The most elaborate project undertaken during the Sui dynasty was the construction of the Grand Canal, which was one of the world's largest waterworks projects before modern times. The second emperor, Sui Yangdi (reigned 604–618 C.E.), completed work on the canal to facilitate trade between northern and southern China, particularly to make the abundant supplies of rice and other food crops from the Yangzi River valley available to residents of northern regions. The only practical and economical way to transport food crops in large quantities was by water. But since Chinese rivers generally flow from west to east, only an artificial waterway could support a large volume of trade between north and south.

The Grand Canal was really a series of artificial waterways that ultimately reached from Hangzhou in the south to the imperial capital of Chang'an in the west to a terminus near modern Beijing in the north. Sui Yangdi used canals dug as early as the Zhou dynasty, but he linked them into a network that served much of China. When completed, the Grand Canal extended almost 2,000 kilometers (1,240 miles) and reportedly was forty paces wide, with roads running parallel to the waterway on either side.

Though expensive to construct, Sui Yangdi's investment in the Grand Canal paid dividends for more than a thousand years. It integrated the economies of northern and southern China, thereby establishing an economic foundation for political and cultural unity. Until the arrival of railroads in the twentieth century, the Grand Canal served as the principal conduit for internal trade. Indeed, the canal continues to function even today, although mechanical transport has diminished its significance as a trade route.

Sui Yangdi's construction projects served China well over a long term, but their dependence on high taxes and forced labor generated hostility toward his rule. The

In a painting that dates probably from about the seventeenth century, workers build dikes to hold back a river. Construction of the Grand Canal also involved heavy work by large numbers of conscripted laborers.

Grand Canal alone required the services of conscripted laborers by the millions. Military reverses in Korea prompted discontented subjects to revolt against Sui rule. During the late 610s, rebellions broke out in northern China when Sui Yangdi sought additional resources for his Korean campaign. In 618 a disgruntled minister assassinated the emperor and brought the dynasty to an end.

The Tang Dynasty

Soon after Sui Yangdi's death, a rebel leader seized Chang'an and proclaimed himself emperor of a new dynasty that he named Tang after his hereditary title. The dynasty survived for almost three hundred years (618–907 C.E.), and Tang rulers organized China into a powerful, productive, and prosperous society.

Tang Taizong

Much of the Tang's success was due to the energy, ability, and policies of the dynasty's second emperor, Tang Taizong (reigned 627–649 C.E.). Taizong was both ambitious and ruthless: in making his way to the imperial throne, he murdered two of his brothers and pushed his father aside. Once on the throne, however, he displayed a high sense of duty and strove conscientiously to provide an effective, stable government. He built a splendid capital at Chang'an, and he saw himself as a Confucian ruler who heeded the interests of his subjects. Contemporaries reported that banditry ended during his reign, that the price of rice remained low, and that taxes levied on peasants amounted to only one-fortieth of the annual harvest—a 2.5 percent tax rate—although required rent payments and compulsory labor services meant that the effective rate of taxation was somewhat higher. These reports suggest that China enjoyed an era of unusual stability and prosperity during the reign of Tang Taizong.

Three policies in particular help to explain the success of the early Tang dynasty: maintenance of a well-articulated transportation and communications network, distribution of land according to the principles of the equal-field system, and reliance on a bureaucracy based on merit. All three policies originated in the Sui dynasty, but Tang rulers applied them more systematically and effectively than their predecessors had.

Transportation and Communications

Apart from the Grand Canal, which served as the principal route for long-distance transportation within China, Tang rulers maintained an extensive communications network based on roads, horses, and sometimes human runners. Along the main routes, Tang officials maintained inns, postal stations, and stables, which provided rest and refreshment for travelers, couriers, and their mounts. Using couriers traveling by horse, the Tang court could communicate with the most distant cities in the empire in about eight days. Even human runners provided impressively speedy services: relay teams of some 9,600 runners supplied the Tang court at Chang'an with seafood delivered fresh from Ningbo, more than 1,000 kilometers (620 miles) away!

The Equal-Field System

The equal-field system governed the allocation of agricultural land. Its purpose was to ensure an equitable distribution of land and to avoid the concentration of landed property that had caused social problems during the Han dynasty. The system allotted land to individuals and their families according to the land's fertility and the recipients' needs. About one-fifth of the land became the hereditary possession of the recipients, while the rest remained available for redistribution when the original recipients' needs and circumstances changed.

For about a century, administrators were able to apply the principles of the equal-field system relatively consistently. By the early eighth century, however, the system showed signs of strain. A rapidly rising population placed pressure on the land available for distribution. Meanwhile, through favors, bribery, or intimidation of administrators, influential families found ways to retain land scheduled for redistribution. Furthermore, large parcels of land fell out of the system altogether when Buddhist monasteries acquired them. Nevertheless, during the first half of the Tang dynasty, the system provided a foundation for stability and prosperity in the Chinese countryside.

Bureaucracy of Merit

The Tang dynasty also relied heavily on a bureaucracy based on merit, as reflected by performance on imperial civil service examinations. Following the example of the Han dynasty, Sui and Tang rulers recruited government officials from the ranks of candidates who had progressed through the Confucian educational system and had mastered a sophisticated curriculum concentrating on the classic works of Chinese literature and philosophy. Although powerful families used their influence to place relatives in positions of authority, most officeholders won their posts because of intellectual ability. Members of this talented class were generally loyal to the dynasty, and they worked to preserve and strengthen the state. The Confucian educational system and the related civil service served Chinese governments so well that with modifications and an occasional interruption, they survived for thirteen centuries, disappearing only after the collapse of the Qing dynasty in the early twentieth century.

Military Expansion

Soon after its foundation, the powerful and dynamic Tang state began to flex its military muscles. In the north, Tang forces brought Manchuria under imperial authority and forced the Silla kingdom in Korea to acknowledge the Tang emperor as overlord. To the south, Tang armies conquered the northern part of Vietnam. To the west they extended Tang authority as far as the Aral Sea and brought a portion of the high plateau of Tibet under Tang control. Territorially, the Tang empire ranks among the largest in Chinese history.

Tang Foreign Relations

In an effort to fashion a stable diplomatic order, the Tang emperors revived the Han dynasty's practice of maintaining tributary relationships between China and neighboring lands. According to Chinese political theory, China was the Middle Kingdom, a powerful realm with the responsibility to bring order to subordinate lands through a system of tributary relationships. Neighboring lands and peoples would recognize Chinese emperors as their overlords. As tokens of their subordinate status, envoys from these states would regularly deliver gifts to the court of the Middle Kingdom and would perform the kowtow—a ritual prostration during which subordinates knelt before the emperor and touched their foreheads to the ground. In return, tributary states received confirmation of their authority as well as lavish gifts. Because Chinese authorities often had little real influence in these supposedly subordinate lands, there was always something of a fictional quality to the system. Nevertheless, it was extremely important throughout east Asia and central Asia because it institutionalized relations between China and neighboring lands, fostering trade and cultural exchanges as well as diplomatic contacts.

Tang Decline

Under able rulers such as Taizong, the Tang dynasty flourished. During the mid-eighth century, however, casual and careless leadership brought the dynasty to a crisis from which it never fully recovered. In 755, while the emperor neglected public affairs in favor of music and his favorite concubine, one of the dynasty's foremost military commanders, An Lushan, mounted a rebellion and captured the capital at Chang'an, as well as the secondary capital at Luoyang. His revolt was short-lived: in 757 a soldier murdered An Lushan, and by 763 Tang forces had suppressed An Lushan's army and recovered their capitals. But the rebellion left the dynasty in a gravely weakened state. Tang commanders had to invite a nomadic Turkish people,

In this wall painting from the tomb of a Tang prince, three Chinese officials (at left) receive envoys from foreign lands who pay their respects to representatives of the Middle Kingdom. The envoys probably come from the Byzantine empire, Korea, and Siberia.

Sources from the Past

The Poet Du Fu on Tang Dynasty Wars

The eighth century was a golden age of Chinese poetry. Among the foremost writers of the era was Du Fu (712–770 C.E.), often considered China's greatest poet. Born into a prominent Confucian family, Du Fu wrote in his early years about the beauty of the natural world. After the rebellion of An Lushan, however, he fell into poverty and experienced difficulties. Not surprisingly, poetry of his later years lamented the chaos of the late eighth century. In the following verses, Du Fu offered a bitter perspective on the wars that plagued China in the 750s and 760s.

A Song of War Chariots

The war-chariots rattle,
The war-horses whinny.
Each man of you has a bow and a quiver at his belt.
Father, mother, son, wife, stare at you going,
Till dust shall have buried the bridge beyond Chang'an.
They run with you, crying, they tug at your sleeves,
And the sound of their sorrow goes up to the clouds;
And every time a bystander asks you a question,
You can only say to him that you have to go.
. . . We remember others at fifteen sent north to guard the river
And at forty sent west to cultivate the camp-farms.
The mayor wound their turbans for them when they started out.
With their turbaned hair white now, they are still at the border,
At the border where the blood of men spills like the sea—
And still the heart of Emperor Wu is beating for war.
. . . Do you know that, east of China's mountains, in two hundred districts
And in thousands of villages, nothing grows but weeds,
And though strong women have bent to the ploughing,
East and west the furrows all are broken down?
. . . Men of China are able to face the stiffest battle,
But their officers drive them like chickens and dogs.
Whatever is asked of them,
Dare they complain?
For example, this winter
Held west of the gate,
Challenged for taxes,
How could they pay?
. . . We have learned that to have a son is bad luck—
It is very much better to have a daughter
Who can marry and live in the house of a neighbour,
While under the sod we bury our boys.
. . . Go to the Blue Sea, look along the shore
At all the old white bones forsaken—
New ghosts are wailing there now with the old,
Loudest in the dark sky of a stormy day.

SOURCE: Cyril Birch, ed. *Anthology of Chinese Literature,* 2 vols. New York: Grove Press, 1965, pp. 1:240–41.

Assess the effects of war in the late Tang dynasty from the viewpoints of imperial rulers and individual subjects.

the Uighurs, to bring an army into China to oust An Lushan from the imperial capitals. In return for their services, the Uighurs demanded the right to sack Chang'an and Luoyang after the expulsion of the rebels.

The Tang imperial house never regained control of affairs after this crisis. The equal-field system deteriorated, and dwindling tax receipts failed to meet dynastic needs. Imperial armies were unable to resist the encroachments of Turkish peoples in the late eighth century. During the ninth century a series of rebellions devastated the Chinese countryside. One uprising, led by the military commander Huang Chao, embroiled much of eastern China for almost a decade from 875 to 884. Huang Chao's revolt reflected and fueled popular discontent: he routinely pillaged the wealthy and distributed a portion of his plunder among the poor. In an effort to control the rebels, the Tang emperors granted progressively greater power and authority to regional military commanders, who gradually became the effective rulers of China. In 907 the last Tang emperor abdicated his throne, and the dynasty came to an end.

The Song Dynasty

Following the Tang collapse, warlords ruled China until the Song dynasty reimposed centralized imperial rule in the late tenth century. Though it survived for more than three centuries, the Song dynasty (960–1279 C.E.) never built a very powerful state. Song rulers mistrusted military leaders, and they placed much more emphasis on civil administration, industry, education, and the arts than on military affairs.

Song Taizu

The first Song emperor, Song Taizu (reigned 960–976 C.E.), himself inaugurated this policy. Song Taizu began his career as a junior military officer serving one of the most powerful warlords in northern China. He had a reputation for honesty and effectiveness, and in 960 his troops proclaimed him emperor. During the next several years, he and his army subjected the warlords to their authority and consolidated Song control throughout China. He then persuaded his generals to retire honorably to a life of leisure so that they would not seek to displace him, and he set about organizing a centralized administration that placed military forces under tight supervision.

Song Taizu regarded all state officials, even minor functionaries in distant provinces, as servants of the imperial government. In exchange for their loyalty, Song rulers rewarded these officials handsomely. They vastly expanded the bureaucracy based on merit by creating more opportunities for individuals to seek a Confucian education and take civil service examinations. They accepted many more candidates into the bureaucracy than their Sui and Tang predecessors, and they provided generous salaries for those who qualified for government appointments. They even placed civil bureaucrats in charge of military forces.

Song Weaknesses

The Song approach to administration resulted in a more centralized imperial government than earlier Chinese dynasties had enjoyed. But it caused two big problems that weakened the dynasty and eventually brought about its fall. The first problem was financial: the enormous Song bureaucracy devoured China's surplus production. As the number of bureaucrats and the size of their rewards grew, the imperial treasury came under tremendous pressure. Efforts to raise taxes aggravated the peasants, who mounted two major rebellions in the early twelfth century. By that time, however, bureaucrats dominated the Song administration to the point that it was impossible to reform the system.

The second problem was military. Scholar bureaucrats generally had little military education and little talent for military affairs, yet they led Song armies in the field and made military decisions. It was no coincidence that nomadic peoples flourished along China's northern border throughout the Song dynasty. From the early tenth through the early twelfth century, the Khitan, a seminomadic people from Manchuria, ruled a vast empire stretching from northern Korea to Mongolia. During the first half of the Song dynasty, the Khitan demanded and received large tribute payments of silk and silver from the Song state to the south. In the early twelfth century, the nomadic Jurchen conquered the Khitan, overran northern China, captured the Song capital at Kaifeng, and proclaimed establishment of the Jin empire. Thereafter the Song dynasty moved its capital to the prosperous port city of Hangzhou and survived only in southern China so that the latter part of the dynasty is commonly known as the Southern Song. This

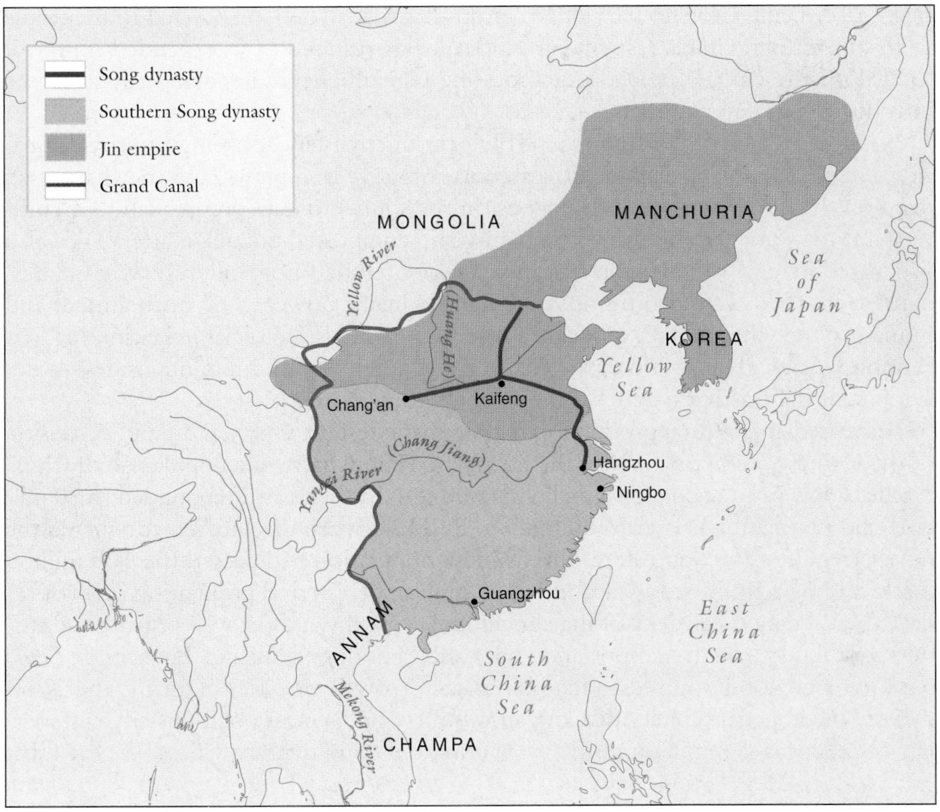

MAP [15.2]
The Song dynasty, 960–1279 C.E.

For an interactive version of this map, go to www.mhhe.com/bentley3ch15maps.

truncated Southern Song shared a border with the Jin empire about midway between the Yellow River and the Yangzi River until 1279, when Mongol forces ended the dynasty and incorporated southern China into their empire.

The Economic Development of Tang and Song China

Although the Song dynasty did not develop a particularly strong military capacity, it benefited from a remarkable series of agricultural, technological, industrial, and commercial developments that transformed China into the economic powerhouse of Eurasia. This economic development originated in the Tang dynasty, but its results became most clear during the Song, which presided over a land of enormous prosperity. The economic surge of Tang and Song times had implications that went well beyond China, since it stimulated trade and production throughout much of the eastern hemisphere for more than half a millennium, from about 600 to 1300 C.E.

Agricultural Development

Fast-Ripening Rice

The foundation of economic development in Tang and Song China was a surge in agricultural production. Sui and Tang armies prepared the way for increased agricultural productivity when they imposed their control over southern China and ventured into Vietnam. In Vietnam they encountered new strains of fast-ripening rice that enabled cultivators to harvest two crops per year. When introduced to the fertile fields of southern China, fast-ripening rice quickly resulted in an expanded supply of food. Like the *dar al-Islam,* Tang and Song China benefited enormously from the introduction of new food crops.

New Agricultural Techniques

Chinese cultivators also increased their productivity by adopting improved agricultural techniques. They made increased use of heavy iron plows, and they harnessed oxen (in the north) and water buffaloes (in the south) to help prepare land for cultivation. They enriched the soil with manure and composted organic matter. They also organized extensive irrigation systems. These included not only reservoirs, dikes, dams, and canals but also pumps and water wheels, powered by both animal and human energy, that moved water into irrigation systems. Artificial irrigation made it possible to extend cultivation to new lands, including terraced mountainsides—a development that vastly expanded China's agricultural potential.

Population Growth

Increased agricultural production had dramatic results. One was a rapid expansion of the Chinese population. After the fall of the Han dynasty, the population of China reached a low point at about 45 million in 600 C.E. By 800 it had rebounded to 50 million, and two centuries later to 60 million. By 1127, when the Jurchen conquered the northern half of the Song state, the Chinese population had passed the 100 million mark, and by 1200 it stood at about 115 million. This rapid population growth reflected both the productivity of the agricultural economy and the well-organized distribution of food through transportation networks built during Sui and Tang times.

Urbanization

Increased food supplies encouraged the growth of cities. During the Tang dynasty the imperial capital of Chang'an was the world's most populous city with perhaps as many as two million residents. During the Song dynasty, China was the most

A wall painting in a Buddhist cave depicts a peasant plowing his field in the rain with the aid of an ox and a heavy plow. Other peasants have found shelter from the rain and consume a midday meal brought to them by their wives.

urbanized land in the world. In the late thirteenth century, Hangzhou, capital of the Southern Song dynasty, had more than one million residents. They supported hundreds of restaurants, taverns, teahouses, brothels, music halls, theaters, clubhouses, gardens, markets, craft shops, and specialty stores dealing in silk, gems, porcelain, lacquerware, and other goods. Hangzhou residents, like those in most cities, observed peculiar local customs. Taverns often had several floors, for example, and patrons gravitated to higher or lower stories according to their plans: those desiring only a cup or two of wine sat at street level, whereas those planning an extended evening of revelry sought tables on the higher floors.

As a capital, Hangzhou was something of a special case among cities, but during the Tang and Song eras, scores of Chinese cities boasted populations of one hundred thousand or more. Li Bo (701–761 C.E.), who was perhaps the most popular poet of the Tang era, took the social life of these Chinese cities as one of his principal themes. Li Bo mostly wrote light, pleasing verse celebrating life, friendship, and especially wine. (Tradition holds that he died by drowning when the drunken poet fell out of a boat while attempting to embrace the moon's reflection in the water.) The annual spring festival was an occasion dear to the heart of urban residents, who flocked to the streets to shop for new products, have their fortunes told, and eat tasty snacks from food vendors.

Another result of increased food production was the emergence of a commercialized agricultural economy. Because fast-ripening rice yielded bountiful harvests, many cultivators could purchase inexpensive rice and raise vegetables and fruits for sale on the commercial market. Cultivators specialized in crops that grew well in their own regions, and they often exported their harvests to distant regions. By the twelfth century, for example, the wealthy southern province of Fujian imported rice and devoted its land to the production of lychees, oranges, and sugarcane, which fetched high prices in northern markets. Indeed, market-oriented cultivation went so far that

A twelfth-century painting depicts the spring festival as observed in the northern Song capital of Kaifeng. Porters, shopkeepers, peddlers, fortune tellers, and Confucian scholars deep in conversation are all in view.

authorities tried—with only limited success—to require Fujianese to grow rice so as to avoid excessive dependence on imports.

Patriarchal Social Structures

Alongside increasing wealth and agricultural productivity, Tang and especially Song China experienced a tightening of patriarchal social structures, which perhaps represented an effort to preserve family fortunes through enhanced family solidarity. During the Song dynasty the veneration of family ancestors became much more elaborate than before. Instead of simply remembering ancestors and invoking their aid in rituals performed at home, descendants diligently sought the graves of their earliest traceable forefathers and then arranged elaborate graveside rituals in their honor. Whole extended families often traveled great distances to attend annual rituals venerating deceased ancestors—a practice that strengthened the sense of family identity and cohesiveness.

Foot Binding

Strengthened patriarchal authority also helps to explain the popularity of foot binding, which spread among privileged classes during the Song era. Foot binding involved the tight wrapping of young girls' feet with strips of cloth that prevented natural growth of the bones and resulted in tiny, malformed, curved feet. Women with bound feet could not walk easily or naturally. Usually they needed canes to walk by themselves, and sometimes they depended on servants to carry them around in litters. Foot binding never became universal in China—it was impractical for peasants or lower-class working women in the cities—but wealthy families often bound the feet of their daughters to enhance their attractiveness, display their high social standing, and gain increased control over the girls' behavior. Like the practice of veiling women in the Islamic world, foot binding placed women of privileged classes under tight supervision of their husbands or other male guardians, who then managed the women's affairs in the interests of the larger family.

Technological and Industrial Development

Porcelain

Abundant supplies of food enabled many people to pursue technological and industrial interests. During the Tang and Song dynasties, Chinese crafts workers generated a remarkable range of technological innovations. During Tang times they discovered techniques of producing high-quality porcelain, which was lighter, thinner, and adaptable to more uses than earlier pottery. When fired with glazes, porcelain could also become an aesthetically appealing utensil and even a work of art. Porcelain technology gradually diffused to other societies, and Abbasid crafts workers in particular produced porcelain in large quantities. Yet demand for Chinese porcelain remained high, and the Chinese exported vast quantities of porcelain during the Tang and Song dynasties. Archaeologists have turned up Tang and Song porcelain at sites all along the trade networks of the postclassical era: Chinese porcelain graced the tables of wealthy and refined households in southeast Asia, India, Persia, and the port cities of east Africa. Tang and Song products gained such a reputation that fine porcelain has come to be known generally as *chinaware*.

Metallurgy

Tang and Song craftsmen also improved metallurgical technologies. Production of iron and steel surged during this era, due partly to techniques that resulted in stronger and more useful metals. Chinese craftsmen discovered that they could use coke instead of coal in their furnaces and produce superior grades of metal. Between the early ninth and the early twelfth century, iron production increased almost tenfold according to official records, which understate total production. Most of the increased supply of iron and steel went into weaponry and agricultural tools: during the early Song dynasty, imperial armaments manufacturers produced 16.5 million iron arrowheads per year. Iron and steel also went into construction projects involving large structures such as bridges and pagodas. As in the case of porcelain technology, metallurgical techniques soon diffused to lands beyond China. Indeed, Song military difficulties stemmed partly from the fact that nomadic peoples quickly learned Chinese techniques and fashioned their own iron weapons for use in campaigns against China.

Gunpowder

Quite apart from improving existing technologies, Tang and Song craftsmen also invented entirely new products, tools, and techniques, most notably gunpowder, printing, and naval technologies. Daoist alchemists discovered how to make gunpowder during the Tang dynasty, as they tested the properties of various experimental concoctions while seeking elixirs to prolong life. They soon learned that it was unwise to mix charcoal, saltpeter, sulphur, and arsenic, because the volatile compound often resulted in singed beards and destroyed buildings. Military officials, however, recognized opportunity in the explosive mixture. By the mid-tenth century they were using gunpowder in bamboo "fire lances," a kind of flamethrower, and by the eleventh century they had fashioned primitive bombs.

The earliest gunpowder weapons had limited military effectiveness: they probably caused more confusion because of noise and smoke than damage because of their destructive potential. Over time, however, refinements enhanced their effectiveness. Knowledge of gunpowder chemistry quickly diffused through Eurasia, and by the late thirteenth century peoples of southwest Asia and Europe were experimenting with metal-barreled cannons.

Printing

The precise origins of printing lie obscured in the mists of time. Although some form of printing may have predated the Sui dynasty, only during the Tang era did printing become common. The earliest printers employed block-printing techniques: they carved a reverse image of an entire page into a wooden block, inked the block, and then pressed a sheet of paper on top. By the mid-eleventh century, printers had begun to experiment with reusable, movable type: instead of carving images into blocks, they fashioned dies in the shape of ideographs, arranged them in a frame, inked them, and pressed the frame over paper sheets. Because formal writing in the Chinese language involved as many as forty thousand different characters, printers often found movable type to be unwieldy and inconvenient, so they continued to print from wooden blocks long after movable type became available.

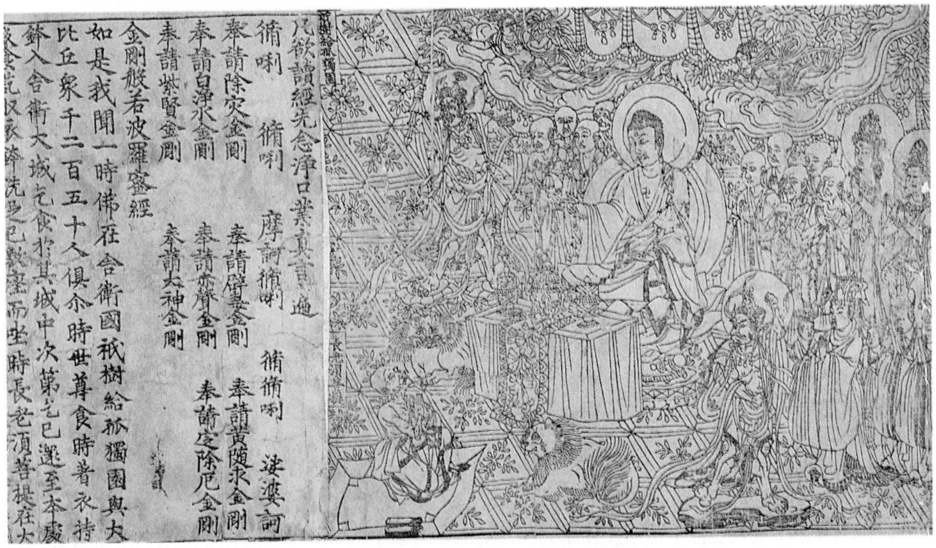

A printed book from the twelfth century presents a Chinese translation of a Buddhist text along with a block-printed illustration of the Buddha addressing his followers.

Contexts & Connections

The Spread of Printing Technology

It is not surprising that China was the birthplace of printing. Paper had been in use there at least since the second century C.E., so early Chinese artisans had a strong but cheap material to use as a surface for printed characters and images. For many centuries Chinese had also fashioned seals from wood, stone, metal, and clay to make impressions of names or words on paintings, letters, and documents. It was a relatively short step from the impressment of individual characters onto paper with a seal to the printing of whole pages, documents, and books from carved blocks of wood.

By the ninth century, printing had made its way to Japan and Korea. Buddhism favored the adoption of printing throughout east Asia because Mahayana Buddhists regarded the copying and distribution of sacred texts as a highly meritorious act. Indeed, in Japan printers worked only in monasteries and produced only religious texts until the late sixteenth century.

Beyond east Asia, however, printing won acceptance only gradually. Knowledge of Chinese printing did not reach Christian Europe until the thirteenth century. In any event, printing was not a practical possibility there until the arrival of paper-making technology. The principal material used in early European book production was parchment or vellum, a very expensive writing surface specially prepared from the skins of young sheep, calves, or goats. If they had only parchment or vellum to work with, Europeans would not have been able to afford the quantities of books that printing presses were capable of churning out. Paper production reached Islamic Spain about 1150 but did not come into widespread use in Christian Europe until the fifteenth century. About 1450 the German craftsman Johannes Gutenberg independently invented a system of printing with movable type. From that time forward, the European printing press and paper-making industry mutually reinforced one another, and Europe was soon awash in a sea of books, pamphlets, announcements, flyers, news sheets, and other printed matter.

What about the Islamic world? Paper was in use in Muslim central Asia at least from the eighth century, and the Abbasid caliph Harun al-Rashid built a paper mill in Baghdad about 794. Paper quickly displaced parchment and vellum as a writing material in the Islamic world, yet printing did not come into widespread use there until the nineteenth century, at least partly because of aesthetic considerations. Among the most highly prized art forms in the Islamic world was calligraphy: for many readers, printing presses offered a very poor substitute for elegant, handwritten texts. Muslims expected their copies of the Quran in particular to be finely crafted volumes, not cheap, mass-produced books. The absence of printing meant that many texts were inaccessible to Muslim readers. Yet thousands of manuscript books circulated throughout the realm of Islam and served the needs of Muslim societies tolerably well. Only in the context of political, military, and financial difficulties in modern times did the efficiencies of printing come to outweigh the aesthetics of calligraphy in the Islamic world.

Printing made it possible to produce texts quickly, cheaply, and in huge quantities. By the late ninth century, printed copies of Buddhist texts, Confucian works, calendars, agricultural treatises, and popular works appeared in large quantities, particularly in southwestern China (modern Sichuan province). Song dynasty officials disseminated printed works broadly by visiting the countryside with pamphlets that outlined effective agricultural techniques.

Naval Technology

Chinese inventiveness extended also to naval technology. Before Tang times, Chinese mariners did not venture very far from land. They traveled the sea lanes to Korea, Japan, and the Ryukyu Islands but relied on Persian, Arab, Indian, and Malay mariners for long-distance maritime trade. During the Tang dynasty, however, Chinese consumers developed a taste for the spices and exotic products of southeast Asian islands, and Chinese mariners increasingly visited those lands in their own ships. By the time of the Song dynasty, Chinese seafarers sailed ships fastened with iron nails, waterproofed with oils, furnished with watertight bulkheads, driven by canvas and bamboo sails, steered by rudders, and navigated with the aid of the "south-pointing needle"—the magnetic compass. Larger ships sometimes even had small rockets powered by gunpowder. Chinese ships mostly plied the waters between Japan and the Malay peninsula, but some of them ventured into the Indian Ocean and called at ports in India, Ceylon, Persia, and east Africa. These long-distance travels helped to diffuse elements of Chinese naval technology, particularly the compass, which soon became the common property of mariners throughout the Indian Ocean basin.

The Emergence of a Market Economy

Increased agricultural production, improved transportation systems, population growth, urbanization, and industrial production combined to stimulate the Chinese economy. China's various regions increasingly specialized in the cultivation of particular food crops or the production of particular manufactured goods, trading their own products for imports from other regions. The market was not the only influence on the Chinese economy: government bureaucracies played a large role in the distribution of staple foods such as rice, wheat, and millet, and dynastic authorities closely watched militarily sensitive enterprises such as the iron industry. Nevertheless, millions of cultivators produced fruits and vegetables for sale on the open market, and manufacturers of silk, porcelain, and other goods supplied both domestic and foreign markets. The Chinese economy became more tightly integrated than ever before, and foreign demand for Chinese products fueled rapid economic expansion.

Financial Instruments

Indeed, trade grew so rapidly during Tang and Song times that China experienced a shortage of the copper coins that served as money for most transactions. To alleviate the shortage, Chinese merchants developed alternatives to cash that resulted in even more economic growth. Letters of credit came into common use during the early Tang dynasty. Known as "flying cash," they enabled merchants to deposit goods or cash at one location and draw the equivalent in cash or merchandise elsewhere in China. Later developments included the use of promissory notes, which pledged payment of a given sum of money at a later date, and checks, which entitled the bearer to draw funds against cash deposited with bankers.

Paper Money

The search for alternatives to cash also led to the invention of paper money. Wealthy merchants pioneered the use of printed paper money during the late ninth century. In return for cash deposits from their clients, they issued printed notes that the clients could redeem for merchandise. In a society short of cash, these notes greatly facilitated commercial transactions. Occasionally, however, because of temporary economic reverses or poor management, merchants were not able to honor their notes. The resulting discontent among creditors often led to disorder and sometimes even to riots.

By the eleventh century, however, the Chinese economy had become so dependent on alternatives to cash that it was impractical to banish paper money altogether. To preserve its convenience while forestalling public disorder, government authorities forbade private parties from issuing paper money and reserved that right for the state. The first paper money printed under government auspices appeared in 1024 in Sichuan province, the most active center of early printing. By the end of the century, government authorities throughout most of China issued printed paper money—complete with serial numbers and dire warnings against the printing of counterfeit notes. Rulers of nomadic peoples in central Asia soon began to adopt the practice in their own states.

Sources from the Past

The Arab Merchant Suleiman on Business Practices in Tang China

The Arab merchant Suleiman made several commercial ventures by ship to India and China during the early ninth century C.E. In 851 an Arab geographer wrote an account of Suleiman's travels, describing India and China for Muslim readers in southwest Asia. His report throws particularly interesting light on the economic conditions and business practices of Tang China.

Young and old Chinese all wear silk clothes in both winter and summer, but silk of the best quality is reserved for the kings. . . . During the winter, the men wear two, three, four, five pairs of pants, and even more, according to their means. This practice has the goal of protecting the lower body from the high humidity of the land, which they fear. During the summer, they wear a single shirt of silk or some similar material. They do not wear turbans. . . .

In China, commercial transactions are carried out with the aid of copper coins. The Chinese royal treasury is identical to that of other kings, but only the king of China has a treasury that uses copper coins as a standard. These copper coins serve as the money of the land. The Chinese have gold, silver, fine pearls, fancy silk textiles, raw silk, and all this in large quantities, but they are considered commodities, and only copper coins serve as money.

Imports into China include ivory, incense, copper ingots, shells of sea turtles, and rhinoceros horn, with which the Chinese make ornaments. . . .

The Chinese conduct commercial transactions and business affairs with equity. When someone lends money to another person, he writes up a note documenting the loan. The borrower writes up another note on which he affixes an imprint of his index finger and middle finger together. Then they put the two notes together, roll them up, and write a formula at the point where one touches the other [so that part of the written formula appears on each note]. Next, they separate the notes and entrust to the lender the one on which the borrower recognizes his debt. If the borrower denies his debt later on, they say to him, "Present the note that the lender gave to you." If the borrower maintains that he has no such note from the lender, and denies that he ever agreed to the note with his fingerprints on it, and if the lender's note has disappeared, they say to him, "Declare in writing that you have not contracted this debt, but if later the lender brings forth proof that you have contracted this debt that you deny, you will receive twenty blows of the cane on the back and you will be ordered to pay a penalty of twenty million copper coins." This sum is equal to about 2,000 dinars [gold coins used in the Abbasid empire]. Twenty blows of the cane brings on death. Thus no one in China dares to make such a declaration for fear of losing at the same time both life and fortune. We have seen no one who has agreed when invited to make such a declaration. The Chinese are thus equitable to each other. No one in China is treated unjustly.

SOURCE: Gabriel Ferrand, trans. *Voyage du marchand arabe Sulayman en Inde et en Chine.* Paris, 1922, pp. 45, 53–54, 60–61. (Translated into English by Jerry H. Bentley.)

In what ways might Chinese policies have encouraged business and trade during the Tang dynasty?

Printed paper money caused serious problems for several centuries after its appearance. Quite apart from contamination of the money supply by counterfeit notes, government authorities frequently printed currency representing more value than they actually possessed in cash reserves—a practice not unknown in more recent times. The result was a partial loss of public confidence in paper money. By the late eleventh century, some notes of paper money would fetch only 95 percent of their face value in cash. Not until the Qing dynasty (1644–1911 C.E.) did Chinese authorities place the issuance of printed money under tight fiscal controls. In spite of abuses, however, printed paper money provided a powerful stimulus to the Chinese economy.

A Cosmopolitan Society

Trade and urbanization transformed Tang and Song China into a prosperous, cosmopolitan society. Trade came to China both by land and by sea. Muslim merchants from the Abbasid empire and central Asia helped to revive the silk roads network and flocked to large Chinese trading centers. Even subjects of the Byzantine empire made their way across the silk roads to China. Residents of large Chinese cities like Chang'an and Luoyang became quite accustomed to merchants from foreign lands. Indeed, musicians and dancers from Persia became popular entertainers in the cosmopolitan cities of the Tang dynasty. Meanwhile, Arab, Persian, Indian, and Malay mariners arriving by way of the Indian Ocean and South China Sea established sizable merchant communities in the bustling southern Chinese port cities of Guangzhou and Quanzhou. Contemporary reports said that the rebel general Huang Chao massacred 120,000 foreigners when he sacked Guangzhou and subjected it to a reign of terror in 879.

China and the Hemispheric Economy

Indeed, high productivity and trade brought the Tang and Song economy a dynamism that China's borders could not restrain. Chinese consumers developed a taste for exotic goods that stimulated trade throughout much of the eastern hemisphere. Spices from the islands of southeast Asia made their way to China, along with products as diverse as kingfisher feathers and tortoise shell from Vietnam, pearls and incense from India, and horses and melons from central Asia. These items became symbols of a refined, elegant lifestyle—in many cases because of attractive qualities inherent in the commodities themselves but sometimes simply because of their scarcity and foreign provenance. In exchange for such exotic items, Chinese sent abroad vast quantities of silk, porcelain, and laquerware. In central Asia, southeast Asia, India, Persia, and the port cities of east Africa, wealthy merchants and rulers wore Chinese silk and set their tables with Chinese porcelain. China's economic surge during the Tang and Song dynasties thus promoted trade and economic growth throughout much of the eastern hemisphere.

Foreign music and dance were very popular in the large cities of Tang China. This ceramic model depicts a troupe of musicians from southwest Asia performing on a platform mounted on a camel. Many such models survive from Tang times.

Cultural Change in Tang and Song China

Interactions with peoples of other societies encouraged cultural change in postclassical China. The Confucian and Daoist traditions did not disappear. But they made way for a foreign religion—Mahayana Buddhism—and they developed along new lines that reflected the conditions of Tang and Song society.

The Establishment of Buddhism

Buddhist merchants traveling the ancient silk roads visited China as early as the second century B.C.E. During the Han dynasty their faith attracted little interest there: Confucianism, Daoism, and cults that honored family ancestors were the most popular cultural alternatives. After the fall of the Han, however, the Confucian tradition suffered a loss of credibility. The purpose and rationale of Confucianism was to maintain public order and provide honest, effective government. But in an age of warlords and nomadic invasions, it seemed that the Confucian tradition had simply failed. Confucian educational and civil service systems went into decline, and rulers sometimes openly scorned Confucian values.

Foreign Religions in China

During the unsettled centuries following the fall of the Han dynasty, several foreign religions established communities in China. Nestorian Christians and Manichaeans settled in China, followed later by Zoroastrians fleeing the Islamic conquerors of Persia. Nestorians established communities in China by the late sixth century. The emperor Tang Taizong himself issued a proclamation praising their doctrine, and he allowed them to open monasteries in Chang'an and other cities. By the mid-seventh century, Arab and Persian merchants had also established Muslim communities in the port cities of south China. Indeed, legend holds that an uncle of Muhammad himself built a small red mosque in the port city of Guangzhou. These religions of salvation mostly served the needs of foreign merchants trading in China and converts from nomadic societies. Sophisticated residents of Chinese cities appreciated foreign music and dance as well as foreign foods and trade goods, but most foreign religious faiths attracted little interest.

Dunhuang

Yet Mahayana Buddhism gradually found a popular following in Tang and Song China. Buddhism came to China over the silk roads. Residents of oasis cities in central Asia had converted to Buddhism as early as the first or second century B.C.E., and the oases became sites of Buddhist missionary efforts. By the fourth century C.E., a sizable Buddhist community had emerged at Dunhuang in western China (modern Gansu province). Between about 600 and 1000 C.E., Buddhists built hundreds of cave temples in the vicinity of Dunhuang and decorated them with murals depicting events in the lives of the Buddha and the *boddhisatvas* who played prominent roles in Mahayana Buddhism. They also assembled libraries of religious literature and operated scriptoria to produce Buddhist texts. Missions supported by establishments such as those at Dunhuang helped Buddhism to establish a foothold in China.

Buddhism in China

Buddhism attracted Chinese interest partly because of its high standards of morality, its intellectual sophistication, and its promise of salvation. Practical concerns also help to account for its appeal. Buddhists established monastic communities in China and accumulated sizable estates donated by wealthy converts. They cultivated these lands intensively and stored a portion of their harvests for distribution among local residents during times of drought, famine, or other hardship. Buddhist monasteries thus became important elements in the local economies of Chinese communities.

In some ways Buddhism posed a challenge to Chinese cultural and social traditions. Buddhist theologians typically took written texts as points of departure for elaborate, speculative investigations into metaphysical themes such as the nature of the soul. Among Chinese intellectuals, however, only the Confucians placed great emphasis on written texts, and they devoted their energies mostly to practical rather than metaphysical issues. Meanwhile, Daoists had limited interest in written texts of any kind. Buddhist morality called for individuals to strive for perfection by observing an ascetic ideal, and it encouraged serious Buddhists to follow a celibate, monastic lifestyle. By contrast, Chinese morality centered on the family unit and the obligations of filial piety, and it strongly encouraged procreation so that generations of offspring would be available to venerate family ancestors. Some Chinese held that Buddhist monasteries were economically harmful, since they paid no taxes, whereas others scorned Buddhism as an inferior creed because of its foreign origins.

Buddhism and Daoism

Because of these differences and concerns, Buddhist missionaries sought to tailor their message to Chinese audiences. They explained Buddhist concepts in vocabulary borrowed from Chinese cultural traditions, particularly Daoism. They translated the Indian term *dharma* (the basic Buddhist doctrine) as *dao* ("the way" in the Daoist sense of the term), and they translated the Indian term *nirvana* (personal salvation

A tenth-century painting in a cave at Dunhuang depicts a monastery on Mt. Wutai in southern China, reputedly the earthly home of an influential *boddhisatva* and the site of numerous Buddhist monasteries.

that comes after an individual soul escapes from the cycle of incarnation) as *wuwei* (the Daoist ethic of noncompetition). While encouraging the establishment of monasteries and the observance of celibacy, they also recognized the validity of family life and offered Buddhism as a religion that would benefit the extended Chinese family: one son in the monastery, they taught, would bring salvation for ten generations of his kin.

Chan Buddhism

The result was a syncretic faith, a Buddhism with Chinese characteristics. One of the more popular schools of Buddhism in China, for example, was the Chan (also known by its Japanese name, Zen). Chan Buddhists had little interest in written texts but, instead, emphasized intuition and sudden flashes of insight in their search for spiritual enlightenment. In this respect they resembled Daoists as much as they did Buddhists.

During the Tang and Song dynasties, this syncretic Buddhism became an immensely popular and influential faith in China. Monasteries appeared in all the major cities, and stupas dotted the Chinese landscape. The monk Xuanzang (602–664) was only one of many devout pilgrims who traveled to India to visit holy sites and learn about Buddhism in its homeland. Many of these pilgrims returned with copies of treatises that deepened the understanding of Buddhism in China. Xuanzang and other pilgrims played roles of enormous significance in establishing Buddhism as a popular faith in China.

Hostility to Buddhism

In spite of its popularity, Buddhism met determined resistance from Daoists and Confucians. Daoists resented the popular following that Buddhists attracted, which resulted in diminished resources available for their own tradition. Confucians despised Buddhists' exaltation of celibacy, and they denounced the faith as an alien superstition. They also condemned Buddhist monasteries as wasteful, unproductive burdens on society.

Persecution

During the late Tang dynasty, Daoist and Confucian critics of Buddhism found allies in the imperial court. Beginning in the 840s the Tang emperors ordered the

This scroll painting depicts the return of the monk Xuanzang to China. His baggage included 657 books, mostly Buddhist treatises but also a few works on grammar and logic, as well as hundreds of relics and images.

closure of monasteries and the expulsion of Buddhists as well as Zoroastrians, Nestorian Christians, and Manichaeans. Motivated largely by a desire to seize property belonging to foreign religious establishments, the Tang rulers did not implement their policy in a thorough way. While it discouraged further expansion, Tang policy did not eradicate foreign faiths from China. Buddhism in particular enjoyed popular support that enabled it to survive. Indeed, it even influenced the development of the Confucian tradition during the Song dynasty.

Neo-Confucianism

The Song emperors did not persecute Buddhists, but they actively supported native Chinese cultural traditions in hopes of limiting the influence of foreign religions. They contributed particularly generously to the Confucian tradition. They sponsored the studies of Confucian scholars, for example, and subsidized the printing and dissemination of Confucian writings.

Confucians and Buddhism

Yet the Confucian tradition of the Song dynasty differed from that of earlier times. The earliest Confucians had concentrated resolutely on practical issues of politics and morality, since they took the organization of a stable social order as their principal concern. Confucians of the Song dynasty studied the classic works of their tradition, but they also became familiar with the writings of Buddhists. They found much to admire in Buddhist thought. Buddhism not only offered a tradition of logical thought and argumentation but also dealt with issues, such as the nature of the soul and the individual's relationship with the cosmos, not systematically explored by Confucian thinkers. Thus Confucians of the Song dynasty drew a great deal of inspiration from Buddhism. Because their thought reflected the influence of Buddhism as well as original Confucian values, it has come to be known as neo-Confucianism.

Zhu Xi

The most important representative of Song neo-Confucianism was the philosopher Zhu Xi (1130–1200 C.E.). A prolific writer, Zhu Xi maintained a deep commitment to Confucian values emphasizing proper personal behavior and social harmony. Among his writings was an influential treatise entitled *Family Rituals* that provided detailed instructions for weddings, funerals, veneration of ancestors, and other family ceremonies. As a good Confucian, Zhu Xi considered it a matter of the highest importance that individuals play their proper roles both in their family and in the larger society.

Yet Zhu Xi became fascinated with the philosophical and speculative features of Buddhist thought. He argued in good Confucian fashion for the observance of high moral standards, and he believed that academic and philosophical investigations were important for practical affairs. But he concentrated his own efforts on abstract and abstruse issues of more theoretical than practical significance. He wrote extensively on metaphysical themes such as the nature of reality. He argued in a manner reminiscent of Plato that two elements accounted for all physical being: *li,* a principle somewhat similar to Plato's Forms or Ideas that defines the essence of the being, and *qi,* its material form.

Neo-Confucian Influence

Neo-Confucianism ranks as an important cultural development for two reasons. First, it illustrates the deep influence of Buddhism in Chinese society. Even though the neo-Confucians rejected Buddhism as a faith, their writings adapted Buddhist themes and reasoning to Confucian interests and values. Second, neo-Confucianism influenced east Asian thought over a very long term. In China, neo-Confucianism enjoyed the status of an officially recognized creed from the Song dynasty until the early twentieth century, and in lands that fell within China's cultural orbit—particularly Korea, Vietnam, and Japan—neo-Confucianism shaped philosophical, political, and moral thought for half a millennium and more.

Chinese Influence in East Asia

Like societies in Byzantium and the *dar al-Islam,* Chinese society influenced the development of neighboring lands during postclassical times. Chinese armies periodically invaded Korea and Vietnam, and Chinese merchants established commercial relations with Japan as well as with Korea and Vietnam. Chinese techniques of government and administration helped shape public life in Korea, Vietnam, and Japan, and Chinese values and cultural traditions won a prominent place alongside native traditions. By no means did these lands become absorbed into China: all maintained distinctive identities and cultural traditions. Yet they also drew deep inspiration from Chinese examples and built societies that reflected their participation in a larger east Asian society revolving around China.

Korea and Vietnam

Chinese armies ventured into Korea and Vietnam on campaigns of imperial expansion as early as the Qin and Han dynasties. As the Han dynasty weakened, however, local aristocrats organized movements that ousted Chinese forces from both lands. Only during the powerful Tang dynasty did Chinese resources once again enable military authorities to mount large-scale campaigns. Although the two lands responded differently to Chinese imperial expansion, both borrowed Chinese political and cultural traditions and used them in their own societies.

The Silla Dynasty

During the seventh century, Tang armies conquered much of Korea before the native Silla dynasty rallied to prevent Chinese domination of the peninsula. Both Tang and Silla authorities preferred to avoid a long and costly conflict, so they agreed to a political compromise: Chinese forces withdrew from Korea, and the Silla king recognized the Tang emperor as his overlord. In theory, Korea was a vassal state in a vast Chinese empire. In practice, however, Korea was in most respects an independent kingdom, although the ruling dynasty prudently maintained cordial relations with its powerful neighbor.

Thus Korea entered into a tributary relationship with China. Envoys of the Silla kings regularly delivered gifts to Chinese emperors and performed the kowtow, but these concessions brought considerable benefits to the Koreans. In return for their recognition of Chinese supremacy, they received gifts more valuable than the tribute they delivered to China. Moreover, the tributary relationship opened the doors for Korean merchants to trade in China.

Chinese Influence in Korea

Meanwhile, the tributary relationship facilitated the spread of Chinese political and cultural influences to Korea. Embassies delivering tribute to China included Korean royal officials who observed the workings of the Chinese court and bureaucracy and then organized the Korean court on similar lines. The Silla kings even built a new capital at Kumsong modeled on the Tang capital at Chang'an. Alongside royal officials, tribute embassies included scholars who studied Chinese thought and literature and who took copies of Chinese writings back to Korea. Their efforts helped to build Korean interest in the Confucian tradition, particularly among educated aristocrats. While Korean elite classes turned to Confucius, Chinese schools of Buddhism attracted widespread popular interest. Chan Buddhism, which promised individual salvation, won the allegiance of peasants and commoners.

China and Korea differed in many respects. Most notably, perhaps, aristocrats and royal houses dominated Korean society much more than was the case in China. Although the Korean monarchy sponsored Chinese schools and a Confucian examination system, Korea never established a bureaucracy based on merit such as that of Tang and Song China. Political initiative remained firmly in the hands of the ruling classes. Nevertheless, extensive dealings with its powerful neighbor ensured that Korea reflected the influence of Chinese political and cultural traditions.

China and Vietnam

Chinese relations with Vietnam were far more tense than with Korea. When Tang armies ventured into the land that Chinese called Nam Viet, they encountered spirited resistance on the part of the Viet people, who had settled in the region around the Red River. Tang forces soon won control of Viet towns and cities, and they launched efforts to absorb the Viets into Chinese society, just as their predecessors had absorbed the indigenous peoples of the Yangzi River valley. The Viets readily adopted Chinese agricultural methods and irrigation systems as well as Chinese schools and administrative techniques. Like their Korean counterparts, Viet elites studied Confucian texts and took examinations based on a Chinese-style education, and Viet traders marketed their wares in China. Vietnamese authorities even entered into tributary relationships with the Chinese court. Yet the Viets resented Chinese efforts to dominate the southern land, and they mounted a series of revolts against Tang authorities. As the Tang dynasty fell during the early tenth century, the Viets won their independence and successfully resisted later Chinese efforts at imperial expansion to the south.

Tang dynasty pottery figure of a Vietnamese dancer. Commercial and tributary relationships introduced southeast Asian performers to China, where sophisticated urban communities appreciated their exotic entertainment.

Like Korea, Vietnam differed from China in many ways. Many Vietnamese retained their indigenous religions in preference to Chinese cultural traditions. Women played a much more prominent role in Vietnamese society and economy than did their Chinese counterparts. Southeast Asian women had dominated local and regional markets for centuries, and they participated actively in business ventures closed to women in the more rigidly patriarchal society of China.

Chinese Influence in Vietnam

Nevertheless, Chinese traditions found a place in the southern land. Vietnamese authorities established an administrative system and bureaucracy modeled on that of China, and Viet ruling classes prepared for their careers by pursuing a Confucian education. Furthermore, Buddhism came to Vietnam from China as well as India and won a large popular following. Thus, like Korea, Vietnam absorbed political and cultural influence from China and reflected the development of a larger east Asian society centered on China.

Early Japan

Chinese armies never invaded Japan, but Chinese traditions deeply influenced Japanese political and cultural development. The earliest inhabitants of Japan were nomadic peoples from northeast Asia. They migrated to Japan, perhaps across land bridges that formed during an ice age, about two hundred thousand years ago. Their language, material culture, and religion derived from their parent society in northeast Asia. Later migrants, who arrived in several waves from the Korean peninsula, introduced cultivation of rice, bronze and iron metallurgy, and horses into Japan. As the population of the Japanese islands grew and built a settled agricultural society, small states dominated by aristocratic clans emerged. By the middle of the first millennium C.E., several dozen states ruled small regions.

Nara Japan

The establishment of the powerful Sui and Tang dynasties in China had repercussions in Japan, where they suggested the value of centralized imperial government. One of the aristocratic clans in Japan insisted on its precedence over the others, although in fact it had never wielded effective authority outside its own territory in central Japan. Inspired by the Tang example, this clan claimed imperial authority and introduced a series of reforms designed to centralize Japanese politics. The imperial house established a court modeled on that of the Tang, instituted a Chinese-style bureaucracy, implemented an equal-field system, provided official support for Confucianism and Buddhism, and in the year 710 moved to a new capital city at Nara (near modern Kyoto) that was a replica of the Tang capital at Chang'an. Never was Chinese influence more prominent in Japan than during the Nara period (710–794 C.E.).

Yet Japan did not lose its distinctive characteristics or become simply a smaller model of Chinese society. While adopting Confucian and Buddhist traditions from China, for example, the Japanese continued to observe the rites of Shinto, their indigenous religion, which revolved around the veneration of ancestors and a host of nature spirits and deities. Japanese society reflected the influence of Chinese traditions but still developed along its own lines.

The experiences of the Heian, Kamakura, and Muromachi periods clearly illustrate this point. In 794 the emperor of Japan transferred his court from Nara to a newly constructed capital at nearby Heian (modern Kyoto). During the next four centuries, Heian became the seat of a refined and sophisticated society that drew inspiration from China but also elaborated distinctively Japanese political and cultural traditions.

Heian Japan

During the Heian period (794–1185 C.E.), local rulers on the island of Honshu mostly recognized the emperor as Japan's supreme political authority. Unlike their Chinese counterparts, however, Japanese emperors rarely ruled but, rather, served as ceremonial figureheads and symbols of authority. Effective power lay in the hands of the Fujiwara family, an aristocratic clan that controlled affairs from behind the throne through its influence over the imperial house and manipulation of its members.

Since the ninth century the Japanese political order has almost continuously featured a split between a publicly recognized imperial authority and a separate agent of effective rule. This pattern helps to account for the remarkable longevity of the Japanese imperial house. Because emperors have not ruled, they have not been subject to deposition during times of turmoil: ruling parties and factions have come and gone, but the imperial house has survived.

The cultural development of Heian Japan also reflected both the influence of Chinese traditions and the elaboration of peculiarly Japanese ways. Most literature imitated Chinese models and indeed was written in the Chinese language. Boys and young men who received a formal education in Heian Japan learned Chinese, read the classic works of China, and wrote in the foreign tongue. Officials at court conducted business and kept records in Chinese, and literary figures wrote histories and treatises in the style popular in China. Even Japanese writing reflected Chinese influence, since scholars borrowed many Chinese characters and used them to represent Japanese words. They also adapted some Chinese characters into a Japanese syllabic script, in which symbols represent whole syllables rather than a single sound, as in an alphabetic script.

The Tale of Genji

Because Japanese women rarely received a formal Chinese-style education, in Heian times aristocratic women made the most notable contributions to literature in the Japanese language. Of the many literary works that have survived from this era, none reflects Heian court life better than *The Tale of Genji*. Composed by Murasaki Shikibu, a lady-in-waiting at the Heian court who wrote in Japanese syllabic script rather than Chinese characters, this sophisticated work relates the experiences of a fictitious imperial prince named Genji. Living amid gardens and palaces, Genji and his friends devoted themselves to the cultivation of an ultrarefined lifestyle, and they became adept at mixing subtle perfumes, composing splendid verses in fine calligraphic hand, and wooing sophisticated women.

The Tale of Genji also offers a meditation on the passing of time and the sorrows that time brings to sensitive human beings. As Genji and his friends age, they reflect

Samurai depart from a palace in Kyoto after capturing it, murdering the guards, seizing an enemy general there, and setting the structure ablaze. The armor and weaponry of the samurai bespeak the militarism of the Kamakura era.

on past joys and relationships no longer recoverable. Their thoughts suffuse *The Tale of Genji* with a melancholy spirit that presents a subtle contrast to the elegant atmosphere of their surroundings at the Heian court. Due to her limited command of Chinese, Lady Murasaki created one of the most remarkable literary works in the Japanese language.

Decline of Heian Japan

As the charmed circle of aristocrats and courtiers led elegant lives at the imperial capital, the Japanese countryside underwent fundamental changes that brought an end to the Heian court and its refined society. The equal-field system gradually fell into disuse in Japan as it had in China, and aristocratic clans accumulated most of the islands' lands into vast estates. By the late eleventh century, two clans in particular—the Taira and the Minamoto—overshadowed the others. During the mid-twelfth century the two engaged in outright war, and in 1185 the Minamoto emerged victorious. The Minamoto did not seek to abolish imperial authority in Japan but, rather, claimed to rule the land in the name of the emperor. They installed the clan leader as *shogun*—a military governor who ruled in place of the emperor—and established the seat of their government at Kamakura, near modern Tokyo, while the imperial court remained at Kyoto. For most of the next four centuries, one branch or another of the Minamoto clan dominated political life in Japan.

Medieval Japan

Historians refer to the Kamakura and Muromachi periods as Japan's medieval period—a middle era falling between the age of Chinese influence and court domination of political life in Japan, as represented by the Nara and Heian periods, and the modern age, inaugurated by the Tokugawa dynasty in the sixteenth century, when a centralized government unified and ruled all of Japan. During this middle era, Japanese society and culture took on increasingly distinctive characteristics.

Political Decentralization

In the Kamakura (1185–1333 C.E.) and Muromachi (1336–1573 C.E.) periods, Japan developed a decentralized political order in which provincial lords wielded effective power and authority in local regions where they controlled land and economic affairs. As these lords and their clans vied for power and authority in the countryside, they found little use for the Chinese-style bureaucracy that Nara and Heian rulers had instituted in Japan and still less use for the elaborate protocol and refined conduct that prevailed at the courts. In place of etiquette and courtesy, they valued military talent and discipline. The mounted warrior, the *samurai,* thus played the most distinctive role in Japanese political and military affairs.

The Samurai

The samurai were professional warriors, specialists in the use of force and the arts of fighting. They served the provincial lords of Japan, who relied on the samurai both to enforce their authority in their own territories and to extend their claims to other lands. In return for these police and military services, the lords supported the samurai from the agricultural surplus and labor services of peasants working under their jurisdiction. Freed of obligations to feed, clothe, and house themselves and their families, samurai devoted themselves to hunting, riding, archery, and martial arts.

Thus, although it had taken its original inspiration from the Tang empire in China, the Japanese political order developed along lines different from those of the Middle Kingdom. Yet Japan clearly had a place in the larger east Asian society centered on China. Japan borrowed from China, among other things, Confucian values, Buddhist religion, a system of writing, and the ideal of centralized imperial rule. Though somewhat suppressed during the Kamakura and Muromachi periods, these elements of Chinese society not only survived in Japan but also decisively influenced Japanese development during later periods.

The revival of centralized imperial rule in China had profound implications for all of east Asia and indeed for most of the eastern hemisphere. When the Sui and Tang dynasties imposed their authority throughout China, they established a powerful state that guided political affairs throughout east Asia. Tang armies extended Chinese influence to Korea, Vietnam, and central Asia. They did not invade Japan, but the impressive political organization of China prompted the islands' rulers to imitate Tang examples. Moreover, the Sui and Tang dynasties laid a strong political foundation for rapid economic development. Chinese society prospered throughout the postclassical era, partly because of technological and industrial innovation. Tang and Song prosperity touched all of China's neighbors, since it encouraged surging commerce in east Asia. Chinese silk, porcelain, and lacquerware were prized commodities among trading peoples from southeast Asia to east Africa. Chinese inventions such as paper, printing, gunpowder, and the magnetic compass found a place in societies throughout the eastern hemisphere as they diffused across the silk roads and sea lanes. The postclassical era was an age of religious as well as commercial and technological exchanges: Nestorian Christians, Zoroastrians, Manichaeans, and Muslims all maintained communities in Tang China, and Buddhism became the most popular religious faith in all of east Asia. During the postclassical era, Chinese social organization and economic dynamism helped to sustain interactions between the peoples of the eastern hemisphere on an unprecedented scale.

CHRONOLOGY

589–618	Sui dynasty (China)
602–664	Life of Xuanzang
604–618	Reign of Sui Yangdi
618–907	Tang dynasty (China)
627–649	Reign of Tang Taizong
669–935	Silla dynasty (Korea)
710–794	Nara period (Japan)
755–757	An Lushan's rebellion
794–1185	Heian period (Japan)
875–884	Huang Chao's rebellion
960–1279	Song dynasty (China)
960–976	Reign of Song Taizu
1024	First issuance of government-sponsored paper money
1130–1200	Life of Zhu Xi
1185–1333	Kamakura period (Japan)
1336–1573	Muromachi period (Japan)

FOR FURTHER READING

Kenneth Ch'en. *Buddhism in China: A Historical Survey.* Princeton, 1964. A clear and detailed account by an eminent scholar.

Hugh R. Clark. *Community, Trade, and Networks: Southern Fujian Province from the Third to the Thirteenth Century.* Cambridge, 1991. Excellent scholarly study exploring the transformation of a region by trade and market forces.

Peter Duus. *Feudalism in Japan.* 2nd ed. New York, 1976. A brief survey of early Japanese political history, concentrating on the Kamakura and Muromachi periods.

Patricia Buckley Ebrey. *Chinese Civilization: A Sourcebook.* 2nd ed. New York, 1993. A splendid collection of documents in translation.

Patricia Buckley Ebrey and Peter N. Gregory, eds. *Religion and Society in T'ang and Sung China.* Honolulu, 1993. Important collection of scholarly essays dealing with the early entry of Buddhism in China.

Mark Elvin. *The Pattern of the Chinese Past.* Stanford, 1973. A brilliant analysis of Chinese history, concentrating particularly on economic, social, and technological themes.

Jacques Gernet. *Buddhism in Chinese Society: An Economic History from the Fifth to the Tenth Century.* Trans. by F. Verellen. New York, 1995. An important study emphasizing the economic and social significance of Buddhist monasteries in the Chinese countryside.

———. *Daily Life in China on the Eve of the Mongol Invasion, 1250–1276.* Trans. by H. M. Wright. New York, 1962. Rich portrait of Southern Song China, emphasizing social history.

Ivan Morris. *The World of the Shining Prince: Court Life in Ancient Japan.* Harmondsworth, 1964. Vividly reconstructs the court life of Heian Japan.

Joseph Needham. *Science in Traditional China.* Cambridge, Mass., 1981. Essays on the history of Chinese science and technology.

Edward H. Schafer. *The Golden Peaches of Samarkand: A Study of T'ang Exotics.* Berkeley, 1963. Deals with relations between China and central Asian lands during the Tang dynasty.

———. *The Vermilion Bird: T'ang Images of the South.* Berkeley, 1967. Evocative study of relations between China and Vietnam during the Tang dynasty.

Murasaki Shikibu. *The Tale of Genji.* 2 vols. Trans. by E. Seidensticker. New York, 1976. Fresh and readable translation of Lady Murasaki's classic work.

H. Paul Varley. *Japanese Culture.* 4th ed. Honolulu, 2000. An authoritative analysis of Japanese cultural development from early times to the present.

Susan Whitfield. *Life along the Silk Road.* Berkeley, 1999. Focuses on the experiences of ten individuals who lived or traveled on the silk roads during the postclassical era.

Sally Hovey Wriggins. *Xuanzang: A Buddhist Pilgrim on the Silk Road.* Boulder, 1996. A fascinating and well-illustrated account of Xuanzang's journey to India and his influence on the development of Buddhism in China.

Arthur F. Wright. *Buddhism in Chinese History.* Stanford, 1959. A brief and incisive study of Buddhism in China by an eminent scholar.

———. *The Sui Dynasty: The Unification of China,* A.D. 581–617. New York, 1978. A useful survey that places the Sui dynasty in its larger historical context.

OLC

See our **Online Learning Center at www.mhhe.com/bentley3** for additional readings, practice maps, quizzes, and internet activities.

PSI

Unfamiliar words? Check out the **Primary Source Investigator CD-ROM** for an interactive glossary, interactive maps, more images, and primary sources.

Kabir, the blind guru, weaves cloth while discussing religious matters with disciples.

CHAPTER 16

India and the Indian Ocean Basin

Buzurg ibn Shahriyar was a tenth-century shipmaster from Siraf, a prosperous and bustling port city on the Persian Gulf coast. He probably sailed frequently to Arabia and India, and he may have ventured also to Malaya, the islands of southeast Asia, China, and east Africa. Like all sailors, he heard stories about the distant lands that mariners had visited, the different customs they observed, and the adventures that befell them during their travels. About 953 C.E. he compiled 136 such stories in his *Book of the Wonders of India.*

Buzurg's collection included a generous proportion of tall tales. He told of a giant lobster that seized a ship's anchor and dragged the vessel through the water, of mermaids and sea dragons, of creatures born from human fathers and fish mothers who lived in human society but had flippers that enabled them to swim through the water like fish, of serpents that ate cattle and elephants, of birds so large that they crushed houses, of a monkey that seduced a sailor, and of a talking lizard. Yet alongside the tall tales, many of Buzurg's stories accurately reflected the conditions of his time. One recounted the story of a king from northern India who converted to Islam and requested translations of Islamic law. Others reported on Hindu customs, shipwrecks, encounters with pirates, and slave trading.

Several of Buzurg's stories tempted readers with visions of vast wealth attainable through maritime trade. Buzurg mentioned fine diamonds from Kashmir, pearls from Ceylon, and a Jewish merchant who left Persia penniless and returned from India and China with a shipload of priceless merchandise. Despite their embellishments and exaggerations, his stories faithfully reflected the trade networks that linked the lands surrounding the Indian Ocean in the tenth century. While Buzurg clearly thought of India as a distinct land with its own customs, he also recognized a larger world of trade and communication that extended from east Africa to southeast Asia and beyond to China.

Just as China served as the principal inspiration of a larger east Asian society in the postclassical era, India influenced the development of a larger cultural zone in south and southeast Asia. Yet China and India played different roles in their respective spheres of influence. In east Asia, China was the dominant power, even if it did not always exercise authority directly over its neighbors. In south and southeast Asia, however, there emerged no centralized imperial authority like the Tang dynasty in China. Indeed, although several states organized large regional kingdoms, no single state was able to extend its authority to all parts of the Indian subcontinent, much less to the mainland and islands of southeast Asia.

Though politically disunited, India remained a coherent and distinct society as a result of powerful social and cultural traditions: the caste system and the Hindu religion shaped human experiences and values throughout the subcontinent during the postclassical era. Beginning in the seventh century Islam also began to attract a popular following in India, and after the eleventh century Islam deeply influenced Indian society alongside the caste system and Hinduism.

Beyond the subcontinent Indian traditions helped to shape a larger cultural zone extending to the mainland and islands of southeast Asia. Throughout most of the region, ruling classes adopted Indian forms of political organization and Indian techniques of statecraft. Indian merchants took their Hindu and Buddhist faiths to southeast Asia, where they first attracted the interest of political elites and then of the popular masses. Somewhat later, Indian merchants also helped introduce Islam to southeast Asia.

While Indian traditions influenced the political and cultural development of southeast Asia, the entire Indian Ocean basin began to move toward economic integration during the postclassical era, as Buzurg ibn Shahriyar's stories suggest. Lands on the rim of the Indian Ocean retained distinctive political and cultural traditions inherited from times past. Yet innovations in maritime technology, development of a well-articulated network of sea lanes, and the building of port cities and entrepôts enabled peoples living around the Indian Ocean to trade and communicate more actively than ever before. As a result, peoples from east Africa to southeast Asia and China increasingly participated in the larger economic, commercial, and cultural life of the Indian Ocean basin.

Islamic and Hindu Kingdoms

Like the Han and Roman empires, the Gupta dynasty came under severe pressure from nomadic invaders. From the mid-fourth to the mid-fifth century C.E., Gupta rulers resisted the pressures and preserved order throughout much of the Indian subcontinent. Beginning in 451 C.E., however, White Huns from central Asia invaded India and disrupted the Gupta administration. By the mid-sixth century the Gupta state had collapsed, and effective political authority quickly devolved to invaders, local allies of the Guptas, and independent regional power brokers. From the end of the Gupta dynasty until the sixteenth century, when a Turkish people known as the Mughals extended their authority and their empire to most of the subcontinent, India remained a politically divided land.

The Quest for Centralized Imperial Rule

Northern and southern India followed different political trajectories after the fall of the Gupta empire. In the north, politics became turbulent and almost chaotic. Local states contested for power and territory, and northern India became a region of continuous tension and intermittent war. Nomadic Turkish-speaking peoples from central Asia frequently took advantage of this unsettled state of affairs to cross the Khyber Pass and force their way into India. They eventually found niches for themselves in the caste system and became completely absorbed into Indian society. Until processes of social absorption worked themselves out, however, the arrival of nomadic peoples caused additional disruption in northern India.

Harsha

Even after the collapse of the Gupta dynasty, the ideal of centralized imperial rule did not entirely disappear. During the first half of the seventh century, King Harsha (reigned 606–648 C.E.) temporarily restored unified rule in most of northern India and sought to revive imperial authority. Harsha came to the throne of his kingdom in the lower Ganges valley at the age of sixteen. Full of energy and ambition, he led his army throughout northern India. His forces included twenty thousand cavalry, fifty thousand infantry, and five thousand war elephants, and by about 612 he had subdued those who refused to recognize his authority.

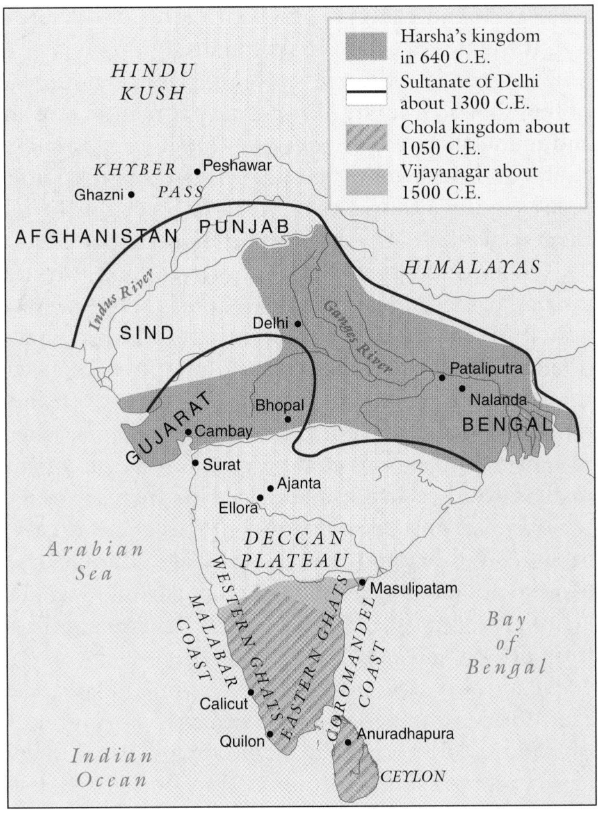

MAP [16.1]
Major states of postclassical India, 600–1600 C.E.

For an interactive version of this map, go to www.mhhe.com/bentley3ch16maps.

Harsha enjoyed a reputation for piety, liberality, and even scholarship. He was himself a Buddhist, but he looked kindly on other faiths as well. He built hospitals and provided free medical care for his subjects. The Chinese pilgrim Xuanzang lived in northern India during his reign and reported that Harsha liberally distributed wealth to his subjects. On one occasion, Xuanzang said, the king and his aides doled out resources continuously for seventy-five days, making gifts to half a million people. Harsha also generously patronized scholars and even wrote three plays.

Collapse of Harsha's Kingdom

Despite his energy and his favorable reputation, Harsha was unable to restore permanent centralized rule. Since the fall of the Gupta dynasty, local rulers had established their authority too securely in India's regions for Harsha to overcome them. Harsha spent much of his reign on horseback traveling throughout his realm to solidify alliances with local rulers, who were virtually kings in their own lands. He managed to hold his loose empire together mainly by the force of his personality and his constant attention to political affairs. Ultimately, however, he fell victim to an assassin and left no heir to maintain his realm. His empire immediately disintegrated, and local rulers once again turned northern India into a battleground as they sought to enlarge their realms at the expense of their neighbors.

The Introduction of Islam to Northern India

The Conquest of Sind

Amid nomadic incursions and contests for power, northern India also experienced the arrival of Islam and the establishment of Islamic states. Islam reached India by several routes. One was military: Arab forces entered India as early as the mid-seventh century, even before the establishment of the Umayyad caliphate, although their first expeditions were exploratory ventures rather than campaigns of conquest. In 711, however, a well-organized expedition conquered Sind, the Indus River valley in northwestern India, and incorporated it as a province of the expanding Umayyad empire. At mid-century, along with most of the rest of the *dar al-Islam,* Sind passed into the hands of the Abbasid caliphs.

Sind stood on the fringe of the Islamic world, well beyond the effective authority of the Abbasid caliphs. Much of its population remained Hindu, Buddhist, or Parsee, and it also sheltered a series of unorthodox Islamic movements. Infighting between Arab administrators eventually offered opportunities for local political elites to reassert Hindu authority over much of Sind. Yet the region remained nominally under the jurisdiction of the caliphs until the collapse of the Abbasid dynasty in 1258.

Merchants and Islam

While conquerors brought Islam to Sind, Muslim merchants took their faith to coastal regions in both northern and southern India. Arab and Persian mariners had visited Indian ports for centuries before Muhammad, and their Muslim descendants dominated trade and transportation networks between India and western lands from the seventh through the fifteenth centuries. Muslim merchants formed small communities in all the major cities of coastal India, where they played a prominent role in Indian business and commercial life. They frequently married local women, and in many cases they also found places for themselves in Indian society. Thus Islam entered India's port cities in a more gradual but no less effective way than was the case in Sind. Well before the year 1000, for example, the Gujarat region housed a large Muslim population. Muslim merchants congregated there because of the port city of Cambay, the most important trading center in India throughout the millennium from 500 to 1500 C.E.

Turkish Migrants and Islam

Islam also entered India by a third route: the migrations and invasions of Turkish-speaking peoples from central Asia. During the tenth century, several Turkish groups had become acquainted with Islam through their dealings with the Abbasid caliphate and had converted to the faith. Some of these Muslim Turks entered the Abbasid realm as mercenary soldiers or migrated into Byzantine Anatolia, while others moved into Afghanistan, where they established an Islamic state.

Mahmud of Ghazni

Mahmud of Ghazni, leader of the Turks in Afghanistan, soon turned his attention to the rich land to the south. Between 1001 and 1027 he mounted seventeen raiding expeditions into India. Taking advantage of infighting between local rulers, he annexed several states in northwestern India and the Punjab. For the most part, however, Mahmud had less interest in conquering and ruling India than in plundering the wealth stored in its many well-endowed temples. Mahmud and his forces demolished hundreds of sites associated with Hindu or Buddhist faiths, and their campaigns hastened the decline of Buddhism in the land of its birth. They frequently established mosques or Islamic shrines on the sites of Hindu and Buddhist structures that they destroyed. Not surprisingly, however, Mahmud's raids did not encourage Indians to turn to Islam.

The Sultanate of Delhi

During the late twelfth century, Mahmud's successors mounted a more systematic campaign to conquer northern India and place it under Islamic rule. By the early thirteenth century, they had conquered most of the Hindu kingdoms in northern India and established an Islamic state known as the sultanate of Delhi. The sultans established their capital at Delhi, a strategic site controlling access from the Punjab to the Ganges valley, and they ruled northern India at least in name for more than three centuries, from 1206 to 1526.

During the fourteenth century the sultans of Delhi commanded an army of three hundred thousand, and their state ranked among the most powerful in the Islamic world. Yet for the most part, the authority of the sultans did not extend far beyond Delhi. They often conducted raids in the Deccan region of southern India, but they never overcame Hindu resistance there. They had no permanent bureaucracy or administrative apparatus. Even in northern India, they imposed a thin veneer of Islamic

A fourteenth-century painting depicts the Turkish conqueror Mahmud of Ghazni as he dons a robe bestowed upon him as a gift by the Abbasid caliph. Although Mahmud pursued independent policies, he always recognized the caliph as his overlord.

political and military authority on a land populated mostly by Hindus, and they depended on the goodwill of Hindu kings to carry out their policies and advance their interests in local regions. Indeed, they did not even enjoy comfortable control of their own court: of the thirty-five sultans of Delhi, nineteen perished at the hands of assassins. Nevertheless, the sultans prominently sponsored Islam and helped to establish a secure place for their faith in the cultural landscape of India.

The Hindu Kingdoms of Southern India

Although it too remained politically divided, the southern part of the Indian subcontinent largely escaped the invasions, chronic war, and turmoil that troubled the north. Most Hindu rulers in the south presided over small, loosely administered states. Competition between states sometimes resulted in regional wars, but southern conflicts were less frequent, less intense, and less damaging than those that plagued the north.

The Chola Kingdom

While many regional states organized affairs in local jurisdictions, two kingdoms expanded enough to exercise at least nominal rule over much of southern India. The first was the Chola kingdom, situated in the deep south, which ruled the Coromandel coast for more than four centuries, from 850 to 1267 C.E. At its high point, during the eleventh century, Chola forces conquered Ceylon and parts of southeast Asia. Financed by the profits of trade, the Chola navy dominated the waters from the South China Sea to the Arabian Sea.

Chola rulers did not build a tightly centralized state: they allowed considerable autonomy for local and village institutions as long as they maintained order and delivered tax revenues on time. By the twelfth century, however, the Chola state was in decline. Native Sinhalese forces expelled Chola officials from Ceylon, and revolts erupted within southern India. The Chola realm did not entirely collapse, but by the early thirteenth century, much reduced in size and power, it had reverted to the status of one regional kingdom among many others in southern India.

The kings of Vijayanagar endowed their capital with splendid buildings and even provided these handsome domed stables for their elephants.

The Kingdom of Vijayanagar

The second state that dominated much of southern India was the kingdom of Vijayanagar, based in the northern Deccan. The kingdom owed its origin to efforts by the sultans of Delhi to extend their authority to southern India. Exploratory forays by Turkish forces provoked a defensive reaction in the south. Officials in Delhi dispatched two brothers, Harihara and Bukka, to represent the sultan and implement court policies in the south. Although they had converted from their native Hinduism to Islam, Harihara and Bukka recognized an opportunity to establish themselves as independent rulers. In 1336 they renounced Islam, returned to their original Hindu faith, and proclaimed the establishment of an independent empire of Vijayanagar (meaning "city of victory"). Their unusual coup did not lead to hostilities between Muslims and Hindus: Muslim merchants continued to trade unmolested in the ports of southern India, as they had for more than half a millennium. But the Hindu kingdom of Vijayanagar was the dominant state in southern India from the mid-fourteenth century until 1565 when it fell to Mughal conquerors from the north.

As in northern India, then, political division and conflict between states in southern India characterized its political history in postclassical times. India did not generate the sort of large-scale, centralized, imperial state that guided the fortunes of postclassical societies in the eastern Mediterranean, southwest Asia, or China. States like the sultanate of Delhi in northern India and the kingdoms of Chola and Vijayanagar in the south were not powerful enough to organize political life throughout the subcontinent. Nevertheless, on the basis of trade, common social structures, and inherited cultural traditions, a coherent and distinctive society flourished in postclassical India.

Production and Trade in the Indian Ocean Basin

As in the Mediterranean, southwest Asia, and China, agricultural yields increased significantly in postclassical India, enabling large numbers of people to devote themselves to trade and manufacturing rather than the production of food. Trade forged links between the various regions of the subcontinent and fostered economic development in southern India. Trade also created links between India and distant lands, as merchants and manufacturers transformed the Indian Ocean basin into a vast zone of communication and exchange. The increasing prominence of trade and industry brought change to Indian society, as merchant and artisan guilds became stronger and more influential than before. Yet caste identities and loyalties also remained strong, and the caste system continued to serve as the most powerful organizing feature of Indian society.

Agriculture in the Monsoon World

The Monsoons

Because of the rhythms of the monsoons, irrigation was essential for the maintenance of a large, densely populated, agricultural society. During the spring and summer, warm, moisture-laden winds from the southwest bring most of India's rainfall. During the autumn and winter, cool and very dry winds blow from the northeast. To achieve their agricultural potential, Indian lands required a good watering by the southern monsoon, supplemented by irrigation during the dry months. Light rain during the spring and summer months or short supplies of water for irrigation commonly led to drought, reduced harvests, and widespread famine.

Irrigation Systems

In northern India, irrigation had been a fixture of the countryside since Harappan times, when cultivators tapped the waters of the Indus River. Later, as Aryans migrated into the Ganges River valley, they found plentiful surface water and abundant opportunities to build irrigation systems. For the most part, however, southern India is an arid land without rivers like the Indus or Ganges that can serve as sources for large-scale irrigation. Thus, as southern India became more densely populated, irrigation systems became crucial, and a great deal of energy and effort went into the construction of waterworks. Dams, reservoirs, canals, wells, and tunnels appeared in large numbers. Particularly impressive were monumental reservoirs lined with brick or stone that captured the rains of the spring and summer months and held them until the dry season, when canals carried them to thirsty fields. One such reservoir—actually an artificial lake constructed near Bhopal during the eleventh century—covered some 650 square kilometers (250 square miles). Projects of this size required enormous investments of human energy, both for their original construction and for continuing maintenance, but they led to significant increases in agricultural productivity.

Population Growth

As a result of this increased productivity, India's population grew steadily throughout the postclassical era. In 600 C.E., shortly after the fall of the Gupta dynasty, the subcontinent's population stood at about 53 million. By 800 it had increased almost 20 percent to 64 million, and by 1000 it had grown by almost another 25 percent to 79 million. During the following centuries the rate of growth slowed, as Indian numbers increased by 4 to 5 million individuals per century. Toward 1500, however, the rate of growth increased again, and by 1500 the subcontinent's population had reached 105 million.

Urbanization

This demographic surge encouraged the concentration of people in cities. During the fourteenth century, the high point of the sultanate of Delhi, the capital city had a population of about four hundred thousand, which made it second only to Cairo among Muslim cities. Many other cities—particularly ports and trading centers like Cambay, Surat, Calicut, Quilon, and Masulipatam—had populations well over one hundred thousand. Cities in southern India grew especially fast, partly as a result of increasing agricultural productivity in the region.

Trade and the Economic Development of Southern India

Political fragmentation of the subcontinent did not prevent robust trade between the different states and regions of India. As the population grew, opportunities for specialized work became more numerous. Increased trade was a natural result of this process.

Internal Trade

Most regions of the Indian subcontinent were self-sufficient in staple foods such as rice, wheat, barley, and millet. The case was different, however, with iron, copper, salt, pepper, spices, condiments, and specialized crops that grew well only in certain regions. Iron came mostly from the Ganges River valley near Bengal, copper mostly from the Deccan Plateau, salt mostly from coastal regions, and pepper from southern India. These and other commodities sometimes traveled long distances to consumers in remote parts of the subcontinent. Pepper, saffron, and sugar were popular commodities in subcontinental trade, and even rice sometimes traveled as a trade item to northern and mountainous regions where it did not grow well.

Southern India and Ceylon benefited especially handsomely from this trade. As invasions and conflicts disrupted northern India, southern regions experienced rapid economic development. The Chola kingdom provided relative stability in the south, and Chola expansion in southeast Asia opened markets for Indian merchants and producers. Coastal towns like Calicut and Quilon flourished, and they attracted increasing numbers of residents.

Temples and Society

The Chola rulers allowed considerable autonomy to their subjects, and the towns and villages of southern India largely organized their own affairs. Public life revolved around Hindu temples that served as economic and social centers. Southern Indians used their growing wealth to build hundreds of elaborate Hindu temples, which organized agricultural activities, coordinated work on irrigation systems, and maintained reserves of surplus production for use in times of need. These temples also provided basic schooling for boys in the community, and larger temples offered advanced instruction as well. Temples often possessed large tracts of agricultural land, and they sometimes employed hundreds of people, including brahmins, attendants, musicians, servants, and slaves. To meet their financial obligations to employees, temple administrators collected a portion of the agricultural yield from lands subject to temple authority. Administrators were also responsible for keeping order in their communities and delivering tax receipts to the Cholas and other political authorities.

Temple authorities also served as bankers, made loans, and invested in commercial and business ventures. As a result, temples promoted the economic development of southern India by encouraging production and trade. Temple authorities cooperated closely with the leaders of merchant guilds in seeking commercial opportunities to exploit. The guilds often made gifts of land or money to temples by way of consolidating their relationship with the powerful economic institutions. Temples thus grew prosperous and became crucial to the economic health of southern India.

Cross-Cultural Trade in the Indian Ocean Basin

Indian prosperity sprang partly from the productivity of Indian society, but it depended also on the vast wealth that circulated in the commercial world of the Indian Ocean basin. Trade in the Indian Ocean was not new in postclassical times: Indian merchants had already ventured to southeast Asia during the classical era, and they dealt regularly with mariners from the Roman empire who traveled to India in search of pepper. During the postclassical era, however, larger ships and improved commercial organization supported a dramatic surge in the volume and value of trade in the Indian Ocean basin.

Dhows and Junks

The earliest voyaging in the Indian Ocean followed the coastlines, but already in classical times mariners recognized the rhythms of the monsoons. Over time they built larger ships, which enabled them to leave the coasts behind and ply the blue waters of the Indian Ocean: the dhows favored by Indian, Persian, and Arab sailors averaged about one hundred tons burden in 1000 and four hundred tons in 1500. After the naval and commercial expansion of the Song dynasty, large Chinese and

During the eighth century C.E., workers carved a massive temple out of sheer rock at Ellora in central India. Temple communities like the one that grew up at Ellora controlled enormous resources in postclassical India.

southeast Asian junks also sailed the Indian Ocean: some of them could carry one thousand tons of cargo.

As large, stable ships came into use, mariners increasingly entrusted their crafts and cargoes to the reasonably predictable monsoons and sailed directly across the Arabian Sea and the Bay of Bengal. In the age of sail, it was impossible to make a round trip across the entire Indian Ocean without spending months at distant ports waiting for the winds to change, so merchants usually conducted their trade in stages.

Emporia

Because India stood in the middle of the Indian Ocean basin, it was a natural site for emporia and warehouses. Merchants coming from east Africa or Persia exchanged their cargoes at Cambay, Calicut, or Quilon for goods to take back west with the winter monsoon. Mariners from China or southeast Asia called at Indian ports and traded their cargoes for goods to ship east with the summer monsoon. Merchants also built emporia outside India: the storytelling mariner Buzurg ibn Shahriyar came from the emporium of Siraf on the Persian Gulf, a port city surrounded by desert that nevertheless enjoyed fabulous wealth because of its trade with China, India, and east Africa. Because of their central location, however, Indian ports became the principal clearinghouses of trade in the Indian Ocean basin, and they became remarkably cosmopolitan centers. Hindus, Buddhists, Muslims, Jews, and others who inhabited the Indian port cities did business with counterparts from all over the eastern hemisphere and swapped stories like those recounted by Buzurg ibn Shahriyar.

Dhows fitted with lateen sails skim across the Indian Ocean much like their ancestors of the postclassical era.

Particularly after the establishment of the Umayyad and Abbasid dynasties in southwest Asia and the Tang and Song dynasties in China, trade in the Indian Ocean surged. Indian merchants and mariners sometimes traveled to distant lands in search of marketable goods, but the carrying trade between India and points west fell mostly into Arab and Persian hands. During the Song dynasty, Chinese junks also ventured into the western Indian Ocean and called at ports as far away as east Africa. In the Bay of Bengal and the China seas, Malay and Chinese vessels were most prominent.

Specialized Production

As the volume of trade in the Indian Ocean basin increased, lands around the ocean began to engage in specialized production of commodities for the commercial market. For centuries Indian artisans had enjoyed a reputation for the manufacture of fine cotton textiles, which they produced in small quantities for wealthy consumers. In postclassical times their wares came into high demand throughout the trading world of the Indian Ocean basin. In response to that demand, Indian artisans built thriving local industries around the production of high-quality cotton textiles. These industries influenced the structure of the Indian economy: they created a demand for specific agricultural products, provided a livelihood for thousands of artisans, and enabled consumers to import goods from regions that specialized in the production of other commodities.

Alongside textiles other specialized industries that emerged in postclassical India included sugar refining, leather tanning, stone carving, and carpet weaving. Iron and steel production also emerged as prominent industries. Indian artisans became well known especially for the production of high-carbon steel that held a lethal cutting edge and that consequently came into high demand for use in knives and swords. Other lands concentrated on the production of different manufactured goods and agricultural commodities: China produced silk, porcelain, and lacquerware, southeast Asian lands provided fine spices, while incense, horses, and dates came from southwest Asia, and east Africa contributed gold, ivory, and slaves. Thus trade en-

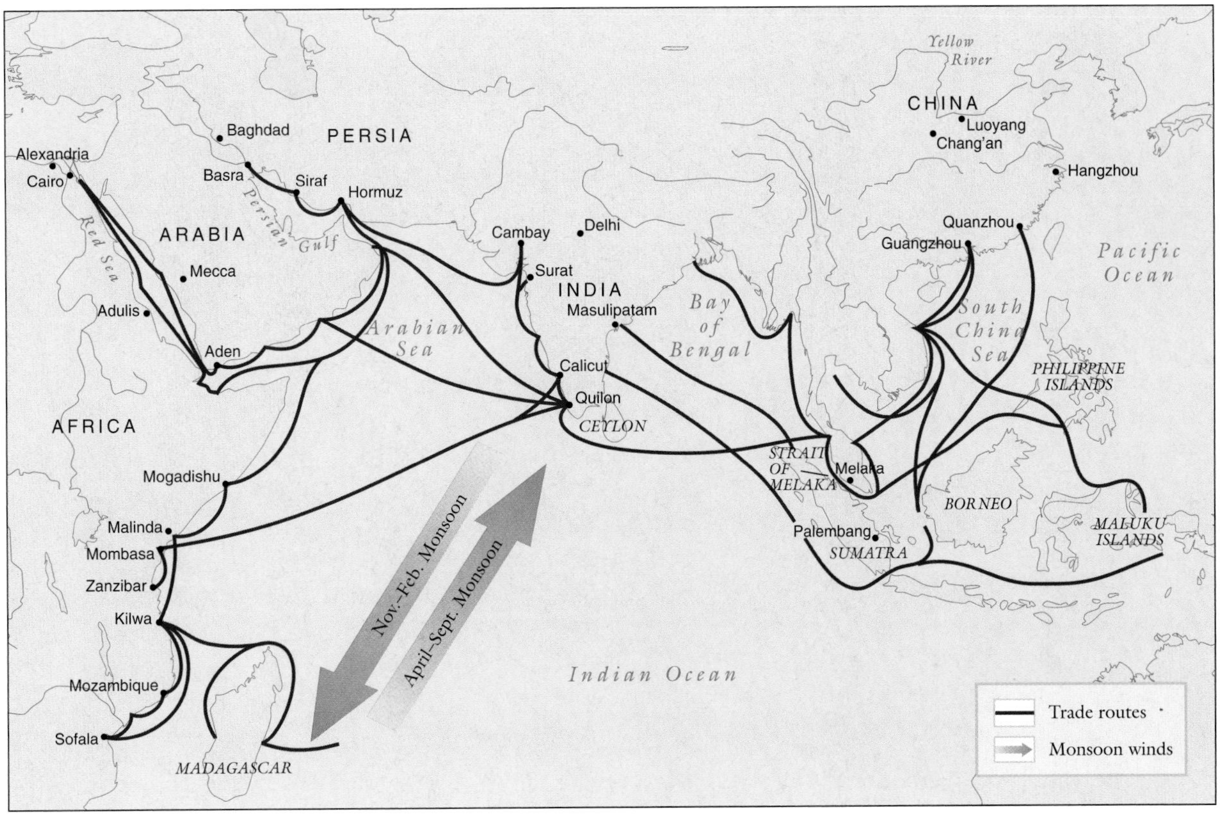

MAP [16.2]
The trading world of the Indian Ocean basin, 600–1600 C.E.

couraged specialized production and economic development in all lands participating in the trade networks of the Indian Ocean basin: cross-cultural trade in postclassical times influenced the structure of economies and societies throughout much of the eastern hemisphere.

The Kingdom of Axum

The experience of the kingdom of Axum (sometimes spelled Aksum) well illustrates the potential of trade to support political as well as economic development. Founded in the highlands of northern Ethiopia about the first century C.E., Axum was originally a small kingdom whose merchants traded from the port of Adulis on the Red Sea. Axum soon displaced Kush as Egypt's principal link to southern lands and sent the Nubian kingdom into economic and political decline: about 360 C.E. Axumite forces even invaded Kush and destroyed the capital city of Meroë. During the fourth and fifth centuries, Axumites adopted Christianity and established a distinctive church that maintained relations with Christian communities in Egypt and the Mediterranean basin. During the sixth century Axum embarked on a round of territorial expansion, building an empire that included most of modern-day Ethiopia as well as Yemen in southern Arabia. Indeed, an Axumite army and elephant corps campaigned as far north as Mecca in the year 571 C.E., birth year of the prophet Muhammad.

During the seventh and eighth centuries, Arab conquerors sought to bring Axum into the expanding realm of Islam, but the kingdom maintained its independence and its Christian religion. Because neighboring lands mostly adopted Islam, Axum fell out of communication with other Christian societies. Nevertheless, Axumite merchants

Mealtime for a Persian merchant and his two companions served by three women attendants in this ceiling decoration from the Ajanta caves in central India.

not only maintained commercial ties with distant lands, as ships from Adulis routinely sailed for India and the islands of southeast Asia, but also traded regularly with Muslim merchants in neighboring lands. From the sixth to ninth centuries C.E., Adulis was perhaps the most prominent port in east Africa, funneling gold, ivory, and slaves from sub-Saharan Africa to Egypt, the eastern Mediterranean region, and the Indian Ocean basin. Thus, even though challenged by Muslim forces, Axum was able to maintain its independence and prosperity, largely because of its participation in trading networks of the Indian Ocean and Mediterranean Sea.

Caste and Society

The political, economic, and social changes of the postclassical era brought a series of challenges for India's caste system. Migrations, the growing prominence of Islam, economic development, and urbanization all placed pressures on the caste system as it had developed during the Vedic and classical eras. But the caste system has never been a rigid, unchanging structure. Rather, individuals and groups have continuously adjusted it and adapted it to new circumstances. Adjustments and adaptations of the postclassical era resulted in a caste system that was more complex than in earlier ages and that also extended its geographic reach deeper into southern India than ever before. In the absence of strong central governments, the caste system helped

Sources from the Past

Cosmas Indicopleustes on Trade in Southern India

Cosmas Indicopleustes was a Christian monk from Egypt who lived during the sixth century C.E. *and traveled widely throughout north Africa and southwest Asia. On one of his trips, he ventured as far as India and Ceylon, which he described at some length in a work entitled* The Christian Topography. *Cosmas's account clearly shows that sixth-century India and Ceylon played prominent roles in the larger economy of the Indian Ocean basin.*

Ceylon lies on the other side of the pepper country [southern India]. Around it are numerous small islands all having fresh water and coconut trees. They nearly all have deep water close up to their shores. . . . Ceylon is a great market for the people in those parts. The island also has a church of Persian Christians who have settled there, and a priest who is appointed from Persia, and a deacon and a complete ecclesiastical ritual. But the natives and their kings are heathens. . . .

Since the island of Ceylon is in a central position, it is much frequented by ships from all parts of India and from Persia and Ethiopia, and it likewise sends out many of its own. And from the remotest countries—I mean China and other trading places—it receives silk, aloes, cloves, sandalwood, and other products, and these again are passed on to markets on this side, such as Male [the western coast of southern India], where pepper grows, and to Calliana [a port city near modern Bombay], which exports copper and sesame logs and cloth for making dresses, for it also is a great place of business. And also to Sind [Gujarat], where musk and castor and spice are procured, and to Persia and the Homerite country [Anatolia], and to Adule [in Ethiopia]. And this island [Ceylon] receives imports from all these markets that we have mentioned and passes them on to the remoter ports, while at the same time exporting its own produce in both directions. . . .

The kings of various places in India keep elephants. . . . They may have six hundred each, or five hundred, some more, some fewer. Now the king of Ceylon gives a good price both for the elephants and for the horses that he has. The elephants he pays for by the cubit [a unit of measurement equivalent to about half a meter or twenty inches]. For the height is measured from the ground, and the price is reckoned at so many gold coins for each cubit—fifty [coins] it may be, or a hundred, or even more. Horses they bring to him from Persia, and he buys them, exempting the importers of them from paying custom duties. The kings of the Indian subcontinent tame their elephants, which are caught wild, and employ them in war.

SOURCE: Cosmas Indicopleustes. *The Christian Topography of Cosmas, an Egyptian Monk.* Trans. by J. W. McCrindle. London: Hakluyt Society, 1897, pp. 364–72. (Translation slightly modified.)

How did Ceylon compare as a commercial center with Constantinople and Baghdad, as described by Benjamin of Tudela?

maintain to order in local communities by providing guidance on individuals' roles in society and their relationships with others.

Caste and Migration

The caste system closely reflected changes in Indian society. It adapted to the arrival of migrants, for example, and helped to integrate them into Indian society. As Turkish peoples or Muslim merchants pursued opportunities in India, they gained recognition as distinct groups under the umbrella of the caste system. They established codes of conduct both for the regulation of behavior within their own groups and for guidance in dealing with members of other castes. Within a few generations their descendants had become absorbed into Indian society.

Caste and Social Change

The caste system also accommodated the social changes brought about by trade and economic development. Indeed, the caste system influenced the lives of most people by helping to order their work and their relationships with other workers. The castes that individuals most closely identified with were the subcastes *(jati)*, which often took the form of workers' guilds. As merchants and manufacturers became increasingly important in the larger economy, they organized powerful guilds to represent their interests. Merchant guilds in particular wielded political and economic influence, since their members enjoyed access to considerable wealth and contributed in large measure to the economic health of their states. Guild members forged group identities by working within the caste system. Merchants specializing in particular types of commerce, such as the silk, cotton, or spice trade, established themselves as distinct subcastes, as did artisans working in particular industries, such as the iron, steel, or leather business.

Expansion of the Caste System

Besides becoming more complex, the caste system also extended its geographic reach. Caste distinctions first became prominent in northern India following Aryan migrations into the subcontinent. During the postclassical era, the caste system became securely established in southern India as well. Economic development aided this process by encouraging commercial relationships between southern merchants and their caste-conscious counterparts in the north. The emergence of merchant and craft guilds in southern regions strengthened the caste system, since guild members usually organized as a subcaste. Powerful temples also fostered caste distinctions. Caste-conscious brahmins who supervised the temples were particularly effective promoters of the system, since temples provided the only formal education available in most regions and also served as centers of local social life. By about the eleventh century C.E., caste had become the principal basis of social organization in southern India.

The Meeting of Hindu and Islamic Traditions

The Indian cultural landscape underwent a thorough transformation during the postclassical era. Jainism and Buddhism lost much of their popular following. Neither belief completely disappeared from India, and indeed, a small community continues to observe each faith there even today. After 1000 C.E., however, Hindu and Islamic traditions increasingly dominated the cultural and religious life of India.

Hinduism and Islam differed profoundly as religious traditions. The Hindu pantheon made places for numerous gods and spirits, for example, whereas Islamic theology stood on the foundation of a firm and uncompromising monotheism. Yet both religions attracted large popular followings throughout the subcontinent, with Hinduism predominating in southern India and Islam in the north.

The Development of Hinduism

Toward the end of the first millennium C.E., Buddhism flourished in east Asia, central Asia, and parts of southeast Asia but came under great pressure in India. Like Mahayana Buddhism, both Hinduism and Islam promised salvation to devout individuals, and they gradually attracted Buddhists to their own communities. Invasions of India by Turkish peoples hastened the decline of Buddhism because the invaders looted and destroyed Buddhist stupas and shrines. In 1196 Muslim forces overran the city of Nalanda and ravaged the schools where Xuanzang and other foreign pilgrims had studied with the world's leading Buddhist philosophers and theologians. The conquerors torched Buddhist libraries and either killed or exiled thousands of monks living at Nalanda. Buddhism soon became a minor faith in the land of its birth.

Vishnu and Shiva

Hinduism benefited from the decline of Buddhism. One reason for the increasing popularity of Hinduism was the remarkable growth of devotional cults, particularly those dedicated to Vishnu and Shiva, two of the most important deities in the Hindu pantheon. Vishnu was the preserver of the world, a god who observed the universe from the heavens and who occasionally entered the world in human form in order to resist evil or communicate his teachings. By contrast, Shiva was both a god of fertility and a destructive deity: he brought life but also took it away when its season had passed. Hindus associated many gods and goddesses with Vishnu and Shiva, and they recognized other cults that were altogether independent of these two. But the most popular devotional cults focused on veneration of Vishnu or Shiva.

Devotional Cults

Hindus embraced the new cults warmly because they promised salvation. Devotional cults became especially popular in southern India, where individuals or family groups went to great lengths to honor their chosen deities. Often cults originated when individuals identified Vishnu or Shiva with a local spirit or deity associated with a particular region or a prominent geographic feature. The famous cult of Shiva as lord of the dancers arose, for example, about the fifth or sixth century C.E. when devotees identified a stone long venerated locally in a southern Indian village as a symbol of Shiva. In the tenth century Chola kings took the dancing Shiva as their family god and spread the cult's popularity throughout southern India. By venerating images of Vishnu or Shiva, offering them food and drink, and meditating on the deities and their qualities, Hindus hoped to achieve a mystic union with the gods that would bring grace and salvation. As the cults proliferated, temples and shrines dotted the landscape of southern India. Veneration of Vishnu and Shiva gradually became popular among Hindus in northern as well as southern India.

Southern Indian artists often portrayed Shiva in bronze sculptures as a four-armed lord of dancers. In this figure from the Chola dynasty, Shiva crushes with his foot a dwarf demon symbolizing ignorance. One hand holds a bell to awaken his devotees, another bears the fire used by Shiva as creator and destroyer of the world, and a third gestures Shiva's benevolence toward his followers.

Shankara

The significance of Hinduism extended well beyond popular religion: it also influenced philosophy. Just as Buddhism, Christianity, and Islam influenced moral thought and philosophy in other lands, devotional Hinduism guided

An elaborate open-air rock carving at Mamallapuram, south of modern Madras, celebrates the Ganges River as a gift from Shiva and other gods.

the efforts of the most prominent philosophers in postclassical India. Brahmin philosophers such as Shankara and Ramanuja took the Upanishads as a point of departure for subtle reasoning and sophisticated metaphysics. Shankara, a southern Indian devotee of Shiva who was active during the early ninth century C.E., took it upon himself to digest all sacred Hindu writings and harmonize their sometimes contradictory teachings into a single, consistent system of thought. In a manner reminiscent of Plato, Shankara held that the physical world was illusion—a figment of the imagination—and that ultimate reality lay beyond the physical senses. Although he was a worshiper of Shiva, Shankara mistrusted emotional services and ceremonies, insisting that only by disciplined logical reasoning could human beings understand the ultimate reality of Brahman, the impersonal world-soul of the Upanishads. Only then could they appreciate the fundamental unity of the world, which Shankara considered a perfectly understandable expression of ultimate reality, even though to human physical senses that same world appears chaotic and incomprehensible.

Ramanuja

Ramanuja, a devotee of Vishnu who was active during the eleventh and early twelfth centuries C.E., challenged Shankara's uncompromising insistence on logic. Also a brahmin philosopher from southern India, Ramanuja's thought reflected the deep influence of devotional cults. According to Ramanuja, intellectual understanding of ultimate reality was less important than personal union with the deity. Ramanuja granted that intellectual efforts could lead to comprehension of reality, but he held that genuine bliss came from salvation and identification of individuals with their gods. He followed the *Bhagavad Gita* in recommending intense devotion to Vishnu, and he taught that by placing themselves in the hands of Vishnu, devotees would win the god's grace and live forever in his presence. Thus, in contrast to Shankara's consistent, intellectual system of thought, Ramanuja's philosophy pointed toward a Hindu theology of salvation. Indeed, his thought inspired the development of devotional cults throughout India, and it serves even today as a philosophical foundation for Hindu popular religion.

Islam and Its Appeal

The Islamic faith did not attract much immediate interest among Indians when it arrived in the subcontinent. It won gradual acceptance in merchant communities where foreign Muslim traders took local spouses and found a place in Indian society. Elsewhere, however, circumstances did not favor its adoption, since it often arrived in the cultural baggage of conquering peoples. Muslim conquerors generally reserved important political and military positions for their Arab, Persian, and Turkish companions. Only rarely did they allow Indians—even those who had converted to Islam—to hold sensitive posts. Thus, quite apart from the fact that they introduced a foreign religion radically different from those of the subcontinent, conquerors offered little incentive for Indians to convert to Islam.

Conversion to Islam

Gradually, however, many Indians converted to Islam. By 1500 C.E. Indian Muslims numbered perhaps twenty-five million—about one-quarter of the subcontinent's population. Some Indians adopted Islam in hope of improving their positions in society:

Sources from the Past

The *Bhagavata Purana* on Devotion to Vishnu

With the development of devotional Hinduism in the postclassical era, religious leaders produced a body of literature known as the puranas, *texts that told stories about the gods and offered instructions in proper methods of worship. The most influential of these works is the* Bhagavata Purana ("Purana of the Lord"), *composed about the eighth or ninth century C.E. In the following selection the god Vishnu sometimes refers to himself in the third person as "the lord" and sometimes speaks in the first person while instructing devotees how to worship him and support his cult.*

The teachers consider the utterance of the Lord's name as destructive of sin completely, even when the utterance is due to the name being associated with something else, or is done jocularly, or as a result of involuntary sound, or in derision. . . .

One should therefore resort to a teacher, desiring to know what constitutes the supreme welfare. . . . Taking the teacher as the deity, one should learn from him the practices characteristic of the Lord's devotees. . . . First, detachment from all undesirable associations, then, association with the good souls, compassion, friendliness, and due humility toward all beings, purity, penance, forbearance, silence, study of sacred writings, straighforwardness, continence, nonviolence, equanimity, seeing one's own Self and the Lord everywhere, seeking solitude, freedom from home, wearing clean recluse robes, satisfying oneself with whatever comes to one, faith in the scriptures of devotion and refraining from censure of those of other schools, subjugation of mind, speech, and action, truthfulness, quietude, restraint, listening to accounts of the Lord's advents, exploits, and qualities, singing of the Lord, contemplation of the Lord of wonderful exploits, engaging in acts only for His sake, dedicating unto the Lord everything—the rites one does, gifts, penance, sacred recital, righteous conduct and whatever is dear to one like one's wife, son, house, and one's own life—cultivating friendship with those who consider the Lord as their soul and master, service to the Lord and to the world and especially to the great and good souls, sharing in the company of fellow devotees the sanctifying glory of the Lord, sharing with them one's delight, satisfaction and virtues of restraint, remembering oneself and reminding fellow-worshipers of the Lord who sweeps away all sin; bearing a body thrilled with devotion and ecstatic experience of the Lord, now in tears with some thought of the Lord, now laughing, now rejoicing, now speaking out, now dancing, now singing, now imitating the Lord acts, and now becoming quiet with the blissful experience of the Supreme—such are the devotees, who behave like persons not of this world. . . .

One should engage himself in singing of Me, praising Me, dancing with My themes, imitating My exploits and acts, narrating My stories or listening to them.

With manifold hymns of praise of Me, taken from the *Puranas* or from the local languages . . . , the devotee should praise and pray to Me that I bless him and prostrate himself completely before Me. With his head and hands at My feet, he should pray, "My lord, from the clutches of death [i.e., the cycle of birth and death], save me who have taken refuge under You." . . .

Whenever and wherever one feels like worshiping Me in images, etc., one should do so; I am, however, present in oneself and in all beings; for I am the Soul of everything. . . .

Having consecrated an image of Me one should build a firm temple for Me, and beautiful flower gardens around for conducting daily worship and festivals. For the maintenance of My worship, etc., in special seasons as well as every day, one should bestow fields, bazaars, townships, and villages, and thereby attain to My own lordship.

SOURCE: Ainslie T. Embree and Stephen Hay, eds. *Sources of Indian Tradition,* 2 vols., 2nd ed. New York: Columbia University Press, 1988, 1: 325–26, 328.

Assess the extent to which the Bhagavata Purana *builds on devotional teachings offered in the* Bhagavad Gita *discussed earlier.*

Hindus of lower castes, for example, hoped to escape discrimination by converting to a faith that recognized the equality of all believers. In fact, Hindus rarely improved their social standing by conversion. Often members of an entire caste or subcaste adopted Islam en masse, and after conversion they continued to play the same social and economic roles that they had before.

Sufis

In India as elsewhere, the most effective agents of conversion to Islam were Sufi mystics. Sufis encouraged a personal, emotional, devotional approach to Islam. They did not insist on fine points of doctrine, and they sometimes even permitted their followers to observe rituals or venerate spirits not recognized by the Islamic faith. Because of their piety and sincerity, however, Sufi missionaries attracted individuals searching for a faith that could provide comfort and meaning for their personal lives.

In India as in other lands, Sufi mystics were the most effective Muslim missionaries. This eighteenth-century painting depicts the Sufi Khwaja Khidr, beloved in Muslim communities throughout northern India as one associated with springtime, fertility, and happiness.

Thus, like Hinduism, Indian Islam emphasized piety and devotion. Even though Hinduism and Islam were profoundly different religions, they encouraged the cultivation of similar spiritual values that transcended the social and cultural boundary lines of postclassical India.

The Bhakti Movement

In some ways the gap between Hinduism and Islam narrowed in postclassical India because both religions drew on long-established and long-observed cultural traditions. Sufis, for example, often attracted schools of followers in the manner of Indian gurus, spiritual leaders who taught Hindu values to disciples who congregated around them. Even more important was the development of the *bhakti* movement, a cult of love and devotion that ultimately sought to erase the distinction between Hinduism and Islam. The bhakti movement emerged in southern India during the twelfth century, and it originally encouraged a traditional piety and devotion to Hindu values. As the movement spread to the north, bhakti leaders increasingly encountered Muslims and became deeply attracted to certain Islamic values, especially monotheism and the notion of spiritual equality of all believers.

Guru Kabir

The bhakti movement gradually rejected the exclusive features of both Hinduism and Islam. Thus guru Kabir (1440–1518), a blind weaver who was one of the most famous bhakti teachers, went so far as to teach that Shiva, Vishnu, and Allah were all manifestations of a single, universal deity, whom all devout believers could find within their own hearts. The bhakti movement did not succeed in harmonizing Hinduism and Islam. Nevertheless, like the Sufis, bhakti teachers promoted values that helped to build bridges between India's social and cultural communities.

The Influence of Indian Society in Southeast Asia

Just as China stood at the center of a larger east Asian society, India served as the principal source of political and cultural traditions widely observed throughout south and southeast Asia. For a millennium and more, southeast Asian peoples adapted Indian political structures and religions to local needs and interests. Although Indian armed forces rarely ventured into the region, southeast Asian lands reflected the influence of Indian society, as merchants introduced Hinduism, Buddhism, Sanskrit writings, and Indian forms of political organization. Beginning about the twelfth century, Islam also found solid footing in southeast Asia, as Muslim merchants, many of them Indians, established trading communities in the important port cities of the region. During the next five hundred years, Islam attracted a sizable following and became a permanent feature in much of southeast Asia.

The States of Southeast Asia

Indian Influence in Southeast Asia

Indian merchants visited the islands and mainland of southeast Asia from an early date, perhaps as early as 500 B.C.E. By the early centuries C.E., they had become familiar figures throughout southeast Asia, and their presence brought opportunities for the native ruling elites of the region. In exchange for spices and exotic products such as pearls, aromatics, and animal skins, Indian merchants brought textiles, beads, gold, silver, manufactured metal goods, and objects used in political or religious rituals. Southeast Asian rulers used the profits from this trade to consolidate their political control.

Meanwhile, southeast Asian ruling elites became acquainted with Indian political and cultural traditions. Without necessarily giving up their own traditions, they borrowed Indian forms of political organization and accepted Indian religious faiths. On the model of Indian states, for example, they adopted kingship as the principal form of political authority. Regional kings in southeast Asia surrounded themselves with courts featuring administrators and rituals similar to those found in India.

Ruling elites also sponsored the introduction of Hinduism or Buddhism—sometimes both—into their courts. They embraced Indian literature like the *Ramayana* and the *Mahabharata,* which promoted Hindu values, as well as treatises that explained Buddhist views on the world. They did not show much enthusiasm for the Indian caste system and continued to acknowledge the deities and nature spirits that southeast Asian peoples had venerated for centuries. But ruling elites readily adopted Hinduism and Buddhism, which they found attractive because the Indian faiths reinforced the principle of monarchical rule.

Funan

The first state known to have reflected Indian influence in this fashion was Funan, which dominated the lower reaches of the Mekong River (including parts of modern Cambodia and Vietnam) between the first and the sixth century C.E. The rulers of Funan consolidated their grip on the Mekong valley and built a capital city at the port of Oc Eo. Funan grew wealthy because it dominated the Isthmus of Kra, the narrow portion of the Malay peninsula where merchants transported trade goods between China and India. (The short portage enabled them to avoid a long voyage around the Malay peninsula.) The rulers of Funan drew enormous wealth by controlling trade between China and India. They used their profits to construct an elaborate system of water storage and irrigation—so extensive that aerial photography still reveals its lines—that served a productive agricultural economy in the Mekong delta.

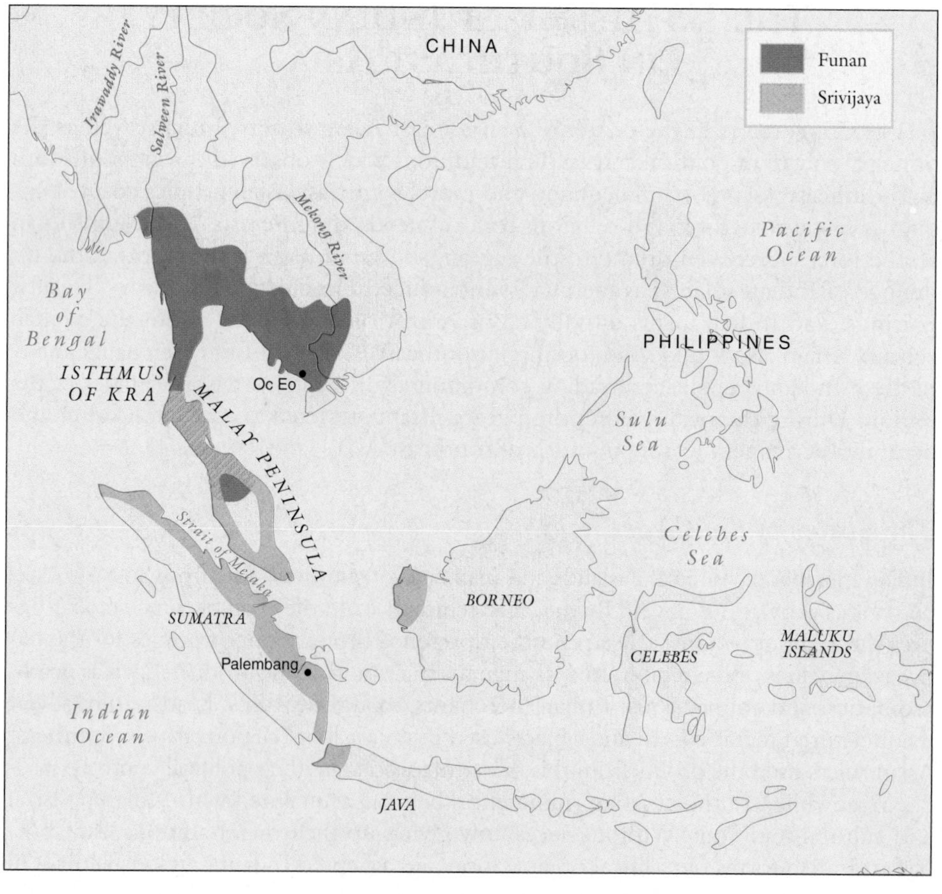

MAP [16.3]
Early states of southeast Asia: Funan and Srivijaya, 100–1025 C.E.

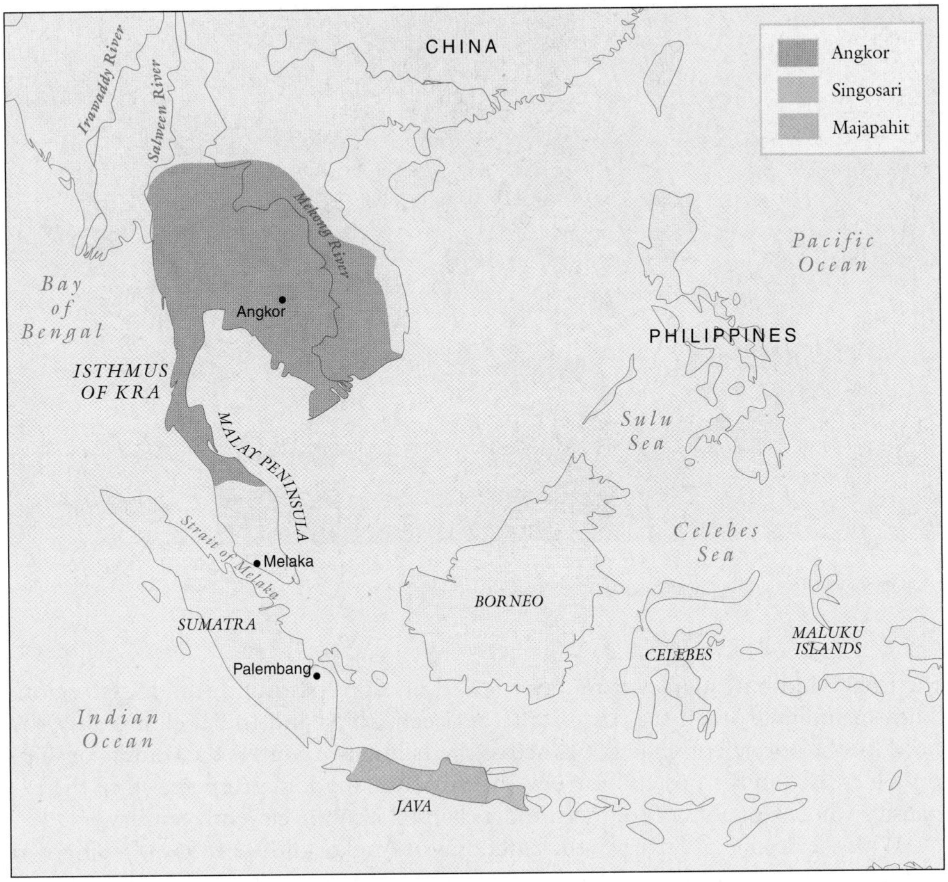

MAP [16.4]
Later states of southeast Asia: Angkor, Singosari, and Majapahit, 889–1520 C.E.

As trade with India became an increasingly important part of Funan's economy, the ruling classes adopted Indian political, cultural, and religious traditions. They took the Sanskrit term *raja* ("king") for themselves and claimed divine sanction for their rule in the manner of Hindu rulers in India. They established positions for administrators and bureaucrats such as those found at Indian courts and conducted official business in Sanskrit. They introduced Indian ceremonies and rituals and worshiped Vishnu, Shiva, and other Hindu deities. They continued to honor local deities, particularly water spirits venerated widely throughout southeast Asia, but they eagerly welcomed Hinduism, which offered additional recognition and divine legitimacy for their rule. At first, Indian cultural and religious traditions were most prominent and most often observed at ruling courts. Over the longer term, however, these traditions extended well beyond ruling elites and won a secure place in southeast Asian society.

During the sixth century C.E., a bitter power struggle weakened Funan internally. Peoples from the north took advantage of this weakness, migrated to the lower Mekong valley in large numbers, and overwhelmed Funan. Chams settled in the southern portion of modern Vietnam, and Khmers dominated in the region occupied by modern Cambodia. By the late sixth century, Funan's intricate irrigation system had fallen into ruins, and Funan itself soon passed into oblivion.

Srivijaya

After the fall of Funan, political leadership in southeast Asia passed to the kingdom of Srivijaya (670–1025 C.E.) based on the island of Sumatra. The kings of Srivijaya built a powerful navy and controlled commerce in southeast Asian waters. They compelled port cities in southeast Asia to recognize their authority, and they financed

Maritime trade flourished in southeast Asia during postclassical times. This ninth-century relief carving from the Buddhist temple at Borobodur in Java depicts a typical southeast Asian ship.

their navy and bureaucracy from taxes levied on ships passing through the region. They maintained an all-sea trade route between China and India, eliminating the need for the portage of trade goods across the Isthmus of Kra. As the volume of shipping increased in the postclassical era, the Srivijaya kingdom prospered until the expansive Chola kingdom of southern India eclipsed it in the eleventh century.

With the decline of Srivijaya, the kingdoms of Angkor (889–1431 C.E.), Singosari (1222–1292 C.E.), and Majapahit (1293–1520 C.E.) dominated affairs in southeast Asia. Many differences characterized these states. Funan had its base of operations in the Mekong valley, Srivijaya at Palembang in southern Sumatra, Angkor in Cambodia, and Singosari and Majapahit on the island of Java. Funan and Angkor were land-based states that derived most of their wealth from productive agricultural economies, whereas Srivijaya, Singosari, and Majapahit were island-based states that prospered because they controlled maritime trade. Funan and Majapahit were largely Hindu states, but the kings of Srivijaya and Angkor made deep commitments to Buddhism. Native southeast Asian traditions survived in all these states, and at the court of Singosari, religious authorities fashioned a cultural blend of Hindu, Buddhist, and indigenous values. Sculptures at the Singosari court depicted Hindu and Buddhist personalities, for example, but used them to honor local deities and natural spirits rather than Indian deities.

Angkor

The magnificent monuments of Angkor testify eloquently to the influence of Indian traditions in southeast Asia. Beginning in the ninth century, kings of the Khmers began to build a capital city at Angkor Thom. With the aid of brahmin advisors from India, the kings designed the city as a microcosmic reflection of the Hindu world order. At the center, they built a temple representing the Himalayan Mount Meru, the sacred abode of Shiva, and surrounded it with numerous smaller temples representing other parts of the Hindu universe.

As the Khmers turned to Buddhism during the twelfth and thirteenth centuries, they added Buddhist temples to the complex, though without removing the earlier structures inspired by Hinduism. The entire complex formed a square with sides of about three kilometers (two miles), surrounded by a moat filled from the nearby Tonle Sap River. During the twelfth century the Khmer kings constructed a smaller

General view of the temple complex dedicated to Vishnu at Angkor Wat.

but even more elaborate temple center at Angkor Wat, about one kilometer (just over half a mile) from Angkor Thom.

The Khmers abandoned Angkor in 1431 after Thai peoples invaded the capital and left much of it in ruins. Soon the jungle reclaimed both Angkor Thom and Angkor Wat, which remained largely forgotten until French missionaries and explorers rediscovered the sites in the mid-nineteenth century. Rescued from the jungle, the temple complexes of Angkor stand today as vivid reminders of the influence of Indian political, cultural, and religious traditions in southeast Asia.

The Arrival of Islam

Muslim merchants had ventured into southeast Asia by the eighth century, but only during the tenth century did they become prominent in the region. Some came from southern Arabia or Persia, but many were Indians from Gujarat or the port cities of southern India. Thus Indian influence helped to establish Islam as well as Hinduism and Buddhism in southeast Asia.

Conversion to Islam

For several centuries Islam maintained a quiet presence in southeast Asia. Small communities of foreign merchants observed their faith in the port cities of the region but attracted little interest on the part of the native inhabitants. Gradually, however, ruling elites, traders, and others who had regular dealings with foreign Muslims became interested in the faith. During the late thirteenth century, the Venetian traveler Marco Polo visited the island of Sumatra and noted that many residents of the towns and cities had converted to Islam, while those living in the countryside and the hills retained their inherited traditions.

Like Hinduism and Buddhism, Islam did not enter southeast Asia as an exclusive faith. Ruling elites who converted to Islam often continued to honor Hindu, Buddhist, or native southeast Asian traditions. They adopted Islam less as an exclusive and absolute creed than as a faith that facilitated their dealings with foreign Muslims and provided additional divine sanction for their rule. Rarely did they push their subjects to convert to Islam, although they allowed Sufi mystics to preach their faith before popular audiences. As in India, Sufis in southeast Asia appealed to a large public because of their reputation for sincerity and holiness. They allowed converts to retain inherited customs while adapting the message of Islam to local needs and interests.

Melaka

During the fifteenth century the spread of Islam gained momentum in southeast Asia, largely because the powerful state of Melaka sponsored the faith throughout the region. Founded during the late fourteenth century by Paramesvara, a rebellious prince from Sumatra, Melaka took advantage of its strategic location in the Strait of Melaka, near modern Singapore, and soon became prominent in the trading world of southeast Asia. During its earliest days Melaka was more a lair of pirates than a legitimate state. By the mid-fifteenth century, however, Melaka had built a substantial navy that patrolled the waters of southeast Asia and protected the region's sea lanes. Melakan fleets compelled ships to call at the port of Melaka, where ruling authorities levied taxes on the value of their cargoes. Thus, like southeast Asian states of earlier centuries, Melaka became a powerful state through the control of maritime trade.

In one respect, though, Melaka differed significantly from the earlier states. Although it began as a Hindu state, Melaka soon became predominantly Islamic. About the mid-fifteenth century the Melakan ruling class converted to Islam. It welcomed theologians, Sufis, and other Islamic authorities to Melaka and sponsored missionary campaigns to spread Islam throughout southeast Asia. By the end of the fifteenth century, mosques had begun to define the urban landscapes of Java, Sumatra, and the Malay peninsula, and Islam had made its first appearance in the spice-bearing islands of Maluku and in the southern islands of the Philippine archipelago.

Thus, within several centuries of its arrival, Islam was a prominent feature in the cultural landscape of southeast Asia. Along with Hinduism and Buddhism, Islam helped link southeast Asian lands to the larger cultural world of India and to the larger commercial world of the Indian Ocean basin.

With respect to political organization, India differed from postclassical societies in China, southwest Asia, and the eastern Mediterranean basin: India did not experience a return of centralized imperial rule such as that provided by the Tang and Song dynasties, the Umayyad and Abbasid dynasties, and the Byzantine empire. In other respects, however, India's development was similar to that of other postclassical societies. Increased agricultural production fueled population growth and urbanization while trade encouraged specialized industrial production and rapid economic growth. The vigorous and voluminous commerce of the Indian Ocean basin influenced the structure of economies and societies from east Asia to east Africa. It brought prosperity especially to India, which not only contributed cotton, pepper, sugar, iron, steel, and other products to the larger hemispheric economy but also served as a major clearinghouse of trade. Like contemporary societies, postclassical India experienced cultural change, and Indian traditions deeply influenced the cultural development of other lands. Hinduism and Islam emerged as the two most popular religious faiths within the subcontinent, while Indian merchants helped to establish Hinduism, Buddhism, and Islam in southeast Asian lands. Throughout the postclassical era, India participated fully in the larger hemispheric zone of cross-cultural communication and exchange.

CHRONOLOGY

	CHRONOLOGY
1st to 6th century	Kingdom of Funan
606–648	Reign of Harsha
670–1025	Kingdom of Srivijaya
711	Conquest of Sind by Umayyad forces
early 9th century	Life of Shankara
850–1267	Chola kingdom
889–1431	Kingdom of Angkor
1001–1027	Raids on India by Mahmud of Ghazni
11th to 12th century	Life of Ramanuja
12th century	Beginning of the bhakti movement
1206–1526	Sultanate of Delhi
1336–1565	Kingdom of Vijayanagar
1440–1518	Life of guru Kabir

FOR FURTHER READING

Aziz Ahmad. *Studies in Islamic Culture in the Indian Environment.* Oxford, 1964. A scholarly analysis of the arrival of Islam and its effects in India.

A. L. Basham. *The Wonder That Was India.* New York, 1954. A popular survey by a leading scholar of ancient India.

Al-Biruni. *Alberuni's India.* 2 vols. Trans. by E. Sachau. London, 1910. English translation of al-Biruni's eleventh-century description of Indian customs, religion, philosophy, geography, and astronomy.

Buzurg ibn Shahriyar. *The Book of the Wonders of India: Mainland, Sea and Islands.* Trans. by G. S. P. Freeman-Grenville. London, 1981. Stories and tall tales of a tenth-century mariner who sailed frequently between Persia and India.

K. N. Chaudhuri. *Asia before Europe: Economy and Civilisation of the Indian Ocean from the Rise of Islam to 1750.* Cambridge, 1990. Controversial and penetrating analysis of economic, social, and cultural structures shaping societies of the Indian Ocean basin.

———. *Trade and Civilisation in the Indian Ocean: An Economic History from the Rise of Islam to 1750.* Cambridge, 1985. Brilliant analysis of the commercial life of the Indian Ocean basin by a prominent scholar.

Georges Coedès. *The Indianized States of Southeast Asia.* Trans. by S. B. Cowing. Honolulu, 1968. A careful survey that is still useful, though somewhat dated.

Ainslie T. Embree and Stephen Hay, eds. *Sources of Indian Tradition.* 2 vols. 2nd ed. New York, 1988. An important collection of primary sources in English translation.

Bernard Groslier and Jacques Arthaud. *Angkor: Art and Civilization.* Rev. ed. Trans. by E. E. Smith. New York, 1966. Well-illustrated summary, concentrating on the magnificent temple complexes at Angkor.

Kenneth R. Hall. *Maritime Trade and State Development in Early Southeast Asia.* Honolulu, 1985. Examines the link between long-distance trade and state building in southeast Asia.

Charles Higham. *The Civilization of Angkor.* London, 2001. Draws usefully on recent archaeological research in placing Angkor in historical context.

S. M. Ikram. *Muslim Civilization in India.* Ed. by A. T. Embree. New York, 1964. Important survey of Islam and its impact in India.

Hermann Kulke and Dietmar Rothermund. *A History of India.* Totowa, N.J., 1986. A valuable interpretative synthesis of Indian history.

Eleanor Mannikka. *Angkor Wat: Time, Space, and Kingship.* Honolulu, 1996. A detailed analysis of the magnificent Cambodian temple complex from an architectural point of view.

Patricia Risso. *Merchants and Faith: Muslim Commerce and Culture in the Indian Ocean.* Boulder, 1995. Surveys the activities of Muslim merchants in the Indian Ocean basin from the seventh to the nineteenth centuries.

Kernial Singh Sandhu. *Early Malaysia.* Singapore, 1973. Survey concentrating on the periods of Indian and Islamic influence in southeast Asia.

Burton Stein. *Vijayanagara.* Cambridge, 1989. A study of the southern Hindu kingdom concentrating on political and economic history.

Romila Thapar. *A History of India.* Harmondsworth, 1966. A sound, popular survey by one of the world's leading students of early Indian history.

OLC

See our **Online Learning Center at www.mhhe.com/bentley3** for additional readings, practice maps, quizzes, and internet activities.

PSI

Unfamiliar words? Check out the **Primary Source Investigator CD-ROM** for an interactive glossary, interactive maps, more images, and primary sources.

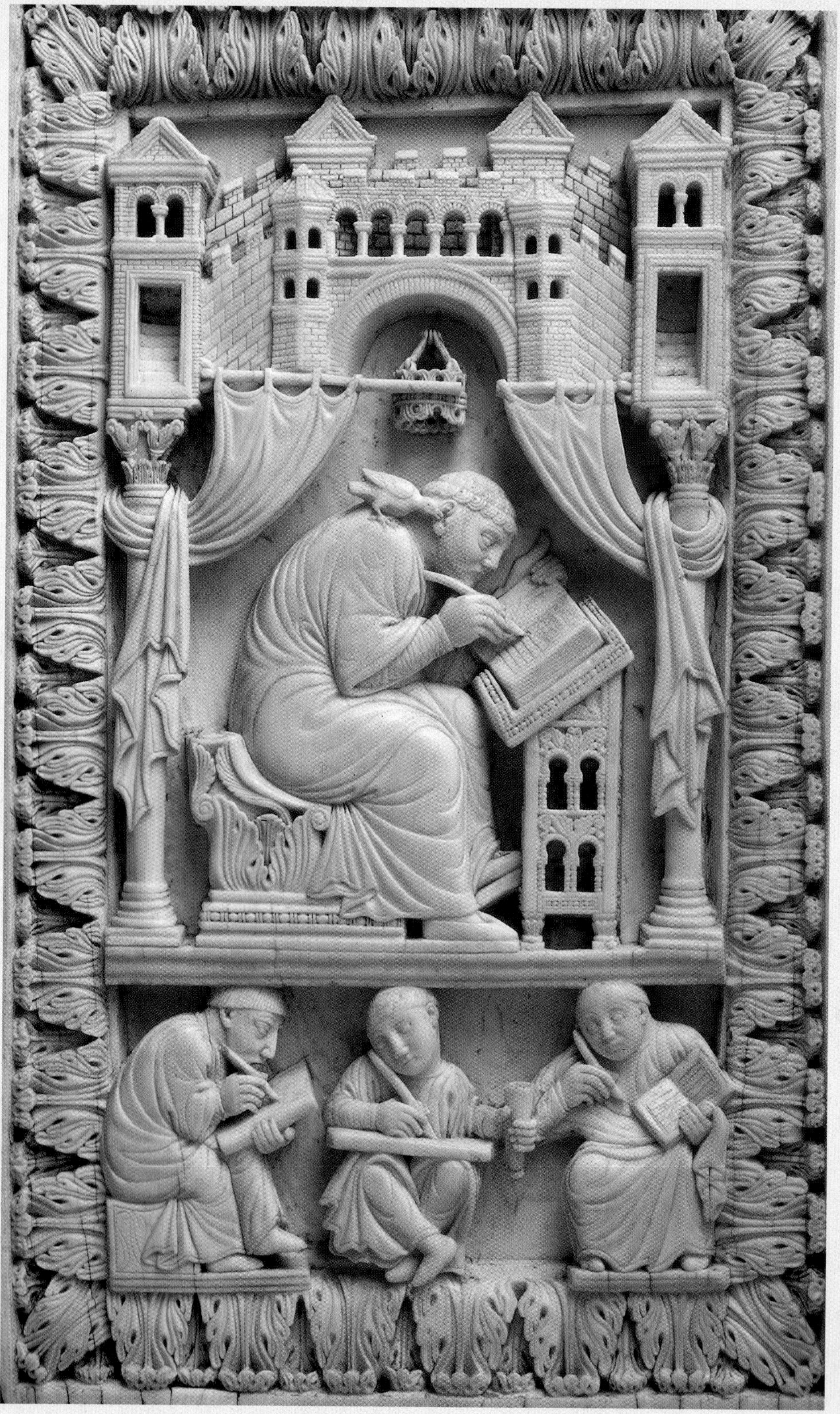

An ivory book cover carved in the tenth century depicts Pope Gregory I at his writing desk.

CHAPTER 17

THE FOUNDATIONS OF CHRISTIAN SOCIETY IN WESTERN EUROPE

In 802 C.E. a most unusual traveler made his way from Baghdad to Aachen (in modern Germany), capital of the western European empire ruled by Charlemagne. The traveler was an albino elephant, a diplomatic gift from the Abbasid caliph Harun al-Rashid to Charlemagne. The elephant—whom Harun named Abu al-Abbas, in honor of the Abbasid dynasty's founder—was born in India and went to Baghdad as a present from an Indian king. From Baghdad the animal accompanied an embassy overland to Syria, then traveled by ship from Beirut to Malta and Rome, and finally went overland north to Charlemagne's court. Abu al-Abbas must have shivered through the cold, damp winters of western Europe, yet he overawed and amazed all who beheld him until his death in 810.

Charlemagne was not friendly to Islam. At the battle of Tours (732 C.E.) his grandfather, Charles Martel, had defeated a Muslim army that ventured into Frankish territory after Muslim forces had conquered most of the Iberian peninsula. Charlemagne himself fought Muslim forces in northern Spain. One of the battles from his campaign—in a much fictionalized version—provided the story line in later centuries for a popular poetic work called the *Song of Roland*. Nevertheless, in spite of his personal religious preferences, Charlemagne found it both necessary and convenient to have diplomatic dealings with Harun al-Rashid.

Charlemagne dispatched at least three embassies to Baghdad and received three in return. The embassies dealt with several issues: the safety of Christian pilgrims and merchants traveling in Abbasid-controlled Syria and Palestine, relations between Charlemagne's realm and neighboring Muslim Spain, and policy toward the Byzantine empire, which stood between western Europe and the Abbasid caliphate. Charlemagne's realm was weak and poor compared to the Abbasid empire, and by the mid-ninth century it was well on the way to dissolution. For about half a century, however, it seemed that Charlemagne and his successors might be able to establish a centralized imperial state in western Europe. His dealings with Harun al-Rashid—and the unusual odyssey of the elephant Abu al-Abbas—indicated that Charlemagne had the potential and the ambition to establish a western European empire similar to the Byzantine and Abbasid realms.

Historians refer to the era from about 500 to 1500 C.E. as the medieval period of European history—the "middle ages" falling between the classical era and modern times. During the early medieval period, from about 500 to 1000 C.E., European peoples recovered from the invasions that brought the Roman empire to an end and laid the political, economic, and cultural foundations for a new society. Europeans did not rebuild a powerful society as quickly as did the Abbasids in southwest Asia or the Tang and Song emperors of China: like India during the postclassical era, early medieval Europe was a politically disunited and disorganized region. Unlike India, though, Europe mostly disengaged from hemispheric communication and exchange. Only about the tenth century, after the establishment of effective political authority and a productive agricultural economy, were western European peoples able to reenter the larger trading world of the eastern hemisphere.

Three developments of the early medieval era served as foundations for the development of the powerful European society that emerged after 1000 C.E. First, following the disruption caused by invasions and depopulation, the peoples of western Europe restored political order. Unlike their counterparts in southwest Asia and China, they did not return to centralized imperial rule but, instead, resorted to a decentralized political order that vested public authority mostly in local and regional rulers. Second, European peoples began a process of economic recovery. They did not build large cities or generate a powerful industrial economy like those of the Byzantine, Abbasid, Tang, and Song empires. But they boosted agricultural production by increasing the amount of land under cultivation and introducing new tools and techniques, thus laying an agricultural foundation for trade and rapid economic development after the tenth century. Third, European peoples built an institutional framework that enabled the Christian church based in Rome to provide religious leadership and maintain cultural unity throughout western Europe. Thus, just as Confucianism, Buddhism, Hinduism, Islam, and eastern Christianity shaped cultural values in other lands, western Christianity emerged as the principal source of cultural authority in western Europe.

The Quest for Political Order

After toppling Rome's authority in the late fifth century C.E., Germanic invaders established successor states throughout the western Roman empire. From the fifth through the eighth century, continuing invasions and conflicts among the invaders themselves left western Europe in shambles. For a brief moment during the late eighth and early ninth centuries, it looked as though one group of Germanic invaders, the Franks, might reestablish imperial authority in western Europe. If they had succeeded, they might have played a role similar to that of the Sui and Tang dynasties in China by reviving centralized imperial rule after a hiatus of several centuries. By the late ninth century, however, the Frankish empire had fallen victim to internal power struggles and a fresh series of invasions by Muslims, Hungarian Magyars, and Vikings. Political authority in early medieval Europe then devolved to local and regional jurisdictions, and Europeans fashioned a decentralized political order.

Germanic Successor States

In 476 C.E. the Germanic general Odoacer deposed the last of the western Roman emperors, but the administrative apparatus of the Roman empire did not immediately disappear. Provincial governors continued to rule in their territories, aided by Roman bureaucrats and tax collectors, and Roman generals continued to field armies throughout the crumbling empire. Cities of the western Roman empire, however, lost population during the fifth century, as invasions and contests for power disrupted trade and manufacturing. This decay of Roman cities hastened imperial decline. De-

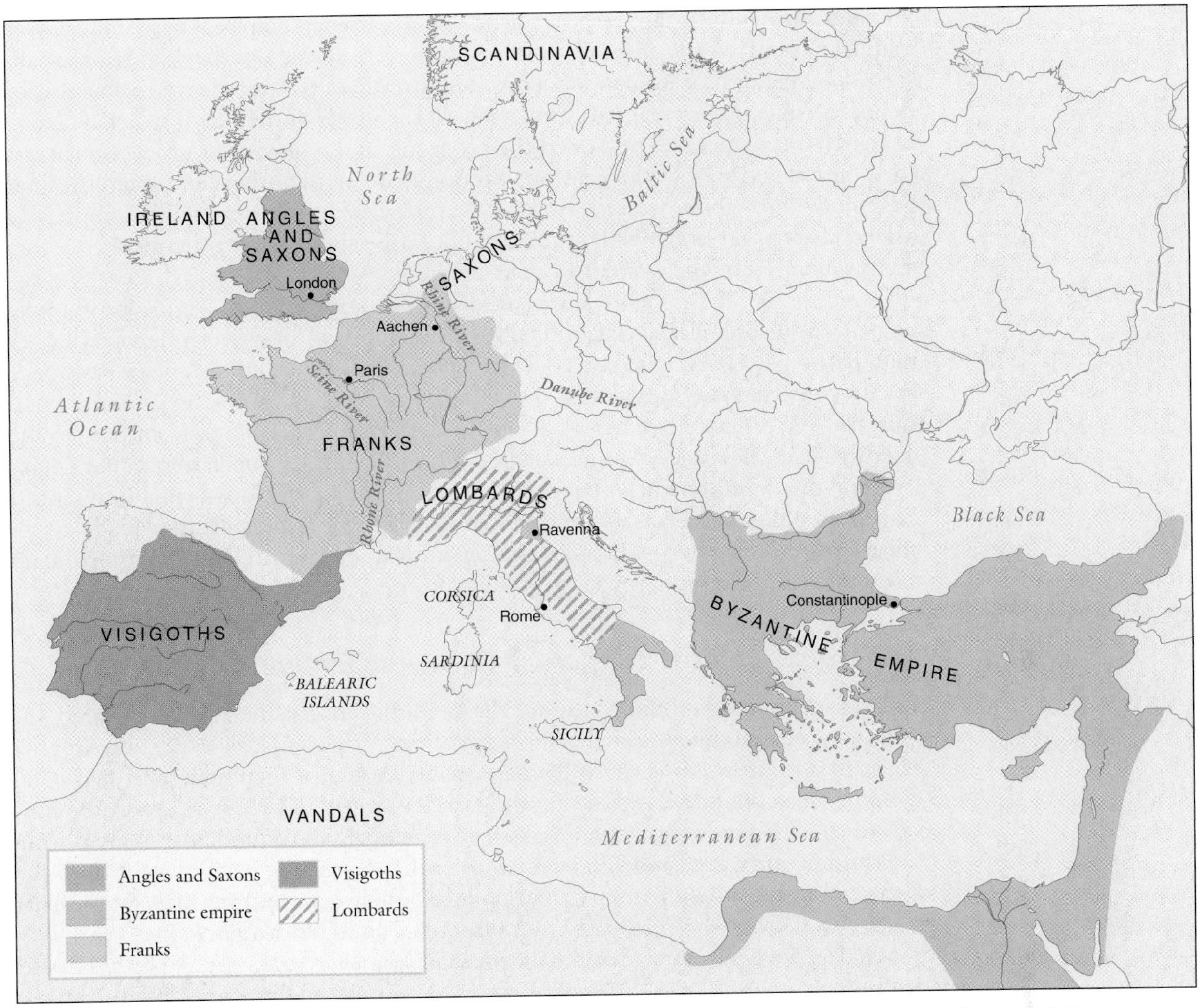

MAP [17.1]
Successor states to the Roman empire, ca. 600 C.E.

prived of legitimacy and resources supplied from Rome and the other major cities of the empire, imperial institutions progressively weakened.

Germanic Kingdoms

By the late fifth century, the invaders had organized a series of Germanic kingdoms as successor states in place of the Roman empire. Visigoths conquered Spain during the 470s, for example, and established a kingdom there that survived until the Muslim invasions of the early eighth century. Ostrogoths dominated Italy from the fifth century until Justinian's forces reasserted imperial authority there during the 530s. The departure of Byzantine armies from Italy created a power vacuum, which the Lombard people quickly moved to fill. Although they did not establish a tightly centralized monarchy, the Lombards maintained their hegemony throughout most of Italy from the mid-sixth until the mid-eighth century. Meanwhile, beginning about the mid-fifth century, Gaul fell under the control of other Germanic peoples, including the Burgundians, who settled in the southern and eastern regions, and the Franks, who brought the more northerly and westerly regions under their control. Angles, Saxons, and other Germanic peoples from Germany and Denmark crossed the English Channel and established regional kingdoms in Britain.

Thus, throughout the western portion of the Roman empire, Germanic peoples gradually displaced the authority and institutions of Rome. As they did so, they absorbed a great deal of Roman influence. Many of them converted to Christianity, for example, while others adapted Roman law to the needs of their own societies. None of the Germanic peoples possessed the economic and military resources—much less the political and social organization—to dominate all the others and establish their hegemony throughout western Europe. Nevertheless, the Franks built an impressive imperial state that organized, at least temporarily, about half of the territories formerly embraced by the western Roman empire.

The Franks

Even though their empire survived for only a short time, the Franks profoundly influenced the political, social, and cultural development of western Europe. Rather than participate actively in the commercial world of the Mediterranean basin, the Franks constructed a society that drew on the agricultural resources of continental Europe. As a result, the center of gravity in western Europe shifted from Italy to the northern lands of France, Germany, and the Low Countries. Furthermore, the Franks oversaw the development of decentralized political institutions, which influenced European politics and society for a millennium and more. Finally, they made a firm alliance with the western Christian church and helped Roman Christianity maintain its cultural and religious primacy in western Europe.

The Franks and the Temporary Revival of Empire

As Roman authority crumbled during the late fifth century, the Franks appeared unlikely to play a prominent role in European affairs. They had little experience in government and little exposure to Roman society. Some of their ancestors had lived within Roman boundaries since about the third century, and a few had probably converted to Christianity. But the Franks had developed a group identity only during the third century C.E., much later than the other Germanic peoples. Not until the fifth century did a strong military and political leader emerge from their midst. That leader was Clovis, who ruled the Franks from 481 until his death in 511.

Clovis

Under Clovis the Franks became the preeminent military and political power in western Europe. In 486 Clovis led Frankish forces on a campaign that wiped out the last vestiges of Roman authority in Gaul. Then he imposed his authority on the Franks themselves. Finally, he organized campaigns against other Germanic peoples whose states bordered the Frankish realm in Gaul. By the time of his death, Clovis had thoroughly transformed the Franks. No longer were they just one among many Germanic peoples inhabiting a crumbling Roman empire. Instead, they ranked as the most powerful and dynamic of the peoples building new states in western Europe.

A manuscript illustration depicts the baptism of Clovis witnessed by church officials (left) and Frankish nobles (right), while a dove descends from above, indicating divine approval of the event.

Clovis's Conversion

One reason for the Franks' rapid rise had to do with religion. Originally, all the Germanic invaders of the Roman empire were polytheists who honored a pantheon of warlike gods and other deities representing elements of nature such as the sun, moon, and wind. As they settled in and around the Roman empire, many Germanic peoples converted to Christianity. Most of them accepted Arian Christianity, which was popular in much of the eastern Roman empire. In both Rome and Constantinople, however, church authorities followed the decisions of church councils at Nicaea and Constantinople and condemned Arian views as heretical. Unlike other Germanic peoples, the Franks remained mostly pagan until the time of Clovis, who converted to Roman rather than to Arian Christianity along with his army. Clovis's conversion probably reflected the influence of his wife, Clotilda, a devout Christian who had long urged her husband to adopt her faith.

The Franks' conversion had large political implications. By adopting Roman rather than Arian Christianity, the Franks attracted the allegiance of the Christian population of the former Roman empire as well as recognition and support from the pope and the hierarchy of the western Christian church. Alliance with the church of Rome greatly strengthened the Franks, who became the most powerful of the Germanic peoples between the fifth and ninth centuries.

The Carolingians

After Clovis's death the Frankish kings lost much of their authority, as aristocratic warriors seized effective control of affairs in their own regions. Nevertheless, Clovis's successors ruled the Frankish kingdom until the early eighth century, when the aristocratic clan of the Carolingians displaced the line of Clovis and asserted the authority of the central government. The Carolingian dynasty takes its name from its founder, Charles (*Carolus* in Latin)—known as Charles Martel ("Charles the Hammer") because of his military prowess. In 732 at the battle of Tours (in the central part of modern France), he turned back a Muslim army that had ventured from Spain—recently conquered by Muslim warriors from north Africa—in order to reconnoiter lands north of the Pyrenees mountains. His victory helped persuade Muslim rulers of Spain that it was not worthwhile for them to seek further conquests in western Europe. Charles Martel himself never ruled as king of the Franks but, rather, served as deputy to the last of Clovis's descendants. In 751, however, Charles's son claimed the throne for himself.

Charlemagne

The Frankish realm reached its high point under Charles Martel's grandson Charlemagne ("Charles the Great"), who reigned from 768 to 814. Like King Harsha in India, Charlemagne temporarily reestablished centralized imperial rule in a society disrupted by invasion and contests for power between ambitious local rulers. Like Harsha again, Charlemagne possessed enormous energy, and the building of the Carolingian empire was in large measure his personal accomplishment. Although barely literate, Charlemagne was extremely intelligent. He spoke Latin, understood some Greek, and regularly conversed with theologians and other learned men. He maintained diplomatic relations with the Byzantine empire and the Abbasid caliphate. The

A bronze statue depicts Charlemagne riding a horse and carrying an orb symbolizing his imperial authority.

Sources from the Past

Gregory of Tours on the Conversion of Clovis

St. Gregory (538–594 C.E.) was bishop of Tours in central Gaul for the last twenty-one years of his life. During this period he composed a History of the Franks, *which is the chief source of information about the early Franks. Gregory clearly embellished the story of Clovis's conversion to Christianity, but his account indicates the significance of the event both for Clovis and for the Roman church.*

The queen [Clotilda] did not cease to urge him [Clovis] to recognize the true God and cease worshiping idols. But he could not be influenced in any way to this belief, until at last a war arose with the Alamanni, in which he was driven by necessity to confess what before he had of his free will denied. It came about that as the two armies were fighting fiercely, there was much slaughter, and Clovis's army began to be in danger of destruction. He saw it and raised his eyes to heaven, and with remorse in his heart he burst into tears and cried: "Jesus Christ, whom Clotilda asserts to be the son of the living God, who art said to give aid to those in distress and to bestow victory on those who hope in thee, I beseech the glory of thy aid, with the vow that if thou wilt grant me victory over these enemies, and I shall know that power which she says that people dedicated in thy name have had from thee, I will believe in thee and be baptized in thy name. For I have invoked my own gods, but, as I see, they have withdrawn from aiding me; and therefore I believe that they possess no power, since they do not help those who obey them. I now call upon thee, I desire to believe thee, only let me be rescued from my adversaries." And when he said this, the Alamanni turned their backs, and began to disperse in flight. And when they saw that their king was killed, they submitted to the dominion of Clovis, saying: "Let not the people perish further, we pray; we are yours now." And he stopped the fighting, and after encouraging his men retired in peace and told the queen how he had had merit to win the victory by calling on the name of Christ. . . .

Then the queen asked saint Remi, bishop of Rheima, to summon Clovis secretly, urging him to introduce the king to the word of salvation. And the bishop sent for him secretly and began to urge him to believe in the true God, maker of heaven and earth, and to cease worshiping idols, which could help neither themselves nor any one else. But the king said: "I gladly hear you, most holy father; but there remains one thing: the people who follow me cannot endure to abandon their gods; but I shall go and speak to them according to your words." He met with his followers, but before he could speak, the power of God anticipated him, and all the people cried out together: "O pious king, we reject our mortal gods, and we are ready to follow the immortal God whom Remi preaches." This was reported to the bishop, who was greatly rejoiced, and bade them get ready the baptismal font. . . . And the king was the first to ask to be baptized by the bishop. . . . And so the king confessed all-powerful God in the Trinity and was baptized in the name of the Father, Son, and Holy Spirit, and was anointed with the holy ointment with the sign of the cross of Christ. And of his army more than 3,000 were baptized.

SOURCE: Gregory of Tours. *History of the Franks.* Trans. by E. Brehaut. New York: Columbia University Press, 1916, pp. 39–41. (Translation slightly modified.)

To what extent was Clovis's conversion a case of religious transformation and to what extent a political act?

gift of the white elephant Abu al-Abbas symbolized relations between the Carolingian and Abbasid empires, and the animal accompanied Charlemagne on many of his travels until its death.

When Charlemagne inherited the Frankish throne, his realm included most of modern France as well as the lands that now form Belgium, the Netherlands, and southwestern Germany. Charlemagne was a conqueror in the mold of the Germanic peoples who invaded the Roman empire. By the time of his death in 814, Charlemagne had extended his authority to northeastern Spain, Bavaria, and Italy as far south as Rome. He campaigned for thirty-two years to impose his rule on the Saxons of northern Germany and repress their rebellions. Beyond the Carolingian empire proper, rulers in eastern Europe and southern Italy paid tribute to Charlemagne as imperial overlord.

Charlemagne's Administration

Charlemagne established a court and capital at Aachen (in modern Germany), but like Harsha in India, he spent most of his reign traveling throughout his realm in order to maintain his authority. Such constant travel was necessary because Charlemagne did not have the financial resources to maintain an elaborate bureaucracy or an administrative apparatus that could implement his policies. Instead, Charlemagne relied on aristocratic deputies, known as counts, who held political, military, and legal authority in local jurisdictions.

The counts often had their own political ambitions, and they sometimes pursued policies contrary to the interests of the central government. In an effort to bring the counts under tighter control, Charlemagne instituted a new group of imperial officials known as *missi dominici* ("envoys of the lord ruler"), who traveled every year to all local jurisdictions and reviewed the accounts of local authorities.

Charlemagne built the Frankish kingdom into an empire on the basis of military expeditions and began to outfit it with some centralized institutions. Yet he hesitated

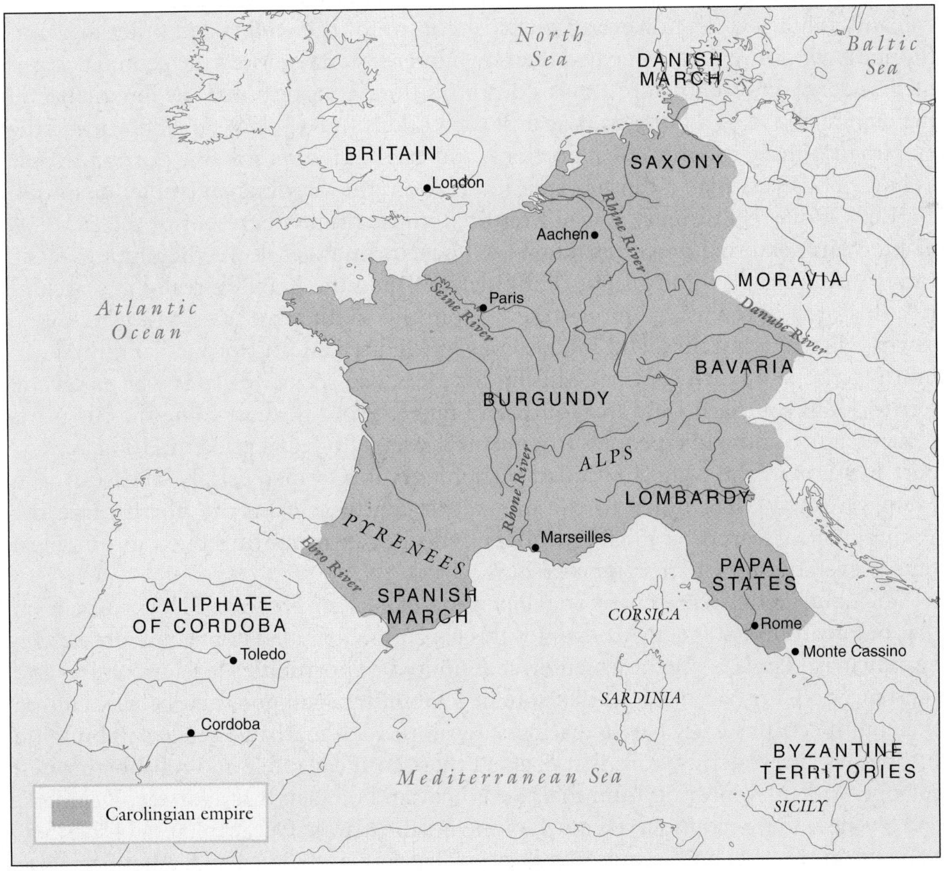

MAP [17.2]
The Carolingian empire, 814 C.E.

For an interactive version of this map, go to www.mhhe.com/bentley3ch17maps.

to call himself emperor because the imperial title would constitute a direct challenge to the authority of the Byzantine emperors, who regarded themselves as the sole and legitimate successors of the Roman emperors.

Charlemagne as Emperor

Only in the year 800 did Charlemagne accept the title of emperor. While campaigning in Italy, Charlemagne attended religious services on Christmas Day conducted by Pope Leo III. During the services, the pope proclaimed Charlemagne emperor and placed an imperial crown on his head. It is not certain, but it is at least possible that Charlemagne did not know of the pope's plan and that Leo surprised him with an impromptu coronation: Charlemagne had no desire for strained relations with Byzantine emperors, who deeply resented the use of the imperial title in western Europe as a pretentious affront to their own dignity and authority. In any case, Charlemagne had already built an imperial state, and his coronation constituted public recognition of his accomplishments.

Decline and Dissolution of the Carolingian Empire

If Charlemagne's empire had endured, Carolingian rulers might well have built a bureaucracy, used the *missi dominici* to enhance the authority of the central government, and permanently reestablished centralized imperial rule in western Europe. As it happened, however, internal disunity and external invasions brought the Carolingian empire to an early end.

Louis the Pious

Charlemagne's only surviving son, Louis the Pious (reigned 814–840), succeeded his father and kept the Carolingian empire together. Lacking Charlemagne's strong will and military skills, however, Louis lost control of the counts and other local authorities, who increasingly pursued their own interests and ignored the central government. Moreover, even before Louis's death his three sons disputed the inheritance of the empire and waged bitter wars against each other. In 843 they agreed to divide the empire into three roughly equal portions, and each of them took one portion to rule as king. Thus, less than a century after its creation, the Carolingian empire dissolved.

Invasions

Even if internal disunity had not resulted in the dismemberment of the Carolingian empire, external pressures might well have brought it down. Beginning in the early ninth century, three groups of invaders pillaged the Frankish realm in search of wealth stored in towns and monasteries. From the south came Muslims, who raided towns, villages, churches, and monasteries in Mediterranean Europe from the mid-ninth to the late tenth century. Muslim invaders also seized Sicily as well as several territories in southern Italy and southern France. From the east came the Magyars, descendants of nomadic peoples from central Asia who had settled in Hungary. Expert horsemen, the Magyars raided settlements in Germany, Italy, and southern France from the late ninth to the mid-tenth century. From the north came the Vikings, most feared of all the invaders, who began mounting raids in northern France even during Charlemagne's reign.

Norse Expansion

Viking invasions represented one dimension of a larger process of Norse expansion that began around 800 C.E. Motives for this expansion included population pressure in Scandinavian lands, some of which offered limited opportunities for agriculture, and resistance to Christian missions that sought to abolish pagan gods and beliefs. During the eighth century C.E., Norse mariners developed a remarkable set of shipbuilding techniques and seafaring skills that enabled them to travel safely and reliably through the open ocean. Venturing from their Scandinavian homelands of Norway, Denmark, and Sweden, they reconnoitered much of the north Atlantic Ocean and established settlements in the Shetland Islands, the Faeroes, Iceland, and Greenland. About the year 1000 C.E., a small group even established a colony at Newfoundland in modern Canada and explored the Atlantic coast of North America at least as far south as modern-day Maine in the United States. Norse colonies in North America survived no more than a few decades, and even the colony in Greenland eventually disappeared around 1500 C.E. after a cooling global climate made it difficult to cultivate food crops there. Nevertheless, the colonies in Greenland and North America demonstrate the ability of Norse peoples to travel safely over long stretches of open ocean. These remarkable seafaring skills made it possible for Norse cultivators to migrate from their homelands and establish new agricultural communities in the north Atlantic basin.

Danish Vikings prepare to invade England in this manuscript illustration produced at an English monastery about 1130.

The Vikings

Most Norse seafarers were merchants seeking commercial opportunities or migrants seeking lands to settle and cultivate. Some, however, turned their maritime skills more toward raiding and plundering than trading or raising crops. These were the Vikings. The term *Viking* originally referred to a group that raided the British Isles from their home at Vik in southern Norway. Over time, however, the term came to refer more generally to Norse mariners who mounted invasions and plundered settlements from eastern Europe to Mediterranean lands.

The Vikings sailed shallow-draft boats that could cross heavy seas, but then could also navigate the many rivers offering access to interior regions of Europe. Viking sailors carefully coordinated their ships' movements and timed their attacks to take advantage of the tides. Fleets of Viking boats with ferocious dragon heads mounted on their prows could sail up a river, arrive unexpectedly at a village or monastery far from the sea, and then spill

The Oseberg ship, pictured here, is the best-preserved Viking vessel from the early middle ages. Built around 800 C.E., it served as a royal tomb until its discovery in 1903. A ship this size would accommodate about forty men.

MAP [17.3]
The dissolution of the Carolingian empire (843 C.E.) and the invasions of early medieval Europe in the ninth and tenth centuries.

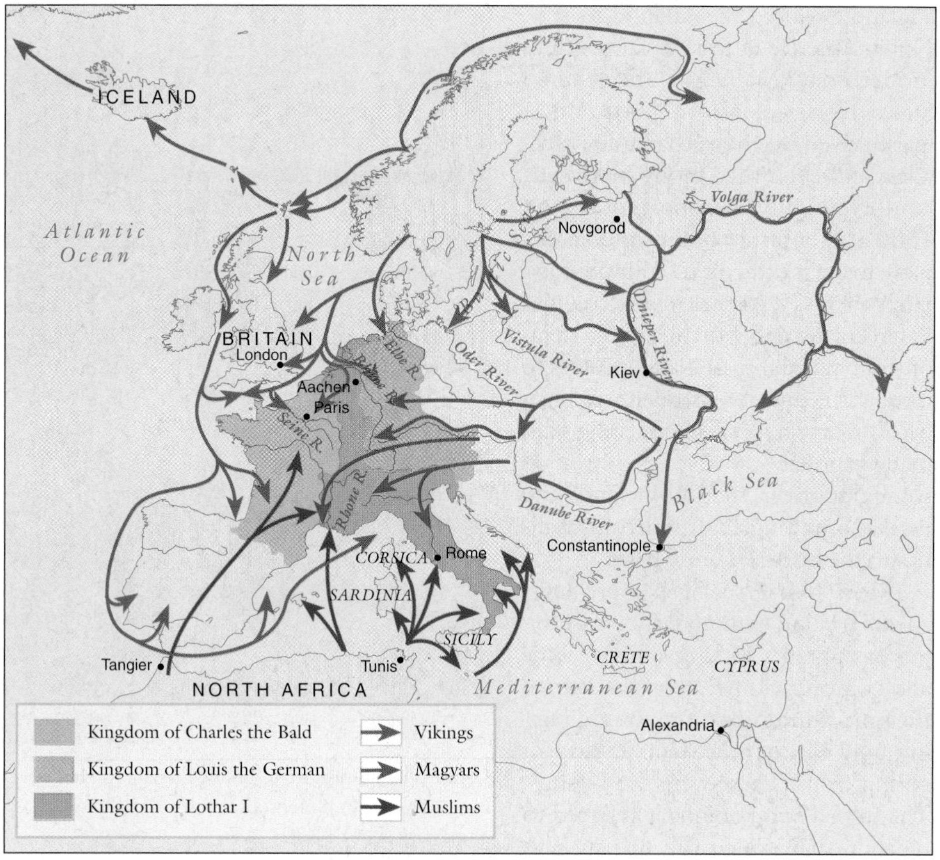

out crews of warriors who conducted lightning raids on unprepared victims. In 844 C.E. more than 150 Viking ships sailed up the Garonne River in southern France, plundering settlements along the way. Sometimes large fleets of Viking ships even attacked sizable cities. In 845 a menacing fleet of some 800 vessels materialized without warning before the city of Hamburg in northern Germany; in 885 a Viking force consisting of at least 700 ships sailed up the Seine River and besieged Paris; and in 994 an armada of about 100 ships sprinted up the Thames River and raided London. Bypassing relatively close targets in Russia, Germany, England, Ireland, France, and Spain, some Vikings ventured into the Mediterranean, where they plundered sites in the Balearic Islands, Sicily, and southern Italy. By following the Russian rivers to the Black Sea, other Vikings made their way to Constantinople, which they raided at least three times during the ninth and tenth centuries.

The Establishment of Regional Authorities

The Carolingians had no navy, no means to protect vulnerable sites, and no way to predict the movements of Viking raiders. Defense against the Magyars and Muslims as well as the Vikings rested principally with local forces that could respond rapidly to invasions. Because imperial authorities were unable to defend their territory, the Carolingian empire became the chief casualty of the invasions. After the ninth century, political and military initiative in western Europe passed increasingly to regional and local authorities.

England

Responses to ninth-century invasions took different forms in different lands. In England, which bore the brunt of the earliest Viking raids, invasions prompted the series of small kingdoms established earlier by Angles, Saxons, and other Germanic peoples to merge into a single larger realm. The leader of this effort was King Alfred (reigned 871–899), who expanded from his base in southern England to territories farther north held by Danish invaders. Alfred built a navy to challenge the Vikings at sea and constructed fortresses on land to secure areas that he conquered from the invaders. Danish settlers continued to occupy agricultural lands, but by the mid-tenth century Alfred's successors had established themselves as kings of all England.

Germany

In Germany the response to invasion brought the end of Carolingian rule and the formation of a more effective state under a new dynasty. When Carolingian authorities were unable to prevent invasions by the Magyars, local lords took matters into their own hands. The most successful of them was King Otto I of Saxony (reigned 936–973). In 955 he faced a large Magyar army at Lechfeld near Augsburg and inflicted a crushing defeat that effectively ended the Magyar threat. Otto also imposed his authority throughout Germany, and twice he led armies into Italy to support the papacy against Lombard magnates. On his second venture there in 962, the pope proclaimed him emperor and bestowed an imperial crown upon him. Otto's realm was really a German kingdom rather than an empire, but the imperial title survived until the nineteenth century, and later rulers of the Holy Roman Empire dated the foundation of their state to Otto's coronation in 962. In Germany, as in England, then, response to ninth-century invasions led to the organization of an effective regional state.

France

In France the end of Carolingian rule led to the proliferation of local authorities. Counts and other subordinates of the Carolingians withdrew allegiance from the central government, ruled their territories in their own interests, and usurped royal rights and prerogatives for themselves. They collected taxes, organized armed forces, built castles, and provided justice without reference to the Carolingians or other central authorities. Meanwhile, Vikings established many settlements in northern France, where they carved out small, independent states. The devolution of political and military responsibility to local authorities in tenth-century France encouraged the development of a decentralized political order.

The emergence of effective regional kingdoms and local authorities prevented the return of centralized imperial rule like that of the Carolingians or postclassical societies in China, southwest Asia, and the eastern Mediterranean region. Like postclassical India, medieval Europe became a society of competing regional states. By putting an end to the ninth-century invasions and establishing a stable political order, these states laid a foundation for social, economic, and cultural development.

EARLY MEDIEVAL SOCIETY

Historians once used the term *feudalism* to refer to the political and social order of medieval Europe. They spoke of a "feudal system" based on a neat hierarchy of lords and vassals, who collectively took charge of political and military affairs. Increasingly, however, scholars are abandoning the term *feudalism* because it distorts and oversimplifies the understanding of a complicated society. It is more helpful to view early medieval Europe as a society in which local political and military elites worked out various ad hoc ways to organize their territories and maintain order in the absence of effective central authorities. The arrangements they adopted had deep implications for the lives of political and military elites themselves and also for their relationships with commoners.

Organizing a Decentralized Society

After the dissolution of the Carolingian empire, European nobles built a decentralized society as they sought to protect their lands and maintain public order during a period of weak central authority and periodic invasions from outside. Local nobles, such as the Carolingian counts or other authorities, took responsibility for maintaining order in their own territories. These nobles usually owed at least nominal allegiance to a higher authority, most often a Carolingian king descended from Louis the Pious. In fact, though, the nobles acted with growing independence: they collected rents and fees, administered local affairs, mobilized armed forces, decided legal disputes, and sought to enhance their own authority at the expense of their superiors.

Lords and Retainers

To organize their territories the local nobles built military and political relationships with other prominent individuals in their territories. In doing so, they drew on military talent during the later Roman empire and the early Frankish kingdom, and they mobilized small private armies by attracting armed retainers into their service with grants of land or money. During the ninth and tenth centuries, as the Carolingian empire dissolved, local authorities revived these recruitment practices. Local lords provided grants that enabled their retainers to support themselves and their families. Usually these grants were parcels of land, but they sometimes took other forms, such as the right to income generated by a mill, the right to receive rents or payments from a village, or even a payment of money. These grants enabled retainers to devote their time and energy to the service of their lords rather than the domestic tasks of cultivating food and providing for families. The grants also provided resources that retainers needed to maintain horses and acquire expensive military equipment such as armor and weapons. In exchange for their grants, retainers owed loyalty, obedience, respect, counsel, and military service to their lords.

Military retainers receive swords that indicate their close relationship with a local lord who accepts them as partners in authority.

Indeed, relationships between lords and retainers became stronger because political leaders increasingly attracted followers by offering them rights over land and they increasingly recognized the prerogative of their supporters to pass these rights along to their heirs. In effect, these ties established close relationships between local political and military authorities. These relationships became extremely important for the larger social order because retainers increasingly exercised political and legal rights over their holdings. Retainers became responsible for the organizations of local public works projects, the resolution of disputes, and the administration of justice. As a result, political authorities and military specialists merged into a hereditary noble class that lived off the surplus agricultural production that it extracted from cultivators.

Potential for Instability

This decentralized political order developed into a complicated and sometimes even confusing network of relationships between lords and retainers. A lord with several retainers might himself be a retainer to a higher lord, who in turn might be one of several retainers to a yet greater lord in a web of relationships extending from local communities to a king. In some ways, dependence on the personal relationship between lord and retainer introduced an element of instability into the political order, since retainers—particularly those with many retainers of their own—sometimes decided unpredictably to pursue their own interests rather than those of their lords. Unless lords could discipline and control their retainers, this decentralized political order had strong potential to lead to political chaos, as in post–Carolingian France, where ambitious local authorities largely ignored central authorities and pursued their own interests.

Yet it was also possible for high-ranking lords to build powerful states on the foundation of relationships between lords and retainers. The tenth-century rulers of England and Germany, for example, monitored their retainers and prevented them from becoming too independent. And during the high middle ages (discussed in chapter 20), the kings of both England and France depended on relationships with their retainers in building powerful, centralized monarchies.

Serfs and Manors

Military, political, and legal affairs were the business of a small governing elite composed of lords and their retainers. But the establishment of a decentralized political order in early medieval Europe had important implications for the lives of all classes of people. Benefices held by political elites consisted most often of land cultivated by peasants who lived on the land and delivered a portion of their production to their superiors. Only by tapping this surplus agricultural production could lords and their retainers secure the material resources they needed to maintain their control over military, political, and legal affairs.

Serfs

The development of a decentralized political order accompanied fundamental changes in European society, particularly for slaves and free peasants. Both Roman and Germanic societies had recognized enslaved and free classes, and for several centuries after the fall of the western Roman empire the population of western Europe consisted mostly of slaves and free peasants. As European society regained stability following the collapse of the Roman empire and the Germanic invasions, these slaves and free peasants worked at the same kinds of agricultural tasks and frequently intermarried. Free peasants often sought protection from a lord and pledged their labor and obedience in exchange for security and land to cultivate. Beginning about the mid-seventh century, rulers and administrators recognized intermediate categories of individuals neither fully slave nor fully free. Though not chattel slaves subject to sale on a master's whim, these semifree individuals, known as *serfs,* owed obligations to the lords whose lands they cultivated.

Serfs' Obligations

Serfs usually had the right to work certain lands and to pass rights to those lands along to their heirs, so long as they observed their obligations to landlords. These obligations included both labor services and payments of rents in kind, such as a portion of a serf's own harvest, a chicken, or a dozen eggs, at specified times during the year. Male serfs typically worked three days a week in the fields of their lords and provided additional labor services during planting and harvesting seasons, while women churned butter, made cheese, brewed beer, spun thread, wove cloth, or sewed clothes for the lords and their families. Some women also kept sheep and cattle, and their obligations to lords included products from their herds. Because landlords provided them with land to cultivate and sometimes with tools and animals as well, serfs had little opportunity to move to different lands. Indeed, they were able to do so only with the permission of their lord. They even had to pay fees for the right to marry a serf who worked for a different lord.

Manors

During the early middle ages, the institution of serfdom encouraged the development of the manor as the principal form of agricultural organization in western Europe. A manor was a large estate consisting of fields, meadows, forests, agricultural tools, domestic animals, and sometimes lakes or rivers, as well as serfs bound to the land. The lord of the manor was a prominent political or military figure. He and his deputies provided government, administration, police services, and justice for the manor. If a dispute arose between serfs, for example, the lord and his deputies restored order, conducted an investigation, and determined how to resolve the conflict. Many lords had the authority to execute serfs for serious misconduct such as murder or other violent crimes.

By the Carolingian era, manors dominated rural regions in much of France, western Germany, and the Low Countries, as well as southern England and northern Italy. In the absence of thriving cities, manors became largely self-sufficient communities. Lords of the manors maintained mills, bakeries, breweries, and wineries, and serfs produced most of the iron tools, leather goods, domestic utensils, and textiles that the manorial community needed. Small local markets, often organized near monasteries, supplied the products that residents of manors could not conveniently manufacture for themselves. During the high middle ages, craft skills developed on manors would help fuel an impressive round of economic development in western Europe.

The Economy of Early Medieval Europe

During the early middle ages, economic activity in western Europe was considerably slower than in China, India, southwest Asia, and the eastern Mediterranean region. Agricultural production suffered from repeated invasions by Germanic peoples, Magyars, Muslims, and Vikings, which seriously disrupted European economy and society. The decay of urban centers resulted in diminished industrial production and trade. By the tenth century, however, political stability served as a foundation for economic recovery, and western Europeans began to participate more actively in the larger trading world of the eastern hemisphere.

Agriculture

With the establishment of the Frankish kingdom and the Carolingian empire, the European center of gravity shifted from the Mediterranean to more northern lands, particularly France. But the agricultural tools and techniques inherited from the classical Mediterranean world did not transfer very well. In light, well-drained Mediterranean soils, cultivators used small wooden plows that basically broke the surface of the soil, created a furrow, and disrupted weeds. This type of plow made little headway in the heavy, moist soils of the north.

Heavy Plows

After the eighth century a more serviceable plow became available: a heavy tool equipped with iron tips that dug into the earth and with a mould-board that turned the soil so as to aerate it thoroughly and break up the root networks of weeds. Though known as early as the second century, this heavy northern plow did not see widespread use until the Carolingian era. The heavy plow was a more expensive piece of equipment than the light Mediterranean plow, and it required cultivators to harness much more energy to pull it through moist northern soils. Once hitched to oxen or draft horses, however, the heavy plow contributed to significantly increased agricultural production.

In this twelfth-century manuscript illustration, a peasant guides a heavy, wheeled plow while his wife prods the oxen that pull the plow.

As the heavy plow spread throughout western Europe, cultivators took several additional steps that increased agricultural production. Under the direction of their lords, serfs cleared new lands for cultivation. They constructed watermills, which enabled them to take advantage of a ready and renewable source of inanimate energy, thus freeing human and animal energy for other work. They developed a special horse collar, which enabled them to rely less on slow-moving oxen and more on much speedier horses to draw their heavy plows. As a result, they were able to increase the amount of land under cultivation. They also experimented with new methods of rotating crops that enabled them to cultivate land more intensively than before.

A Rural Society

The agricultural surplus of early medieval Europe was sufficient to sustain political elites like lords and their retainers, but not substantial enough to support cities with large populations of artisans, crafts workers, merchants, and professionals. Whereas cities had thrived and trade had linked all regions of the Roman empire, early medieval Europe was almost entirely a rural society that engaged in little commerce. Manors and local communities produced most of the manufactured goods that they needed, including textiles and heavy tools, and they provided both the materials and the labor for construction and other large-scale projects. Towns were few and sparsely populated, and they served as economic hubs for the areas immediately surrounding them rather than as vibrant centers integrating the economic activities of distant regions.

Mediterranean Trade

By no means did trade entirely disappear from western Europe. Local markets and fairs offered opportunities for small-scale exchange, while itinerant peddlers shopped their wares from one settlement to another. Maritime trade flourished in the Mediterranean despite Muslim conquests in the region. Christian merchants from Italy and Spain regularly traded across religious boundary lines with Muslims of Sicily, Spain, and north Africa, who linked Europe indirectly with the larger Islamic world of communication and exchange. By the end of the early medieval era, about 1000 C.E., food crops that in earlier centuries had made their way throughout much of the Islamic world were beginning to take root also in Mediterranean Europe. Hard durum

Sources from the Past

Life on an Early Medieval Manor

Some useful insights into the lives and experiences of common people come from a decree known as the "Capitulary de Villis" issued by the emperor Charlemagne in 807 C.E. as a guide for stewards of Carolingian estates. The decree envisions a community with sophisticated agricultural and craft skills. Probably few estates observed all provisions of Charlemagne's decree, but the capitulary nonetheless communicates clearly how lords hoped to control their manors and profit from their production.

Each steward shall make an annual statement of all our income: an account of our lands cultivated by the oxen which our ploughmen drive and of our lands which the tenants of farms ought to plough; an account of the pigs, of the rents, of the obligations and fines; of the game taken in our forests without our permission; . . . of the mills, of the forest, of the fields, of the bridges, and ships; of the free men and the hundreds who are under obligations to our treasury; of markets, vineyards, and those who owe wine to us; of the hay, firewood, torches, planks, and other kinds of lumber; of the waste lands; of the fruits of the trees, of the nut trees, larger and smaller; of the grafted trees of all kinds; of the gardens; of the turnips; of the fish ponds; of the hides, skins, and horns; of the honey, wax; of the fat, tallow and soap; of the mulberry wine, cooked wine, mead, vinegar, beer, wine new and old; of the new grain and the old; of the hens and eggs; of the geese; the number of fishermen, [metal] smiths, sword-makers, and shoemakers; . . . of the forges and mines, that is iron and other mines; of the lead mines; . . . of the colts and fillies; they shall make all these known to us, set forth separately and in order, at Christmas, in order that we may know what and how much of each thing we have. . . .

[Stewards] must provide the greatest care, that whatever is prepared or made with the hands, that is, lard, smoked meat, salt meat, partially salted meat, wine, vinegar, mulberry wine, cooked wine . . . mustard, cheese, butter, malt, beer, mead, honey, wax, flour, all should be prepared and made with the greatest cleanliness. . . .

[Stewards should ensure] that in each of our estates, the chambers [living quarters] shall be provided with counterpanes, cushions, pillows, bed clothes, coverings for the tables and benches; vessels of brass, lead, iron and wood; andirons, chains, pot-hooks, adzes, axes, augers, cutlasses and all other kinds of tools, so that it shall never be necessary to go elsewhere for them, or to borrow them. And the weapons, which are carried against the enemy, shall be well cared for, so as to keep them in good condition; and when they are brought back they shall be placed in the chamber.

For our women's work they are to give at the proper time, as has been ordered, the materials, that is the linen, wool, woad, vermillion, madder, wool-combs, teasels, soap, grease, vessels and the other objects which are necessary.

Of the food products other than meat, two-thirds shall be sent each year for our own use, that is of the vegetables, fish, cheese, honey, mustard, vinegar, millet, panic [a grain similar to millet], dried and green herbs, radishes, and in addition of the wax, soap and other small products; and they shall tell us how much is left by a statement, as we have said above; and they shall not neglect this as in the past; because from those two-thirds, we wish to know how much remains.

Each steward shall have in his district good workmen, namely, blacksmiths, goldsmiths, silversmiths, shoemakers, [wood] turners, carpenters, sword-makers, fishermen, foilers [fine metalworkers], soap-makers, men who know how to make beer, cider, berry, and all other kinds of beverages, bakers to make pastry for our table, net-makers who know how to make nets for hunting, fishing and fowling, and the others who are too numerous to be designated.

SOURCE: *Translations and Reprints from the Original Sources of European History,* vol. 2. Philadelphia: University of Pennsylvania Press, 1900. (Translation slightly modified.)

On the basis of the "Capitulary de Villis," how would you characterize the conditions of material life in the Carolingian countryside?

wheat, rice, spinach, artichokes, eggplant, lemons, limes, oranges, and melons all made their way to Sicily, southern Italy, and Spain because of European participation in the larger trading world of the eastern hemisphere, even if western European merchants were not nearly so prominent as their Byzantine, Arab, Persian, Indian, Malay, and Chinese counterparts.

Norse Merchant-Mariners

Maritime trade flourished also in the North Sea and the Baltic Sea. Most active among the early medieval merchants in the northern seas were Norse seafarers, kinsmen of the Vikings who raided lands from eastern Europe to the Mediterranean. Norse traders followed the same routes as Viking raiders, and many individual mariners no doubt turned from commerce to plunder and back again as opportunities arose. Norse merchants called at ports from Russia to Ireland, carrying cargoes of fish and furs from Scandinavia, honey from Poland, wheat from England, wine from France, beer from the Low Countries, and swords from Germany. By traveling down the Russian rivers to the Black Sea, they were able to trade actively in both the Byzantine and Abbasid empires. Thus, like Mediterranean merchants, Norse mariners linked western Europe with the Islamic world. Indeed, the Carolingian empire depended heavily on this connection: Norse merchants took Scandinavian products to the Abbasid empire and brought back silver, which they traded at Carolingian ports for wine, jugs, glassware, and other products. This silver transported from the Abbasid empire by Norse merchants was a principal source of bullion used for minting coins in early medieval Europe and hence a crucially important element of the western European economy.

Population

By 900 the results of political stability and agricultural innovation were clearly evident in population figures as well as trade. In 200 C.E., before the Roman empire began to experience serious difficulties, the European population stood at about thirty-six million. It fell sharply over the next four centuries, to thirty-one million in 400 and twenty-six million in 600—a decline that reflected both the ravages of epidemic diseases and the unsettled conditions of the early middle ages. Then, gradually, the population recovered, edging up to twenty-nine million in 800 and thirty-two million in 900. By 1000 European population once again amounted to thirty-six million—the level it had reached some eight centuries earlier. By the end of the early middle ages, western Europe was poised to experience remarkable economic and demographic expansion that vastly increased European influence in the eastern hemisphere.

THE FORMATION OF CHRISTIAN EUROPE

By the time the Roman empire collapsed, Christianity was the principal source of religious, moral, and cultural authority throughout the Mediterranean basin. In the northern lands of Gaul, Germany, the British isles, and Scandinavia, however, Christianity had attracted few converts. Germanic invaders of the Roman empire sometimes embraced Arian Christianity, but not until the conversion of Clovis and the Franks did Roman Christianity enjoy a powerful and energetic sponsor in lands beyond the Mediterranean rim. One of the most important developments of the early middle ages was the conversion of western Europe to Roman Christianity. The Franks, the popes, and the monasteries played important roles in bringing about this conversion. The adoption of Roman Christianity ensured that medieval Europe would inherit crucial cultural elements from classical Roman society, including the Latin language and the institutional Roman church.

The Politics of Conversion

Clovis and the Franks won the support of the church hierarchy as well as the Christian population of the former Roman empire when they converted to the Roman faith. Their alliance with the Roman church also provided them with access to educated and literate individuals who could provide important political services. Scribes, secretaries, and record keepers for the Frankish kingdom came largely from the ranks of churchmen—priests, monks, bishops, and abbots—since very few others received a formal education during the early middle ages.

The Franks and the Church

A deep commitment to Roman Christianity became a hallmark of Frankish policy. Clovis, his successors, and the Carolingians viewed themselves as protectors of the papacy. Charlemagne mounted a military campaign that destroyed the power of the Lombards, who had threatened the popes and the city of Rome since the sixth century, and brought most of central and northern Italy into the expanding Carolingian empire. In exchange for this military and political support, the Carolingians received recognition and backing from the popes, including the award of Charlemagne's imperial crown at the hands of Pope Leo III.

Charlemagne not only supported the church in Italy but also worked to spread Christianity in northern lands. He maintained a school at his court in Aachen where he assembled the most prominent scholars from all parts of his empire. They corrected texts, made careful copies of the Bible and classical Latin literature, and taught Christian doctrine to men preparing for careers as priests or church officials. Charlemagne ordered monasteries throughout his empire to establish elementary schools, and he even tried to persuade village priests to provide free instruction in reading and writing. These efforts had limited success, but they certainly increased literacy in the Latin language as well as popular understanding of basic Christian doctrine. Charlemagne's efforts also resulted in an explosion of writing: not since the fall of the Roman empire had western Europe produced so much writing.

The Spread of Christianity

Charlemagne sometimes promoted the spread of Christianity by military force. Between 772 and 804 he waged a bitter campaign against the Saxons, a pagan people inhabiting northern Germany. Alongside his claim to political hegemony, he insisted that the Saxons adopt Roman Christianity. The Saxons violently resisted both the political and the religious dimensions of Charlemagne's campaign. In the end, though, Charlemagne prevailed: the Saxons not only acknowledged Charlemagne as their political lord but also replaced their pagan traditions with Christianity.

Pagan ways did not immediately disappear from western Europe. Even within the Carolingian empire, pockets of paganism survived for several centuries after the arrival of Christianity, particularly in out-of-the-way areas that did not attract the immediate attention of conquerors or missionaries. Moreover, beyond the Carolingian empire were the Scandinavian lands, whose peoples resisted Christianity until the end of the millennium. By the year 1000, however, Christianity had won the allegiance of most people throughout western Europe and even in the Nordic lands. By sponsoring the Roman church and its missionaries, Charlemagne helped establish Christianity as the dominant religious and cultural tradition in western Europe.

The Papacy

Apart from the political support it received from the Franks, the Roman church benefited from strong papal leadership. When the western Roman empire collapsed, the papacy survived and claimed spiritual authority over all the lands formerly embraced by the empire. For a century after the dissolution of the western Roman empire, the popes cooperated closely with the Byzantine emperors, who seemed to be the nat-

Pope Leo III crowns Charlemagne emperor in a manuscript illustration. The coronation symbolized the firm alliance between the Franks and the western Christian church.

ural heirs to the emperors of Rome. Beginning in the late sixth century, however, the popes acted more independently and devoted their efforts to strengthening the western Christian church based at Rome and clearly distinguishing it from the eastern Christian church based at Constantinople. The two churches differed on many issues by the eleventh century, and in 1054 the pope and patriarch mutually excommunicated each other. After the eleventh century the two branches of Christianity formed distinct identities as the Roman Catholic and Eastern Orthodox churches.

Pope Gregory I

The individual most important for providing the Roman church with its sense of direction was Pope Gregory I (590–604 C.E.), also known as Gregory the Great. As pope, Gregory faced an array of difficult challenges. During the late sixth century the Lombards consolidated their hold on the Italian peninsula, menacing Rome and the Roman church in the process. Gregory ensured the survival of both the city and the church by mobilizing local resources and organizing the defense of Rome. He also faced difficulties within the church, since bishops frequently acted independently of the pope, as though they were supreme ecclesiastical authorities within their own dioceses. To regain the initiative, Gregory reasserted papal primacy—the claim that the bishop of Rome was the ultimate authority in the Christian church. Gregory also made contributions as a theologian: he strongly emphasized the sacrament of penance, which required individuals to confess their sins to their priests and then to atone for their sins by penitential acts prescribed by the priests—a practice that enhanced the influence of the Roman church in the lives of individuals.

The Conversion of England

Gregory strengthened the Roman church further by extending its appeal and winning new converts in western Europe. The most important of his many missionary campaigns was one directed at England, recently conquered by Angles, Saxons, and other Germanic peoples. He aimed his efforts at the kings who ruled the various regions of England, hoping that their conversion would induce their subjects to adopt Christianity. This tactic largely succeeded: by the early seventh century Christianity had established a stable foothold in England, and by 800 England was securely within the fold of the Roman church.

Gregory's successors continued his policy of expanding the Roman church through missionary activity. France and Germany offered plentiful opportunities to win converts, particularly as the Frankish kingdom and the Carolingians brought those lands under their control. Some of the popes' most effective missionaries were monks. Pope Gregory himself was a monk, and he relied heavily on the energies of his fellow monks in seeking converts in England and elsewhere.

Monasticism

Christian monasticism had its origin in Egypt. During the second and third centuries, many devout Christians sought to lead ascetic and holy lives in the deserts of Egypt. Some lived alone as hermits, and others formed communes where they devoted themselves to the pursuit of holiness rather than worldly success. When Christianity became legal during the fourth century, the monastic lifestyle became an increasingly popular alternative throughout the Roman empire. Monastic communities cropped up in Italy, Spain, Gaul, and the British isles as well as in the eastern Mediterranean region.

Monastic Rules

During the early days of monasticism, each community developed its own rules, procedures, and priorities. Some communities demanded that their inhabitants follow extremely austere lifestyles that sapped the energy of the monks. Other communities did not establish any clear expectations of their recruits, with the result that monks frittered away their time or wandered aimlessly from one monastic house to another. These haphazard conditions prevented monasteries from mounting effective Christian missions.

A fourteenth-century manuscript illustration shows St. Benedict presenting his rule to a group of nuns.

St. Benedict

St. Benedict of Nursia (480–547 C.E.) strengthened the early monastic movement by providing it with discipline and a sense of purpose. In 529 St. Benedict prepared a set of regulations known as Benedict's *Rule* for the monastic community that he had founded at Monte Cassino, near Rome. The *Rule* did not permit extreme asceticism, but it required monks to take vows to lead communal, celibate lives under the absolute direction of the abbot who supervised the monastery: poverty, chastity, and obedience became the prime virtues for Benedictine monks. The *Rule* also called for monks to spend their time in prayer, meditation, and work. At certain hours monks came together for religious services and prayer, and they divided the remainder of the day into periods for study, reflection, and manual labor.

St. Scholastica

Monasteries throughout Europe began to adopt Benedict's *Rule* as the standard for their own houses. Through the influence of St. Benedict's sister, the nun St. Scholastica (482–543), an adaptation of the *Rule* soon provided guidance for the religious life of women living in convents. Within a century most European monasteries and convents observed the Benedictine *Rule*. During the following centuries the Roman church generated many alternatives to Benedictine monasticism. Yet even today most Roman Catholic monasteries observe rules that reflect the influence of the Benedictine tradition.

Strengthened by the discipline that the Benedictine *Rule* introduced, monasteries became a dominant feature in the social and cultural life of western Europe throughout the middle ages. Monasteries helped to provide order in the countryside, for example, and to expand agricultural production. Monasteries accumulated large landholdings—as well as authority over serfs working their lands—from the bequests of wealthy individuals seeking to contribute to the church's work and thereby to merit salvation. Particularly in France and Germany, abbots of monasteries dispatched teams of monks and serfs to clear forests, drain swamps, and prepare lands for cultivation. Indeed, monasteries organized much of the labor that brought about the expansion of agricultural production in early medieval Europe.

Monasteries were the principal centers of literacy in western Europe during the early middle ages. In this manuscript illustration, one monk copies a manuscript, another makes geometric calculations, a third cuts parchment, while two work on the building, and one more rings the bells that call monks and members of the surrounding community to religious services.

Monasticism and Society

Like Buddhist monasteries in Asian lands and charitable religious foundations in Muslim lands, European monasteries provided a variety of social services. They served as inns for travelers and places of refuge for individuals suffering from natural or other calamities. They served as orphanages and provided medical treatment for the ill and injured. They often set up schools and offered at least some rudimentary educational services for local regions, and large monasteries provided more advanced instruction for those preparing for the priesthood or high ecclesiastical positions. Some monasteries maintained libraries and scriptoria, where monks copied works of classical literature and philosophy as well as the scriptures and other Christian writings. Almost all works of Latin literature that have come down to the present survive because of copies made by medieval monks. Finally, monasteries served as a source of literate, educated, and talented individuals whose secretarial and administrative services were crucial for the organization of effective government in early medieval Europe.

Because of the various roles they played in the larger society, monasteries were particularly effective agents in the spread of Christianity. While they organized life in the countryside and provided social services, monks also zealously preached Christianity and tended to the spiritual needs of rural populations. For many people a neighboring monastery was the only source of instruction in Christian doctrine, and a local monastic church offered the only practical opportunity for them to take part in religious services. Monks patiently and persistently served the needs of rural populations, and over the decades and centuries they helped to instill Christian values in countless generations of European peasants.

Like societies in China, India, southwest Asia, and the eastern Mediterranean region, western European society experienced massive change during the postclassical era. In some ways western Europe had the most difficult experience of all the postclassical societies. In China, southwest Asia, and the eastern Mediterranean, societies were able to preserve or reestablish centralized imperial rule that maintained order and stability while also facilitating trade and encouraging economic development. India did not generate an imperial form of government, but because of the subcontinent's geographic location and productive capacity, India participated actively in the larger economic and commercial life of the eastern hemisphere. In contrast, rulers of early medieval Europe did not reinstate an imperial form of government—except for the short-lived Carolingian empire—and western Europeans did not participate actively in the larger trading world of the eastern hemisphere. The standards of material life in early medieval Europe—as measured by agricultural and industrial production, volume of trade, and the extent of urban settlement—stood well below those of other postclassical societies.

Yet, just as postclassical developments deeply influenced the evolution of societies in other lands, the early medieval era was a crucial period for the development of western Europe. In the absence of a durable centralized empire, western Europeans found ways to maintain relative order and stability by decentralizing political responsibilities and relying on local authorities for political organization. Over the longer term the decentralized political order of medieval Europe discouraged the revival of empire and encouraged the emergence of regional states that organized their communities into powerful societies. During the early middle ages, western Europeans experimented with agricultural techniques that enabled them to expand production dramatically, conduct increased trade, and rebuild urban centers. Finally, western Christianity preserved elements of classical Roman society and established a foundation for cultural unity in western Europe, just as Buddhism, Hinduism, Islam, and eastern Christianity served as sources of cultural authority in other societies.

CHRONOLOGY

476	Fall of the western Roman empire
480–547	Life of St. Benedict of Nursia
481–511	Reign of Clovis
482–543	Life of St. Scholastica
590–604	Reign of Pope Gregory I
751–843	Carolingian kingdom
768–814	Reign of Charlemagne
800	Coronation of Charlemagne as emperor
814–840	Reign of Louis the Pious
843	Dissolution of the Carolingian empire
871–899	Reign of King Alfred
936–973	Reign of King Otto I of Saxony
955	Battle of Lechfeld
962	Coronation of Otto I

FOR FURTHER READING

Geoffrey Barraclough. *The Crucible of Europe.* Berkeley, 1976. A brilliant, brief analysis of early medieval Europe concentrating on the Carolingian era and its aftermath.

Robert-Henri Bautier. *The Economic Development of Medieval Europe.* New York, 1971. An excellent and well-illustrated survey, which examines the economic and social history of western Europe in the context of the larger Mediterranean basin.

Marc Bloch. *Feudal Society.* 2 vols. Trans. by L. A. Manyon. Chicago, 1961. A classic interpretation concentrating on social and economic history that has decisively influenced the way historians think about medieval Europe.

Peter Brown. *The Rise of Western Christendom: Triumph and Diversity, A.D. 200–1000.* 2nd ed. Oxford, 2003. A landmark analysis of early Christian history that incorporates the findings of recent scholarship.

Einhard and Notker the Stammerer. *Two Lives of Charlemagne.* Ed. and trans. by Lewis Thorpe. New York, 1969. Excellent translations of two early biographies of Charlemagne.

F. L. Ganshof. *Frankish Institutions under Charlemagne.* Trans. by B. and M. Lyon. New York, 1970. Concise synthesis of research on Charlemagne's government.

Patrick J. Geary. *Before France and Germany: The Creation and Transformation of the Merovingian World.* 2nd ed. New York, 1997. Draws usefully on recent research in reconstructing early medieval Europe.

———, ed. *Readings in Medieval History.* Lewiston, N.Y., 1989. Offers substantial English translations of primary sources.

Louis Halphen. *Charlemagne and the Carolingian Empire.* Trans. by G. de Nie. Amsterdam, 1977. Thorough discussion of Charlemagne's imperial creation and its larger importance in European history.

David Herlihy. *Opera Muliebra: Women and Work in Medieval Europe.* New York, 1990. Examines women's roles both in their own households and in the larger society of medieval Europe.

Richard Hodges and David Whitehouse. *Mohammed, Charlemagne, and the Origins of Europe: Archaeology and the Pirenne Thesis.* Ithaca, 1983. Draws on archaeological discoveries in placing the early medieval European economy in hemispheric context.

Edward James. *The Franks.* Oxford, 1988. A concise account.

Gwyn Jones. *A History of the Vikings.* Rev. ed. Oxford, 1984. The best general work on Viking society and Viking expansion.

Ferdinand Lot. *The End of the Ancient World and the Beginnings of the Middle Ages.* Trans. by P. and M. Leon. New York, 1961. A masterful survey of the Germanic invasions and their results for western Europe.

Michael McCormick. *Origins of the European Economy: Communications and Commerce, A.D. 300–900.* Cambridge, Mass., 2001. A thorough and comprehensive analysis that emphasizes the participation of early medieval Europe in a larger Mediterranean economy.

Rosamond McKitterick. *The Frankish Kingdoms under the Carolingians, 751–987.* New York, 1983. Comprehensive survey of the Carolingian dynasty with special attention to political, cultural, and religious developments.

Susan Reynolds. *Fiefs and Vassals: The Medieval Evidence Reinterpreted.* Oxford, 1994. A powerful scholarly critique of the concept of feudalism.

———. *Kingdoms and Communities in Western Europe, 900–1300.* Oxford, 1984. An imaginative study focusing on the political and social values that undergirded western European society.

J. M. Wallace-Hadrill. *The Barbarian West: The Early Middle Ages, A.D. 400–1000.* New York, 1962. A powerful and insightful synthesis by a leading scholar.

OLC

See our **Online Learning Center at www.mhhe.com/bentley3** for additional readings, practice maps, quizzes, and internet activities.

PSI

Unfamiliar words? Check out the **Primary Source Investigator CD-ROM** for an interactive glossary, interactive maps, more images, and primary sources.

PART IV

An Age of Cross-Cultural Interaction, 1000 to 1500 C.E.

The half millennium from 1000 to 1500 C.E. differed markedly from earlier eras. During classical and postclassical times, large, regional societies situated in China, India, southwest Asia, and the Mediterranean basin dominated the eastern hemisphere. Peoples of these lands built extensive networks of trade and communication that spanned the eastern hemisphere and influenced the development of all its societies. From 1000 to 1500 C.E., however, nomadic Turkish and Mongol peoples overran settled societies and established vast transregional empires from China to eastern Europe.

Nomadic peoples toppled several postclassical states, most notably the Song empire in China and the Abbasid realm in southwest Asia. By building empires that transcended the boundaries of postclassical states, however, nomadic Turks and Mongols laid a political foundation for sharply increased trade and communication between peoples of different societies and cultural regions. Indeed, their empires prompted the peoples of the eastern hemisphere to forge closer links than ever before in history. By the mid-fourteenth century, merchants, diplomats, and missionaries traveled frequently between lands as far removed as Italy and China.

Increased trade in the Indian Ocean basin also promoted more intense cross-cultural communications. Maritime trade built on the political stability, economic expansion, and demographic growth of the postclassical era. By the fourteenth century, mariners called at ports throughout the Indian Ocean basin from southeast Asia to India, Ceylon, Arabia, and east Africa, while sea lanes through the South China Sea offered access to ports in the islands of southeast Asia, China, Japan, and Korea. Commercial goods traveled over the Indian Ocean in larger quantities than ever before. From the eleventh century forward, cargoes increasingly consisted of bulky commodities like timber, coral, steel, building materials, grains, dates, and other foodstuffs. This trade in bulk goods indicated a movement toward economic integration as societies of the Indian Ocean basin concentrated increasingly on cultivating crops or producing goods for export while importing foods or goods that they could not produce very well themselves.

Demographic growth, increased agricultural production, and economic expansion helped to underwrite rapid political development in sub-Saharan Africa and western Europe. Powerful regional states and centralized empires emerged in west Africa and central Africa while a series of wealthy city-states dominated the east African coast. In western Europe the decentralized states of the early middle ages evolved into more tightly centralized regional states. Rulers in several of these states were able to organize networks of military retainers and political supporters who strengthened the claims of central authorities against local challengers. Increasing volumes of trade favored this movement toward centralization in sub-Saharan Africa and western Europe, since taxes levied on trade helped to finance the professional bureaucrats and armed forces that centralized states required.

Although they did not participate in the demographic and economic expansion of the eastern hemisphere, the indigenous peoples of the Americas and Oceania also built larger and more centralized societies from 1000 to 1500 C.E. Centralized empires appeared in Mesoamerica and Andean South America while agricultural societies emerged in several regions of North America. Even in the absence of large domesticated animals, trade networks linked peoples as far distant as Mexico and the Great Lakes region. Pacific island societies also moved toward tighter political organization. Because they lived on small land bases distributed irregularly throughout a vast ocean, Pacific islanders had no realistic possibility of building large imperial states. Within their own agricultural and fishing societies, however, they established tightly centralized kingdoms that organized public affairs and sponsored distinctive cultural traditions.

During the fourteenth and fifteenth centuries C.E., much of the eastern hemisphere experienced difficulties not only because of warfare arising from the conquests of nomadic peoples but also because of epidemic bubonic plague and global climatic changes that brought cooler temperatures. In building their transregional empires, nomadic peoples sometimes devastated the lands that they conquered, throwing societies and economies into turmoil. While facilitating trade and travel, nomadic empires also made it possible for diseases to spread rapidly over long distances, and during the fourteenth century, epidemic bubonic plague became a hemispheric phenomenon. Meanwhile, cooler weather resulted in lower agricultural yields in many lands, and in some far northern lands, it made agriculture impractical. Together with military destruction and pandemic plague, reduced agricultural production led to political, social, and economic problems throughout much of the eastern hemisphere.

Nevertheless, by the mid-fifteenth century, peoples from China to western Europe were recovering from these difficulties and rebuilding prosperous societies. In their own quest for prosperity, western European peoples unwittingly laid the foundations of a new era in world history. While searching for sea routes to Asian markets, European mariners happened upon the continents of North and South America. They soon ventured into the Pacific Ocean, where they encountered Australia and the Pacific islands. Their voyages brought the world's various peoples for the first time into permanent and sustained communication with one another, and their interactions triggered a series of consequences that profoundly influenced modern world history. The European voyages that gave rise to this interdependent and interconnected world took place precisely because of the movement toward increasing interaction in the eastern hemisphere during the centuries following 1000 C.E. The period from 1000 to 1500 C.E. set the stage for the modern era of world history.

Chabi, a Nestorian Christian and the favorite wife of Khubilai Khan, wearing the distinctive headgear reserved for Mongol women of the ruling class.

CHAPTER 18

NOMADIC EMPIRES AND EURASIAN INTEGRATION

TURKISH MIGRATIONS AND IMPERIAL EXPANSION

Nomadic Economy and Society

Turkish Empires in Persia, Anatolia, and India

THE MONGOL EMPIRES

Chinggis Khan and the Making of the Mongol Empire

The Mongol Empires after Chinggis Khan

The Mongols and Eurasian Integration

Decline of the Mongols in Persia and China

AFTER THE MONGOLS

Tamerlane the Whirlwind

The Foundation of the Ottoman Empire

Guillaume Boucher was a goldsmith who lived during the early and middle decades of the thirteenth century. At some point, perhaps during the 1230s, he left his native Paris and went to Budapest, which was then a part of the kingdom of Hungary. There he was captured by Mongol warriors campaigning in Hungary. The Mongols noticed and appreciated Boucher's talents, and when they left Hungary in 1242, they took him along with other skilled captives to their central Asian homeland.

For at least the next fifteen years, Boucher lived at the Mongol capital at Karakorum. Though technically a slave, he enjoyed some prestige. He supervised fifty assistants in a workshop that produced decorative objects of gold and silver for the Mongol court. His most ingenious creation was a spectacular silver fountain in the form of a tree. Four pipes, concealed by the tree's trunk, carried wines and other intoxicating drinks to the top of the tree and then dispensed them into silver bowls from which courtiers and guests filled their cups. Apart from his famous fountain, Boucher also produced statues in gold and silver, built carriages, designed buildings, and even sewed ritual garments for Roman Catholic priests who conducted services for Christians living at Karakorum and sought converts in the Mongol empire.

Boucher was by no means the only European living at the Mongol court. His wife was a woman of French ancestry whom Boucher had met and married in Hungary. The Flemish missionary William of Rubruck visited Karakorum in 1254, and during his sojourn there he encountered a French woman named Paquette who was an attendant to a Mongol princess, an artisan from Russia (Paquette's husband), an unnamed nephew of a French bishop, a Greek soldier, and an Englishman named Basil. Other European visitors to the Mongol court found Germans, Slavs, and Hungarians as well as Chinese, Koreans, Turks, Persians, and Armenians, among others. Many thirteenth-century roads led to Karakorum.

Nomadic peoples had made their influence felt throughout much of Eurasia as early as classical times. The Xiongnu confederation dominated central Asia and posed a formidable threat to the Han dynasty in China from the third to the first century B.C.E. During the second and third centuries C.E., the Huns and other nomadic peoples from central Asia launched the migrations that helped bring down the western Roman empire, and later migrations of the White Huns destroyed the Gupta state in India. Turkish peoples ruled a large central Asian empire from the sixth through the ninth centuries, and the Uighur Turks even seized the capital cities of the Tang dynasty in the mid-seventh century.

Between the eleventh and fifteenth centuries, nomadic peoples became more prominent than ever before in Eurasian affairs. Turkish peoples migrated to Persia, Anatolia, and India, where they overcame existing authorities and established new states. During the thirteenth and fourteenth centuries, the Mongols established themselves as the most powerful people of the central Asian steppes and then turned on settled societies in China, Persia, Russia, and eastern Europe. By the early fourteenth century, the Mongols had built the largest empire the world has ever seen, stretching from Korea and China in the east to Russia and Hungary in the west.

Most of the Mongol states collapsed during the late fourteenth and fifteenth centuries, but the decline of the Mongols did not signal the end of nomadic peoples' influence on Eurasian affairs. Although a native Chinese dynasty replaced the Mongol state in China, the possibility of a Mongol revival forced the new dynasty to focus attention and resources on its central Asian frontier. Moreover, from the fourteenth through the seventeenth centuries, Turkish peoples embarked on new campaigns of expansion that eventually brought most of India, much of central Asia, all of Anatolia, and a good portion of eastern Europe under their domination.

The military campaigns of nomadic peoples were sometimes exceedingly destructive. Nomadic warriors often demolished cities, slaughtered urban populations, and ravaged surrounding agricultural lands. Yet these same forces also encouraged systematic peaceful interaction between peoples of different societies. Between the eleventh and fifteenth centuries, the imperial campaigns of Turkish and Mongol peoples forged closer links than ever before between Eurasian lands. By fostering cross-cultural communication and exchange on an unprecedented scale, the nomadic empires integrated the lives of peoples and the experiences of societies throughout much of the eastern hemisphere.

Turkish Migrations and Imperial Expansion

Turkish peoples never formed a single, homogeneous group but, rather, organized themselves into clans and tribes that often fought bitterly with one another. Turkish clans and identities probably emerged after the Xiongnu confederation broke apart in the first and second centuries C.E. All Turkish peoples spoke related languages, and all were nomads or descendants of nomads. From modest beginnings they expanded their influence until they dominated not only the steppes of central Asia but also settled societies in Persia, Anatolia, and India.

Nomadic Economy and Society

Nomadic societies in central Asia developed by adapting to the ecological conditions of arid lands. Central Asia does not receive enough rain to support large-scale agriculture. Oases permit intense cultivation of limited regions, but for the most part only grasses and shrubs grow on the central Asian steppe lands, and there are no large rivers or other sources of water to support large-scale irrigation systems. Humans cannot survive on grasses and shrubs, but grazing animals thrive on them. To take advantage of the vast open spaces of central Asia, nomads herded grazing animals, especially sheep and horses, but also cattle, goats, and camels.

Nomadic Peoples and Their Animals

Nomadic peoples drove their herds and flocks to lands with abundant grass and then moved them along as the animals thinned the vegetation. They did not wander aimlessly through the steppes but, rather, followed migratory cycles that took account of the seasons and local climatic conditions. They lived mostly off the meat, milk, and hides of their animals. They used animal bones for tools and animal dung as fuel for fires. They made shoes and clothes out of wool from their sheep and skins from their other animals. Wool was also the source of the felt that they used to fashion large tents called *yurts* in which they lived. They even prepared an alcoholic drink from animal products by fermenting mare's milk into a potent concoction known as *kumiss*.

The aridity of the climate and the nomadic lifestyle limited the development of human societies in central Asia. Only at oases did agriculture make it possible for dense populations to congregate. Settlements were few and small—and often temporary as well, since nomads carried their collapsible felt yurts with them as they drove their herds. Nomads often engaged in small-scale cultivation of millet or vegetables when they found sources of water, but the harvests were sufficient only to supplement animal products, not to sustain whole societies. Nomads also produced limited amounts of pottery, leather goods, iron weapons, and tools. Given their migratory habits, however, both intensive agriculture and large-scale craft production were practical impossibilities.

Nomadic and Settled Peoples

Thus nomads avidly sought opportunities to trade with settled peoples, and as early as the classical era brisk trade linked nomadic and settled societies. Much of this commerce took place on a small scale as nomads sought agricultural products and manufactured goods to satisfy their immediate needs. Often, however, nomads also participated in long-distance trade networks. Because of their mobility and their familiarity with large regions of central Asia, nomadic peoples were ideally suited to organize and lead the caravans that crossed central Asia and linked settled societies from China to the Mediterranean basin. During the postclassical era and later, Turkish peoples were especially prominent on the caravan routes of central Asia.

Nomadic Society

Nomadic society generated two social classes: nobles and commoners. Charismatic leaders won recognition as nobles and thereby acquired the prestige needed to organize clans and tribes into alliances. Normally, nobles did little governing, since clans and tribes looked after their own affairs and resented interference. During times of war, however, nobles wielded absolute authority over their forces, and they dealt swiftly and summarily with those who did not obey orders.

The nobility was a fluid class. Leaders passed noble status along to their heirs, but the heirs could lose their status if they did not continue to provide appropriate leadership for their clans and tribes. Over the course of a few generations, nobles could return to the status of commoners who tended their own herds and followed new leaders. Meanwhile, commoners could win recognition as nobles by outstanding conduct, particularly by courageous behavior during war. Then, if they were clever diplomats, they could arrange alliances between clans and tribes and gain enough support to displace established leaders.

Nomadic Religion

The earliest religion of the Turkish peoples revolved around shamans—religious specialists who possessed supernatural powers, communicated with the gods and nature spirits, invoked divine aid on behalf of their communities, and informed their companions of their gods' will. Yet many Turkish peoples became attracted to the religious and cultural traditions they encountered when trading with peoples of settled societies. They did not abandon their inherited beliefs or their shamans, but by the sixth century C.E. many Turks had converted to Buddhism, Nestorian Christianity, or Manichaeism. Partly because of their newly adopted religious and cultural traditions and partly because of their prominence in Eurasian trade networks, Turkish peoples also developed a written script.

Turkish Conversion to Islam

In the tenth century Turks living near the Abbasid empire began to turn to Islam. Their conversion had great significance. When Turkish peoples began to migrate into settled societies in large numbers, they helped spread Islam to new lands, particularly

A wall painting from a cave at Dunhuang, a major oasis on the silk roads, depicts a band of sword-wielding thieves (left) holding up a party of Turkish merchants (right). According to convention, the artist represented the Turks with pale skins, long noses, and deep-set eyes.

Anatolia and northern India. The boundaries of the Islamic world thus expanded along with the political and military influence of Turkish peoples.

Military Organization

This expansion took place when nomadic leaders organized vast confederations of peoples all subject, at least nominally, to a *khan* ("ruler"). In fact, khans rarely ruled directly but, rather, through the leaders of allied tribes. Yet when organized on a large scale, nomadic peoples wielded massive military power due mostly to their outstanding cavalry forces. Nomadic warriors learned to ride horses as children, and they had superior equestrian skills. Their arrows flew with deadly accuracy even when launched from the backs of galloping horses. Moreover, units of warriors coordinated their movements to outmaneuver and overwhelm their opponents.

Few armies were able to resist the mobility and discipline of well-organized nomadic warriors. When they found themselves at a disadvantage, they often were able to beat a hasty retreat and escape from their less speedy adversaries. With this military background, several groups of Turkish nomads began in the tenth century C.E. to seize the wealth of settled societies and build imperial states in the regions surrounding central Asia.

Turkish Empires in Persia, Anatolia, and India

Saljuq Turks and the Abbasid Empire

Turkish peoples entered Persia, Anatolia, and India at different times and for different purposes. They approached Abbasid Persia much as Germanic peoples had earlier approached the Roman empire. From about the mid-eighth to the mid-tenth century,

Turkish peoples lived mostly on the borders of the Abbasid realm, which offered abundant opportunities for trade. By the mid to late tenth century, large numbers of Saljuq Turks served in Abbasid armies and lived in the Abbasid realm itself. By the mid-eleventh century the Saljuqs overshadowed the Abbasid caliphs. Indeed, in 1055 the caliph recognized the Saljuq leader Tughril Beg as *sultan* ("chieftain"). Tughril first consolidated his hold on the Abbasid capital at Baghdad, then he and his successors extended Turkish rule to Syria, Palestine, and other parts of the realm. For the last two centuries of the Abbasid state, the caliphs served as figureheads of authority while actual governance lay in the hands of the Turkish sultans.

A carved statuette depicts a Turkish sultan of the thirteenth century, perhaps Tughril II or Tughril III, while at prayer.

Saljuq Turks and the Byzantine Empire

While some Turkish peoples established themselves in Abbasid Persia, others turned their attention to the rich land of Anatolia, breadbasket of the Byzantine empire. Led by the Saljuqs, Turkish peoples began migrating into Anatolia in large numbers in the early eleventh century. In 1071 Saljuq forces inflicted a devastating defeat on the Byzantine army at Manzikert in eastern Anatolia and even took the Byzantine emperor captive. Following this victory Saljuqs and other Turkish groups entered Anatolia almost at will. The peasants of Anatolia, who mostly resented their Byzantine overlords, often looked upon the Saljuqs as liberators rather than conquerors.

The migrants thoroughly transformed Anatolia. Turkish groups displaced Byzantine authorities and set up their own political and social institutions. They levied taxes on the Byzantine church, restricted its activities, and sometimes confiscated church property. Meanwhile, they welcomed converts to Islam and made political, social, and economic opportunities available to them. By 1453, when Ottoman Turks captured the Byzantine capital at Constantinople, Byzantine and Christian Anatolia had become largely a Turkish and Islamic land.

Ghaznavid Turks and the Sultanate of Delhi

While the Saljuqs spearheaded Turkish migrations in Abbasid Persia and Byzantine Anatolia, Mahmud of Ghazni led the Turkish Ghaznavids of Afghanistan in raids on lucrative sites in northern India. When the Ghaznavids began their campaigns in the early eleventh century, their principal goal was plunder. Gradually, though, they became more interested in permanent rule. They asserted their authority first over the Punjab and then over Gujarat and Bengal. By the thirteenth century, the Turkish sultanate of Delhi claimed authority over all of northern India. Several of the Delhi sultans conceived plans to conquer southern India and extend Muslim rule there, but none was able to realize these ambitious. The sultans faced constant challenges from Hindu princes in neighboring lands, and they periodically had to defend their northern frontiers from new Turkish or Mongol invaders. They maintained an enormous army with a large elephant corps, but these forces enabled them to hold on to their territories rather than to expand their empire.

Turkish rule had great social and cultural implications in India, like it did in Anatolia. Mahmud of Ghazni was a zealous foe of Buddhism and Hinduism alike, and he launched frequent raids on shrines, temples, and monasteries. His forces stripped Buddhist and Hindu establishments of their wealth, destroyed their buildings, and often slaughtered their residents and attendants as well. As Turkish invaders repressed Buddhism and Hinduism, they encouraged conversion to Islam and enabled their faith to establish a secure presence in northern India.

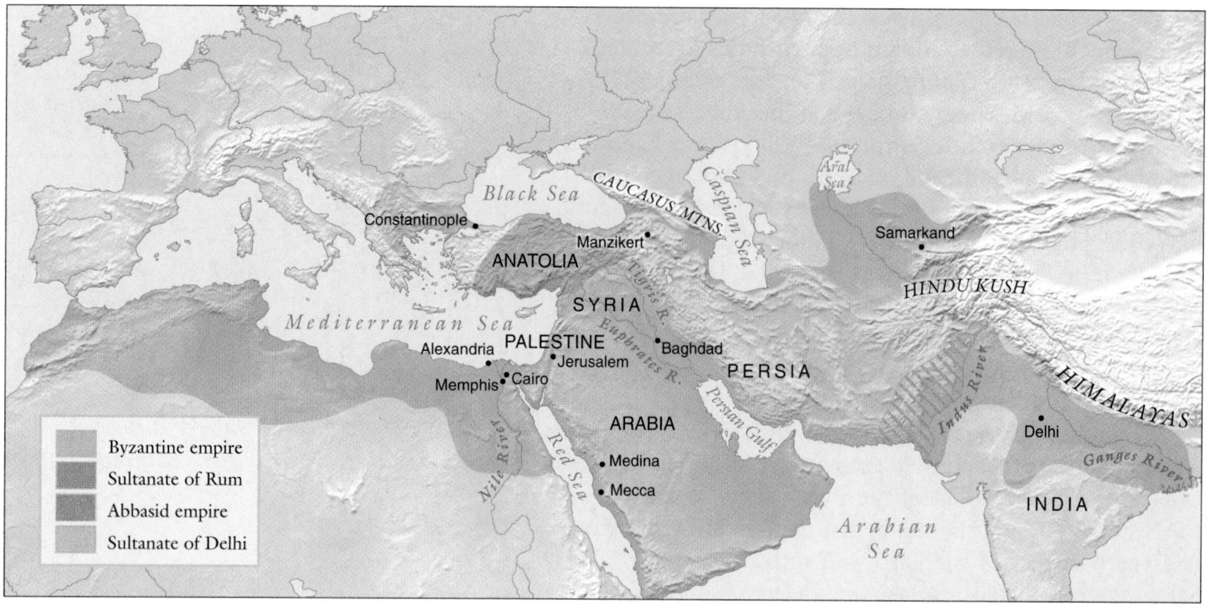

MAP [18.1]
Turkish empires and their neighbors about 1210 C.E.

Though undertaken by different groups, for different reasons, and by different means, the Turkish conquests of Persia, Anatolia, and India represented part of a larger expansive movement by nomadic peoples. In all three cases the formidable military prowess of Turkish peoples enabled them to move beyond the steppe lands of central Asia and dominate settled societies. By the thirteenth century, the influence of nomadic peoples was greater than ever before in Eurasian history. Yet the Turkish conquests represented only a prelude to an astonishing round of empire building launched by the Mongols during the thirteenth and fourteenth centuries.

THE MONGOL EMPIRES

For most of history the nomadic Mongols lived on the high steppe lands of eastern central Asia. Like other nomadic peoples, they displayed deep loyalty to kin groups organized into families, clans, and tribes. They frequently allied with Turkish peoples who built empires on the steppes, but they rarely played a leading role in the organization of states before the thirteenth century. Strong loyalties to kinship groups made it difficult for the Mongols to organize a stable society on a large scale. During the early thirteenth century, however, Chinggis Khan (sometimes spelled "Genghis Khan") forged the various Mongol tribes into a powerful alliance that built the largest empire the world has ever seen. Although the vast Mongol realm soon dissolved into a series of smaller empires—most of which disappeared within a century—the Mongols' imperial venture brought the societies of Eurasia into closer contact than ever before.

Chinggis Khan and the Making of the Mongol Empire

The unifier of the Mongols was Temüjin, born about 1167 into a noble family. His father was a prominent warrior who forged an alliance between several Mongol clans and seemed likely to become a powerful leader. When Temüjin was about ten years old, however, rivals poisoned his father and destroyed the alliance. Abandoned by his

This painting by a Chinese artist depicts Chinggis Khan at about age sixty. Though most of his conquests were behind him, Chinggis Khan's focus and determination are readily apparent in this portrait.

father's allies, Temüjin led a precarious existence for some years. He lived in poverty, since rivals seized the family's animals, and several times eluded enemies seeking to eliminate him as a potential threat to their own ambitions. A rival once captured him and imprisoned him in a wooden cage, but Temüjin made a daring midnight escape and regained his freedom.

Chinggis Khan's Rise to Power

During the late twelfth century, Temüjin made an alliance with a prominent Mongol clan leader. He also mastered the art of steppe diplomacy, which called for displays of personal courage in battle, combined with intense loyalty to allies—as well as a willingness to betray allies or superiors to improve one's position—and the ability to entice previously unaffiliated tribes into cooperative relationships. Temüjin gradually strengthened his position, sometimes by forging useful alliances, often by conquering rival contenders for power, and occasionally by turning suddenly against a troublesome ally. He eventually brought all the Mongol tribes into a single confederation, and in 1206 an assembly of Mongol leaders recognized Temüjin's supremacy by proclaiming him Chinggis Khan ("universal ruler").

Mongol Political Organization

Chinggis Khan's policies greatly strengthened the Mongol people. Earlier nomadic state builders had ruled largely through the leaders of allied tribes. Because of his personal experiences, however, Chinggis Khan mistrusted the Mongols' tribal organization. He broke up the tribes and forced men of fighting age to join new military units with no tribal affiliations. He chose high military and political officials not on the basis of kinship or tribal status but, rather, because of their talents or their loyalty to him. Although he spent most of his life on horseback, Chinggis Khan also established a capital at Karakorum—present-day Har Horin, located about 300 kilometers (186 miles) west of the modern Mongolian capital of Ulaanbaatar—where he built a luxurious palace. As command center of Chinggis Khan's empire, Karakorum symbolized a source of Mongol authority superior to the clan or tribe. Chinggis Khan's policies created a Mongol state that was not only much stronger than any earlier nomadic confederation but also less troubled by conflicts between clans and tribes.

The most important institution of the Mongol state was the army, which magnified the power of the small population. In the thirteenth century the Mongol population stood at about one million people—less than 1 percent of China's numbers. During Chinggis Khan's life, his army numbered only 100,000 to 125,000 Mongols, although allied peoples also contributed forces. How was it possible for so few people to conquer the better part of Eurasia?

Mongol Arms

A Persian manuscript illustration depicts Chinggis Khan and his cavalry in hot pursuit of retreating forces.

Like earlier nomadic armies, Mongol forces relied on outstanding equestrian skills. Mongols grew up riding horses, and they honed their skills by hunting and playing competitive games on horseback. Their bows, short enough for archers to use while riding, were also stiff, firing arrows that could fell enemies at 200 meters (656 feet). Mongol horsemen were among the most mobile forces of the premodern world, sometimes traveling more than 100 kilometers (62 miles) per day to surprise an enemy. Furthermore, the Mongols understood the psychological dimensions of warfare and used them to their advantage. If enemies surrendered without resistance, the Mongols usually spared their lives, and they provided generous treatment for artisans, crafts workers, and those with military skills. In the event of resistance, however, the Mongols ruthlessly slaughtered whole populations, sparing only a few, whom they sometimes drove before their armies as human shields during future conflicts.

Once he had united the Mongols, Chinggis Khan turned his army and his attention to other parts of central Asia and particularly to nearby settled societies. He attacked the various Turkish peoples ruling in Tibet, northern China, Persia, and the central Asian steppes. His conquests in central Asia were important because they protected him against the possibility that other nomadic leaders might challenge his rule. But the Mongol campaigns in China and Persia had especially far-reaching consequences.

Mongol Conquest of Northern China

Chinggis Khan himself extended Mongol rule to northern China, dominated since 1127 C.E. by the nomadic Jurchen people, while the Song dynasty continued to rule in southern China. The conquest of China began in 1211 C.E. when Mongol raiding parties invaded the Jurchen realm. Raids quickly became more frequent and intense, and soon they developed into a campaign of conquest. By 1215 the Mongols had captured the Jurchen capital near modern Beijing, which under the new name of Khanbaliq ("city of the khan") served also as the Mongol capital in China. Fighting between Mongols and Jurchen continued until 1234, but by 1220 the Mongols had largely established control over northern China.

Mongol Conquest of Persia

While part of his army consolidated the Mongol hold on northern China, Chinggis Khan led another force to Afghanistan and Persia, ruled at that time by a successor to the Saljuqs known as the Khwarazm shah. In 1218 Chinggis Khan sought to open trade and diplomatic relations with the Khwarazm shah. The shah despised the Mongols, however, and he ordered his officials to murder Chinggis Khan's envoys and the merchants accompanying them. The following year Chinggis Khan took his army west to seek revenge. Mongol forces pursued the Khwarazm shah to an island in the Caspian Sea where he died. Meanwhile, they shattered the shah's army and seized control of his realm.

To forestall any possibility that the shah's state might survive and constitute a challenge to his own empire, Chinggis Khan wreaked destruction on the conquered land. The Mongols ravaged one city after another, demolishing buildings and massacring hundreds of thousands of people. Some cities never recovered. The Mongols also destroyed the delicate *qanat* irrigation systems that sustained agriculture in the

Sources from the Past

Marco Polo on Mongol Military Tactics

The Venetian Marco Polo traveled extensively through central Asia and China in the late thirteenth century, when Mongol empires dominated Asia. His book of travel writings is an especially valuable source of information about the Mongol age. Among other things, he described the Mongol way of making war.

Their arms are bows and arrows, sword and mace; but above all the bow, for they are capital archers, indeed the best that are known. . . .

When a Mongol prince goes forth to war, he takes with him, say, 100,000 men. Well, he appoints an officer to every ten men, one to every hundred, one to every thousand, and one to every ten thousand, so that his own orders have to be given to ten persons only, and each of these ten persons has to pass the orders only to another ten, and so on, no one having to give orders to more than ten. And every one in turn is responsible only to the officer immediately over him; and the discipline and order that comes of this method is marvellous, for they are a people very obedient to their chiefs. . . .

When they are going on a distant expedition they take no gear with them except two leather bottles for milk, a little earthenware pot to cook their meat in, and a little tent to shelter them from rain. And in case of great urgency they will ride ten days on end without lighting a fire or taking a meal. On such an occasion they will sustain themselves on the blood of their horses, opening a vein and letting the blood jet into their mouths, drinking till they have had enough, and then staunching it. . . .

When they come to an engagement with the enemy, they will gain the victory in this fashion. They never let themselves get into a regular medley, but keep perpetually riding round and shooting into the enemy. And as they do not count it any shame to run away in battle, they will sometimes pretend to do so, and in running away they turn in the saddle and shoot hard and strong at the foe, and in this way make great havoc. Their horses are trained so perfectly that they will double hither and thither, just like a dog, in a way that is quite astonishing. Thus they fight to as good purpose in running away as if they stood and faced the enemy because of the vast volleys of arrows that they shoot in this way, turning round upon their pursuers, who are fancying that they have won the battle. But when the Mongols see that they have killed and wounded a good many horses and men, they wheel round bodily and return to the charge in perfect order and with loud cries, and in a very short time the enemy are routed. In truth they are stout and valiant soldiers, and inured to war. And you perceive that it is just when the enemy sees them run, and imagines that he has gained the battle, that he has in reality lost it, for the Mongols wheel round in a moment when they judge the right time has come. And after this fashion they have won many a fight.

SOURCE: Marco Polo. *The Book of Ser Marco Polo,* 3rd ed. Trans. and ed. by Henry Yule and Henri Cordier. London: John Murray, 1921, pp. 260–63. (Translation slightly modified.)

In what ways do the military practices described by Marco Polo reflect the influence of the steppe environment on the Mongols?

arid region, resulting in severely reduced agricultural production. For centuries after the Mongol conquest, Persian chroniclers cursed the invaders and the devastation they visited upon the land.

By the time of his death in 1227, Chinggis Khan had laid the foundation of a vast and mighty empire. He had united the Mongols, established Mongol supremacy in central Asia, and extended Mongol control to northern China in the east and Persia in the west. Chinggis Khan was a conqueror, however, not an administrator. He ruled the Mongols themselves through his control over the army, but he did not establish a central government for the lands that he conquered. Instead, he assigned Mongol overlords to supervise local administrators and to extract a generous tribute for the Mongols' own uses. Chinggis Khan's heirs continued his conquests, but they also undertook the task of designing a more permanent administration to guide the fortunes of the Mongol empire.

The Mongol Empires after Chinggis Khan

Chinggis Khan's death touched off a struggle for power among his sons and grandsons, several of whom had ambitions to succeed the great khan. Eventually, his heirs divided Chinggis Khan's vast realm into four regional empires. The great khans ruled China, the wealthiest of Mongol lands. Descendants of Chaghatai, one of Chinggis Khan's sons, ruled the khanate of Chaghatai in central Asia. Persia fell under the authority of rulers known as the ilkhans, and the khans of the Golden Horde dominated Russia. The great khans were nominally superior to the others, but they were rarely able to enforce their claims to authority. In fact, for as long as the Mongol empires survived, ambition fueled constant tension and occasional conflict among the four khans.

Khubilai Khan

The consolidation of Mongol rule in China came during the reign of Khubilai (sometimes spelled Qubilai), one of Chinggis Khan's grandsons. Khubilai was perhaps the most talented of the great conqueror's descendants. He unleashed ruthless attacks against his enemies, but he also took an interest in cultural matters and worked to improve the welfare of his subjects. He actively promoted Buddhism, and he provided support also for Daoists, Muslims, and Christians in his realm. The famous Venetian traveler Marco Polo, who lived almost two decades at Khubilai's court, praised him for his generosity toward the poor and his efforts to build roads. Though named great khan in 1260, Khubilai spent four years fighting off contenders. From 1264 until his death in 1294, Khubilai Khan presided over the Mongol empire at its height.

For an interactive version of this map, go to www.mhhe.com/bentley3ch18maps.

MAP [18.2]
The Mongol empires about 1300 C.E.

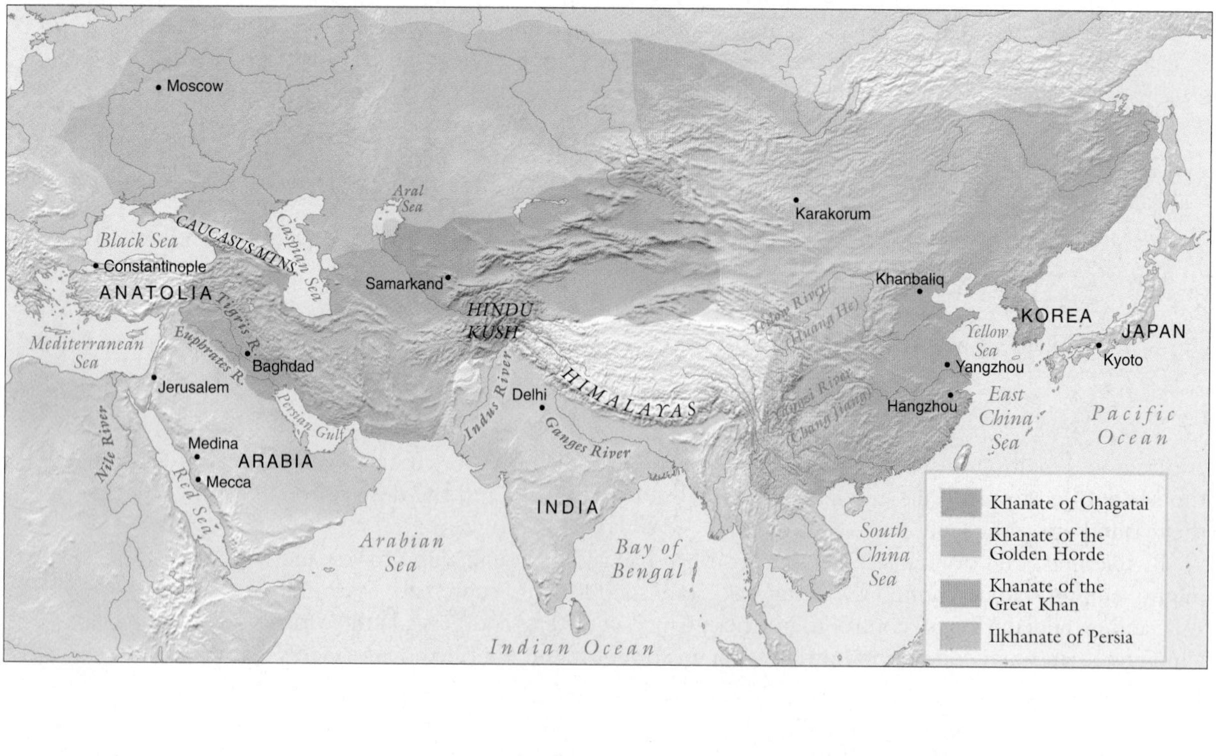

Mongol Conquest of Southern China

Khubilai extended Mongol rule to all of China. From his base at Khanbaliq, he relentlessly attacked the Song dynasty in southern China. The Song capital at Hangzhou fell to Mongol forces in 1276, and within three years Khubilai had eliminated resistance throughout China. In 1279 he proclaimed himself emperor and established the Yuan dynasty, which ruled China until its collapse in 1368.

Beyond China, Khubilai had little success as a conqueror. During the 1270s and 1280s, he launched several invasions of Vietnam, Cambodia, and Burma as well as a naval expedition against Java involving five hundred to one thousand ships and twenty thousand troops. But Mongol forces did not adapt well to the humid, tropical jungles of southeast Asia. Pasturelands were inadequate for their horses, and the fearsome Mongol horsemen were unable to cope with the guerrilla tactics employed by the defenders. In 1274 and again in 1281, Khubilai also attempted seaborne invasions of Japan, but on both occasions typhoons thwarted his plans. The storm of 1281 was especially vicious: it destroyed about 4,500 Mongol vessels carrying more than one hundred thousand armed troops—the largest seaborne expedition before World War II. Japanese defenders attributed their continued independence to the *kamikaze* ("divine winds").

The Golden Horde

As Khubilai consolidated his hold on east Asia, his cousins and brothers tightened Mongol control on lands to the west. Mongols of the group known as the Golden Horde overran Russia between 1237 and 1241 and then mounted exploratory expeditions into Poland, Hungary, and eastern Germany in 1241 and 1242. Mongols of the Golden Horde prized the steppes north of the Black Sea as prime pastureland for their horses. They maintained a large army on the steppes from which they mounted raids into Russia. They did not occupy Russia, which they regarded as an unattractive land of forests, but they extracted tribute from the Russian cities and agricultural provinces. The Golden Horde maintained its hegemony in Russia until the mid-fifteenth century, when the princes of Moscow rejected its authority while building a powerful Russian state. By the mid-sixteenth century Russian conquerors had extended their control to the steppes, but Mongol khans descended from the Golden Horde continued to rule the Crimea until the late eighteenth century.

The Ilkhanate of Persia

While the Golden Horde established its authority in Russia, Khubilai's brother Hülegü toppled the Abbasid empire and established the Mongol ilkhanate in Persia.

In 1280 a famous Chinese court painter, Liu Guandao, depicted Khubilai Khan (center) with a hunting party. The emperor wears Chinese silks under Mongolian furs, while the hunters' equipment includes Mongolian bows, arrows, and satchels.

In 1258 he captured the Abbasid capital of Baghdad after a brief siege. His troops looted the city, executed the caliph, and massacred more than two hundred thousand residents by Hülegü's own estimate. From Persia, Hülegü's army ventured into Syria, but Muslim forces from Egypt soon expelled them and placed a limit on Mongol expansion to the southwest.

When the Mongols crushed ruling regimes in large settled societies, particularly in China and Persia, they discovered that they needed to become governors as well as conquerors. The Mongols had no experience administering complex societies, where successful governance required talents beyond the equestrian and military skills esteemed on the steppes. They had a difficult time adjusting to their role as administrators. Indeed, they never became entirely comfortable in the role, and most of their conquests fell out of their hands within a century.

Mongol Rule in Persia

The Mongols adopted different tactics in the different lands that they ruled. In Persia they made important concessions to local interests. Although Mongols and their allies occupied the highest administrative positions, Persians served as ministers, provincial governors, and state officials at all lower levels. The Mongols basically allowed the Persians to administer the ilkhanate as long as they delivered tax receipts and maintained order.

Over time, the Mongols even assimilated to Persian cultural traditions. The early Mongol rulers of Persia mostly observed their native shamanism, but they tolerated all religions—including Islam, Nestorian Christianity, Buddhism, and Judaism—and they ended the privileges given Muslims during the Abbasid caliphate. Gradually, however, the Mongols themselves gravitated toward Islam. In 1295 Ilkhan Ghazan publicly converted to Islam, and most of the Mongols in Persia followed his example. Ghazan's conversion sparked large-scale massacres of Christians and Jews, and it signaled the return of Islam to a privileged position in Persian society. It also indicated the absorption of the Mongols into Muslim Persian society.

Mongol Rule in China

In China, by contrast, the Mongol overlords stood aloof from their subjects, whom they scorned as mere cultivators. They outlawed intermarriage between Mongols and Chinese and forbade the Chinese from learning the Mongol language. Soon after their conquest some of the victors went so far as to suggest that the Mongols exterminate the Chinese people and convert China itself into pastureland for their horses. Cooler heads eventually prevailed, and the Mongols decided simply to extract as much revenue as possible from their Chinese subjects. In doing so, however, they did not make as much use of native administrative talent as did their counterparts in Persia. Instead, they brought foreign administrators into China and placed them in charge. Along with their nomadic allies, the Mongols' administrative staff included Arabs, Persians, and perhaps even Europeans: Marco Polo may have served as an administrator in the city of Yangzhou during the reign of Khubilai Khan.

The Mongols also resisted assimilation to Chinese cultural traditions. They ended the privileges enjoyed by the Confucian scholars, and they dismantled the Confucian educational and examination system, which had produced untold generations of civil servants for the Chinese bureaucracy. They did not persecute Confucians, but they allowed the Confucian tradition to wither in the absence of official support. Meanwhile, to remain on good terms with subjects of different faiths, the Mongols allowed the construction of churches, temples, and shrines, and they even subsidized some religious establishments. They tolerated all cultural and religious traditions in China, including Confucianism, Daoism, Buddhism, and Christianity. Of Khubilai Khan's four wives, his favorite was Chabi, a Nestorian Christian.

The Mongols and Buddhism

For their part the Mongols mostly continued to follow their native shamanist cults, although many of the ruling elite became enchanted with the Lamaist school

The siege of Baghdad: a Persian manuscript illustration depicts Mongol forces camped outside the city walls while residents huddle within.

of Buddhism that developed in Tibet. Lamaist Buddhism held several attractions for the Mongols. It made a prominent place for magic and supernatural powers, and in that respect it resembled the Mongols' shamanism. Moreover, Lamaist Buddhist leaders officially recognized the Mongols as legitimate rulers and went out of their way to court the Mongols' favor. They numbered the Mongols in the ranks of universal Buddhist rulers and even recognized the Mongol khans as incarnations of the Buddha himself. Thus it is not surprising that the Mongol ruling elites would find Lamaist Buddhism attractive.

The Mongols and Eurasian Integration

In building their vast empire, the Mongols brought tremendous destruction to lands throughout much of the Eurasian landmass. Yet they also sponsored interaction among peoples of different societies and linked Eurasian lands more directly than ever before. Indeed, Mongol rulers positively encouraged travel and communication over long distances. Recognizing the value of regular communications for their vast empire, Chinggis Khan and his successors maintained a courier network that rapidly relayed news, information, and government orders. The network included relay stations with fresh horses and riders so that messages could travel almost nonstop throughout Mongol territories. The Mongols' encouragement of travel and communication facilitated trade, diplomatic travel, missionary efforts, and movements of peoples to new lands.

The Mongols and Trade

As a nomadic people dependent on commerce with settled agricultural societies, the Mongols worked to secure trade routes and ensure the safety of merchants passing through their territories. The Mongol khans frequently fought among themselves, but they maintained reasonably good order within their realms and allowed merchants to travel unmolested through their empires. As a result, long-distance travel and trade became much less risky than in earlier times. Merchants increased their commercial investments, and the volume of long-distance trade across central Asia dwarfed that of earlier eras. Lands as distant as China and western Europe became directly linked for the first time because of the ability of individuals to travel across the entire Eurasian landmass.

Diplomatic Missions

Like trade, diplomatic communication was essential to the Mongols, and their protection of roads and travelers benefited ambassadors as well as merchants. Chinggis Khan destroyed the Khwarazm shah in Persia because the shah unwisely murdered the Mongol envoys Chinggis Khan dispatched in hopes of opening diplomatic and commercial relations. Throughout the Mongol era the great khans in China, the ilkhans in Persia, and the other khans maintained close communications by means of diplomatic embassies. They also had diplomatic dealings with rulers in Korea, Vietnam, India, western Europe, and other lands as well. Some diplomatic travelers crossed the entire Eurasian landmass. Several European ambassadors traveled to Mongolia and China to deliver messages from authorities seeking to ally with the Mongols against Muslim states in southwest Asia. Diplomats also traveled west: Rabban Sauma, a Nestorian Christian monk born in Khanbaliq, visited Italy and France as a representative of the Persian ilkhan.

Missionary Efforts

Like the silk roads in earlier times, Eurasian routes during the era of the Mongol empires served as highways for missionaries as well as merchants and diplomats. Sufi missionaries helped popularize Islam among Turkish peoples in central Asia, while Lamaist Buddhism from Tibet attracted considerable interest among the Mongols. Nestorian Christians, who had long been prominent in oasis communities throughout central Asia, found new opportunities to win converts when they went to China to serve as administrators for Mongol rulers there. Roman Catholic Christians also mounted missionary campaigns in China. (See chapter 22 for further discussion of travel during the Mongol era.)

Resettlement

Another Mongol policy that encouraged Eurasian integration was the practice of resettling peoples in new lands. As a nomadic people, the Mongols had limited numbers of skilled artisans and educated individuals, but the more their empire expanded, the more they needed the services of specialized crafts workers and literate administrators. Mongol overlords recruited the talent they needed largely from the ranks of their allies and the peoples they conquered, and they often moved people far from their homelands to sites where they could best make use of their services. Among the most important of the Mongols' allies were the Uighur Turks, who lived mostly in oasis cities along the silk roads. The Uighurs were literate and often highly educated, and they provided not only many of the clerks, secretaries, and administrators who ran the Mongol empires but also units of soldiers who bolstered Mongol garrisons. Arab and Persian Muslims were also prominent among those who administered the Mongols' affairs far from their homelands.

Conquered peoples also supplied the Mongols with talent. When they overcame a city, Mongol forces routinely surveyed the captured population, separated out those with specialized skills, and sent them to the capital at Karakorum or some other place where there was demand for their services. From the ranks of conquered peoples came soldiers, bodyguards, administrators, secretaries, translators, physicians, armor makers, metalsmiths, miners, carpenters, masons, textile workers, musicians, and jewelers. After the 1230s the Mongols often took censuses of lands they conquered, partly to levy taxes and conscript military forces and partly to locate talented individuals. The Parisian goldsmith Guillaume Boucher was only one among thousands of foreign-born individuals who became permanent residents of the Mongol capital at Karakorum because of their special talents. Like their protection of trade and diplomacy, the Mongols' policy of resettling allies and conquered peoples promoted Eurasian integration by increasing communication and exchange between peoples of different societies.

Decline of the Mongols in Persia and China

Collapse of the Ilkhanate

Soon after the long and prosperous reign of Khubilai Khan, the Mongols encountered serious difficulties governing Persia and China. In Persia excessive spending strained the treasury, and overexploitation of the peasantry led to reduced revenues. In the early 1290s the ilkhan tried to resolve his financial difficulties by introducing paper money and ordering all subjects to accept it for payment of all debts. The purpose of this measure was to drive precious metals into the hands of the government, but the policy was a miserable failure: rather than accept paper that they regarded as worthless, merchants simply closed their shops. Commerce ground to a halt until the ilkhan rescinded his order. Meanwhile, factional struggles plagued the Mongol leadership. The regime went into steep decline after the death of Ilkhan Ghazan in 1304. When the last of the Mongol rulers died without an heir in 1335, the ilkhanate itself simply collapsed. Government in Persia devolved to local levels until late in the fourteenth century when Turkish peoples reintroduced effective central government.

Decline of the Yuan Dynasty

Mongol decline in China was a more complicated affair. As in Persia, it had an economic dimension. The Mongols continued to use the paper money that the Chinese had introduced during the Tang and Song dynasties, but they did not maintain adequate reserves of the bullion that backed up paper notes. The general population soon lost confidence in paper money, and prices rose sharply as a reflection of its diminished value. As in Persia, too, factions and infighting hastened Mongol decline in China. As the richest of the Mongol empires, China attracted the attention of ambitious warriors. Beginning in the 1320s power struggles, imperial assassinations, and civil war convulsed the Mongol regime in China.

Bubonic Plague

Apart from financial difficulties and factional divisions, the Mongol rulers of China also faced an onslaught of epidemic disease. By facilitating trade and communications throughout Eurasia, the Mongols unwittingly expedited the spread of bubonic plague (discussed in chapter 22). During the 1330s plague erupted in southwestern China. From there it spread throughout China and central Asia, and by the late 1340s it had reached southwest Asia and Europe, where it became known as the Black Death. Bubonic plague sometimes killed half or more of an exposed population, particularly during the furious initial years of the epidemic, and it seriously disrupted economies and societies throughout much of Eurasia. In China depopulation and labor shortages that followed on the heels of epidemic plague weakened the Mongol regime. (Plague would also have caused serious problems for the Mongol rulers of Persia had the ilkhanate not collapsed before its arrival.)

The Mongols also faced a rebellious subject population in China. The Mongols stood apart from their Chinese subjects, who returned the contempt of their conquerors. Beginning in the 1340s southern China became a hotbed of peasant rebellion and banditry, which the Mongols could not control. In 1368 rebel forces captured Khanbaliq, and the Mongols departed China en masse and returned to the steppes.

Surviving Mongol Khanates

Despite the collapse of the Mongol regimes in Persia and China, Mongol states did not completely disappear. The khanate of Chaghatai continued to prevail in central Asia, and Mongols posed a threat to the northwestern borders of China until the eighteenth century. Meanwhile, the khanate of the Golden Horde continued to dominate the Caucasus and the steppe lands north of the Black Sea and Caspian Sea until the mid-sixteenth century when a resurgent Russian state brought the Golden Horde down. Like Mongols in China, however, Mongols in Russia continued to threaten until the eighteenth century, and Mongols who had settled in the Crimean peninsula retained their identity until Josef Stalin forcibly moved them to other parts of the Soviet Union in the mid-twentieth century.

After the Mongols

By no means did the decline of the Mongols signal the end of nomadic peoples' influence in Eurasia. As Mongol strength waned, Turkish peoples resumed the expansive campaigns that the Mongols had interrupted. During the late fourteenth and early fifteenth centuries, the Turkish conqueror Tamerlane built a central Asian empire rivaling that of Chinggis Khan himself. Although Tamerlane's empire foundered soon after his death, it deeply influenced three surviving Turkish Muslim states—the Mughal empire in India, the Safavid empire in Persia, and the Ottoman empire based in Anatolia—and also embraced much of southwest Asia, southeastern Europe, and north Africa.

Tamerlane the Whirlwind

The Lame Conqueror

The rapid collapse of the Mongol states left gaping power vacuums in China and Persia. While the native Ming dynasty filled the vacuum in China, a self-made Turkish conqueror named Timur moved on Persia. Because he walked with a limp, contemporaries referred to him as Timur-i lang—"Timur the Lame," an appellation that made its way into English as Tamerlane.

Born about 1336 near Samarkand, Tamerlane took Chinggis Khan as his model. Like Chinggis Khan, Tamerlane came from a family of the minor nobility and had to make his own way to power. Like Chinggis Khan, too, he was a charismatic leader and a courageous warrior, and he attracted a band of loyal followers. During the 1360s he eliminated rivals to power, either by persuading them to join him as allies or by defeating their armies on the battlefield, and he won recognition as leader of his own tribe. By 1370 he had extended his authority throughout the khanate of Chaghatai and begun to build a magnificent imperial capital in Samarkand.

Spoils from Tamerlane's campaigns and raids enriched the conqueror's capital at Samarkand. They financed, among other buildings, the magnificent tomb where Tamerlane's remains still rest.

Tamerlane's Conquests

For the rest of his life, Tamerlane led his armies on campaigns of conquest. He turned first to the region between Persia and Afghani-

MAP [18.3]
Tamerlane's empire about 1405 C.E.

stan, and he took special care to establish his authority in the rich cities so that he could levy taxes on trade and agricultural production. Next he attacked the Golden Horde in the Caucasus region and Russia, and by the mid-1390s he had severely weakened it. During the last years of the century, he invaded India and subjected Delhi to a ferocious sack: contemporary chroniclers reported, with some exaggeration, that for a period of two months after the attack not even birds visited the devastated city. Later Tamerlane campaigned along the Ganges, although he never attempted to incorporate India into his empire. He opened the new century with campaigns in southwest Asia and Anatolia. In 1404 he began preparations for an invasion of China, and he was leading his army east when he fell ill and died in 1405.

Like his model Chinggis Khan, Tamerlane was a conqueror, not a governor. He spent almost his entire adult life planning and fighting military campaigns: he even had himself carried around on a litter during his final illness, as he prepared to invade China. He did not create an imperial administration but, rather, ruled through tribal leaders who were his allies. He appointed overlords in the territories he conquered, but they relied on existing bureaucratic structures and simply received taxes and tributes on his behalf.

Tamerlane's Heirs

Given its loose organization, it is not surprising that Tamerlane's empire experienced stresses and strains after the conqueror's death. Tamerlane's sons and grandsons engaged in a long series of bitter conflicts that resulted in the contraction of his empire and its division into four main regions. For a century after Tamerlane's death, however, they maintained control over the region from Persia to Afghanistan. When the last vestiges of Tamerlane's imperial creation disappeared, in the early sixteenth century, the Mughal, Safavid, and Ottoman empires that replaced it all clearly reflected the Turkish Muslim legacy of the lame conqueror.

Contexts & Connections

Nomadic Conquerors and Their Contemporary Appeal

Chinggis Khan and Tamerlane were among the most violent individuals ever to walk the earth. While building massive empires and protecting trade routes, they also destroyed thriving cities and massacred defenseless populations. They often resorted to calculated cruelties to intimidate or humiliate their opponents.

Yet these unsavory conquerors have found devoted followings in later centuries and even in the present day. Tamerlane, for example, was a hero to the Turco-Mongolian Mughals, who drew on his memory as both inspiration and legitimation for their conquest of India in the sixteenth century. In the mid-twentieth century, the Soviet ruler Josef Stalin felt such gnawing curiosity about the lame conqueror that he had Tamerlane's body exhumed and studied. More recently, the people of independent Uzbekistan have taken Tamerlane as a symbol of national identity and glory—even though the Uzbeks descend from a nomadic Turkish group that migrated to the land now called Uzbekistan only in the sixteenth century, long after the conqueror's death.

Stalin would have exhumed the corpse of Chinggis Khan as well as Tamerlane if he had been able to find it. He sent several expeditions to search for Chinggis Khan's grave, but the Mongol conqueror had taken precautions to have his body interred in a secret resting place in the mountains rather than a grandiose tomb. Unable to lay hands on Chinggis Khan's body, Stalin had to content himself with learning Mongol military secrets through the historical record. In some ways he was successful: during World War II, he adapted a classic Mongol military tactic by luring German invaders deep into Soviet territory, then picking off units that could not adequately supply themselves or support one another.

While Stalin admired Chinggis Khan the individual as a conqueror, the official Soviet view held that the Mongols in general were violent thugs who saddled Russia with an oppressive and parasitic regime. Quite apart from their historical views, Soviet leaders were also wary about the possibility that memories of Chinggis Khan might serve as a focus for the organization of resistance in Outer Mongolia, the northern region of Mongolia that the Soviet Union controlled as a buffer zone between its own territory and China. Soviet officials hunted down all known descendants of Chinggis Khan and sent some off to the infamous prison camps while marching others into the woods for summary execution. As late as 1964, the official Soviet newspaper *Pravda* denounced Chinggis Khan as a "bloodthirsty barbarian" and bluntly warned against any effort "to place him on a pedestal as a historically progressive personage."

Since the collapse of the Soviet Union in 1991 and the establishment of an independent Mongolia, Chinggis Khan has emerged as a symbol of Mongolian national identity and independence from both Russia and China. His name, which was dangerous to utter publicly in Soviet times, is now prominent throughout Mongolia: popular brands of vodka, cigarettes, and candy bars all bear the name Chinggis Khan, as does Mongolia's foremost rock group, while the conqueror's likeness appears on postage stamps and paper money. In Mongolia as in Uzbekistan, contemporary political interests have transformed a brutal conqueror into a national icon.

The Foundation of the Ottoman Empire

Chapter 28 will discuss the Mughal empire in India and the Safavid empire in Persia, both of which emerged during the early sixteenth century as Tamerlane's empire finally dissolved. The early stages of Ottoman expansion predated Tamerlane, however, and the foundation of the Ottoman empire throws additional light on the influence of nomadic peoples during the period 1000 to 1500 C.E.

Osman

After the Mongol conquest of Persia, large numbers of nomadic Turks migrated from central Asia to the ilkhanate and beyond to the territories in Anatolia that the Saljuq Turks had seized from the Byzantine empire. There they followed charismatic leaders who organized further campaigns of conquest. Among these leaders was

Osman, who during the late thirteenth and early fourteenth centuries carved a small state for himself in northwestern Anatolia. In 1299 Osman declared independence from the Saljuq sultan and launched a campaign to build a state at the expense of the Byzantine empire. After every successful operation Osman attracted more and more followers, who came to be known as Osmanlis or Ottomans.

Although besieged by Ottoman forces, Constantinople received supplies from the sea for almost two months before Ottomans destroyed the city walls and completed their conquest of the Byzantine empire.

Ottoman Conquests

During the 1350s the Ottomans gained a considerable advantage over their Turkish rivals when they established a foothold across the Dardanelles at Gallipoli in the Balkan peninsula. The Ottomans quickly moved to expand the boundaries of their Balkan holdings. Byzantine forces resisted Ottoman incursions, but because of political fragmentation, ineffective government, and exploitation of the peasantry, the Ottomans found abundant local support. By the 1380s the Ottomans had become by far the most powerful people in the Balkan peninsula, and by the end of the century they were poised to capture Constantinople and take over the Byzantine empire.

Tamerlane temporarily delayed Ottoman expansion in the Byzantine realm. In 1402 Tamerlane's forces crushed the Ottoman army, captured the sultan, and subjected the Ottoman state to the conqueror's authority. After Tamerlane's death, Ottoman leaders had to reestablish their rule in their own realm. This undertaking involved both the repression of ambitious local princes who sought to build power bases at Ottoman expense and the defense of Ottoman territories against Byzantine, Venetian, and other Christian forces that sought to turn back the advance of the Turkish Muslims. By the 1440s the Ottomans had recovered their balance and begun again to expand in the Byzantine empire.

The Capture of Constantinople

The campaign culminated in 1453 when Sultan Mehmed II, known as Mehmed the Conqueror, captured the Byzantine capital of Constantinople. After subjecting it to a sack, he made the city his own capital under the Turkish name of Istanbul. With Istanbul as a base, the Ottomans quickly absorbed the remainder of the Byzantine empire. By 1480 they controlled all of Greece and the Balkan region. They continued to expand throughout most of the sixteenth century as well, extending their rule to southwest Asia, southeastern Europe, Egypt, and north Africa. Once again, then, a nomadic people asserted control over a long-settled society and quickly built a vast empire.

During the half millennium from 1000 to 1500 C.E., nomadic peoples of central Asia played a larger role than ever before in world history. As early as the second millennium B.C.E., they had periodically threatened states from China to the eastern Mediterranean region, and from classical times they had traded regularly and actively with peoples of settled societies. From 1000 to 1500 their relations with neighboring peoples changed, as they dominated affairs in most of Eurasia through their conquests and their construction of vast transregional empires. Turkish peoples built the most durable of the nomadic empires, but the spectacular conquests of the Mongols most clearly demonstrated the potential of nomadic peoples to project their formidable military power to settled agricultural societies. By establishing connections that spanned the Eurasian landmass, the nomadic empires laid the foundation for increasing communication, exchange, and interaction among peoples of different societies and thereby fostered the integration of the eastern hemisphere. The age of nomadic empires from 1000 to 1500 C.E. foreshadowed the integrated world of modern times.

CHRONOLOGY

1055	Tughril Beg named sultan
1071	Battle of Manzikert
1206–1227	Reign of Chinggis Khan
1211–1234	Mongol conquest of northern China
1219–1221	Mongol conquest of Persia
1237–1241	Mongol conquest of Russia
1258	Mongol capture of Baghdad
1264–1279	Mongol conquest of southern China
1264–1294	Reign of Khubilai Khan
1279–1368	Yuan dynasty
1295	Conversion of Ilkhan Ghazan to Islam
1336–1405	Life of Tamerlane
1453	Ottoman capture of Constantinople

FOR FURTHER READING

S. A. M. Adshead. *Central Asia in World History.* New York, 1993. A provocative essay on central Asia and its place in the larger world.

Thomas T. Allsen. *Mongol Imperialism: The Policies of the Grand Qan Möngke in China, Russia, and the Islamic Lands, 1251–1259.* Berkeley, 1987. Scholarly analysis of Mongol empire building by Chinggis Khan's successors.

Thomas J. Barfield. *The Nomadic Alternative.* Englewood Cliffs, N.J., 1993. A sensitive study of nomadic societies in Africa and Eurasia by a leading anthropologist.

———. *The Perilous Frontier: Nomadic Empires and China.* Cambridge, Mass., 1989. Scholarly examination of the relationship between nomadic empires and Chinese society.

Vladimir N. Basilov, ed. *Nomads of Eurasia.* Trans. by M. F. Zirin. Los Angeles, 1989. Lavishly illustrated volume that presents translations of essays by Russian scholars on nomadic societies.

René Grousset. *Conqueror of the World: The Life of Chingis-khan.* Trans. by M. McKellar and D. Sinor. New York, 1966. Lively account of Chinggis Khan's life and career.

———. *The Empire of the Steppes: A History of Central Asia.* Trans. by N. Walford. New Brunswick, 1970. A popular account, still useful though somewhat dated, of nomadic empires in central Asia.

Charles J. Halperin. *Russia and the Golden Horde: The Mongol Impact on Medieval Russian History.* Bloomington, 1985. An insightful study of the Golden Horde and its influence on Russian society.

Halil Inalcik. *The Ottoman Empire: The Classical Age, 1300–1600.* Trans. by N. Itzkowitz and C. Imber. New York, 1973. The best short introduction to early Ottoman history.

Paul Kahn, ed. *The Secret History of the Mongols: The Origin of Chingis Khan.* Adapted from the translation of F. W. Cleaves. San Francisco, 1984. A translation of the Mongols' history of their own society, adapted for modern readers.

Adam T. Kessler. *Empires beyond the Great Wall: The Heritage of Genghis Khan.* Los Angeles, 1993. Well-illustrated survey of nomadic states in central Asia from the Xiongnu to the Mongols.

Beatrice Forbes Manz. *The Rise and Rule of Tamerlane.* Cambridge, 1989. Scholarly analysis of Tamerlane's career and his empire.

David Morgan. *Medieval Persia, 1040–1797.* London, 1988. A brief and insightful survey concentrating on the eras of Turkish and Mongol dominance in Persia.

———. *The Mongols.* Oxford, 1986. Lucid and witty study: the best short work on the Mongols.

Michael Prawdin. *The Mongol Empire: Its Rise and Legacy.* 2nd ed. Trans. by E. and C. Paul. New York, 1961. A vivid and detailed study examining Mongol history from Chinggis Khan to Tamerlane.

Tamara Talbot Rice. *The Seljuks in Asia Minor.* London, 1961. Well-illustrated survey of Saljuq history and society, concentrating on the Saljuqs in Anatolia.

Morris Rossabi. *Khubilai Khan: His Life and Times.* Berkeley, 1988. Excellent scholarly study of the greatest of the great khans.

Arthur Waldron. *The Great Wall of China: From History to Myth.* Cambridge, 1989. Examines the role of defensive walls, including the Great Wall, in Chinese efforts to forestall raids by nomadic peoples of central Asia.

OLC

See our **Online Learning Center at www.mhhe.com/bentley3** for additional readings, practice maps, quizzes, and internet activities.

PSI

Unfamiliar words? Check out the **Primary Source Investigator CD-ROM** for an interactive glossary, interactive maps, more images, and primary sources.

A bronze plaque from the kingdom of Benin depicts a local chief flanked by warriors and attendants.

CHAPTER 19

STATES AND SOCIETIES OF SUB-SAHARAN AFRICA

A remarkable oral tradition preserves the story of the lion prince Sundiata, thirteenth-century founder of the Mali empire in west Africa. Oral traditions include stories, histories, epics, and other accounts transmitted by professional singers and storytellers known in Africa as griots. Until scholars began to collect and publish African oral traditions about the middle of the twentieth century, the story of Sundiata was available only when a griot recited it.

According to the oral tradition, Sundiata's father ruled a small west African kingdom in the northeastern part of what is now Guinea. Despite his royal parentage, Sundiata had a difficult childhood, since a congenitally defective leg left him partially crippled. When the old king died, his enemies invaded the kingdom and killed the royal offspring, sparing the child Sundiata because they thought his physical condition would prevent him from posing a threat to their ambitions. But Sundiata overcame his injury, learned to use the bow and arrow, and strengthened himself by hunting in the forest. As Sundiata grew stronger, his enemies began to fear him, and they forced him to seek refuge in a neighboring kingdom. While in exile, Sundiata distinguished himself as a warrior and assembled a powerful cavalry force staffed by loyal followers and allies.

About 1235 Sundiata returned to his homeland and claimed the throne. His cavalry slashed through the countryside, defeating his enemies almost at will. Within a few years he had overcome resistance, established the Mali empire, and consolidated his rule throughout the valley of the Niger River. Although he respected traditional religious beliefs and magical powers, Sundiata was also a Muslim, and he welcomed Muslim merchants from north Africa into his realm. He built a capital city at Niani, which soon became a thriving commercial center. Indeed, as a result of its control of the gold trade—and the political stability provided by Sundiata—the Mali empire became probably the wealthiest land in sub-Saharan Africa. For two centuries after Sundiata's death about 1260, the lion prince's legacy shaped the lives of west African peoples and linked west Africa with north Africa and the Mediterranean basin.

From the classical era forward, peoples from east Asia to the Mediterranean basin established extensive networks of trade and communication. African peoples living south of the Sahara desert participated in the larger economy of the eastern hemisphere, though not so fully as their counterparts in north Africa, who from ancient times were prominent in the trading world of the Mediterranean basin. Geographic conditions help to explain why trade and communication networks did not embrace sub-Saharan Africa as readily as they did other regions: the Sahara desert poses a formidable challenge to overland travelers from the north, the African coastlines offer few good natural harbors, and cataracts complicate travel up the continent's major rivers.

Nevertheless, like their Eurasian and north African counterparts, peoples of sub-Saharan Africa organized productive societies, built powerful states, and participated in large-scale networks of communication and exchange. Internal African processes drove much of this development. Between 1000 and 1500 C.E., in the wake of the Bantu and other migrations (discussed in chapter 3), peoples of sub-Saharan Africa continued to expand the amount of territory under cultivation and to establish agricultural societies. Furthermore, as their population increased, they organized states, developed centers of economic specialization, and carried on interregional trade. Alongside these internal processes, relations with other peoples of the eastern hemisphere also profoundly influenced the development of African societies. From the early centuries C.E. to 1500 and later as well, trade with lands of the Mediterranean and the Indian Ocean basins encouraged African peoples to organize their societies so as to produce commodities desired by consumers throughout much of the eastern hemisphere. This trade promoted urban development, the organization of large states and empires, and the introduction of new food crops and new religious beliefs into sub-Saharan Africa.

Effects of Early African Migrations

By 1000 C.E. Bantu-speaking peoples had settled in most parts of Africa south of the equator, while Kushite, Sudanese, Mande, and other peoples had also established communities in lands far from their original homes. Some African peoples undertook small-scale migrations long thereafter, even into the nineteenth century. By about 1000, however, most of the migrations were complete, and for the next several centuries, African peoples built societies on the foundation of small communities that the Bantu and other migrations had generated.

Agriculture and Population Growth

The principal early result of the Bantu and other migrations was to spread agriculture and herding to almost all parts of Africa, excluding deserts and dense, equatorial rain forests. As they established agricultural societies, cultivators and herders displaced many of the hunting, gathering, and fishing peoples who previously inhabited sub-Saharan Africa and absorbed them into their own societies. After about 500 B.C.E., most Bantu peoples possessed iron metallurgy, which enabled them to fashion iron axes, adzes, and hoes that facilitated further clearing of lands and extension of agriculture. By the early centuries C.E., cultivation and herding had reached the southernmost parts of Africa. Yams, sorghum, and millet were the dietary staples of many peoples in south Africa, and the indigenous Khoi people themselves adopted cattle raising even before Bantu and Kushite herders moved into the region. These developments resulted in increased agricultural production, rising population, and pressure for continuing migration to new territories.

Bananas

The introduction of bananas to Africa encouraged a fresh migratory surge. First domesticated in southeast Asia, bananas entered Africa by way of sea lanes across the Indian Ocean. During the late centuries B.C.E., Malay seafarers from the islands that make up modern Indonesia sailed west beyond India, and by the early centuries C.E. they were exploring the east African coasts. Between about 300 and 500 C.E., they colonized the island of Madagascar and established banana cultivation there. (Apart from bananas, they also brought Asian yams, taro, chickens, and southeast Asian cultural traditions. Malagasy, the language spoken on Madagascar even today, belongs to the Austronesian family of languages.) From Madagascar, bananas easily made the jump to the east African mainland. By 500 C.E. several varieties of bananas had become well established in Africa. They provided a nutritious supplement to Bantu diets and enabled the Bantu to expand into heavily forested regions where yams and millet did not grow well. Thus cultivation of bananas increased the supply of food available to the Bantu, enriched their diets, and allowed them to expand more rapidly than before.

Population Growth

The population history of sub-Saharan Africa clearly reflects the significance of iron metallurgy and bananas. In 400 B.C.E., before iron working had deeply influenced the continent's societies, the population of sub-Saharan Africa stood at about 3.5 million. By the turn of the millennium, human numbers exceeded 11 million. By 800 C.E., after banana cultivation had spread throughout the continent, the sub-Saharan population had climbed to 17 million. And by 1000, when the Bantu migrations had introduced agriculture and iron metallurgy to most regions of sub-Saharan Africa, the population had passed 22 million.

African Political Organization

By 1000 C.E., after more than two millennia of migrations, the Bantu had approached the limits of their expansion. Because agricultural peoples already occupied most of the continent, migrating into new territories and forming new settlements was much more difficult than in previous centuries. Instead of migrating in search of new lands to cultivate, then, African peoples developed increasingly complex forms of government that enabled them to organize their existing societies more efficiently.

Kin-Based Societies

Scholars have sometimes used the terms *stateless society* and *segmentary society* to refer to one form of social organization widely prevalent in Africa during and after the Bantu migrations. Although somewhat misleading, since they seem to imply that Bantu societies had little or no government, these terms accurately reflect the fact that early Bantu societies did not depend on an elaborate hierarchy of officials or a bureaucratic apparatus to administer their affairs. Instead, Bantu peoples governed themselves mostly through family and kinship groups.

Bantu peoples usually settled in villages with populations averaging about one hundred people. Male heads of families constituted a village's ruling council, which decided the public affairs for the entire group. The most prominent of the family heads presided over the village as a chief and represented the settlement when it dealt with neighboring peoples. A group of villages constituted a district, which became the principal focus of ethnic loyalties. Usually there was no chief or larger government for the district. Instead, village chiefs negotiated on matters concerning two or more villages. Meanwhile, within individual villages, family and kinship groups disciplined their own members as necessary.

This type of organization lends itself particularly well to small-scale communities, but kin-based societies often grew to large proportions. Some networks of villages and districts organized the public affairs of several hundred thousand people. By the nineteenth century, for example, the Tiv people of Nigeria, numbering almost one million, conducted their affairs in a kin-based society built on a foundation of family and clan groups.

Chiefdoms

After about 1000 C.E., however, kin-based societies faced difficult challenges. Population growth strained resources, but few lands were available for migrants to settle. Conflicts between villages and districts became more frequent and more intense. Increased conflict encouraged Bantu communities to organize military forces

According to legend, this handsome terra-cotta head represents an ambitious warrior who usurped power in the small state of Ife (in modern Nigeria). Produced shortly after 1000 C.E., it testifies to the increasing tensions in sub-Saharan politics after the turn of the millennium.

for both offensive and defensive purposes, and military organization in turn encouraged the development of more formal structures of government. Many districts fell under the leadership of powerful chiefs, who overrode kinship networks and imposed their own authority on their territories. Some of these chiefs conquered their neighbors and consolidated their lands into small kingdoms. These local kingdoms emerged in several regions of sub-Saharan Africa after about 1000 C.E. The kingdoms of Ife and Benin arose in the forested regions of west Africa. Both realms were city-states in which the court and urban residents controlled the surrounding countryside through family relationships and political alliances. Both Ife and Benin also produced magnificent sculptures that put human faces and figures to the early history of sub-Saharan Africa. Local kingdoms appeared also in southern Africa and central Africa.

Kingdom of Kongo

One of the most active areas of political development was the basin of the Congo River (also known as the Zaire River), a region where brisk economic development supported the emergence of large as well as small kingdoms. After about 1000 C.E. population pressures and military challenges encouraged kin-based societies in the Congo region to form small states embracing a few villages each. By 1200 conflict between these small states had resulted in the organization of larger, regional principalities that could resist political and military pressures better than small kingdoms could. One of the more prosperous of the Congolese states was the Kingdom of Kongo, which participated actively in trade networks involving copper, raffia cloth, and nzimbu shells from the Atlantic Ocean. During the fourteenth century the Kingdom of Kongo came to embrace much of the modern-day Republic of the Congo and Angola.

The central government of Kongo included the king and officials who oversaw military, judicial, and financial affairs. Beneath the central government were six provinces administered by governors, each of whom supervised several districts administered by subordinate officials. Within the districts, villages ruled by chiefs provided local government. Though not the only kingdom in sub-Saharan Africa, Kongo was perhaps the most tightly centralized of the early Bantu kingdoms. In most cases the king or other central administrators could appoint or replace local officials at will, and the central government maintained a royal currency system based on cowries, seashells that came from the Indian Ocean. The kingdom of Kongo provided effective organization from the fourteenth until the mid-seventeenth century when Portuguese slave traders undermined the authority of the kings and the central government.

Kin-based societies did not disappear with the emergence of formal states. To the contrary, they survived into the nineteenth century in much of sub-Saharan Africa. Yet regional states and large kingdoms became increasingly prominent during the centuries after 1000 C.E. as Bantu and other African peoples responded to population pressures and military challenges facing their societies.

Islamic Kingdoms and Empires

While Bantu peoples organized societies on the basis of African traditions, merchants from north Africa and southwest Asia introduced their Islamic faith to sub-Saharan Africa. Islam arrived by two routes: it went to west Africa overland by trans-Saharan camel caravans, and it traveled to coastal east Africa over the sea lanes of the Indian Ocean in the vessels of merchant mariners. After the eighth century C.E., Islam profoundly influenced the political, social, and economic development of sub-Saharan Africa as well as its cultural and religious development.

Trans-Saharan Trade and Islamic States in West Africa

The Sahara desert has never served as an absolute barrier to communication between human societies. Small numbers of nomadic peoples have lived in the desert itself ever since a process of desiccation created the Sahara beginning about 5000 B.C.E. These nomads migrated around the desert and had dealings with other peoples settled on its fringes. Even in ancient and classical times, merchants occasionally organized commercial expeditions across the desert, although the value and volume of trade in the Mediterranean basin greatly exceeded that crossing the Sahara.

In this engraving by a German artist of the mid-nineteenth century, a small caravan approaches Timbuktu. Camels and donkeys serve as beasts of burden, and horse-mounted escorts accompany the party.

Camels

The arrival of the camel quickened the pace of communication and transportation across the Sahara. Camels came to north Africa from Arabia, by way of Egypt and the Sudan, about the seventh century B.C.E. During the late centuries B.C.E., a special camel saddle, which took advantage of the animals' distinctive physical structure, also made its way to north Africa. Because a caravan took seventy to ninety days to cross the Sahara and because camels could travel long distances before needing water, they proved to be useful beasts of burden in an arid region. After about 300 C.E. camels increasingly replaced horses and donkeys as the preferred transport animals throughout the Sahara as well as in the deserts of central Asia.

When Arab conquerors established their Islamic faith in north Africa during the seventh and eighth centuries, they also integrated the region into a rapidly expanding zone of commerce and communication. Thus it was natural for Muslims in north Africa to explore the potential of trade across the Sahara. By the late eighth century, Islamic merchants had trekked across the desert and established commercial relations with societies in sub-Saharan west Africa. There they found a series of long-established trading centers such as Gao, a terminus of caravan routes across the Sahara that offered access to the Niger River valley, which was a flourishing market for copper, ironware, cotton textiles, salt, grains, and carnelian beads.

The Kingdom of Ghana

The principal state of west Africa at the time of the Muslims' arrival there was the kingdom of Ghana (not related to the modern state of Ghana), situated between the Senegal and Niger rivers in a region straddling the border between the modern states of Mali and Mauritania. Ghana emerged as a kingdom at an uncertain but early date: according to legends preserved by Arab travelers, as many as twenty-two kings ruled in Ghana before Muhammad and his companions embarked on the *hijra*. Ghana probably developed as a state during the fourth or fifth century C.E. when settled, agricultural peoples sought to protect their societies from the raids of camel-riding nomads who increasingly came out of the Sahara. When Muslims arrived in west Africa, the kingdom of Ghana was a regional state much like others that were emerging or soon would appear elsewhere in sub-Saharan Africa.

Gold Trade

As trade and traffic across the desert increased, Ghana underwent a dramatic transformation. It became the most important commercial site in west Africa because it was the center for trade in gold, which was in high demand because of economic development and surging trade throughout the eastern hemisphere. Muslim merchants flocked to camel caravans traveling across the Sahara to Ghana in search of gold for consumers in the Mediterranean basin and elsewhere in the Islamic world. Ghana itself did not produce gold, but the kings procured nuggets from lands to the south—probably from the region around the headwaters of the Niger, Gambia, and Senegal rivers, which enjoyed the world's largest supply of gold available at the time. By controlling and taxing trade in the precious metal, the kings both enriched and strengthened their realm. Apart from gold, merchants from Ghana also provided ivory and slaves for traders from north Africa. In exchange, they received horses, cloth, small manufactured wares, and salt—a crucial commodity in the tropics, but one that local sources could not supply in large quantities.

Koumbi-Saleh

Integration into trans-Saharan trade networks brought enormous wealth and considerable power to Ghana. The kingdom's capital and principal trading site stood at Koumbi-Saleh, a small town today but a thriving commercial center with a population of some fifteen thousand to twenty thousand people when the kingdom was at its height, from the ninth to the twelfth century. Al-Bakri, a Spanish Muslim traveler of the mid-eleventh century, described Koumbi-Saleh as a flourishing site with buildings of stone and more than a dozen mosques. Koumbi-Saleh's wealth also supported

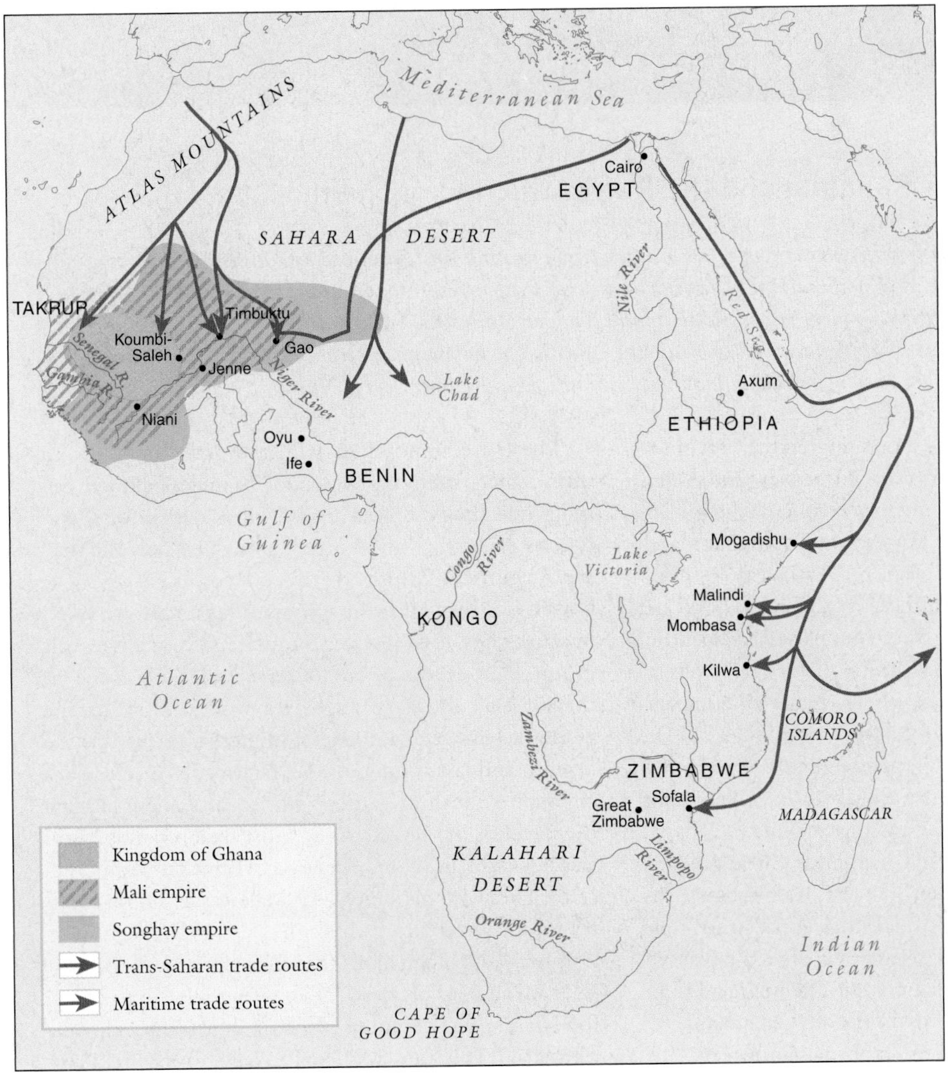

MAP [19.1]
Kingdoms, empires, and city-states of sub-Saharan Africa, 800–1500 C.E.

For an interactive version of this map, go to www.mhhe.com/bentley3ch19maps.

a large number of *qadi* and Muslim scholars. From taxes levied on trade passing through Ghana, the kings financed a large army—al-Bakri reported that they could field two hundred thousand warriors—that protected the sources of gold, maintained order in the kingdom, kept allied and tributary states in line, and defended Ghana against nomadic incursions from the Sahara.

Islam in West Africa

By about the tenth century, the kings of Ghana had converted to Islam. Their conversion led to improved relations with Muslim merchants from north Africa as well as Muslim nomads from the desert who transported trade goods across the Sahara. It also brought them recognition and support from Muslim states in north Africa. The kings of Ghana made no attempt to impose Islam forcibly on their society—unlike the neighboring kings of Takrur, who zealously campaigned for the conversion of their entire kingdom—nor did they accept Islam exclusively even for their own purposes. Instead, they continued to observe traditional religious customs: al-Bakri mentioned,

Sources from the Past

Sundiata and the Reconstruction of Niani

African griots tell many different versions of an oral tradition dealing with Sundiata and his establishment of the Mali empire. Some dwell on Sundiata's cunning and clever strategy, others on his courage and physical valor. After recounting his birth, childhood, and campaign to conquer Mali, some oral traditions emphasize Sundiata's connections with his birthplace and capital city, Niani. The following selection deals with Sundiata's restoration of stability and prosperity and especially his services to Niani.

The troops were marching along singing the "Hymn to the Bow," which the crowd took up. New songs flew from mouth to mouth. Young women offered the soldiers cool water and cola nuts. And so the triumphal march across Mali ended outside Niani, Sundiata's city.

It was a ruined town which was beginning to be rebuilt by its inhabitants. A part of the ramparts had been destroyed and the charred walls still bore the marks of fire. From the top of the hill, Djata [a nickname for Sundiata] looked on Niani, which looked like a dead city. . . . The survivors of the catastrophe were standing in rows on the Mali road. The children were waving branches, a few young women were singing, but the adults were mute. . . .

With Sundiata peace and happiness entered Niani. Lovingly Sogolon's son [i.e., Sundiata] had his native city rebuilt. He restored in the ancient style his father's old enclosure where he had grown up. People came from all the villages of Mali to settle in Niani. The walls had to be destroyed to enlarge the town, and new quarters were built for each kin group in the enormous army. . . .

In their new-found peace the villages knew prosperity again, for with Sundiata happiness had come into everyone's home. Vast fields of millet, rice, cotton, indigo, and fonio surrounded the villages. Whoever worked always had something to live on. Each year long caravans carried the taxes in kind [in the form of grains] to Niani. You could go from village to village without fearing brigands. A thief would have his right hand chopped off and if he stole again he would be put to the sword [in accordance with Islamic law].

New villages and new towns sprang up in Mali and elsewhere. "Dyulas," or traders, became numerous and during the reign of Sundiata the world knew happiness.

There are some kings who are powerful through their military strength. Everybody trembles before them, but when they die nothing but ill is spoken of them. Others do neither good nor ill and when they die they are forgotten. Others are feared because they have power, but they know how to use it and they are loved because they love justice. Sundiata belonged to this group. He was feared, but loved as well. He was the father of Mali and gave the world peace. After him the world has not seen a greater conqueror, for he was the seventh and last conqueror. He had made the capital of an empire out of his father's village, and Niani became the navel of the earth. In the most distant lands Niani was talked of and foreigners said, "Travellers from Mali can tell lies with impunity," for Mali was a remote country for many peoples.

The griots, fine talkers that they were, used to boast of Niani and Mali saying: "If you want salt, go to Niani, for Niani is the camping place of the [trans-Saharan] caravans. If you want gold, go to Niani, for Bouré, Bambougou, and Wagadou [sources of west African gold] work for Niani. If you want fine cloth, go to Niani, for the Mecca road passed by Niani. If you want fish, go to Niani, for it is there that the fishermen of Maouti and Djenné come to sell their catches. If you want meat, go to Niani, the country of the great hunters, and the land of the ox and the sheep. If you want to see an army, go to Niani, for it [is] there that the united forces of Mali are to be found. If you want to see a great king, go to Niani, for it is there that the son of Sogolon lives, the man with two names."

SOURCE: D. T. Niane, ed. *Sundiata: An Epic of Old Mali.* Trans. by G. D. Pickett. Harlow, England: Longman, 1965, pp. 80–82.

To what extent was Sundiata's support for Islam an issue in the shaping of his reputation?

for example, that native religious specialists practiced magic and kept idols in the woods surrounding the royal palace at Koumbi-Saleh. Even in the absence of efforts to impose Islam on Ghana, however, the faith attracted converts, particularly among those engaged in trade with Muslim merchants from the north.

As the kingdom expanded to the north, it became vulnerable to attacks by nomadic peoples from the Sahara who sought to seize some of the kingdom's wealth. During the early thirteenth century, raids from the desert weakened the kingdom, and it soon collapsed. Several successor states took over portions of Ghana's territory, but political leadership in west Africa fell to the powerful Mali empire, which emerged just as the kingdom of Ghana dissolved.

Sundiata

The lion prince Sundiata (reigned 1230–1255) built the Mali empire during the first half of the thirteenth century after his return from exile. While away from home, he made astute alliances with local rulers, gained a reputation for courage in battle, and assembled a large army dominated by cavalry. By about 1235 he had consolidated his hold on the Mali empire, which embraced Ghana as well as other, neighboring kingdoms in the regions surrounding the Senegal and Niger rivers. The empire included most of the modern state of Mali and extended also to lands now known as Mauritania, Senegal, Gambia, Guinea-Bissau, Guinea, and Sierra Leone.

The Mali Empire and Trade

Mali benefited from trans-Saharan trade on an even larger scale than Ghana did. From the thirteenth until the late fifteenth century, Mali controlled and taxed almost all trade passing through west Africa. Enormous caravans with as many as twenty-five thousand camels linked Mali to north Africa. The capital city of Niani attracted merchants seeking to enter the gold trade, and market cities on the caravan routes like Timbuktu, Gao, and Jenne became prosperous centers featuring buildings of brick and stone. Like the later kings of Ghana, the rulers of Mali honored Islam and provided protection, lodging, and comforts for Muslim merchants from the north. Although they did not force Islam on their realm, they encouraged its spread on a voluntary basis.

Mansa Musa

The significance of trade and Islam for west Africa became clearest during the reign of Sundiata's grand-nephew Mansa Musa, who ruled Mali from 1312 to 1337, during the high point of the empire. Mansa Musa observed Islamic tradition by making his pilgrimage to Mecca in 1324–1325. His party formed a gargantuan caravan that included thousands of soldiers, attendants, subjects, and slaves as well as a hundred camels carrying satchels of gold. Mansa Musa bestowed lavish gifts on those who hosted him along the way, and during his three-month visit to Cairo, he distributed so much gold that the metal's value declined by as much as 25 percent on local markets.

This terra-cotta sculpture from the thirteenth or fourteenth century depicts a helmeted and armored warrior astride a horse with elaborate harness and head protection.

Mansa Musa and Islam

Mansa Musa drew great inspiration from his pilgrimage to Mecca, and upon return to Mali he took his religion even more seriously than before. He built mosques, particularly in the trading cities frequented by Muslim merchants, and he sent promising students to study with distinguished Islamic scholars in north Africa. He also established religious schools and brought in Arabian and north African teachers, including four descendants of Muhammad himself, to make Islam better known in Mali.

Within a century of Mansa Musa's reign, Mali would be in serious decline: factions crippled the central government, provinces seceded from the empire, and military pressures came both from neighboring kingdoms and from desert nomads. By the late fifteenth century, the Songhay empire had completely overcome Mali. Yet Mansa Musa and other Mali rulers had established a tradition of centralized government that the Songhay realm itself would continue, and they had ensured that Islam would have a prominent place in west African society over the long term.

The Indian Ocean Trade and Islamic States in East Africa

While trans-Saharan caravan traffic linked west Africa to the larger trading world of the eastern hemisphere, merchant mariners sailing the sea lanes of the Indian Ocean performed a similar service for coastal east Africa. Indian and Persian sailors had visited the east African coasts after about 500 B.C.E., and Hellenistic and Roman mariners sailed through the Red Sea en route to the same coasts. After the late centuries B.C.E., Malay seafarers also ventured into the western Indian Ocean from their island homelands in southeast Asia, and by the fourth and fifth centuries C.E. they had established colonies on the island of Madagascar. These early visitors had limited opportunities to trade,

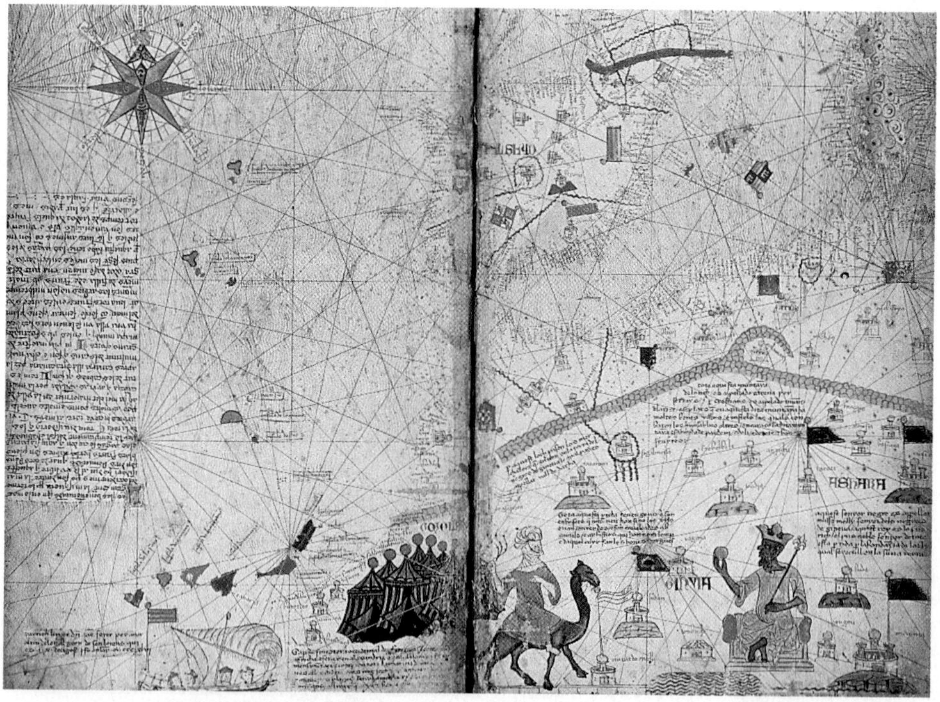

Mansa Musa enjoyed a widespread reputation as the wealthiest king in the world. On this map, prepared in 1375 by a cartographer from the Mediterranean island of Majorca, Mansa Musa holds a gold nugget about the size of a grapefruit.

however, since east African populations consisted mostly of hunting, gathering, and fishing peoples.

By the second century C.E., Bantu peoples had populated much of east Africa. They introduced agriculture, cattle herding, and iron metallurgy to the region, and here, as elsewhere in sub-Saharan Africa, they founded complex societies governed by small, local states. As their population increased, Bantu peoples founded settlements on the coasts and offshore islands as well as the interior regions of east Africa. These coast dwellers supplemented their agricultural production with ocean fishing and maritime trade. They were the builders of Swahili society.

The Swahili

Swahili is an Arabic term meaning "coasters," referring to those who engaged in trade along the east African coast. The Swahili dominated the east African coast from Mogadishu in the north to Kilwa, the Comoro Islands, and Sofala in the south. They spoke Swahili, a Bantu language supplemented with words and ideas borrowed from Arabic. Swahili peoples developed different dialects, but they communicated readily among themselves because individuals frequently visited other Swahili communities in their oceangoing craft. Indeed, all along the east African coast, Swahili society underwent similar patterns of development with respect to language, religion, architecture, and technology.

By the tenth century, Swahili society attracted increasing attention from Islamic merchants. From the interior regions of east Africa, the Swahili obtained gold, slaves, ivory, and exotic local products such as tortoise shells and leopard skins, which they traded for pottery, glass, and textiles that Muslim merchants brought from Persia, India, and China. The rapidly increasing volume and value of trade had large repercussions for Swahili states and societies, just as such changes did for west African societies.

The Swahili City-States

By the eleventh and twelfth centuries, trade had brought tremendous wealth to coastal east Africa. By controlling and taxing trade within their jurisdictions, local chiefs strengthened their own authority and increased the influence of their communities. Gradually, trade concentrated at several coastal and island port cities that enjoyed sheltered or especially convenient locations: Mogadishu, Lamu, Malindi, Mombasa, Zanzibar, Kilwa, Mozambique, and Sofala. Each of these sites developed into a powerful city-state governed by a king who supervised trade and organized public life in the region.

The cities themselves underwent an impressive transformation. Villages in the interior regions of east Africa had buildings made of wood and dried mud, the principal materials used even for prominent structures like mosques. By about the twelfth century, however, Swahili peoples began to construct much larger buildings of coral, and by the fifteenth century the main Swahili towns boasted handsome stone mosques and public buildings. Meanwhile, the ruling elites and wealthy merchants of Swahili trading cities dressed in silk and fine cotton clothes, and they set their tables with porcelain imported from China.

This fine piece of Chinese porcelain, probably produced in the fifteenth century, found its way into a Swahili tomb in modern Dar es Salaam, Tanzania.

Kilwa

Ruins of Kilwa's Great Mosque, built during the thirteenth century, testify to the wealth that Indian Ocean trade brought to the city.

Travelers' reports and recent archaeological discoveries have thrown especially clear light on the development of Kilwa, one of the busiest city-states on the east African coast. The earliest Bantu inhabitants of Kilwa relied mostly on fishing and engaged in a limited amount of trade between about 800 and 1000 C.E. During the next two centuries, they imported pottery and stoneware from other regions in east Africa and began to rely more on agriculture to support their growing numbers. By the early thirteenth century, Kilwans were prosperous enough to erect multistory stone buildings, and they used copper coins to facilitate economic transactions. Between 1300 and 1505, when Portuguese mariners subjected the city to a devastating sack, Kilwa enjoyed tremendous prosperity. The Moroccan traveler Ibn Battuta visited the city in 1331 and reported that Muslim scholars from Arabia and Persia lived at Kilwa and consulted regularly with the local ruler.

With a population of about twelve thousand, Kilwa was a thriving city with many stone buildings and mosques. Residents imported cotton and silk textiles as well as perfumes and pearls from India, and archaeologists have unearthed a staggering amount of Chinese porcelain. Merchants of Kilwa imported these products in exchange for gold, slaves, and ivory obtained from interior regions. By the late fifteenth century, Kilwa exported about a ton of gold per year. Participation in Indian Ocean trade networks brought similar experiences to the other major Swahili cities.

In fact, the influence of long-distance trade passed well beyond the coasts to the interior regions of east Africa. Villagers in the interior did not enjoy the sumptuous lifestyles of the Swahili elites, but trade and the wealth that it brought underwrote the establishment of large and powerful kingdoms in east and central Africa.

Zimbabwe

The best known of these kingdoms was Zimbabwe. The term *zimbabwe* refers simply to the dwelling of a chief. As early as the fifth and sixth centuries C.E., the region occupied by the modern states of Zimbabwe and Mozambique featured many wooden residences known throughout the land as *zimbabwe*. By the ninth century, chiefs had begun to build their *zimbabwe* of stone—indicating an increasingly complex and well-organized society that could invest resources in expensive construction projects. About the early thirteenth century, a magnificent stone complex known as Great Zimbabwe began to arise near Nyanda in the modern state of Zimbabwe. Within stone walls 5 meters (16 feet) thick and 10 meters (32 feet) tall, Great Zimbabwe was a city of stone towers, palaces, and public buildings that served as the capital of a large kingdom situated between the Zambesi and the Limpopo Rivers. At the time of its greatest extent, during the late fifteenth century, up to eighteen thousand people may have lived in the vicinity of the stone complex at Great Zimbabwe, and the kingdom stretched from the outskirts of the Swahili city of Sofala deep into the interior of south-central Africa.

Sources from the Past

Ibn Battuta on Muslim Society at Mogadishu

During the fourteenth century the Moroccan jurist Ibn Battuta traveled throughout much of the eastern hemisphere. Twice he visited sub-Saharan Africa: in 1331 when he traveled along the Swahili coast, and in 1351–1352 when he visited the Mali empire. His account of his visit to the Swahili city of Mogadishu offers insight into the mercantile and social customs of the city as well as the hospitality accorded to distinguished visitors.

[Mogadishu] is a town endless in its size. Its people have many camels, of which they slaughter hundreds every day and they have many sheep. Its people are powerful merchants. In it are manufactured the cloths named after it which have no rival, and are transported as far as Egypt and elsewhere.

One of the customs of the people of this city is that when a ship arrives at the anchorage, the *sunbuqs* (these are small boats) come out to it. In every *sunbuq* is a group of young people of the town, and every one of them brings a covered dish with food in it. He offers it to one of the merchants of the ship and says, "This is my guest." Each one of them does similarly. When the merchant disembarks from the ship he goes nowhere but to the house of his host from among these young people. But a man who has frequented the place a good deal and obtained a knowledge of its people may lodge where he wishes. When he lodges with his host, he [the host] sells his goods for him and buys on his behalf. [Anyone] who buys from [the merchant] at too low a price or sells to him without the presence of his host—that transaction is considered as rejected. There is a profit for them in this custom.

When the young people came to the ship on which I was, one of them came to me. My companions told him, "This is not a merchant but a *faqih* [legal scholar]." He shouted to his companions and said to them, "This is the guest of the *qadi* [Islamic judge]." One of the *qadi*'s people was among them and he informed him of that. The *qadi* came to the shore of the sea with a group of students and sent one of them to me. I disembarked with my travelling companions and saluted the *qadi* and his company. He said to me, "In the name of God, let us go to greet the shaikh." And I said: "Who is the shaikh?" He said, "The sultan." And it is their custom to speak of the sultan as the shaikh. . . .

When I arrived with the *qadi* . . . at the house of the sultan, one of the young men came out and greeted the *qadi* who said to him, "Take this message with which you are entrusted and let the *mawlana* [our master] the shaikh know that this man has come from the land of al-Hijaz [in Arabia]." He did so, then returned bringing with him a dish with some betel leaves and areca nuts on it. He gave me ten leaves and a small quantity of nuts. He gave similarly to the *qadi* and what remained on the dish to my travelling companions and the students of the *qadi*. And he brought a sprinkler of Damascene rose water which he sprinkled over me and the *qadi*. And he said, "*Mawlana* commands that he lodge in the Scholars' House." (This is the house prepared for students of Religious Studies.) . . .

We stayed three days and food was brought to us thrice a day, for that is their custom. When it was the fourth day, a Friday, the *qadi* and the students and one of the *wazirs* of the shaikh came to me. They brought me a suit of their clothing—a silk wrapper to tie around the middle instead of trousers (which they do not know), an upper garment of Egyptian linen with markings, a lined gown of Jerusalem material, and an Egyptian turban with embroideries. They also brought garments for my companions befitting their circumstances. We went to the grand mosque and prayed behind the *maqsura* [private box for the sultan]. When the shaikh came out of the gate of *maqsura,* I greeted him together with the *qadi*. He welcomed me and spoke in their language to the *qadi*. Then he said [to me] in the Arabic language, "You are most welcome. You have honoured our country and given us pleasure."

SOURCE: Said Hamdun and Noel King, eds. *Ibn Battuta in Black Africa*. Princeton: Markus Wiener, 1998, pp. 15–19.

From Ibn Battuta's report, how could you characterize the role of hospitality on the Swahili coast?

Kings residing at Great Zimbabwe controlled and taxed the trade between the interior and coastal regions. They organized the flow of gold, ivory, slaves, and local products from sources of supply to the coast. Their control over these products enabled them to forge alliances with local leaders and to profit handsomely from commercial transactions. Just as the trans-Saharan trade encouraged the building of states and empires in west Africa, the Indian Ocean trade generated wealth that financed the organization of city-states on the coast and large kingdoms in the interior regions of east and central Africa.

Islam in East Africa

In east Africa, again like in west Africa, trade brought cultural as well as political changes. Like their counterparts in west Africa, the ruling elites and the wealthy merchants of east Africa converted to the Islamic faith. They did not necessarily give up their religious and cultural traditions but, rather, continued to observe them for purposes of providing cultural leadership in their societies. By adopting Islam, however, they laid a cultural foundation for close cooperation with Muslim merchants trading in the Indian Ocean basin. Moreover, Islam served as a fresh source of legitimacy for their rule, since they gained recognition from Islamic states in southwest Asia, and their conversion opened the door to political alliances with Muslim rulers in other lands. Even though the conversion of elite classes did not bring about the immediate spread of Islam throughout their societies, it enabled Islam to establish a presence in east Africa under the sponsorship of some particularly influential patrons. The faith eventually attracted interest in larger circles and became one of the principal cultural and religious traditions of east Africa.

African Society and Cultural Development

By the eleventh century C.E., Africa was a land of enormous diversity. The peoples of sub-Saharan Africa spoke some eight hundred different languages, and the continent supported a wide variety of societies and economies: mobile bands of hunting and gathering peoples, fishing peoples who lived alongside the continent's lakes and coasts, nomadic herders, subsistence farmers who migrated periodically to fresh lands, settled cultivators, and city-based societies that drew their livelihoods from mining, manufacturing, and trade. Although this diversity makes it difficult to speak of African society and cultural development in general terms, certain social forms and cultural patterns appeared widely throughout sub-Saharan Africa.

Social Classes

In kingdoms, empires, and city-states, such as Kongo, Mali, and Kilwa, respectively, African peoples developed complex societies with clearly defined classes: ruling elites, military nobles, administrative officials, religious authorities, wealthy merchants, artisans, business entrepreneurs, common people, peasants, and slaves. These societies more or less resembled those found in other settled, agricultural lands of Eurasia organized by powerful states.

In the small states and kin-based societies of sub-Saharan Africa, however, social structures were different. Small states often generated an aristocratic or ruling elite, and they always recognized a class of religious authorities. Outside the larger states and empires, however, generally speaking, kinship, sex and gender expectations, and age groupings were the principal considerations that determined social position in sub-Saharan Africa.

Kinship Groups

Extended families and clans served as the main foundation of social and economic organization in small-scale agricultural societies. Unlike most societies in north Africa

An illustration from a seventeenth-century missionary account shows an African blacksmith (seated at right) working at his forge while an attendant (seated at left) uses a bellows to pump air into the furnace.

and Eurasia, the institution of privately owned property did not exist in sub-Saharan Africa. Instead, communities claimed rights to land and used it in common. The villages of sub-Saharan Africa, where most of the population lived, generally consisted of several extended family groups. Male heads of families jointly governed the village and organized the work of their own groups. They allocated portions of the communal lands for their relatives to cultivate and were responsible for distributing harvests equitably among all members of their groups. Thus most villagers functioned in society first as members of a family or clan.

Sex and Gender Relations

Sex and gender relations also influenced the roles individuals played in society. Sex largely determined work roles. Workers with special skills were mostly men. Leather tanning, for example, was the work of men who carefully guarded knowledge of their techniques and tanning compounds, which they passed down to their heirs. Iron working was a highly prestigious skill in many African societies because blacksmiths knew the secrets of turning ores into useful objects such as knives, hoes, spearheads, and swords. Blacksmiths often served as community leaders, and like leather tanners, they passed knowledge of their craft down to their heirs. Women in blacksmith families often served as potters for their communities. They too enjoyed special prestige because of their ability to transform ingredients from the earth into useful pottery vessels. Men usually undertook the heavy labor of clearing land and preparing it for cultivation. Both men and women participated in the planting and harvesting of crops, and women also tended to domestic chores and took primary responsibility for child rearing.

Women's Roles

As in other societies, men largely monopolized public authority. Yet women in sub-Saharan Africa generally had more opportunities open to them than did their counterparts in other lands. Women enjoyed high honor as the sources of life. On at least a few occasions, women made their ways to positions of power, and aristocratic

The massive stone complex of Great Zimbabwe, which featured very fine construction techniques, required the services of numerous expert masons and other craftsmen.

women often influenced public affairs by virtue of their prominence within their own families. Women merchants commonly traded at markets, and they participated actively in both local and long-distance trade in Africa. Sometimes women even engaged in combat and organized all-female military units.

The arrival of Islam did not change the status of women in sub-Saharan Africa as dramatically as it did in Arabia and southwest Asia. South of the Sahara, early converts to Islam came mostly from the ranks of the ruling elites and the merchant classes. Because it did not become a popular faith for several centuries after its introduction, Islam did not deeply influence the customs of most Africans. Even at royal courts where Islam attracted eager converts, Muslims of sub-Saharan Africa simply did not honor the same social codes as their counterparts in Arabia, southwest Asia, and north Africa. In a few societies upper-class Muslim women wore veils and led secluded lives. For the most part, however, Muslim women in sub-Saharan Africa socialized freely with men outside their immediate families, and they continued to appear and work openly in society in ways not permitted to women in other Islamic lands. Thus Islam did relatively little to curtail the opportunities available to women or to compromise their status in sub-Saharan Africa.

Age Grades

Apart from kinship and expectations based on sex and gender roles, African society also made a place for age groups that included all individuals within a given community born within a few years of one another. Historical linguistic analysis suggests that the recognition of these age grades, or age sets, arose in the early days of agricultural society in the Sudan, and it is clear that in many African societies the practice of grouping individuals into age grades has continued into recent times. Members of age grades performed tasks appropriate for their levels of development, and they often bonded with one another to form tight circles of friends and political allies. Members of an age grade might provide labor for community projects, for example, or take joint responsibility for looking after village elders. They aided members who experienced adversities and helped one another at crucial junctures, such as marriage and the building of a new household. Thus age grades had the effect of establishing social ties that crossed the lines of family and kinship.

Slavery

One class of individuals stood apart from the other social groups: slaves. As in other lands, the institution of slavery had a place in Africa since remote antiquity. Most slaves were captives of war. Others came from the ranks of debtors, suspected witches, and criminals. Within Africa most slaves probably worked as agricultural laborers, although many also worked as construction laborers, miners, or porters.

Slaves were an important form of personal wealth in sub-Saharan Africa. Although the absence of private property prevented people from becoming wealthy through the accumulation of landholdings, the accumulation of slaves enabled individuals or families to increase their agricultural production and also to enhance their positions in society. Thus slave trading and slave holding were prominent features of sub-Saharan African society.

Slave Trading

After about the ninth century C.E., the expansion of the trans-Saharan and Indian Ocean trade networks stimulated increased traffic in African slaves. Muslim merchants provided access to markets in India, Persia, southwest Asia, and the Mediterranean basin where the demand for slaves outstripped the supply available from eastern Europe, previously the main source of slaves. As a result, merchants from northern lands traded in sub-Saharan Africa not only for gold, ivory, and exotic local products but also for slaves.

In response to this demand, slave raiding became an increasingly prominent activity within Africa itself. Rulers of large-scale states and empires began to make war on smaller states and kin-based societies, which could not defend themselves effectively against better organized neighbors, in search of captives destined for northern slave markets. In some years, ten thousand to twenty thousand Africans left their homes as slaves. During the mid-fourteenth century, the Moroccan traveler Ibn Battuta crossed the Sahara desert in a caravan that included six hundred slaves bound for north Africa and the Mediterranean basin. Mansa Musa of Mali set out on his pilgrimage to Mecca with five hundred slaves, many of whom he distributed along the way as gifts to his hosts. Other slaves departed from the coastal cities of east Africa for destinations in Persia and India.

The Zanj Revolt

Records of this slave trade are scarce, but a lengthy uprising known as the Zanj revolt throws light on the nature of African slavery in Muslim lands. The term *Zanj* referred to black slaves from the Swahili coast. At least by the seventh century C.E., many Zanj slaves labored under extremely difficult conditions in southern Mesopotamia, where they worked on sugarcane plantations or cleared land of salt deposits to prepare it for cultivation. On several occasions they mounted revolts, which Muslim authorities promptly snuffed. Following a series of riots, in about 869 a rebel slave named Ali bin Muhammad organized about fifteen thousand Zanj slaves into a massive force that captured Basra, the most important city of southern Mesopotamia, and even established a rebel state in the region. Distracted by other threats, the Abbasid rulers of Mesopotamia turned their full attention to the rebellion only in 879, a full decade after it had begun. By 883 they had crushed the revolt, killed Ali bin Muhammad, and executed the other rebel leaders. Despite its ultimate collapse, the fourteen-year Zanj revolt clearly demonstrated that African slavery was a prominent feature of Muslim society.

Though smaller than the Atlantic slave trade of modern times, the Islamic slave trade was a sizable affair: between 750 and 1500 C.E. the number of African slaves transported to foreign lands may have exceeded ten million. The high demand led to the creation of networks within Africa that supplied slaves and served as a foundation for the Atlantic slave trade in later centuries.

African Religion

Peoples of sub-Saharan Africa developed a wide range of languages, societies, and cultural traditions. Religious beliefs and practices in particular took many forms. The continent's peoples referred to their deities by different names, told different stories about them, and honored them with different rituals. Yet certain features were common to many religions of sub-Saharan Africa. In combination, these features offer considerable insight into the cultural and religious climate of sub-Saharan Africa in premodern times.

Creator God

Many African peoples had held monotheistic beliefs from the early days of Sudanic agriculture. Their beliefs did not persist unchanged through the centuries. To the contrary, they underwent considerable development as individual peoples learned about deities honored in other societies or as they sought their own improved understandings of the gods and their roles in the world. Nevertheless, many peoples recognized a single divine force or male god as the agent responsible for setting the world in motion and providing it with order. Some peoples believed that this god also sustained the world, intervening indirectly, through spirits, to influence the course of human affairs. Some considered this deity to be all-powerful, others regarded him as all-knowing, and many considered him both omnipotent and omniscient.

Lesser Gods and Spirits

Apart from the superior creator god, Africans recognized many lesser gods and spirits often associated with the sun, wind, rain, trees, rivers, and other natural features. Unlike the creator god, these lesser deities participated actively in the workings of the world. They could confer or withhold benefits and bring favor or injury to humans. Similarly, most Africans believed that the souls of departed ancestors had the power to intervene in the lives and experiences of their descendants: the departed could shape events to the advantage of descendants who behaved properly and honored their ancestors and bring misfortune as punishment for evil behavior and neglect of their ancestors' memory. Much of the ritual of African religions focused on honoring of deities, spirits, or ancestors' souls to win their favor or regain their goodwill.

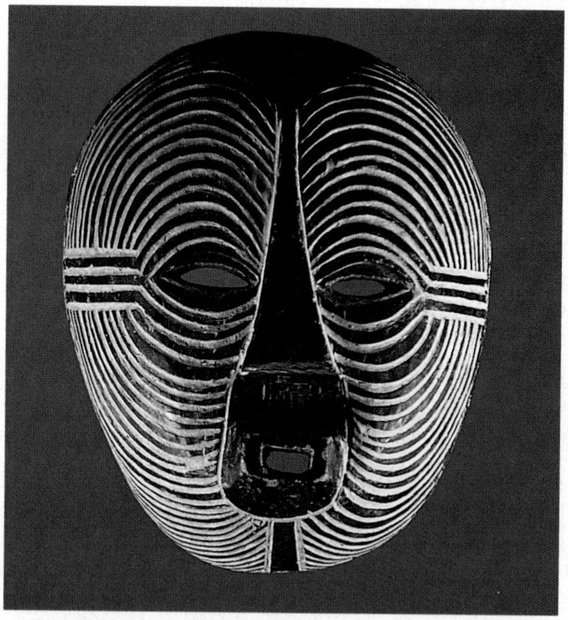

Entrancing and enthralling masks like this one from Congo were essential to the proper observance of religious rituals, which often involved communicating with natural or animal spirits. Masks transformed diviners and provided them with powers not accessible to normal humans.

The rituals included prayers, animal sacrifices, and ceremonies marking important stages of life—such as birth, circumcision, marriage, and death.

Diviners

Like other peoples of the world, Africans recognized classes of religious specialists—individuals who by virtue of their innate abilities or extensive training had the power to mediate between humanity and supernatural beings. Often referred to as diviners, they were intelligent people, usually men though sometimes women as well, who understood clearly the networks of political, social, economic, and psychological relationships within their communities. When afflicted by illness, sterility, crop failure, or some other disaster, individuals or groups consulted diviners to learn the cause of their misfortune. Diviners then consulted oracles, identified the causes of the trouble, and prescribed medicine, rituals, or sacrifices designed to eliminate the problem and bring about a return to normality.

For the most part, African religion did not concern itself with matters of theology but, rather, with the more practical business of explaining, predicting, and controlling the experiences of individuals and groups in the world. Thus African religion strongly emphasized morality and proper behavior as essential to the maintenance of an orderly world. Failure to observe high moral standards would lead to disorder, which would displease deities, spirits, and departed ancestors and ensure that misfortune befell the negligent parties. Because proper moral behavior was so important to their fortunes, family and kinship groups took responsibility for policing their members and disciplining those who fell short of expected standards.

The Arrival of Christianity and Islam

Alongside religions that concentrated on the practical matter of maintaining an orderly world, two religions of salvation won converts in sub-Saharan Africa—Christianity and Islam. Both arrived in Africa as foreign faiths introduced by foreign peoples, and in

The church of St. George at Lalibela, Ethiopia, a massive structure in the form of a cross constructed by excavating the earth and rock surrounding the church itself.

The magnificent mosque at Jenne, constructed in the fourteenth century, served as a principal center of Islamic education and scholarship in the Mali empire.

time the sub-Saharan adherents adapted both faiths to the needs and interests of their societies.

Early Christianity in North Africa

Christianity reached Egypt and north Africa during the first century C.E., soon after the faith's appearance, as it attracted converts throughout the Mediterranean basin. Alexandria in Egypt became one of the most prominent centers of early Christian thought, and north Africa was the home of St. Augustine, among many other leaders of the fledgling church. Yet for several centuries Christianity remained a Mediterranean faith whose appeal did not reach sub-Saharan Africa.

The Christian Kingdom of Axum

About the middle of the fourth century C.E., Christianity established a foothold in the kingdom of Axum, located in the highlands of modern Ethiopia. The first Axumite converts were probably local merchants who traded with Mediterranean Christians calling at the port of Adulis on the Red Sea. As missionaries visited Ethiopia, the kings of Axum also converted to Christianity, possibly in hopes of improving relations with their powerful neighbors to the north in Christian Egypt. Indeed, the kings of Axum were some of the first royal converts to Christianity, adopting the faith shortly after the Roman emperor Constantine himself. Missionaries later established monasteries, translated the Bible into the Ethiopian language, and worked to popularize Christianity throughout the kingdom.

The fortunes of Christianity in Ethiopia reflected the larger political experience of the region. In the late seventh century C.E., the ruling house of Axum fell into decline, and during the next several centuries the expansion of Islam left an isolated island of Christianity in the Ethiopian highlands. During the twelfth century, however, a new ruling dynasty undertook a centralizing campaign and enthusiastically promoted Christianity as a faith that could provide cultural unity for the land. From the twelfth through the sixteenth century, Christianity enjoyed particular favor in Ethiopia. During the twelfth century, the Ethiopian kings ordered the carving of eleven massive churches out of solid rock—a monumental work of construction that required enormous resources and untold hours of labor. During the thirteenth century, rulers of Ethiopia's Solomonic dynasty claimed descent from the Israelite kings David and Solomon in an effort to lend additional biblical luster to their authority. The fictional work *Kebra Negast (The*

Glory of Kings), which undertook to trace this lineage, has recently become popular among Rastafarians and devotees of reggae music in Ethiopia, Jamaica, and other lands as well. Meanwhile, Christianity retained its privileged status in Ethiopia until it fell out of favor following the socialist revolution of 1974.

Ethiopian Christianity

During the centuries after the Islamic conquests of Egypt, the Sudan, and northern Africa, Ethiopian Christians had little contact with Christians in other lands. As a result, although Ethiopian Christianity retained basic Christian theology and rituals, it increasingly reflected the interests of its African devotees. Ethiopian Christians believed that a large host of evil spirits populated the world, for example, and carried amulets or charms for protection against these menacing spirits. The twelfth-century carved-rock churches themselves harked back to pre-Christian values, since rock shrines had been a prominent feature in Ethiopian religion from the second or perhaps even third millennium B.C.E. The rock churches absorbed this tradition into Ethiopian Christianity. Not until the sixteenth century, when Portuguese mariners began to visit Ethiopia en route to India, did Ethiopians reestablish relations with Christians from other lands. By that time the Portuguese had introduced their Roman Catholic faith to the kingdom of Kongo, and Christianity began to win a place for itself elsewhere in sub-Saharan Africa.

Meanwhile, Islam appealed strongly to ruling elites and merchants in sub-Saharan west Africa and coastal east Africa because it served as a cultural foundation for their business relationships with Muslim merchants from north Africa and southwest Asia. Nonetheless, African ruling elites and merchants did not convert to Islam purely for mercenary reasons. To the contrary, the converts often took their new faith seriously. They built mosques, founded religious schools, invited experts in Islamic law into their lands, and displayed real enthusiasm for their adopted faith. Mansa Musa's pilgrimage to Mecca and his support of Islam in Mali represented a devotion to Islam shared by untold numbers of sub-Saharan Muslims.

African Islam

Like Christianity, Islam in sub-Saharan Africa reflected the interests of local converts. Thus as in India, southeast Asia, and other lands, Islam in sub-Saharan Africa made a place for the inherited traditions and beliefs of sub-Saharan Muslims. Africans who converted to Islam continued to take protective measures against the workings of evil spirits and witches, for example, and to participate in rituals designed to please nature deities and the spirits of departed ancestors.

Islam and African Society

Islam also had to accommodate African notions of proper relations between the sexes. When Ibn Battuta visited Mali in the mid-fourteenth century, he took deep offense at casual conversations that women had with men other than their husbands, and he became especially incensed when he observed women going about in public, even at the imperial court, dressed only in loincloths. Yet his hosts, even those who considered themselves pious Muslims, paid no heed to his railings and the lectures he delivered about the proper behavior and dress of women in Islamic society.

Indeed, during the early centuries after its introduction to the region, Islam supplemented rather than replaced the traditional religions of sub-Saharan Africa. West African merchants sometimes adopted Islam when they engaged actively in trade, since a common faith facilitated their dealings with Muslim merchants from other lands, but returned to their inherited traditions when they turned from mercantile to other pursuits. And ruling elites routinely continued to honor inherited religious traditions, which provided powerful sanctions for their rule, long after adopting Islam for the various advantages that it made available to them.

States and societies of sub-Saharan Africa differed considerably from those in other parts of the eastern hemisphere. The foundations of most sub-Saharan societies were the agricultural economy and iron-working skills that Bantu and other peoples spread throughout most of the African continent. As these peoples migrated to new regions and established new communities, they usually based their societies on kin groups rather than state structures that predominated elsewhere in the eastern hemisphere. When different societies came into conflict with one another, however, they increasingly established formal political authorities to guide their affairs. African peoples organized states of various sizes, some very small and others quite large. When they entered into commercial relationships with Muslim peoples in southwest Asia and north Africa, they also built formidable imperial states in west Africa and bustling city-states in coastal east Africa. These states had far-reaching implications for sub-Saharan societies because they depended on a regular and reliable flow of trade goods—particularly gold, ivory, and slaves—and they encouraged African peoples to organize themselves politically and economically to satisfy the demands of foreign Muslim merchants. Trade also had cultural implications because it facilitated the introduction of Islam, which together with native African traditions profoundly influenced the development of sub-Saharan societies. After the eighth century, ruling elites in both west Africa and coastal east Africa mostly accepted Islam and strengthened its position in their societies by building mosques, consulting Muslim advisors, and supporting Islamic schools. By 1500 C.E. African traditions and Islamic influences had combined to fashion a series of powerful, productive, and distinctive societies in sub-Saharan Africa.

CHRONOLOGY

4th century C.E.	Introduction of bananas to Africa
11th to 13th century	Kingdom of Ghana
11th to 15th century	Swahili cities
12th to 15th century	Kingdom of Great Zimbabwe
12th to 16th century	Christian kingdom of Axum
13th to 15th century	Mali empire
1230–1255	Reign of Sundiata
14th to 17th century	Kingdom of Kongo
1312–1337	Reign of Mansa Musa
1324–1325	Mansa Musa's pilgrimage to Mecca

FOR FURTHER READING

Ibn Battuta. *Ibn Battuta in Black Africa.* Ed. and trans. by Said Hamdun and Noel King. Princeton, 1998. Translations of travel accounts of visits to coastal east Africa and the empire of Mali by a famous fourteenth-century Moroccan traveler.

Paul Bohannan and Philip D. Curtin. *Africa and Africans.* 3rd ed. Prospect Heights, Ill., 1988. Exploration of themes in African history, society, and culture by an anthropologist and a historian.

E. W. Bovill. *The Golden Trade of the Moors.* 2nd ed. London, 1968. Popular history of west Africa concentrating on the trans-Saharan caravan trade.

Basil Davidson. *A History of East and Central Africa to the Late Nineteenth Century.* Garden City, N.Y., 1969. Brief survey by a leading popular historian of sub-Saharan Africa.

———. *The Lost Cities of Africa.* Rev. ed. Boston, 1987. Excellent popular account that examines cities of sub-Saharan Africa in the light of archaeological discoveries.

Christopher Ehret. *An African Classical Age: Eastern and Southern Africa in World History, 1000 B.C. to A.D. 400.* Charlottesville, Va., 1998. A path-breaking volume focusing on eastern and southern Africa and drawing on both linguistic and archaeological evidence.

———. *The Civilizations of Africa: A History to 1800.* Charlottesville, Va., 2002. An important contribution that views Africa in the context of world history.

G. S. P. Freeman-Grenville, ed. *The East African Coast: Select Documents from the First to the Nineteenth Century.* Oxford, 1962. Translations of documents illustrating the history of trade and political development in coastal east Africa.

J. F. P. Hopkins and N. Levtzion, eds. *Corpus of Early Arabic Sources for West African History.* Princeton, 2000. Translations of numerous important accounts by Muslim merchants and geographers who reported on conditions in west Africa before modern times.

Mark Horton and John Middleton. *The Swahili: The Social Landscape of a Mercantile Society.* Oxford, 2000. Useful survey that draws on both archaeological and written evidence.

E. Bolaji Idowu. *African Traditional Religion: A Definition.* Maryknoll, N.Y., 1973. Brief survey of traditional African religious beliefs from an African perspective.

Robert W. July. *Precolonial Africa: An Economic and Social History.* New York, 1975. Excellent short analysis of African social and economic history.

Nehemia Levtzion. *Ancient Ghana and Mali.* London, 1973. Concentrates on the political, social, and cultural history of west African kingdoms and empires.

Ali A. Mazrui. *The Africans: A Triple Heritage.* Boston, 1986. Emphasizes the legacies of indigenous, Islamic, and western influences on African history.

John S. Mbiti. *African Religions and Philosophy.* 2nd ed. London, 1990. A thorough and systematic study of traditional African religions in their cultural context.

Roderick James McIntosh. *The Peoples of the Middle Niger: The Island of Gold.* Oxford, 1998. Fascinating volume emphasizing the environmental context of west African history.

John Middleton. *The World of the Swahili: An African Mercantile Civilization.* New Haven, 1992. Rich scholarly analysis that places modern Swahili society and culture in its historical context.

D. T. Niane, ed. *Sundiata: An Epic of Old Mali.* Trans. by G. D. Pickett. London, 1965. Translation of the story of Sundiata, founder of the Mali empire, as preserved in African oral tradition.

Derek Nurse and Thomas Spear. *The Swahili: Reconstructing the History and Language of an African Society, 800–1500.* Philadelphia, 1985. A short but solid and insightful survey of Swahili history.

Roland Oliver and J. D. Fage. *A Short History of Africa.* 6th ed. London, 1988. Brief survey from paleolithic times to the present.

Alexandre Popovic. *The Revolt of African Slaves in Iraq.* Trans. by L. King. Princeton, 1999. Important study of the Zanj revolt of the ninth century.

Jan Vansina. *Paths in the Rainforests: Toward a History of Political Tradition in Equatorial Africa.* Madison, 1990. A brilliant synthesis of early African history by one of the world's foremost historians of Africa.

OLC

See our **Online Learning Center at www.mhhe.com/bentley3** for additional readings, practice maps, quizzes, and internet activities.

PSI

Unfamiliar words? Check out the **Primary Source Investigator CD-ROM** for an interactive glossary, interactive maps, more images, and primary sources.

Cloth merchants cut and sew woolen fabrics in a town market while customers shop and a man receives a shave.

CHAPTER 20

Western Europe during the High Middle Ages

In 1260 C.E. two brothers, Niccolò and Maffeo Polo, traveled from their native Venice to Constantinople. The Polo brothers were jewel merchants, and while in Constantinople, they decided to pursue opportunities farther east. They went first to Soldaia (modern Sudak), near Caffa on the Black Sea, and then to the trading cities of Sarai and Bulghar on the Volga River. At that point they might have returned home except that a war broke out behind them and prevented them from retracing their steps, so they joined a caravan and continued east. They spent three years in the great central Asian trading city of Bokhara, where they received an invitation to join a diplomatic embassy going to the court of Khubilai Khan. They readily agreed and traveled by caravan to the Mongol court, where the great khan received them and inquired about their land, rulers, and religion.

Khubilai was especially interested in learning more about Roman Catholic Christianity, most likely because he ruled a multicultural empire and wished to maintain harmony among the cultural and religious groups inhabiting his realm. Thus he asked the Polo brothers to return to Europe and request the pope to send learned theologians who could serve as authoritative sources of information on Christian doctrine. They accepted the mission and returned to Italy in 1269 as envoys of the great khan.

The Polo brothers were not able to satisfy the great khan's desire for expertise in Christian doctrine. The pope designated two missionaries to accompany the Polos, and the party set out in 1271, together with Niccolò's seventeen-year-old son Marco Polo. Soon, however, the missionaries became alarmed at fighting along the route, and they decided to abandon the embassy and return to Europe. Thus only the Polos completed the journey, arriving at the Mongol court of Shangdu in 1274. Although they presented Khubilai with presents and letters from the pope rather than the requested missionaries, the great khan received them warmly and welcomed them to his court. In fact, they remained in China in the service of the great khan for the next seventeen years. Their mission gave rise to Marco Polo's celebrated account of his travels, and it signaled the reintegration of Europe into the political and economic affairs of the larger eastern hemisphere.

During the early middle ages, western Europe was a violent and disorderly land. The collapse of the western Roman empire and invasions by migratory peoples wrecked European society and economy. The Carolingian empire provided order only for a short time before a new series of invasions brought it down. As a result of the turmoil and disarray that plagued Europe during the half millennium from 500 to 1000 C.E., western Europeans played little role in the development of a hemispheric economy during the era dominated by the Tang, Song, Abbasid, and Byzantine empires.

During the early middle ages, however, Europeans laid the foundations of a more dynamic society. Regional states became the basis for a stable political order. New tools and technologies led to increased agricultural production and economic growth. The missionary efforts of the western Christian church brought cultural and religious unity to most of Europe. During the "high middle ages" of European history—the period from about 1000 to 1300 C.E.—European peoples built a vibrant and powerful society on the political, economic, and cultural foundations laid during the early middle ages.

Although the idea of empire continued to fascinate political thinkers and leaders, empire builders of the high middle ages did not manage to bring all of Europe under their control. Instead, local rulers organized powerful regional states. Increased agricultural production fueled rapid population growth. Economic expansion led to increased long-distance trade, enriched cities, and supported the establishment of new towns. Cultural and religious affairs also reflected the dynamism of the high middle ages, as European philosophers and theologians reconsidered traditional doctrines in light of fresh knowledge.

Political organization, demographic increase, and economic growth pushed Europeans once again into the larger world. European merchants began to participate directly in the commercial economy of the eastern hemisphere, sometimes traveling as far as China in search of luxury goods. Ambitious military and political leaders expanded the boundaries of Christendom by seizing Muslim-held territories in Spain and the Mediterranean islands. European forces even mounted a series of military crusades that sought to bring Islamic lands of the eastern Mediterranean basin under Christian control. They ultimately failed, but the crusades clearly demonstrated that Europeans were beginning to play a much larger role in the world than they had for the previous half millennium.

THE ESTABLISHMENT OF REGIONAL STATES

Long after its disappearance the Roman empire inspired European philosophers, theologians, and rulers, who dreamed of a centralized political structure embracing all of Christian Europe. Beginning in the late tenth century, German princes formed the so-called Holy Roman Empire, which they viewed as a Christian revival of the earlier Roman empire. In fact, however, the Roman empire returned only in name. Whenever the medieval emperors attempted to extend their influence beyond Germany, they faced stiff resistance from the popes and the princes of other European lands. Meanwhile, independent monarchies emerged in France and England, and other authorities ruled in the various regions of Italy and Spain. Thus medieval Europe was a political mosaic of independent and competing regional states. These states frequently clashed with one another, and they all faced perennial challenges from within. Yet they also organized their own territories efficiently, and they laid the political foundations for the emergence of powerful national states in a later era.

The Holy Roman Empire

Otto I

As the Carolingian empire faded during the ninth century, counts, dukes, and other local authorities took responsibility for providing order in their own regions. Gradually, some of them extended their influence beyond their own jurisdictions and built

MAP [20.1]
The regional states of medieval Europe, 1000–1300 C.E.

For an interactive version of this map, go to www.mhhe.com/bentley3ch20maps.

larger states. Otto of Saxony was particularly aggressive. By the mid-tenth century, he had established himself as king in northern Germany. He campaigned east of the Elbe River in lands populated by Slavic peoples (in what is now eastern Germany, western Poland, and the Czech Republic), and twice he ventured into Italy to quell political disturbances, protect the church, and seek opportunities in the south. In appreciation for his aid to the church, Pope John XII proclaimed Otto emperor in 962 C.E. Thus was born the Holy Roman Empire.

The imperial title had considerable cachet, and on several occasions energetic emperors almost transformed the Holy Roman Empire into a hegemonic state that might have reintroduced imperial unity to Europe. Conflict with the papacy, however, prevented the emperors from building a strong and dynamic state. Although the popes crowned the medieval emperors, their relations were usually tense, since both popes and emperors made large claims to authority in Christian Europe. Relations became especially strained when emperors sought to influence the selection of church officials, which the popes regarded as their own prerogative, or when emperors sought to extend their authority into Italy, where the popes had long provided political leadership.

Investiture Contest

Neither the popes nor the emperors were strong enough to dominate the other, but the popes were able to prevent the emperors from building a powerful imperial state that would threaten the papacy as Europe's principal spiritual authority. The capacity of the papacy to weaken the empire became apparent during the Investiture Contest, a controversy over the appointment of church officials in the late eleventh and early twelfth centuries. From the earliest days of the Holy Roman Empire, imperial authorities had named important church officials to their positions, since the higher clergy provided political as well as religious services. In an effort to regain control of the clergy and ensure that church officials met appropriate spiritual criteria, Pope Gregory VII (1073–1085 C.E.) ordered an end to the practice of lay investiture—the selection and installation of church officials by lay rulers such as the emperors. When Emperor Henry IV (1056–1106 C.E.) challenged the pope's policy, Gregory excommunicated him and released his subjects from their duty to obey him. The German princes then took the opportunity to rebel against the emperor. Henry eventually regained control of the empire but only after beseeching Gregory's mercy while standing barefoot in the snow. Because of the pope's intervention in imperial affairs, however, the German princes won concessions that enhanced their independence and diminished the emperor's authority.

Frederick Barbarossa

Popes and emperors clashed over their conflicting interests in Italy as well as over the appointment of church officials. Among the most vigorous of the medieval emperors was Frederick I, known as Frederick Barbarossa—"the red beard"—a vigorous and gallant man who reigned from 1152 to 1190 C.E. Working from his ancestral lands in southern Germany, Barbarossa sought to absorb the wealthy and increasingly urban region of Lombardy in northern Italy. Integration of Lombardy with his German holdings would have provided Barbarossa with the resources to control the German princes, build a powerful state, and dominate much of Europe. This prospect did not appeal to the popes, who marshaled support from other European states on behalf of the Italian cities. By the end of Barbarossa's reign, the papal coalition had forced the emperor to relinquish his rights in Lombardy. Once again, papal policies forestalled the transformation of the Holy Roman Empire into a powerful state.

Voltaire, the eighteenth-century French writer, once quipped that the Holy Roman Empire was "neither holy, nor Roman, nor an empire." Indeed, the Holy Roman Empire was an empire principally in name. In reality, it was a regional state ruling Germany, though it also wielded influence intermittently in eastern Europe and Italy. In no sense, however, did the Holy Roman Empire restore imperial unity to western Europe.

Regional Monarchies in France and England

In the absence of an effective imperial power, regional states emerged throughout medieval Europe. In France and England, princes established regional monarchies on the basis of relationships between lords and their retainers.

Capetian France

The French monarchy grew slowly from humble beginnings. When the last of the Carolingians died, in 987 C.E., the lords of France elected a minor noble named Hugh Capet to serve as king. Capet held only a small territory around Paris, and he was in no position to challenge his retainers, some of whom were far more powerful than the king himself. During the next three centuries, however, his descendants, known as the Capetian kings, gradually added to their resources and expanded their political influence. Relying on relationships between lords and retainers, they absorbed the territories of retainers who died without heirs and established the right to administer justice throughout the realm. By the early fourteenth century, the Capetian kings had gradually centralized power and authority in France.

King Louis IX (reigned 1226–1270), also known as St. Louis, helped to consolidate the Capetian hold on the French monarchy. In this fourteenth-century manuscript illustration, he hears the petitions of humble subjects (right), while hanged criminals (left) serve as a reminder of felony's results.

The Normans

The English monarchy developed quite differently. Its founders were Normans—descendants of Vikings who carved out a state on the peninsula of Normandy in France during the ninth century. Though nominally subject to Carolingian and later to Capetian rulers, the dukes of Normandy in fact pursued their own interests with little regard for their lords. Within Normandy the dukes built a tightly centralized state in which all authority stemmed from the dukes themselves. The dukes also retained title to all land in Normandy, and in an effort to forestall conflicts of interest they strictly limited the right of their retainers to grant land to others.

Norman England

In 1066 Duke William of Normandy invaded England, then ruled by descendants of the Angles, Saxons, and other Germanic peoples who had migrated there during the fifth and sixth centuries. Following a speedy military victory, the duke, now known as William the Conqueror, introduced Norman principles of government and land tenure to England. While retaining many institutions of their Anglo-Saxon predecessors, the Norman kings of England ruled over a much more tightly centralized realm than did the Capetian kings of France.

Both the Capetians and the Normans faced challenges from retainers seeking to pursue independent policies or enlarge their powers at the expense of the monarchs. Both dynasties also faced external challenges: indeed, they often battled each other, since the Normans periodically sought to expand their possessions in France. On the basis of relationships between lords and retainers, however, both the Capetians and the Normans managed to organize regional monarchies that maintained order and provided reasonably good government.

The Bayeux tapestry, a magnificent mural of woven linen about 70 meters (230 feet) long, depicts the Norman invasion and conquest of England in 1066. In this section Norman warriors sail across the English Channel and disembark in southern England.

Regional States in Italy and Iberia

Church Influence in Italy

Regional states emerged also in other lands of medieval Europe, though not on such a large scale as the monarchies of France and England. In Italy, for example, no single regime controlled the entire peninsula. Rather, a series of ecclesiastical states, city-states, and principalities competed for power and position. In central Italy the popes had provided political leadership since the Carolingian era. Indeed, although the papacy was a spiritual rather than a political post, the popes ruled a good-sized territory in central Italy known as the Papal State. In northern Italy, too, the church influenced political affairs, since bishops of the major cities took much of the initiative in organizing public life in their regions. During the high middle ages, however, as the cities grew wealthy from trade and manufacturing, lay classes challenged the bishops and eventually displaced them as ruling authorities.

Italian States

By about the twelfth century, a series of prosperous city-states—including Florence, Bologna, Genoa, Milan, and Venice—dominated not only their own urban districts but also the surrounding hinterlands. Meanwhile, in southern Italy, Norman adventurers—cousins of those who conquered Anglo-Saxon England—invaded territories still claimed by the Byzantine empire and various Muslim states. With papal approval and support, they overcame Byzantine and Muslim authorities, brought southern Italy into the orbit of Roman Catholic Christianity, and laid the foundations for the emergence of the powerful kingdom of Naples.

The Italian city-state of Florence grew rapidly during the high middle ages. This portrait of the city concentrates on the space enclosed by walls completed in the early fourteenth century.

Christian and Muslim States in Iberia

As in Italy, a series of regional states competed for power in the Iberian peninsula. From the eighth to the eleventh centuries, Muslim conquerors ruled most of the peninsula. Only in northern Spain did small Christian states survive the Muslim conquest. Beginning in the mid-eleventh century, though, Christian adventurers from these states began to attack Muslim territories and enlarge their own domains. By the late thirteenth century, the Christian kingdoms of Castile, Aragon, and Portugal controlled most of the Iberian peninsula, leaving only the small kingdom of Granada in Muslim hands.

With its Holy Roman Empire, regional monarchies, ecclesiastical principalities, city-states, and new states founded on conquest, medieval Europe might seem to present a chaotic and confusing political spectacle, particularly when compared to a land such as China, reunified by centralized imperial rule. Moreover, European rulers rarely sought to maintain the current state of affairs but, rather, campaigned constantly to enlarge their holdings at the expense of their neighbors. As a result, the political history of medieval Europe was a complicated affair. Yet the regional states of the high middle ages effectively tended to public affairs in limited regions. In doing so, they fashioned alternatives to a centralized empire as a form of political organization.

Economic Growth and Social Development

As regional states provided increasingly effective political organization, medieval Europe experienced dramatic economic growth and social development. The economic revival closely resembled the processes that in an earlier era had strengthened China, India, and the Islamic world. Increased agricultural production, urbanization, manufacturing, and trade transformed Europe into a powerful society and drew it once again into commercial relationships with distant lands.

Growth of the Agricultural Economy

As in China, India, and the Islamic world during the early postclassical era, a dramatic increase in agricultural yields was the foundation of economic growth and social development in medieval Europe. Several developments help to account for this increased agricultural production: the opening of new lands to cultivation, improved agricultural techniques, the use of new tools and technologies, and the introduction of new crops.

Expansion of Arable Land

Beginning in the late tenth century, as local lords pacified their territories and put an end to invasions, Europe began to experience population pressure. In response serfs and monks cleared forests, drained swamps, and increased the amount of land devoted to agriculture. At first the lords opposed these efforts, since they reduced the amount of land available for game preserves, where nobles enjoyed hunting wild animals. Gradually, however, the lords realized that expanding agricultural production would yield higher taxes and increase their own wealth. By the early twelfth century, lords were encouraging the expansion of cultivation, and the process gathered momentum.

Improved Agricultural Techniques

Meanwhile, reliance on improved methods of cultivation and better agricultural technology led to significantly higher productivity. During the high middle ages, European cultivators refined and improved their techniques in the interests of larger yields. They experimented with new crops and with different cycles of crop rotation to ensure the most abundant harvests possible without compromising the fertility of the soil. They increased cultivation especially of beans, which not only provided dietary protein but also enriched the land because of their property of fixing nitrogen in the soils where they grow. They kept more domestic animals, which not only served as beasts of burden and sources of food but also enriched fields with their droppings. They dug ponds in which they raised fish, which provided yet another dietary supplement. By the thirteenth century, observation and experimentation with new crops and new techniques had vastly increased understanding of agricultural affairs. News of these discoveries circulated widely throughout Europe in books and treatises on household economics and agricultural methods. Written in vernacular languages for lay readers, these works helped to publicize innovations, which in turn led to increased agricultural productivity.

New Tools and Technologies

During the high middle ages, European peoples expanded their use of watermills and heavy plows, which had appeared during the early middle ages, and also introduced new tools and technologies. Two simple items in particular—the horseshoe and the horse collar—made it possible to increase sharply the amount of land that cultivators could work. Horseshoes helped to prevent softened and split hooves on horses that tramped through moist European soils. Horse collars placed the burden of a heavy load on an animal's chest and shoulders rather than its neck and enabled horses to pull heavy plows without choking. Thus Europeans could hitch their plows to horses rather than to slower oxen and bring more land under the plow.

New Crops

Expansion of land under cultivation, improved methods of cultivation, and the use of new tools and technologies combined to increase both the quantity and the quality of food supplies. During the early middle ages, the European diet consisted almost entirely of grains and grain products such as gruel and bread. During the centuries from 1000 to 1300, meat, dairy products, fish, vegetables, and legumes such as beans and peas became much more prominent in the European diet, though without displacing grains as staple foods. Spain, Italy, and other Mediterranean lands benefited also from widespread cultivation of crops that had earlier been disseminated through the Islamic world: hard durum wheat, rice, spinach, artichokes, eggplant, lemons, limes, oranges, and melons all became prominent items in Mediterranean diets during the high middle ages.

Population Growth

As in other lands, increased agricultural productivity supported rapid population growth in medieval Europe. In 800 C.E., during the Carolingian era, European population stood at about twenty-nine million. By 1000, when regional states had ended invasions and restored order, it had edged up to thirty-six million. During the next few centuries, as the agricultural economy expanded, population burgeoned. By 1100 it had reached forty-four million; by 1200 it had risen to fifty-eight million, an increase of more than 30 percent within one century; and by 1300 it had grown an additional 36 percent to seventy-nine million. During the fourteenth century, epidemic plague severely reduced populations and disrupted economies in Europe as well as Asia and north Africa—a development discussed in chapter 22. Between 1000 and 1300, however, rapid demographic growth helped stimulate a vigorous revival of towns and trade in medieval Europe.

The Revival of Towns and Trade

Urbanization

With abundant supplies of food, European society was able to support large numbers of urban residents—artisans, crafts workers, merchants, and professionals. Attracted by urban opportunities, peasants and serfs from the countryside flocked to established

Venice, home of Marco Polo and a legion of merchants, drew enormous prosperity from trade. Street vendors, shopkeepers, and merchant ships figure prominently in this illustration from a fourteenth-century manuscript.

cities and founded new towns at strategically located sites. Cities founded during Roman times, such as Paris, London, and Toledo, became thriving centers of government and business, and new urban centers emerged from Venice in northern Italy to Bergen on the west coast of Norway. Northern Italy and Flanders (the northwestern part of modern Belgium) experienced especially strong urbanization. For the first time since the fall of the western Roman empire, cities began to play a major role in European economic and social development.

Textile Production

The growth of towns and cities brought about increasing specialization of labor, which in turn resulted in dramatic expansion of manufacturing and trade. Manufacturing concentrated especially on the production of wool textiles. The cities of Italy and Flanders in particular became lively centers for the spinning, weaving, and dyeing of wool. Trade in wool products helped to fuel economic development throughout Europe. By the twelfth century the counts of Champagne in northern France sponsored fairs that operated almost year-round and that served as vast marketplaces where merchants from all parts of Europe compared and exchanged goods.

Genoese bankers change money and check the accounts of their clients in this fourteenth-century manuscript illustration.

Mediterranean Trade

The revival of urban society was most pronounced in Italy, which was geographically well situated to participate in the trade networks of the Mediterranean basin. During the tenth century the cities of Amalfi and Venice served as ports for merchants engaged in trade with Byzantine and Muslim partners in the eastern Mediterranean. During the next century the commercial networks of the Mediterranean widened to embrace Genoa, Pisa, Naples, and other Italian cities. Italian merchants exchanged salt, olive oil, wine, wool fabrics, leather products, and glass for luxury goods such as gems, spices, silk, and other goods from India, southeast Asia, and China that Muslim merchants brought to eastern Mediterranean markets.

As trade expanded, Italian merchants established colonies in the major ports and commercial centers of the Mediterranean and the Black Sea. By the thirteenth century, Venetian and Genoese

Sources from the Past

Francesco Balducci Pegolotti on Trade between Europe and China

Francesco Balducci Pegolotti was an employee of a Florentine banking company. He traveled as far as London and Cyprus on bank business. Although he probably did not travel to Asia, Pegolotti learned about conditions that long-distance traders faced from many merchants who ventured far from home. About 1340 Pegolotti compiled their reports into a book of information and advice for merchants traveling to China from the port of Tana (modern Rostov) on the Sea of Azov.

In the first place, you must let your beard grow long and not shave. And at Tana you should furnish yourself with a dragoman [guide and interpreter]. And you must not try to save money in the matter of dragomen by taking a bad one instead of a good one. For the additional wages of the good one will not cost you so much as you will save by having him. And besides the dragoman it will be well to take at least two good men servants who are acquainted with the [Turkish] Cumanian tongue. . . .

The road you travel from Tana to Cathay [China] is perfectly safe, whether by day or by night, according to what the merchants say who have used it. Only if the merchant, in going or coming, should die upon the road, everything belonging to him will become the perquisite of the lord of the country in which he dies, and the officers of the lord will take possession of all. And in like manner if he die in Cathay. But if his brother be with him, or an intimate friend and comrade calling himself his brother, then to him they will surrender the property of the deceased, and so it will be rescued. . . .

Cathay is a province which contains a multitude of cities and towns. Among others there is one in particular, that is to say the capital city, to which is great resort of merchants, and in which there is a vast amount of trade; and this city is called Khanbaliq. And the said city hath a circuit of one hundred miles, and is all full of people and houses and of dwellers in the said city.

You may calculate that a merchant with a dragoman and two men servants and with goods to the value of twenty-five thousand golden florins should spend on his way to Cathay from sixty to eighty ingots of silver, and not more if he manages well; and for all the road back again from Cathay to Tana, including the expenses of living and the pay of servants, and all other charges, the cost will be about five ingots per head of pack animals, or something less. And you may reckon the ingot to be worth five golden florins. . . .

Anyone from Genoa or Venice wishing to go to the places above named and to make the journey to Cathay should carry linens with him, and if he visits Urgench [in modern Uzbekistan] he will dispose of these well. In Urgench he should purchase ingots of silver, and with these he should proceed without making any further investment, unless it be some bales of the very finest stuffs which go in small bulk, and cost no more for carriage than coarser stuffs would do.

Whatever silver the merchants may carry with them as far as Cathay the lord of Cathay will take from them and put into his treasury. And to merchants who thus bring silver they give that paper money of theirs in exchange. This is of yellow paper, stamped with the seal of the lord aforesaid. And this money is called balishi; and with this money you can readily buy silk and all other merchandise that you have a desire to buy. And all the people of the country are bound to receive it. And yet you shall not pay a higher price for your goods because your money is of paper. And of the said paper money there are three kinds, one being worth more than another, according to the value which has been established for each by that lord.

SOURCE: Henry Yule and Henri Cordier, eds. *Cathay and the Way Thither*, 2nd ed., 4 vols. London: Hakluyt Society, 1913–16, 3:151–55. (Translation slightly modified.)

On the basis of Pegolotti's report, how could you characterize the various commercial, financial, and economic risks faced by European merchants traveling to China and trading there?

merchants maintained large communities in Constantinople, Alexandria, Cairo, Damascus, and the Black Sea ports of Tana, Caffa, and Trebizond. Caffa was the first destination of the Venetian brothers Niccolò and Maffeo Polo when they embarked on their commercial venture of 1260. These trading posts enabled them to deal with Muslim merchants engaged in the Indian Ocean and overland trade with India, southeast Asia, and China. By the mid-thirteenth century the Polos and a few other Italian merchants were beginning to venture beyond the eastern Mediterranean region to central Asia, India, and China in search of commercial opportunities.

The Hanseatic League

Although medieval trade was most active in the Mediterranean basin, a lively commerce grew up also in the northern seas. The Baltic Sea and the North Sea were sites of a particularly well-developed trade network known as the Hanseatic League, or more simply as the Hansa—an association of trading cities stretching from Novgorod to London and embracing all the significant commercial centers of Poland, northern Germany, and Scandinavia. The Hansa dominated trade in grain, fish, furs, timber, and pitch from northern Europe. The fairs of Champagne and the Rhine, Danube, and other major European rivers linked the Hansa trade network with that of the Mediterranean.

Improved Business Techniques

As in postclassical China and the Islamic world, a rapidly increasing volume of trade encouraged the development of credit, banking, and new forms of business organization in Europe. Bankers issued letters of credit to merchants traveling to distant markets, thus freeing them from the risk and inconvenience of carrying cash or bullion. Having arrived at their destinations, merchants exchanged their letters of credit for merchandise or cash in the local currency. In the absence of credit and banking, it would have been impossible for merchants to trade on a large scale.

Meanwhile, merchants devised new ways of spreading and pooling the risks of commercial investments. They entered into partnerships with other merchants, and they limited the liability of partners to the extent of their individual investments. The limitation on individual liability encouraged the formation of commercial partnerships, thus further stimulating the European economy.

Social Change

The Three Estates

Medieval social commentators frequently held that European society embraced three estates or classes: "those who pray, those who fight, and those who work." Those who prayed were clergy of the Roman Catholic church. From lowly parish priests to bishops, cardinals, and popes, the clergy constituted a spiritual estate owing its loyalty to the church rather than secular rulers. The fighters came from the ranks of nobles. They inherited their positions in society and received an education that concentrated on equestrian skills and military arts. Finally, there were those who worked—the vast majority of the population—who mostly cultivated land as peasants dependent for protection on their lords, those who fought.

The formula dividing society neatly into three classes captures some important truths about medieval Europe. It clearly reflects a society marked by political, social, and economic inequality: although they did not necessarily lead lives of luxury, those who prayed and those who fought enjoyed rights and honors denied to those who worked. Though bound by secular law, for example, clerics were members of an international spiritual society before they were subjects of a lord, and if they became involved in legal difficulties, they normally faced courts of law administered by the church rather than secular rulers. For their part the nobles mostly lived off the surplus production of dependent peasants and serfs.

Chivalry

Yet, while expressing some truths, the formula overlooks processes that brought considerable change to medieval European society. Within the ranks of the nobles, for example, an emphasis on chivalry and courtly behavior gradually introduced expectations of high ethical standards and refined manners that encouraged warriors to become cultivated leaders of society. Chivalry was an informal but widely recognized code of ethics and behavior considered appropriate for nobles. Church officials originally promoted the chivalric code in an effort to curb fighting within Christendom. By the twelfth century the ritual by which a young man became initiated into the nobility as a knight commonly called for the candidate to place his sword upon a church altar and pledge his service to God. Thus, rather than seeking wealth and power, the noble who observed the chivalric code would devote himself to the causes of order, piety, and the Christian faith.

Troubadours

Aristocratic women found the chivalric code much to their liking, and they went to some lengths to spread its values. Instead of emphasizing the code's religious dimensions, however, they promoted refined behavior and tender, respectful relations between the sexes. Reflections of their interests survive in the songs and poems of the troubadours, a class of traveling poets, minstrels, and entertainers whom aristocratic women enthusiastically patronized. The troubadours, who were most active in southern France and northern Italy, drew inspiration from a long tradition of love poetry produced in nearby Muslim Spain. Many troubadours visited the expanding Christian kingdoms of Spain, where they heard love poems and songs from servants, slaves, and musicians of Muslim ancestry. Enchanted by this refined literature, they began to produce similar verses for their own aristocratic patrons.

Eleanor of Aquitaine

During the late twelfth and thirteenth centuries, troubadours traveled from one aristocratic court to another, where noblewomen rewarded them for singing songs and reciting verses that celebrated passionate love between a man and a woman. Troubadours flocked especially to Poitiers where Eleanor of Aquitaine (1122–1204) liberally supported romantic poets and entertainers. Eleanor was the most celebrated woman of her day, and she used her influence to encourage the cultivation of good manners, refinement, and romantic love. The troubadours' performances did not instantly transform rough warriors into polished courtiers. Over a long term, however, the code of chivalry and the romantic poetry and song presented at aristocratic courts gradually softened the manners of the nobility.

Independent Cities

Social change also touched those who worked. By the twelfth century the ranks of workers included not only peasants but also increasing numbers of merchants, artisans, crafts workers, and professionals such as physicians and lawyers who filled the growing towns of medieval Europe. The expansion of the urban working population promoted the development of towns and cities as jurisdictions that fit awkwardly in the framework of the medieval political order. Because of their military power, lords could dominate small towns and tax their wealth. As towns grew larger, however, urban populations were increasingly able to resist the demands of nobles and guide their own affairs. By the late eleventh century, inhabitants of prosperous towns were demanding that local lords grant them charters of incorporation that exempted them from political regulation, allowed them to manage their own affairs, and abolished taxes and tolls on commerce within the urban district. Sometimes groups of cities organized leagues to advance their commercial interests, as in the case of the Hansa, or to protect themselves against the encroachments of political authorities.

Guilds

The cities of medieval Europe were by no means egalitarian societies: cities attracted noble migrants as well as peasants and serfs, and urban nobles often dominated city affairs. Yet medieval towns and cities also reflected the interests and contributions

Women were prominent in the markets of medieval Europe and sometimes worked as bankers or tailors, as in this manuscript illustration.

of the working classes. Merchants and workers in all the arts, crafts, and trades organized guilds that regulated the production and sale of goods within their jurisdictions. By the thirteenth century the guilds had come to control much of the urban economy of medieval Europe. They established standards of quality for manufactured goods, sometimes even requiring members to adopt specific techniques of production, and they determined the prices at which members had to sell their products. In an effort to maintain a balance between supply and demand—and to protect their members' interests—they also regulated the entry of new workers into their groups.

Guilds had social as well as economic significance. They provided a focus for friendship and mutual support in addition to work. Guild members regularly socialized with one another, and prosperous guilds often built large halls where members held meetings, banquets, and sometimes boisterous drinking parties. Guilds often came to the aid of members and their families by providing financial and moral support for those who fell ill. They also arranged funeral services for their deceased and provided support for survivors. Quite apart from regulating work, then, guilds constituted a kind of social infrastructure that made it possible for medieval cities to function.

Urban Women

Women who lived in the countryside continued to perform the same kinds of tasks that their ancestors tended to in the early middle ages: household chores, weaving, and the care of domestic animals. But medieval towns and cities offered fresh opportunities for women as well as for men. In the patriarchal society of medieval Europe, few routes to public authority were open to women, but in the larger towns and cities women worked alongside men as butchers, brewers, bakers, candle makers, fishmongers, shoemakers, gemsmiths, innkeepers, launderers, money changers, merchants, and occasionally physicians and pharmacists. Women dominated some occupations, particularly those involving textiles and decorative arts, such as sewing, spinning, weaving, and the making of hats, wigs, and fur garments.

Most guilds admitted women into their ranks, and some guilds had exclusively female memberships. In thirteenth-century Paris, for example, there were approximately one hundred guilds. Six of them admitted only women, but another eighty included women as well as men among their members. The increasing prominence of women in European society illustrates the significance of towns and cities as agents of social change in medieval Europe.

European Christianity during the High Middle Ages

Roman Catholic Christianity guided European thought on religious, moral, and ethical matters. Representatives of the Roman church administered the rituals associated with birth, marriage, and death. Most of the art, literature, and music of the high middle ages drew inspiration from Christian doctrines and stories. Just as mosques and minarets defined the skylines of Muslim cities, the spires of churches and cathedrals dominated the landscape of medieval Europe, testifying visually to the importance of religion and the pervasive presence of the Roman Catholic church.

Western Christianity changed in several ways between 1000 and 1300. As the Roman Catholic church developed an identity distinct from the Eastern Orthodox church, western theologians became reacquainted with the works of Aristotle—mostly unknown to European scholars of the early middle ages—and they produced an impressive synthesis of Aristotelian philosophy and Christian values. Meanwhile, lay classes elaborated a rich tradition of popular religion. Some popular religious movements posed challenges to Roman Catholicism by advocating theological and institutional changes that would have thoroughly transformed the established church. For the most part, however, popular religion remained within the bounds of Roman Catholic orthodoxy and represented an effort to express Christianity in terms meaningful to the laity of medieval Europe.

Schools, Universities, and Scholastic Theology

During the early middle ages, European society was not stable and wealthy enough to support institutions of advanced education. Monasteries sometimes maintained schools that provided a rudimentary education, and political leaders occasionally supported scholars who lived at their courts, but very few schools offered formal education beyond an elementary level. In the absence of a widely observed curriculum or course of study, early medieval scholars drew their inspiration from the Bible and from major spokesmen of the early Christian church such as St. Augustine of Hippo.

Cathedral Schools

During the high middle ages, economic development sharply increased the wealth of Europe and made more resources available for education. Meanwhile, an increasingly complex society created a demand for educated individuals who could deal with complicated political, legal, and theological issues. Beginning in the early eleventh century, bishops and archbishops in France and northern Italy organized schools in their cathedrals and invited well-known scholars to serve as master teachers. Schools in the cathedrals of Paris, Chartres, and Bologna in particular attracted students from all parts of Europe.

A manuscript illustration depicts a professor, at top left, lecturing in a medieval German university. About half the students listen and take notes diligently, while the others catch up on their sleep or chat with friends.

By the twelfth century the cathedral schools had established formal curricula based on writings in Latin, the official language of the Roman Catholic church. Instruction concentrated on the liberal arts, especially literature and philosophy. Students read the Bible and the writings of the church fathers, such as St. Augustine, St. Jerome, and St. Ambrose, as well as classical Latin literature and the few works of Plato and Aristotle that were available in Latin translation. Some cathedral schools also offered advanced instruction in law, medicine, and theology.

Universities

About the mid-twelfth century, students and teachers organized academic guilds and persuaded political authorities to grant charters guaranteeing their rights. Student guilds demanded fair treatment for students from townspeople, who sometimes charged excessive rates for room and board, and called on their teachers to provide rigorous, high-quality instruction. Faculty guilds sought to vest teachers with the right to bestow academic degrees, which served as licenses to teach in other cities, and to control the curriculum in their own institutions. These guilds had the effect of transforming cathedral schools into universities. The first universities were those of Bologna, Paris, and Salerno—noted for instruction in law, theology, and medicine, respectively—but by the late thirteenth century, universities had appeared also in Rome, Naples, Seville, Salamanca, Oxford, Cambridge, and other cities throughout Europe.

The Influence of Aristotle

The evolution of the university coincided with the rediscovery of the works of Aristotle. European scholars of the early middle ages knew only a few of Aristotle's minor works that were available in Latin translation. Byzantine scholars knew Aristotle in the original Greek, but they rarely had any dealings with their Roman Catholic counterparts. During the high middle ages, as commerce and communication increased between Byzantine Orthodox and Roman Catholic Christians, western Europeans learned about Artistotle's thought and obtained Latin translations from Byzantine philosophers. Western European scholars learned about Aristotle also through Muslim philosophers who appreciated the power of his thought and had most of his works translated into Arabic. Christian and Jewish scholars in Sicily and Spain became aware of these Arabic translations, which they retranslated into Latin. Although the resulting works had their flaws—since they filtered Aristotle's original Greek through both Arabic and Latin—they made Aristotle's thought accessible to European Christian scholars.

Scholasticism: St. Thomas Aquinas

During the thirteenth century, understanding of Aristotle's thought and Latin translations of his works spread throughout Europe, and they profoundly influenced almost all branches of thought. The most notable result was the emergence of scholastic theology, which sought to synthesize the beliefs and values of Christianity with the logical rigor of Greek philosophy. The most famous of the scholastic theologians was St. Thomas Aquinas (1225–1274), who spent most of his career teaching at the University of Paris. While holding fervently to his Christian convictions, St. Thomas believed that Aristotle had understood and explained the workings of the world better than any other thinker of any era. St. Thomas saw no contradiction between Aristotle and Christian revelation but, rather, viewed them as complementary authorities: Aristotle provided the most powerful analysis of the world according to human reason while Christianity explained the world and human life as the results of a divine plan. By combining Aristotle's rational power with the teachings of Christianity, St. Thomas expected to formulate the most truthful and persuasive system of thought possible.

In St. Thomas's view, for example, belief in the existence of God did not depend exclusively on an individual's faith. By drawing on Aristotle, St. Thomas believed, it was possible to prove rationally that God exists. Aristotle himself never recognized a personal deity such as the Jewish and Christian God, but he argued that a conscious agent had set the world in motion. St. Thomas borrowed Aristotle's arguments and identified the conscious agent with the Jewish and Christian God, who outlined his plan for the world in the Hebrew scriptures and the Christian New Testament. Thus, as expressed in the thought of St. Thomas Aquinas, scholastic theology represented the harmonization of Aristotle with Christianity and the synthesis of reason and faith.

Like the neo-Confucianism of Zhu Xi or the Islamic philosophy of Ibn Rushd, scholastic theology reinterpreted inherited beliefs in light of the most advanced knowledge of the time.

Popular Religion

St. Thomas and the other scholastic theologians addressed a sophisticated, intellectual elite, not the common people of medieval Europe. The popular masses neither knew nor cared much about Aristotle. For their purposes, Christianity was important primarily as a set of beliefs and rituals that gave meaning to individual lives and that bound them together into coherent communities. Thus formal doctrine and theology did not appeal to popular audiences as much as the ceremonies and observances that involved individuals in the life of a larger community.

Sacraments

Popular piety generally entailed observance of the sacraments and devotion to the saints recognized by the Roman Catholic church. Sacraments are holy rituals that bring spiritual blessings on the observants. The church recognized seven sacraments, including baptism, matrimony, penance, and the Eucharist. By far the most popular was the Eucharist, during which priests offered a ritual meal commemorating Jesus' last meal with his disciples before his trial and execution by Roman authorities. Because the sacrament kept individuals in good standing with the church, conscientious believers observed it weekly, and the especially devout on a daily basis. In addition to preparing individuals for salvation and symbolizing their membership in a holy community, the Eucharist had mundane uses: popular beliefs held that the sacrament would protect individuals from sudden death and advance their worldly interests.

Devotion to Saints

Popular religion also took the form of devotion to the saints. According to church teachings, saints were human beings who had led such exemplary lives that God held them in special esteem. As a result, they enjoyed special influence with heavenly authorities and were able to intervene on behalf of individuals living in the world. Medieval Europeans constantly prayed for saints to look after their spiritual interests and to ensure them of admission to heaven. Often they also invoked the aid of saints who had reputations for helping living people as well as souls of the dead. Tradition held that certain saints could cure diseases, relieve toothaches, and guide sailors through storms to a port.

The Virgin Mary

During the high middle ages, the most popular saint was always the Virgin Mary, mother of Jesus, who personified the Christian ideal of womanhood, love, and sympathy, and who reportedly lavished aid on her devotees. According to a widely circulated story, the Virgin once even spared a criminal from hanging when he called upon her name. During the twelfth and thirteenth centuries, Europeans dedicated hundreds of churches and cathedrals to the Virgin, among them the splendid cathedral of Notre Dame ("Our Lady") of Paris.

Saints' Relics

Medieval Europeans went to great lengths to express their adoration of the Virgin and other saints through veneration of their relics and physical remains, widely believed to retain the powers associated with the holy individuals themselves. Churches assembled vast collections of relics, such as clothes, locks of hair, teeth, and bones of famous saints. Especially esteemed were relics associated with Jesus or the Virgin, such as the crown of thorns that Jesus reportedly wore during his crucifixion or drops of the Virgin's milk miraculously preserved in a vial. The practice of assembling relics clearly opened the door to fraud, but medieval Europeans avidly continued to admire and venerate saints' relics.

Pilgrimage

Some collections of relics became famous well beyond their own regions. Like Muslims making the hajj, pilgrims trekked long distances to honor the saints the

Architects and laborers sometimes worked more than a century to construct the massive gothic cathedrals of medieval Europe. Built during the twelfth and thirteenth centuries, the magnificent cathedral of Notre Dame in Paris honors the Virgin Mary.

relics represented. Throughout the high middle ages, streams of pilgrims visited two European cities in particular—Rome in Italy and Compostela in Spain—and some ventured even farther to Jerusalem and the holy land of Christian origins. Rome was the spiritual center of western Christian society: apart from the popes and the central administration of the Roman Catholic church, the relics of St. Peter and St. Paul, the two most prominent apostles of early Christianity, rested in the churches of Rome. Compostela stood on the very periphery of Christian society, in a remote corner of northwestern Spain. Yet the relics of St. James preserved in the cathedral of Santiago de Compostela exercised a powerful attraction for the pious, who made Compostela the second-most popular pilgrimage destination of medieval Europe. Some devoted pilgrims also visited Jerusalem and the sites associated with the origins of Christianity: spiritual as well as commercial interests called Europeans into the larger world.

The making of pilgrimages became so common during the high middle ages that a travel industry emerged to serve the needs of pilgrims. Inns dotted the routes leading to popular churches and shrines, and guides shepherded groups of pilgrims to religious sites and explained their significance. There were even guide books that pointed out the major attractions along pilgrims' routes and warned them of difficult terrain and unscrupulous scoundrels who took advantage of visitors.

Reform Movements and Popular Heresies

Although veneration of the saints and the making of pilgrimages indicated a deep reservoir of piety, popular religion also reflected the social and economic development of medieval Europe. As Europe's wealth increased, several groups of particularly devout individuals feared that European society was becoming excessively materialistic. Even the Roman Catholic church seemed tainted by materialism. Benedictine monasteries, in which monks originally observed the virtues of poverty, chastity, and obedience, had in many cases become comfortable retreats where privileged individuals led leisurely lives. Meanwhile, the central administration of the Roman church expanded dramatically as lawyers and bureaucrats ran the church's affairs and sought ways to swell its treasury.

Dominicans and Franciscans

The devout responded to this state of affairs in several ways. Working within the Roman church, some individuals organized movements designed to champion spiritual over materialistic values. Most prominent of them were St. Dominic (1170–1221) and St. Francis (1182–1226). During the thirteenth century St. Dominic and St. Francis founded orders of mendicants ("beggars"), known as the Dominican and Franciscan friars, who would have no personal possessions and would have to beg for their food and other needs from audiences to whom they preached. Mendicants were especially active in towns and cities, where they addressed throngs of recently arrived migrants whose numbers were so large that existing urban churches and clergy could not serve them well. The Dominicans and Franciscans also worked zealously to combat heterodox movements and to persuade heretics to return to the Roman Catholic church.

St. Francis of Assisi was the son of a wealthy merchant in central Italy, but he abandoned the comforts that he inherited and pledged himself to a life of poverty and preaching. Stories represented in this fresco from the basilica of St. Francis at Assisi report that he preached to the birds and encouraged them to sing in praise of God.

Popular Heresy

Whereas the Dominicans and Franciscans worked within the church, others rejected the Roman Catholic church altogether and organized alternative religious movements. During the twelfth and thirteenth centuries in particular, several popular movements protested the increasing materialism of European society. The Waldensians, who were most active in southern France and northern Italy, despised the Roman Catholic clergy as immoral and corrupt, and they advocated modest and simple lives. They asserted the right of the laity to preach and administer sacraments—functions that the church reserved

Sources from the Past

Thomas of Celano on St. Francis of Assisi

Thomas of Celano was an early disciple of St. Francis. He joined the Franciscan Order about 1215, and in 1228, at the request of Pope Gregory IX, he composed a biography of St. Francis. His account emphasizes the transformation of St. Francis from a spoiled rich brat to a man of deep spirituality who made special efforts to help the poor.

In the city of Assisi, which lies at the edge of the Spoleto valley, there was a man by the name of Francis, who from his earliest years was brought up by his parents proud of spirit, in accordance with the vanity of the world; and imitating their wretched life and habits for a long time, he became even more vain and proud. . . .

These are the wretched circumstances among which the man whom we venerate today as a saint, for he truly is a saint, lived in his youth; and almost up to the twenty-fifth year of his age, he squandered and wasted his time miserably. Indeed, he outdid all his contemporaries in vanities and he came to be a promoter of evil and was more abundantly zealous for all kinds of foolishness. He was the admiration of all and strove to outdo the rest in the pomp of vainglory, in jokes, in strange doings, in idle and useless talk, in songs, in soft and flowing garments, for he was very rich, not however avaricious but prodigal, not a hoarder of money but a squanderer of his possession, a cautious business man but a very unreliable steward. On the other hand, he was a very kindly person, easy and affable, even making himself foolish because of it; for because of these qualities many ran after him, doers of evil and promoters of crime. . . .

[After his conversion] his greatest concern was to be free from everything of this world, lest the serenity of his mind be disturbed even for an hour by the taint of anything that was mere dust. He made himself insensible to all external noise, and bridling his external senses with all his strength and repressing the movements of his nature, he occupied himself with God alone. . . . He therefore frequently chose solitary places so that he could direct his mind completely to God; yet he was not slothful about entering into the affairs of his neighbors, when he saw the time was opportune, and he willingly took care of things pertaining to their salvation. For his safest haven was prayer; not prayer of a single moment, or idle or presumptuous prayer, but prayer of long duration, full of devotion, serene in humility. If he began late, he would scarcely finish before morning. Walking, sitting, eating, or drinking, he was always intent upon prayer. . . .

The father of the poor, the poor Francis, conforming himself to the poor in all things, was grieved when he saw some one poorer than himself, not because he longed for vainglory, but only from a feeling of compassion. And, though he was content with a tunic that was quite poor and rough, he very frequently longed to divide it with some poor person. But that this very rich poor man, drawn on by a great feeling of affection, might be able to help the poor in some way, he would ask the rich of this world, when the weather was cold, to give him a mantle or some furs. And when, out of devotion, they willingly did what the most blessed father asked of them, he would say to them: "I will accept this from you with the understanding that you do not expect ever to have it back again." And when he met the first poor man, he would clothe him with what he had received with joy and gladness. He bore it very ill if he saw a poor person reproached or if he heard a curse hurled upon any creature by anyone. . . .

For, he was accustomed to say: "Who curses a poor man does an injury to Christ, whose noble image he wears, the image of him who made himself poor for us in this world." Frequently, therefore, when he found the poor burdened down with wood or other things, he offered his own shoulders to help them, though his shoulders were very weak.

SOURCE: Marion A. Habig, ed. *St. Francis of Assisi's Writings and Early Biographies: English Omnibus Sources for the Life of St. Francis.* Chicago: Franciscan Herald Press, 1972, pp. 229–31, 288–92.

In what ways did St. Francis's life experiences—his dissolute youth and his later concern for the poor—reflect the social and economic conditions of medieval Europe?

exclusively for priests—and they did not hesitate to criticize the church on the basis of biblical teachings. Although church authorities declared them heretical, the Waldensians continued to attract enthusiastic participants: a few Waldensians survive even today.

The Cathars

The Cathars, sometimes called Albigensians, went even further than the Waldensians. As Europeans participated more actively in long-distance trade networks, they encountered ideas popular in the Byzantine empire and elsewhere in the Mediterranean basin. Most active in southern France and northern Italy, the Cathars adopted the teachings of heretical groups in eastern Europe, like the Bogomils, who viewed the world as the site of an unrelenting, cosmic struggle between the forces of good and evil. They considered the material world evil and advocated an ascetic, pure, spiritual existence. Those who sought spiritual perfection renounced wealth and marriage and adopted a strict vegetarian diet. They also rejected the Roman Catholic church, which they considered hopelessly corrupt, along with its priests and sacraments.

Their teachings and rapidly growing numbers posed such a direct challenge to the Roman Catholic church that Pope Innocent III called for a military campaign to destroy the Cathars. During the early thirteenth century, warriors from northern France undertook the so-called Albigensian crusade, which ruthlessly crushed Cathar communities in southern France. Although a few Cathars survived in remote regions, by the fifteenth century they had almost entirely disappeared.

The Medieval Expansion of Europe

During the high middle ages, the relationship between western European peoples and their neighbors underwent dramatic change. Powerful states, economic expansion, and demographic growth all strengthened European society while church officials encouraged the colonization of pagan and Muslim lands as a way to extend the influence of Roman Catholic Christianity. Beginning about the mid-eleventh century, Europeans embarked upon expansive ventures on several fronts: Atlantic, Baltic, and Mediterranean. Scandinavian seafarers ventured into the Atlantic Ocean, establishing colonies in Iceland, Greenland, and even for a short time in North America. In the Baltic region Europeans conquered and introduced Christianity to Prussia, Livonia, Lithuania, and Finland. In the Mediterranean basin Europeans recaptured Spain and the Mediterranean islands that Muslims had conquered between the eighth and tenth centuries. Finally, knights from all over Europe mounted enormous campaigns designed to seize the holy land of Palestine from Muslims and place it under Christian authority. As military ventures, the crusades achieved limited success, since they brought the holy land into Christian hands only temporarily. Nevertheless, the crusades signaled clearly that Europeans were beginning to play a much larger role in the affairs of the eastern hemisphere than they had during the early middle ages.

Atlantic and Baltic Colonization

Vinland

When regional states began to emerge and protect western Europe from Viking raids during the ninth and tenth centuries, Scandinavian seafarers turned their attention to the islands of the North Atlantic Ocean. They occupied Iceland beginning in the late ninth century, and at the end of the tenth century a party led by Eric the Red discovered Greenland and established a small colony there. About 1000 C.E. his son Leif Ericsson led another exploratory party south and west of Greenland, arriving eventually at modern Newfoundland in Canada. There the party found plentiful supplies of fish and timber. Because of the wild grapes growing in the region, Leif called it Vinland. During the

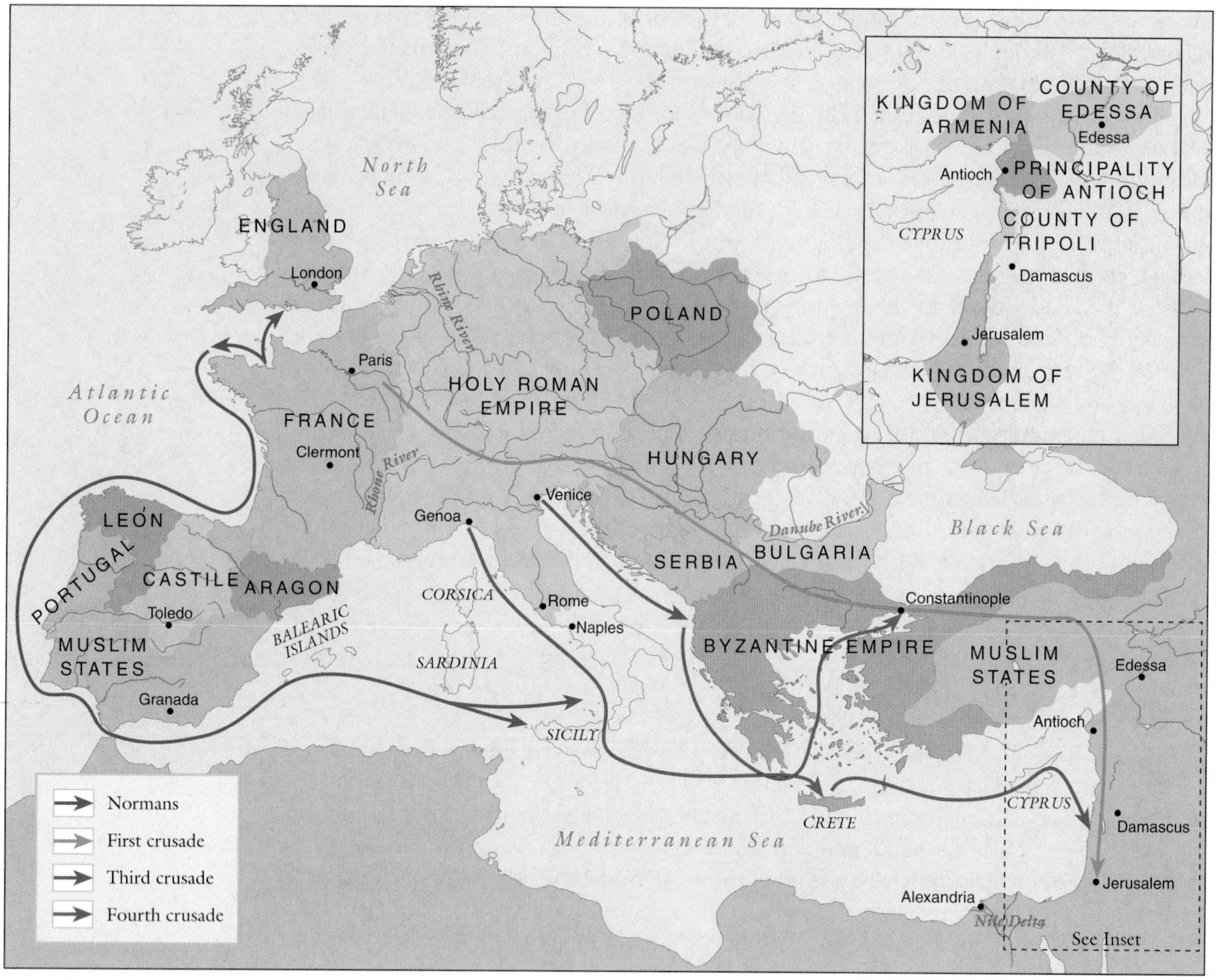

MAP [20.2]
The medieval expansion of Europe, 1000–1250 C.E.

years following Leif's voyage, Greenlanders made several efforts to establish permanent colonies in Vinland.

Since the 1960s, archaeologists in northern Newfoundland have uncovered Scandinavian tools and building foundations dating to the early eleventh century. From this evidence and the stories of maritime ventures preserved in Scandinavian sagas, it is clear that the Greenlanders founded a colony in Newfoundland and maintained it for several decades. Ultimately they left Vinland—or died there—since they did not have the resources to sustain a settlement over the stormy seas of the North Atlantic Ocean. Nonetheless, the establishment of even a short-lived colony indicated a growing capacity of Europeans to venture into the larger world.

Christianity in Scandinavia

While Scandinavians explored the North Atlantic, the Roman Catholic church drew Scandinavia itself into the community of Christian Europe. The kings of Denmark and Norway converted to Christianity in the tenth century. Conversion of their subjects came gradually and with considerable resistance, since most held tightly to their inherited traditions. Yet royal support for the Roman Catholic church ensured that Christianity would have a place in Danish and Norwegian societies. In 999 or 1000 the Norwegian colony in Iceland also formally adopted Christianity. Between the twelfth and fourteenth centuries, Sweden and Finland followed their neighbors into the Christian faith.

Crusading Orders and Baltic Expansion

In the Baltic lands of Prussia, Livonia, and Lithuania, Christian authority arrived in the wake of military conquest. During the era of crusades, zealous Christians formed a series of hybrid, military-religious orders. The most prominent were the Templars, Hospitallers, and Teutonic Knights, who not only took religious vows but also pledged to devote their lives and efforts to the struggle against Muslims and pagans. The Teutonic Knights were most active in the Baltic region, where they waged military campaigns against the pagan Slavic peoples during the twelfth and thirteenth centuries. Aided by German missionaries, the Knights founded churches and monasteries in the territories they subdued. By the late thirteenth century, the Roman Catholic church had established its presence throughout the Baltic region, which progressively became absorbed into the larger society of Christian Europe.

The Reconquest of Sicily and Spain

The boundaries of Christian Europe also expanded in the Mediterranean basin. There Europeans came into conflict with Muslims, whose ancestors had conquered the major Mediterranean islands and most of the Iberian peninsula between the eighth and tenth centuries. As their society became stronger, Europeans undertook to reconquer those territories and reintegrate them into Christian society.

The Reconquest of Sicily

Most important of the islands was Sicily, which Muslims had conquered in the ninth century. During the eleventh century, Norman warriors returned Sicily to Christian hands. The Norman adventurer Robert Guiscard carved out a state for himself in southern Italy while his brother Roger undertook the conquest of Sicily. By 1090, after almost twenty years of conflict, Roger had established his authority throughout the island. Missionaries and clergy soon appeared and reintroduced Roman Catholic Christianity to Sicily. Islam did not disappear immediately: Muslims continued to practice their faith privately, and Muslim scholars in Sicily introduced their Christian counterparts to the Arabic translations of Aristotle that inspired the scholastic philosophers. Over the longer term, however, as Muslims either left Sicily or converted to Christianity, Islam gradually disappeared from the island.

The Reconquista *of Spain*

The reconquest of Spain—known as the *reconquista*—took a much longer time than did the recapture of Sicily. Following the Muslim invasion and conquest of the early eighth century, the caliphate of Córdoba ruled almost all of the Iberian peninsula. A small Christian state survived in Catalonia in the far northeast, and the kingdom of León resisted Muslim advances in the far northwest. The process of *reconquista* began in the 1060s from these Christian toeholds. By 1085 Christian forces had pushed as far south as Toledo, and by 1150 they had recaptured Lisbon and established their authority over half of the peninsula. Their successes lured reinforcements from France and England, and in the first half of the thirteenth century a new round of campaigns brought most of Iberia as well as the Balearic Islands into Christian hands. Only the kingdom of Granada in the far south of the peninsula remained Muslim. It survived as an outpost of Islam until 1492, when Christian forces mounted a campaign that conquered Granada and completed the *reconquista*.

The political, economic, and demographic strength of Christian Europe helps to explain the reconquests of Sicily and Spain as military ventures. Especially in the case of Spain, however, it is clear that religious concerns also helped to drive the *reconquista*. The popes and other leading clergy of the Roman Catholic church regarded Islam as an affront to Christianity, and they enthusiastically encouraged campaigns against the Muslims. When reconquered territories fell into Christian hands, church officials immediately established bishoprics and asserted Christian authority. They also organized campaigns to convert local populations. Dominican friars were especially active in Spain. They appealed to learned audiences by explaining Christianity in the terms of scholastic theology and arguments derived from Aristotle, whom Muslim intellectuals held in high esteem. When addressing popular audiences, they simply outlined the basic teachings of Christianity and urged their listeners to convert. With the establishment of Christian rule, the Roman Catholic church began to displace Islam in conquered Spain.

The Crusades

The term *crusade* refers to a holy war. It derives from the Latin word *crux,* meaning "cross," the device on which Roman authorities had executed Jesus. When a pope declared a crusade, warriors would "take up the cross" as a symbol of their faith, sew strips of cloth in the form of a cross on the backs of their garments, and venture forth to fight on behalf of Christianity. The wars that Christians fought against pagans in the Baltic and Muslims in the Mediterranean were crusades in this sense of the term, as was the campaign waged by Roman Catholic Christians against Cathar heretics in southern France. In popular usage, though, the crusades generally refer to the massive expeditions that Roman Catholic Christians mounted in an effort to recapture Palestine, the land of Christian origins, and the holy city of Jerusalem from Muslim authorities.

Urban II

Pope Urban II launched the crusades in 1095. While meeting with bishops at the Council of Clermont, he called for Christian knights to take up arms and seize the holy land, promising salvation for those who fell during the campaign. The response to Urban's appeal was immediate and enthusiastic. A zealous preacher named Peter the Hermit traveled throughout France, Germany, and the Low Countries whipping up support among popular audiences. Within a year of Pope Urban's call, the Hermit had organized a ragtag army of poor knights and enthusiastic peasants—including women as well as men—and set out for Palestine without proper training, discipline, weapons, supplies, or plans. Not surprisingly, the campaign was a disaster: participants fought

The crusades involved brutal conflict and atrocities from all sides. In this twelfth-century manuscript illustration, crusaders lob severed enemy heads at Muslims defending a fortress.

Another manuscript illustration depicts Muslims burning captured crusaders at the stake.

not only with Greeks and Turks they met on the road to Palestine but also among themselves. Many members of Peter's band died in these conflicts, and Turkish forces captured others and forced them into slavery. Few made it beyond Anatolia or back to Europe. Yet the campaign indicated the high level of interest that the crusading idea generated among the European public.

The First Crusade

Shortly after Peter's ill-fated venture, French and Norman nobles organized a more respectable military expedition to the holy land. In late 1096 the crusading armies began the long trek to Palestine. In 1097 and 1098 they captured Edessa, Antioch, and other strategic sites. In 1099 Jerusalem itself fell to the crusaders, who then proceeded to extend their conquests and carve conquered territories into Christian states.

Although the crusaders did not realize it, hindsight shows that their quick victories came largely because of division and disarray in the ranks of their Muslim foes. The crusaders' successes, however, encouraged Turks, Egyptians, and other Muslims to settle their differences, at least temporarily, in the interests of expelling European Christians from the eastern Mediterranean. By the mid-twelfth century the crusader communities had come under tremendous pressure. The crusader state of Edessa fell to Turks in 1144, and the Muslim leader Salah al-Din, known to Europeans as Saladin, recaptured Jerusalem in 1187. Crusaders maintained several of their enclaves for another century, but Saladin's victories sealed the fate of Christian forces in the eastern Mediterranean.

Later Crusades

Europeans did not immediately concede Palestine to the Muslims. By the mid-thirteenth century they had launched five major crusades, but none of the later ventures succeeded in reestablishing a Christian presence in Palestine. The fourth crusade (1202–1204) went badly astray when the crusaders conquered Constantinople, subjected the city to a ruthless sack, and installed a Roman Catholic regime that survived until 1261. The Byzantine empire never fully recovered from this blow and lumbered along in serious decline until Ottoman Turks toppled it in 1453. Even though the later crusades failed in their principal objective, the crusading idea inspired European dreams of conquest in the eastern Mediterranean until the late sixteenth century.

Consequences of the Crusades

As holy wars intended to reestablish Roman Catholic Christianity in the eastern Mediterranean basin, the crusades were wars of military and political expansion. Yet in the long run, the crusades were much more important for their social, economic, commercial, and cultural consequences. Even as European armies built crusader states in Palestine and Syria, European scholars and missionaries dealt with Muslim philosophers and theologians, and European merchants traded eagerly with their Muslim counterparts. The result was a large-scale exchange of ideas, technologies, and trade goods that profoundly influenced European development. Through their sojourns in Palestine and their regular dealings with Muslims throughout the Mediterranean basin, European Christians became acquainted with the works of Aristotle, Islamic science and astronomy, "Arabic" numerals (which Muslims had borrowed from India), and techniques of paper production (which Muslims had learned from China). They also learned to appreciate new food and agricultural products such as spices, granulated sugar, coffee, and dates as well as trade goods like silk products, cotton textiles, carpets, and tapestries.

In the early days of the crusades, Europeans had little to exchange for these products other than rough, wool textiles, furs, and timber. During the crusading era, however, demand for the new commodities increased throughout western Europe as large numbers of people developed a taste for goods previously available only to wealthy elites. Seeking to meet the rising demand for luxury goods, Italian merchants developed new products and marketed them in commercial centers and port cities like Constantinople, Alexandria, Cairo, Damascus, Tana, Caffa, and Trebizond. Thus Niccolò, Maffeo, and Marco Polo traded in gems and jewelry, while other merchants marketed fine woolen textiles or glassware. By the thirteenth century, large numbers of Italian merchants had begun to travel well beyond Egypt, Palestine, and Syria to avoid Muslim intermediaries and to deal directly with the producers of silks and spices in India, China, and southeast Asia. Thus, although the crusades largely failed as military ventures, they helped encourage the reintegration of western Europe into the larger economy of the eastern hemisphere.

From 1000 to 1300 western Europe underwent thorough political and economic reorganization. Building on foundations laid during the early middle ages, political leaders founded a series of independent regional states. Despite the establishment of the Holy Roman Empire, they did not revive central imperial authority in western Europe. Regional states maintained good order and fostered rapid economic growth. Agricultural improvements brought increased food supplies, which encouraged urbanization, manufacturing, and trade. By the thirteenth century, European peoples traded actively throughout the Mediterranean, Baltic, and North Sea regions, and a few plucky merchants even ventured as far away as China in search of commercial opportunities. In the high middle ages, as in the early middle ages, Roman Catholic Christianity was the cultural foundation of European society. The church prospered during the high middle ages, and advanced educational institutions like cathedral schools and universities reinforced the influence of Roman Catholic Christianity throughout Europe. Christianity even played a role in European political and military expansion, since church officials encouraged crusaders to conquer pagan and Muslim peoples in Baltic and Mediterranean lands. Thus between 1000 and 1300, western European peoples strengthened their own society and began in various ways to interact regularly with their counterparts in other regions of the eastern hemisphere.

CHRONOLOGY

962	Coronation of Otto I as Holy Roman Emperor
1056–1106	Reign of Emperor Henry IV
1066	Norman invasion of England
1073–1085	Reign of Pope Gregory VII
1096–1099	First crusade
1122–1204	Life of Eleanor of Aquitaine
1152–1190	Reign of Emperor Frederick Barbarossa
1170–1221	Life of St. Dominic
1182–1226	Life of St. Francis
1187	Recapture of Jerusalem by Saladin
1202–1204	Fourth crusade
1225–1274	Life of St. Thomas Aquinas
1271–1295	Marco Polo's trip to China

FOR FURTHER READING

Robert Bartlett. *The Making of Europe: Conquest, Colonization, and Cultural Change, 950–1350.* Princeton, 1993. A well-documented examination of European expansion from a cultural point of view.

Robert-Henri Bautier. *The Economic Development of Medieval Europe.* New York, 1971. An excellent and well-illustrated survey that puts the economic and social history of western Europe in the context of the larger Mediterranean basin.

Marc Bloch. *Feudal Society.* 2 vols. Trans. by L. A. Manyon. Chicago, 1961. A classic interpretation concentrating on social and economic history that has decisively influenced the way historians think about medieval Europe.

Rosalind Brooke and Christopher Brooke. *Popular Religion in the Middle Ages: Western Europe, 1000–1300.* London, 1984. Well-illustrated essays on the faith of the masses.

Georges Duby. *Rural Economy and Country Life in the Medieval West.* Trans. by C. Postan. Columbia, S.C., 1968. Authoritative and well-documented study of the medieval agrarian world by a distinguished scholar.

Patrick J. Geary, ed. *Readings in Medieval History.* Lewiston, N.Y., 1989. Offers substantial English translations of primary sources.

Jean Gimpel. *The Medieval Machine: The Industrial Revolution of the Middle Ages.* New York, 1976. Explores the role of science and technology in the economy and society of medieval Europe.

David Herlihy. *Opera Muliebra: Women and Work in Medieval Europe.* New York, 1990. Examines women's roles both in their own households and in the larger society of medieval Europe.

Benjamin Z. Kedar. *Crusade and Mission: European Approaches toward the Muslims.* Princeton, 1984. Insightful scholarly analysis of European policies toward Muslims during the crusading era.

Robert S. Lopez. *The Commercial Revolution of the Middle Ages, 950–1350.* Englewood Cliffs, N.J., 1971. A succinct account of economic development during the high middle ages.

Robert S. Lopez and I. W. Raymond, eds. *Medieval Trade in the Mediterranean World.* New York, 1955. Offers translations of documents illustrating patterns and problems of trade in the medieval Mediterranean.

Hans Eberhard Mayer. *The Crusades.* 2nd ed. Oxford, 1988. Perhaps the best short history of the crusades.

J. R. S. Phillips. *The Medieval Expansion of Europe.* Oxford, 1988. Excellent survey of European ventures in the larger world during the high and late middle ages.

Joshua Prawer. *The Crusaders' Kingdom: European Colonialism in the Middle Ages.* New York, 1972. A comprehensive study that views crusaders' states as expressions of medieval European colonialism.

Susan Reynolds. *Fiefs and Vassals: The Medieval Evidence Reinterpreted.* Oxford, 1994. A powerful scholarly critique of the concept of feudalism.

———. *Kingdoms and Communities in Western Europe, 900–1300.* Oxford, 1984. An imaginative study focusing on the political and social values that undergirded western European society.

Jonathan Riley-Smith. *The Crusades: A Short History.* New Haven, 1987. Synthesizes a great deal of scholarship on the crusades.

Armando Sapori. *The Italian Merchant in the Middle Ages.* Trans. by P. A. Kennen. New York, 1970. Spirited account of medieval Italian merchants and their activities.

Shulamith Shahar. *The Fourth Estate: A History of Women in the Middle Ages.* Trans. by C. Galai. London, 1983. Well-documented study of women and their status in medieval society.

Lynn White Jr. *Medieval Technology and Social Change.* Oxford, 1962. Pioneering study of technological diffusion and the role of technology in European economy and society.

OLC

See our **Online Learning Center at www.mhhe.com/bentley3** for additional readings, practice maps, quizzes, and internet activities.

PSI

Unfamiliar words? Check out the **Primary Source Investigator CD-ROM** for an interactive glossary, interactive maps, more images, and primary sources.

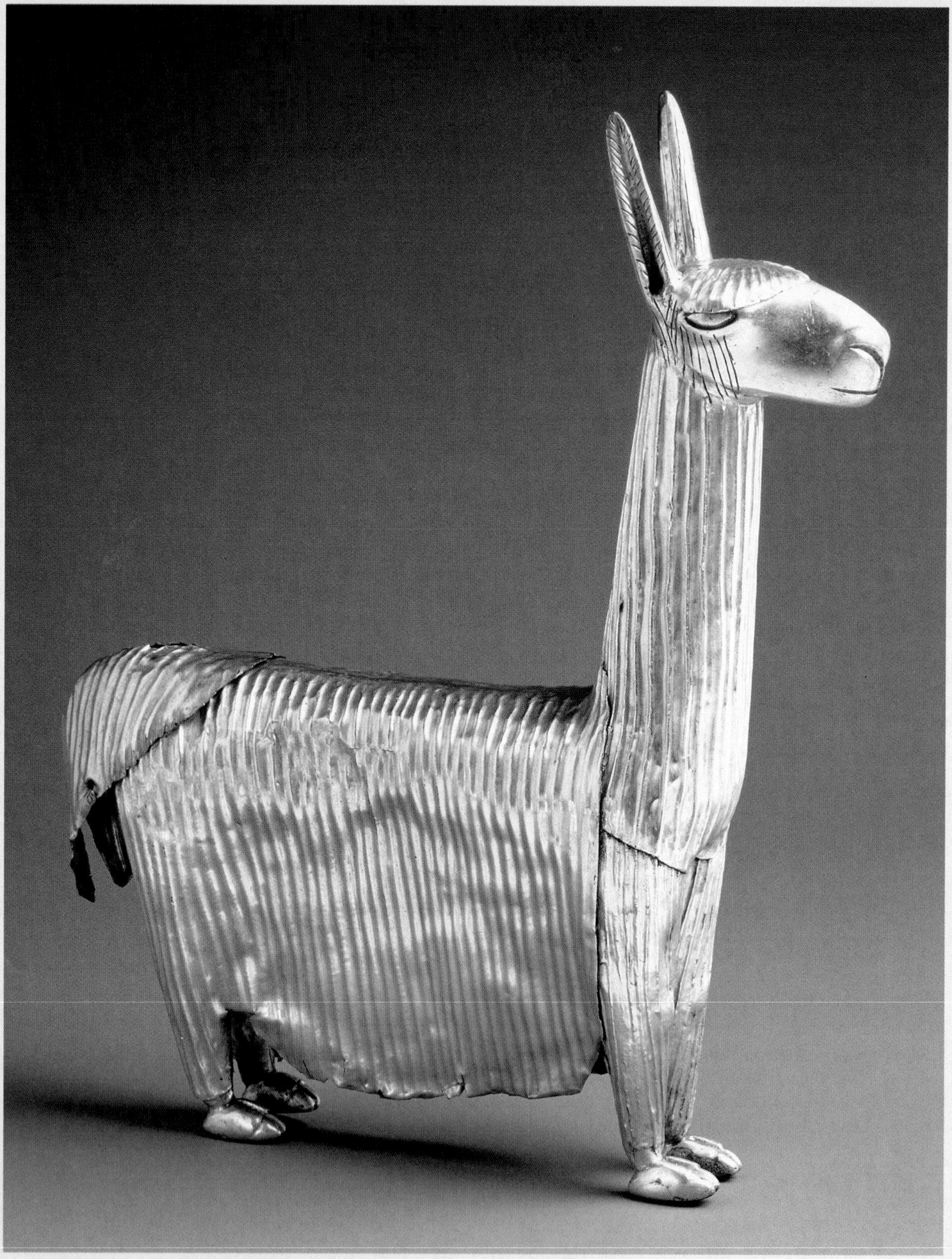

A handsome llama fashioned from silver sheet from Inca Peru.

CHAPTER 21

WORLDS APART: THE AMERICAS AND OCEANIA

In November 1519 a small Spanish army entered Tenochtitlan, capital city of the Aztec empire. The Spanish forces came in search of gold, and they had heard many reports about the wealth of the Aztec empire. Yet none of these reports prepared them adequately for what they saw.

Years after the conquest of the Aztec empire, Bernal Díaz del Castillo, a soldier in the Spanish army, described Tenochtitlan at its high point. The city itself sat in the water of Lake Texcoco, connected to the surrounding land by three broad causeways, and as in Venice, canals allowed canoes to navigate to all parts of the city. The imperial palace included many large rooms and apartments. Its armory, well stocked with swords, lances, knives, bows, arrows, slings, armor, and shields, attracted Bernal Díaz's professional attention. The aviary of Tenochtitlan included eagles, hawks, parrots, and smaller birds in its collection, and jaguars, mountain lions, wolves, foxes, and rattlesnakes were noteworthy residents of the zoo.

To Bernal Díaz the two most impressive sights were the markets and temples of Tenochtitlan. The markets astonished him because of their size, the variety of goods they offered, and the order that prevailed there. In the principal market at Tlatelolco, a district of Tenochtitlan, Bernal Díaz found gold and silver jewelry, gems, feathers, embroidery, slaves, cotton, cacao, animal skins, maize, beans, vegetables, fruits, poultry, meat, fish, salt, paper, and tools. It would take more than two days, he said, to walk around the market and investigate all the goods offered for sale. His well-traveled companions-in-arms compared the market of Tlatelolco favorably to those of Rome and Constantinople.

The temples also struck Bernal Díaz, though in a different way. Aztec temples were the principal sites of rituals involving human sacrifice. Bernal Díaz described his ascent to the top of the main pyramidal temple in Tenochtitlan, where fresh blood lay pooled around the stone that served as a sacrificial altar. He described priests with hair entangled and matted with blood. Interior rooms of the temple were so encrusted with blood, Bernal Díaz reported, that their walls and floors had turned black, and the stench overcame even professional Spanish soldiers. Some of the interior rooms held the dismembered limbs of sacrificial victims, while others were resting places for thousands of human skulls and bones.

The contrast between Tenochtitlan's markets and temples challenged Bernal Díaz and his fellow soldiers. In the markets they witnessed peaceful and orderly exchange of the kind that took place all over the world. In the temples, however, they saw signs of human sacrifice on a scale rarely matched, if ever, anywhere in the world. Yet by the cultural standards of the Aztec empire, there was no difficulty reconciling the commercial activity of the marketplaces with the human sacrifice of the temples. Both had a place in the maintenance of the world: trade enabled a complex society to function while sacrificial rituals pleased the gods and persuaded them to keep the world going.

Although the peoples of Africa, Asia, and Europe interacted regularly before modern times, the indigenous peoples of the Americas had only sporadic dealings with their contemporaries across the oceans. Scandinavian seafarers established a short-lived colony in Newfoundland, and occasional ships from Europe and west Africa may have made their way to the western hemisphere. Before 1492, however, interaction between peoples of the eastern and western hemispheres was fleeting and random rather than a sustained and regular affair. During the period from 1000 to 1500 C.E., however, the peoples of North and South America, like their counterparts in the eastern hemisphere, organized large empires with distinctive cultural and religious traditions, and they created elaborate trade networks touching most regions of the American continents.

The indigenous peoples of Australia and the Pacific islands had irregular and sporadic dealings with peoples outside Oceania. Asian trade networks extended to the Philippines, the islands of Indonesia, and New Guinea, but they did not reach far into the Pacific Ocean. They touched a few regions of northern Australia and the Mariana Islands, including Guam, but they did not extend to the more distant island societies of the Pacific Ocean. Pacific islanders themselves often sailed over the open ocean, creating and sustaining links between the societies of various island groups. They also had some dealings with the inhabitants of Asian and American lands bordering the Pacific Ocean. To a greater extent than their counterparts in the eastern hemisphere, however, the indigenous peoples of Australia and the Pacific islands built self-sufficient societies that tended to their own needs. Even though they had extremely limited amounts of land and other natural resources to work with, by the thirteenth century C.E. they had established well-organized agricultural societies and chiefly states throughout the Pacific islands.

STATES AND EMPIRES IN MESOAMERICA AND NORTH AMERICA

Mesoamerica entered an era of war and conquest in the eighth century C.E. Great stores of wealth had accumulated in Teotihuacan, the largest early city in Mesoamerica. When Teotihuacan declined, it became a target for less-prosperous but well-organized forces from the countryside and northern Mexico. Attacks on Teotihuacan opened a long era of militarization and empire building in Mesoamerica that lasted until Spanish forces conquered the region in the sixteenth century. Most prominent of the peoples contesting for power in Mesoamerica were the Mexica, the architects of the Aztec empire.

The Toltecs and the Mexica

During the ninth and early tenth centuries, after the collapse of Teotihuacan, several regional states dominated portions of the high central valley of Mexico, the area surrounding Mexico City where agricultural societies had flourished since the late centuries B.C.E. Although these successor states and their societies shared the religious and cultural traditions of Teotihuacan, they fought relentlessly among themselves.

Their capital cities all stood on well-defended hill sites, and warriors figured prominently in their works of art.

Toltecs

With the emergence of the Toltecs and later the Mexica, much of central Mexico again came under unified rule. The Toltecs began to migrate into the area about the eighth century. They came from the arid land of northwestern Mexico, and they settled mostly at Tula, about 50 kilometers (31 miles) northwest of modern Mexico City. Though situated in a corner of the valley of Mexico that possesses thin soil and receives little rainfall, the Toltecs tapped the waters of the nearby River Tula to irrigate crops of maize, beans, peppers, tomatoes, chiles, and cotton. At its high point, from about 950 to 1150 C.E., Tula supported an urban population that might have reached sixty thousand people. Another sixty thousand lived in the surrounding region.

The Toltecs maintained a large and powerful army that campaigned periodically throughout central Mexico. They built a compact regional empire and maintained fortresses far to the northwest to protect their state from invasion by nomadic peoples. From the mid-tenth through the mid-twelfth centuries, they exacted tribute from subject peoples and transformed their capital into a wealthy city. Residents lived in spacious houses made of stone, adobe, or mud and sometimes covered their packed-earth floors with plaster.

Tula

The city of Tula became an important center of weaving, pottery, and obsidian work, and residents imported large quantities of jade, turquoise, animal skins, exotic bird feathers, and other luxury goods from elsewhere in Mesoamerica. The Toltecs maintained close relations with societies on the Gulf coast as well as with the Maya of Yucatan. Indeed, Tula shared numerous architectural designs and art motifs with the Maya city of Chichén Itzá some 1,500 kilometers (932 miles) to the east.

Beginning about 1125 C.E. the Toltec empire faced serious difficulties as conflicts between the different ethnic groups living at Tula led to civil strife. By the mid-twelfth century large numbers of migrants—mostly nomadic peoples from northwestern Mexico—had entered Tula and settled in the surrounding area. By 1175 the combination of civil conflict and nomadic incursion had destroyed the Toltec state. Archaeological evidence suggests that fire destroyed much of Tula about the same time. Large numbers of people continued to inhabit the region around Tula, but by the end of the twelfth century the Toltecs no longer dominated Mesoamerica.

The Mexica

Among the migrants drawn to central Mexico from northwestern regions was a people who called themselves the Mexica, often referred to as Aztecs because they dominated the alliance that built the Aztec empire in the fifteenth century. (The term *Aztec* derives from *Aztlán,* "the place of the seven legendary caves," which the Mexica remembered as the home of their ancestors.) The Mexica arrived in central Mexico about the middle of the thirteenth century. They had a reputation for making trouble by kidnapping women from nearby communities and seizing land already cultivated by others. On several occasions their neighbors became tired of their disorderly behavior and forced them to move. For a century they migrated around central Mexico, jostling and fighting with other peoples and sometimes surviving only by eating fly eggs and snakes.

Tenochtitlan

About 1345 the Mexica settled on an island in a marshy region of Lake Texcoco and founded the city that would become their capital—Tenochtitlan, on top of which Spanish conquerors later built Mexico City. Though inconvenient at first, the site offered several advantages. The lake harbored plentiful supplies of fish, frogs, and waterfowl. Moreover, the lake enabled the Mexica to develop the *chinampa* system of agriculture. The Mexica dredged a rich and fertile muck from the lake's bottom and built it up into small plots of land known as *chinampas.* During the dry season, cultivators tapped water from canals leading from the lake to their plots, and in the temperate climate they grew crops

Although the lakes of central Mexico have largely disappeared, a few *chinampas* survive, such as this one in Xochimilco, near modern Mexico City.

of maize, beans, squashes, tomatoes, peppers, and chiles year-round. *Chinampas* were so fertile and productive that cultivators were sometimes able to harvest seven crops per year from their gardens. Finally, the lake served as a natural defense: waters protected Tenochtitlan on all sides, and Mexica warriors patrolled the three causeways that eventually linked their capital to the surrounding mainland.

The Aztec Empire

By the early fifteenth century, the Mexica were powerful enough to overcome their immediate neighbors and demand tribute from their new subjects. During the middle decades of the century, prodded by the military elite that ruled Tenochtitlan, the Mexica launched ambitious campaigns of imperial expansion. Under the rule of "the Obsidian Serpent" Itzcóatl (1428–1440) and Motecuzoma I (1440–1469), also known as Moctezuma or Montezuma, they advanced first against Oaxaca in southwestern Mexico. After conquering the city and slaying many of its inhabitants, they populated Oaxaca with colonists, and the city became a bulwark for the emerging Mexica empire.

The Mexica next turned their attention to the Gulf coast, whose tropical products made welcome tribute items in Tenochtitlan. Finally, they conquered the cities of the high plateaus between Tenochtitlan and the Gulf coast. About the mid-fifteenth century the Mexica joined forces with two neighboring cities, Texcoco and Tlacopan (modern Tacuba), to create a triple alliance that guided the Aztec empire. Dominated by the Mexica and Tenochtitlan, the allies imposed their rule on about twelve million people and most of Mesoamerica, excluding only the arid northern and western regions and a few small pockets where independent states resisted the expanding empire.

Tribute and Trade

The main objective of the triple alliance was to exact tribute from subject peoples. From nearby peoples the Mexica and their allies received food crops and manufactured items such as textiles, rabbit-fur blankets, embroidered clothes, jewelry, and obsidian knives. Tribute obligations were sometimes very oppressive for subject peoples. The annual tribute owed by the state of Tochtepec on the Gulf coast, for example, included 9,600 cloaks, 1,600 women's garments, 200 loads of cacao, and 16,000 rubber balls, among other items. Ruling elites entrusted some of these tribute items to officially recognized merchants, who took them to distant lands and exchanged them for local products. These included luxury items such as translucent jade, emeralds, tortoise shells, jaguar skins, parrot feathers, seashells, and game animals. The tropical lowlands also supplied vanilla beans and cacao—the source of cocoa and chocolate—from which Mexica elites prepared tasty beverages.

Unlike imperial states in the eastern hemisphere, the Aztec empire had no elaborate bureaucracy or administration. The Mexica and their allies simply conquered their subjects and assessed tribute, leaving local governance and the collection of tribute in the hands of the conquered peoples themselves. The allies did not even maintain military garrisons throughout their empire. Nor did they keep a permanent, standing army. They simply assembled forces as needed when they launched

MAP [21.1]
The Toltec and Aztec empires, 950–1520 C.E.

campaigns of expansion or mounted punitive expeditions against insubordinate subjects. Nevertheless, the Mexica in particular had a reputation for military prowess, and fear of reprisal kept most subject peoples in line.

At the high point of the Aztec empire in the early sixteenth century, tribute from some 489 subject territories flowed into Tenochtitlan, which was an enormously wealthy city. The Mexica capital had a population of about two hundred thousand people, and another three hundred thousand lived in nearby towns and suburban areas. The principal market had separate sections for merchants dealing in gold, silver, slaves, henequen and cotton cloth, shoes, animal skins, turkeys, dogs, wild game, maize, beans, peppers, cacao, and fruits.

For an interactive version of this map, go to www.mhhe.com/bentley3ch21maps.

The Spanish soldier Bernal Díaz del Castillo marveled at the sight before him when he first laid eyes on Tenochtitlan:

> And when we saw so many cities and villages built in the water and other great towns on dry land and that straight and level causeway going towards Mexico [Tenochtitlan], we were amazed . . . on account of the great towers and [temples] and buildings rising from the water, and all built of masonry. And some of our soldiers even asked whether the things that we saw were not a dream? It is not to be wondered at that I here write it down in this manner, for there is so much to think over that I do not know how to describe it, seeing things as we did that had never been heard of or seen before, not even dreamed about.

Mexica Society

More information survives about the Mexica and their subjects than about any other people of the pre-Columbian Americas. A few Mexica books survived the Spanish conquest of the Aztec empire, and they offer direct testimony about the Mexica way of life. Moreover, a great deal of information survives from lengthy interviews conducted by Spanish missionaries with priests, elders, and other leaders of the Mexica during the mid-sixteenth century. Their reports fill many thick volumes and shed considerable light on Mexica society.

Social Structure

Mexica society was rigidly hierarchical, with public honors and rewards going mostly to the military elite. The Mexica looked upon all males as potential warriors,

A Spanish copy of a Mexica list records tribute owed by six northwestern towns to the ruler Motecuzoma II. Each two years the towns delivered, among other items, women's skirts and blouses, men's shirts, warriors' armor and shields, an eagle, and various quantities of maize, beans, and other foods.

and individuals of common birth could distinguish themselves on the battlefield and thereby improve their social standing. For the most part, however, the military elite came from the Mexica aristocracy. Men of noble birth received the most careful instruction and intense training in military affairs, and they enjoyed the best opportunities to display their talents on the battlefield.

Warriors

The Mexica showered wealth and honors on the military elite. Accomplished warriors received extensive land grants as well as tribute from commoners for their support. The most successful warriors formed a council whose members selected the ruler, discussed public issues, and filled government positions. They ate the best foods—turkey, pheasant, duck, deer, boar, and rabbit—and they consumed most of the luxury items like vanilla and cacao that came into Mexica society by way of trade or tribute. Even dress reflected social status in Mexica society. Sumptuary laws required commoners to wear coarse, burlap-like garments made of henequen but permitted aristocrats to drape themselves in cotton. Warriors enjoyed the right to don brightly colored capes and adorn themselves with lip plugs and eagle feathers after they captured enemies on the battlefield and brought them back to Tenochtitlan.

Mexica Women

Women played almost no public role in a society so dominated by military values, but they wielded influence within their families and enjoyed high honor as mothers of warriors. Mexica women did not inherit property or hold official positions, and the law subjected them to the strict authority of their fathers and husbands. Women were prominent in the marketplaces, as well as in crafts involving embroidery and needlework. Yet Mexica society prodded them toward motherhood and homemaking.

With the exception of a few who dedicated themselves to the service of a temple, all Mexica women married. Mexica values taught that their principal function was to bear children, especially males who might become distinguished warriors, and society recognized the bearing of children as equal to a warrior's capture of enemy in battle. Indeed, women who died in childbirth won the same fame as warriors who died valiantly on the battlefield. Even among the elite classes, Mexica women had the responsibilities of raising young children and preparing food for their families.

Sources from the Past

Mexica Expectations of Boys and Girls

Bernardino de Sahagún was a Franciscan missionary who worked to convert the native peoples of Mesoamerica to Christianity in the mid-sixteenth century. He interviewed Mexica elders and assembled a vast amount of information about their society before the arrival of Europeans. His records include the speeches made by midwives as they delivered infants to aristocratic families. The speeches indicate clearly the roles men and women were expected to play in Mexica society.

[To a newborn boy the midwife said:] "Heed, hearken: thy home is not here, for thou art an eagle, thou art an ocelot; thou art a roseate spoonbill, thou art a troupial. Thou art the serpent, the bird of the lord of the near, of the nigh. Here is only the place of thy nest. Thou hast only been hatched here; thou hast only come, arrived. Thou art only come forth on earth here. Here dost thou bud, blossom, germinate. Here thou becomest the chip, the fragment [of thy mother]. Here are only the cradle, thy cradle blanket, the resting place of thy head: only thy place of arrival. Thou belongest out there; out there thou hast been consecrated. Thou hast been sent into warfare. War is thy desert, thy task. Thou shalt give drink, nourishment, food to the sun, the lord of the earth. Thy real home, thy property, thy lot is the home of the sun there in the heavens. . . . Perhaps thou wilt receive the gift, perhaps thou wilt merit death [in battle] by the obsidian knife, the flowered death by the obsidian knife. . . ."

And if it were a female, the midwife said to her when she cut her umbilical cord: "My beloved maiden, my beloved noblewoman, thou has endured fatigue! Our lord, the lord of the near, of the nigh, hath sent thee. Thou hast come to arrive at a place of weariness, a place of anguish, a place of fatigue where there is cold, there is wind. . . . Thou wilt be in the heart of the home, thou wilt go nowhere, thou wilt nowhere become a wanderer, thou becomest the banked fire, the hearth stones. Here our lord planteth thee, burieth thee. And thou wilt become fatigued, thou wilt become tired; thou art to provide water, to grind maize, to drudge; thou art to sweat by the ashes, by the hearth."

Then the midwife buried the umbilical cord of the noblewoman by the hearth. It was said that by this she signified that the little woman would nowhere wander. Her dwelling place was only within the house; her home was only within the house; it was not necessary for her to go anywhere. And it meant that her very duty was drink, food. She was to prepare drink, to prepare food, to grind, to spin, to weave.

SOURCE: Bernardino de Sahagún. *Florentine Codex: General History of the Things of New Spain,* 13 vols. Trans. by Charles E. Dibble and Arthur J. O. Anderson. Salt Lake City: University of Utah Press, 1950–82, 7:171–73 (book 6, chapter 31).

How did gender roles and expectations of Mexica society compare with those of other settled, agricultural societies such as China, India, the Islamic world, sub-Saharan Africa, and Europe?

Priests

Alongside the military aristocracy, a priestly class also ranked among the Mexica elite. Priests received a special education in calendrical and ritual lore, and they presided over religious ceremonies that the Mexica viewed as crucial to the continuation of the world. Priests read omens and explained the forces that drove the world, thereby wielding considerable influence as advisers to Mexica rulers. On a few occasions, priests even became supreme rulers of the Aztec empire: the ill-fated Motecuzoma II (reigned 1502–1520), ruler of the Aztec empire when Spanish invaders appeared in 1519, was a priest of the most popular Mexica cult.

Cultivators and Slaves

The bulk of the Mexica population consisted of commoners who lived in hamlets cultivating *chinampas* and fields allocated to their families by community groups known as *calpulli*. Originally, *calpulli* were clans or groups of families claiming descent from common ancestors. With the passage of time, ancestry became less important to the nature of the *calpulli* than the fact that groups of families lived together in communities, organized their own affairs, and allocated community property to individual families. Apart from cultivating plots assigned by their *calpulli*, Mexica commoners also worked on lands awarded to aristocrats or prominent warriors and contributed labor services to public works projects involving the construction of palaces, temples, roads, and irrigation systems. Cultivators delivered periodic tribute payments to state agents, who distributed a portion of what they collected to the elite classes and stored the remainder in state granaries and warehouses. In addition to these cultivators of common birth, Mexica society included a large number of slaves, who usually worked as domestic servants. Most slaves were not foreigners, but Mexica. Families sometimes sold younger members into servitude out of financial distress, while other Mexica were forced into slavery because of criminal behavior.

Artisans and Merchants

Skilled artisans, particularly those who worked with gold, silver, cotton textiles, tropical bird feathers, and other items destined for consumption by the elite, enjoyed considerable prestige in Mexica society. Merchants specializing in long-distance trade occupied an important but somewhat more tenuous position in Mexica society. Merchants supplied the exotic products such as gems, animal skins, and tropical bird feathers consumed by the elites and provided political and military intelligence about the lands they visited. Yet they often fell under suspicion as greedy profiteers, and aristocratic warriors frequently extorted wealth and goods from merchants who lacked powerful patrons or protectors.

Mexica Religion

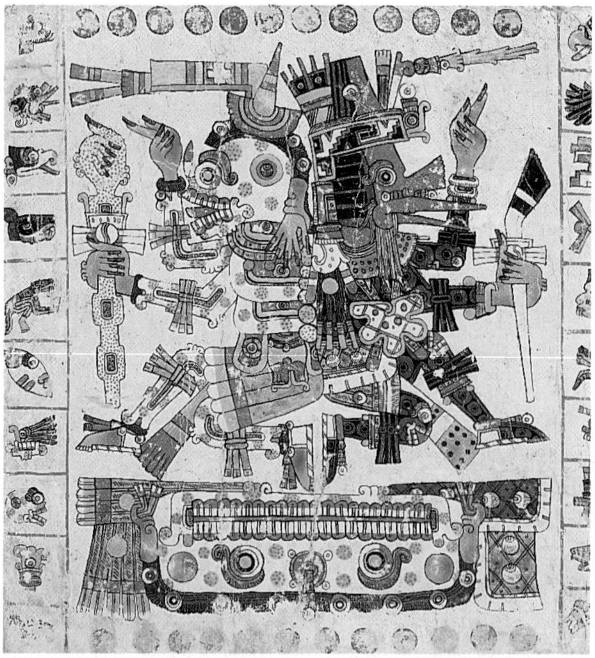

A Mexica manuscript known as the Codex Borgia depicts Quetzalcóatl (left) as the lord of life and Tezcatlipoca (right) as the god of death.

When they migrated to central Mexico, the Mexica already spoke the Nahuatl language, which had been the prevalent tongue in the region since the time of the Toltecs. The Mexica soon adopted other cultural and religious traditions, some of which dated from the time of the Olmecs, shared by all the peoples of Mesoamerica. Most Mesoamerican peoples played a ball game in formal courts, for example, and maintained a complicated calendar based on a solar year of 365 days and a ritual year of 260 days. The Mexica enthusiastically adopted the ball game, and they kept a sophisticated calendar, although it was not as elaborate as the Maya calendar.

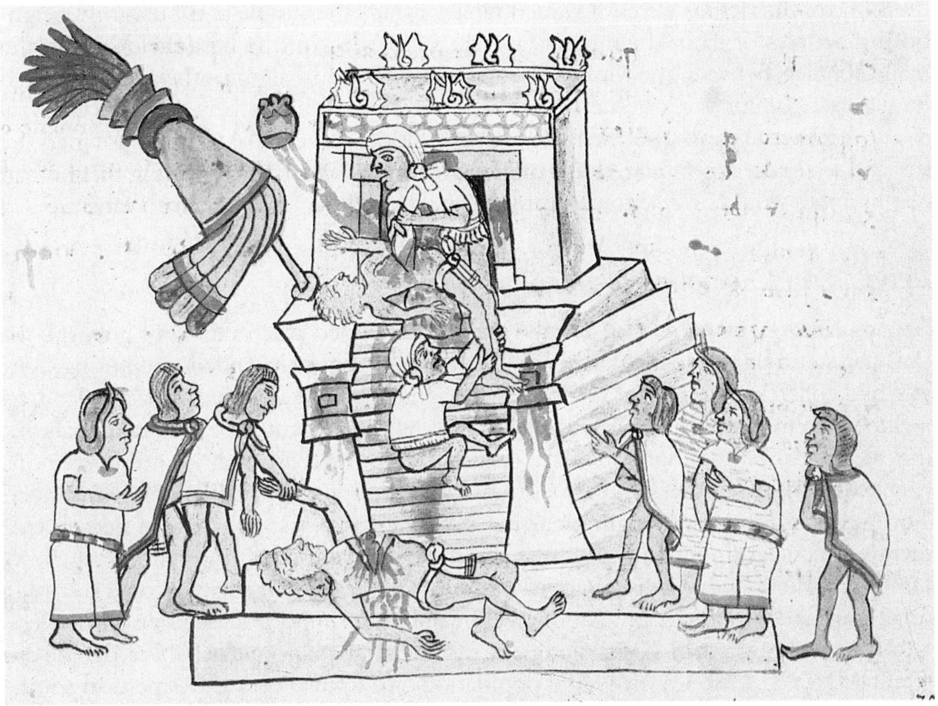

In this manuscript illustration an aide stretches a victim over a sacrificial altar while a priest opens his chest, removes the still-beating heart, and offers it to Huitzilopochtli. At the bottom of the structure, attendants remove the body of an earlier victim.

Mexica Gods

The Mexica also absorbed the religious beliefs common to Mesoamerica. Two of their principal gods—Tezcatlipoca, "the Smoking Mirror," and Quetzalcóatl, "the Feathered Serpent"—had figured in Mesoamerican pantheons at least since the time of Teotihuacan, although different peoples knew them by various names. Tezcatlipoca was a powerful figure, the giver and taker of life and the patron deity of warriors, whereas Quetzalcóatl had a reputation for supporting arts, crafts, and agriculture.

Ritual Bloodletting

Like their predecessors, the Mexica believed that their gods had set the world in motion through acts of individual sacrifice. By letting their blood flow, the gods had given the earth the moisture it needed to bear maize and other crops. To propitiate the gods and ensure the continuation of the world, the Mexica honored their deities through sacrificial bloodletting. Mexica priests regularly performed acts of self-sacrifice, piercing their earlobes or penises with cactus spines in honor of the primeval acts of their gods. The religious beliefs and bloodletting rituals clearly reflected the desire of the Mexica to keep their agricultural society going.

Huitzilopochtli

Mexica priests also presided over the sacrificial killing of human victims. From the time of the Olmecs, and possibly even earlier, Mesoamerican peoples had regarded the ritual sacrifice of human beings as essential to the world's survival. The Mexica, however, placed much more emphasis on human sacrifice than their predecessors did. To a large extent the Mexica enthusiasm for human sacrifice followed from their devotion to the god Huitzilopochtli. Mexica warriors took Huitzilopochtli as their patron deity in the early years of the fourteenth century as they subjected neighboring peoples to their rule. Military success persuaded them that Huitzilopochtli especially favored the Mexica, and as military successes mounted, the priests of Huitzilopochtli's cult demanded sacrificial victims to keep the war god appeased.

Some of the victims were Mexica criminals, while others came as tribute from neighboring peoples or from the ranks of warriors captured on the battlefield during the many conflicts between the Mexica and their neighbors. In all cases the Mexica viewed human sacrifice not as a gruesome form of entertainment but, rather, as a ritual essential to the world's survival. They believed that the blood of sacrificial victims sustained the sun and secured a continuing supply of moisture for the earth, thus ensuring that human communities would be able to cultivate their crops and perpetuate their societies.

Peoples and Societies of the North

Beyond Mexico the peoples of North America developed a rich variety of political, social, and cultural traditions. Many North American peoples depended on hunting, fishing, and collecting edible plants. In the arctic and subarctic regions, for example, diets included sea mammals like whale, seal, and walrus supplemented by land mammals like moose and caribou. Peoples in coastal regions consumed fish, but in interior regions such as the North American plains, they hunted large animals like bison and deer. Throughout the continent nuts, berries, roots, and grasses such as wild rice supplemented the meat provided by hunters and fishers. Like their counterparts elsewhere, hunting, fishing, and foraging peoples of North America built societies on a relatively small scale, since food resources in the wild would not support dense populations.

Pueblo and Navajo Societies

In several regions of North America, agricultural economies enabled peoples to maintain settled societies with large populations. In what is now the American southwest, for example, Pueblo and Navajo peoples tapped river waters to irrigate crops of maize, which constituted as much as 80 percent of their diets. They also cultivated beans, squashes, and sunflowers, and they supplemented their crops with wild plants and small game such as rabbit. The hot and dry environment periodically brought drought and famine. Nevertheless, by about 700 C.E. the Pueblo and Navajo began to construct permanent stone and adobe buildings. Archaeologists have discovered about 125 sites where agricultural peoples built such communities.

Iroquois Peoples

Large-scale agricultural societies emerged also in the woodlands east of the Mississippi River. Woodlands peoples began to cultivate maize and beans during the early centuries C.E., and after about 800 these cultivated foods made up the bulk of their diets. They lived in settled communities, and they often surrounded their larger settlements with wooden palisades, which served as defensive walls. By 1000, for example, the Owasco people had established a distinct society in what is now upstate New York, and by about 1400 the five Iroquois nations (Mohawk, Oneida, Onondaga, Cayuga, and Seneca) had emerged from Owasco society. Women were in charge of Iroquois villages and longhouses, in which several related families lived together, and supervised cultivation of fields surrounding their settlements. Men took responsibility for affairs beyond the village—hunting, fishing, and war.

Mound-Building Peoples

The most impressive structures of the woodlands were the enormous earthen mounds that dotted the countryside throughout the eastern half of North America. Woodlands peoples used these mounds sometimes as stages for ceremonies and rituals, often as platforms for dwellings, and occasionally as burial sites. Modern agriculture, road building, and real estate development have destroyed most of these mounds, but several surviving examples demonstrate that they sometimes reached gigantic proportions.

Cahokia

The largest surviving structure is a mound at Cahokia near East St. Louis, Illinois. More than 30 meters (100 feet) high, 300 meters (1,000 feet) long, and 200 meters (650 feet) wide, it was the third-largest structure in the western hemisphere before the arrival of Europeans. Only the temple of the sun in Teotihuacan and the temple of

Originally constructed about 1000 C.E., the Great Serpent Mound sits atop a ridge in modern Ohio. The serpent's coiled tail is visible at the left, while its open mouth holds an egg on the right.

Quetzalcóatl in Cholula were larger. When the Cahokia society was at its height, from approximately 900 to 1250 C.E., more than one hundred smaller mounds stood within a few kilometers of the highest and most massive mound. Scholars have estimated that during the twelfth century, fifteen thousand to thirty-eight thousand people lived in the vicinity of the Cahokia mounds.

Trade

Because peoples north of Mexico had no writing, information about their societies comes almost exclusively from archaeological discoveries. Burial sites reveal that mound-building peoples recognized various social classes, since they bestowed grave goods of differing quality and quantities on their departed kin. Archaeologists have shown, too, that trade linked widely separated regions and peoples of North America. An elaborate network of rivers—notably the Mississippi, Missouri, Ohio, and Tennessee rivers, along with their many tributaries—facilitated travel and trade by canoe in the eastern half of North America. Throughout the eastern woodlands, archaeologists have turned up stones with sharp cutting edges from the Rocky Mountains, copper from the Great Lakes region, seashells from Florida, minerals from the upper reaches of the Mississippi River, and mica from the southern Appalachian mountains. Indeed, the community at Cahokia probably owed its size and prominence to its location at the hub of North American trade networks. Situated near the confluence of the Mississippi, Missouri, and Ohio rivers, Cahokia was most likely the center of trade and communication networks linking the eastern woodlands of North America with the lower Mississippi valley and lands bordering the Gulf of Mexico.

States and Empires in South America

South American peoples had no script and no tradition of writing before the arrival of Spanish invaders in the early sixteenth century. As a result, the experiences of early South

Contexts & Connections

Mounds and Their Interpreters

The societies of mound-building peoples declined after about 1400, but neither the peoples nor their works disappeared. The Spanish explorer Hernando de Soto was one of the first Europeans to visit the mound-building regions while leading an expedition (1539–1543) through territory now occupied by the states of Florida, Georgia, South Carolina, Tennessee, Alabama, Mississippi, Louisiana, Texas, and Arkansas. During its travels the expedition came across large populations and scores of towns, many of them protected by wooden palisades, as well as hundreds of mounds.

During the next two centuries the native population of the region dramatically declined in the wake of epidemics fueled by smallpox and other diseases introduced to the western hemisphere by European peoples. When Anglo-American settlers ventured into the eastern woodlands and the Mississippi valley after the American revolution, they encountered small native communities with sparse populations. Not realizing that the native population had been much larger in earlier times, the settlers found it difficult to account for the massive mounds that dotted the region by the thousands.

Early Anglo-American commentators could not imagine that the mounds were the work of North America's indigenous peoples, whom they considered backward and brutish. In any case, they had no interest in recognizing talent and skill among native peoples, whose lands they sought to appropriate for their own purposes. Accordingly, they advanced a series of theories to explain the presence of the mounds. The favorite early theory was that the mound builders were the descendants of lost tribes of Israel, which had left Palestine after the Assyrian conquest of their kingdom in the eighth century B.C.E. and had somehow made their way across the Atlantic Ocean to North America. Other theories suggested that the mounds were the work of Phoenicians, Vikings, or Welshmen who had come across the Atlantic Ocean. A somewhat less fanciful view attributed the mounds to Toltecs who had come north from Mexico. More inventive hypotheses imagined survivors from the lost continent of Atlantis or an extinct race of giants as mound builders. Twentieth-century theories held that intelligent creatures from outer space had visited the earth and left the mounds as part of their work.

Modern archaeological studies have shown definitively that there is no need to imagine exiled Israelites, Phoenicians, or space aliens as mound builders. It is quite clear that the native peoples of North America themselves not only constructed the mounds but also built flourishing settlements around them and relied on them as nodes in wide-ranging networks of communication and exchange. It is also clear that the mounds themselves were the products of careful engineering and architecture: studies of surviving mounds have revealed that their builders used different kinds of soil at different parts of their structures to improve drainage and increase stability. During the past two centuries, Euro-American settlers have displaced native communities and destroyed most of the mounds that native peoples constructed. Those that survive, however, testify eloquently to the record of the native peoples as builders of complex societies as well as earthen mounds.

American societies are much more difficult to recover than those of Mesoamerica, where writing had been in use since the fifth century B.C.E. Yet, from archaeological evidence and information recorded by Spanish conquerors, it is possible to reconstruct much of the historical experience of Andean South America, which had been the site of complex societies since the first millennium B.C.E. As in Mesoamerica, cities and secular government in South America began to overshadow ceremonial centers and priestly regimes during the centuries from 1000 to 1500 C.E. Toward the end of the period, like the Mexica in Mesoamerica, the Incas built a powerful state, extended their authority over a vast region, and established the largest empire South America had ever seen.

The Coming of the Incas

After the disappearance of the Chavín and Moche societies, a series of autonomous regional states organized public affairs in Andean South America. The states frequently clashed, but rarely did one of them gain a long-term advantage over the others. For the most part they controlled areas either in the mountainous highlands or in the valleys and coastal plains.

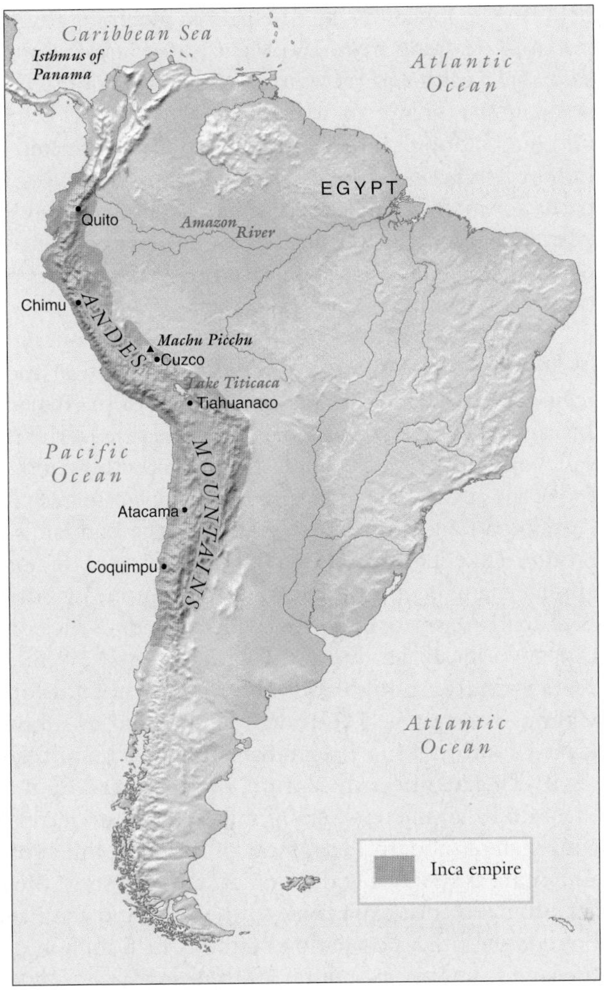

MAP [21.2]
The Inca empire, 1471–1532 C.E.

Chucuito

After the twelfth century, for example, the kingdom of Chucuito dominated the highlands region around Lake Titicaca, which straddles the border between modern Peru and Bolivia at about 4,000 meters (13,000 feet) of elevation. Chucuito depended on the cultivation of potatoes and the herding of llamas and alpacas—camel-like beasts that were the only large domesticated animals anywhere in the Americas before the sixteenth century. In elaborately terraced fields built with stone retaining walls, cultivators harvested potatoes of many different colors, sizes, and tastes. Like maize in Mesoamerica, potatoes served as the staple of the highlanders' diet, which revolved around a potato-based stew enlivened by maize, tomatoes, green vegetables, peppers, chiles, and meat from llamas, alpacas, or tender, domesticated guinea pigs.

Apart from meat, llamas and alpacas provided the highlanders with wool, hides, and dung, widely used as fuel in a land with few trees. In exchange for potatoes and woolen textiles, the highlanders obtained maize and coca leaves from societies in lower valleys. They used maize to enhance their diet and to brew a beerlike beverage, and they chewed the coca leaves, which worked as a mild stimulant and enhanced stamina in the thin air of the high Andes. (When processed, coca leaves yield a much more powerful stimulant with addictive properties—cocaine.)

Chimu

In the lowlands the powerful kingdom of Chimu (sometimes referred to as Chimor) emerged in the tenth century and expanded to dominate some 900 kilometers (560 miles) of the Peruvian coast for about a century before the arrival of the Incas in the mid-fifteenth century. Chimu governed a large and thriving society. Irrigation networks tapped the rivers and streams flowing from the Andes mountains, watered fields in the lowlands, and helped to generate abundant yields of maize and sweet potatoes. Judging from goods excavated at grave sites, Chimu society enjoyed considerable wealth and recognized clear distinctions between social classes.

Chimu's capital city, Chanchan, whose ruins lie close to the modern city of Trujillo, had a population that exceeded fifty thousand and may have approached one hundred thousand. Chanchan featured massive brick buildings, which indicated a capacity for mobilizing large numbers of people and resources for public purposes. The city's geography itself reflected a well-defined social order: each block belonged to an individual clan that supervised the affairs of its own members and coordinated their efforts with those of other clans.

For several centuries, regional states like Chucuito and Chimu maintained order in Andean South America. Yet, within a period of about thirty years, these and other regional states fell under the domination of the dynamic and expansive society of the Incas. The word *Inca* originally was the title of the rulers of a small kingdom in the valley of Cuzco, but in modern usage the term refers more broadly to those who spoke the Incas' Quechua language, or even to all subjects of the Inca empire.

The Inca Empire

After a long period of migration in the highlands, the Incas settled in the region around Lake Titicaca about the mid-thirteenth century. At first they lived as one among many peoples inhabiting the region. About 1438, however, the Inca ruler Pachacuti (reigned 1438–1471) launched a series of military campaigns that vastly expanded the Incas' authority. Pachacuti first extended Inca control over the southern and northern highlands and then turned his forces on the coastal kingdom of Chimu. Though well defended, Chimu had to submit to the Incas when Pachacuti gained control of the waters that supplied Chimu's irrigation system.

By the late fifteenth century, the Incas had built a huge empire stretching more than 4,000 kilometers (2,500 miles) from modern Quito to Santiago. It embraced almost all of modern Peru, most of Ecuador, much of Bolivia, and parts of Chile and Argentina as well. Only the tropical rain forests of the Amazon and other river valleys set a limit to Inca expansion to the east, and the Pacific Ocean defined its western boundary. With a population of about 11.5 million, the Inca empire easily ranked as the largest state ever built in South America.

The Incas ruled as a military and administrative elite. They led armies composed mostly of conquered peoples, and they staffed the bureaucracy that managed the empire's political affairs. But the Incas themselves were not numerous enough to overwhelm their subjects. They routinely sought to encourage obedience among subject peoples by taking hostages from their ruling classes and forcing them to live at the Inca capital. When conquered peoples became restive or uncooperative, the Incas sent loyal subjects as colonists, provided them with choice land and economic benefits, and established them in garrisons to maintain order. When conquered peoples rebelled, Inca armies forced them to leave their homes and resettle in distant parts of the empire.

Quipu and Inca Administration

Administration of the Inca empire rested with a large class of bureaucrats. In the absence of a script, bureaucrats relied on a mnemonic aid known as *quipu* to keep track of their responsibilities. Quipu consisted of an array of small cords of various colors and lengths, all suspended from one large, thick cord. Experts tied a series of knots in the small cords, which sometimes numbered a hundred or more, to help them remember certain kinds of information. Most quipu recorded statistical information having to do with population, state property, taxes, and labor services that communities owed to the central government. Occasionally, though, quipu also helped experts to remember historical information having to do with the establishment of the Inca empire, the Inca rulers, and their deeds. Although much more unwieldy and less flexible than writing, quipu enabled Inca bureaucrats to keep track of information well enough to run an orderly empire.

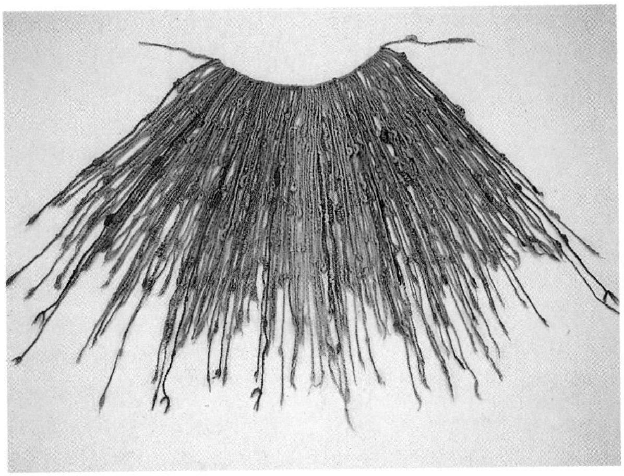

The different colors of quipu threads designated the different items recorded: population, animals, textiles, weapons, and perhaps even rulers and notable events of their reigns. People needed an advanced education to record and "read" information by quipu.

Cuzco

The Inca capital at Cuzco served as the administrative, religious, and ceremonial center of the empire. Cuzco's population exceeded one hundred thousand and may have reached three hundred thousand at the high point of the Inca empire in the late fifteenth century. Most prominent of the residents were the Inca rulers and high nobility, the high priests of the various religious cults, and the hostages of conquered peoples who lived with their families under the watchful eyes of Inca guardians. Cuzco had many handsome buildings of red stone, and the most important temples and palaces sported gold facings.

Inca Roads

A magnificent and extensive road system enabled the central government at Cuzco to communicate with all parts of the far-flung Inca empire and to dispatch large military forces rapidly to distant trouble spots. Two roads linked the Inca realm from north to south—one passing through the mountains, the other running along the coast. Scholars have estimated the combined length of these roads at 16,000 kilometers (9,944 miles). During the early sixteenth century, Spanish conquerors marveled at the roads—paved with stone, shaded by trees, and wide enough to accommodate eight horsemen riding abreast. A corps of official runners carried messages along the roads so that news and information could travel between Cuzco and the most distant parts of the empire within a few days. When the Inca rulers desired a meal of fresh fish, they dispatched runners from Cuzco to the coast more than 320 kilometers (200 miles) away and had their catch within two days. Like roads in empires in other parts of the world, the Incas' roads favored their efforts at centralization. Their roads even facilitated the spread of the Quechua language and their religious cult focusing on the sun, both of which became established throughout their empire.

Inca Society and Religion

Trade

Despite these splendid roads, Inca society did not generate large classes of merchants and skilled artisans. On the local level the Incas and their subjects bartered surplus agricultural production and handcrafted goods among themselves. Long-distance trade, however, fell under the supervision of the central government. Administrators organized exchanges of agricultural products, textiles, pottery, jewelry, and craft goods, but the Inca state did not permit individuals to become independent merchants. In the absence of a market economy, there was no opportunity for a large class of professional, skilled artisans to emerge. Many individuals produced pottery, textiles, and tools for local consumption, and a few produced especially fine goods for the ruling, priestly,

Descendants prepare a ritual meal for a mummified Inca ruler (depicted in the background).

and aristocratic classes. But skilled craftsworkers were much less prominent among the Incas than among the Mexica and the peoples of the eastern hemisphere.

Ruling Elites

The main classes in Inca society were the rulers, aristocrats, priests, and peasant cultivators of common birth. The Incas considered their chief ruler a deity descended from the sun. In theory, this god-king owned all land, livestock, and property in the Inca realm, which he governed as an absolute and infallible ruler. Inca rulers retained their prestige even after death. Their descendants mummified the royal remains and regarded departed kings as intermediaries with the gods. Succeeding rulers often deliberated state policy in the presence of royal mummies so as to benefit from their counsel. Indeed, on the occasion of certain festivals, rulers brought out the mummified remains of their ancestors, dressed them in fine clothes, adorned them with gold and silver jewelry, honored them, and presented them with offerings of food and drink in order to maintain cordial relations with former rulers. Meanwhile, by way of tending to the needs of their living subjects, the Inca god-kings supervised a class of bureaucrats, mostly aristocrats, who allocated plots of land for commoners to cultivate on behalf of the state.

Aristocrats and Priests

Like the ruling elites, Inca aristocrats and priests led privileged lives. Aristocrats consumed fine foods and dressed in embroidered clothes provided by common subjects. Aristocrats also had the right to wear large ear spools that distended their lobes so much that Spanish conquerors referred to them as "big ears." Priests often came from royal and aristocratic families. They led celibate and ascetic lives, but they deeply influenced Inca society because of their education and their responsibility for overseeing religious rituals. The major temples supported hundreds of priests, along with attendants and virgin women devoted to divine service who prepared ceremonial meals and wove fine ritual garments for the priestly staff.

Peasants

The cultivators were mostly peasants of common birth who lived in communities known as *ayllu,* similar to the Mexicas' *calpulli,* which were the basic units of rural society. Ranging in size from small villages to larger towns, each *ayllu* consisted of several families who lived together, sharing land, tools, animals, crops, and work. Peasants supported themselves by working on lands allocated to individual families by their *ayllu.* Instead of paying taxes or tribute, peasants also worked on state lands administered by aristocrats. Much of the production from these state lands went to support the ruling, aristocratic, and priestly classes. The rest went into state storehouses for public relief in times of famine and for the support of widows, orphans, and others unable to cultivate land for themselves. Apart from agricultural work, peasants also owed compulsory labor services to the Inca state. Men provided the heavy labor required for the construction, maintenance, and repair of roads, buildings, and irrigation systems. Women delivered tribute in the form of textiles, pottery, and jewelry. With the aid of quipu, Inca bureaucrats kept track of the labor service and tribute owed by local communities.

Inca Gods: Inti and Viracocha

Members of the Inca ruling class venerated the sun as a god and as their major deity, whom they called Inti. They also recognized the moon, stars, planets, rain, and other natural forces as divine. Some Incas, including the energetic ruler Pachacuti, also showed special favor to the god Viracocha, creator of the world, humankind, and all else in the universe. The cult of the sun, however, outshone all the others. In Cuzco alone some four thousand priests, attendants, and virgin devotees served Inti, whose temple attracted pilgrims from all parts of the Inca empire. Priests of all cults honored their deities with sacrifices, which in Inca society usually took the form of agricultural produce or animals such as llamas and guinea pigs rather than humans.

Fulfilling her tribute duty, an Inca woman weaves woolen fabric on a loom attached to a tree.

Moral Thought

Alongside sacrifices and ritual ceremonies, Inca religion had a strong moral dimension. The Incas taught a concept of sin as a violation of the established social or natural order, and they believed in a life beyond death during which individuals would receive rewards or punishments based on the quality of their earthly lives. Sin, they believed, would bring divine disaster both for individuals and for their larger communities. The Incas also observed rituals of confession and penance by which priests absolved individuals of their sins and returned them to the good graces of the gods.

The Societies of Oceania

Inhabitants of Oceania did not interact with peoples of different societies as frequently or systematically as did their counterparts in the eastern hemisphere, but they built and maintained flourishing societies of their own. The aboriginal peoples of Australia ventured over vast stretches of their continent and created networks of trade and exchange between hunting and gathering societies. Only in the far north, however, did they deal with peoples beyond Australia as they traded sporadically with merchants from New Guinea and the islands of southeast Asia. Meanwhile, throughout the Pacific Ocean, islanders built complex agricultural societies. By the time European mariners sailed into the Pacific Ocean in the sixteenth century, the larger island groups had sizable populations, hierarchical social orders, and hereditary chiefly rulers. In the central and western Pacific, mariners sailed regularly between island groups and established elaborate trade networks. Islanders living toward the eastern and western edge of the Pacific Ocean also had occasional dealings with American and Asian peoples, sometimes with significant consequences for Pacific islands societies themselves.

The Nomadic Foragers of Australia

After the aboriginal peoples of Australia learned how to exploit the resources of the continent's varied regions, they led lives that in some ways changed little over the centuries.

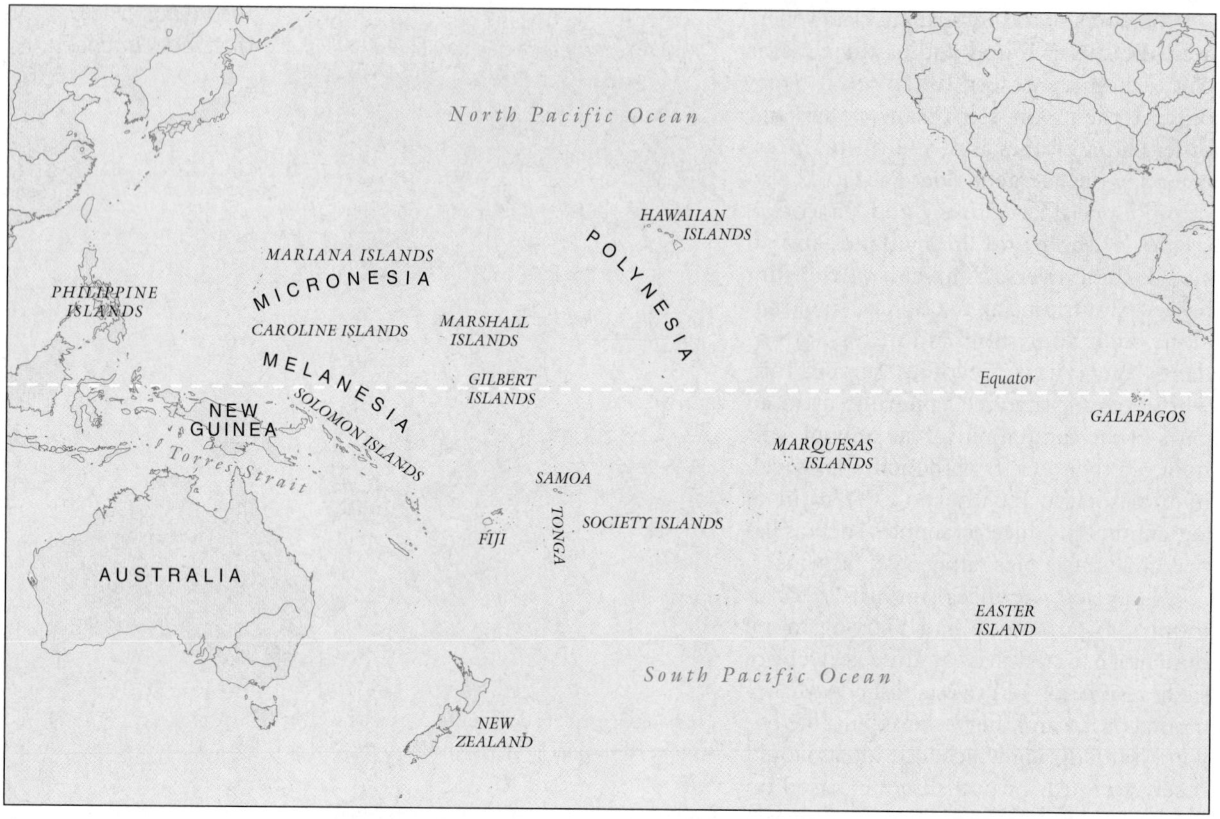

MAP [21.3]
The societies of Oceania.

Unlike their neighbors to the north, they did not turn to agriculture. The inhabitants of New Guinea began to herd swine and cultivate root crops about 5000 B.C.E., and the inhabitants of islands in the Torres Strait (which separates Australia from New Guinea) took up gardening soon thereafter. Although aboriginal peoples of northern Australia must have known about foods cultivated in neighboring lands, they maintained nomadic, foraging societies until European peoples migrated to Australia in large numbers during the nineteenth and twentieth centuries.

Trade

As a result of their mobile and nomadic way of life, aboriginal Australians frequently met and interacted with peoples of neighboring societies. Because Australia is a continent of enormous climatic and ecological diversity, different peoples enjoyed access to food and other resources unknown to others they encountered during their seasonal migrations. Even though as nomads they did not accumulate large quantities of material goods, groups regularly exchanged surplus food and small items when they met.

This sort of small-scale exchange eventually enabled trade goods to spread throughout most of Australia. Individuals did not travel along all the trade routes. Instead, trade goods passed from one aboriginal community to another until they came to rest in regions often distant from their origins. Pearly oyster shells were among the most popular trade items. Archaeologists have turned up many of these shells fashioned into jewelry more than 1,600 kilometers (1,000 miles) from the waters where the oysters bred. From interior regions came stone axe heads, spears, boomerangs, furs, skins, and fibers.

Aboriginal peoples occasionally traded foodstuffs, but with the exception of some root vegetables, these items were generally too perishable for exchange. Peoples on the north coast also engaged in a limited amount of trade with mariners from New Guinea and the islands of southeast Asia. Australian spears and highly prized pearly shells went north in exchange for exotic items like the striking flowers of the bird-of-paradise plant, stone clubs, decorative trinkets—and occasionally iron axes, much coveted by aboriginal peoples who had no tradition of metallurgy.

Cultural and Religious Traditions

In spite of seasonal migrations, frequent encounters with peoples from other aboriginal societies, and trade over long distances, the cultural traditions of Australian peoples mostly did not diffuse much beyond the regions inhabited by individual societies. Aboriginal peoples paid close attention to the prominent geographic features of the lands around them. Rocks, mountains, forests, mineral deposits, and bodies of water were crucial for their survival, and they related stories and myths about these and other geographic features. Often they conducted religious observances designed to ensure continuing supplies of animals, plant life, and water. Given the intense concern of aboriginal peoples with their immediate environments, their cultural and religious traditions focused on local matters and did not appeal to peoples from other regions.

The Development of Pacific Island Societies

By the early centuries C.E., human migrants had established agricultural societies in almost all the island groups of the Pacific Ocean. About the middle of the first millennium C.E., they ventured to the large islands of New Zealand—the last large, habitable region of the earth to receive members of the human species. After 1000 C.E. Polynesians inhabiting the larger Pacific islands grew especially numerous, and their surging population prompted remarkable social and political development.

Trade between Island Groups

In the central and western regions of the Pacific, where several clusters of islands are relatively close to each other, mariners linked island societies. Regional trade networks facilitated exchanges of useful goods like axes and pottery, exotic items like shells and decorative ornaments, and sometimes even foodstuffs like yams. Regional trade within individual island groups served social and political as well as economic functions, since it helped ruling elites establish and maintain harmonious relations with each other. In some cases, trade crossed longer distances and linked different island groups. Inhabitants of the Tonga, Samoa, and Fiji islands traded mats and canoes, for example, and also intermarried, thus creating political and social relationships.

Long-Distance Voyaging

Elsewhere in Polynesia, vast stretches of deep blue water made it much more complicated to travel between different island groups and societies. As a result, regular trade networks did not emerge in the eastern Pacific Ocean. Nevertheless, mariners undertook lengthy voyages on an intermittent basis, sometimes with momentous results. After the original settlement of Easter Island about 300 C.E., for example, Polynesian mariners probably ventured to the western coast of South America, where they learned about the cultivation of sweet potatoes. Between about 400 and 700 C.E., mariners spread sweet potatoes throughout Polynesia and beyond to New Caledonia and Vanuatu. The new crop quickly became a prominent source of food in all the islands it reached. Sweet potatoes were especially important for the Maori population of New Zealand because the staple crops of the tropical Pacific did not flourish in the temperate climes of New Zealand. Thus long-distance voyages were responsible for the dissemination of sweet potatoes to remote islands situated thousands of kilometers from the nearest inhabited lands.

Another case of long-distance voyaging prompted social changes in the Hawaiian Islands. For centuries after the voyages that brought the original settlers to the islands in the early centuries C.E., there was little travel or communication between Hawai`i and other Polynesian societies. During the twelfth and thirteenth centuries,

A painting from 1825 shows several fishponds in active use near Honolulu in Hawai`i.

however, a series of two-way voyages linked Hawai`i with Tahiti and the Marquesas Islands. Memories of these voyages survive in oral traditions that relate the introduction into Hawai`i of new chiefly and priestly lines from Tahiti. Evidence for the voyages comes also from Hawaiian adoption of fishhook styles from Tahiti and words from the Tahitian language.

Population Growth

While undertaking regular or intermittent voyages over long distances, islanders throughout the Pacific Ocean also built productive agricultural and fishing societies. They cultivated taro, yams, sweet potatoes, bananas, breadfruit, and coconuts, and they kept domesticated pigs and dogs. They also fed on abundant supplies of fish, which they caught by spear, net, and hook. After about the fourteenth century, as their population increased, the inhabitants of Hawai`i built ingenious fishponds that allowed small fry to swim from the ocean through narrow gates into rock-enclosed spaces but prevented larger fish from escaping. Fishponds enabled Hawaiians to harvest large quantities of mature fish with relative ease and thus contributed to the islanders' food supplies. The establishment of agricultural and fishing societies led to rapid population growth in all the larger Pacific island groups—Samoa, Tonga, the Society Islands (including Tahiti), and Hawai`i. In Hawai`i, the most heavily populated of the Polynesian island groups, the human population may have exceeded five hundred thousand when European mariners arrived in the late eighteenth century.

Dense populations sometimes led to environmental degradation and social strife on small islands with limited resources. Easter Island in particular was the site of dramatic problems arising from overpopulation. Polynesian migrants originally settled Easter Island in the early centuries C.E., and during the era from about 1100 to 1500, their descendants numbered about ten thousand. This population placed tremendous pressure on the island's resources and also competed fiercely among themselves for those resources. By 1500, having divided into hostile camps, islanders fought one another ferociously, engaging in brutal massacres of their enemies and the desecration of their bodies. As their society disintegrated, they sometimes resorted to cannibalism for lack of sufficient food.

A massive wall constructed of basalt rock protects a burial site at Nan Madol in Pohnpei.

Nan Madol

In other lands, dense populations promoted social organization on a scale never before seen in Oceania. On Pohnpei in the Caroline Islands, for example, the Sandeleur dynasty built a powerful state and organized construction of a massive stone palace and administrative center at Nan Madol. Built mostly during the period from 1200 to 1600, the complex included ninety-three artificial islets protected by seawalls and breakwaters on three sides.

Development of Social Classes

Indeed, beginning about the thirteenth century, expanding populations prompted residents of many Pacific islands to develop increasingly complex social and political structures. Especially on the larger islands, workers became more specialized: some concentrated on cultivating certain crops while others devoted their efforts to fishing, producing axes, or constructing large, seagoing canoes. Distinct classes emerged as aristocratic and ruling elites decided the course of public affairs in their societies and extracted surplus agricultural production from those of common birth. The islands of Tonga, Tahiti, and Hawai`i had especially stratified societies with sharp distinctions between various classes of high chiefs, lesser chiefs, and commoners. Hawaiian society also recognized distinct classes of priests and skilled artisans, such as adze makers and canoe builders, ranking between the chiefly and common classes.

The Formation of Chiefly States

In addition to distinct social classes, island societies generated strong political leadership. Ruling chiefs generally oversaw public affairs in portions of an island, sometimes in an entire island, and occasionally in several islands situated close to each other. In Tonga and Hawai`i, high chiefs frequently launched campaigns to bring additional islands under their control and create large centralized states. Rarely, however, were these militant chiefs able to overcome geographic and logistic difficulties and realize their expansionist ambitions before the nineteenth century.

Nevertheless, high chiefs guided the affairs of complex societies throughout Polynesia. They allocated lands to families, mobilized labor for construction projects, and organized men into military forces. They commanded enormous respect within their societies. In Hawai`i, for example, the classes of high chiefs known as *ali`i nui* intermarried, ate the best fish and other foods that were *kapu* ("taboo") to commoners, and had the right to wear magnificent cloaks adorned with thousands of bright red and yellow bird feathers. Indeed, a *kapu* forbade commoners from approaching or even casting a shadow on the *ali`i nui*.

Polynesian Religion

High chiefs worked closely with priests, who served as intermediaries between human communities and the gods. Gods of war and agriculture were common throughout the Pacific islands, but individual islands and island groups recognized deities particular to their own regions and interests. The most distinctive architecture of early Pacific societies was the ceremonial precinct and temple structure known as *marae* (or *heiau* in Hawaiian). *Marae* often had several terraced floors with a rock or coral wall designating the boundaries of the sacred space. In Tonga and Samoa, temples made of timber and

Sources from the Past

Mo`ikeha's Migration from Tahiti to Hawai`i

A group of Polynesian oral traditions preserve memories of numerous two-way voyages between Tahiti and Hawai`i in the twelfth and thirteenth centuries. One of them has to do with Mo`ikeha, a high chief who left Tahiti because of domestic difficulties and migrated to Hawai`i, where he founded a new chiefly line. The legend recounts several voyages between Tahiti and Hawai`i. The following excerpts deal with Mo`ikeha's establishment as a chief in Hawai`i and the later arrival of his Tahitian son La`amaikahiki, who is credited with the introduction of Tahitian religious and cultural traditions to Hawai`i.

It was dark by the time they arrived [at the Hawaiian island of Kaua`i], so they did not land, instead, mooring their canoe offshore. Early the next morning the people saw this double-hulled canoe floating offshore with the kapu sticks of a chief aboard. The canoe was brought ashore and the travellers got off. Meanwhile the locals were gathering in a crowd to go surf-riding. . . . Among them were the two daughters of the ali`i nui [chief] of Kaua`i, Ho`oipoikamalanai and Hinauu.

Mo`ikeha and his companions saw the crowd and followed along to take part in the morning exercise. Mo`ikeha was a handsome man with dark reddish hair and a tall, commanding figure.

When Ho`oipoikamalanai and her sister saw Mo`ikeha, they immediately fell in love with him, and they decided to take him for their husband. Mo`ikeha in the meantime was also struck with the beauty and grace of the two sisters, and he, too, fell in love with them and decided to take one of them to be his wife. After enjoying the surf for a time, Ho`oipoikamalanai and her sister returned home and told their father about the new arrival and said: "We wish to take that young chief as a husband for one of us." The father approved.

Orders were issued that Mo`ikeha be brought to the house of the two ali`i women. Mo`ikeha and his company were sent for and brought in the presence of the king [the ali`i nui of Kaua`i]. The love of these young people being mutual, Ho`oipoikamalanai and Hinauu took Mo`ikeha to be their husband. Mo`ikeha became ali`i nui of Kaua`i after the death of his father-in-law. . . .

Mo`ikeha worked to make his two wives and five children happy, giving his undivided attention to the bringing up of his boys. He thought no more of Lu`ukia [his lover in Tahiti], but after a while, he began to feel a yearning desire to see his son La`amaikahiki, his child by his first wife Kapo. So he called his five sons together and said to them: "I'm thinking of sending one of you boys to bring your elder brother to Hawai`i.". . .

[After Mo`ikeha's son Kila sailed to Tahiti and found his elder half-brother] La`amaikahiki immediately prepared to accompany his brother to Hawai`i, as Mo`ikeha wished. La`amaikahiki took his priests and his god Lonoika`ouali`i, and set sail for Hawai`i with the men who had come with Kila. When they were approaching Kaua`i, La`amaikahiki began beating his drum. Mo`ikeha heard his drum and ordered everything, the land as well as the house, to be made ready for the reception of the chief La`amaikahiki. Upon the arrival of La`amaikahiki and Kila, the high priest of Kaua`i, Poloahilani, took La`amaikahiki and his god Lonoila`ouali`i ("Lono at the Chiefly Supremacy") to the heiau [temple]. It is said that La`amaikahiki was the first person to bring a god (akua) to Hawai`i. . . .

[After returning to Tahiti, then sailing again to Hawai`i, La`amaikahiki] set sail again, going up the Kona coast [of Hawai`i Island]. . . . It was on this visit that La`amaikahiki introduced hula dancing, accompanied by the drum, to Hawai`i. . . .

La`amaikahiki stayed a long time on Kaua`i teaching the people the art of dancing. From Kaua`i La`amaikahiki visited all the other islands of this group and thus the drum dance (hula ka`eke) spread to the other islands.

SOURCE: Teuira Henry and others. *Voyaging Chiefs of Havai`i.* Ed. by Dennis Kawaharada. Honolulu: Kalamaku Press, 1995, pp. 138–39, 144–46.

How would you characterize the political, social, and cultural significance of two-way voyaging between Tahiti and Hawai`i?

thatched roofs served as places of worship, sacrifice, and communication between priests and the gods, whereas in eastern Polynesia religious ceremonies took place on platforms in open-air courtyards. The largest of these structures, the *marae* Mahaiatea on Tahiti, took the form of a step pyramid about 15 meters (49 feet) high with a base measuring 81 by 22 meters (266 by 72 feet).

Pacific island societies did not enjoy access to the range of technologies developed by continental peoples until the sixteenth and later centuries. Yet Pacific islanders cleverly exploited their environments, established productive agricultural economies, built elaborate, well-organized societies, and reached out when possible to engage in trade with their neighbors. Their achievements testify anew to the human impulses toward densely populated communities and interaction with other societies.

The original inhabitants of the Americas and Oceania lived in societies that were considerably smaller than those of the eastern hemisphere. They did not possess the metallurgical technologies that enabled their counterparts to exploit the natural environment, nor did they possess the transportation technologies based on wheeled vehicles and domesticated animals that facilitated trade and communication among peoples of the eastern hemisphere. Nevertheless, long before they entered into sustained interaction with European and other peoples, they built complex societies and developed sophisticated cultural and religious traditions. Indigenous peoples established foraging, fishing, and agricultural societies throughout the Americas, and they fashioned tools from wood, stone, and bone that enabled them to produce enough food to support sizable communities. In Mesoamerica and Andean South America, they also built imperial states that organized public affairs on a large scale. The cultural and religious traditions of these imperial societies reflected their concern for agricultural production and the maintenance of complex social structures.

The original inhabitants of Australia and the Pacific islands built societies on a smaller scale than did the peoples of the Americas, but they too devised effective means of exploiting the natural environment and organizing flourishing communities. Australia was a continent of foraging nomadic peoples, whereas the Pacific islands supported densely populated agricultural societies. Although they had limited communication with peoples of the Americas or the eastern hemisphere, the peoples of Oceania traded and interacted regularly with their neighbors, and inhabitants of the Pacific islands sometimes undertook lengthy voyages to trade with distant island groups.

CHRONOLOGY

	AMERICAS
950–1150	High point of the Toltec empire
1175	Collapse of the Toltec empire
1250	Inca settlement near Cuzco
1345	Foundation of Tenochtitlan by the Mexica
1400	Emergence of the five Iroquois nations
1428–1440	Reign of the Aztec ruler Itzcóatl
1438–1471	Reign of the Inca ruler Pachacuti
1440–1469	Reign of the Aztec ruler Motecuzoma I
1502–1520	Reign of the Aztec ruler Motecuzoma II
1519	Arrival of Spanish conquerors in Mexico
	OCEANIA
eleventh century	Beginning of population growth in Pacific islands
twelfth century	Beginning of two-way voyages between Hawai`i and Tahiti and the Marquesas islands
thirteenth century	Emergence of distinct social classes and chiefly states
fourteenth century	Construction of fishponds in Hawai`i

FOR FURTHER READING

Peter Bellwood. *The Polynesians: Prehistory of an Island People.* Rev. ed. London, 1987. Well-illustrated popular account emphasizing the origins and early development of Polynesian societies.

Geoffrey Blainey. *Triumph of the Nomads: A History of Aboriginal Australia.* Melbourne, 1975. A sympathetic account of Australia before European arrival, well informed by archaeological discoveries.

Inga Clendinnen. *Aztecs: An Interpretation.* Cambridge, 1991. A brilliant recreation of the Mexica world, concentrating on cultural and social themes.

George A. Collier, Renato I. Rosaldo, and John D. Wirth, eds. *The Inca and Aztec States, 1400–1800: Anthropology and History.* New York, 1982. Seventeen well-focused essays represent approaches that scholars have taken to the Inca and Aztec empires.

Nigel Davies. *The Ancient Kingdoms of Mexico.* Harmondsworth, 1983. Reliable popular account.

Hans Dietrich Disselhoff. *Daily Life in Ancient Peru.* Trans. by A. Jaffa. New York, 1967. A well-illustrated volume concentrating on social history that places Inca society in larger historical context.

Ben Finney. *Voyage of Rediscovery: A Cultural Odyssey through Polynesia.* Berkeley, 1994. Fascinating account of efforts to understand ancient Polynesian techniques of seafaring and to chart the courses of Polynesian migrations.

Ross Hassig. *Aztec Warfare: Imperial Expansion and Political Control.* Norman, Okla., 1988. A solid scholarly study of Mexica military affairs and their role in the building of the Aztec empire.

Jesse D. Jennings, ed. *The Prehistory of Polynesia.* Cambridge, Mass., 1979. Brings together essays by prominent scholars on Polynesia before the arrival of Europeans in the Pacific Ocean.

Friedrich Katz. *The Ancient American Civilizations.* Trans. by K. M. L. Simpson. New York, 1972. Detailed survey that compares the experiences of Mesoamerica and Andean South America.

Patrick V. Kirch. *The Evolution of the Polynesian Chiefdoms.* Cambridge, 1984. Examines the development of Polynesian societies in light of archaeological discoveries.

———. *On the Road of the Winds: An Archaeological History of the Pacific Islands before European Contact.* Berkeley, 2000. A valuable synthesis of recent scholarship by the foremost contemporary archaeologist of the Pacific islands.

Miguel León-Portilla. *The Aztec Image of Self and Society: An Introduction to Nahua Culture.* Salt Lake City, 1992. An excellent guide to Mexica social and cultural history by the foremost student of the Mexica.

David Lewis. *We, the Navigators: The Ancient Art of Landfinding in the Pacific.* Honolulu, 1973. Fascinating reconstruction of traditional methods of noninstrumental navigation used by seafaring peoples of the Pacific islands.

Alfred Métraux. *The History of the Incas.* Trans. by G. Ordish. New York, 1969. A well-illustrated and well-informed popular account.

Lynda Norene Shaffer. *Native Americans before 1492: The Moundbuilding Centers of the Eastern Woodlands.* Armonk, N.Y., 1992. Places the societies of mound-building peoples in larger historical context.

Muriel Porter Weaver. *The Aztecs, Maya, and Their Predecessors: Archaeology of Mesoamerica.* 3rd ed. New York, 1993. An up-to-date survey based on historical and archaeological research.

Eric Wolf. *Sons of the Shaking Earth.* Chicago, 1959. Thoughtful analysis of Mesoamerican history by a leading anthropologist and historian.

OLC

See our **Online Learning Center at www.mhhe.com/bentley3** for additional readings, practice maps, quizzes, and internet activities.

PSI

Unfamiliar words? Check out the **Primary Source Investigator CD-ROM** for an interactive glossary, interactive maps, more images, and primary sources.

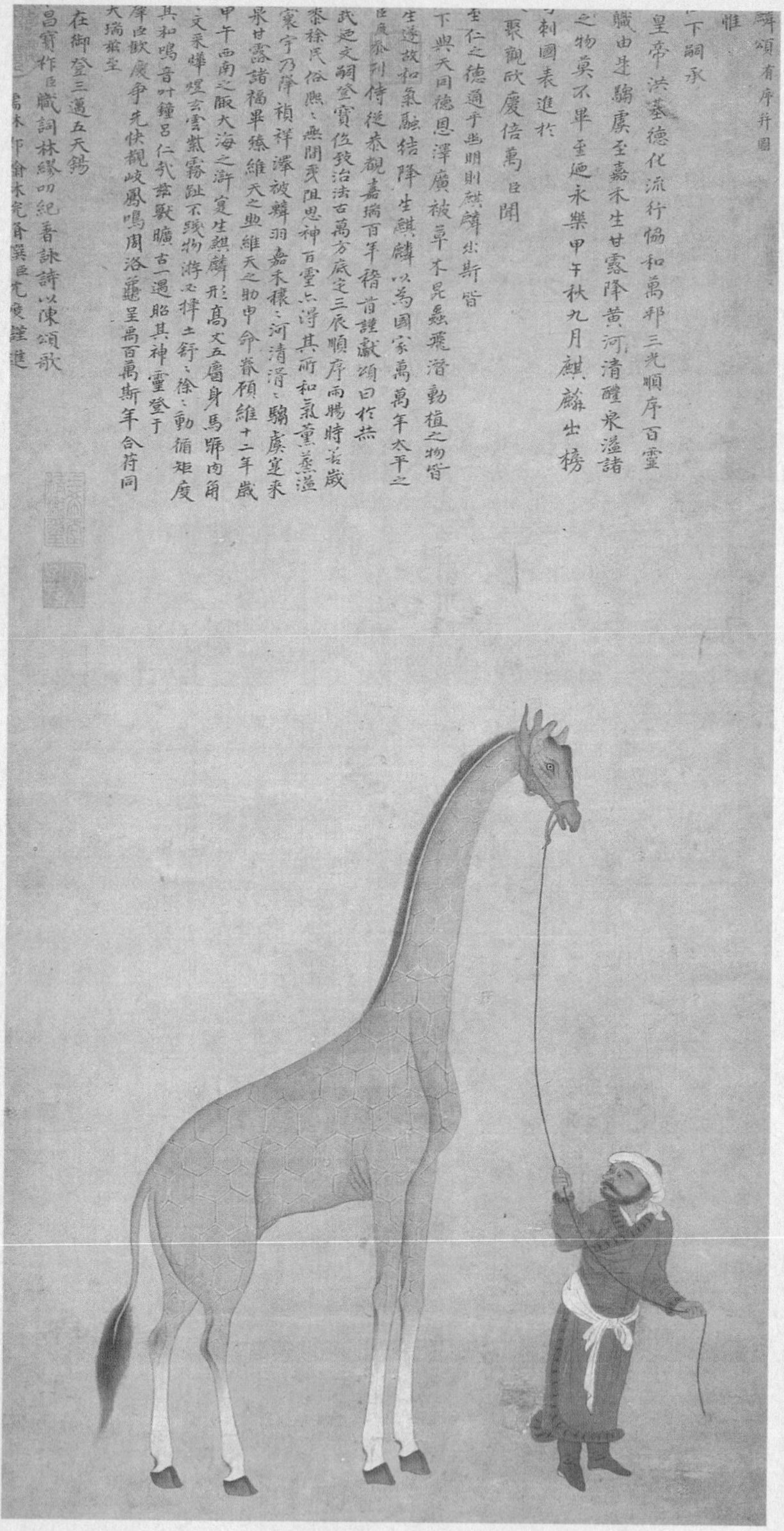

A giraffe from east Africa sent as a present to China in 1414 and painted by a Chinese artist at the Ming zoo.

CHAPTER 22

Reaching Out: Cross-Cultural Interactions

One of the great world travelers of all time was the Moroccan legal scholar Ibn Battuta. Born in 1304 at Tangier, Ibn Battuta followed family tradition and studied Islamic law. In 1325 he left Morocco, perhaps for the first time, to make a pilgrimage to Mecca. He traveled by caravan across north Africa and through Egypt, Palestine, and Syria, arriving at Mecca in 1326. After completing his hajj Ibn Battuta did not head for home, but spent a year visiting Mesopotamia and Persia, then traveled by ship through the Red Sea and down the east African coast as far south as Kilwa. By 1330 he had returned to Mecca, but he did not stay there long. When he learned that the sultan of Delhi offered handsome rewards to foreign legal scholars, he set off for India. Instead of traveling there directly by sailing across the Arabian Sea, however, he followed a long and circuitous land route that took him through Egypt, Syria, Anatolia, Constantinople, the Black Sea, and the great trading cities of central Asia, Bokhara and Samarkand. Only in 1333 did he arrive in Delhi from the north.

For the next eight years, Ibn Battuta remained in India, serving mostly as a *qadi* (judge) in the government of Muhammad ibn Tughluq, the sultan of Delhi. In 1341 Muhammad appointed him to head an enormous embassy to China, but a violent storm destroyed the party's ships as they prepared to depart Calicut for the sea voyage to China. All personal goods and diplomatic presents sank with the ships, and many of the passengers drowned. (Ibn Battuta survived because he was on shore attending Friday prayers at the mosque when the storm struck.) For the next several years, Ibn Battuta made his way around southern India, Ceylon, and the Maldive Islands, where he served as a *qadi* for the recently founded Islamic sultanate, before continuing to China on his own about 1345. He visited the bustling southern Chinese port cities of Quanzhou and Guangzhou, where he found large communities of Muslim merchants, before returning to Morocco in 1349 by way of southern India, the Persian Gulf, Syria, Egypt, and Mecca.

Still, Ibn Battuta's travels were not complete. In 1350 he made a short trip to the kingdom of Granada in southern Spain, and in 1353 he joined a camel caravan across the Sahara desert to visit the Mali empire, returning to Morocco in 1355. During his travels Ibn Battuta visited the equivalent of forty-four modern countries and logged more than 117,000 kilometers (73,000 miles). His account of his adventures stands with Marco Polo's book among the classic works of travel literature.

Between 1000 and 1500 C.E., the peoples of the eastern hemisphere traveled, traded, communicated, and interacted more regularly and intensively than ever before.

The large empires of the Mongols and other nomadic peoples provided a political foundation for this cross-cultural interaction. When they conquered and pacified vast regions, nomadic peoples provided safe roads for merchants, diplomats, missionaries, and other travelers. Quite apart from the nomadic empires, improvements in maritime technology led to increased traffic in the sea lanes of the Indian Ocean and the South China Sea. As a result, long-distance travel became much more common than in earlier eras, and individual travelers like Ibn Battuta and Marco Polo sometimes ventured throughout much of the eastern hemisphere.

Merchants and travelers exchanged more than trade goods. They diffused technologies and spread religious faiths. They also exchanged diseases and facilitated the spread of pathogens that caused massive and deadly epidemics. During the middle decades of the fourteenth century, bubonic plague traveled the trade routes from western China to central Asia, southwest Asia, north Africa, and Europe. During its initial, furious onslaught, bubonic plague ravaged societies wherever it struck, and it continued to cause epidemics for three centuries and more.

Gradually, however, societies recovered from the plague. By the early fifteenth century, Chinese and western European peoples in particular had restabilized their societies and begun to renew cross-cultural contacts. In Europe, this effort had profound consequences for modern world history. As they sought entry to the markets of Asia, European mariners not only established direct connections with African and Asian peoples but also sailed to the western hemisphere and the Pacific Ocean. Their voyages brought the peoples of the eastern hemisphere, the western hemisphere, and Oceania into permanent and sustained interaction with one another. Thus cross-cultural interactions of the period 1000 to 1500 pointed toward global interdependence, a principal characteristic of modern world history.

LONG-DISTANCE TRADE AND TRAVEL

Travelers embarked on long-distance journeys for a variety of reasons. Nomadic peoples ranged widely in the course of migrations and campaigns of conquest. East European and African slaves traveled involuntarily to the Mediterranean basin, southwest Asia, India, and sometimes even southern China. Buddhist, Christian, and Muslim pilgrims undertook extraordinary journeys to visit holy shrines. Three of the more important motives for long-distance travel between 1000 and 1500 C.E. were trade, diplomacy, and missionary activity. The cross-cultural interactions that resulted helped spread technological innovations throughout the eastern hemisphere.

Patterns of Long-Distance Trade

Merchants engaged in long-distance trade relied on two principal networks of trade routes. Luxury goods of high value relative to their weight, such as silk textiles and precious stones, often traveled overland on the silk roads used since classical times. Bulkier commodities, such as steel, stone, coral, and building materials, traveled the sea lanes of the Indian Ocean, since it would have been unprofitable to transport them overland. The silk roads linked all of the Eurasian landmass, and trans-Saharan caravan routes drew west Africa into the larger economy of the eastern hemisphere. The sea lanes of the Indian Ocean served ports in southeast Asia, India, Arabia, and east Africa while also offering access via the South China Sea to ports in China, Japan, Korea, and the spice-bearing islands of southeast Asia. Thus, in combination, land and sea routes touched almost every corner of the eastern hemisphere.

Trading Cities

As the volume of trade increased, the major trading cities and ports grew rapidly, attracting buyers, sellers, brokers, and bankers from parts near and far. Khanbaliq (modern Beijing), Hangzhou, Quanzhou, Melaka, Cambay, Samarkand, Hormuz, Baghdad, Caffa, Cairo, Alexandria, Kilwa, Constantinople, Venice, Timbuktu, and many other cities had large quarters occupied by communities of foreign merchants. When a trading or port city enjoyed a strategic location, maintained good order, and resisted the temptation to levy excessive customs fees, it had the potential to become a major emporium serving long-distance trade networks. A case in point is Melaka (in modern Malaysia). Founded in the 1390s, within a few decades Melaka became the principal clearinghouse of trade in the eastern Indian Ocean. The city's authorities policed the strategic Strait of Melaka and maintained a safe market that welcomed all merchants and levied reasonable fees on goods exchanged there. By the end of the fifteenth century, Melaka had a population of some fifty thousand people, and in the early sixteenth century the Portuguese merchant Tomé Pires reported that more than eighty languages could be heard in the city's streets.

The magnificent twelfth-century caravanserai at Tercan in eastern Anatolia provided food, lodging, and protection for merchants traveling with camels, donkeys, and horses. The Saljuqs built caravanserais throughout Anatolia.

During the early and middle decades of the thirteenth century, the Mongols' campaigns caused economic disruption throughout much of Eurasia—particularly in China and southwest Asia, where Mongol forces toppled the Song and Abbasid dynasties. Mongol conquests inaugurated a long period of economic decline in southwest Asia where the conquerors destroyed cities and allowed irrigation systems to fall into disrepair. As the Mongols consolidated their hold on conquered lands, however, they laid the political foundation for a surge in long-distance trade along the silk roads. Merchants traveling the silk roads faced less risk of banditry or political turbulence than in previous times. Meanwhile, strong economies in China, India, and western Europe fueled demand for foreign commodities. Many merchants traveled the whole distance from Europe to China in pursuit of profit.

Marco Polo

The best-known long-distance traveler of Mongol times was the Venetian Marco Polo (1253–1324). Marco's father Niccolò and uncle Maffeo were among the first European merchants to visit China. Between 1260 and 1269 they traveled and traded throughout Mongol lands, and they met Khubilai Khan as he was consolidating his hold on China. When they returned to China in 1271, seventeen-year-old Marco Polo accompanied them. The great khan took a special liking to Marco, who was a marvelous conversationalist and storyteller. Khubilai allowed Marco to pursue his mercantile interests in China and also sent him on numerous diplomatic missions, partly because Marco regaled him with stories about the distant parts of his realm. After seventeen years in China, the Polos decided to return to Venice, and Khubilai granted them permission to leave. They went back on the sea route by way of Sumatra, Ceylon, India, and Arabia, arriving in Venice in 1295.

A historical accident has preserved the story of Marco Polo's travels. After his return from China, Marco was captured and made a prisoner of war during a conflict between his native Venice and its commercial rival, Genoa. While imprisoned, Marco related tales of his travels to his fellow prisoners. One of them was a writer of romances, and he compiled the stories into a large volume that circulated rapidly throughout Europe.

In spite of occasional exaggerations and tall tales, Marco's stories deeply influenced European readers. Marco always mentioned the textiles, spices, gems, and other goods he observed during his travels, and European merchants took note, eager to participate

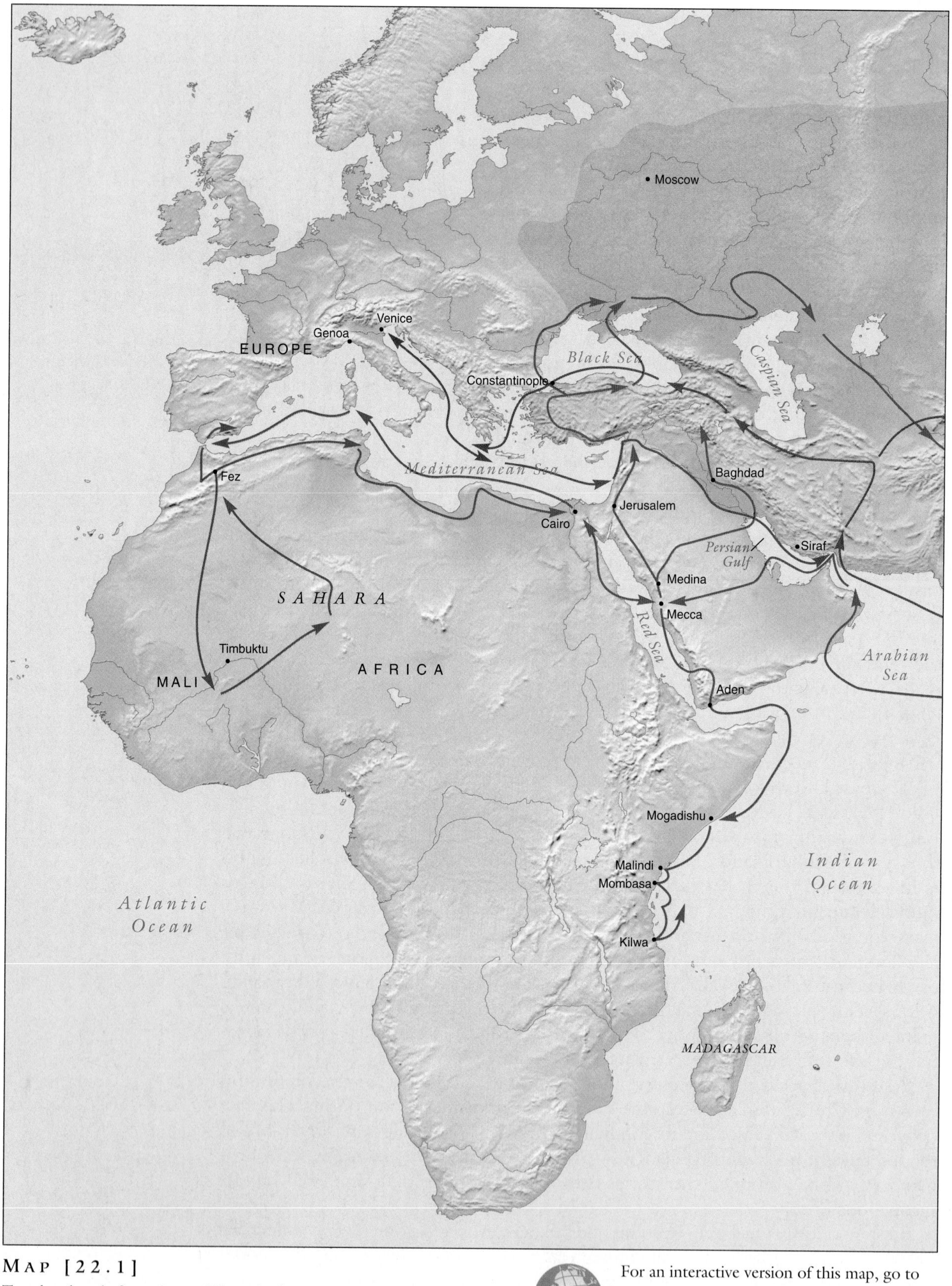

MAP [22.1]
Travel and trade from the twelfth to the fourteenth century.

For an interactive version of this map, go to www.mhhe.com/bentley3ch22maps.

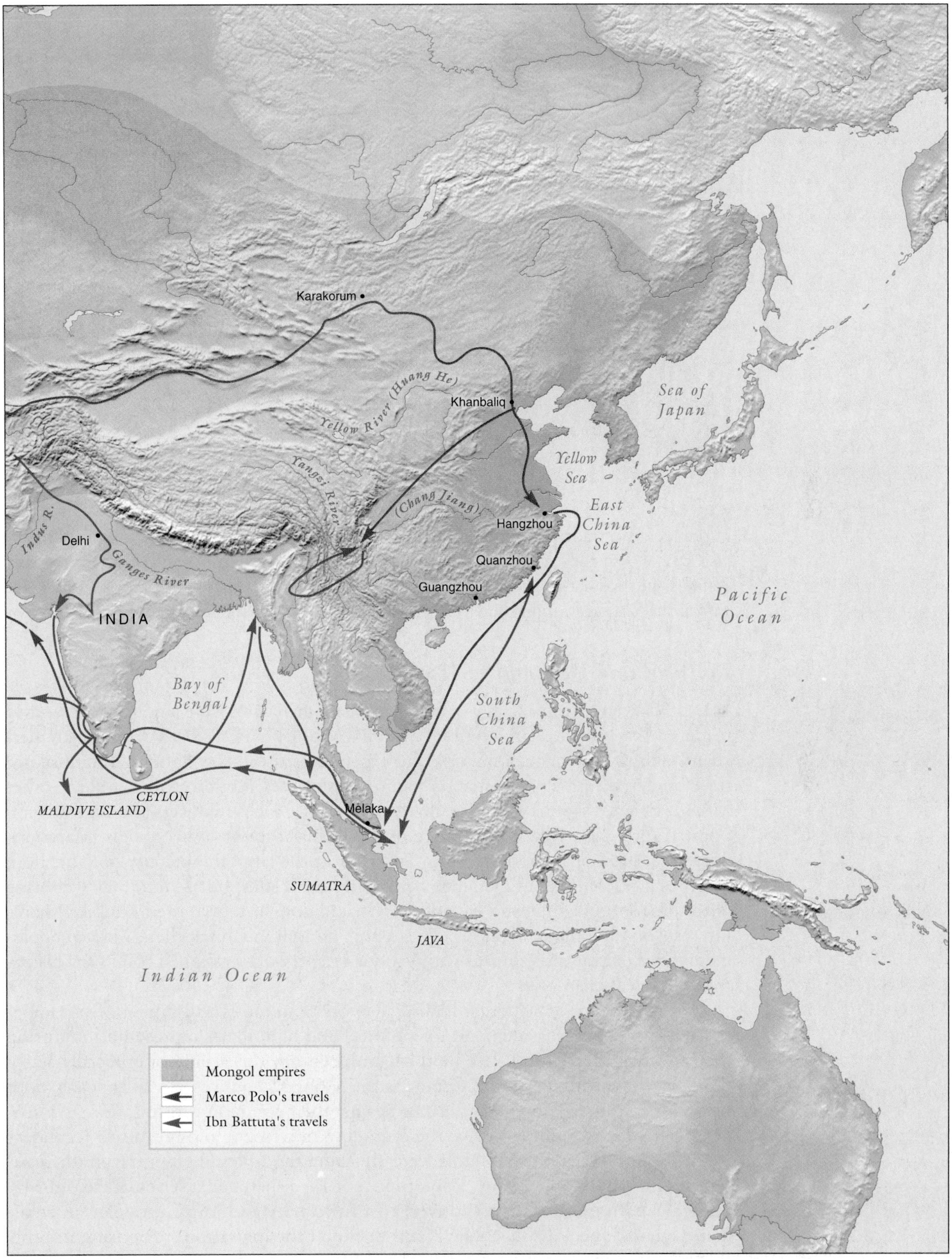
Karakorum
Khanbaliq
Yellow River (Huang He)
Yangzi River
(Chang Jiang)
Hangzhou
Quanzhou
Guangzhou
Sea of Japan
Yellow Sea
East China Sea
Pacific Ocean
Indus R.
Delhi
Ganges River
INDIA
Bay of Bengal
South China Sea
CEYLON
MALDIVE ISLAND
Melaka
SUMATRA
JAVA
Indian Ocean
Mongol empires
Marco Polo's travels
Ibn Battuta's travels

An illustration from a fourteenth-century French manuscript depicts Marco Polo picking pepper with local workers in southern India.

in the lucrative trade networks of Eurasia. The Polos were among the first Europeans to visit China, but they were not the last. In their wake came hundreds of others, mostly Italians. In most cases their stories do not survive, but their travels helped to increase European participation in the larger economy of the eastern hemisphere.

Political and Diplomatic Travel

Marco Polo came from a family of merchants, and merchants were among the most avid readers of his stories. Marco himself most likely collaborated closely with Italian merchants during his years in China. Yet his experiences also throw light on long-distance travel undertaken for political and diplomatic purposes. Khubilai Khan and the other Mongol rulers of China did not entirely trust their Chinese subjects and regularly appointed foreigners to administrative posts. In his account of his travels, Marco reported that Khubilai appointed him governor of the large trading city of Yangzhou. There is no independent evidence to confirm this claim, but Marco may well have filled some sort of administrative position. In addition, he represented Khubilai Khan's interests on diplomatic missions. To support himself in China, then, Marco supplemented his mercantile ventures with various official duties assigned to him by his patron, the great khan.

Mongol-Christian Diplomacy

The emergence of elaborate trading networks and the establishment of vast imperial states created great demand for political and diplomatic representation during the centuries after 1000 C.E. The thirteenth century was a time of especially active diplomacy involving parties as distant as the Mongols and western Europeans, both of whom considered a military alliance against their common Muslim foes. As European Christians sought to revive the crusading movement and recapture Jerusalem from Muslim forces, the Mongols were attacking the Abbasid empire from the east. During the 1240s and 1250s, Pope Innocent IV dispatched a series of envoys who invited the Mongol khans to convert to Christianity and join Europeans in an alliance against the Muslims. The khans declined the invitation, proposing in reply that the pope and European Christians submit to Mongol rule or face destruction.

Rabban Sauma

Although the early round of Mongol-European diplomacy offered little promise of cooperation, the Mongols later initiated another effort. In 1287 the Mongol ilkhan of Persia planned to invade the Muslim-held lands of southwest Asia, capture Jerusalem, and crush Islam as a political force in the region. In hopes of attracting support for the project, he dispatched Rabban Sauma, a Nestorian Christian priest born in the Mongol capital of Khanbaliq but of Turkish ancestry, as an envoy to the pope and European political leaders.

Rabban Sauma met with the kings of France and England, the pope, and other high officials of the Roman Catholic church. He enjoyed a fine reception, but he did not succeed in attracting European support for the ilkhan. Only a few years later, in 1295, Ghazan, the new ilkhan of Persia, converted to Islam, thus precluding any further possibility of an alliance between the Mongols of Persia and European Christians. Nevertheless, the flurry of diplomatic activity illustrates the complexity of political affairs in the eastern hemisphere and the need for diplomatic consultation over long distances.

The expansion of Islamic influence in the eastern hemisphere encouraged a different kind of politically motivated travel. Legal scholars and judges played a crucial role in Islamic societies, since the *sharia* prescribed religious observances and social relationships based on the Quran. Conversions to Islam and the establishment of Islamic states in India, southeast Asia, and sub-Saharan Africa created a demand for Muslims educated in Islamic law. After about the eleventh century, educated Muslims from southwest Asia and north Africa regularly traveled to recently converted lands to help instill Islamic values.

Ibn Battuta

Best known of the Muslim travelers was Ibn Battuta (1304–1369). Islamic rulers governed most of the lands Ibn Battuta visited—including India, the Maldive Islands, the Swahili city-states of east Africa, and the Mali empire—but very few Muslims educated in the law were available in those lands. With his legal credentials Ibn Battuta had little difficulty finding government positions. As *qadi* and advisor to the sultan of Delhi, he supervised the affairs of a wealthy mosque and heard cases at law, which he strictly enforced according to Islamic standards of justice. On one occasion Ibn Buttuta sentenced a man to receive eighty lashes because he had drunk wine eight years earlier.

After leaving northern India, Ibn Battuta obtained a post as *qadi* in the Maldive Islands. There he heard cases at law and worked zealously to promote proper observance of Islam. He ordered lashings for men who did not attend Friday prayers, and he once sentenced a thief to lose his right hand in accordance with punishment prescribed by the *sharia*. He also attempted, unsuccessfully, to persuade island women to meet the standards of modesty observed in other Islamic lands by covering their breasts. In both east and west Africa, Ibn Battuta consulted with Muslim rulers and offered advice about government, women's dress, and proper relationships between the sexes. Like many other legal scholars whose stories went unrecorded, Ibn Battuta provided guidance in the ways of Islam in societies recently converted to the faith.

Missionary Campaigns

Sufi Missionaries

Islamic values spread not only through the efforts of legal scholars, but also through the missionary activities of Sufi mystics. As in the early days of Islam, Sufis in the period from 1000 to 1500 ventured to recently conquered or converted lands and sought to win a popular following for the faith in India, southeast Asia, and sub-Saharan Africa. Sufis did not insist on a strict, doctrinally correct understanding of Islam but, rather, emphasized piety and devotion to Allah. They even tolerated continuing

Sources from the Past

Ibn Battuta on Customs in the Mali Empire

Long-distance travelers often encountered unfamiliar customs in foreign societies. The Moroccan traveler Ibn Battuta approved heartily when staying with hosts who honored the values of his own Muslim society, but he had little tolerance for those who did not. Here he describes what he witnessed at the sultan's court in the Mali empire.

The blacks are the most humble of men before their king and the most extreme in their self-abasement before him. They swear by his name, saying "Mansa Sulaimanki" [the law of Mansa Sulaiman, the Mali sultan]. When he calls one of them while he is in session . . . the man invited takes off his clothes and wears patched clothes, takes off his turban, puts on a dirty cap, and goes in raising his clothes and trousers up his legs halfway to his knees. He advances with humility looking like a beggar. He hits the ground with his elbows, he hits it hard. He stands bowed, like one . . . in prayer, listening to what the king says. When one of them speaks to the sultan and he gives him an answer, he removes his clothes from his back and throws dust on his head and back, as a person does when bathing with water. I used to wonder how they do not blind their eyes. . . .

Sometimes one of them would stand before him and recall what he had done in his [the sultan's] service, saying, "I did such and such on such a day," and, "I killed so and so on such a day." Those who know this confirm that he is telling the truth. Their confirmation is by pulling the strings of their bows and letting them go, as one does when one is shooting. If the sultan says to him that he has spoken the truth or thanks him, he takes off his clothes and dusts. This is good manners among them. . . .

Amongst their good qualities is the small amount of injustice amongst them, for of all people they are the furthest from it. . . .

Another of the good habits amongst them is the way they meticulously observe the times of the prayers and attendance at them, so also it is with regard to their congregational services and their beating of their children to instill these things in them.

When it is Friday, if a man does not come early to the mosque he will not find a place to pray because of the numbers of the crowd. It is their custom for every man to send his boy [i.e., servant] with his prayer mat. He spreads it for him in a place commensurate with his position and keeps the place until he comes to the mosque. . . .

Among their good qualities is their putting on of good white clothes on Friday. If a man among them has nothing except a tattered shirt, he washes and cleans it and attends the Friday prayer in it. Another of their good qualities is their concern for learning the sublime Quran by heart. . . .

Among the bad things which they do—their serving women, slave women and little daughters appear before people naked, exposing their private parts. I used to see many of them in this state in [the fasting month of] Ramadan, for it was the custom of the *farariyya* [commanders] to break the fast in the sultan's house. Everyone of them has his food carried in to him by twenty or more of his slave girls and they are naked, every one. Also among their bad customs is the way women will go into the presence of the sultan naked, without any covering; and the nakedness of the sultan's daughters—on the night of the twenty-seventh of Ramadan, I saw about a hundred slave girls coming out of his palace with food, with them were two of his daughters, they had full breasts and no clothes on. Another of their bad customs is their putting of dust and ashes on their heads as a sign of respect. . . . And another is that many of them eat animals not ritually slaughtered, and dogs and donkeys.

SOURCE: Said Hamdun and Noel King, eds. *Ibn Battuta in Black Africa*. Princeton: Markus Wiener, 1998, pp. 49–50, 58–59.

Discuss the various ways in which Islamic influences and established local customs came together in the Mali empire.

reverence of traditional deities, whom the Sufis treated as manifestations of Allah and his powers. By taking a flexible approach to their missions, the Sufis spread Islamic values without facing the resistance that unyielding and doctrinaire campaigns would likely have provoked.

Christian Missionaries

Meanwhile, Roman Catholic missionaries also traveled long distances in the interests of spreading Christianity. Missionaries accompanied the crusaders and other forces to all the lands where Europeans extended their influence after the year 1000. In lands where European conquerors maintained a long-term presence—such as the Baltic lands, the Balkan region, Sicily, and Spain—missionaries attracted converts in large numbers, and Roman Catholic Christianity became securely established. In the eastern Mediterranean region, however, where crusaders were unable to hold their conquests permanently, Christianity remained a minority faith.

The most ambitious missions sought to convert Mongols and Chinese to Roman Catholic Christianity. Until the arrival of European merchants and diplomats in the thirteenth century, probably no Roman Catholic Christian had ever ventured as far east as China, although Nestorian Christians from central Asia had maintained communities there since the seventh century. As more Europeans traveled to China, their expatriate communities created a demand for Roman Catholic services. Many of the Roman Catholic priests who traveled to China probably intended to serve the needs of these communities, but some of them also sought to attract converts.

John of Montecorvino

Most active of the Roman Catholic missionaries in China was John of Montecorvino, an Italian Franciscan who went to China in 1291, became the first archbishop of Khanbaliq in 1307, and died there in 1328. While serving the community of Roman Catholic expatriates in China, John worked energetically to establish Christianity in the host society. He translated the New Testament and the Book of Psalms into Turkish, a language commonly used at the Mongol court, and he built several churches in China. He took in young boys from Mongol and Chinese families, baptized them, and taught them Latin and Roman Catholic rituals. By 1305 he claimed to have baptized six thousand individuals, and he invited the great khan himself to convert to Christianity. Although popular and widely respected among Europeans, Chinese, and Mongols alike, John attracted few Asian peoples to Christianity.

Caterina Vilioni, daughter of the Venetian merchant Domenico Vilioni, died in the Chinese trading city of Yangzhou in 1342. Her tombstone, which shows she was part of the Roman Catholic community in Yangzhou, came to light during a construction project in 1951.

Roman Catholic authorities in Europe dispatched many other priests and missionaries to China during the early fourteenth century, but like John of Montecorvino, they won few converts. Missions successfully established Christian communities in Scandinavia, eastern Europe, Spain, and the Mediterranean islands that European armies recaptured from Muslims during the centuries after 1000 C.E., but east Asia was too distant for the resources available to the Roman Catholic church. Moreover, east Asian peoples already possessed sophisticated religious and cultural traditions, so Christianity had little appeal. Nevertheless, Christian missions to China continued until

Sources from the Past

John of Montecorvino on His Mission in China

The Franciscan John of Montecorvino (1247–1328) served as a Roman Catholic missionary in Armenia, Persia, and India before going to China in 1291. There he served as priest to expatriate European Christians, and he sought to attract converts to Christianity from the Mongol and Chinese communities. In a letter of 8 January 1305 asking for support from his fellow Franciscans in Italy, John outlined some of his activities during the previous thirteen years.

[After spending thirteen months in India] I proceeded on my further journey and made my way to China, the realm of the emperor of the Mongols who is called the great khan. To him I presented the letter of our lord the pope and invited him to adopt the Catholic faith of our Lord Jesus Christ, but he had grown too old in idolatry. However, he bestows many kindnesses upon the Christians, and these two years past I have gotten along well with him. . . .

I have built a church in the city of Khanbaliq, in which the king has his chief residence. This I completed six years ago; and I have built a bell tower to it and put three bells in it. I have baptized there, as well as I can estimate, up to this time some 6,000 persons. . . . And I am often still engaged in baptizing.

Also I have gradually bought one hundred and fifty boys, the children of pagan parents and of ages varying from seven to eleven, who had never learned any religion. These boys I have baptized, and I have taught them Greek and Latin after our manner. Also I have written out Psalters for them, with thirty hymnals and breviaries [prayer books]. By help of these, eleven of the boys already know our service and form a choir and take their weekly turn of duty as they do in convents, whether I am there or not. Many of the boys are also employed in writing out Psalters and other suitable things. His Majesty the Emperor moreover delights much to hear them chanting. I have the bells rung at all the canonical hours, and with my congregation of babes and sucklings I perform divine service, and the chanting we do by ear because I have no service book with the notes. . . .

Indeed if I had but two or three comrades to aid me, it is possible that the emperor khan himself would have been baptized by this time! I ask then for such brethren to come, if any are willing to come, such I mean as will make it their great business to lead exemplary lives. . . .

I have myself grown old and grey, more with toil and trouble than with years, for I am not more than fifty-eight. I have got a competent knowledge of the language and script which is most generally used by the Tartars. And I have already translated into that language and script the New Testament and the Psalter and have caused them to be written out in the fairest penmanship they have, and so by writing, reading, and preaching, I bear open and public testimony to the law of Christ.

SOURCE: Henry Yule and Henri Cordier, eds. *Cathay and the Way Thither,* 4 vols. London: Hakluyt, 1913–16, 3:45–50. (Translation slightly modified.)

To what extent did John of Montecorvino's missionary work reflect conditions different from those that motivated St. Francis of Assisi to found a mendicant order?

the mid-fourteenth century, when the collapse of the Mongols' Yuan dynasty and the eruption of epidemic disease temporarily disrupted long-distance travel across Eurasia.

Long-Distance Travel and Cross-Cultural Exchanges

Cultural Exchanges

Long-distance travel of all kinds, whether for commercial, political, diplomatic, or missionary purposes, encouraged cultural exchanges between peoples of different soci-

A thirteenth-century manuscript illustration depicts two lute players: Muslim (left) and Christian (right). Muslim artists deeply influenced Christian poetry and music during the middle ages.

eties. Songs, stories, religious ideas, philosophical views, and scientific knowledge all passed readily among travelers who ventured into the larger world during the era from 1000 to 1500 C.E. The troubadours of western Europe, for example, drew on the poetry, music, and love songs of Muslim performers when developing the literature of courtly love. Similarly, European scientists avidly consulted their Muslim and Jewish counterparts in Sicily and Spain to learn about their understanding of the natural world.

Large numbers of travelers also facilitated agricultural and technological diffusion during the period from 1000 to 1500. Indeed, technological diffusion sometimes facilitated long-distance travel itself. The magnetic compass, for example, invented in China during the Tang or Song dynasty, spread throughout the Indian Ocean basin during the eleventh century, and by the mid-twelfth century European mariners used compasses in the Mediterranean and the Atlantic Ocean. Diffusion of the compass was a boon to maritime trade, since it allowed mariners to sail over long stretches of deep water with confidence in their ability to find their destinations and return home safely.

Spread of Crops

Long-distance journeys enabled Muslim travelers to introduce new food and commercial crops to sub-Saharan Africa. Food crops included citrus fruits and Asian strains of rice, which enriched diets in west Africa after the eleventh century. Muslims also introduced cotton to west Africa, and by 1100 cotton fabrics had become popular with the ruling elites and wealthy merchants of the west African kingdoms. Cotton grew well in the savannas, and by 1500 it was the principal textile produced in sub-Saharan Africa.

Sugarcane

Muslims were also instrumental in the continuing diffusion of sugarcane. Muslim merchants and other travelers had begun large-scale cultivation of sugarcane in southwest Asia and north Africa during the Abbasid caliphate. They experimented with the plant in west Africa but had limited success because of adverse environmental conditions.

After the twelfth century, however, Muslims facilitated the westward spread of sugarcane by acquainting European crusaders with crystallized sugar refined from cane. Up to that time Europeans had little access to refined sugar, and they relied on honey and fruits as sweeteners. They immediately appreciated the convenience of refined sugar. Italian entrepreneurs began to organize sugarcane plantations on Mediterranean islands such as Sicily, Cyprus, Crete, and Rhodes. Rapidly increasing demand for refined sugar encouraged investors to seek suitable locations throughout the Mediterranean basin. The cultivation of sugarcane had deep social and economic implications. Besides influencing local economic development in lands where it spread, it touched distant societies as well. Like their Muslim predecessors, European sugar producers often staffed their plantations with slave laborers, and the growth of plantations fueled an increasing demand for Muslim war captives and black Africans who could supply labor services.

Gunpowder Technologies

Although Muslim merchants and travelers were especially prominent agents of diffusion, Mongols also contributed to the process, notably by helping to spread gunpowder technologies west from China. Mongol invaders learned about gunpowder from Chinese military engineers in the early thirteenth century and soon incorporated gunpowder-based weapons into their arsenal: as early as 1214 Chinggis Khan's armies included an artillery unit. During the 1250s, as they campaigned in Persia and southwest Asia, the Mongols used catapults and trebuchets to lob gunpowder bombs into cities under siege. Muslim armies soon developed similar weapons in response.

By the mid-thirteenth century gunpowder had reached Europe—possibly by way of Mongol-ruled Russia—and Europeans had begun to experiment with gunpowder-fueled rockets. By the early fourteenth century, armies from China to Europe possessed primitive cannons. Although not especially accurate, the weapons were powerful enough to blow holes in the defensive walls of cities under siege. Thus, with the assistance of Mongol warriors, gunpowder technology rapidly spread from its homeland in China across the entire Eurasian landmass.

Agricultural and technological diffusions of the era 1000 to 1500 were by no means unique processes in world history. For millennia, agricultural crops and technological skills had spread widely whenever peoples of different societies interacted with one another. Because of the particularly intense interactions of the period from 1000 to 1500, however, agricultural and technological diffusion profoundly influenced the lives of peoples throughout the eastern hemisphere. The spread of food crops enriched diets and supported increasing populations while the spread of industrial crops like cotton promoted economic development. The diffusion of the magnetic compass enabled mariners to sail the seas more safely and effectively, and the spread of gunpowder technology changed forever the nature of war.

Crisis and Recovery

As Eurasian peoples traveled over long distances, they not only exchanged trade goods, agricultural crops, and technological expertise, but also unwittingly helped disease pathogens to spread. When diseases broke out among previously unexposed populations, they often caused massive epidemics that severely disrupted whole societies. During the fourteenth century, bubonic plague erupted in epidemics that ravaged societies throughout most of Asia, Europe, and north Africa. Epidemic plague struck intermittently until the seventeenth century, but by the fifteenth century Chi-

English forces besiege a French citadel during the Hundred Years' War (1337–1453). Note that the besiegers on the left side of this manuscript illustration employ cannons and smaller firearms that launch gunpowder bombs.

nese and western European societies had begun to recover from its effects and wield their influence in the larger world.

Bubonic Plague

The Little Ice Age

About 1300 C.E. a process of global climatic change caused temperatures to decline significantly and abruptly throughout the world. For more than five hundred years, the earth experienced a "little ice age," when temperatures were much cooler than in the era from 1000 to 1300 C.E. With markedly cooler temperatures and shorter growing seasons, agricultural production declined in many lands, leading to famine and sometimes even starvation. In some northerly lands, agriculture ceased to be a practical possibility: after the onset of the little ice age, Norse settlers gradually abandoned the colonies they had occupied in Greenland since the tenth century.

Origins of Epidemic Bubonic Plague

As they struggled to cope with the cooling climate, peoples in much of the eastern hemisphere suddenly encountered a new challenge in the form of devastating epidemic disease. Bubonic plague spread from the Yunnan region of southwestern China where it probably had been endemic for centuries. The plague bacillus infects rodents such as rats, squirrels, and prairie dogs, and fleas transmit the pathogen from one rodent to another. If rodent populations decline, fleas seek other hosts and sometimes spread the disease to human victims. In the early fourteenth century, Mongol military campaigns helped spread plague from Yunnan to China's interior: an epidemic in 1331 reportedly killed 90 percent of the population in Hebei province in northeastern China, near modern Beijing. During the 1350s epidemics broke out in widely scattered regions of China, and contemporaries reported that plague carried away two-thirds of the population in some afflicted areas.

Spread of Plague

During the 1340s Mongols, merchants, and other travelers helped to spread the disease along trade routes to points west of China. It thrived in the oases and trading cities of central Asia where domestic animals and rodents provided abundant breeding

A painting of 1503 graphically communicates the horror felt by medieval Europeans when bubonic plague struck their communities. Here death takes away a cartload of victims, while others die beside the road.

grounds for fleas and the plague bacillus. By 1346 it had reached the Black Sea ports of Caffa and Tana. In 1347 Italian merchants fled plague-infected Black Sea ports and unwittingly spread the disease throughout the Mediterranean basin. By 1348, following the trade routes, plague had sparked epidemics in most of western Europe.

Wherever it appeared, bubonic plague struck with frightful effects. Victims developed inflamed lymph nodes particularly in the neck, armpit, and groin areas, and most died within a few days after the onset of symptoms. Internal hemorrhaging often discolored the inflammations known as buboes—which gave rise to the term *bubonic* plague—and because of the black or purple swellings, Europeans referred to the plague as the "Black Death." Bubonic plague typically killed 60 to 70 percent of its human victims and had the potential to ravage a society within a few months. In some small villages and towns, disease wiped out the entire population. A spate of new births generally followed outbreaks of plague as societies tried to replenish their numbers, but plague also returned and claimed new victims. In Europe plague erupted intermittently from the 1340s until the late seventeenth century.

Some parts of the eastern hemisphere did not suffer directly from plague epidemics. The long, cold winters of Scandinavia discouraged the proliferation of plague-bearing rodents and fleas, so the northernmost parts of Europe escaped the plague's worst effects. For reasons unknown, India also seems to have avoided serious difficulties. In fact, Indian population grew from 91 million in the year 1300 to 97 million a century later and 105 million in 1500. Epidemics also largely bypassed sub-Saharan Africa, even though plague had long been endemic in the Great Lakes region of east Africa.

Population Decline

In lands hard hit by plague, however, it took a century and more to begin recovery from the demographic consequences of epidemic disease. In 1300 China's population, already reduced by conflicts with the Mongols since the early thirteenth century, stood at eighty-five million. In 1400, after about seventy years of epidemic plague, Chinese numbers amounted to only seventy-five million. A century later demographic recovery was under way, and China's population rebounded to one hundred million. European society also reeled from the effects of bubonic plague. From seventy-nine million in 1300, European population dropped by almost 25 percent to sixty million in 1400. As in China, demographic recovery in Europe was under way in 1500 when European population climbed to eighty-one million. Islamic societies in southwest Asia, Egypt, and north Africa also suffered devastating population losses, and demographic recovery took much longer there than in China and Europe. In Egypt human population probably did not reach preplague levels until the nineteenth century.

Social and Economic Effects

Because of the heavy demographic toll that it levied, bubonic plague disrupted societies and economies throughout Eurasia and north Africa. Epidemics killed the young, the weak, and the old in especially high numbers, but they spared no group. Peasants and laborers, artisans and crafts workers, merchants and bankers, priests and nuns, rulers and bureaucrats all fell before the plague's onslaught. The disease caused massive labor shortages, which in turn generated social unrest.

In western Europe, for example, urban workers demanded higher wages, and many left their homes in search of better conditions. Political authorities responded by freezing wages and forbidding workers to leave their homes. For their part, peasants in the countryside also sought to improve their circumstances by moving to regions where landlords offered better terms. Landlords responded to this challenge by restricting the freedom of peasants to move and by reimposing labor requirements: in effect, the lords sought to reinstate conditions of serfdom that they had allowed to lapse before the arrival of plague. As a result of sharply conflicting interests, disgruntled workers and peasants mounted a series of rebellions that rocked both the towns and the countryside of western Europe. Authorities eventually extinguished the revolts but only after considerable social disruption and loss of life.

By the seventeenth century the plague had lost much of its ferocity. Epidemics occurred more sporadically, and they did not seriously diminish human populations. Since the 1940s antibiotic drugs have brought the disease largely under control among human populations, although it survives in rodent communities throughout much of the world.

Recovery in China: The Ming Dynasty

By the mid-fourteenth century the Mongol's Yuan dynasty was experiencing very difficult times. Financial mismanagement led to serious economic difficulties, and political conflicts led to assassinations and factional fighting among the Mongols themselves. In 1368, with bubonic plague raging, the Yuan dynasty collapsed, and the Mongols departed China en masse and returned to the steppes, leaving China in a state of both demographic and political turmoil. An increasing birthrate soon helped to replenish human numbers. Political recovery accompanied the demographic rebound.

Hongwu

When the Yuan dynasty fell, the governance of China returned to Chinese hands. The new emperor came from a family so poor that he spent much of his youth as a beggar. Orphaned, he entered a Buddhist monastery to assure himself of food, clothing, and shelter. Because of his size and strength, he came to the notice of military commanders, and he made his way through the ranks to lead the rebellious forces that toppled the Yuan dynasty. In 1368 he became Emperor Hongwu, and he proclaimed the establishment of the Ming ("brilliant") dynasty, which lasted until 1644.

Ming Centralization

Hongwu immediately set about eliminating all traces of Mongol rule and establishing a government on the model of traditional Chinese dynasties. Like the founders of several earlier Chinese dynasties, Hongwu had little interest in scholarly matters, but he reestablished the Confucian educational and civil service systems to ensure a supply of talented officials and bureaucrats. At the same time, he moved to centralize authority more tightly than ever before in Chinese history. In 1380, when he suspected his chief minister of involvement in a treasonous plot, Hongwu executed the minister and his bureaucratic allies and also abolished the minister's position altogether. From that time forward the Ming emperors ruled directly, without the aid of chief ministers, and they closely supervised imperial affairs.

Mandarins and Eunuchs

The Ming emperors insisted on absolute obedience to the policies and initiatives of the central government. They relied heavily on the mandarins, a special class of powerful officials sent out as emissaries of the central government to ensure that local officials implemented imperial policy. The Ming emperors also turned to eunuchs for governmental services. Earlier Chinese emperors, as well as rulers of other lands, had long relied on eunuchs, since they could not generate families and build power bases

Ming artisans won worldwide fame for their blue-and-white porcelain, which inspired the founders of the Delft porcelain factory in the Netherlands. This covered jar dates from the early fifteenth century.

that might challenge ruling houses. In keeping with their centralizing policy, however, the Ming emperors employed eunuchs much more extensively than any of their predecessors, in the expectation that servants whose fortunes depended exclusively on the emperors' favor would work especially diligently to advance the emperors' interests.

The employment of mandarins and eunuchs enhanced the authority of the central government. The tightly centralized administration instituted by the early Ming emperors lasted more than five hundred years. Although the dynasty fell in 1644 to Manchu invaders, who founded the Qing dynasty, the Manchus retained the administrative framework of the Ming state, which largely survived until the collapse of the Qing dynasty in 1911.

Economic Recovery

While building a centralized administration, the Ming emperors also worked toward economic recovery from nomadic rule and epidemic disease. The new rulers conscripted laborers to rebuild irrigation systems that had fallen into disrepair during the previous century, and agricultural production surged as a result. At the same time, they promoted the manufacture of porcelain, lacquerware, and fine silk and cotton textiles. They did not actively promote trade with other lands, but private Chinese merchants eagerly sought commercial opportunities and conducted a thriving business marketing Chinese products in ports and trading cities from Japan to the islands of southeast Asia. Meanwhile, domestic trade surged within China, reflecting increasing productivity and prosperity.

Cultural Revival

Alongside political and economic recovery, the Ming dynasty also sponsored a kind of cultural revival in China. Emperor Hongwu tried to eradicate all signs of the recent nomadic occupation by discouraging the use of Mongol names and the wearing of Mongol dress. Ming emperors actively promoted Chinese cultural traditions, particularly the Confucian and neo-Confucian schools. Hongwu's successor, Yongle, organized the preparation of a vast encyclopedia that compiled all significant works of Chinese history, philosophy, and literature. This *Yongle Encyclopedia* ran to almost twenty-three thousand manuscript rolls, each equivalent to a medium-size book. The government originally planned to issue a printed edition of the encyclopedia, but abandoned the project because of its enormous expense. Nevertheless, the *Yongle Encyclopedia* was a remarkable anthology, and it signaled the Ming rulers' interest in supporting native Chinese cultural traditions.

Recovery in Western Europe: State Building

Demographic recovery strengthened states in western Europe as it did in China. In Europe, however, political authority rested with a series of regional states rather than a centralized empire. By the late fifteenth century, states in Italy, Spain, France, and England had devised techniques of government that vastly enhanced their power.

During the later middle ages (1300–1500), internal problems as well as bubonic plague complicated European political affairs. The Holy Roman Empire survived in name, but after the mid-thirteenth century effective authority lay with the German princes and the Italian city-states rather than the emperor. In Spain descendants of Muslim conquerors held the kingdom of Granada in the southern portion of the Iberian peninsula. The kings of France and England sparred constantly over lands claimed by both. Their hostilities eventually resulted in the Hundred Years' War (1337–1453), a protracted series of intermittent campaigns in which the warring factions sought control of lands in France.

Taxes and Armies

By the late fifteenth century, however, regional states in western Europe had greatly strengthened their societies, and some had also laid the foundations for the emergence of powerful monarchies. The state-building efforts of the later middle ages involved two especially important elements. The first was the development of fresh sources of finance, usually through new taxes levied directly on citizens and subjects, which supplemented the income that rulers received from their subordinates. The second was the maintenance of large standing armies, often composed of mercenary forces and equipped with gunpowder weapons, supported by state funds.

Italian States

The state-building process began in Italy, where profits from industrial production and trade enriched the major cities. The principal Italian states—the city-states of Milan, Venice, and Florence, the papal state based in Rome, and the kingdom of Naples—needed large numbers of officials to administer their complex affairs. They also needed ready access to military forces that could protect their interests. Beginning as early as the thirteenth century, the Italian city-states financed these needs by levying direct taxes and issuing long-term bonds that they repaid from treasury receipts. With fresh sources of finance, the principal Italian states strengthened their authority within their own boundaries and between them controlled public affairs in most of the Italian peninsula.

France and England

During the fourteenth and fifteenth centuries, Italian administrative methods made their way beyond the Alps. Partly because of the enormous expenses they incurred during the Hundred Years' War, the kings of France and England began to levy direct taxes and assemble powerful armies. The French kings taxed sales, hearths, and salt; their English counterparts instituted annual taxes on hearths, individuals, and plow teams. Rulers in both lands asserted the authority of the central government over the nobility. The English kings did not establish a standing army, but they were able to raise powerful forces when rebellion threatened public order. In France, however, King Louis XI (reigned 1461–1483) maintained a permanent army of about fifteen thousand troops, many of them professional mercenary soldiers equipped with firearms. Because the high expense of maintaining such forces was beyond the means of the nobility, Louis and his successors enjoyed a decisive edge over ambitious subordinates seeking to challenge royal authority or build local power bases.

Spain

The process of state building was most dramatic in Spain where the marriage in 1469 of Fernando of Aragon and Isabel of Castile united the two wealthiest and most important Iberian realms. Receipts from the sales tax, the primary source of royal income, supported a powerful standing army. Under Fernando and Isabel, popularly known as the Catholic Kings, Christian forces completed the *reconquista* by conquering the kingdom of Granada and absorbing it into their state. The Catholic Kings also projected their authority beyond Iberia. When a French army threatened the kingdom of Naples in 1494, they seized southern Italy, and by 1559 Spanish forces had established their hegemony throughout most of the Italian peninsula. Fernando and Isabel also sought to make a place for Spain in the markets of Asia by sponsoring Christopher Columbus's quest for a western route to China.

The Florentine painter Masaccio was a pioneer of Renaissance art. His fresco *Tribute Money,* produced about 1427, relies on the technique of linear perspective to depict figures in realistic relationship to one another and their surroundings.

Competition between European states intensified as they tightened their authority in their territories. This competition led to frequent small-scale wars between European states, and it encouraged the rapid development of military and naval technology. As states sought technological advantages over their neighbors, they encouraged the refinement and improvement of weapons, ships, and sails. When one state acquired powerful weapons—such as personal firearms or ships equipped with cannons—neighboring states sought more advanced devices in the interests of security. Thus technological innovations vastly strengthened European armies just as they began to venture again into the larger world.

Recovery in Western Europe: The Renaissance

Demographic recovery and state-building efforts in western Europe coincided with a remarkable cultural flowering known as the Renaissance. The French word *renaissance* means "rebirth," and it refers to a round of artistic and intellectual creativity that took place from the fourteenth to the sixteenth century and that reflected the continuing development of a sophisticated urban society in western Europe. Painters, sculptors, and architects of the Renaissance era drew inspiration from classical Greek and Roman artists rather than from their medieval predecessors. They admired the convincing realism of classical sculpture and the stately simplicity of classical architecture. In their efforts to revive classical aesthetic standards, they transformed European art. Meanwhile, Renaissance scholars known as humanists looked to classical rather than medieval literary models, and they sought to update medieval moral thought and adapt it to the needs of a bustling urban society.

Italian Renaissance Art

Just as they pioneered new techniques of statecraft, the Italian city-states also sponsored Renaissance innovations in art and architecture. In search of realistic depictions, Italian artists studied the human form and represented the emotions of their subjects. Italian painters like Masaccio (1401–1428) and Leonardo da Vinci (1452–1519) relied on the technique of linear perspective to represent the three dimensions of real life on flat, two-dimensional surfaces. Sculptors like Donatello (1386–1466) and Michelangelo Buonarotti (1475–1564) sought to depict their subjects in natural poses that reflected the actual workings of human muscles rather than in the awkward and rigid postures often found in earlier sculptures.

Brunelleschi's magnificent dome on the cathedral of Florence dominates the city's skyline even today.

Renaissance Architecture

Renaissance architects designed buildings in the simple, elegant style preferred by their classical Greek and Roman predecessors. Their most impressive achievement was the construction of domed buildings—awesome structures that enclosed large spaces but kept them open and airy under massive domes. Roman architects had built domes, but their technology and engineering did not survive the collapse of the Roman empire. Inspired by the Pantheon, a handsome Roman temple constructed in the second century C.E., the Florentine architect Filippo Brunelleschi (1377–1446) reinvented equipment and designs for a large dome. During the 1420s and 1430s, he oversaw the construction of a magnificent dome on the cathedral of Florence. Residents of Florence took Brunelleschi's dome as a symbol of the city's wealth and its leadership in artistic and cultural affairs.

The Humanists

Like Renaissance artists and architects, scholars and literary figures known as humanists also drew inspiration from classical models. The term *humanist* referred to scholars interested in the humanities—literature, history, and moral philosophy. They had nothing to do with the secular and often antireligious interests of movements that go under the name humanism today: to the contrary, Renaissance humanists were deeply committed to Christianity. Several humanists worked diligently to prepare accurate texts and translations of the New Testament and other important Christian writings. Most notable of them was Desiderius Erasmus of Rotterdam (1466–1536), who in 1516 published the first edition of the Greek New Testament along with a revised Latin translation and copious annotations. Other humanists drew inspiration from the intense spirituality and high moral standards of early Christianity and promoted those values in their own society.

Humanists scorned the dense and often convoluted writing style of the scholastic theologians. Instead, they preferred the elegant and polished language of classical Greek and Roman authors and the early church fathers, whose works they considered more engaging and more persuasive than the weighty tomes of medieval philosophers and theologians. Thus humanists such as the Florentine Francesco Petrarca, also known in English as Petrarch, (1304–1374) traveled throughout Europe searching for manuscripts of classical works. In the monastic libraries of Italy, Switzerland, and southern France, they found hundreds of Latin writings that medieval scholars had overlooked. During the fifteenth century, Italian humanists became acquainted with Byzantine scholars and enlarged the body of classical Greek as well as Latin works available to scholars.

Humanist Moral Thought

Classical Greek and Latin values encouraged the humanists to reconsider medieval ethical teachings. Medieval moral philosophers had taught that the most honorable calling was that of monks and nuns who withdrew from the world and dedicated their lives to prayer, contemplation, and the glorification of God, but the humanists drew inspiration from classical authors like Cicero, who demonstrated that it was possible to lead a morally virtuous life while participating actively in the affairs of the world. Renaissance humanists argued that it was perfectly honorable for Christians to enter into marriage, business relationships, and public affairs, and they offered a spirited defense for those who rejected the cloister in favor of an active life in society. Humanist moral thought thus represented an effort to reconcile Christian values and ethics with the increasingly urban and commercial society of Renaissance Europe.

Renaissance Europe and the Larger World

Quite apart from their conscious effort to draw inspiration from classical antiquity, Renaissance art and thought also reflected increasing European participation in the affairs of the eastern hemisphere. As merchants linked Europe to the larger hemispheric economy, European peoples experienced increased prosperity that enabled them to invest resources in artistic production and support for scholarship. Renaissance painters filled their canvases with images of silk garments, ceramic vessels, lacquered wood, spice jars, foreign peoples, and exotic animals that had recently come to European attention. Princes and wealthy patrons commissioned hundreds of these paintings that brought a cosmopolitan look to their palaces, residences, and places of business.

This enchantment with the larger world extended also into the realm of ideas. The Italian humanist Giovanni Pico della Mirandola (1463–1494) perhaps best reflected the enthusiasm of Renaissance scholars to comprehend the world beyond western Europe. In his exuberant *Oration on the Dignity of Man* (1486), Pico made a spirited effort to harmonize the divergent teachings of Plato, Aristotle, Judaism, Christianity, and Islam, not to mention Zoroastrianism and various occult and mystical traditions. His ambitious endeavor was ultimately unsuccessful: Pico had limited information about several of the traditions he sought to reconcile, and he sometimes offered superficial interpretations of doctrines that he imperfectly understood. Nevertheless, his *Oration* gave eloquent voice to the burning desire of many European scholars to understand the larger world. It is not surprising that just as Pico and other

A painting by Venetian artists Gentile and Giovanni Bellini reflects Renaissance interests in the Muslim world. The painting depicts St. Mark (standing in the pulpit, left) preaching in Alexandria, Egypt. The audience includes Egyptians, Berbers, Turks, Persians, Ethiopians, and Mongols.

Renaissance humanists were undertaking this effort, European mariners were organizing expeditions to explore the lands and seas beyond Christendom.

Exploration and Colonization

As peoples of the eastern hemisphere recovered from demographic collapse and restored order to their societies, they also sought to revive the networks of long-distance trade and communication that epidemic plague had disrupted. Most active in this effort were China and western Europe—the two societies that recovered most rapidly from the disasters of the fourteenth century. During the early Ming dynasty, Chinese ports accommodated foreign traders, and mariners mounted a series of enormous naval expeditions that visited almost all parts of the Indian Ocean basin. Meanwhile, Europeans ventured from the Mediterranean into the Atlantic Ocean, which served as a highway to sub-Saharan Africa and the Indian Ocean basin. By the end of the fifteenth century, Europeans not only had established sea lanes to India but also had made several return voyages to the American continents, thus inaugurating a process that brought all the world's peoples into permanent and sustained interaction.

The Chinese Reconnaissance of the Indian Ocean Basin

Having ousted the Mongols, the early Ming emperors were not eager to have large numbers of foreigners residing in China. Yet the emperors permitted foreign merchants to trade in the closely supervised ports of Quanzhou and Guangzhou, where they obtained Chinese silk, porcelain, and manufactured goods in exchange for pearls, gems, spices, cotton fabrics, and exotic products like tortoise shells and animal skins. The early Ming emperors also refurbished the large Chinese navy built during the Song dynasty, and they allowed Chinese merchants to participate in overseas trading ventures in Japan and southeast Asia.

Zheng He's Expeditions

Moreover, for almost thirty years, the Ming government sponsored a series of seven massive naval expeditions designed to establish a Chinese presence in the Indian Ocean basin. Emperor Yongle organized the expeditions for two main purposes: to impose imperial control over foreign trade with China and to impress foreign peoples with the power and might that the Ming dynasty had restored to China. Indeed, he might well have hoped to extend the tributary system, by which Chinese dynasties traditionally recognized foreign peoples, to lands in the Indian Ocean basin.

The expeditions took place between 1405 and 1433. Leading them was the eunuch admiral Zheng He, a Muslim from Yunnan in southwestern China who rose through the ranks of eunuch administrators to become a trusted advisor of Yongle. Zheng He embarked on each voyage with an awesome fleet of vessels complemented by armed forces large enough to overcome resistance at any port where the expedition called. On the first voyage, for example, Zheng He's fleet consisted of 317 ships accompanied by almost twenty-eight thousand armed troops. Many of these vessels were mammoth, nine-masted "treasure ships" with four decks capable of accommodating five hundred or more passengers, as well as massive stores of cargo. Measuring up to 124 meters (408 feet) long and 51 meters (166 feet) wide, these treasure ships were by far the largest marine craft the world had ever seen.

On the first three voyages, Zheng He took his fleet to southeast Asia, India, and Ceylon. The fourth expedition went to the Persian Gulf and Arabia, and later expeditions ventured down the east African coast, calling at ports as far south as Malindi in modern Kenya. Throughout his travels, Zheng He liberally dispensed gifts of Chinese silk, porcelain, and other goods. In return he received rich and unusual presents from his hosts, including African zebras and giraffes that ended their days in the Ming imperial zoo. Zheng He and his companions paid respect to the local deities and customs they encountered, and in Ceylon they erected a monument honoring Buddha, Allah, and Vishnu.

Chinese Naval Power

Zheng He generally sought to attain his goals through diplomacy. For the most part his large contingents of armed troops overawed his hosts, and he had little need to engage in hostilities. But a contemporary reported that Zheng He walked like a tiger, and he did not shrink from violence when he considered it necessary to impress foreign peoples with China's military might. He ruthlessly suppressed pirates who had long plagued Chinese and southeast Asian waters. He also intervened in a civil disturbance in order to establish his authority in Ceylon, and he made displays of military force when local officials threatened his fleet in Arabia and east Africa. The seven expeditions established a Chinese presence and reputation in the Indian Ocean basin. Returning from his fourth voyage, Zheng He brought envoys from thirty states who traveled to China and paid their respects at the Ming court.

End of the Voyages

Yet suddenly, in the mid-1430s, the Ming emperors decided to end the expeditions. Confucian ministers, who mistrusted Zheng He and the eunuchs who supported the voyages, argued that resources committed to the expensive expeditions would go to better uses if devoted to agriculture. Moreover, during the 1420s and 1430s the Mongols mounted a new military threat from the northwest, and land forces urgently needed financial support.

Thus in 1433, after Zheng He's seventh voyage, the expeditions ended. Chinese merchants continued to trade in Japan and southeast Asia, but imperial officials destroyed most of the nautical charts that Zheng He had carefully prepared and gave up any plans to maintain a Chinese presence in the Indian Ocean. The decommissioned treasure ships sat in harbors until they rotted away, and Chinese craftsmen forgot the technology of building such large vessels. Yet Zheng He's voyages demonstrated clearly that China could exercise military, political, and economic influence throughout the Indian Ocean basin.

European Exploration in the Atlantic and Indian Oceans

As Chinese fleets reconnoitered the Indian Ocean, European mariners were preparing to enter both the Atlantic and the Indian Ocean basins. Unlike Zheng He and his companions, Europeans did not venture onto the seas in the interests of diplomacy or in hopes of establishing a political and military reputation in foreign lands. Instead, they acted on two different but complementary motives: the desire to expand the boundaries of Roman Catholic Christianity and the desire to profit from commercial opportunities.

Portuguese Exploration

The experience of Portugal illustrates this mixture of motives. Though Portuguese merchants were not especially prominent in trading circles, Portuguese fishermen had a long tradition of seafaring in the stormy Atlantic Ocean. Building on this experience, Portuguese mariners emerged as the early leaders in both Atlantic exploration and the search for a sea route to Asian markets through the Indian Ocean. During the fifteenth century Prince Henrique of Portugal, often called Prince Henry the Navigator, embarked on an ambitious campaign to spread Christianity and increase Portuguese influence on the seas. In 1415 he watched as Portuguese forces seized the Moroccan city of Ceuta, which guarded the Strait of Gibraltar from the south. He regarded his victory both as a blow against Islam and as a strategic move enabling Christian vessels to move freely between the Mediterranean and the Atlantic.

Colonization of the Atlantic Islands

Following the capture of Ceuta, Henrique encouraged Portuguese mariners to venture into the Atlantic. During their voyages they discovered the Madeiras and Azores Islands, all uninhabited, which they soon colonized. They also made an unsuccessful effort to occupy the Canary Islands, inhabited by indigenous peoples but claimed since the early fifteenth century by the kingdom of Castile. Later discoveries included the Cape Verde islands, Fernando Po, São Tomé, and Principe off the west African coast. Because these Atlantic islands enjoyed fertile soils and a Mediterranean climate, Portuguese entrepreneurs soon began to cultivate sugarcane there, often in collaboration with Italian investors. Italians had financed sugar plantations in the Mediterranean islands since the twelfth century, and their commercial networks provided a ready means to distribute sugar to Europeans who were rapidly developing a taste for sweets.

Slave Trade

During the middle decades of the fifteenth century, a series of Portuguese fleets also explored the west African coast, each expedition proceeding a bit farther than its predecessor. Originally, the Portuguese traded guns, textiles, and other manufactured items for African gold and slaves. Portuguese traders took full advantage of the long-established African commerce in slaves, but they also changed the nature of the slave trade by dramatically increasing its volume and by sending slaves to new destinations. By the mid-fifteenth century the Portuguese dispatched thousands of slaves annually from their forts on islands off the African coast. They delivered most of their human cargo to recently founded plantations in the Atlantic islands, where the slaves worked as laborers, although some worked as domestic servants in Europe. The use of African slaves to perform heavy labor on commercial plantations soon became common practice, and it fueled the development of a huge, Atlantic-wide trade that delivered as many as twelve million enslaved Africans to destinations in North America, South America, and the Caribbean region.

Indian Ocean Trade

While some Portuguese mariners traded profitably in west Africa, others sought to enter the lucrative trade in Asian silk and spices. A sea route to Asian markets would enable Portuguese merchants to avoid Muslim and Italian intermediaries, through whom almost all Asian luxury goods reached European markets, and participate directly in the flourishing commercial world of the Indian Ocean basin. Toward the end of the fifteenth century, Portuguese mariners began to search seriously for a sea lane from Europe around Africa and into the Indian Ocean. By 1488 Bartolomeu Dias had sailed around the Cape of Good Hope and entered the Indian Ocean. Restless because of the long journey and distance from home, the crew forced Dias to return immediately to Portugal, but his voyage proved that it was possible to sail from Europe to the Indian Ocean. In 1497 Vasco da Gama departed Portugal with the intention of sailing to India. After rounding the Cape of Good Hope, he cruised up the east African coast and found a Muslim pilot who showed him how to take advantage of the seasonal monsoon winds to sail across the Arabian Sea to India. In 1498 he arrived at Calicut, and by 1499 he had returned to Lisbon with a hugely profitable cargo of pepper and spices.

For most of the following century, Portuguese merchants and mariners dominated trade between Europe and Asia. Indeed, they attempted to control all shipping in the Indian Ocean. Their ships, armed with cannons, were able to overpower the vessels of Arabs, Persians, Indians, southeast Asians, and others who sailed the Indian Ocean. They did not have enough ships to oversee all trade in the region, but the entry of Portuguese mariners into the Indian Ocean signaled the beginning of European imperialism in Asia.

Christopher Columbus

While Portuguese seafarers sought a sea route around Africa to India, the Genoese mariner Cristoforo Colombo, known in English as Christopher Columbus,

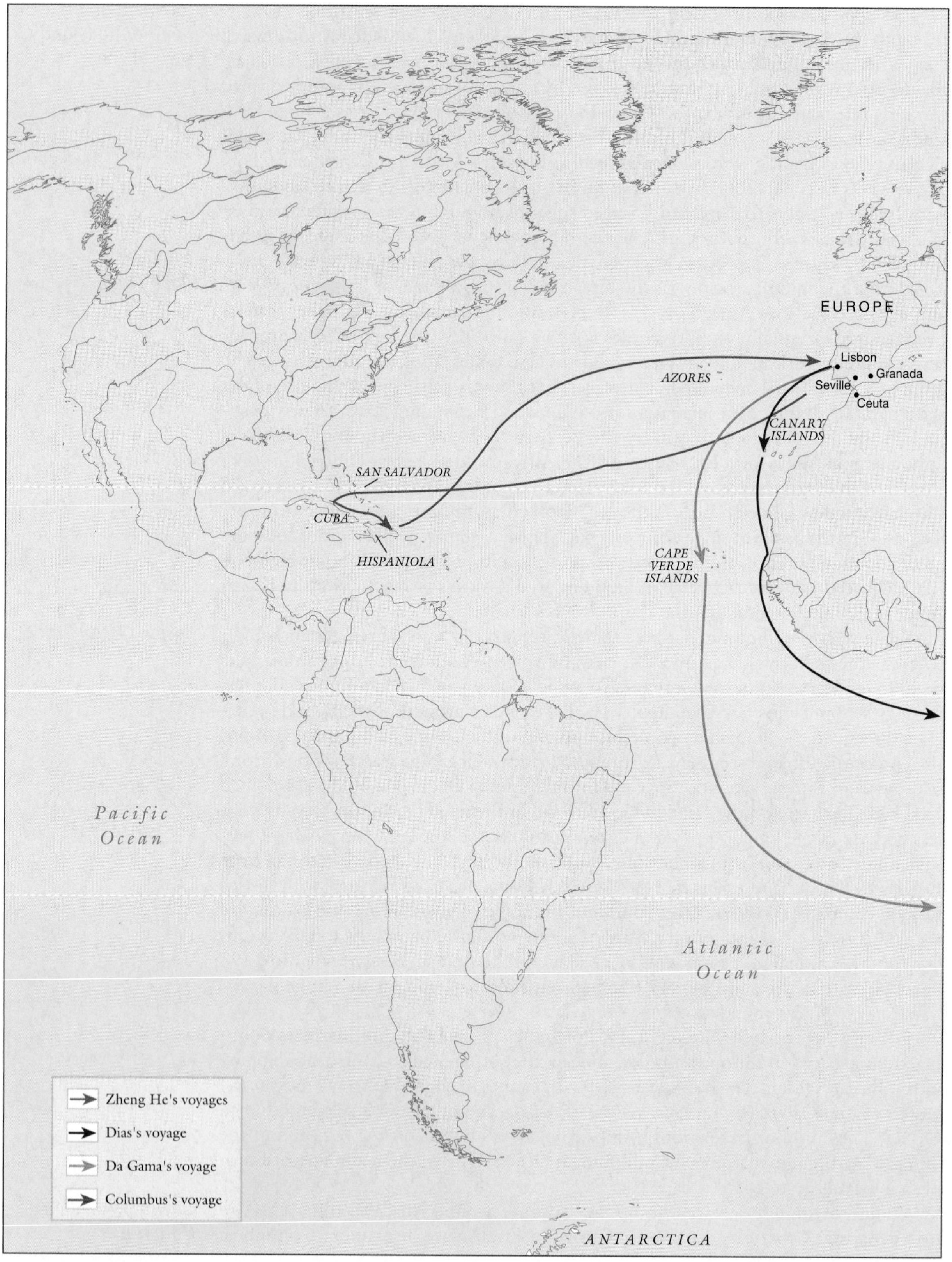

MAP [22.2]
Chinese and European voyages of exploration, 1405–1498.

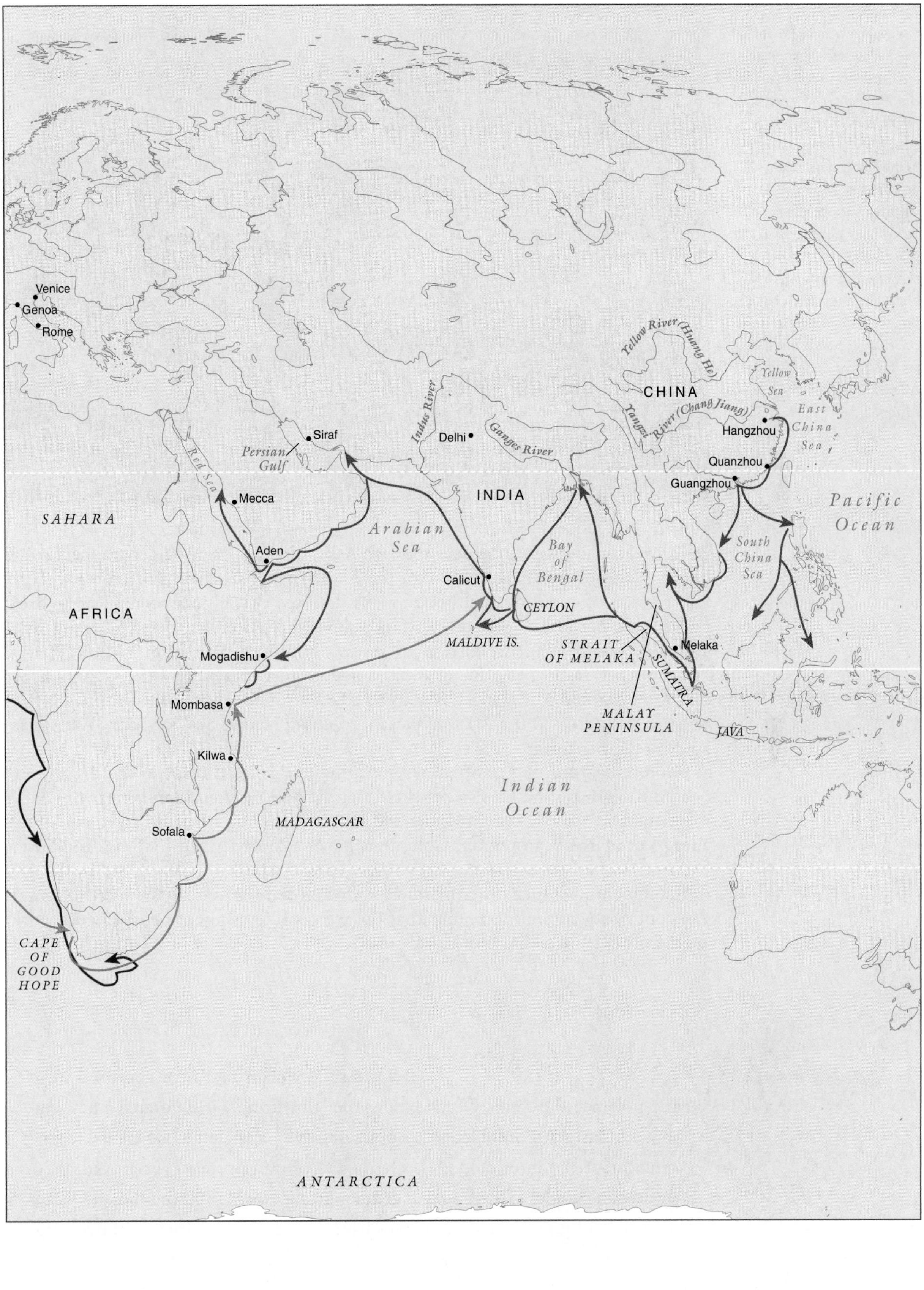
Venice
Genoa
Rome
SAHARA
AFRICA
Red Sea
Mecca
Siraf
Persian Gulf
Aden
Mogadishu
Mombasa
Kilwa
Sofala
MADAGASCAR
CAPE OF GOOD HOPE
Arabian Sea
Indus River
Delhi
Ganges River
INDIA
Calicut
MALDIVE IS.
CEYLON
Bay of Bengal
STRAIT OF MELAKA
Melaka
SUMATRA
MALAY PENINSULA
JAVA
Yellow River (Huang He)
CHINA
Yangzi River (Chang Jiang)
Yellow Sea
East China Sea
Hangzhou
Quanzhou
Guangzhou
Pacific Ocean
South China Sea
Indian Ocean
ANTARCTICA

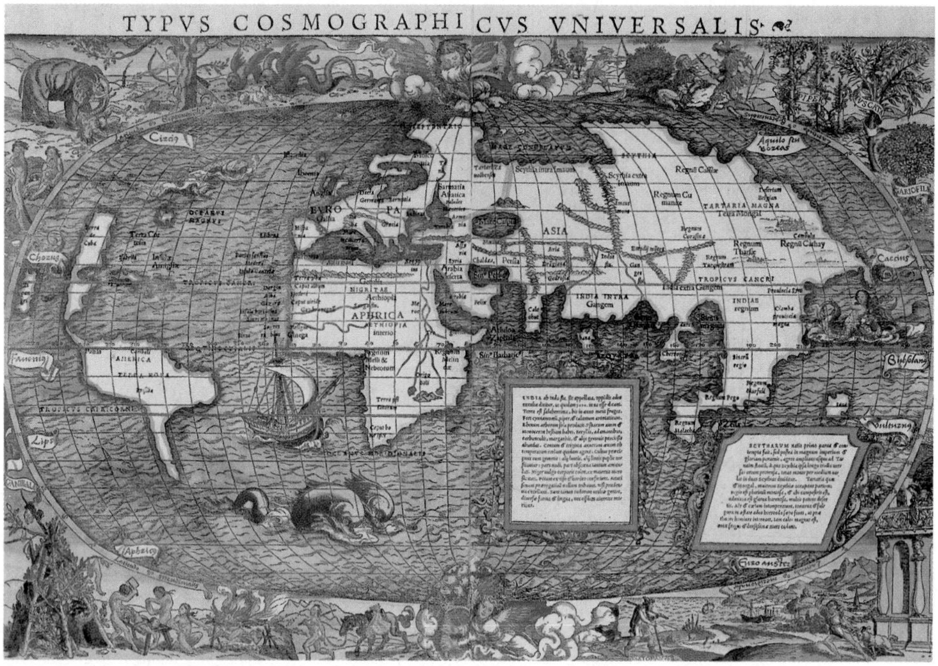

Although Christopher Columbus believed that he had sailed into Asian waters, later mariners soon realized that the Americas were continents unknown to geographers of the eastern hemisphere. This map, prepared in 1532 by the German cartographer Sebastian Münster, shows that by the early sixteenth century, European geographers had acquired a rough but accurate understanding of South America but had reconnoitered only the Atlantic coastline of North America.

conceived the idea of sailing west to reach Asian markets. Because geographers in the eastern hemisphere knew nothing of the Americas, Columbus's notion made a certain amount of good sense, although many doubted that his plan could lead to profitable trade because of the long distances involved. After the king of Portugal declined to sponsor an expedition to test Columbus's plan, the Catholic Kings, Fernando and Isabel of Spain, agreed to underwrite a voyage. In 1492 Columbus set sail. After a stop in the Canary Islands to take on supplies and make repairs, his fleet of three ships crossed the Atlantic Ocean, reaching land at San Salvador (Watling Island) in the Bahamas.

Columbus returned to Spain without the gold, silk, and spices that he had expected to find, but he persistently held that he had reached islands near the Asian mainland and the markets of China and Japan. Although he made three more voyages to the Caribbean region, Columbus never acknowledged that his expeditions had not reached Asia. News of his voyages spread rapidly, however, and by the end of the fifteenth century other mariners had explored the Caribbean and the American continents enough to realize that the western hemisphere constituted a world apart from Europe, Asia, and Africa.

As European mariners ventured into the Indian and Atlantic Ocean basins, they unwittingly inaugurated a new era in world history. For millennia, peoples of different societies had traded, communicated, and interacted. As technologies of transportation improved, they dealt with peoples at increasingly greater distances. By 1500 the Indian Ocean served as a highway linking peoples from China to east Africa, and overland traffic kept the silk roads busy from China to the Mediterranean Sea. Trade goods, diplomatic missions, religious faiths, technological skills, agricultural crops, and disease pathogens all moved readily over the sea lanes and the silk roads, and they profoundly influenced the development of societies throughout the eastern hemisphere. In the western hemisphere, trading networks linked lands as distant as Mexico and the Great Lakes region while Pacific islanders regularly traveled and traded between island groups.

Never before, however, had peoples of the eastern hemisphere, the western hemisphere, and Oceania dealt with one another on a regular and systematic basis. The voyages of European mariners during the fifteenth and following centuries initiated a long-term process—one that continues in the present day—that brought all regions and peoples of planet earth into permanent and sustained interaction. The formation and reconfiguration of global networks of power, communication, and exchange that followed from these interactions rank among the most prominent themes of modern world history.

CHRONOLOGY

1214	Creation of a Mongol artillery unit
1253–1324	Life of Marco Polo
1287–1288	Rabban Sauma's embassy to Europe
1291–1328	John of Montecorvino's mission to China
1304–1369	Life of Ibn Battuta
1304–1374	Life of Francesco Petrarca
1330s	First outbreaks of bubonic plague in China
1337–1453	Hundred Years' War
1347	Arrival of bubonic plague in the Mediterranean basin
1368–1644	Ming dynasty
1405–1433	Zheng He's expeditions in the Indian Ocean
1466–1536	Life of Desiderius Erasmus of Rotterdam
1488	Bartolomeu Dias's voyage around Africa
1492	Christopher Columbus's first voyage to the western hemisphere
1497–1498	Vasco da Gama's voyage to India

FOR FURTHER READING

Janet L. Abu-Lughod. *Before European Hegemony: The World System, A.D. 1250–1350.* New York, 1989. An important study of long-distance trade networks during the Mongol era.

Jerry H. Bentley. *Humanists and Holy Writ: New Testament Scholarship in the Renaissance.* Princeton, 1983. Examines Renaissance humanists' efforts to prepare accurate texts, translations, and commentaries on the New Testament.

———. *Old World Encounters: Cross-Cultural Contacts and Exchanges in Pre-Modern Times.* New York, 1993. Studies cultural and religious exchanges in the eastern hemisphere before 1500 C.E.

Luce Boulnois. *The Silk Road.* Trans. by D. Chamberlain. New York, 1966. Popular account of trade and travel over the silk roads.

Jerry Brotton. *The Renaissance Bazaar: From the Silk Road to Michelangelo.* Oxford, 2002. A provocative and well-illustrated study arguing that encounters in the larger world deeply influenced Renaissance cultural development in Europe.

Kenneth Chase. *Firearms: A Global History to 1700.* Cambridge, 2003. Offers a fresh interpretation of the invention and early diffusion of gunpowder weapons.

K. N. Chaudhuri. *Asia before Europe: Economy and Civilisation of the Indian Ocean from the Rise of Islam to 1750.* Cambridge, 1990. Controversial and penetrating analysis of economic, social, and cultural structures shaping societies of the Indian Ocean basin.

———. *Trade and Civilisation in the Indian Ocean: An Economic History from the Rise of Islam to 1750.* Cambridge, 1985. Brilliant analysis of the commercial life of the Indian Ocean basin by a prominent scholar.

Philip D. Curtin. *Cross-Cultural Trade in World History.* Cambridge, 1984. Groundbreaking analysis of patterns of long-distance trade concentrating on merchant communities in foreign lands.

Christopher Dawson, ed. *Mission to Asia.* Toronto, 1980. Translations of travel accounts and letters by European missionaries in central Asia and China during the Mongol era.

Michael W. Dols. *The Black Death in the Middle East.* Princeton, 1977. Careful, scholarly investigation of bubonic plague and its effects in southwest Asia.

Ross E. Dunn. *The Adventures of Ibn Battuta: A Muslim Traveler of the 14th Century.* Berkeley, 1986. Fascinating reconstruction of Ibn Battuta's travels and experiences.

Mark Elvin. *The Pattern of the Chinese Past.* Stanford, 1973. Brilliant analysis of Chinese history concentrating on social and economic developments.

Brian Fagan. *The Little Ice Age: How Climate Made History, 1300–1850.* New York, 2000. Popular account of the little ice age, with emphasis on its effects in Europe and North America.

Felipe Fernández-Armesto. *Before Columbus: Exploration and Colonisation from the Mediterranean to the Atlantic, 1229–1492.* London, 1987. Scholarly survey of early European ventures in the Atlantic Ocean.

Robert S. Gottfried. *The Black Death: Natural and Human Disaster in Medieval Europe.* New York, 1983. The best general study of bubonic plague and its effects in Europe.

Margaret L. King. *Women of the Renaissance.* Chicago, 1991. A lively and imaginative discussion of women's roles and experiences in Renaissance Europe.

John Larner. *Marco Polo and the Discovery of the World.* New Haven, 1999. Excellent study of Marco Polo and his significance, based on a thorough review of both textual evidence and recent scholarship.

Louise L. Levathes. *When China Ruled the Seas: The Treasure Fleet of the Dragon Throne, 1405–1433.* New York, 1994. Excellent popular account of Zheng He's voyages.

Lauro Martines. *Power and Imagination: City States in Renaissance Italy.* New York, 1979. An attractive and thoughtful analysis of the Italian Renaissance.

William H. McNeill. *Plagues and Peoples.* Garden City, N.Y., 1976. A pioneering study of infectious and contagious diseases and their effects in world history.

Arnold Pacey. *Technology in World Civilization: A Thousand-Year History.* Oxford, 1990. A brief and insightful study that concentrates on processes of technological diffusion.

J. R. S. Phillips. *The Medieval Expansion of Europe.* Oxford, 1988. Surveys European ventures into the larger world during the high and late middle ages.

William D. Phillips Jr. and Carla Rahn Phillips. *The Worlds of Christopher Columbus.* New York, 1992. The best general work on Christopher Columbus.

Marco Polo. *The Travels.* Trans. by R. Latham. Harmondsworth, 1958. An accurate translation of Marco Polo's work based on reliable scholarship.

Sanjay Subrahmanyam. *The Career and Legend of Vasco da Gama.* Cambridge, 1997. Solid and thoughtful study of the important Portuguese navigator.

Frances Wood. *The Silk Road: Two Thousand Years in the Heart of Asia.* Berkeley, 2002. A brilliantly illustrated volume discussing the history of the silk roads from antiquity to the twentieth century.

See our **Online Learning Center at www.mhhe.com/bentley3** for additional readings, practice maps, quizzes, and internet activities.

Unfamiliar words? Check out the **Primary Source Investigator CD-ROM** for an interactive glossary, interactive maps, more images, and primary sources.

PART V

THE ORIGINS OF GLOBAL INTERDEPENDENCE, 1500–1800

By 1500 C.E. peoples throughout the world had built well-organized societies with distinctive cultural traditions. Powerful agricultural societies dominated most of Asia, the Mediterranean basin, Europe, much of sub-Saharan Africa, Mexico, and the central Andean region. Pastoral nomads thrived in the dry grassy regions of central Asia and Africa, and hunting and gathering societies with small populations survived in lands where cultivation and herding were not practical possibilities. The vast majority of the world's peoples, however, lived in agricultural societies that observed distinctive political, social, and cultural traditions.

By 1500 peoples of the world had also established intricate transportation networks that supported travel, communication, and exchange between their societies. For more than a millennium, merchants had traveled the silk roads that linked lands from China to the Mediterranean basin, and mariners had plied the Indian Ocean and neighboring waters in connecting lands from Japan to east Africa. Caravan routes across the Sahara desert brought sub-Saharan west Africa into the larger economy of the eastern hemisphere. Although pioneered by merchants in the interests of trade, these transportation networks also supported cultural and biological exchanges. Several religious traditions—most notably Buddhism, Christianity, and Islam—traveled along the trade routes and attracted followers in distant lands. Similarly, food crops, animal stocks, and disease pathogens spread throughout much of the eastern hemisphere in premodern times. Transportation networks in the Americas and Oceania were not as extensive as those in the eastern hemisphere, but they also supported communication and exchange over long distances. Trade linked societies throughout North America, and seafarers routinely sailed between island groups in the central and western Pacific Ocean.

Commercial, cultural, and biological exchanges of premodern times prefigured much more intense cross-cultural interactions after 1500. These later interactions followed the establishment of new transportation networks in the form of sea lanes linking the lands of the Indian, Atlantic, and Pacific Ocean basins. Beginning in the fifteenth century, European mariners sought new, all-sea routes to the markets of Asia. As a result of their exploratory voyages, they established trade routes throughout the world's oceans and entered into dealings with many of the world's peoples. The new sea lanes not only fostered direct contact between Europeans and the peoples of sub-Saharan Africa and Asia but also facilitated interaction between the peoples of the eastern hemisphere, the western hemisphere, and Oceania. In short, European mariners created globe-girdling networks of transportation, communication, and exchange that supported cross-cultural interactions much more systematic and intense than those of earlier times.

The establishment of links between all the world's regions and peoples gave rise to the early modern era of world history, approximately 1500 to 1800 C.E. The early modern era differed from the period from 1000 to 1500, when there were only sporadic contacts between peoples of the eastern hemisphere, the western hemisphere, and Oceania. It also differed from the modern era from 1800 to the present, when national states, heavy industry, powerful weapons, and efficient technologies of transportation and communication enabled peoples of European ancestry to achieve political and economic dominance in the world.

During the early modern era, several global processes touched peoples in all parts of the world and influenced the development of their societies. One involved biological exchange: plants, animals, diseases, and human communities crossed the world's oceans and established themselves in new lands where they dramatically affected both the natural environment and established societies. Another involved commercial exchange: merchants took advantage of newly established sea lanes to inaugurate a genuinely global economy in which agricultural products, manufactured goods, and other commodities reached markets in distant lands. Yet another process involved the diffusion of technologies and cultural traditions: printing and gunpowder spread throughout the world, and Christianity and Islam attracted increasing numbers of converts in widely spread regions of the world.

These global processes had different effects for different peoples. The indigenous peoples of the Americas and Oceania experienced turmoil and disruption: diseases introduced from the eastern hemisphere ravaged their populations and sometimes led to the collapse of their societies. Europeans by contrast largely flourished during the early modern era: they traded profitably throughout the world and claimed vast stretches of land in the Americas, where they founded colonies and cultivated crops for sale on the open market. Africans benefited from the introduction of new food crops and the opportunity to obtain trade goods from abroad, but these benefits came at a terrible cost: millions of enslaved individuals from sub-Saharan Africa underwent a forced migration to the western hemisphere, where they performed hard labor, lived in poverty, and suffered both physical and psychological abuse. East Asian and Islamic peoples sought to limit the influence of global processes in their lands: they prospered from increased trade but restricted the introduction of foreign ideas and technologies into their societies.

European peoples drew most benefit from global processes of the period 1500 to 1800, but by no means did they dominate world affairs in early modern times. They established empires and settler colonies in the Americas, but most of the western hemisphere lay beyond their control until the nineteenth century. They established a series of fortified trading posts and the colony of Angola in Africa, but they traded in Africa at the sufferance of local authorities and rarely wielded direct influence beyond the coastlines. They conquered the Philippines and many Indonesian islands but posed no threat at all to the powerful states that ruled China, India, southwest Asia, and Anatolia, or even to the island state of Japan. Although they did not achieve global hegemony in early modern times, European peoples nevertheless played a more prominent role in world affairs than any of their ancestors, and their efforts fostered the development of an increasingly interdependent world.

Europeans, Javanese, Chinese, and African slaves come together in this painting of the fish market at Batavia (1661) by the Dutch artist Andries Beeckman.

CHAPTER 23

TRANSOCEANIC ENCOUNTERS AND GLOBAL CONNECTIONS

On 8 July 1497 the Portuguese mariner Vasco da Gama led a small fleet of four armed merchant vessels with 170 crewmen out of the harbor at Lisbon. His destination was India, which he planned to reach by sailing around the continent of Africa and through the Indian Ocean. He carried letters of introduction from the king of Portugal as well as cargoes of gold, pearls, wool textiles, bronzeware, iron tools, and other goods that he hoped to exchange for pepper and spices in India.

Before there would be an opportunity to trade, however, da Gama and his crew had a prolonged voyage through two oceans. They sailed south from Portugal to the Cape Verde Islands off the west coast of Africa, where they took on water and fresh provisions. On 3 August they headed southeast into the Atlantic Ocean to take advantage of the prevailing winds. For the next ninety-five days, the fleet saw no land as it sailed through some six thousand nautical miles of open ocean. By October, da Gama had found westerly winds in the southern Atlantic, rounded the Cape of Good Hope, and entered the Indian Ocean. The fleet slowly worked its way up the east coast of Africa, engaging in hostilities with local authorities at Mozambique and Mombasa, as far as Malindi, where da Gama secured the services of an Indian Muslim pilot to guide his ships across the Arabian Sea. On 20 May 1498—more than ten months after its departure from Lisbon—the fleet anchored at Calicut in southern India.

In India the Portuguese fleet found a wealthy, cosmopolitan society. Upon its arrival local authorities in Calicut dispatched a pair of Tunisian merchants who spoke Spanish and Italian to serve as translators for the newly arrived party. The markets of Calicut offered not only pepper, ginger, cinnamon, and spices but also rubies, emeralds, gold jewelry, and fine cotton textiles. Alas, apart from gold and some striped cloth, the goods that da Gama had brought attracted little interest among merchants at Calicut. Nevertheless, da Gama managed to exchange gold for a cargo of pepper and cinnamon that turned a handsome profit when the fleet returned to Portugal in August 1499. Da Gama's expedition opened the door to direct maritime trade between European and Asian peoples and helped to establish permanent links between the world's various regions.

Cross-cultural interactions have been a persistent feature of historical development. Even in ancient times mass migration, campaigns of imperial expansion, and long-distance trade deeply influenced societies throughout the world. As a result of these interactions, Buddhism, Islam, and Christianity spread from their places of birth to the distant corners of the eastern hemisphere. Long before modern times, arteries of long-distance trade served also as the principal conduits for exchanges of plants, animals, and diseases.

After 1500 C.E. cross-cultural interactions took place on a much larger geographic scale, and encounters were often more disruptive than in earlier centuries. Equipped with advanced technologies and a powerful military arsenal, western European peoples began to cross the world's oceans in large numbers during the early modern era. At the same time, Russian adventurers built an enormous Eurasian empire and ventured tentatively into the Pacific Ocean.

Europeans were not the only peoples who actively explored the larger world during the early modern era. In the early fifteenth century the Ming emperors of China sponsored a series of seven massive maritime expeditions that visited all parts of the Indian Ocean basin. Although state-sponsored expeditions came to an end after 1435, Chinese merchants and mariners were prominent figures in east Asian and southeast Asian lands throughout the early modern era. In the sixteenth century Ottoman mariners also ventured into the Indian Ocean. Following the Ottoman conquest of Egypt in 1517, both merchant and military vessels established an Ottoman presence throughout the Indian Ocean basin. Ottoman subjects traveled as far as China, but they were most active in Muslim lands from east Africa and Arabia to India and southeast Asia, where they enjoyed especially warm receptions.

While other peoples also made their way into the larger world, only Europeans linked the lands and peoples of the eastern hemisphere, the western hemisphere, and Oceania. Because only they traveled regularly between the world's major geographic regions, European peoples benefited from unparalleled opportunities to increase their power, wealth, and influence. The projection of European influence brought about a decisive shift in the global balance of power. During the millennium 500 to 1500 C.E., the world's most powerful societies were those organized by imperial states such as the Tang dynasty of China, the Abbasid dynasty in southwest Asia, the Byzantine empire in the eastern Mediterranean region, and the Mongol empires that embraced much of Eurasia. After 1500, however, European peoples became much more prominent than before in the larger world, and they began to establish vast empires that by the nineteenth century ruled most of the world.

The expansion of European influence also resulted in the establishment of global networks of transportation, communication, and exchange. A worldwide diffusion of plants, animals, diseases, and human communities followed European ventures across the oceans, and intricate trade networks gave birth to a global economy. Although epidemic diseases killed millions of people, the spread of food crops and domesticated animals led to a dramatic surge in global population. The establishment of global trade networks ensured that interactions between the world's peoples would continue and intensify.

The European Reconnaissance of the World's Oceans

Between 1400 and 1800, European mariners launched a remarkable series of exploratory voyages that took them to all the earth's waters, with the exception of those in extreme polar regions. These voyages were very expensive affairs. Yet private investors and government authorities had strong motives to underwrite the expeditions and outfit them with advanced nautical technology. The voyages of exploration paid large dividends: they enabled European mariners to chart the world's ocean basins and develop an accurate understanding of world geography. On the basis of this knowledge, European merchants and mariners established global networks of communication, transportation, and exchange—and profited handsomely from their efforts.

Motives for Exploration

A complex combination of motives prompted Europeans to explore the world's oceans. Most important of these motives were the search for basic resources and lands suitable for the cultivation of cash crops, the desire to establish new trade routes to Asian markets, and the aspiration to expand the influence of Christianity.

Portuguese Exploration

Mariners from the relatively poor and hardscrabble kingdom of Portugal were most prominent in the search for fresh resources to exploit and lands to cultivate. Beginning in the thirteenth century, Portuguese seamen ventured away from the coasts and into the open Atlantic Ocean. They originally sought fish, seals, whales, timber, and lands where they could grow wheat to supplement the meager resources of Portugal. By the early fourteenth century, they had discovered the uninhabited Azores and Madeiras Islands. They called frequently at the Canary Islands, inhabited by the indigenous Guanche people, which Italian and Iberian mariners had visited since the early fourteenth century. Because European demand for sugar was strong and increasing, the prospect of establishing sugar plantations on the Atlantic islands was very tempting. Italian entrepreneurs had organized sugar plantations in Palestine and the Mediterranean islands since the twelfth century, and in the fifteenth century Italian investors worked with Portuguese mariners to establish plantations in the Atlantic islands. Continuing Portuguese voyages also led to the establishment of plantations on more southerly Atlantic islands, including the Cape Verde Islands, São Tomé, Principe, and Fernando Po.

The Lure of Trade

Even more alluring than the exploitation of fresh lands and resources was the goal of establishing maritime trade routes to the markets of Asia. During the era of the Mongol empires, European merchants often traveled overland as far as China in order to trade in silk, spices, porcelain, and other Asian goods. In the fourteenth century, however, with the collapse of the Mongol empires and the spread of bubonic plague, travel on the silk roads became much less safe than before. Muslim mariners continued to bring Asian goods through the Indian Ocean and the Red Sea to Cairo, where Italian merchants purchased them for distribution in western Europe. But prices at Cairo were high, and Europeans sought ever-larger quantities of Asian goods, particularly spices.

By the fourteenth century the wealthy classes of Europe regarded Indian pepper and Chinese ginger as expensive necessities, and they especially prized cloves and nutmeg from the spice islands of Maluku. Merchants and monarchs alike realized that by offering direct access to Asian markets and eliminating Muslim intermediaries, new maritime trade routes would increase the quantities of spices and other Asian goods available in Europe—and would also yield enormous profits.

African trade also beckoned to Europeans and called them to the sea. Since the twelfth century, Europeans had purchased west African gold, ivory, and slaves delivered by the trans-Saharan camel caravans of Muslim merchants to north African ports. Gold was an especially important commodity because the precious metal from west Africa was their principal form of payment for Asian luxury goods. As in the case of Asian trade, maritime routes that eliminated Muslim intermediaries and offered more direct access to African markets would benefit European merchants.

Missionary Efforts

Alongside material incentives, the goal of expanding the boundaries of Christianity also drove Europeans into the larger world. Like Buddhism and Islam, Christianity is a missionary religion. The New Testament specifically urged Christians to spread

A detail from the Catalan Atlas, a magnificent illustrated representation of the known world produced about 1375, depicts a camel caravan traveling from China to Europe across the silk roads.

their faith throughout the world. Efforts to spread the faith often took peaceful forms. During the era of the Mongol empires, Franciscan and Dominican missionaries had traveled as far as India, central Asia, and China in search of converts. Yet the expansion of Christianity was by no means always a peaceful affair. Beginning in the eleventh century, western Europeans had launched a series of crusades and holy wars against Muslims in Palestine, the Mediterranean islands, and Iberia. Crusading zeal remained especially strong in Iberia, where the *reconquista* came to an end in 1492: the Muslim kingdom of Granada fell to Spanish Christian forces just weeks before Christopher Columbus set sail on his famous first voyage to the western hemisphere. Whether through persuasion or violence, overseas voyages offered fresh opportunities for western Europeans to spread their faith.

In practice, the various motives for exploration combined and reinforced each other. Dom Henrique of Portugal, often called Prince Henry the Navigator, promoted voyages of exploration in west Africa specifically to enter the gold trade, discover profitable new trade routes, gain intelligence about the extent of Muslim power, win converts to Christianity, and make alliances against the Muslims with any Christian rulers he might find. When the Portuguese mariner Vasco da Gama reached the Indian port of Calicut in 1498, local authorities asked him what he wanted there. His reply: "Christians and spices." The goal of spreading Christianity thus became a powerful justification and reinforcement for the more material motives for the voyages of exploration.

The Technology of Exploration

Without advanced nautical technology and navigational skills, even the strongest motives would not have enabled European mariners to reconnoiter the world's oceans. Embarking on voyages that would keep them out of the sight of land for weeks at a time, mariners needed sturdy ships, navigational equipment, and sailing techniques that would permit them to make their way across the seas and back again. They inherited much of their nautical technology from Mediterranean and northern European maritime traditions and combined it imaginatively with elements of Chinese or Arabic origin.

Ships and Sails

From their experiences in the coastal waters of the Atlantic, European sailors learned to construct ships strong enough to brave most adverse conditions. Beginning about the twelfth century, they increased the maneuverability of their craft by building a rudder onto the stern. (The sternpost rudder was a Chinese invention that had diffused across the Indian Ocean and probably became known to Europeans through Arab ships in the Mediterranean.) They outfitted their vessels with two main types of sail, both of which Mediterranean mariners had used since classical times. Square sails enabled them to take full advantage of a following wind (a wind blowing from behind), although these sails did not work well in crosswinds. Triangular lateen sails, on the other hand, were very maneuverable and could catch winds from the side as well as from behind. With a combination of square and lateen sails, European ships were able to use whatever winds arose. Their ability to tack—to advance against the wind by sailing across it—was crucial for the exploration of regions with uncooperative winds.

Navigational Instruments

The most important navigational equipment on board these vessels were magnetic compasses and astrolabes (soon replaced by cross staffs and back staffs). The compass was a Chinese invention of the Tang or Song dynasty that had diffused throughout the Indian Ocean basin in the eleventh century. By the mid-twelfth century, European mariners used compasses to determine their heading in Mediterranean and Atlantic waters. The astrolabe was a simplified version of an instrument used by Greek and Persian astronomers to determine latitude by measuring the angle of the sun or the pole star above the horizon. Portuguese mariners visiting the Indian Ocean in the late fifteenth century encountered Arab sailors using simpler and more serviceable instruments for determining latitude, which the Portuguese then used as models for the construction of cross staffs and back staffs.

European mariners' ability to determine direction and latitude enabled them to assemble a vast body of data about the earth's geography and to find their way around the world's oceans with tolerable accuracy and efficiency. (The measurement of longitude requires the ability to measure time precisely and so had to wait until the late eighteenth century, when dependable, spring-driven clocks became available.)

Knowledge of Winds and Currents

Equipped with advanced technological hardware, European mariners ventured into the oceans and gradually compiled a body of practical knowledge about the winds and currents that determined navigational possibilities in the age of sail. In both the Atlantic and Pacific Oceans, strong winds blow regularly to create giant "wind wheels" both north and south of the equator, and ocean currents follow a similar pattern. Between about five and twenty-five degrees of latitude north and south of the equator, trade winds blow from the east. Between about thirty and sixty degrees north and south, westerly winds prevail. Winds and currents in the Indian

By using cross staffs to measure the angle of the sun or pole star above the horizon, mariners could determine latitude.

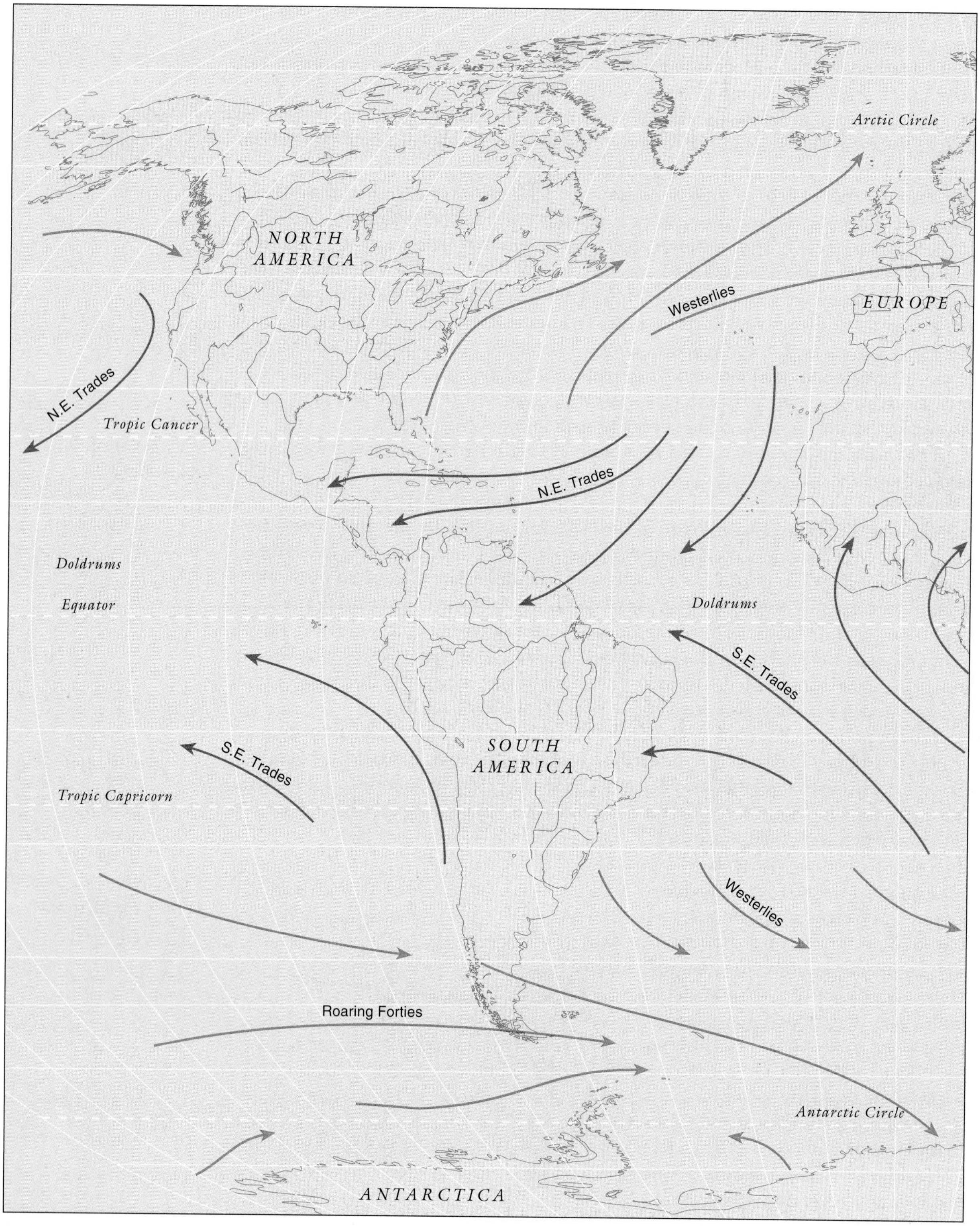

MAP [23.1]
Wind and current patterns in the world's oceans.

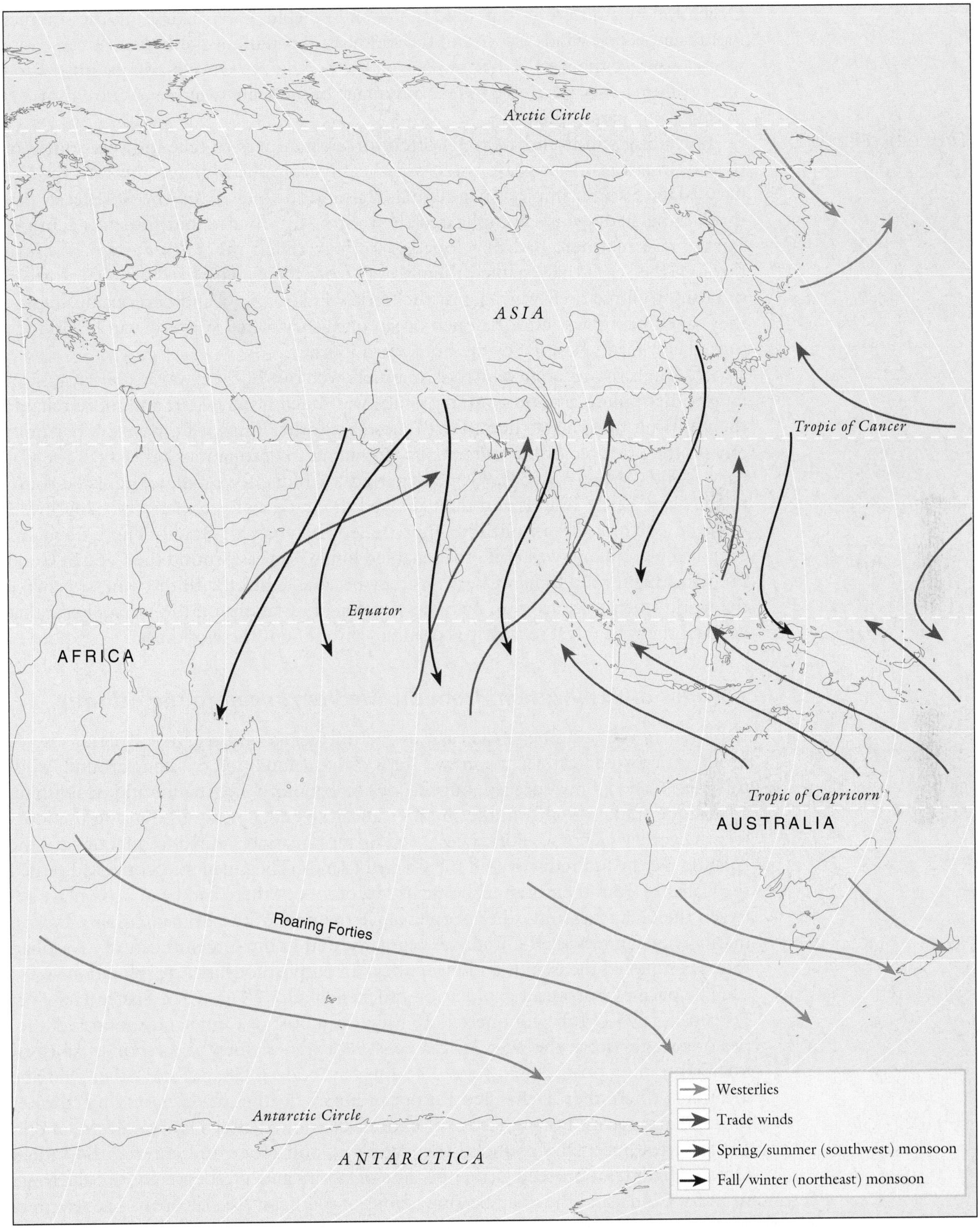
Arctic Circle
ASIA
Tropic of Cancer
Equator
AFRICA
Tropic of Capricorn
AUSTRALIA
Roaring Forties
Antarctic Circle
ANTARCTICA
Westerlies
Trade winds
Spring/summer (southwest) monsoon
Fall/winter (northeast) monsoon

Ocean follow a different, but still regular and reliable, pattern. During the summer months monsoon winds blow from the southeast throughout the Indian Ocean basin, whereas during the winter they blow from the northwest. Once mariners understood these patterns, they were able to take advantage of prevailing winds and currents to sail to almost any part of the earth.

The volta do mar

Prevailing winds and currents often forced mariners to take indirect routes to their destinations. European vessels sailed easily from the Mediterranean to the Canary Islands, for example, since regular trade winds blew from the northeast. But those same trade winds complicated the return trip. By the mid-fifteenth century, Portuguese mariners had developed a strategy called the *volta do mar* ("return through the sea") that enabled them to sail from the Canaries to Portugal. Instead of trying to force their way against the trade winds—a slow and perilous business—they sailed northwest into the open ocean until they found westerly winds and then turned east for the last leg of the homeward journey.

Although the *volta do mar* took mariners well out of their way, experience soon taught that sailing around contrary winds was much faster, safer, and more reliable than butting up against them. Portuguese and other European mariners began to rely on the principle of the *volta do mar* in sailing to destinations other than the Canary Islands. When Vasco da Gama departed for India, for example, he sailed south to the Cape Verde Islands and then allowed the trade winds to carry him southwest into the Atlantic Ocean until he approached the coast of Brazil. There da Gama caught the prevailing westerlies that enabled him to sail east, round the Cape of Good Hope, and enter the Indian Ocean. As they became familiar with the wind systems of the world's oceans, European mariners developed variations on the *volta do mar* that enabled them to travel reliably to coastlines throughout the world.

Voyages of Exploration: from the Mediterranean to the Atlantic

Exploratory voyaging began as early as the thirteenth century. In 1291 the Vivaldi brothers departed from Genoa in two ships with the intention of sailing around Africa to India. They did not succeed, but the idea of exploring the Atlantic and establishing a maritime trade route from the Mediterranean to India persisted. During the fourteenth century Genoese, Portuguese, and Spanish mariners sailed frequently into the Atlantic Ocean and rediscovered the Canary Islands. The Guanche people had settled the Canaries from their original home in Morocco, but there had been no contact between the Guanches and other peoples since the time of the Roman empire. Iberian mariners began to visit the Canaries regularly, and in the fifteenth century Castilian forces conquered the islands and made them an outpost for further exploration.

Prince Henry of Portugal

The pace of European exploration quickened after 1415 when Prince Henry of Portugal (1394–1460) conquered the Moroccan port of Ceuta and sponsored a series of voyages down the west African coast. Portuguese merchants soon established fortified trading posts at São Jorge da Mina (in modern Ghana) and other strategic locations. There they exchanged European horses, leather, textiles, and metalwares for gold and slaves. Portuguese explorations continued after Henry's death, and in 1488 Bartolomeu Dias rounded the Cape of Good Hope and entered the Indian Ocean. He did not proceed farther because of storms and a restless crew, but the route to India, China, and the spice-bearing islands of southeast Asia lay open. The sea route to the Indian Ocean offered European merchants the opportunity to buy silk, spices, and pepper at the source, rather than through Muslim intermediaries, and to take part in the flourishing trade of Asia described by Marco Polo.

Vasco da Gama

Portuguese mariners did not immediately follow up Dias's voyage, because domestic and foreign problems distracted royal attention from voyages to Asia. In 1497,

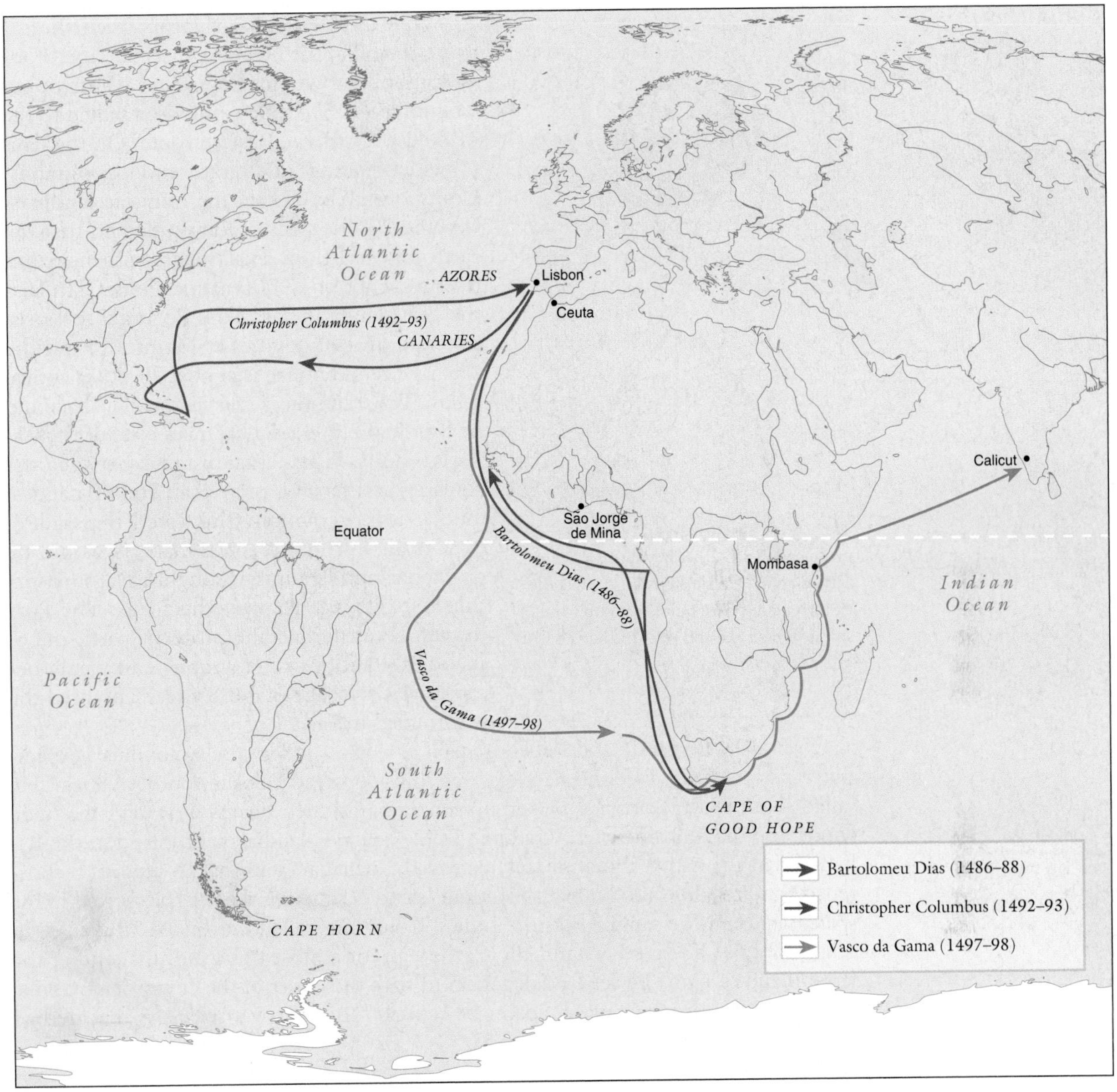

MAP [23.2]
European exploration in the Atlantic Ocean, 1486–1498.

however, Vasco da Gama departed Lisbon with a fleet of four armed merchant ships bound for India. His experience was not altogether pleasant. His fleet went more than three months without seeing land, and his cargoes excited little interest in Indian markets. His return voyage was especially difficult, and less than half of his crew made it safely back to Portugal. Yet his cargo of pepper and cinnamon was hugely profitable, and Portuguese merchants began immediately to organize further expeditions. By 1500 they had built a trading post at Calicut, and Portuguese mariners soon called at ports throughout India and the Indian Ocean basin. By the late sixteenth century, English and Dutch mariners had followed the Portuguese into the Indian Ocean basin.

For an interactive version of this map, go to www.mhhe.com/bentley3ch23maps.

Christopher Columbus

The earliest surviving world globe, produced in 1492 by the German cartographer Martin Behaim, depicts the eastern hemisphere quite accurately but shows almost no land west of Iberia except for east Asia.

While Portuguese navigators plied the sea route to India, the Genoese mariner Cristoforo Colombo, known in English as Christopher Columbus (1451–1506), proposed sailing to the markets of Asia by a western route. On the basis of wide reading of literature on geography, Columbus believed that the Eurasian landmass covered 270 degrees of longitude and that the earth was a relatively small sphere with a circumference of about 17,000 nautical miles. (In fact, the Eurasian landmass from Portugal to Korea covers only 140 degrees of longitude, and the earth's circumference is almost 25,000 nautical miles.) By Columbus's calculations, Japan should be less than 2,500 nautical miles west of the Canary Islands. (The actual distance between the Canaries and Japan is more than 10,000 nautical miles.) This geography suggested that sailing west from Europe to Asian markets would be profitable, and Columbus sought royal sponsorship for a voyage to prove his ideas. The Portuguese court declined his proposal, partly out of skepticism about his geography and partly because Dias's voyage of 1488 already pointed the way toward India.

Eventually Fernando and Isabel of Spain agreed to underwrite Columbus's expedition, and in August 1492 his fleet of three ships departed Palos in southern Spain. He sailed south to the Canaries, picked up supplies, and then turned west with the trade winds. On the morning of 12 October 1492, he made landfall at an island in the Bahamas that the native Taino inhabitants called Guanahaní and that Columbus rechristened San Salvador (also known as Watling Island). Thinking that he had arrived in the spice islands known familiarly as the Indies, Columbus called the Tainos "Indians." In search of gold he sailed around the Caribbean for almost three months, and at the large island of Cuba he sent a delegation to seek the court of the emperor of China. When Columbus returned to Spain, he reported to his royal sponsors that he had reached islands just off the coast of Asia.

Hemispheric Links

Columbus never reached the riches of Asia, and despite three additional voyages across the Atlantic Ocean, he obtained very little gold in the Caribbean. Yet news of his voyage spread rapidly throughout Europe, and hundreds of Spanish, English, French, and Dutch mariners soon followed in his wake. Particularly in the early sixteenth century, many of them continued to seek the passage to Asian waters that Columbus himself had pursued. Over a longer term, however, it became clear that the American continents and the Caribbean islands themselves held abundant opportunities for entrepreneurs. Thus Columbus's voyages to the western hemisphere had unintended but momentous consequences, since they established links between the eastern and western hemispheres and paved the way for the conquest, settlement, and exploitation of the Americas by European peoples.

Voyages of Exploration: from the Atlantic to the Pacific

While some Europeans sought opportunities in the Americas, others continued to seek a western route to Asian markets. The Spanish military commander Vasco Nuñez

Sources from the Past

Christopher Columbus's First Impressions of American Peoples

Christopher Columbus kept journals of his experiences during his voyages to the western hemisphere. The journal of his first voyage survives mostly in summary, but it clearly communicates Columbus's first impressions of the peoples he met in the Caribbean islands. The following excerpts show that Columbus, like other European mariners, had both Christianity and commerce in mind when exploring distant lands.

Thursday, 11 October [1492]. . . .

I . . . in order that they would be friendly to us—because I recognized that they were people who would be better freed [from error] and converted to our Holy Faith by love than by force—to some of them I gave red caps, and glass beads which they put on their chests, and many other things of small value, in which they took so much pleasure and became so much our friends that it was a marvel. Later they came swimming to the ships' launches where we were and brought us parrots and cotton thread in balls and javelins and many other things, and they traded them to us for other things which we gave them, such as small glass beads and bells. In sum, they took everything and gave of what they had willingly.

But it seemed to me that they were a people very poor in everything. All of them go as naked as their mothers bore them; and the women also, although I did not see more than one quite young girl. And all those that I saw were young people, for none did I see of more than 30 years of age. They are very well formed, with handsome bodies and good faces. Their hair [is] coarse—almost like the tail of a horse—and short. They wear their hair down over their eyebrows except for a little in the back which they wear long and never cut. . . .

They do not carry arms nor are they acquainted with them, because I showed them swords and they took them by the edge and through ignorance cut themselves. They have no iron. Their javelins are shafts without iron and some of them have at the end a fish tooth and others of other things. All of them alike are of good-sized stature and carry themselves well. I saw some who had marks of wounds on their bodies and I made signs to them asking what they were; and they showed me how people from other islands nearby came there and tried to take them, and how they defended themselves and I believed and believe that they come here from *tierra firme* [the continent] to take them captive. They should be good and intelligent servants, for I see that they say very quickly everything that is said to them; and I believe that they would become Christians very easily, for it seemed to me that they had no religion. . . .

Monday, 12 November. . . .

They are very gentle and do not know what evil is; nor do they kill others, nor steal; and they are without weapons and so timid that a hundred of them flee from one of our men even if our men are teasing them. And they are credulous and aware that there is a God in heaven and convinced that we come from the heavens; and they say very quickly any prayer that we tell them to say, and they make the sign of the cross. So that Your Highnesses ought to resolve to make them Christians: for I believe that if you begin, in a short time you will end up having converted to our Holy Faith a multitude of peoples and acquiring large dominions and great riches and all of their peoples for Spain. Because without doubt there is in these lands a very great quantity of gold; for not without cause do these Indians that I bring with me say that there are in these islands places where they dig gold and wear it on their chests, on their ears, and on their arms, and on their legs; and they are very thick bracelets. And also there are stones, and there are precious pearls and infinite spicery. . . . And also here there is probably a great quantity of cotton; and I think that it would sell very well here without taking it to Spain but to the big cities belonging to the Grand [Mongol] Khan.

SOURCE: Christopher Columbus. *The* Diario *of Christopher Columbus's First Voyage to America.* Trans. by Oliver Dunn and James E. Kelley Jr. Norman: University of Oklahoma Press, 1989, pp. 65–69, 143–45.

On the basis of Columbus's account, what inferences can you draw about his plans for American lands and peoples?

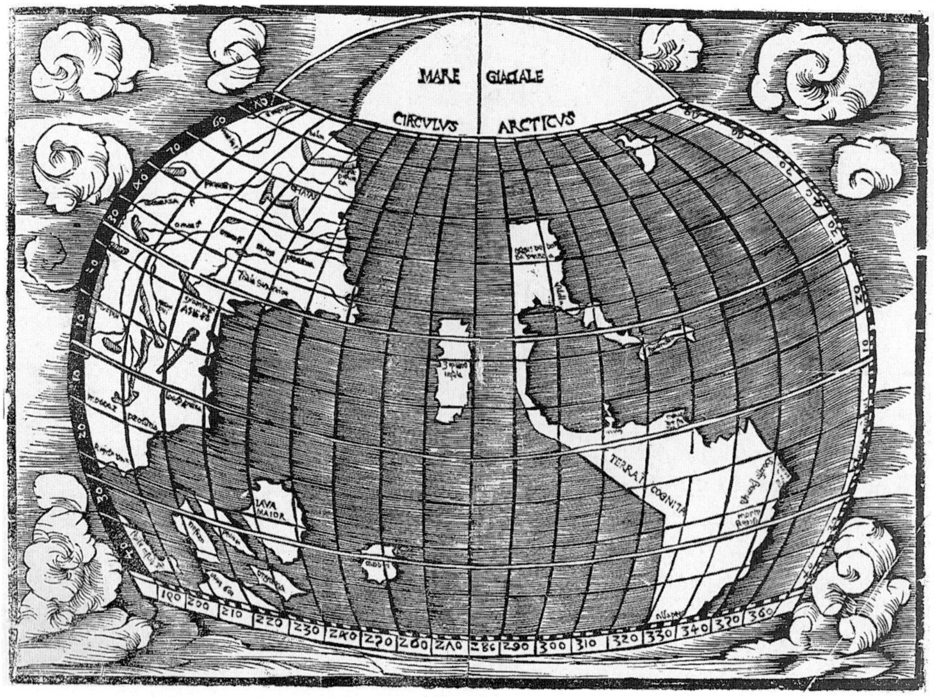

A map prepared about 1512 by the Polish cartographer Jan Stobnicza shows eloquently that it took a long time for geographers to realize the extent of the Americas and the Pacific Ocean. Here "Cipangu" (Japan) lies just west of Mexico, with the Asian mainland nearby.

de Balboa sighted the Pacific Ocean in 1513 while searching for gold in Panama, but in the early sixteenth century no one knew how much ocean lay between the Americas and Asia. Indeed, no one even suspected the vast size of the Pacific Ocean, which covers one-third of the earth's surface.

Ferdinand Magellan

The reconnaissance of the Pacific Ocean basin began with the Portuguese navigator Fernão de Magalhães (1480–1521), better known as Ferdinand Magellan. While sailing in the service of Portugal, Magellan had visited ports throughout the Indian Ocean basin and had traveled east as far as the spice islands of Maluku. He believed that the spice islands and Asian markets lay fairly close to the western coast of the Americas, and he decided to pursue Christopher Columbus's goal of establishing a western route to Asian waters. Because Portuguese mariners had already reached Asian markets through the Indian Ocean, they had little interest in Magellan's proposed western route. Thus, on his Pacific expedition and circumnavigation of the world (1519–1522), Magellan sailed in the service of Spain.

The Circumnavigation

Magellan's voyage was an exercise in endurance. He began by probing the eastern coast of South America in search of a strait leading to the Pacific. Eventually he found and sailed through the tricky and treacherous Strait of Magellan near the southern tip of South America. After exiting the strait, his fleet sailed almost four months before taking on fresh provisions at Guam. During that period crewmen survived on worm-ridden biscuits, leather that they had softened in the ocean, and water gone foul. Ship's rats that were unfortunate enough to fall into the hands of famished sailors quickly became the centerpiece of a meal. A survivor reported in his account of the voyage that crewmen even ate ox hides, which they softened by dragging them through the sea for four or five days and then grilled on coals. Lacking fresh fruits and vegetables in their diet, many of the crew fell victim to the dreaded disease of scurvy, which caused painful rotting of the gums, loss of teeth, abscesses, hemorrhaging, weakness, loss of spirit, and in most cases death. Scurvy killed twenty-nine members of Magellan's crew during the Pacific crossing.

Conditions improved after the fleet called at Guam, but its ordeal had not come to an end. From Guam, Magellan proceeded to the Philippine Islands, where he became involved in a local political dispute that took the lives of Magellan himself and 40 of his crew. The survivors continued on to the spice islands of Maluku, where they took on a cargo of cloves. Rather than brave the Pacific Ocean once again, they sailed home through the familiar waters of the Indian Ocean—and thus completed the first circumnavigation of the world—returning to Spain after a voyage of almost exactly three years. Of Magellan's five ships and 280 men, a single ship with 18 of the original crew returned. (Another 17 crewmen returned later by other routes so that 35 members of Magellan's original crew survived the expedition.)

Exploration of the Pacific

The Pacific Ocean is so vast that it took European explorers almost three centuries to chart its features. Spanish merchants built on information gleaned from Magellan's expedition and established a trade route between the Philippines and Mexico, but they did not continue to explore the ocean basin itself. English navigators, however, ventured into the Pacific in search of an elusive northwest passage from Europe to Asia. In fact, a northwest passage exists, but most of its route lies within the Arctic Circle. It is so far north that ice clogs its waters for much of the year, and it was only in the twentieth century that the Norwegian explorer Roald Amundsen traveled from the Atlantic to the Pacific by way of the northwest passage. Nevertheless, while searching for a passage, English mariners established many of the details of Pacific geography. In the sixteenth century, for example, Sir Francis Drake scouted the west coast of North America as far north as Vancouver Island. By the mid-eighteenth century French mariners had joined English seafarers in exploring the Pacific Ocean in search of a northwest passage.

Russian expansion was mostly a land-based affair in early modern times, but by the eighteenth century Russians also were exploring the Pacific Ocean. Russian officials commissioned the Danish navigator Vitus Bering to undertake two maritime expeditions (1725–1730 and 1733–1742) in search of a northeast passage to Asian ports. Bering sailed through the icy Arctic Ocean and the Bering Strait, which separates Siberia from Alaska, and reconnoitered northern Asia as far as the Kamchatka peninsula. Other Russian explorers made their way from Alaska down the western Canadian coast to northern California. By 1800 Russian mariners were scouting the Pacific Ocean as far south as the Hawaiian Islands. Indeed, they built a small fort on the island of Kaua`i and engaged in trade there for a few years in the early nineteenth century.

Captain James Cook

Alongside Magellan, however, the most important of the Pacific explorers was Captain James Cook (1728–1779), who led three expeditions to the Pacific and died in a scuffle with the indigenous people of Hawai`i. Cook charted eastern Australia and New Zealand, and he added New Caledonia, Vanuatu, and Hawai`i to European maps of the Pacific. He probed the frigid waters of the Arctic Ocean and spent months at a time in the tropical islands of Tahiti, Tonga, and Hawai`i, where he showed deep interest in the manners, customs, and languages of Polynesian peoples. By the time Cook's voyages had come to an end, European geographers had compiled a reasonably accurate understanding of the world's ocean basins, their lands, and their peoples.

TRADE AND CONFLICT IN EARLY MODERN ASIA

The voyages of exploration taught European mariners how to sail to almost any coastline in the world and return safely. Once they arrived at their destinations, they sought commercial opportunities. In the eastern hemisphere they built a series of fortified

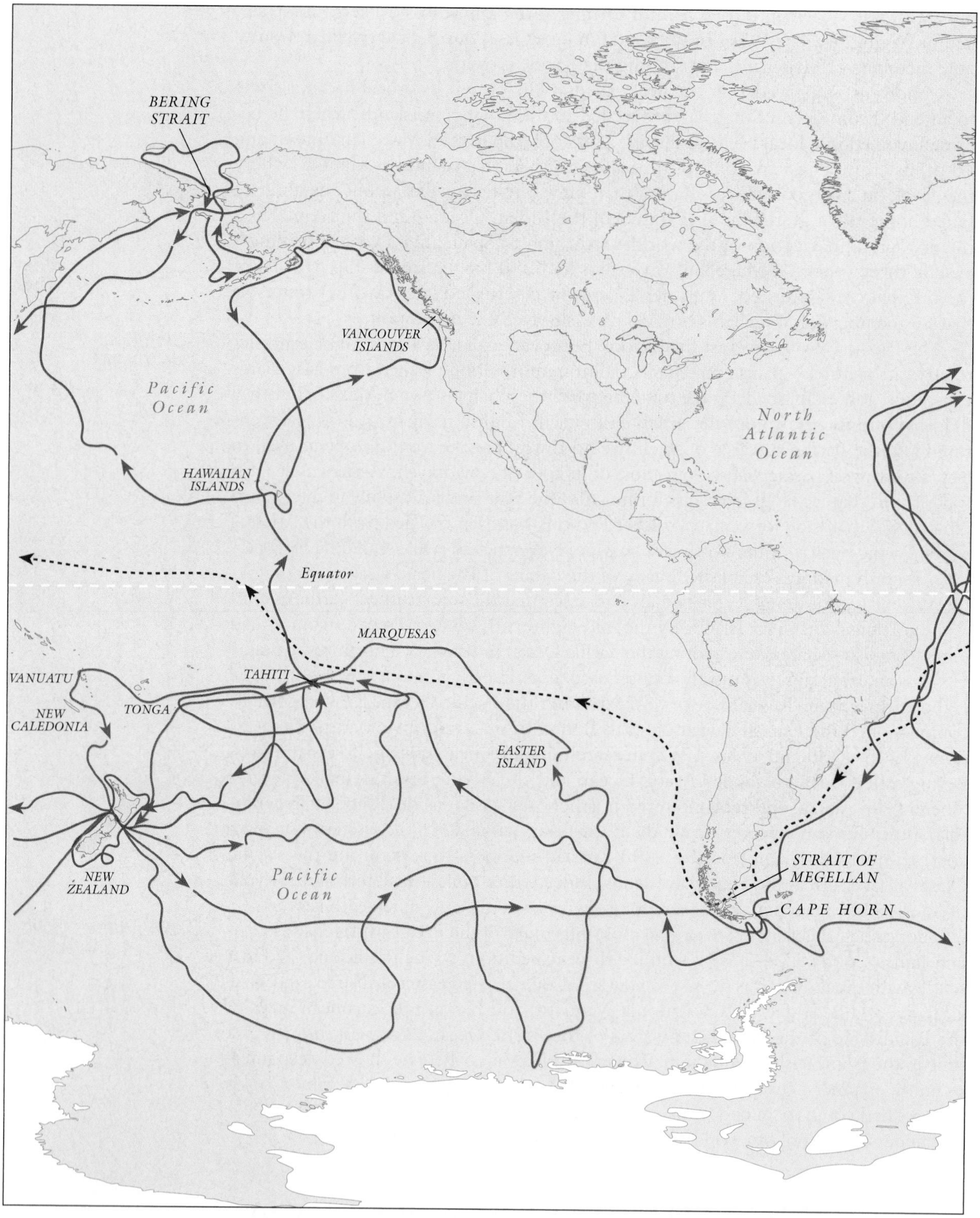

MAP [23.3]
European exploration in the Pacific Ocean, 1519–1780.

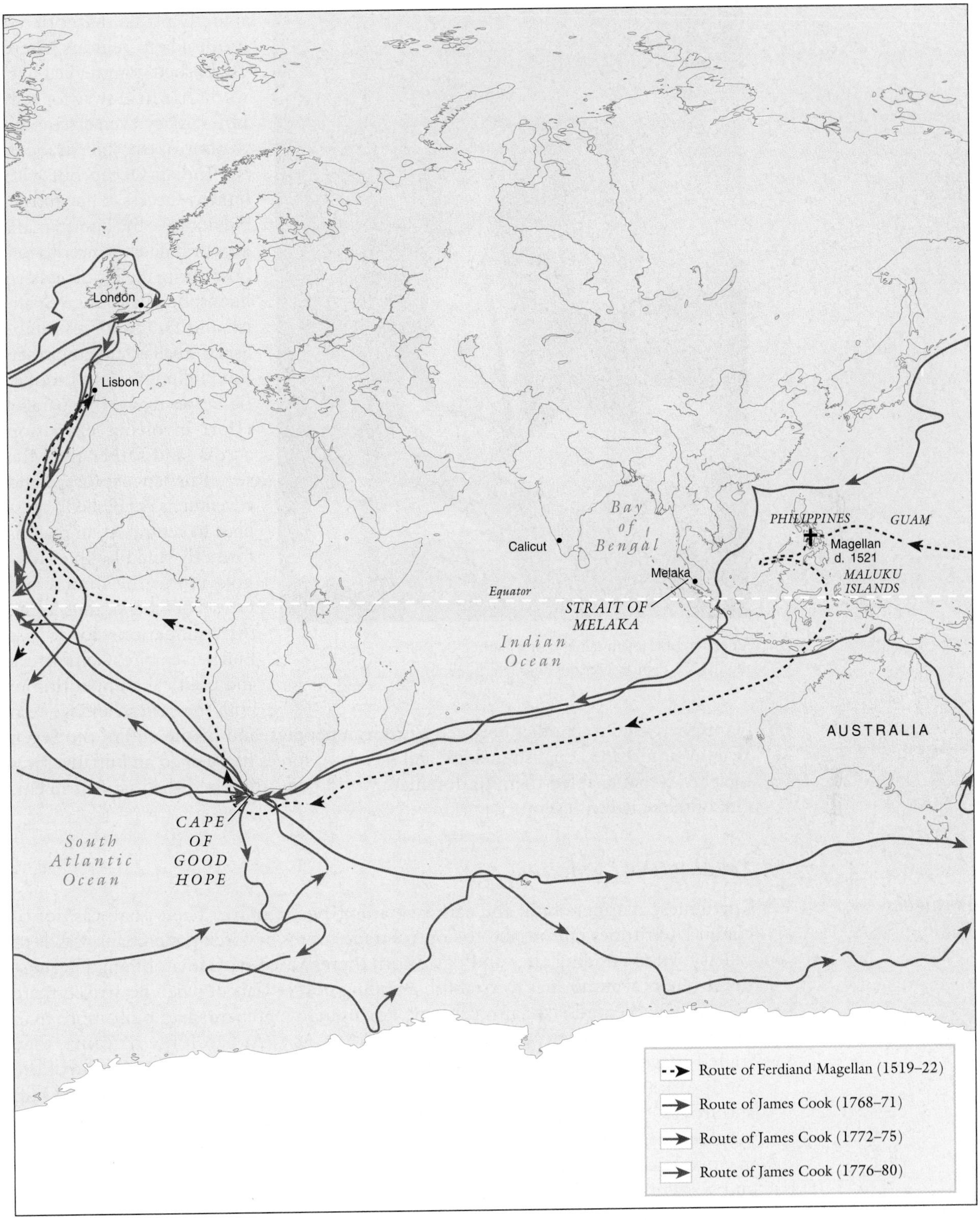
London
Lisbon
Calicut
Bay of Bengal
Melaka
STRAIT OF MELAKA
Equator
Indian Ocean
PHILIPPINES
GUAM
Magellan d. 1521
MALUKU ISLANDS
AUSTRALIA
CAPE OF GOOD HOPE
South Atlantic Ocean
Route of Ferdiand Magellan (1519–22)
Route of James Cook (1768–71)
Route of James Cook (1772–75)
Route of James Cook (1776–80)

A portrait of Captain James Cook painted by William Hodges about 1775 depicts a serious and determined man.

trading posts that offered footholds in regions where established commercial networks had held sway for centuries. They even attempted to control the spice trade in the Indian Ocean but with limited success. They mostly did not have the human numbers or military power to impose their rule in the eastern hemisphere, although Spanish and Dutch forces established small island empires in the Philippines and Indonesia, respectively. In a parallel effort involving expansion across land rather than the sea, Russian explorers and adventurers established a presence in central Asian regions formerly ruled by the Mongols and in the tundra and forests of Siberia, thus laying the foundations for a vast Eurasian empire. Commercial and political competition in both the eastern and western hemispheres led to conflict between European peoples, and by the end of the Seven Years' War in 1763, English military and merchant forces had gained an initiative over their rivals that enabled them to dominate world trade and build the vast British empire of the nineteenth century.

Trading-Post Empires

Portuguese Trading Posts

Portuguese mariners built the earliest trading-post empire. Their goal was not to conquer territories but, rather, to control trade routes by forcing merchant vessels to call at fortified trading sites and pay duties there. Vasco da Gama obtained permission from local authorities to establish a trading post at Calicut when he arrived there in 1498. By the mid-sixteenth century, Portuguese merchants had built more than fifty trading posts between west Africa and east Asia. At São Jorge da Mina, they traded in west African slaves, and at Mozambique they attempted to control the south African gold trade. From Hormuz they controlled access to the Persian Gulf, and from Goa they organized trade in Indian pepper. At Melaka they oversaw shipping between the South China Sea and the Indian Ocean, and they channeled trade in cloves and nutmeg through Ternate in the spice islands of Maluku. Posts at Macau and Nagasaki offered access to the markets of China and Japan.

Afonso d'Alboquerque

Equipped with heavy artillery, Portuguese vessels were able to overpower most other craft that they encountered, and they sometimes trained their cannon effectively onshore. The architect of their aggressive policy was Afonso d'Alboquerque, commander of Portuguese forces in the Indian Ocean during the early sixteenth century. Alboquerque's fleets seized Hormuz in 1508, Goa in 1510, and Melaka in 1511. From these strategic sites, Alboquerque sought to control Indian Ocean trade by forcing all merchant ships to purchase safe-conduct passes and present them at Portuguese trading posts. Ships without passes were subject to confiscation, along with their cargoes. Alboquerque's forces punished violators of his policy by executing them or cutting off their hands. Alboquerque was confident of Portuguese naval superiority and its ability to control trade in the Indian Ocean. After taking Melaka, he boasted that the arrival of Portuguese ships sent other vessels scurrying and that even the birds left the skies and sought cover.

Alboquerque's boast was an exaggeration. Although heavily armed, Portuguese forces did not have enough vessels to enforce the commander's orders. Arab, Indian, and Malay merchants continued to play prominent roles in Indian Ocean commerce, usually without taking the precaution of securing a safe-conduct pass. Portuguese ships transported perhaps half the pepper and spices that Europeans consumed during the early and middle decades of the sixteenth century, but Arab vessels delivered shipments through the Red Sea, which Portuguese forces never managed to control, to Cairo and Mediterranean trade routes.

By the late sixteenth century, Portuguese hegemony in the Indian Ocean was growing weak. Portugal was a small country with a small population—about one million in 1500—and was unable to sustain a large seaborne trading empire for very long. The crews of Portuguese ships often included Spanish, English, and Dutch sailors, who became familiar with Asian waters while in Portuguese service. By the late sixteenth century, investors in other lands began to organize their own expeditions to Asian markets. Most prominent of those who followed the Portuguese into the Indian Ocean were English and Dutch mariners.

English and Dutch Trading Posts

Like their predecessors, English and Dutch merchants built trading posts on Asian coasts and sought to channel trade through them, but they did not attempt to control shipping on the high seas. They occasionally seized Portuguese sites, most notably when a Dutch fleet conquered Melaka in 1641. Yet Portuguese authorities held many of their trading posts into the twentieth century: Goa remained the official capital of Portuguese colonies in Asia until Indian forces reclaimed it in 1961. Meanwhile, English and Dutch entrepreneurs established parallel networks. English merchants concentrated on India and built trading posts at Bombay, Madras, and Calcutta, while the Dutch operated more broadly from Cape Town, Colombo, and Batavia (modern Jakarta on the island of Java).

English and Dutch merchants enjoyed two main advantages over their Portuguese predecessors. They sailed faster, cheaper, and more powerful ships, which offered both an economic and a military edge over their competitors. Furthermore, they conducted trade through an exceptionally efficient form of commercial organization—the joint-stock company—which enabled investors to realize handsome profits while limiting the risk to their investments.

The Trading Companies

English and Dutch merchants formed two especially powerful joint-stock companies: the English East India Company, founded in 1600, and its Dutch counterpart, the United East India Company, known from its initials as the VOC (Vereenigde Oost-Indische Compagnie), established in 1602. Private merchants advanced funds to launch these companies, outfit them with ships and crews, and provide them with commodities and money to trade. Although they enjoyed government support, the companies were privately owned enterprises. Unhampered by political oversight, company agents concentrated strictly on profitable trade. Their charters granted them the right to buy, sell, build trading posts, and even make war in the companies' interests.

Sources from the Past

Afonso D'Alboquerque Seizes Hormuz

Afonso d'Alboquerque the mariner had a son of the same name who in 1557 published a long set of historical Commentaries *on his father's deeds. His account of the battle for Hormuz vividly illustrates the effectiveness of Portuguese artillery as well as the chaos and confusion of sea battles in early modern times.*

As some time had passed since the king [of Hormuz] had received information about the [Portuguese] fleet and the destruction that the great Afonso d'Alboquerque had wrought along the [Arabian] coast, he began to prepare himself to fight with him. For this end he gave orders to detain all the ships that came into the port of Hormuz and added a force of sixty great vessels into which he draughted off many soldiers and much artillery with everything that was required for the undertaking. And among these great vessels there was one belonging to the king of Cambay [in India] . . . and another of the prince of Cambay. . . . And besides these ships there were in the harbor about 200 galleys, which are long ships with many oars. . . . There were also many barks full of small guns and men wearing sword-proof dress and armed from head to foot, most of them being archers. All this fleet was rigged out with flags and standards and colored ensigns, and made a very beautiful appearance. . . .

When Afonso d'Alboquerque perceived the gleaming of the swords and waving of the bucklers and other doings of the Moors [Muslims] on shore, . . . he understood by these signs that the king was determined to give him battle. . . . When morning broke, . . . he ordered a broadside to be fired. The bombardiers took aim so that with the first two shots they fired they sent two large ships which were in front of them, with all their men, to the bottom—one being the prince of Cambay's ship. . . . Afonso Lopez da Costa, who was stationed on the land side, vanquished and sent to the bottom some portion of the galleys and guard boats that his artillery could reach. Manuel Telez, after having caused great slaughter upon some vessels, . . . ran into a large vessel that lay close to him and killed a part of the men in it, while the rest threw themselves into the sea, and those who were heavy-armed went down at once. João da Nova too with his artillery did great execution among the ships that lay along the piles, as did also Antonio do Campo and Francisco de Tavora among the galleys that had surrounded them, and all night long they kept on hooking their anchors together in order to catch the galleys in the middle of them. And although the Moors endeavored to avenge themselves with their artillery, our men were so well fortified with their defenses that they did them no harm, except on the upper deck, and with their arrows they wounded some people.

The fight was so confused on this side and on that, both with artillery and arrows, that it lasted some time without either party seeing each other by reason of the smoke. As soon as this cleared off, . . . and when Afonso saw the discomfiture of the king's fleet and the unexpected victory that Our Lord had sent him and the Moors throwing themselves into the sea from fear of our artillery, thinking that they could escape in that way by swimming, . . . [Afonso] called out to the captains to take to their boats and follow up the victory.

SOURCE: Afonso d'Alboquerque. *Commentaries of the Great Afonso Dalboquerque,* 4 vols. Trans. by Walter de Gray Birch. London: Hakluyt Society, 1875–84, 1:105, 112–14. (Translation slightly modified.)

How might a Muslim commentator have described the battle for Hormuz?

The English and Dutch companies experienced immediate financial success. In 1601, for example, five English ships set sail from London with cargoes mostly of gold and silver coins valued at thirty thousand pounds sterling. When they returned in 1603, the spices that they carried were worth more than one million pounds sterling. The first Dutch expedition did not realize such fantastic profits, but it more

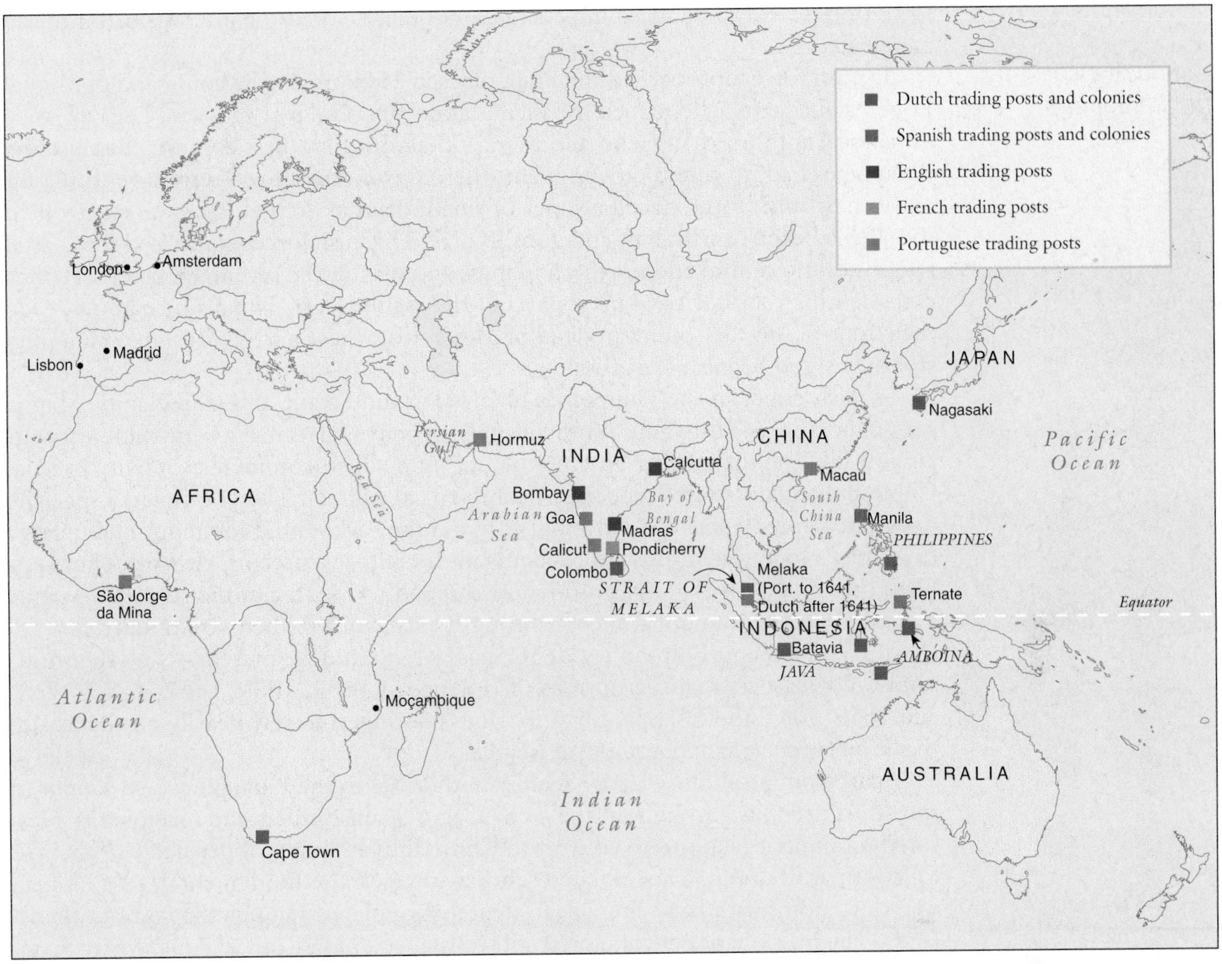

MAP [23.4]
European trading posts in Africa and Asia, about 1700.

than doubled the investments of its underwriters. Because of their advanced nautical technology, powerful military arsenal, efficient organization, and relentless pursuit of profit, the English East India Company and the VOC contributed to the early formation of a global network of trade.

European Conquests in Southeast Asia

Following voyages of exploration to the western hemisphere, Europeans conquered indigenous peoples, built territorial empires, and established colonies settled by European migrants. In the eastern hemisphere, however, they were mostly unable to force their will on large Asian populations and powerful centralized states. With the decline of the Portuguese effort to control shipping in the Indian Ocean, Europeans mostly traded peacefully in Asian waters alongside Arab, Indian, Malay, and Chinese merchants.

Yet in two island regions of southeast Asia—the Philippines and Indonesia—Europeans conquered existing authorities and imposed their rule. Though densely populated, neither the Philippines nor Indonesia had a powerful state when Europeans arrived there in the sixteenth century. Nor did imperial authorities in China or India lay claim to the island regions. Heavily armed ships enabled Europeans to bring massive force to bear and to establish imperial regimes that favored the interests of European merchants.

Conquest of the Philippines

Spanish forces approached the Philippines in 1565 under the command of Miguel López de Legazpi, who named the islands after King Philip II of Spain. Legazpi overcame local authorities in Cebu and Manila in almost bloodless contests. Because the Philippines had no central government, there was no organized resistance to the intrusion. Spanish forces faced a series of small, disunited chiefdoms, most of which soon fell before Spanish ships and guns. By 1575 Spanish forces controlled the coastal regions of the central and northern islands, and during the seventeenth century they extended their authority to most parts of the archipelago. The main region outside their control was the southern island of Mindanao, where a large Muslim community stoutly resisted Spanish expansion.

Manila

Spanish policy in the Philippines revolved around trade and Christianity. Manila soon emerged as a bustling, multicultural port city—an entrepôt for trade particularly in silk—and it quickly became the hub of Spanish commercial activity in Asia. Chinese merchants were especially prominent in Manila. They occupied a specially designated commercial district of the city, and they accounted for about one-quarter of Manila's forty-two thousand residents in the mid-seventeenth century. They supplied the silk goods that Spanish traders shipped to Mexico in the so-called Manila galleons. Their commercial success brought suspicion on their community, and resentful Spanish and Filipino residents massacred Chinese merchants by the thousands in at least six major eruptions of violence in 1603, 1639, 1662, 1686, 1762, and 1819. Nevertheless, Spanish authorities continued to rely heavily on the wealth that Chinese merchants brought to Manila.

Apart from promoting trade, Spanish authorities in the Philippines also sought to spread Christianity throughout the archipelago. Spanish rulers and missionaries pressured prominent Filipinos to convert to Christianity in hopes of persuading others to follow their example. They opened schools to teach the fundamentals of Christian doctrine, along with basic literacy, in densely populated regions throughout the islands. The missionaries encountered stiff resistance in highland regions, where Spanish authority was not as strong as on the coasts, and resistance drew support from opponents of Spanish domination as well as from resentment of the newly arrived faith. Over the long term, however, Filipinos turned increasingly to Christianity, and by the nineteenth century the Philippines had become one of the most fervent Roman Catholic lands in the world.

Conquest of Java

Dutch mariners, who imposed their rule on the islands of Indonesia, did not worry about seeking converts to Christianity, but concentrated instead on the trade in spices, particularly cloves, nutmeg, and mace. The architect of Dutch policy was Jan Pieterszoon Coen, who in 1619 founded Batavia on the island of Java to serve as an entrepôt for the VOC. Batavia occupied a strategic site near the Sunda Strait, and its market attracted both Chinese and Malay vessels. Coen's plan was to establish a VOC monopoly over spice production and trade, thus enabling Dutch merchants to reap enormous profits in European markets. Coen brought his naval power to bear on the small Indonesian islands and forced them to deliver spices only to VOC merchants. On larger islands like Java, he took advantage of tensions between local princes and authorities and extracted concessions from many in return for providing them with aid against the others. By the late seventeenth century, the VOC controlled all the ports of Java as well as most of the important spice-bearing islands throughout the Indonesian archipelago.

Dutch numbers were too few for them to rule directly over their whole southeast Asian empire. They made alliances with local authorities to maintain order in most regions, reserving for direct Dutch rule only Batavia and the most important spice-bearing islands such as clove-producing Amboina and the Banda Islands. They sought less to rule than to control the production of spices. The Dutch did not embark on campaigns of conquest for purposes of adding to their holdings, but they uprooted spice-bearing plants on islands they did not control and mercilessly attacked peoples who sold their spices to merchants not associated with the VOC. Monopoly profits from the spice trade not only enriched the VOC but also made the Netherlands the most prosperous land in Europe throughout most of the seventeenth century.

Harvesting mace on the island of Lontor in the Banda Islands.

Foundations of the Russian Empire in Asia

While western European peoples were building maritime empires, Russians were laying the foundations for a vast land empire that embraced most of northern Eurasia. This round of expansion began in the mid-sixteenth century, as Russian forces took over several Mongol khanates in central Asia. These acquisitions resulted in Russian control over the Volga River and offered opportunities for trade with the Ottoman empire, Iran, and even India through the Caspian Sea. Because of its strategic location on the Volga delta where the river flows into the Caspian Sea, the city of Astrakhan became a bustling commercial center, home to a community of several hundred foreign merchants from as far away as northern India. During the seventeenth and eighteenth centuries, some of the Indian merchants regularly made their way up the Volga River to trade in Moscow and the Russian interior, while others devised plans (which they never realized) to extend their activities to the Baltic Sea and take their business to western Europe. In the eighteenth century, Russian forces extended their presence in the Caspian Sea region by absorbing much of the Caucasus, a vibrant multiethnic region embracing the modern-day states of Georgia, Armenia, and Azerbaijan.

Siberia

Far more extensive were Russian acquisitions in northeastern Eurasia. The frozen tundras and dense forests of Siberia posed formidable challenges, but explorers and merchants made their way into the region in a quest for fur. Throughout the early modern era, fur was a lucrative commodity that lured Russians eastward, just as North American fur attracted the interest of English, French, and Dutch merchants. Russian expansion in northeastern Eurasia began in 1581 when the wealthy Stroganov family hired a freebooting adventurer named Yermak to capture the khanate of Sibir in the Ural Mountains. In the following decades, Russian explorers pushed into the interior regions of Siberia by way of the region's great rivers. By 1639 they had made their way across the Eurasian landmass and reached the Pacific Ocean.

Native Peoples of Siberia

Siberia was home to about twenty-six major ethnic groups that lived by hunting, trapping, fishing, or herding reindeer. These indigenous peoples varied widely in language and religion, and they responded in different ways to the arrival of Russian adventurers who sought to exact tribute from them by coercing them to supply pelts on a regular basis. Some groups readily accepted iron tools, woven cloth, flour, tea, and liquor for the skins of fur-bearing animals such as otter, lynx, marten, arctic fox, and especially the sleek sable. Others resented the ever-increasing demands for tribute and resisted Russian encroachment on their lands. Russian forces then resorted to punishing raids and hostage taking to induce Siberian peoples to deliver furs. The Yakut people of the Lena and Aldan River valleys in central Siberia mounted a revolt against Russian oppression in 1642 and experienced a brutal retribution that continued for forty years, forcing many Yakut out of their settlements and reducing their population by an estimated 70 percent. Quite apart from military violence, the peoples of Siberia also reeled from epidemic diseases that reduced many populations by more than half.

As violence and disease sharply diminished the delivery of furs, the Russian government recognized that its interests lay in protection of the "small peoples," as state officials called the indigenous inhabitants of Siberia. Government-sponsored missionaries sought to convert Siberian peoples to Orthodox Christianity and bring them into Russian society, but they had little success. Few Siberians expressed an interest in Christianity, and those few came mostly from the ranks of criminals, abandoned hostages, slaves, and others who had little status in their own societies. Furthermore, once indigenous peoples converted to Christianity, they were exempt from obligations to provide fur tributes, so the Russian government demonstrated less zeal in its religious mission than did the Spanish monarchs, who made the spread of Roman Catholic Christianity a prime goal of imperial expansion. Although they managed to attract a few Siberian converts, Orthodox missionaries mostly served the needs of Russian merchants, adventurers, and explorers in Siberia. For their part, the indigenous peoples of Siberia continued to practice their inherited religions guided by native shamans.

For an interactive version of this map, go to www.mhhe.com/bentley3ch23maps.

MAP [23.5]
Russian expansion, 1462–1795.

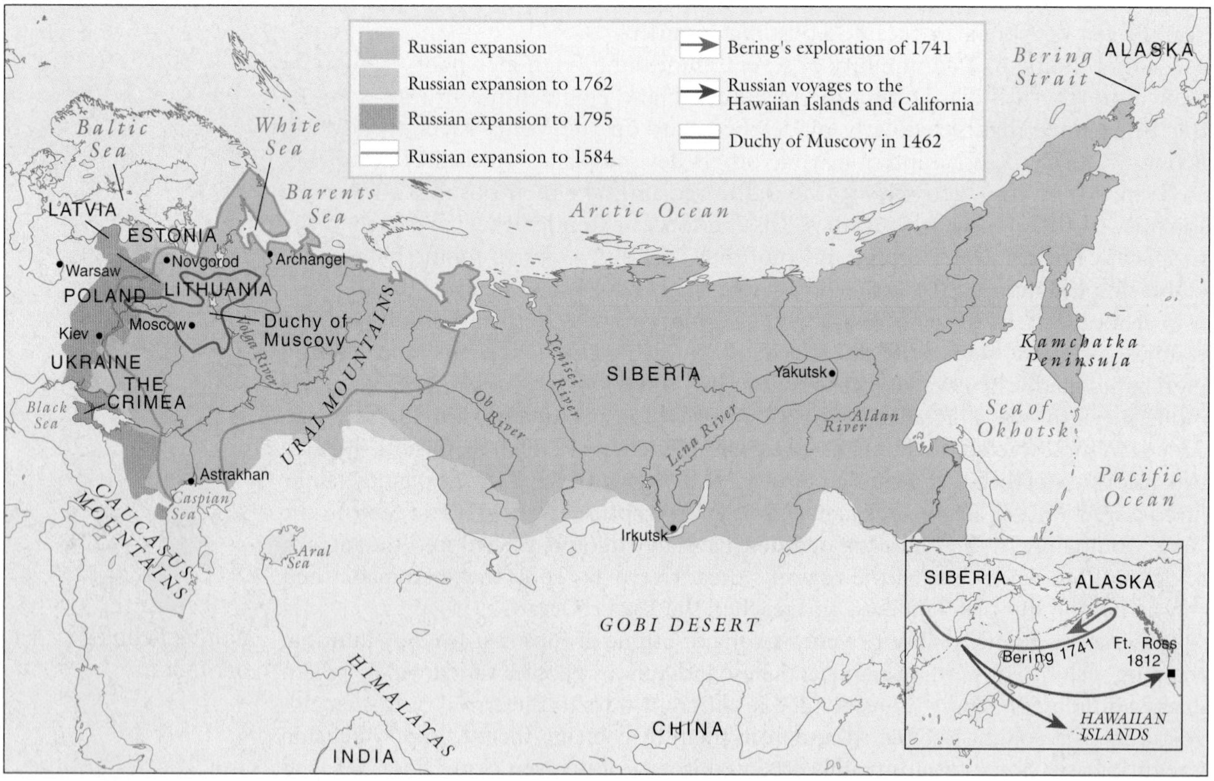

A woodcut illustration depicts indigenous peoples of Siberia delivering fur tribute to Russian merchants in a walled, riverside fort.

The Russian Occupation of Siberia

The settlers who established a Russian presence in Siberia included social misfits, convicted criminals, and even prisoners of war. Despite the region's harsh terrain, Russian migrants gradually filtered into Siberia and thoroughly altered its demographic complexion. Small agricultural settlements grew up near many trading posts, particularly in the fertile Amur River valley. Siberian landowners offered working conditions that were much lighter than those of Russia proper, so disgruntled peasants sometimes fled to settlements east of the Ural Mountains. Over time, Siberian trading posts with their garrisons developed into Russian towns with Russian-speaking populations attending Russian Orthodox churches. By 1763 some 420,000 Russians lived in Siberia, nearly double the number of indigenous inhabitants. In the nineteenth century, large numbers of additional migrants moved east to mine Siberian gold, silver, copper, and iron, and the Russian state was well on the way toward consolidating its control over the region.

Commercial Rivalries and the Seven Years' War

Exploration and imperial expansion led to conflicts not only between Europeans and Asians but also among Europeans themselves. Mariners competed vigorously for trade in Asia and the Americas, and their efforts to establish markets—and sometimes monopolies as well—led frequently to clashes with their counterparts from different lands.

Competition and Conflict

Indeed, throughout the seventeenth and early eighteenth centuries, commercial and political rivalries led to running wars between ships flying different flags. Dutch vessels were most numerous in the Indian Ocean, and they enabled the VOC to dominate the spice trade. Dutch forces expelled most Portuguese merchants from southeast Asia and prevented English mariners from establishing secure footholds there. By the early eighteenth century, trade in Indian cotton and tea from Ceylon had begun to overshadow the spice trade, and English and French merchants working from trading posts in India became the dominant carriers in the Indian Ocean. Fierce competition again generated violence: in 1746 French forces seized the English trading post at Madras, one of the three principal centers of British operations in India.

Commercial competition led to conflict also in the Caribbean and the Americas. English pirates and privateers preyed on Spanish shipping from Mexico, often seizing vessels carrying cargoes of silver. English and French forces constantly skirmished and fought over sugar islands in the Caribbean while also contesting territorial claims in North America. Almost all conflicts between European states in the eighteenth century spilled over into the Caribbean and the Americas.

The Seven Years' War

Commercial rivalries combined with political differences and came to a head in the Seven Years' War (1756–1763). The Seven Years' War was a global conflict in that it took place in several distinct geographic theaters—Europe, India, the Caribbean, and North America—and involved Asian and indigenous American peoples as well as Europeans. Sometimes called "the great war for empire," the Seven Years' War had deep implications for global affairs, since it laid the foundation for 150 years of British imperial hegemony in the world.

In Europe the war pitted Britain and Prussia against France, Austria, and Russia. In India, British and French forces each allied with local rulers and engaged in a contest for hegemony in the Indian Ocean. In the Caribbean, Spanish forces joined with the French in an effort to limit British expansion in the western hemisphere. In North America—where the Seven Years' War merged with a conflict already under way known as the French and Indian War (1754–1763)—British and French armies made separate alliances with indigenous peoples in an effort to outmaneuver each other.

British Hegemony

British forces fought little in Europe, where their Prussian allies held off massive armies seeking to surround and crush the expansive Prussian state. Elsewhere, however, British armies and navies handily overcame their enemies. They ousted French merchants from India and took control of French colonies in Canada, although they allowed French authorities to retain most of their Caribbean possessions. They allowed Spanish forces to retain Cuba but took Florida from the Spanish empire. By no means did these victories make Britain master of the world, or even of Europe: both in Europe and in the larger world powerful states challenged British ambitions. Yet victory in the Seven Years' War placed Britain in a position to dominate world trade for the foreseeable future, and "the great war for empire" paved the way for the establishment of the British empire in the nineteenth century.

Global Exchanges

European explorers and those who followed them established links between all lands and peoples of the world. Interaction between peoples in turn resulted in an unprecedented volume of exchange across the boundary lines of societies and cultural regions. Some of that exchange involved biological species: plants, food crops, animals, human populations, and disease pathogens all spread to regions they had not previously visited. These biological exchanges had differing and dramatic effects on human populations, destroying some of them through epidemic diseases while enlarging others through increased food supplies and richer diets. Commercial exchange also flourished in the wake of the voyages of exploration as European merchants traveled to ports throughout the world in search of trade. By the late sixteenth century, they had built fortified trading posts at strategic sites in the Indian, Atlantic, and Pacific Ocean basins. By the mid-eighteenth century they had established globe-girdling networks of trade and communication.

The Columbian Exchange

Processes of biological exchange were prominent features of world history well before modern times. The early expansion of Islam had facilitated the diffusion of plants and food crops throughout much of the eastern hemisphere during the period from about 700 to 1100 C.E., and transplanted species helped spark demographic and economic growth in all the lands where they took root. During the fourteenth century the spread of bubonic plague caused drastic demographic losses when epidemic disease struck Eurasian and north African lands.

Biological Exchanges

Yet the "Columbian exchange"—the global diffusion of plants, food crops, animals, human populations, and disease pathogens that took place after voyages of exploration by Christopher Columbus and other European mariners—had consequences much more profound than did earlier rounds of biological exchange. Unlike the earlier processes, the Columbian exchange involved lands with radically different flora, fauna, and diseases. For thousands of years the various species of the eastern hemisphere, the western hemisphere, and Oceania had evolved along separate lines. By creating links between these biological zones, the European voyages of exploration set off a round of biological exchange that permanently altered the world's human geography and natural environment.

Beginning in the early sixteenth century, infectious and contagious diseases brought sharp demographic losses to indigenous peoples of the Americas and the Pacific islands. The worst scourge was smallpox, but measles, diphtheria, whooping cough, and influenza also took heavy tolls. Before the voyages of exploration, none of these maladies had reached the western hemisphere or Oceania, and the peoples of those regions consequently had no inherited or acquired immunities to those pathogens. In the eastern hemisphere, these diseases had mostly become endemic: they claimed a certain number of victims from the ranks of infants and small children, but survivors gained immunity to the diseases through exposure at an early age. In some areas of Europe, for example, smallpox was responsible for 10 to 15 percent of deaths, but most victims were age ten or younger. Although its effects were tragic for individual families and communities, smallpox did not pose a threat to European society as a whole because it did not carry away adults, who were mostly responsible for economic production and social organization.

Epidemic Diseases and Population Decline

When infectious and contagious diseases traveled to previously unexposed populations, however, they touched off ferocious epidemics that sometimes destroyed entire societies. Beginning in 1519, epidemic smallpox ravaged the Aztec empire, often in combination with other diseases, and within a century the indigenous population of Mexico had declined by as much as 90 percent, from about 17 million to 1.3 million. By that time Spanish conquerors had imposed their rule on Mexico, and the political, social, and cultural traditions of the indigenous peoples had either disappeared or fallen under Spanish domination.

Imported diseases took their worst tolls in densely populated areas like the Aztec and Inca empires, but they did not spare other regions. Smallpox and other diseases were

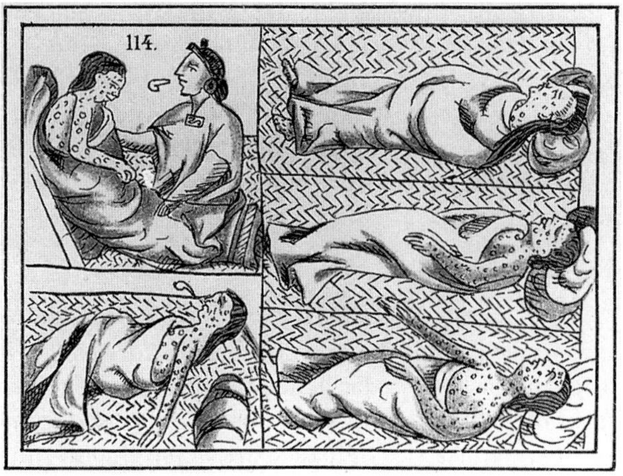

Smallpox victims in the Aztec empire. The disease killed most of those it infected and left disfiguring scars on survivors.

so easily transmissible that they raced to remote areas of North and South America and sparked epidemics even before the first European explorers arrived in those regions. By the 1530s smallpox may have spread as far from Mexico as the Great Lakes in the north and the pampas of Argentina in the south.

When introduced to the Pacific islands, infectious and contagious diseases struck vulnerable populations with the same horrifying effects as in the Americas, albeit on a smaller scale. All told, disease epidemics sparked by the Columbian exchange probably caused the worst demographic calamity in all of world history. Between 1500 and 1800, upwards of one hundred million people may have died of diseases imported into the Americas and Pacific islands.

Food Crops and Animals

Over a longer term, however, the Columbian exchange increased rather than diminished human population because of the global spread of food crops and animals that it sponsored. Wheat, vines, horses, cattle, pigs, sheep, goats, and chickens went from Europe to the Americas where they sharply increased supplies of food and animal energy. Wheat grew well on the plains of North America and on the pampas of Argentina—regions either too dry or too cold for the cultivation of maize—and cattle transformed American grasses into meat and milk that humans could digest.

American Crops

Food crops native to the Americas also played prominent roles in the Columbian exchange. American crops that took root in Africa, Asia, and Europe include maize, potatoes, beans, tomatoes, peppers, peanuts, manioc, papayas, guavas, avocados, pineapples, and cacao, to name only the most important. (A less nutritious transplant was tobacco.) Residents of the eastern hemisphere only gradually developed a taste for American crops, but by the eighteenth century maize and potatoes had contributed to a sharply increased number of calories in Eurasian diets. American bean varieties added protein, and tomatoes and peppers provided vitamins and zesty flavors in lands from western Europe to China. Peanuts and manioc flourished in tropical southeast Asian and west African soils that otherwise would not produce large yields or support large populations.

Population Growth

The Columbian exchange of plants and animals fueled a surge in world population. In 1500, as Eurasian peoples were recovering from epidemic bubonic plague, world population stood at about 425 million. By 1600 it had increased more than 25 percent to 545 million. Human numbers increased less rapidly during the next century, reaching 610 million in 1700. But thereafter they increased at a faster rate than ever before in world history. By 1750 human population stood at 720 million, and by 1800 it had surged to 900 million, having grown by almost 50 percent during the previous century. Much of the rise was due to the increased nutritional value of diets enriched by the global exchange of food crops and animals.

Migration

Alongside disease pathogens and plant and animal species, the Columbian exchange also involved the spread of human populations through transoceanic migra-

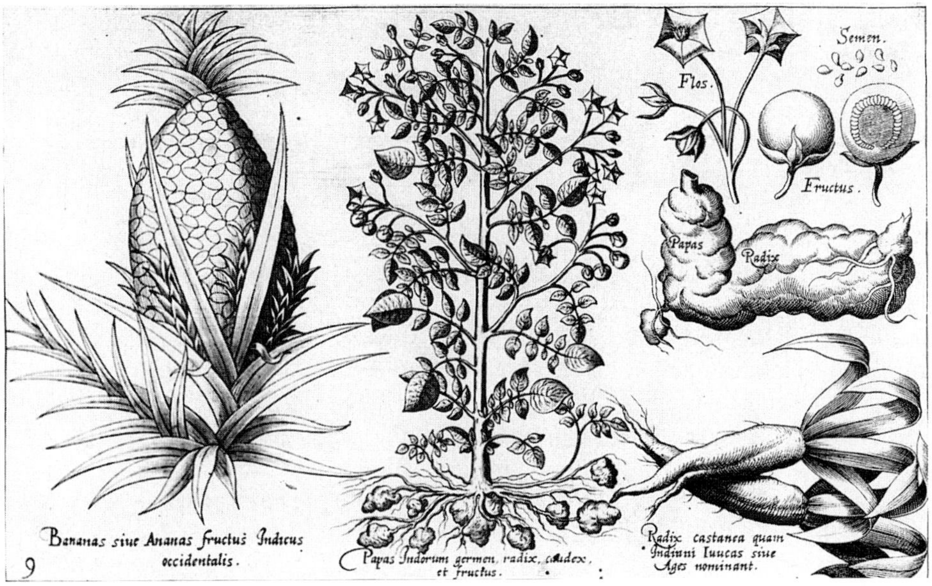

Illustrations in an early-seventeenth-century book depict pineapple, potatoes, and cassava—all plants native to the Americas and unknown to Europeans before the sixteenth century.

tion, whether voluntary or forced. During the period from 1500 to 1800, the largest contingent of migrants consisted of enslaved Africans transported involuntarily to South American, North American, and Caribbean destinations. A smaller but still sizable migration involved Europeans who traveled to the Americas and settled in lands depopulated by infectious and contagious diseases. During the nineteenth century, European peoples traveled in massive numbers mostly to the western hemisphere but also to south Africa, Australia, and Pacific islands where diseases had diminished indigenous populations, and Asian peoples migrated to tropical and subtropical destinations throughout much of the world. In combination, these migrations have profoundly influenced modern world history.

The Origins of Global Trade

The trading-post empires established by Portuguese, Dutch, and English merchants linked Asian markets with European consumers and offered opportunities for European mariners to participate in the carrying trade within Asia. European vessels transported Persian carpets to India, Indian cottons to southeast Asia, southeast Asian spices to India and China, Chinese silks to Japan, and Japanese silver and copper to China and India. By the late sixteenth century, European merchants were as prominent as Arabs in the trading world of the Indian Ocean basin.

Transoceanic Trade

Besides stimulating commerce in the eastern hemisphere, the voyages of European merchant mariners also encouraged the emergence of a genuinely global trading system. As Europeans established colonies in the Caribbean and the Americas, for example, trade networks extended to all corners of the Atlantic Ocean basin. European manufactured goods traveled west across the Atlantic in exchange for silver from Mexican and Peruvian mines and agricultural products such as sugar and tobacco, both of which were in high demand among European consumers. Trade in human beings also figured in Atlantic commerce. European textiles, guns, and other manufactured goods

Contexts & Connections

Vaccination and the Eradication of Smallpox

The introduction of new diseases into the Americas and Oceania caused massive population losses among indigenous peoples and paved the way for European conquest and colonization. Among the ills introduced by Europeans was smallpox, an ancient, highly contagious, and often fatal viral disease. Indeed, smallpox killed more people than any other malady in world history, but vaccination limited its ferocity already in premodern times, and modern medicine eventually eradicated smallpox altogether.

The only cure for smallpox is prevention: once contracted, there is no remedy for this disease. During the course of countless epidemics over several thousand years, observers noticed that those who survived a bout with smallpox did not contract the disease again. This realization prompted premodern physicians to experiment with variolation, the intentional exposure of individuals to a mild form of smallpox so that they would be able to resist the full-blown virus more effectively. The first recorded cases of variolation date to about 600 B.C.E. when Chinese practitioners inoculated individuals either by blowing dried smallpox scabs up a patient's nose or by scratching the patient's arm with a needle dipped in pus from a smallpox lesion. Variolation spread widely to southwest Asia, Europe, and eventually North America, where by the eighteenth century it had won acceptance as a folk practice. While providing years of effective immunity for individuals who survived this early form of inoculation, the technique occasionally infected patients with a fatal dose of smallpox, and variolated individuals were still capable of transmitting virulent smallpox to others.

The experiments of the English physician Edward Jenner dealt a more effective blow against smallpox. Knowing that milkmaids often contracted cowpox, a mild infection that left them immune to smallpox, in 1797 Jenner inoculated eight-year-old James Phipps with cowpox and followed it six weeks later with the smallpox virus. Phipps became ill but soon recovered fully, leading Jenner to deduce that cowpox conferred immunity against smallpox. Later called vaccination (from *vacca,* the Latin word for "cow"), Jenner's procedure not only created a powerful weapon in the war against smallpox but also laid the foundation for scientific immunology. Over time, physicians developed vaccines that prevented sickness and death from polio, tetanus, typhoid, whooping cough, and many other diseases that once plagued humankind.

Yet many people viewed vaccination as an unnatural practice and resisted its introduction to their societies. As late as the twentieth century, smallpox claimed an estimated three hundred million lives. In 1967, however, the World Health Organization (WHO) launched a program to eradicate smallpox through a worldwide campaign of mass vaccination. Within a few years WHO efforts had achieved remarkable success. In 1977 a young man in Somalia had the distinction of being the world's last recorded victim of naturally occurring smallpox, and two years later the WHO certified the eradication of the disease. Today the only officially declared stocks of live smallpox virus survive in two laboratories where medical scientists continue research as needed on this ancient scourge.

went south to west Africa, where merchants exchanged them for African slaves, who then went to the tropical and subtropical regions of the western hemisphere to work on plantations.

The Manila Galleons

The experience of the Manila galleons illustrates the early workings of the global economy in the Pacific Ocean basin. For 250 years, from 1565 to 1815, Spanish galleons—sleek, fast, heavily armed ships capable of carrying large cargoes—regularly plied the waters of the Pacific Ocean between Manila in the Philippines and Acapulco on the west coast of Mexico. From Manila they took Asian luxury goods to Mexico and exchanged them for silver. Most of the precious metal made its way to

Five Spanish galleons stand in the waters off the port of Acapulco on the Pacific coast of Mexico in this sixteenth-century engraving. Smaller craft ferry crewmen ashore, while dockworkers prepare to load cargo on the vessels.

China, where a thriving domestic economy demanded increasing quantities of silver, the basis of Chinese currency. In fact, the demand for silver was so high in China that European merchants exchanged it for Chinese gold, which they later traded profitably for more silver as well as luxury goods in Japan. Meanwhile, some of the Asian luxury goods from Manila remained in Mexico or went to Peru, where they contributed to a comfortable way of life for Spanish ruling elites. Most, however, went overland across Mexico and then traveled by ship across the Atlantic to Spain and European markets.

Environmental Effects of Global Trade

As silver lubricated growing volumes of global trade, pressures fell on several animal species that had the misfortune to become prominent commodities on the world market. Fur-bearing animals came under particularly intense pressure, as hunters sought their pelts for sale to consumers in China, Europe, and North America. During the seventeenth century, an estimated two hundred to three hundred thousand sable pelts flowed annually from Siberia to the global market, and during the eighteenth century, more than sixteen million North American beaver pelts fed consumers' demands for fur hats and cloaks. Wanton hunting of fur-bearing animals soon drove many species into extinction or near-extinction, permanently altering the environments they had formerly inhabited. Quite apart from fur-bearing animals, early modern hunters harvested enormous numbers of deer, codfish, whales, walruses, seals, and other species as merchants sought to supply skins, food, oil, ivory, and other animal products for global consumers.

By the late sixteenth century, conditions favored the relentless human exploitation of the world's natural and agricultural resources, as European mariners had permanently linked the world's port cities and created global trading networks. During the next two centuries, the volume of global trade burgeoned, as English, Dutch, French, and other merchants contributed to the development of global markets. During the seventeenth century, for example, Dutch merchants imported, among other commodities, wheat from south Africa, cowry shells from India, and sugar from Brazil. The wheat fed domestic consumers, who increasingly worked as merchants, bankers, or manufacturers rather than as cultivators. English, Dutch, and other merchants eagerly purchased the cowry shells—which served as currency in much of sub-Saharan Africa—and exchanged them for slaves destined for plantations in the western hemisphere. The sugar went on the market at Amsterdam and found its way to consumers throughout Europe. During the eighteenth century, world trade became even more intricate as mass markets emerged for commodities such as coffee, tea, sugar, and tobacco. By 1750 all parts of the world except Australia participated in global networks of commercial relations in which European merchant mariners played prominent roles.

Global commercial and biological exchanges arose from the efforts of European mariners to explore the world's waters and establish sea lanes that would support long-distance trade. Their search for sea routes to Asia led them to the western hemisphere and the vast expanse of the Pacific Ocean. The geographic knowledge that they accumulated enabled them to link the world's regions into a finely articulated network of trade. But commercial exchange was not the only result of this global network. Food crops, animal stocks, disease pathogens, and human migrants also traveled the sea lanes and dramatically influenced societies throughout the world. Transplanted crops and animal species led to improved nutrition and increasing populations throughout the eastern hemisphere. Epidemics sparked by unfamiliar disease pathogens ravaged indigenous populations in the Americas and the Pacific islands. Massive migrations of human communities transformed the social and cultural landscape of the Americas and encouraged increased mingling of the world's peoples. The European voyages of exploration, transoceanic trade networks, and the Columbian exchange pushed the world's regions toward interdependence and global integration.

CHRONOLOGY

1394–1460	Life of Prince Henry the Navigator of Portugal
1488	Bartolomeu Dias's voyage around the Cape of Good Hope into the Indian Ocean
1492	Christopher Columbus's first voyage to the western hemisphere
1497–1499	Vasco da Gama's first voyage to India
1519–1522	Ferdinand Magellan's circumnavigation of the world
1565–1575	Spanish conquest of the Philippines
1756–1763	Seven Years' War
1768–1780	Captain James Cook's voyages in the Pacific Ocean

FOR FURTHER READING

K. N. Chaudhuri. *Trade and Civilisation in the Indian Ocean: An Economic History from the Rise of Islam to 1750.* Cambridge, 1985. A brilliant analysis that places the European presence in the Indian Ocean in its larger historical context.

———. *The Trading World of Asia and the English East India Company, 1660–1760.* Cambridge, 1978. The best study of the English East India Company and its role in world trade.

Carlo Cipolla. *Guns, Sails, and Empires: Technological Innovation and the Early Phases of European Expansion, 1400–1700.* New York, 1965. A well-written study of the naval and military technology available to European mariners.

Christopher Columbus. *The* Diario *of Christopher Columbus's First Voyage to America.* Trans. by Oliver Dunn and James E. Kelley Jr. Norman, Okla., 1989. A careful translation.

Alfred W. Crosby. *The Columbian Exchange: Biological and Cultural Consequences of 1492.* Westport, Conn., 1972. Focuses on early exchanges of plants, animals, and diseases between Europe and America.

———. *Ecological Imperialism: The Biological Expansion of Europe, 900–1900.* Cambridge, 1986. An important study that examines the establishment of European biological species in the larger world.

Philip D. Curtin. *Cross-Cultural Trade in World History.* New York, 1984. Focuses on the roles of cross-cultural brokers in facilitating trade between different societies.

Stephen Frederic Dale. *Indian Merchants and Eurasian Trade, 1600–1750.* Cambridge, 1994. Scholarly analysis of Indian merchant communities trading in Russia, Persia, and central Asia in early modern times.

Andre Gunder Frank. *ReORIENT: Global Economy in the Asian Age.* Berkeley, 1998. Important and challenging analysis of global economic integration in the early modern world.

Jonathan L. Israel. *Dutch Primacy in World Trade, 1585–1740.* Oxford, 1989. A thorough examination of the Dutch seaborne empire at its height.

Michael Khodarkovsky. *Where Two Worlds Meet: The Russian State and the Kalmyk Nomads, 1600–1771.* Ithaca, 1992. One of the first major studies to look at Russian imperial expansion in Siberia through the eyes of colonized peoples.

William H. McNeill. *Plagues and Peoples.* Garden City, N.Y., 1976. Examines the effects of infectious and contagious diseases in world history.

Anthony Pagden. *European Encounters with the New World: From Renaissance to Romanticism.* New Haven, 1993. Scholarly examination of early European responses to the peoples, societies, and environments they encountered in the Americas.

John H. Parry. *The Age of Reconnaissance.* Berkeley, 1982. Reliable and readable survey of European expansion.

M. N. Pearson. *The Portuguese in India.* Cambridge, 1987. A brief, lively, and up-to-date discussion of the early Portuguese empire in India.

William D. Phillips Jr. and Carla Rahn Phillips. *The Worlds of Christopher Columbus.* Cambridge, 1992. The best general study of Christopher Columbus.

Antonio Pigafetta. *Magellan's Voyage: A Narrative Account of the First Circumnavigation.* 2 vols. Trans. by R. A. Skelton. New Haven, 1969. Valuable account by a crewman on Magellan's circumnavigation of the world.

Kenneth Pomeranz. *The Great Divergence: China, Europe, and the Making of the Modern World Economy.* Princeton, 2000. Pathbreaking scholarly study that illuminates the economic history of the early modern world through comparison of economic development in Asian and European lands.

John F. Richards. *The Unending Frontier: An Environmental History of the Early Modern World.* Berkeley, 2003. Thoroughly explores the environmental effects of the global historical processes that shaped the early modern world.

Stuart B. Schwartz, ed. *Implicit Understandings: Observing, Reporting, and Reflecting on the Encounters between Europeans and Other Peoples in the Early Modern Era.* Cambridge, 1994. Fascinating collection of essays by specialists on cross-cultural perceptions in early modern times.

Yuri Slezkine. *Arctic Mirrors: Russia and the Small Peoples of the North.* Ithaca, N.Y., 1994. Thoughtful analysis of Russian relations with the hunting, fishing, and herding peoples of Siberia.

Sanjay Subrahmanyam. *The Career and Legend of Vasco da Gama.* Cambridge, 1997. The best critical study of the famous Portuguese mariner.

———. *The Portuguese Empire in Asia, 1500–1700: A Political and Economic History.* London, 1993. A sophisticated analysis of the Portuguese trading-post empire.

James D. Tracy, ed. *The Political Economy of Merchant Empires: State Power and World Trade, 1350–1750.* Cambridge, 1991. Essays on the interconnections between political, military, and commercial relationships in early modern times.

———. *The Rise of Merchant Empires: Long-Distance Trade in the Early Modern World, 1350–1750.* Cambridge, 1990. Essays by specialists on global trade in early modern times.

Immanuel Wallerstein. *The Modern World-System.* 3 vols. to date. New York, 1974–. A controversial but influential interpretation of global political and economic development in modern times.

Merry E. Wiesner-Hanks. *Christianity and Sexuality in the Early Modern World: Regulating Desire, Reforming Practice.* London, 2000. Pioneering comparative study of Christian sexuality in global context.

OLC

See our **Online Learning Center at www.mhhe.com/bentley3** for additional readings, practice maps, quizzes, and internet activities.

PSI

Unfamiliar words? Check out the **Primary Source Investigator CD-ROM** for an interactive glossary, interactive maps, more images, and primary sources.

Martin Luther at age forty-two, depicted as a conscientious and determined man by the German painter Lucas Cranach in 1525.

CHAPTER 24

The Transformation of Europe

In 1517 an obscure German monk posed a challenge to the Roman Catholic church. Martin Luther of Wittenberg denounced the church's sale of indulgences, a type of pardon that excused individuals from doing penance for their sins and thus facilitated their entry into heaven. Indulgences had been available since the eleventh century, but in order to raise funds for the reconstruction of St. Peter's basilica in Rome, church authorities began to market indulgences aggressively in the early sixteenth century. From their point of view, indulgences were splendid devices: they encouraged individuals to reflect piously on their behavior while also bringing large sums of money into the church's treasury.

To Martin Luther, however, indulgences were signs of greed, hypocrisy, and moral rot in the Roman Catholic church. Luther despised the pretentiousness of church authorities who arrogated to themselves powers that belonged properly to God alone: no human being had the power to absolve individuals of their sins and grant them admission to heaven, Luther believed, so the sale of indulgences constituted a massive fraud perpetrated on an unsuspecting public. In October 1517, following academic custom of the day, he offered to debate publicly with anyone who wished to dispute his views, and he denounced the sale of indulgences in a document called the *Ninety-Five Theses.*

Luther did not nail his work to the church door in Wittenberg, although a popular legend credited him with this heroic gesture, but news of the *Ninety-Five Theses* spread instantly: within a few weeks, printed copies were available throughout Europe. Luther's challenge galvanized opinion among many who resented the power of the Roman church. It also drew severe criticism from religious and political authorities seeking to maintain the established order. Church officials subjected Luther's views to examination and judged them erroneous, and in 1520 Pope Leo X excommunicated the unrepentant monk. In 1521 the Holy Roman emperor Charles V, a devout Roman Catholic, summoned Luther to an assembly of imperial authorities and demanded that he recant his views. Luther's response: "I cannot and will not recant anything, for it is neither safe nor right to act against one's conscience. Here I stand. I can do no other. God help me. Amen."

Martin Luther's challenge held enormous religious and political implications. Though expelled from the church, Luther still considered himself Christian—indeed, he considered his own faith true Christianity—and he held religious services for a community of devoted followers. Wittenberg became a center of religious dissent, which by the late 1520s had spread through much of Germany and Switzerland. During the 1530s dissidents known as Protestants—because of their protest against the established order—organized movements also in France, England, the Low Countries, and even Italy and Spain. By midcentury Luther's act of individual rebellion had mushroomed into the Protestant Reformation, which shattered the religious unity of western Christendom.

For all of its unsettling effects, the Protestant Reformation was only one of several powerful movements that transformed European society during the early modern era. Another was the consolidation of strong centralized states, which took shape partly because of the Reformation. Between the sixteenth and eighteenth centuries, monarchs in western Europe took advantage of religious quarrels to tighten control over their societies. By curbing the power of the nobility, expanding royal authority, and increasing control over their subjects, they built states much more powerful than the regional monarchies of the middle ages. By the mid-eighteenth century, some rulers had concentrated so much power in their own hands that historians refer to them as absolute monarchs.

Alongside religious conflict and the building of powerful states, capitalism and early modern science also profoundly influenced western European society in early modern times. Early capitalism pushed European merchants and manufacturers into unrelenting competition with one another and encouraged them to reorganize their businesses in search of maximum efficiency. Early modern science challenged traditional ways of understanding the world and the universe. Under the influence of scientific discoveries, European intellectuals sought an entirely rational understanding of human society as well as the natural world, and some sought to base European moral, ethical, and social thought on science and reason rather than Christianity.

Thus between 1500 and 1800, western Europe underwent a thorough transformation. Although the combination of religious, political, social, economic, intellectual, and cultural change was unsettling and often disruptive, it also strengthened European society. The states of early modern Europe competed vigorously and mobilized their human and natural resources in effective fashion. By 1800 several of them had become especially powerful, wealthy, and dynamic. They stood poised to play major roles in world affairs during the nineteenth and twentieth centuries.

The Fragmentation of Western Christendom

In the third century C.E., Christian missionaries began to spread their faith from the Mediterranean basin throughout Europe, and by 1000 C.E. Christianity had established a foothold as far north as Scandinavia and Iceland. Although the peoples of western Europe spoke different languages, ate different foods, and observed different customs, the church of Rome provided them with a common religious and cultural heritage. During the sixteenth and seventeenth centuries, however, revolts against the Roman Catholic church shattered the religious unity of western Europe. Followers of Martin Luther and other Protestant reformers established a series of churches independent of Rome, and Roman Catholic leaders strengthened their own church against the challengers. Throughout early modern times, religious controversies fueled social tensions.

The Protestant Reformation

Martin Luther

Martin Luther (1483–1546) attacked the sale of indulgences as an individual, but he soon attracted enthusiastic support from others who resented the policies of the Roman church. Luther was a prolific and talented writer, and he published scores of works condemning the Roman church. His cause benefited enormously from the printing press, which had first appeared in Europe in the mid-fifteenth century. A sizable literate public inhabited European cities and towns, and readers eagerly consumed printed works on religious as well as secular themes. Printed editions of Luther's writings appeared throughout Europe and sparked spirited debates on indulgences and theological issues. His supporters and critics took their own works to the printers, and religious controversies kept the presses busy churning out pamphlets and treatises for a century and more.

Luther soon moved beyond the issue of indulgences: he attacked the Roman church for a wide range of abuses and called for thorough reform of Christendom. He advocated the closure of monasteries, translation of the Bible from Latin into vernacular languages, and an end to priestly authority, including the authority of the pope himself. When opponents pointed out that his reform program ran counter to church policy, he rejected the authority of the church hierarchy and proclaimed that the Bible was the only source of Christian religious authority.

Luther's works drew an enthusiastic popular response, and in Germany they fueled a movement to reform the church along the lines of Luther's teachings. Lay Christians flocked to hear Luther preach in Wittenberg, and several princes of the Holy Roman Empire warmed to Luther's views—partly because of personal conviction but partly also because religious controversy offered opportunities for them to build their own power bases. During the 1520s and 1530s many of the most important German cities—Strasbourg, Nuremberg, and Augsburg, among others—passed laws prohibiting Roman Catholic observances and requiring all religious services to follow Protestant doctrine and procedures.

Reform outside Germany

By the mid-sixteenth century about half the German population had adopted Lutheran Christianity, and reformers had launched Protestant movements and established alternative churches in other lands as well. By the late 1520s the prosperous cities of Switzerland—Zurich, Basel, and Geneva—had fledgling Protestant churches. The heavily urbanized Low Countries also responded enthusiastically to Protestant appeals. Protestants appeared even in Italy and Spain, although authorities in those lands handily suppressed their challenge to the Roman church.

In England a Reformation took place for frankly political as well as religious reasons. Lutherans and other Protestants worked to build a following in England from the 1520s, but they faced stout government resistance until King Henry VIII (reigned 1509–1547) came into conflict with the pope. Henry wanted to divorce his wife, who had not borne a male heir, but the pope refused to allow him to do so. Henry's response was to sever relations with the Roman church and make himself Supreme Head of the Anglican church—an English pope, as it were. While Henry reigned, the theology of the English church changed little, but under pressure of reformers, his successors replaced Roman Catholic with Protestant doctrines and rituals. By 1560 England had permanently left the Roman Catholic community.

John Calvin

Meanwhile, an even more influential Reformation was taking shape in France and the French-speaking parts of Switzerland. The initiator was a French lawyer, John Calvin (1509–1564), who in the 1530s converted to Protestant Christianity. Because the French monarchy sought to suppress Protestants, Calvin slipped across the border to French-speaking Geneva in Switzerland. There he organized a Protestant community and worked with local officials to impose a strict code of morality and discipline on the city. Calvin also composed an influential treatise, *Institutes of the Christian Religion* (first published in 1536 and frequently reprinted with revisions) that codified Protestant teachings and presented them as a coherent and organized package.

Calvin's Geneva was not only a model Protestant community but also a missionary center. Calvinist missionaries were most active in France, where they attracted strong interest in the cities, but they ventured also to Germany, the Low Countries, England,

Under inspiration of the Catholic Reformation, many devout individuals sought mystic union with God. One of the most famous of the mystics was St. Teresa of Avila (in Spain), who founded a strict order of nuns and often experienced religious visions. A famous sculpture by the Italian artist Gianlorenzo Bernini depicts St. Teresa in an ecstatic trance accompanied by an angel.

Scotland, and even distant Hungary. They established churches in all these lands and worked for reform along Protestant lines. They were most successful in the Netherlands and Scotland. By the late sixteenth century, Lutherans, Anglicans, and Calvinists together had built communities large enough that a return to religious unity in western Christendom was inconceivable.

The Catholic Reformation

In response to the Protestant Reformation, Roman Catholic authorities undertook a massive reform effort within their own church. To some extent their efforts represented a reaction to Protestant success. Yet Roman Catholic authorities also sought to define points of doctrine so as to clarify differences between Roman and Protestant churches, to persuade Protestants to return to the Roman church, and to deepen the sense of spirituality and religious commitment in their own community. Taken together, their efforts constituted the Catholic Reformation.

The Council of Trent

Two institutions were especially important for defining the Catholic Reformation and advancing its goals—the Council of Trent and the Society of Jesus. The Council of Trent was an assembly of bishops, cardinals, and other high church officials who met intermittently between 1545 and 1563 to address matters of doctrine and reform. Drawing heavily on the works of the thirteenth-century scholastic theologian St. Thomas Aquinas, the council defined the elements of Roman Catholic theology in detail. The council acknowledged that abuses had alienated many people from the Roman church, and it took steps to reform the church. The council demanded that church authorities observe strict standards of morality, and it required them to establish schools and seminaries in their districts to prepare priests properly for their roles.

St. Ignatius Loyola

While the Council of Trent dealt with doctrine and reform, the Society of Jesus went on the offensive and sought to extend the boundaries of the reformed Roman church. The society's founder was St. Ignatius Loyola (1491–1556), a Basque nobleman and soldier who in 1521 suffered a devastating leg wound that ended his military career. While recuperating he read spiritual works and popular accounts of saints' lives, and he resolved to put his energy into religious work. In 1540, together with a small band of disciples, he founded the Society of Jesus.

The Society of Jesus

Ignatius required that members of the society, known as Jesuits, complete a rigorous and advanced education. They received instruction not only in theology and philosophy but also in classical languages, literature, history, and science. As a result of this preparation—and their unswerving dedication to the Roman Catholic church—the Jesuits made extraordinarily effective missionaries. They were able to outargue most of their opponents and acquired a reputation for discipline and determination. They often served as counselors to kings and rulers and used their influence to promote policies that benefited the Roman church. They also were the most prominent of the early Christian missionaries outside Europe: in the wake of the European reconnaissance of the world's oceans, Jesuits attracted converts in India, China, Japan, the Philippines, and the Americas, thus making Christianity a genuinely global religion.

Witch-Hunts and Religious Wars

Europeans took religion seriously in the sixteenth century, and religious divisions helped to fuel social and political conflict. Apart from wars, the most destructive violence that afflicted early modern Europe was the hunt for witches, which was especially prominent in regions like the Rhineland where tensions between Protestants and Roman Catholics ran high.

Like many other peoples, Europeans had long believed that certain individuals possessed unusual powers to influence human affairs or discover secret information such as the identity of a thief. During the late fifteenth century, theologians developed a theory that witches derived their powers from the devil. According to this theory, witches made agreements to worship the devil in exchange for supernatural powers, including the ability to fly through the night on brooms, pitchforks, or animals. Theorists believed that the witches regularly flew off to distant places to attend the "witches' sabbath," a gathering that featured devil worship, lewd behavior, and the concoction of secret potions, culminating in sexual relations with the devil himself.

Witch-Hunting

Although the witches' sabbath was sheer fantasy, fears that individuals were making alliances with the devil sparked a massive hunt for witches. Witchcraft became a convenient explanation for any unpleasant turn of events—failure of a crop, outbreak of a fire, an unexpected death, or inability to conceive a child. About 110,000 individuals underwent trial as suspected witches during the sixteenth and seventeenth centuries, and about 60,000 of them died either by hanging or by burning at the stake.

Although men were among the victims, most convicted witches were women. Indeed, women may have accounted for 95 percent or more of the condemned. Many of the women were poor, old, single, or widowed—individuals who lived on the margins of their societies and were easy targets for accusers, since they had few protectors. Witch-hunting was mostly a European affair, but it also spread to European colonies in the Americas. The most intense witch-hunt in the Americas took place in seventeenth-century New England, where a population of about 100,000 colonists tried 234 individuals for witchcraft and executed 36 of them by hanging.

By 1700 the fear of witches had largely diminished. Accusations, trials, and executions occurred only sporadically thereafter. The last legal execution for witchcraft in Europe took place in Switzerland in 1782. For the better part of two centuries, however, the intermittent pursuit of witches revealed clearly the stresses and strains that afflicted European society during early modern times.

Religious Wars

Religious tensions even led to outright war between Protestant and Roman Catholic communities. Religious wars wracked France for thirty-six years (1562–1598), for example, and they also complicated relations between Protestant and Roman Catholic states. In 1588 King Philip II of Spain (reigned 1556–1598) attempted to force England to return to the Roman Catholic church by sending the Spanish Armada—a huge flotilla consisting of 130 ships and 30,000 men—to dethrone the Protestant Queen Elizabeth. The effort collapsed, however, when English forces disrupted the Spanish fleet by sending blazing, unmanned ships into its midst. Then a ferocious gale scattered Spanish vessels throughout the North Sea.

Religious convictions also aggravated relations between the Netherlands and Spain by fueling the revolt of the Dutch provinces from their overlord, the king of Spain. In 1567 Philip sent an army to tighten his control over the provinces and to suppress the Calvinist movement there. Resistance escalated into a full-scale rebellion. By 1610 the seven northern provinces (the modern Netherlands) had won their independence and formed a republic known as the United Provinces, leaving ten southern provinces (modern Belgium) under Spanish and later Austrian rule until the late eighteenth century.

The Thirty Years' War

The religious wars culminated in a massive continental conflict known as the Thirty Years' War (1618–1648). The war opened after the Holy Roman emperor attempted to force his Bohemian subjects to return to the Roman Catholic church, and the main battleground was the emperor's territory in Germany. Other parties soon entered the fray, however, and by the time the war ended Spanish, French, Dutch, German, Swedish, Danish, Polish, Bohemian, and Russian forces had taken part in the conflict.

The motives that prompted these states to enter the war were sometimes political or economic, but religious differences complicated the other issues and made them more difficult to resolve. Regardless of the motives, the Thirty Years' War was the most destructive European conflict before the twentieth century. Quite apart from violence and brutalities committed by undisciplined soldiers, the war damaged economies and societies throughout Europe and led to the deaths of about one-third of the German population. The destructiveness of the Thirty Years' War raised questions about the viability of Europe as a region of strong, independent, well-armed, and intensely competitive states.

The Thirty Years' War offered abundant opportunity for undisciplined mercenary soldiers to prey on civilian populations. Only rarely, as in the mass hanging depicted in this engraving of 1633, did soldiers receive punishment for their criminal acts.

The Consolidation of Sovereign States

Although fundamentally a religious movement, the Reformation had strong political implications, and centralizing monarchs readily made use of religious issues in their efforts to strengthen their states and enhance their authority. Ruling elites had their own religious preferences, and they often promoted a Protestant or Roman Catholic cause out of personal conviction. Religious controversies also offered splendid opportunities for ambitious subordinates who built power bases by appealing to particular religious communities. Over the long run, centralizing monarchs profited most from religious controversy generated by the Reformation. While the Holy Roman Empire fell into disarray because of political and religious quarrels, monarchs in other lands augmented their revenues, enhanced their authority, and created powerful sovereign states. After the devastation of the Thirty Years' War, rulers of these states devised a diplomatic system that sought to maintain order among the many independent and competitive European states.

The Attempted Revival of Empire

After the dissolution of the Carolingian empire in the ninth century C.E., there was no effective imperial government in western Europe. The so-called Holy Roman Empire emerged in the tenth century, but its authority extended only to Germany and northern Italy, and even there the emperors encountered stiff opposition from powerful princes and thriving cities. During the early sixteenth century, it seemed that Emperor Charles V (reigned 1519–1556) might establish the Holy Roman Empire as the preeminent political authority in Europe, but by midcentury it was clear that there would be no revival of empire. Thus, unlike China, India, and Ottoman lands in southwest Asia and north Africa, early modern Europe developed as a region of independent states.

Charles V

After 1438 the Habsburg family, with extensive dynastic holdings in Austria, dominated the Holy Roman Empire. Through marriage alliances with princely and royal families, the Habsburgs accumulated rights and titles to lands throughout Europe and beyond. Charles V inherited authority over the Habsburgs' Austrian domains as well as the duchy of Burgundy (including the wealthy provinces of the Low Countries) and the kingdom of Spain (including its possessions in Italy and the Americas). When he became emperor in 1519, he acquired authority over Germany, Bohemia, Switzerland, and parts of northern Italy. His empire stretched from Vienna in Austria to Cuzco in Peru.

Imperial Fragmentation

In spite of his far-flung holdings, Charles did not extend his authority throughout Europe or even establish a lasting imperial legacy. Throughout his reign Charles had to devote much of his attention and energy to the Lutheran movement and to imperial princes who took advantage of religious controversy to assert their independence. Moreover, Charles did not build an administrative structure for his empire but, instead, ruled each of his lands according to its own laws and customs. He was able to draw on the financial resources of wealthy lands like the Low Countries and Spain to maintain a powerful army. Yet Charles did not have the ambition to extend his authority by military force, but used his army mostly to put down rebellions.

Foreign Challenges

Foreign difficulties also prevented Charles from establishing his empire as the arbiter of Europe. The prospect of a powerful Holy Roman Empire struck fear in the kings of France, and it caused concern among the sultans of the Ottoman empire as well. Charles's holdings surrounded France, and the French kings suspected that the emperor wanted to absorb their realm and extend his authority throughout Europe.

MAP [24.1]
Sixteenth-century Europe.

For an interactive version of this map, go to www.mhhe.com/bentley3ch24maps.

To forestall this possibility, the French kings created every obstacle they could for Charles. Even though they were staunch Roman Catholics, they aided German Lutherans and encouraged them to rebel. The French kings even allied with the Muslim Ottoman Turks against the emperor.

For their part the Ottoman sultans did not want to see a powerful Christian empire threaten their holdings in eastern Europe and their position in the Mediterranean basin. With the encouragement of the French king, Turkish forces conquered Hungary in 1526, and three years later they even laid siege briefly to Vienna. Moreover, during the early sixteenth century Ottoman forces imposed their rule beyond Egypt and embraced almost all of north Africa. By midcentury, Turkish holdings posed a serious threat to Italian and Spanish shipping in the Mediterranean.

Thus numerous domestic and foreign problems prevented Charles V from establishing his vast empire as the supreme political authority in Europe. His inability to suppress the Lutherans was especially disappointing to Charles, and in 1556, after agreeing that imperial princes and cities could determine the religious faith observed in their jurisdictions, the emperor abdicated his throne and retired to a monastery in Spain. His empire did not survive intact. Charles bestowed his holdings in Spain, Italy, the Low Countries, and the Americas on his son, King Philip II of Spain, while his brother Ferdinand inherited the Habsburg family lands in Austria and the imperial throne.

The New Monarchs

In the absence of effective imperial power, guidance of public affairs fell to the various regional states that had emerged during the middle ages. The city-states of Italy were prominent because of their economic power: since the eleventh century they had been Europe's most important centers of trade, manufacturing, and finance. The most powerful European states, however, were the kingdoms of England, France, and Spain. During the late fifteenth and sixteenth centuries, rulers of these lands, known as the "new monarchs," marshaled their resources, curbed the nobility, and built strong centralized regimes.

Finance

The new monarchs included Henry VIII of England, Louis XI and Francis I of France, and Fernando and Isabel of Spain. All the new monarchs sought to enhance their treasuries by developing new sources of finance. The French kings levied direct taxes on sales, households, and the salt trade. A new sales tax dramatically boosted Spanish royal income in the sixteenth century. For fear of provoking rebellion, the English kings did not introduce new taxes, but they increased revenues by raising fines and fees for royal services. Moreover, after Henry VIII severed ties between the English and Roman churches, he dissolved the monasteries and confiscated church wealth in England. This financial windfall enabled Henry to enhance royal power by increasing the size of the state and adding to its responsibilities. After the English Reformation, for example, the state provided poor relief and support for orphans, which previously had been responsibilities of churches and monasteries.

State Power

With their increased income the new monarchs enlarged their administrative staffs, which enabled them to collect taxes and implement royal policies more reliably than before. The French and Spanish monarchs also maintained standing armies that vastly increased their power with respect to the nobility. Their armies with thousands of infantrymen were too large for individual nobles to match, and they equipped their forces with cannons that were too expensive for nobles to purchase. The English kings did not need a standing army to put down the occasional rebellion that flared in their island realm and so did not go to the expense of supporting one. Yet they too increased their power with respect to the nobles by subjecting them to royal justice and forcing them to comply with royal policy.

The debates and disputes launched by the Protestant Reformation helped monarchs increase their power. In lands that adopted Protestant faiths—including England, much of Germany, Denmark, and Sweden—rulers expropriated the monasteries and used church wealth to expand their powers. This option was not open to Roman Catholic kings, but Protestant movements provided them with a justification to mobilize resources, which they used against political as well as religious adversaries.

The Spanish Inquisition

The Spanish Inquisition was the most distinctive institution that relied on religious justifications to advance state ends. Fernando and Isabel founded the Spanish

Inquisition in 1478, and they obtained papal license to operate the institution as a royal agency. Its original task was to ferret out those who secretly practiced Judaism or Islam, but Charles V charged it with responsibility also for detecting Protestant heresy in Spain. Throughout the late fifteenth and sixteenth centuries, however, the Spanish Inquisition served political as well as religious purposes. Moreover, its reach extended well beyond the Iberian peninsula. Just as the fear of witchcraft crossed the Atlantic Ocean and inspired witch-hunts in England's North American colonies, concerns about heresy also made their way to the western hemisphere, where inquisitors worked to protect Spanish colonies from heretical teachings.

Inquisitors had broad powers to investigate suspected cases of heresy. Popular legends have created an erroneous impression of the Spanish Inquisition as an institution running amok, framing innocent victims and routinely subjecting them to torture. In fact, inquisitors usually observed rules of evidence, and they released many suspects after investigations turned up no sign of heresy. Yet, when they detected the scent of heresy, inquisitors could be ruthless. They sentenced hundreds of victims to hang from the gallows or burn at the stake and imprisoned many others in dank cells for extended periods of time. Fear of the inquisition intimidated many into silence, and a strict Roman Catholic orthodoxy prevailed in Spain. The inquisition deterred nobles from adopting Protestant views out of political ambition, and it used its influence on behalf of the Spanish monarchy. From 1559 to 1576, for example, inquisitors imprisoned the archbishop of Toledo—the highest Roman Catholic church official in all of Spain—because of his political independence.

When the Spanish Inquisition detected traces of Protestant heresy, the punishment could be swift and brutal. In this engraving of about 1560, a large crowd observes the execution of heretics (top right) by burning at the stake.

Constitutional States

During the seventeenth and eighteenth centuries, as they sought to restore order after the Thirty Years' War, European states developed along two lines. Rulers in England and the Netherlands shared authority with representative institutions and created constitutional states, whereas monarchs in France, Spain, Austria, Prussia, and Russia concentrated power in their own hands and created a form of state known as absolute monarchy.

Constitutional States

The island kingdom of England and the maritime Dutch republic did not have written constitutions specifying the powers of the state, but during the seventeenth century they evolved governments that claimed limited powers and recognized rights pertaining to individuals and representative institutions. Their constitutional states took different forms: in England a constitutional monarchy emerged, while the Netherlands produced a republic based on representative government. In neither land did constitutional government come easily into being: in England it followed a civil war, while in the Netherlands it emerged after a long struggle for independence. In both lands, however, constitutional government strengthened the state and provided a political framework that enabled merchants to flourish as never before in European experience.

The English Civil War

Constitutional government came to England after political and religious disputes led to the English civil war (1642–1649). From the early seventeenth century, the English kings had tried to institute new taxes without approval of the parliament, which for more than three centuries had traditionally approved new levies. While royal financial policies generated political tensions, religious disagreements aggravated matters further. As Anglicans, the kings supported a church with relatively ornate ceremonies and a hierarchy of bishops working under authority of the monarchs themselves. Meanwhile, however, many of the boldest and most insistent voices within parliament belonged to zealous Calvinists known as Puritans because they sought to purify the English church of any lingering elements, such as ornate ceremonies and a hierarchy of bishops, suggestive of Roman Catholic Christianity. By 1641, King Charles I and parliament were at loggerheads, unable to cooperate or even communicate effectively with one another. Both sides raised armies. In the conflicts that followed, parliamentary forces captured Charles, tried him for tyranny, and in an act that shocked all of Europe, marched him up on a platform and beheaded him in 1649.

The Glorious Revolution

In the absence of a king, a Puritan regime took power but soon degenerated into a disagreeable dictatorship, prompting parliament to restore the monarchy in 1660. King and parliament, however, soon resumed their conflicts. The issue came to a head in a bloodless change of power known as the Glorious Revolution (1688–1689), when parliament deposed King James II and invited his daughter Mary and her Dutch husband, William of Orange, to assume the throne. The resulting arrangement provided that kings would rule in cooperation with parliament, thus guaranteeing that nobles, merchants, and other constituencies would enjoy representation in government affairs.

The Dutch Republic

As in England, a potent combination of political and religious tensions led to conflict from which constitutional government emerged in the Netherlands. In the mid-sixteenth century, authority over the Low Countries, including modern-day Belgium as well as the Netherlands, rested with King Philip II of Spain. In 1566 Philip, a devout Roman Catholic, moved to suppress an increasingly popular Calvinist movement in the Netherlands—a measure that provoked large-scale rebellion against Spanish rule. In 1579 a group of Dutch provinces formed an anti-Spanish alliance, and in 1581 they proclaimed themselves the independent United Provinces. Representative assemblies organized local affairs in each of the provinces, and on this foundation political leaders built a Dutch republic. Spain did not officially recognize the independence of the United Provinces until the end of the Thirty Years' War in

In this contemporary painting, the executioner holds up the just-severed head of King Charles I of England. The prospect of a royal execution overcomes one woman, who faints (at bottom).

1648, but the Dutch republic was effectively organizing affairs in the northern Low Countries by the early seventeenth century.

In many ways, the constitutional governments of England and the Dutch republic represented historical experiments. Apart from the Roman republic in classical times and a few Italian city-states of the medieval and Renaissance eras, European peoples had little experience with representative government. In their responses to political crises, popular leaders in both England and the Netherlands found it possible to mobilize support by appealing to the political and religious interests of broad constituencies and making a place for them in the government. The result was a pair of states that effectively harnassed popular support and used it to magnify state power.

In both England and the Dutch republic, merchants were especially prominent in political affairs, and state policy in both lands favored maritime trade and the building of commercial empires overseas. The constitutional states allowed entrepreneurs to pursue their economic interests with minimal interference from public authorities, and during the late seventeenth and eighteenth centuries both states experienced extraordinary prosperity as a result of these policies. Indeed, in many ways the English and Dutch states represented an alliance between merchants and rulers that worked to the benefit of both. Merchants supported the state with the wealth that they generated through trade—especially overseas trade—while rulers followed policies that looked after the interests of their merchants.

Absolute Monarchies

While constitutional states devised ways to share power and authority, absolute monarchies found other ways to increase state power. Absolutism stood on a theoretical foundation known as the divine right of kings. This theory held that kings derived their authority from God and served as "God's lieutenants upon earth." There was no role in divine-right theory for common subjects or even nobles in public affairs: the king made law and determined policy. Noncompliance or disobedience merited punishment, and rebellion was a despicable act tantamount to blasphemy. In fact, absolute monarchs always relied on support from nobles and other social groups as well, but the claims of divine-right theory clearly reflected efforts at royal centralization.

The most conspicuous absolutist state was the French monarchy. The architect of French absolutism was a prominent church official, Cardinal Richelieu, who served as chief minister to King Louis XIII from 1624 to 1642. Richelieu worked systematically to undermine the power of the nobility and enhance the authority of the king. He destroyed nobles' castles and ruthlessly crushed aristocratic conspiracies. As a counterweight to the nobility, Richelieu built a large bureaucracy staffed by commoners loyal to the king. He also appointed officials to supervise the implementation of royal policy in the provinces. Finally, Richelieu attacked French Calvinists, who often allied with independent nobles, and destroyed their political and military power, although he allowed them to continue observing their faith. By midcentury France was under control of a tightly centralized absolute monarchy.

The Sun King

The ruler who best epitomized royal absolutism was King Louis XIV (reigned 1643–1715), who once reportedly declared that he was himself the state: "*l'état,*

King Louis XIV and his entourage approach the main gate of Versailles (bottom right). Though only partially constructed at the time of this painting (1668), Versailles was already a spacious and luxurious retreat for Louis and his court.

c'est moi." Known as *le roi soleil*—"the sun king"—Louis surrounded himself with splendor befitting one who ruled by divine right. During the 1670s he built a magnificent residence at Versailles, a royal hunting lodge near Paris, and in the 1680s he moved his court there. Louis's palace at Versailles was the largest building in Europe, with 230 acres of formal gardens and 1,400 fountains. Because Louis did not want to wait years for saplings to grow, he ordered laborers to dig up 25,000 fully grown trees and haul them to Versailles for transplanting.

The sun king was the center of attention at Versailles. Court officials hovered around him and tended to his every need. All prominent nobles established residences at Versailles for their families and entourages. Louis strongly encouraged them to live at court, where he and his staff could keep an eye on them, and ambitious nobles gravitated there anyway in hopes of winning influence with the king. Louis himself was the arbiter of taste and style at Versailles, where he lavishly patronized painters, sculptors, architects, and writers whose creations met with his approval.

While nobles living at Versailles mastered the intricacies of court ritual and attended banquets, concerts, operas, balls, and theatrical performances, Louis and his ministers ran the state. In effect, Louis provided the nobility with luxurious accommodations and endless entertainment in exchange for absolute rule. From Versailles Louis and his advisors promulgated laws and controlled a massive standing army that kept order throughout the land. They also promoted economic development by supporting the establishment of new industries, building roads and canals, abolishing internal tariffs, and encouraging exports. Finally, they waged a series of wars designed to enlarge French boundaries and establish France as the preeminent power in Europe.

Absolutism in Russia

Louis XIV was not the only absolute monarch of early modern Europe: Spanish, Austrian, and Prussian rulers embraced similar policies. The potential of absolutism to increase state power was particularly conspicuous in the case of Russia, where tsars of the Romanov dynasty (1613–1917) tightly centralized government functions. (*Tsar,* sometimes spelled *czar,* is a Russianized form of the term *caesar,* which Russian rulers appropriated from Byzantine emperors, who in turn had borrowed it from the classical Roman empire to signify their imperial status.) The Romanovs inherited a state that had rapidly expanded its boundaries since the mid-fourteenth century. Building on the foundation of a small principality around the trading city of Moscow, by 1600 Russia had become a vast empire extending from the Arctic seas in the north to the Caspian Sea in the south, with an increasing presence in the tundra and forests of Siberia as well.

Peter I

Most important of the Romanov tsars was Peter I (reigned 1682–1725), widely known as Peter the Great, who inaugurated a thoroughgoing process of state transformation. Peter had a burning desire to make Russia, a huge but underpopulated land, into a great military power like those that had recently emerged in western Europe. In pursuit of this goal, he worked to transform Russia on the model of western European lands. In 1697–1698 he led a large party of Russian observers on a tour of Germany, the Netherlands, and England to learn about western European administrative methods and military technology. His traveling companions often behaved crudely by western European standards: they consumed beer, wine, and brandy in quantities that astonished their hosts, and King William III sent Peter a bill for damages done by his entourage at the country house where they lodged in England. (Among other things, Peter had ruined the gardens by having his men march through them in military formation.)

Upon return to Moscow, Peter set Russia spinning. He reformed the army by offering better pay and drafting peasants who served for life as professional soldiers. He provided his forces with extensive training and equipped them with modern weapons. He ordered aristocrats to study mathematics and geometry so that they could calcu-

Tsar Peter the Great with a pair of shears, about to remove the beard of a conservative subject.

late how to aim cannons accurately, and he began the construction of a navy with an eye toward domination of the Baltic and other northern seas. He also overhauled the government bureaucracy to facilitate tax collection and improve administrative efficiency. His transformation of Russia even involved a cosmetic makeover, as he commanded his aristocratic subjects to wear western European fashions and ordered men to shave their traditional beards. These measures, which were extremely unpopular among conservative Russians, provoked spirited protest among those who resented the influence of western European ways. Yet Peter insisted on observance of his policies—to the point that he reportedly went into the streets and personally hacked the beards off recalcitrants' faces. Perhaps the best symbol of his policies was St. Petersburg, a newly built seaport that Peter opened in 1703 to serve as a magnificent capital city and haven for Russia's fledgling navy.

Catherine II and the Limits of Reform

The most able of Peter's successors was Catherine II (reigned 1762–1796), also known as Catherine the Great. Like Peter, Catherine sought to make Russia a great power. She worked to improve governmental efficiency by dividing her vast empire into fifty administrative provinces, and she promoted economic development in Russia's towns. For a while, she even worked to improve the conditions of Russia's oppressed peasantry by restricting the punishments that noble landowners could inflict on the serfs who worked their lands. She sought to eliminate common penalties such as torture, beating, and the mutilation of individuals by cutting off their noses, ears, or tongues.

Yet her interest in social reform cooled rapidly when it seemed to inspire challenges to her rule. She faced a particularly unsettling trial in 1773 and 1774, when a disgruntled former soldier named Yemelian Pugachev mounted a rebellion in the steppe lands north of the Caspian Sea. Pugachev raised a motley army of adventurers, exiles, peasants, and serfs who killed thousands of noble landowners and government officials before imperial forces crushed the uprising. Government authorities took the captured Pugachev to Moscow in chains, beheaded him, quartered his body, and displayed his parts throughout the city as a warning against rebellion. Thereafter, Catherine's first concern was the preservation of autocratic rule rather than the transformation of Russia according to western European models.

Thus, in Russia as in other European lands, absolutist policies resulted in tight centralization and considerable strengthening of the state. The enhanced power that flowed from absolutism became dramatically clear in the period 1772 to 1797, when Austria, Prussia, and Catherine II's Russia picked the weak kingdom of Poland apart. In a series of three "partitions," the predatory absolutist states seized Polish territory and absorbed it into their own realms, ultimately wiping Poland entirely off the map. The lesson of the partitions was clear: any European state that hoped to survive needed to construct an effective government that could respond promptly to challenges and opportunities.

The European States System

Whether they relied on absolutist or constitutional principles, European governments of early modern times built states much more powerful than those of their medieval predecessors. This round of state development led to difficulties within Europe, since conflicting interests fueled interstate competition and war. In the absence of an imperial authority capable of imposing and maintaining order in Europe, sovereign states had to find ways to resolve conflicts by themselves.

The Peace of Westphalia

The Thirty Years' War demonstrated the chaos and devastation that conflict could bring. In an effort to avoid tearing their society apart, European states ended the Thirty Years' War with the Peace of Westphalia (1648), which laid the foundations for a system of independent, competing states. Almost all the European states participated in drafting the Peace of Westphalia, and by the treaty's terms they regarded each other as sovereign and equal. They also mutually recognized their rights to organize their own domestic affairs, including religious affairs. Rather than envisioning imperial or papal or some other sort of supreme authority, the Peace of Westphalia entrusted political and diplomatic affairs to states acting in their own interests. European religious unity had disappeared, and the era of the sovereign state had arrived.

The Peace of Westphalia did not bring an end to war. Indeed, war was almost constant in early modern Europe. Most conflicts were minor affairs inaugurated by monarchs seeking to extend their authority to new lands or to reclaim territories seized by others, but they nevertheless disrupted local economies and drained re-

MAP [24.2]
Europe after the Peace of Westphalia, 1648.

For an interactive version of this map, go to www.mhhe.com/bentley3ch24maps.

sources. A few wars, however, grew to sizable proportions. Most notable among them were the wars of Louis XIV and the Seven Years' War. Between 1668 and 1713, the sun king sought to expand his borders east into Germany and to absorb Spain and the Spanish Netherlands into his kingdom. This prospect prompted England, the United Provinces, and Austria to mount a coalition against Louis. Later the Seven Years' War (1756–1763) pitted France, Austria, and Russia against Britain and Prussia, and it merged with conflicts between France and Britain in India and North America to become a global war for imperial supremacy.

The Balance of Power

These shifting alliances illustrate the principal foundation of European diplomacy in early modern times—the balance of power. No ruler wanted to see another state dominate all the others. Thus, when any particular state began to wax strong, others formed coalitions against it. Balance-of-power diplomacy was risky business: it was always possible that a coalition might repress one strong state only to open the door for another. Yet, in playing balance-of-power politics, statesmen prevented the building of empires and ensured that Europe would be a land of independent, sovereign, competing states.

Military Development

Frequent wars and balance-of-power diplomacy drained the resources of individual states but strengthened European society as a whole. European states competed vigorously and sought to develop the most expert military leadership and the most effective weapons for their arsenals. States organized military academies where officers received advanced education in strategy and tactics and learned how to maintain disciplined forces. Demand for powerful weapons stimulated the development of a sophisticated armaments industry that turned out ever more lethal products. Gun foundries manufactured cannons of increasing size, range, power, and accuracy as well as small arms that allowed infantry to unleash withering volleys against their enemies.

In China, India, and Islamic lands, imperial states had little or no incentive to encourage similar technological innovation in the armaments industry. These states possessed the forces and weapons they needed to maintain order within their boundaries, and they rarely encountered foreign threats backed up with superior armaments. In Europe, however, failure to keep up with the latest improvements in arms technology could lead to defeat on the battlefield and decline in state power. Thus Europeans continuously sought to improve their military arsenals, and as a result, by the eighteenth century European armaments outperformed all others.

Early Capitalist Society

While the Protestant Reformation and the emergence of sovereign states brought religious and political change, a rapidly expanding population and economy encouraged the development of capitalism, which in turn led to a restructuring of European economy and society. Technologies of communication and transportation enabled businessmen to profit from distant markets, and merchants and manufacturers increasingly organized their affairs with the market rather than local communities in mind.

Capitalism generated considerable wealth, but its effects were uneven and sometimes unsettling. Economic development and increasing prosperity were noticeable in western Europe, particularly England, France, Germany, and the Netherlands. Yet eastern Europe experienced much less economic ferment, as Poland and Russia increasingly became suppliers of grain and raw materials rather than centers of trade or production. Even in western Europe, early capitalism encouraged social change that sometimes required painful adjustments to new conditions.

Population Growth and Urbanization

American Food Crops

The foundation of European economic expansion in early modern times was a rapidly growing population, which reflected improved nutrition and decreasing mortality. The Columbian exchange enriched European diets by introducing new food crops to European fields and tables. Most notable of the introductions was the potato, which enjoyed the reputation of being an aphrodisiac during the sixteenth and seventeenth centuries. Although potatoes probably did not inspire much romantic ardor, they provided a welcome source of carbohydrates for peasants and laborers who were having trouble keeping up with the rising price of bread. From Ireland to Russia and from Scandinavia to the Mediterranean, cultivators planted potatoes and harvested crops that added calories to European diets. American maize also made its way to Europe. Maize, however, served mostly as feed for livestock rather than a food for human consumption, although peasants sometimes used cornmeal to make bread or porridges like polenta. Other American crops, such as tomatoes and peppers, added vitamins and tangy flavor to European diets.

While recently introduced American crops improved European diets, old diseases lost some of their ferocity. Smallpox continued to carry off about 10 percent of Europe's infants, and dysentery, influenza, tuberculosis, and typhus also claimed victims among young and old, rich and poor alike. Yet better nourished populations were better able to resist these maladies. Bubonic plague, a massive epidemic killer during the fourteenth and fifteenth centuries, receded from European society. After its initial onslaught in the mid-fourteenth century, plague made periodic appearances throughout the early modern era. After the mid-seventeenth century, however, epidemics were rare and isolated events. The last major outbreaks of plague in Europe occurred in London in 1660 and Marseilles in 1720. By the mid-seventeenth century, epidemic disease was almost negligible as an influence on European population.

Population Growth

Although European birthrates did not rise dramatically in early modern times, decreasing mortality resulted in rapid population growth. In 1500 the population of Europe, including Russia, was about 81 million. During the sixteenth century, as Europe recovered from epidemic plague, the population rose to 100 million. The Thirty Years' War—along with the famine and disease that the war touched off—led to population decline from about 1620 to 1650, but by 1700 European population had rallied and risen to 120 million. During the next century it grew by another 50 percent to 180 million.

Urbanization

Rapid population growth drove a process of equally rapid urbanization. Some cities grew because rulers chose them as sites of government. Madrid, for example, was a minor town with a few thousand inhabitants until 1561 when King Philip II decided to locate his capital there. By 1600 the population of Madrid had risen to 65,000, and by 1630 it had reached 170,000. Other cities were commercial and industrial as well as government centers, and their numbers expanded along with the European economy. In the mid-sixteenth century, for example, the population of Paris was about 130,000, and London had about 60,000 inhabitants. A century later the population of both cities had risen to half a million. Other European cities also experienced growth, even if it was not so dramatic as in the cases of Madrid, Paris, and London: Amsterdam, Berlin, Copenhagen, Dublin, Stockholm, Vienna, and others became prominent European cities during the early modern era.

Early Capitalism and Protoindustrialization

The Nature of Capitalism

Population growth and rapid urbanization helped spur a round of remarkable economic development. This economic growth coincided with the emergence of capitalism—an economic system in which private parties make their goods and services available on a free market and seek to take advantage of market conditions to profit from their activities. Whether they are single individuals or large companies, private parties own the land, machinery, tools, equipment, buildings, workshops, and raw materials needed for production. Private parties pursuing their own economic interests hire workers and decide for themselves what to produce: economic decisions are the prerogative of capitalist businessmen, not governments or social superiors. The center of a capitalist system is the market in which businessmen compete with each other, and the forces of supply and demand determine the prices received for goods and services. If businessmen organize their affairs efficiently, they realize handsome profits when they place their goods and services on the market. Otherwise, they incur losses and perhaps even lose their businesses.

The desire to accumulate wealth and realize profits was by no means new. Ever since the introduction of agriculture and the production of surplus crops, some individuals and groups had accumulated great wealth. Indeed, for several thousand years before the early modern era, merchants in China, southeast Asia, India, southwest Asia, the Mediterranean basin, and sub-Saharan Africa had pursued commercial ventures in hopes of realizing profits. Banks, investors, and insurance underwriters had supported privately organized commercial ventures throughout much of the eastern hemisphere since the postclassical era (500–1500 C.E.).

The Old Stock Exchange of Amsterdam, depicted here in a painting of the mid-seventeenth century, attracted merchants, investors, entrepreneurs, and businessmen from all over Europe. There they bought and sold shares in joint-stock companies such as the VOC and dealt in all manner of commodities traded in Amsterdam.

Supply and Demand

During early modern times, however, European merchants and entrepreneurs transformed their society in a way that none of their predecessors had done. The capitalist economic order developed as businessmen learned to take advantage of market conditions by building efficient networks of transportation and communication. Dutch merchants might purchase cheap grain from Baltic lands like Poland or Russia, for example, store it in Amsterdam until they learned about a famine in the Mediterranean and then transport it and sell it in southern France or Spain. Their enormous profits fueled suspicions that they took advantage of those in difficulty, but their activities also supplied hungry communities with the necessities of life, even if the price was high.

Private parties organized an array of institutions and services to support early capitalism. Banks, for example, appeared in all the major commercial cities of Europe: they held funds on account for safekeeping and granted loans to merchants or entrepreneurs launching new business ventures. Banks also published business newsletters—forerunners of the *Wall Street Journal* and *Fortune* magazine—that provided readers with reports on prices, information about demand for commodities in distant markets, and political news that could have an impact on business. Insurance companies mitigated financial losses from risky undertakings like transoceanic voyages. Stock exchanges arose in the major European cities and provided markets where investors could buy and sell shares in joint-stock companies and trade in other commodities as well.

Joint-Stock Companies

Joint-stock companies were especially important institutions in early capitalist society. Large trading companies like the English East India Company and its Dutch counterpart, the Vereenigde Oost-Indische Compagnie (VOC), spread the risks attached to expensive business enterprises and also took advantage of extensive communications and transportation networks. The trading companies organized commercial ventures on a larger scale than ever before in world history. They were the principal foundations of the global economy that emerged in early modern times, and they were the direct ancestors of contemporary multinational corporations.

Politics and Empire

Capitalism did not develop in a political vacuum. To the contrary, it emerged with the active support of government authorities who saw a capitalist order as the one best suited to their individual and collective interests. Merchants were especially influential in the affairs of the English and Dutch states, so it is not surprising that these lands adopted policies that were most favorable to capitalist enterprises throughout the early modern era. The English and Dutch states recognized individuals' rights to possess private property, enforced their contracts, protected their financial interests, and settled disputes between parties to business transactions. They also chartered joint-stock companies and authorized some of them to explore, conquer, and colonize distant lands in search of commercial opportunities. Thus early capitalism developed in the context of imperialism, as European peoples established fortified trading posts in Asia and colonial regimes in both southeast Asia and the Americas. Indeed, imperial expansion and colonial rule were crucial for the development of capitalism, since they enabled European merchants to gain access to the natural resources and commodities that they distributed so effectively through their transportation networks.

Quite apart from its influence on trade and the distribution of goods, capitalism also encouraged European entrepreneurs to organize new ways to manufacture goods. For centuries, craft guilds had monopolized the production of goods such as textiles and metalwares in European towns and cities. Guilds fixed prices and wages, and they regulated standards of quality. They did not seek to realize profits so much as to protect markets and preserve their members' places in society. As a result, they actively discouraged competition and sometimes resisted technological innovation.

The Putting-Out System

Capitalist entrepreneurs seeking profits found the guilds cumbersome and inflexible, so they sidestepped them and moved production into the countryside. Instead

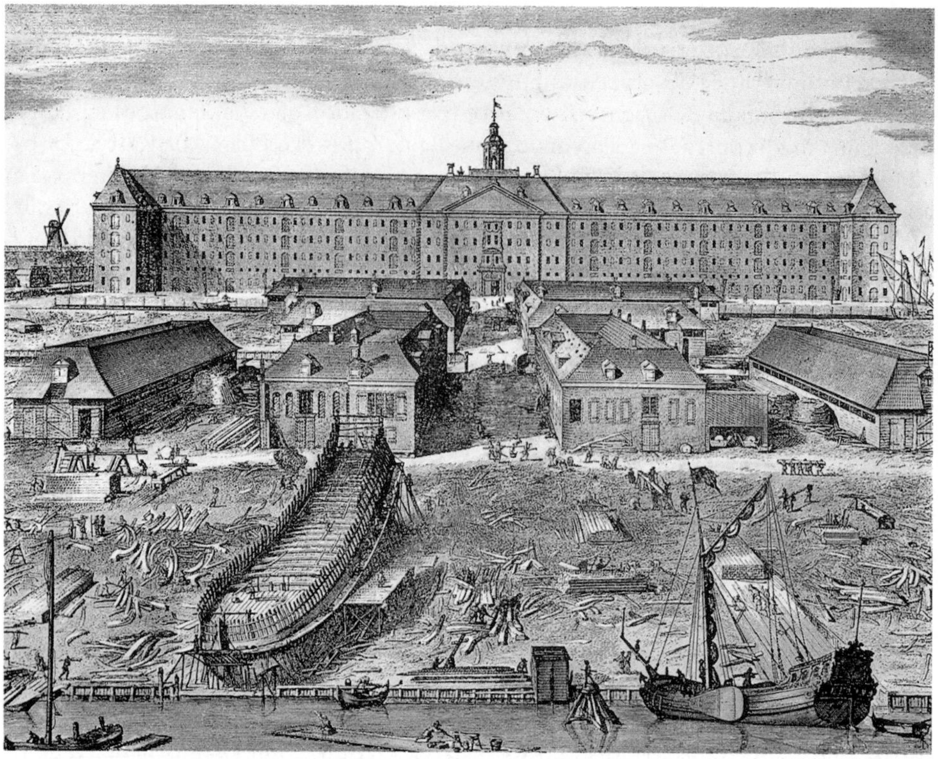

An anonymous engraving depicts activity in a Dutch shipyard where workers build a massive, oceangoing sailing ship. In the seventeenth century, Dutch ships were inexpensive to operate, yet they accommodated abundant cargoes.

of relying on urban artisans to produce cloth, for example, they organized a "putting-out system" by which they delivered unfinished materials like raw wool to rural households. Men and women in the countryside would then spin the wool into yarn, weave the yarn into cloth, cut the cloth according to patterns, and assemble the pieces into garments. The entrepreneur paid workers for their services, picked up the finished goods, and sold them on the market. During the seventeenth and eighteenth centuries, entrepreneurs moved the production of cloth, nails, pins, pots, and many other goods into the countryside through the putting-out system.

Because rural labor was usually plentiful, entrepreneurs spent relatively little on wages and realized handsome profits on their ventures. The putting-out system represented an early effort to organize efficient industrial production. Indeed, some historians refer to the seventeenth and eighteenth centuries as an age of "protoindustrialization." The putting-out system remained a prominent feature of European society until the rise of industrial factories in the nineteenth century.

Social Change in Early Modern Europe

Capitalist economic development brought unsettling change to European lands. The putting-out system, for example, introduced considerable sums of money into the countryside. Increased wealth brought material benefits, but it also undermined long-established patterns of rural life. The material standards of rural life rose dramatically: peasant households acquired more cabinets, furnishings, and tableware, and rural residents wore better clothes, ate better food, and drank better wine. Individuals suddenly acquired incomes that enabled them to pursue their own economic interests and to become financially independent of their families and neighbors. When young adults and women began to earn their own incomes, however, many feared that they might slip out of the control of their families and abandon their kin who continued to work at agricultural tasks.

The putting-out system did not become a prominent feature of production in eastern Europe, but early capitalism prompted deep social change there as well as in lands to the west. Eastern Europe had very few cities in early modern times, so in expansive agrarian states like Poland, Bohemia, and Russia, most people had no alternative to working in the countryside. Landlords took advantage of this situation by forcing peasants to work under extremely harsh conditions.

Serfdom in Russia

Russia in particular was a vast but sparsely populated empire with little trade or manufacturing. Out of a concern to retain the allegiance of the powerful nobles who owned most of Russia's land, the Romanov tsars restricted the freedoms of most Russian peasants and tied them to the land as serfs. The institution of serfdom had emerged in the early middle ages as a labor system that required semifree peasants to provide labor services for landowners and prevented them from marrying or moving away without their landlords' permission. After the fifteenth century, serfdom gradually came to an end in western Europe. In eastern Europe, however, landowners and rulers tightened restrictions on peasants during the sixteenth century, and in Russia the institution of serfdom survived until the nineteenth century. In effect, the Romanovs won the support of the Russian nobles by ensuring them that laborers would be available to work their estates, which otherwise would have been worthless. In 1649 the government promulgated a law code that provided for tight state control over the Russian labor force by establishing a rigid, castelike social order that sharply restricted both occupational and geographic mobility. The law of 1649 did not turn serfs into chattel slaves, but during the late seventeenth and eighteenth centuries, landlords commonly sold serfs to one another as if they were indeed private property. Under these conditions, landlords operated estates with inexpensive labor and derived enormous incomes from the sale of agricultural products on the market.

These arrangements played crucial roles in the emergence of capitalism. In the larger economy of early modern Europe, eastern European lands relied on semifree labor to cultivate grains and provide raw materials such as timber for export to western Europe, where merchants and manufacturers were able to employ free wage labor in building a capitalist economy. Already by the early sixteenth century, consumers in the Netherlands depended for their survival on grains imported from Poland and Russia through the Baltic Sea. Thus it was possible for capitalism to flourish in western Europe only because the peasants and semifree serfs of eastern Europe provided inexpensive foods and raw materials that fueled economic development. From its earliest days, capitalist economic organization had implications for peoples and lands far removed from the centers of capitalism itself.

Profits and Ethics

Capitalism also posed moral challenges. Medieval theologians had regarded profit-making activity as morally dangerous, since profiteers looked to their own advantage rather than the welfare of the larger community. Church officials even attempted to forbid the collection of interest on loans, since they considered interest an unearned and immoral profit. But profit was the lifeblood of capitalism, and bankers were not willing to risk large sums of money on business ventures without realizing handsome returns on their investments in the form of interest. Even as it transformed the European economy, capitalism found advocates who sought to explain its principles and portray it as a socially beneficial form of economic organization. Most important of the early apostles

Sources from the Past

Adam Smith on the Capitalist Market

Adam Smith devoted special thought to the nature of early capitalist society and the principles that made it work. In 1776 he published a lengthy book entitled An Inquiry into the Nature and Causes of the Wealth of Nations, *a vastly influential work that championed free, unregulated markets and capitalist enterprise as the principal ingredients of prosperity. Smith's optimism about capitalism sprang from his conviction that society as a whole benefits when individuals pursue their own economic interests and trade on a free market.*

Every individual is continually exerting himself to find out the most advantageous employment for whatever capital he can command. It is his own advantage, indeed, and not that of the society, which he has in view. . . .

As every individual, therefore, endeavours as much as he can both to employ his capital in the support of domestic industry, and so to direct that industry that its produce may be of the greatest value, every individual necessarily labours to render the annual revenue of the society as great as he can. He generally, indeed, neither intends to promote the public interest, nor knows how much he is promoting it. By preferring the support of domestic to that of foreign industry, he intends only his own security; and by directing that industry in such a manner as its produce may be of the greatest value, he intends only his own gain, and he is in this, as in many other cases, led by an invisible hand to promote an end which was no part of his intention. Nor is it always the worse for the society that it was no part of it. By pursuing his own interest he frequently promotes that of the society more effectually than when he really intends to promote it. I have never known much good done by those who affected to trade for the public good. It is an affectation, indeed, not very common among merchants, and very few words need be employed in dissuading them from it.

What is the species of domestic industry which his capital can employ, and of which the produce is likely to be of the greatest value, every individual, it is evident, can, in his local situation, judge much better than any statesman or lawgiver can do for him. The statesman, who should attempt to direct private people in what manner they ought to employ their capitals, would not only load himself with a most unnecessary attention, but assume an authority which could safely be trusted, not only to no single person, but to no council or senate whatever, and which would nowhere be so dangerous as in the hands of a man who had folly and presumption enough to fancy himself fit to exercise it.

To give the monopoly of the home market to the produce of domestic industry, in any particular art or manufacture, is in some measure to direct private people in what manner they ought to employ their capitals, and must, in almost all cases, be either a useless or a hurtful regulation. If the produce of domestic can be brought there as cheap as that of foreign industry, the regulation is evidently useless. If it cannot, it must generally be hurtful. It is the maxim of every prudent master of a family, never to attempt to make at home what it will cost him more to make than to buy. The tailor does not attempt to make his own shoes, but buys them of the shoemaker. The shoemaker does not attempt to make his own clothes, but employs a tailor. The farmer attempts to make neither the one nor the other, but employs those different artificers. All of them find it for their interest to employ their whole industry in a way in which they have some advantage over their neighbours, and to purchase with a part of its produce, or, what is the same thing, with the price of a part of it, whatever else they have occasion for.

SOURCE: Adam Smith. *An Inquiry into the Nature and Causes of the Wealth of Nations.* Edinburgh: 1863, pp. 198–200.

To what extent do you think Adam Smith's analysis reflected the experiences of his own times, and to what extent did they represent universally valid observations?

of capitalism was the Scottish philosopher Adam Smith (1723–1790), who held that society would prosper when individuals pursued their own economic interests.

Nevertheless, the transition to capitalist society was long and painful. When individuals abandoned the practices of their ancestors and declined to help those who had fallen on hard times, their neighbors readily interpreted their actions as expressions of selfishness rather than economic prudence. Thus capitalist economic practices generated deep social strains, which often manifested themselves in violence. Bandits plagued the countryside of early modern Europe, and muggers turned whole sections of large cities into danger zones. Some historians believe that witch-hunting activities reflected social tensions generated by early capitalism and that accusations of witchcraft represented hostility toward women who were becoming economically independent of their husbands and families.

The Nuclear Family

In some ways capitalism favored the nuclear family as the principal unit of society. For centuries European couples had mostly married late—in their mid-twenties—and set up independent households. Early capitalism offered opportunities for these independent families to increase their wealth by cultivating agricultural crops or producing goods for sale on the market. As nuclear families became more important economically, they also became more socially and emotionally independent. Love between a man and a woman became a more important consideration in the making of marriages than the interests of the larger extended families, and affection between parents and their children became a more important ingredient of family life. Capitalism did not necessarily cause these changes in family life, but it may have encouraged developments that helped to define the nature and role of the family in modern European society.

Science and Enlightenment

While experiencing religious, political, economic, and social change, western Europe also underwent intellectual and cultural transformation. Astronomers and physicists rejected classical Greek and Roman authorities, whose theories had dominated scientific thought during the middle ages, and based their understanding of the natural world on direct observation and mathematical reasoning. During the seventeenth and eighteenth centuries, they elaborated a new vision of the earth and the larger universe. Scholars relied on observation and mathematics to transform the natural sciences in a process known as the scientific revolution. The results of early modern science were so powerful that some European intellectuals sought to overhaul moral, social, and political thought by adapting scientific methods and relying on reason rather than traditional cultural authorities. Their efforts weakened the influence of churches in western Europe and encouraged the development of secular values.

The Reconception of the Universe

The Ptolemaic Universe

Until the seventeenth century, European astronomers based their understanding of the universe on the work of the Greek scholar Claudius Ptolemy of Alexandria. About the middle of the second century C.E., Ptolemy composed a work known as the *Almagest* that synthesized theories about the universe. Ptolemy envisioned a motionless earth surrounded by a series of nine hollow, concentric spheres that revolved around it. Each of the first seven spheres had one of the observable heavenly bodies—the sun, the moon, Mercury, Venus, Mars, Jupiter, and Saturn—embedded in its shell. The eighth sphere held the stars, and an empty ninth sphere surrounded the whole cosmos and provided the spin that kept all the others moving. Beyond the spheres Christian astronomers located heaven, the realm of God.

Following Ptolemy, astronomers believed that the heavens consisted of matter unlike any found on earth. Glowing like perfect jewels in the night skies, heavenly bodies were composed of a pure substance that did not experience change or corruption, and they were not subject to the physical laws that governed the world below the moon. They followed perfect circular paths in making their revolutions around the earth.

Planetary Movement

Although theoretically attractive, this cosmology did not mesh readily with the erratic movements of the planets—a term that comes from the Greek word *planetes,* meaning "wanderer." From the vantage point of the earth, the planets often followed regular courses through the skies, but they sometimes slowed down, stopped, or even turned back on their courses—motions that would be difficult to explain if the planetary spheres revolved regularly around the earth. Astronomers went to great lengths to explain planetary behavior as the result of perfect circular movements. The result was an awkward series of adjustments known as epicycles—small circular revolutions that planets made around a point in their spheres, even while the spheres themselves revolved around the earth.

The Copernican Universe

As astronomers accumulated data on planetary movements, most of them sought to reconcile their observations with Ptolemaic theory by adding increasing numbers of epicycles to their cosmic maps. In 1543, however, the Polish astronomer Nicolaus Copernicus published a treatise *On the Revolutions of the Heavenly Spheres* that broke with Ptolemaic theory and pointed European science in a new direction. Copernicus argued that the sun rather than the earth stood at the center of the universe and that the planets, including the earth, revolved around the sun.

A woodcut illustration depicts the Ptolemaic universe with the earth at the center surrounded by spheres holding the planets and stars.

Compared to Ptolemy's earth-centered universe, this new theory harmonized much better with observational data, but it did not receive a warm welcome. Copernicus's ideas not only challenged prevailing scientific theories but also threatened cherished religious beliefs. His theory implied that the earth was just another planet and that human beings did not occupy the central position in the universe. To some it also suggested the unsettling possibility that there might be other populated worlds in the universe—a notion that would be difficult to reconcile with Christian teachings, which held that the earth and humanity were unique creations of God.

The Scientific Revolution

Although it was unpopular in many quarters, Copernicus's theory inspired some astronomers to examine the heavens in fresh ways. As evidence accumulated, it became clear that the Ptolemaic universe simply did not correspond with reality. Astronomers based their theories on increasingly precise observational data, and they relied on mathematical reasoning to organize the data. Gradually, they abandoned the Ptolemaic in favor of the Copernican model of the universe. Moreover, some of them began to apply their analytical methods to mechanics—the branch of science that deals with moving bodies—and by the mid-seventeenth century accurate observation and mathematical reasoning dominated both mechanics and astronomy. Indeed, reliance on observation and mathematics transformed the study of the natural world and brought about the scientific revolution.

Galileo Galilei

The works of two mathematicians—Johannes Kepler of Germany and Galileo Galilei of Italy—rang the death knell for the Ptolemaic universe. Kepler (1571–1630) demonstrated that planetary orbits are elliptical, not circular as in Ptolemaic theory. Galileo (1564–1642) showed that the heavens were not the perfect, unblemished realm that Ptolemaic astronomers assumed but, rather, a world of change, flux, and many previously unsuspected sights. Galileo took a recently invented instrument—the telescope—turned it skyward, and reported observations that astonished his contemporaries. With his telescope he could see spots on the sun and mountains on the moon—observations that discredited the notion that heavenly bodies were smooth, immaculate, unchanging, and perfectly spherical. He also noticed four of the moons that orbit the planet Jupiter—bodies that no human being had ever before observed—and he caught sight of previously unknown distant stars, which implied that the universe was much larger than anyone had previously suspected.

In addition to his astronomical discoveries, Galileo contributed to the understanding of terrestrial motion. He designed ingenious experiments to show that the velocity of falling bodies depends not on their weight but, rather, on the height from which they fall. This claim brought him scorn from scientists who subscribed to scientific beliefs deriving from Aristotle, but it helped scientists to understand better how moving bodies behave under the influence of earth's gravitational pull. Galileo also anticipated the modern law of inertia, which holds that a moving body will continue to move in a straight line until some force intervenes to check or alter its motion.

Isaac Newton

The new approach to science culminated in the work of the English mathematician Isaac Newton (1642–1727), who depended on accurate observation and mathematical reasoning to construct a powerful synthesis of astronomy and mechanics. Newton outlined his views on the natural world in an epoch-making volume of 1687 entitled *Mathematical Principles of Natural Philosophy.* Newton's work united the heavens and the earth in a vast, cosmic system. He argued that a law of universal gravitation regulates the motions of bodies throughout the universe, and he offered precise mathematical explanations of the laws that govern movements of bodies on the earth. Newton's laws of universal gravitation and motion enabled him to synthesize the sciences of astronomy and mechanics. They also allowed him to explain a vast range of seemingly unrelated phenomena, such as the ebb and flow of the tides, which move according to the gravitational pull of the moon, and the eccentric orbits of planets and comets, which reflect the gravitational influence of the sun, the earth, and other heavenly bodies. Until the twentieth century, Newton's universe served as the unquestioned framework for the physical sciences.

Newton's work symbolized the scientific revolution, but it by no means marked the end of the process by which observation and mathematical reasoning transformed European science. Inspired by the dramatic discoveries of astronomers and physicists, other scientists began to turn away from classical authorities and to construct fresh approaches to the understanding of the natural world. During the seventeenth and eighteenth centuries, anatomy, physiology, microbiology, chemistry, and botany underwent a thorough overhaul, as scientists tested their theories against direct observation of natural phenomena and explained them in rigorous mathematical terms.

An anonymous portrait of Isaac Newton depicts a serious scholar searching intently to discover the principles that govern the universe.

The Enlightenment

Newton's vision of the universe was so powerful and persuasive that its influence extended well beyond science. His work suggested that rational analysis of human behavior and institutions could lead to fresh insights about the human as well as the natural world. From Scotland to Sicily and from Philadelphia to Moscow, European and Euro-American thinkers launched an ambitious project to transform human thought and to use reason to transform the world. Like the early modern scientists, they abandoned Aristotelian philosophy, Christian religion, and other traditionally recognized authorities, and they sought to subject the human world to purely rational analysis. The result of their work was a movement known as the Enlightenment.

Science and Society

Enlightenment thinkers sought to discover natural laws that governed human society in the same way that Newton's laws of universal gravitation and motion regulated the universe. Their search took different forms. The English philosopher John Locke (1632–1704) worked to discover natural laws of politics. He attacked divine-right theories that served as a foundation for absolute monarchy and advocated constitutional government on the grounds that sovereignty resides in the people rather than the state or its rulers. Indeed, he provided much of the theoretical justification for the Glorious Revolution and the establishment of constitutional monarchy in England. The Scottish philosopher Adam Smith turned his attention to economic affairs and held that laws of supply and demand determine what happens in the marketplace. The French nobleman Charles Louis de Secondat, better known as the Baron de Montesquieu (1689–1755), sought to establish a science of politics and discover principles that would foster political liberty in a prosperous and stable state.

The center of Enlightenment thought was France, where prominent intellectuals known collectively as *philosophes* ("philosophers") advanced the cause of reason. The philosophes were not philosophers in the traditional sense of the term so much as public intellectuals. They addressed their works more to the educated public than to scholars: instead of formal philosophical treatises, they mostly composed histories, novels, dramas, satires, and pamphlets on religious, moral, and political issues.

Voltaire

More than any other philosophe, François-Marie Arouet (1694–1778) epitomized the spirit of the Enlightenment. Writing under the pen name Voltaire, he published his first book at age seventeen. By the time of his death at age eighty-four, his published writings included some ten thousand letters and filled seventy volumes. With stinging wit and sometimes bitter irony, Voltaire championed individual freedom and attacked any institution sponsoring intolerant or oppressive policies. Targets of his caustic wit included the French monarchy and the Roman Catholic church. When the king of France sought to save money by reducing the number of horses kept in royal stables, for example, Voltaire suggested that it would be more effective to get rid of the asses who rode the horses. Voltaire also waged a long literary campaign against the Roman Catholic church, which he held responsible for fanaticism, intolerance, and incalculable human suffering. Voltaire's battle cry was *écrasez l'infame*—"crush the damned thing," meaning the church that he considered an agent of oppression.

Deism

Some philosophes were conventional Christians, and a few turned to atheism. Like Voltaire, however, most of them were deists who believed in the existence of a god but denied the supernatural teachings of Christianity, such as Jesus' virgin birth and his resurrection. To the deists the universe was an orderly realm. Deists held that a powerful god set the universe in motion and established natural laws that govern it, but did not take a personal interest in its development or intervene in its affairs. In a favorite simile of the deists, this god was like a watchmaker who did not need to interfere constantly in the workings of his creation, since it operated by itself according to rational and natural laws.

The Theory of Progress

Most philosophes were optimistic about the future of the world and humanity. They expected knowledge of human affairs to advance as fast as modern science, and they believed that rational understanding of human and natural affairs would bring about a new era of constant progress. In fact, progress became almost an ideology of the philosophes, who believed that natural science would lead to greater human control over the world while rational sciences of human affairs would lead to individual freedom and the construction of a prosperous, just, and equitable society.

The philosophes' fond wishes for progress, prosperity, and social harmony did not come to pass. Yet the Enlightenment helped to bring about a thorough cultural transformation of European society. It weakened the influence of organized religion, although it by no means destroyed institutional churches. Enlightenment thought encouraged the replacement of Christian values, which had guided European thought on religious and moral affairs for more than a millennium, with a new set of secular values arising from reason rather than revelation. Furthermore, the Enlightenment encouraged political and cultural leaders to subject society to rational analysis and intervene actively in its affairs in the interests of promoting progress and prosperity. In many ways the Enlightenment legacy continues to influence European and Euro-American societies.

Socially prominent women deeply influenced the development of Enlightenment thought by organizing and maintaining salons—gatherings where philosophes, scientists, and intellectuals discussed the leading ideas of the day. Though produced in 1814, this painting depicts the Parisian salon of Mme. Geoffrin (center left), a leading patron of the French philosophes, about 1775. In the background is a bust of Voltaire, who lived in Switzerland at the time.

During the early modern era, European society experienced a series of profound and sometimes unsettling changes. The Protestant Reformation ended the religious unity of western Christendom, and intermittent religious conflict disrupted European society for a century and more. Centralizing monarchs strengthened their realms and built a society of sovereign, autonomous, and intensely competitive states. Capitalist entrepreneurs reorganized the production and distribution of manufactured goods, and although their methods led to increased wealth, their quest for efficiency and profits clashed with traditional values. Modern science based on direct observation and mathematical explanations emerged as a powerful tool for the investigation of the natural world, and its influence extended even to thought about human affairs. Some people rejected traditional religious beliefs altogether and worked toward the construction of a new moral thought based strictly on science and reason. At just the time that European merchants, colonists, and adventurers were seeking opportunities in the larger world, European society was becoming more powerful, more experimental, and more competitive than ever before.

CHRONOLOGY

1473–1543	Life of Nicolaus Copernicus
1478	Foundation of the Spanish Inquisition
1483–1546	Life of Martin Luther
1491–1556	Life of Ignatius Loyola
1509–1547	Reign of King Henry VIII
1509–1564	Life of John Calvin
1517	Publication of the *Ninety-Five Theses*
1519–1556	Reign of Emperor Charles V
1540	Foundation of the Society of Jesus
1545–1563	Council of Trent
1556–1598	Reign of King Philip II
1564–1642	Life of Galileo Galilei
1571–1630	Life of Johannes Kepler
1588	Spanish Armada
1618–1648	Thirty Years' War
1632–1704	Life of John Locke
1642–1727	Life of Isaac Newton
1643–1715	Reign of King Louis XIV
1648	Peace of Westphalia
1689–1755	Life of the Baron de Montesquieu
1694–1778	Life of Voltaire
1723–1790	Life of Adam Smith

FOR FURTHER READING

William J. Bouwsma. *John Calvin: A Sixteenth-Century Portrait.* New York, 1989. A penetrating examination of one of the principal Protestant reformers.

Fernand Braudel. *Civilization and Capitalism, 15th to 18th Century.* 3 vols. Trans. by S. Reynolds. New York, 1981–84. A rich analysis of early capitalist society by one of the greatest historians of the twentieth century.

Paul Dukes. *The Making of Russian Absolutism, 1613–1801.* 2nd ed. London, 1990. A succinct study of two disparate centuries, the seventeenth and eighteenth, and two influential tsars, Peter and Catherine.

Robert S. Duplessis. *Transitions to Capitalism in Early Modern Europe.* Cambridge, 1997. A valuable synthesis of recent research on early capitalism and protoindustrialization.

Elizabeth L. Eisenstein. *The Printing Press as an Agent of Change.* 2 vols. Cambridge, 1979. An insightful study that examines the significance of printing for the Protestant Reformation and the scientific revolution.

G. R. Elton. *Reformation Europe, 1517–1559.* New York, 1963. An older but insightful analysis of Reformation Europe, with emphasis on religious and political developments.

Peter Gay. *The Enlightenment: An Interpretation.* 2 vols. New York, 1966–69. A classic study making the case for the Enlightenment as a turning point in European cultural history.

Margaret Jacob. *The Cultural Meaning of the Scientific Revolution.* New York, 1989. Explores the larger cultural and social implications of early modern science.

E. L. Jones. *The European Miracle: Environments, Economies, and Geopolitics in the History of Europe and Asia.* 2nd ed. Cambridge, 1987. Examines European politics and economic growth in comparative perspective.

———. *Growth Recurring: Economic Change in World History.* Oxford, 1988. Compares processes of economic growth in China, Europe, and Japan.

Leonard Krieger. *Kings and Philosophers, 1689–1789.* New York, 1970. A thoughtful analysis of European history during an age of absolutism and Enlightenment.

Thomas S. Kuhn. *The Structure of Scientific Revolutions.* 3rd ed. Chicago, 1997. An influential theoretical work that views scientific thought in larger social and cultural context.

Brian P. Levack. *The Witch-Hunt in Early Modern Europe.* New York, 1987. A compact but comprehensive survey of European witchcraft beliefs and pursuit of witches in the sixteenth and seventeenth centuries.

William H. McNeill. *The Pursuit of Power: Technology, Armed Force, and Society since A.D. 1000.* Chicago, 1982. Insightful analysis exploring the influence of sovereign states and early capitalism on military technology and organization.

Heiko A. Oberman. *Luther: Man between God and the Devil.* Trans. by E. Walliser-Schwartzbart. New Haven, 1989. A perceptive study of the first Protestant reformer by a foremost scholar.

Geoffrey Parker. *The Military Revolution: Military Innovation and the Rise of the West, 1500–1800.* Cambridge, 1988. A thoughtful essay on European military affairs in early modern times.

Kenneth Pomeranz. *The Great Divergence: China, Europe, and the Making of the Modern World Economy.* Princeton, 2000. Pathbreaking scholarly study that illuminates the economic history of the early modern world through comparison of economic development in Asian and European lands.

Eugene F. Rice Jr. and Anthony Grafton. *The Foundations of Early Modern Europe, 1460–1559.* 2nd ed. New York, 1994. Excellent introduction to political, social, economic, and cultural developments.

Simon Schama. *The Embarrassment of Riches: An Interpretation of Dutch Culture in the Seventeenth Century.* New York, 1987. A marvelous popular study of the wealthy Dutch republic at its height.

Keith Thomas. *Religion and the Decline of Magic.* New York, 1971. A riveting analysis of popular culture in early modern times, especially strong on the explanation of magic and witchcraft.

See our **Online Learning Center at www.mhhe.com/bentley3** for additional readings, practice maps, quizzes, and internet activities.

Unfamiliar words? Check out the **Primary Source Investigator CD-ROM** for an interactive glossary, interactive maps, more images, and primary sources.

Doña Marina (center) translates for Hernán Cortés (seated at top) as he enters into an alliance with the ruler of Tlaxcala.

CHAPTER 25

New Worlds: The Americas and Oceania

A remarkable young woman played a pivotal role in the Spanish conquest of Mexico. Originally called Malintzin, over the years she has come to be better known as Doña Marina, the name bestowed upon her by Spanish forces. Born about 1500 to a noble family in central Mexico, Doña Marina's mother tongue was Nahuatl, the principal language of the Aztec empire. When she was a girl, Doña Marina's family sent her to the Mexican coast as a slave, and her new family later passed her on to their neighbors in the Yucatan peninsula. During her travels she became fluent in Maya as well as her native Nahuatl language.

When Hernán Cortés arrived on the Mexican coast in 1519, his small army included a Spanish soldier who had learned the Maya language during a period of captivity in the Yucatan. But he had no way to communicate with the Nahuatl-speaking peoples of central Mexico until a Maya chieftain presented him with twelve young women, including Doña Marina, when he entered into an alliance with the foreigner. Doña Marina's linguistic talents enabled Cortés to communicate through an improbable chain of languages—from Spanish to Maya to Nahuatl and then back again—while making his way to the Aztec capital of Tenochtitlan. (Doña Marina soon learned Spanish and thus eliminated the Maya link in the linguistic chain.)

Doña Marina provided Cortés with intelligence and diplomatic as well as linguistic services. On several occasions she learned of plans by native peoples to overwhelm and destroy the tiny Spanish army, and she alerted Cortés to the danger in time for him to forestall an attack. Once she was able to report the precise details of a planned ambush because she played along with an effort to bring her into the scheme. She also helped Cortés negotiate with emissaries from Tenochtitlan and other major cities of central Mexico. Indeed, in the absence of Doña Marina's services, it is difficult to see how Cortés's small band could have survived to see the Aztec capital.

Apart from facilitating the Spanish conquest of the Aztec empire, Doña Marina also played a role in the formation of a new society in Mexico. In 1522, one year after the fall of Tenochtitlan, she gave birth to a son fathered by Cortés, and in 1526 she bore a daughter to a Spanish captain whom she had married. Her offspring were not the first children born in the western hemisphere of indigenous and Spanish parentage, but they symbolize the early emergence of a mestizo population in Mexico. Doña Marina died soon after the birth of her daughter, probably in 1527, but during her short life she contributed to the thorough transformation of Mexican society.

Until 1492 the peoples of the eastern and western hemispheres had few dealings with one another. About 1000 C.E. Norse explorers established a short-lived colony in modern Newfoundland, and sporadic encounters between European fishermen and indigenous peoples of North America probably occurred before Christopher Columbus undertook his first voyage across the Atlantic Ocean. It is likely, too, that an occasional Asian or Austronesian mariner reached the Pacific coast of North or South America before 1492. Yet travel between the eastern hemisphere, the western hemisphere, and Oceania was too irregular and infrequent to generate interaction between peoples of different societies until the fifteenth century.

After 1492, however, the voyages of European mariners led to permanent and sustained contact between the peoples of the eastern hemisphere, the western hemisphere, and Oceania. The resulting encounters brought profound and often violent change to both American and Pacific lands. European peoples possessed powerful military weapons, horses, and sailing ships that provided them with technological advantages over the peoples they encountered in the Americas and the Pacific islands. Moreover, most Europeans also enjoyed complete or partial immunity to diseases that caused demographic disasters when introduced to the western hemisphere and Oceania. Because of their technological advantages and the massive depopulation that followed from epidemic diseases, European peoples were able to establish a presence throughout the Americas and much of the Pacific Ocean basin.

The European presence did not lead to immediate change in Australia and the Pacific islands, although it laid a foundation for dramatic and often traumatic change in the nineteenth and twentieth centuries. In the western hemisphere, however, large numbers of European migrants helped to bring about a profound transformation of American societies in early modern times. In Mexico and Peru, Spanish conquerors established territorial empires that were ruled from Spain. In Brazil, Portuguese entrepreneurs founded sugar plantations and imported African slaves to perform the heavy labor required for their operation. In North America, French, English, and Dutch fur traders allied with indigenous peoples who provided them with animal skins, and their more sedentary compatriots founded settler societies concentrating on the production of cash crops for export. Throughout the western hemisphere, peoples of European, African, and American ancestry interacted to fashion a new world.

Colliding Worlds

When European peoples first sought to establish their presence in the Americas, they brought a range of technology unavailable to the peoples they encountered in the western hemisphere. Even more important than European technology, however, were the divisions between indigenous peoples that Europeans were able to exploit and the effects of epidemic diseases that devastated native societies. Soon after their arrival in the western hemisphere, Spanish conquerors toppled the Aztec and Inca empires and imposed their own rule in Mexico and Peru. In later decades Portuguese planters built sugar plantations on the Brazilian coastline. French, English, and Dutch migrants displaced indigenous peoples in North America and established settler colonies under the rule of European peoples.

The Spanish Caribbean

Tainos

The first site of interaction between European and American peoples was the Caribbean. When Spanish mariners arrived there, the Tainos (also known as Arawaks) were the most prominent people in the region. During the late centuries B.C.E., the ancestors of the Tainos had sailed in canoes from the Orinoco River valley in South

One of the earliest European depictions of Native Americans was this engraving of 1505. The caption informed readers that American peoples lived in communal society, where men took several wives but none had private possessions, and that they routinely smoked and consumed the bodies of slain enemies.

America to the Caribbean islands, and by about 900 C.E. they had settled throughout the region. The Tainos cultivated manioc and other crops, and they lived in small villages under the authority of chiefs who allocated land to families and supervised community affairs. They showed interest in the glass, beads, and metal tools that Spanish mariners brought as trade goods and offered little resistance to the visitors.

Spanish Arrival

Christopher Columbus and his immediate followers made the island of Hispaniola (which embraces modern Haiti and the Dominican Republic) the base of Spanish operations in the Caribbean. There Spanish settlers established the fort of Santo Domingo, which became the capital of the Spanish Caribbean. Columbus's original plan was to build forts and trading posts where merchants could trade with local peoples for products desired by European consumers. Within a few years of Spanish arrival, however, it became clear that the Caribbean region offered no silks or spices for the European market. If Spanish settlers wanted to maintain their presence in the Caribbean, they would need to find some way to make a living.

The settlers first attempted to support their society by mining gold. Spanish settlers were too few in number to mine gold—and in any case they were not inclined to perform heavy physical labor—so the miners came largely from the ranks of the Tainos. Recruitment of labor came through an institution known as the *encomienda,* which gave Spanish settlers (*encomenderos*) the right to compel Tainos to work in their mines or fields. In return for labor, *encomenderos* assumed responsibility to look after their workers' health and welfare and to encourage their conversion to Christianity.

Conscription of Taino labor was a brutal business. *Encomenderos* worked their charges hard and punished them severely when they did not deliver the expected quantities of gold or work sufficiently hard in the fields. Tainos occasionally organized rebellions, but their bows, arrows, and slings had little effect against horse-mounted Spanish forces wielding steel swords and firearms. By about 1515, social disruption and physical abuse had brought decline to Taino populations on the large Caribbean islands—Hispaniola, Jamaica, Puerto Rico, and Cuba—favored by Spanish settlers.

Smallpox

Serious demographic decline set in only after 1518, however, when smallpox reached the Caribbean region and touched off devastating epidemics among the peoples of the western hemisphere. To replace laborers lost to disease, *encomenderos* launched raiding parties to kidnap and enslave Tainos and other peoples. This tactic exposed additional victims to introduced diseases and hastened the decline of indigenous populations.

Under pressure of epidemic disease, the native population of the Caribbean plummeted from about four million in 1492 to a few thousand in the 1540s. Native societies themselves also passed out of existence. Only a few Taino cultural elements survived the sixteenth century: *canoe, hammock, hurricane, barbecue, maize,* and *tobacco* all derive from Taino words, but the society that generated them had largely disappeared by the middle of the sixteenth century.

From Mining to Plantation Agriculture

Deposits of gold were thin in the Caribbean, but optimistic Spanish adventurers continued to seek treasure there for a century and more. After the mid-sixteenth century, however, when Spanish explorers located exceptionally rich sources of silver in Mexico and Peru, the Caribbean became a sleepy backwater of the Spanish empire. English pirates lurked in Caribbean waters hoping to intercept imperial fleets carrying American silver to Spain, but the region was not a center of production. Then, about the 1640s, French, English, and Dutch settlers began to flock to the Caribbean with the intention of establishing plantations. It became clear that even if the Caribbean islands lacked precious metals, they offered ideal conditions for the cultivation of cash crops, particularly sugar, which would fetch high prices in European markets. Later, tobacco also became a prime cash crop of the region. Meanwhile, because indigenous populations were extinct, planters lacked the labor they needed to operate their estates, so they imported several million slaves. By 1700 Caribbean society consisted of a small class of European administrators and large masses of African slaves.

The Conquest of Mexico and Peru

Spanish interest soon shifted from the Caribbean to the American mainland, where settlers hoped to find more resources to exploit. During the early sixteenth century, Spanish *conquistadores* ("conquerors") pressed beyond the Caribbean islands, moving west into Mexico and south into Panama and Peru. Between 1519 and 1521 Hernán Cortés and a small band of men brought down the Aztec empire in Mexico, and between 1532 and 1533 Francisco Pizarro and his followers toppled the Inca empire in Peru. These conquests laid the foundations for colonial regimes that would transform the Americas.

In Mexico and Peru, Spanish explorers found societies quite different from those of the Caribbean islands. Both Mexico and Peru had been sites of agricultural societies, cities, and large states for more than a millennium. In the early fifteenth century, both lands fell under the sway of powerful imperial states: the Mexica people

Sources from the Past

First Impressions of Spanish Forces

As the Spanish army made its way to Tenochtitlan, Motecuzoma dispatched a series of emissaries to communicate with Cortés and learn his intentions. The reports that came back were not reassuring. They brought disturbing news about Spanish weapons, armor, horses, and dogs that were much larger and more aggressive than the small, barkless animals that were native to Mexico.

And when [Motecuzoma] had heard what the messengers reported, he was terrified, he was astounded. . . .

Especially did it cause him to faint away when he heard how the gun, at [the Spaniards'] command, discharged [the shot]; how it resounded as if it thundered when it went off. It indeed bereft one of strength; it shut off one's ears. And when it discharged, something like a round pebble came forth from within. Fire went showering forth; sparks went blazing forth. And its smoke smelled very foul; it had a fetid odor which verily wounded the head. And when [the shot] struck a mountain, it was as if it were destroyed, dissolved. And a tree was pulverized; it was as if it vanished; it was as if someone blew it away.

All iron was their war array. In iron they clothed themselves. With iron they covered their heads. Iron were their swords. Iron were their crossbows. Iron were their shields. Iron were their lances.

And those which bore them upon their backs, their deer [that is, horses], were as tall as roof terraces.

And their bodies were everywhere covered; only their faces appeared. They were very white; they had chalky faces; they had yellow hair, though the hair of some was black. Long were their beards; they also were yellow. They were yellow-headed. [The black men's hair] was kinky, it was curly.

And their food was like fasting food—very large, white, not heavy like [tortillas]; like maize stalks, good-tasting as if of maize stalk flour; a little sweet, a little honeyed. It was honeyed to eat; it was sweet to eat.

And their dogs were very large. They had ears folded over; great dragging jowls. They had fiery eyes—blazing eyes; they had yellow eyes—fiery yellow eyes. They had thin flanks—flanks with ribs showing. They had gaunt stomachs. They were very tall. They were nervous; they went about panting, with tongues hanging out. They were spotted like ocelots; they were varicolored.

And when Motecuzoma heard all this, he was much terrified. It was as if he fainted away. His heart saddened; his heart failed him.

SOURCE: Bernardino de Sahagún. *Florentine Codex: General History of the Things of New Spain,* 13 vols. Trans. by Arthur J. O. Anderson and Charles E. Dibble. Salt Lake City: University of Utah Press, 1950–82, 13:19–20. (Translation slightly modified.)

In light of the reports that he received, what were Motecuzoma's options for dealing with the Spanish threat?

and their allies founded the Aztec empire that expanded to embrace most of Mesoamerica, while the Incas imposed their rule on a vast realm extending from modern Ecuador in the north to modern Chile in the south—the largest state South America had ever seen. The Aztec and Inca empires both had clear lines of political authority, and both had the means to mobilize massive populations, collect taxes or tribute to maintain their societies, and recruit labor for public works projects. (See chapter 21.)

Hernán Cortés

The conquest of Mexico began with an expedition to search for gold on the American mainland. In 1519 Cortés led about 450 soldiers to Mexico and made his way from Veracruz on the Gulf coast to the island city of Tenochtitlan, the stunningly beautiful Aztec capital situated in Lake Texcoco. They seized the emperor Motecuzoma II, who died in 1520 during a skirmish between Spanish forces and residents of Tenochtitlan. Aztec forces soon drove the conquistadores from the capital, but Cortés built a small fleet of ships, placed Tenochtitlan under siege, and in 1521 starved the city into surrender.

Steel swords, muskets, cannons, and horses offered Cortés and his soldiers some advantage over the forces they met and help to account for the Spanish conquest of the Aztec empire. Yet weaponry alone clearly would not enable Cortés's tiny force to overcome a large, densely populated society. Quite apart from military technology, Cortés's expedition benefited from divisions among the indigenous peoples of Mexico. With the aid of Doña Marina, the conquistadores forged alliances with peoples who resented domination by the Mexica, the leaders of the Aztec empire, and who reinforced the small Spanish army with thousands of veteran warriors. Native allies also provided Spanish forces with logistical support and secure bases in friendly territory.

Epidemic Disease

On the mainland, as in the Caribbean, epidemic disease aided Spanish efforts. During the siege of Tenochtitlan, smallpox raged through the city, killing inhabitants by the tens of thousands and fatally sapping the strength of defensive forces. Smallpox rapidly spread beyond the capital, raced through Mexico, and carried off so many people that Aztec society was unable to function. Only in the context of this massive depopulation is it possible to understand the Spanish conquest of Mexico.

Francisco Pizarro

Francisco Pizarro experienced similar results when he led a Spanish expedition from Central America to Peru. Pizarro set out in 1530 with 180 soldiers, later joined by reinforcements to make a force of about 600. The conquistadores arrived in Peru just after a bitter dispute within the Inca ruling house, and it was a simple matter for them to exploit differences between the factions. Already by 1533 they had taken the Inca capital at Cuzco. Under pretext of holding a conference, they called the Inca ruling elites together, seized them, and killed most of them. They spared the Inca ruler Atahualpa until he had delivered a large quantity of gold to Pizarro. Then they strangled him and decapitated his body. The search for treasure continued after the end of Inca rule. Pizarro and his conquistadores looted gold and silver plaques from Cuzco's temples and public buildings, melted down statuettes fashioned from precious metals, and even filched jewelry and ornaments from the embalmed bodies of deceased Inca rulers.

Several considerations help to explain how Pizarro's tiny force was able to topple the Inca empire. Many subjects of the empire despised the Incas as overlords and tax collectors and put up little resistance to Pizarro's forces. Indeed, many allied with the Spanish invaders. Epidemic disease also discouraged resistance: smallpox had spread from Mexico and Central America to Peru in the 1520s, long before Pizarro's arrival, and had already taken a heavy toll among Andean populations. Pizarro and his army actually faced more threats from fresh Spanish interlopers than from native peoples. The conquest of Peru took longer than the conquest of Mexico, but by 1540 Spanish forces had established themselves securely as lords of the land.

In this illustration from Felipe Guaman Poma de Ayala's letter of complaint to the Spanish king, conquistadores decapitate Atahualpa after executing him by strangulation in 1533.

Iberian Empires in the Americas

The conquests of Mexico and Peru were the results not of Spanish royal policy but, rather, of individual efforts by freelance adventurers. During the early days after the conquests, Cortés and Pizarro allocated lands and labor rights to their troops on their own authority. Gradually, however, the Spanish monarchy extended its control over the growing American empire, and by about 1570 the semiprivate regime of the conquistadores had given way to formal rule under the Spanish crown. Bureaucrats charged with the implementation of royal policy and the administration of royal justice replaced the soldiers of fortune who had conquered Mexico and Peru. The conquistadores did not welcome the arrival of the bureaucrats, but with the aid of Spanish lawyers, tax collectors, and military forces, royal officials had their way.

Spanish Colonial Administration

Spanish administrators established two main centers of authority in the Americas—Mexico (which they called New Spain) and Peru (known as New Castile)—each governed by a viceroy who was responsible to the king of Spain. In Mexico they built a new capital, Mexico City, on top of Tenochtitlan. In Peru they originally hoped to rule from the Inca capital of Cuzco, but they considered the high altitude unpleasant and also found the Andean city too inaccessible for their purposes. In 1535 they founded Lima and transferred the government to the coast where it was accessible to Spanish shipping.

The viceroys were the king's representatives in the Americas, and they wielded considerable power. The kings of Spain, attempting to ensure that their viceroys would not build personal power bases and become independent, subjected them to the review of courts known as *audiencias* staffed by university-educated lawyers. The *audiencias* heard appeals against the viceroys' decisions and policies and had the right to address their concerns directly to the Spanish king. Furthermore, the *audiencias* conducted reviews of viceroys' performance at the end of their terms, and negative reviews could lead to severe punishment.

In many ways, Spanish administration in the Americas was a ragged affair. Transportation and communication difficulties limited the ability of viceroys to supervise their territories. In many regions, local administration fell to *audiencias* or town councils. Meanwhile, the Spanish monarchy exercised even less influence on American affairs than the viceroys. It often took two years for the central government in Spain to respond to a query from Mexico or Peru, and many replies simply asked for further information rather than providing firm directives. Even when viceroys received clear orders that they did not like, they found ways to procrastinate: they often responded to the king that "I obey, but I do not enforce," implying that with additional information the king would alter his decision.

New Cities

Spanish rule in the Americas led to the rapid establishment of cities throughout the viceroyalties. Like their compatriots in Spain, colonists preferred to live in cities even when they derived their income from the agricultural production of their landed estates. As the numbers of migrants increased, they expanded the territory under Spanish imperial authority and built a dense network of bureaucratic control based in recently founded cities. The jurisdiction of the viceroyalty of New Spain reached from Mexico City as far as St. Augustine in Florida (founded in 1565). Administrators in Lima oversaw affairs from Panama (founded in 1519) to Concepción (founded in 1550) and Buenos Aires (founded in 1536).

Portuguese Brazil

While Spanish conquistadores and administrators built a territorial empire in Mexico and Peru, Portuguese forces established an imperial presence in Brazil. The Portuguese presence came about by an odd twist of diplomatic convention. In 1494 Spain and Portugal signed the Treaty of Tordesillas, which divided the world along an imaginary north-south line 370 leagues west of the Azores and Cape Verde Islands. According to this agreement, Spain could claim any land west of that line, so long as it was not already under Christian rule, and Portugal gained the same rights for lands east of the line. Thus Portugal gained territory along the northeastern part

MAP [25.1]
European empires and colonies in the Americas about 1700.

For an interactive version of this map, go to www.mhhe.com/bentley3ch25maps.

of the South American continent, a region known as Brazil from the many brazilwood trees that grew along the coast, while the remainder of the western hemisphere fell under Spanish control.

The Portuguese mariner Pero Alvares Cabral sighted Brazil and stopped there briefly in 1500 while making a tack through the Atlantic Ocean en route to India. His compatriots did not display much immediate interest in the land. When French and Dutch mariners began to visit Brazilian shores, however, the Portuguese king decided to consolidate his claim to the land. He made vast land grants to Portuguese nobles in the expectation that they would develop and colonize their holdings, and later he dispatched a governor to oversee affairs and implement royal policy. Portuguese interest in Brazil rose dramatically after midcentury when entrepreneurs established profitable sugar plantations on the coast.

Colonial American Society

The cities of the Iberian empires became centers of European-style society in the Americas: the spires of churches and cathedrals defined their skylines, and Spanish and Portuguese were the languages of government, business, and society. Beyond the urban districts, however, indigenous ways of life persisted. In the Amazon basin and Paraguay, for example, native peoples produced little agricultural surplus, and there were no mineral deposits to attract European migrants. The few Spanish and Portuguese colonists who ventured to those regions learned to adapt to indigenous societies and customs: they ate bread made of manioc flour, made use of native hammocks and canoes, and communicated in the Guaraní and Tupí languages. Indeed, indigenous languages flourish even today throughout much of Latin America: among the more prominent are Nahuatl in Mexico, Quiché in Mexico and Guatemala, Guaraní in Paraguay, and Quechua in the Andean highlands of Peru, Ecuador, and Bolivia.

Spanish and Portuguese peoples saw the western hemisphere more as a land to exploit and administer than as a place to settle and colonize. Nevertheless, sizable contingents of migrants settled permanently in the Americas. Between 1500 and 1800, upwards of five hundred thousand Spanish migrants crossed the Atlantic, alongside one hundred thousand Portuguese. Their presence contributed to the making of a new world—a world characterized by intense interaction between the peoples of Europe, Africa, and the Americas—in the western hemisphere.

Settler Colonies in North America

Throughout the sixteenth century, Spanish explorers sought opportunities north of Mexico and the Caribbean. They established towns, forts, and missions from modern Florida as far north as Virginia on the east coast of North America, and they scouted shorelines off Maine and Newfoundland. On the west coast they ventured into modern Canada and established a fort on Vancouver Island. By midcentury, French, English, and Dutch mariners sailed the North Atlantic in search of fish and a northwest passage to Asia, and by the early seventeenth century they were dislodging Spanish colonists north of Florida. Their search for a northwest passage proved fruitless, but they harvested immense quantities of fish from the cod-filled banks off Labrador, Newfoundland, Nova Scotia, and New England.

Foundation of Colonies

More important, in the early seventeenth century they began to plant permanent colonies on the North American mainland. French settlers established colonies at Port Royal (Nova Scotia) in 1604 and Quebec in 1608, and English migrants founded Jamestown in 1607 and the Massachusetts Bay Colony in 1630. Dutch entrepreneurs built a settlement at New Amsterdam in 1623, but the colony did not remain long in Dutch hands: an English fleet seized it in 1664, rechristened it New York, and absorbed it into English colonial holdings. During the seventeenth and eighteenth centuries, French migrants settled in eastern Canada, and French explorers and traders scouted the St. Lawrence, Ohio, and Mississippi Rivers, building forts all the way to the Gulf of Mexico. Meanwhile, English settlers established colonies along the east coast of the present-day United States of America.

Life in these early settlements was extremely difficult. Most of the settlers did not expect to cultivate food crops but, rather, hoped to sustain their communities by producing valuable commodities such as fur, pitch, tar, or lumber, if not silver and gold. They relied heavily on provisions sent from Europe, and when supply ships did not arrive as expected, they sometimes avoided starvation only because indigenous peoples provided them with food. In Jamestown, food shortages and disease became so severe that only sixty of the colony's five hundred inhabitants survived the winter of 1609–1610. Some settlers went so far as to disinter corpses and consume the flesh of their departed neighbors. One man even slaughtered and ate his wife.

Colonial Government

The French and English colonies in North America differed in several ways from Iberian territories to the south. Whereas Iberian explorations had royal backing, private investors played larger roles in French and English colonial efforts. Individuals put up the money to finance expeditions to America, and they retained much more control over their colonies' affairs than did their Iberian counterparts. Although English colonies were always subject to royal authority, for example, they also maintained their own assemblies and influenced the choice of royal governors: there were no viceroys or *audiencias* in the North American colonies. At the conclusion of the Seven Years' War (1763), the French colony in Canada fell under British control, and it too soon acquired institutions of self-government.

Relations with Indigenous Peoples

French and English colonies differed from Iberian territories also in their relationships with indigenous peoples. French and English migrants did not find large, centralized states like the Aztec and Inca empires. Nor did they encounter agricultural peoples living in densely settled societies. Although most of them spoke Algonquian, Iroquois, or Lakota languages, the peoples of eastern North America had formed dozens of distinct societies. Many of them practiced agriculture, but most also relied on hunting and consequently moved their villages frequently in pursuit of game. They did not claim ownership of precisely bounded territories, but they regularly migrated between well-defined regions.

When European settlers saw forested lands not bearing crops, they staked out farms and excluded the indigenous peoples who had frequently visited the lands dur-

A painting of the English settlement at Jamestown in the early seventeenth century illustrates the precarious relations between European settlers and indigenous peoples. Note the heavy palisades and numerous cannons deployed within the fort, as well as the imposing figure of the native chief Powhatan depicted outside the settlement's walls.

ing the course of their migrations. The availability of fertile farmland soon attracted large numbers of European migrants. Upwards of 150,000 English migrants moved to North America during the seventeenth century alone, and sizable French, German, Dutch, and Irish contingents joined them in the search for land.

European migrants took pains to justify their claims to American lands. English settlers in particular sought to provide legal cover for their expanding communities by negotiating treaties with the peoples whose lands they colonized. Quite apart from legal niceties, migrants also justified their occupation on the grounds that they made productive use of the land, whereas native peoples merely used it as a hunting park. In Europe, hunting was a pastime that only aristocratic and privileged classes could enjoy. Settlers did not recognize that hunting was a way of life, not a sport or hobby, for the peoples of North America.

Conflict

French and English settlers frequently clashed with native peoples who resented intrusions on their hunting grounds, but the conflicts differed from the campaigns of conquest carried out by the conquistadores in Mexico and Peru. English settlers negotiated rights to American lands by treaty, but native peoples did not appreciate the fine points of English law and frequently mounted raids on farms and villages. During an assault of 1622, for example, they massacred almost one-third of the English settlers in the Chesapeake region. Attacks on their communities brought reprisals from settlers, who ruthlessly destroyed the fields and villages of native peoples. Edward Waterhouse, who survived the raid of 1622, went so far as to advocate annihilation of the indigenous population: "Victorie may bee gained many waies: by force, by surprize, by [causing] famine [through] burning their Corne, by destroying and burning their Boats, Canoes, and Houses, by breaking their fishing Weares [nets], by assailing them in their huntings, whereby they get the greatest part of their sustenance in Winter, by pursuing and chasing them with our horses, and blood-Hounds to draw after them, and Mastives [mastiffs] to teare them."

Indeed, a combination of epidemic disease and violent conflict dramatically reduced the indigenous population of North America in early modern times. In 1492 the native population of the territory now embraced by the United States was greater than five million, perhaps as high as ten million. By the mid-sixteenth century, however, smallpox and other diseases had begun to spread north from Mexico and ravage native societies in the plains and eastern woodlands of North America. Between 1600 and 1800 about one million English, French, German, Dutch, Irish, and Scottish migrants crossed the Atlantic and sought to displace native peoples as they pursued economic opportunities in North America. By 1800 indigenous peoples in the territory of the present-day United States numbered only six hundred thousand, as against almost five million settlers of European ancestry and about one million slaves of African ancestry. Although the settler colonies of North America differed markedly from the Iberian territorial empires to the south, they too contributed greatly to the transformation of the western hemisphere.

Colonial Society in the Americas

The European migrants who flooded into the western hemisphere interacted both with the native inhabitants and with African peoples whom they imported as enslaved laborers. Throughout the Americas, relations between individuals of American, European, and African ancestry soon led to the emergence of mestizo populations. Yet European peoples and their Euro-American offspring increasingly dominated political and economic affairs in the Americas. They mined precious metals, cultivated cash crops like sugar and tobacco, and trapped fur-bearing animals to supply capitalist markets that met the voracious demands of European and Asian consumers. Over time they also established their Christian religion as the dominant faith of the western hemisphere.

The Formation of Multicultural Societies

Cabeza de Vaca

Many parts of the Americas remained outside European control until the nineteenth century. Only rarely did Europeans venture into the interior regions of the American continents in the sixteenth century, and those who did, like the adventurer Alvar Nuñez Cabeza de Vaca, often found themselves at the mercy of the native inhabitants. Cabeza de Vaca was a Spanish nobleman who joined an expedition of some three hundred explorers who went from Hispaniola to investigate Florida in 1527. Most members of the expedition soon perished because of inadequate supplies, the harsh environment, and clashes with indigenous forces. Cabeza de Vaca and a small group of survivors built small boats to make their way west across the Gulf of Mexico to New Spain. But disaster struck when the strong current of the Mississippi River pushed the flotilla into the gulf and a fierce storm destroyed the makeshift vessels. The shipwrecked adventurers washed up near modern Galveston, Texas, and soon fell captive to native inhabitants. For the next eight years, Cabeza de Vaca and three companions lived in several different societies, serving sometimes as slaves and sometimes as physicians, before finding their way to Mexico in 1536.

Mestizo Societies

Although their influence reached the American interior only gradually, European migrants radically transformed the social order in the regions where they established imperial states or settler colonies. All European territories became multicultural societies where peoples of varied ancestry lived together under European or Euro-American dominance. Spanish and Portuguese territories soon became not only multicultural but ethnically mixed as well, largely because of migration patterns. Migrants to the Iberian colonies were overwhelmingly men: about 85 percent of the Spanish migrants were men, and the Portuguese migration was even more male-dominated than the Spanish. Because of the small numbers of European women, Spanish and Portuguese migrants entered into relationships with native women, which soon gave rise to an increasingly mestizo (or mixed) society.

Most Spanish migrants went to Mexico, where there was soon a growing population of mestizos—individuals of Spanish and native parentage, like the children of Doña Marina. Women were more prominent among the migrants to Peru than to Mexico, and Spanish colonists there lived mostly in cities, where they maintained a more distinct community than did their counterparts in Mexico. In the colonial cities, Spanish migrants married among themselves and re-created a European-style society. In less settled regions, however, Spanish men associated with native women and gave rise to mestizo society.

With few European women available in Brazil, Portuguese men readily entered into relations both with native women and with African slave women. Brazil soon had large populations not only of mestizos but also of mulattoes born of Portuguese and African parents, *zambos* born of indigenous and African parents, and other combinations arising from these groups themselves. Indeed, marriages between members of different racial and ethnic communities became very common in colonial Brazil and generated a society even more thoroughly mixed than that of mestizo Mexico.

The Social Hierarchy

In both the Spanish and the Portuguese colonies, migrants born in Europe known as *peninsulares* (those who came from the Iberian peninsula) stood at the top of the social hierarchy, followed by *criollos* or creoles, individuals born in the Ameri-

During the eighteenth century, Euro-American artists often depicted families to illustrate the physical characteristics of individuals of different ancestry. The household scene here presents a mestizo father, a Spanish mother, and their daughter, referred to as a *castiza*.

cas of Iberian parents. In the early days of the colonies, mestizos lived on the fringes of society. As time went on, however, the numbers of mestizos grew, and they became essential contributors to their societies, especially in Mexico and Brazil. Meanwhile, mulattoes, zambos, and other individuals of mixed parentage became prominent groups in Brazilian society, although they were usually subordinate to European migrants, Euro-American creoles, and even mestizos. In all the Iberian colonies, imported slaves and conquered peoples stood at the bottom of the social hierarchy.

North American Societies

The social structure of the French and English colonies in North America differed markedly from that of the Iberian colonies. Women were more numerous among the French and especially the English migrants than in Spanish and Portuguese communities, and settlers mostly married within their own groups. French fur traders often associated with native women and generated *métis* (the French equivalent of mestizos) in regions around forts and trading posts. In French colonial cities like Port Royal and Quebec, however, liaisons between French and native peoples were less common.

Mingling between peoples of different ancestry was least common in the English colonies of North America. Colonists disdained the native peoples they encountered and regarded them as lazy heathens who did not recognize private property and did not exert themselves to cultivate the land. Later they also scorned imported African slaves as inferior beings. These attitudes fueled a virulent racism, as English settlers attempted to maintain sharp boundaries between themselves and peoples of American and African ancestry.

Yet even English settlers interacted with American and African peoples, and they readily borrowed useful cultural elements from other communities. They learned about American plants and animals, for example, and they used native terms to refer to unfamiliar animals such as raccoons and opossums or trees such as hickory and pecan. They adapted moccasins and deerskin clothes, and they gave up European military customs of marching in massed ranks and announcing their presence with drums and flying colors. From their slaves they borrowed African food crops and techniques for the cultivation of rice. Yet, unlike their Iberian neighbors to the south, the English settlers strongly discouraged relationships between individuals of different ancestry and mostly refused to accept or even acknowledge offspring of mixed parentage.

Mining and Agriculture in the Spanish Empire

From the Spanish perspective the greatest attractions of the Americas were precious metals, which drew thousands of migrants from all levels of Spanish society. The conquistadores thoroughly looted the easily accessible treasures of the Aztec and Inca empires. Ignoring the artistic or cultural value of artifacts, the conquerors simply melted down silver and gold treasures and fashioned them into ingots. Their followers opened mines to extract the mineral wealth of the Americas in more systematic fashion.

Silver Mining

Gold was not the most abundant American treasure. Silver far outweighed gold in quantity and value, and much of Spain's American enterprise focused on its extraction. Silver production concentrated on two areas: the thinly populated Mexican north, particularly the region around Zacatecas, and the high, cold central Andes,

Mining operations at Potosí gave rise to a large settlement that housed miners and others who supplied food, made charcoal, fashioned tools, and supported the enterprise. In this illustration from the mid-1580s, llamas laden with silver ore descend the mountain (background) while laborers work in the foreground to crush the ore and extract pure silver from it.

particularly the stunningly rich mines of Potosí. Both sites employed large numbers of indigenous laborers. Many laborers went to Zacatecas voluntarily as their home villages experienced the pressures of conquest and disease. Over time they became professional miners, spoke Spanish, and lost touch with the communities of their birth.

Meanwhile, Spanish prospectors discovered a large vein of silver near Potosí in 1545 and began large-scale mining there in the 1580s. By 1600 Potosí was a boomtown with a population of 150,000. Rapid growth created an explosive demand for labor. As in the Mexican mines, Spanish administrators relied mostly on voluntary labor, but they also adapted the Inca practice of requisitioning draft labor, known as the *mita* system, to recruit workers for particularly difficult and dangerous chores that free laborers would not accept. Under the *mita* system, Spanish authorities annually required each native village to send one-seventh of its male population to work for four months in the mines at Potosí. Draft laborers received payment for their work, but wages were very low, and the conditions of work were extremely harsh. Some *mita* laborers hauled heavy baskets of silver ore up steep mine shafts, while others worked with toxic mercury, which miners used to separate the silver from its ore. Death rates of draft laborers were high, and many native men sought to evade *mita* obligations by fleeing to cities or hiding in distant villages. Thus, even though at any given moment draft laborers represented only about 10 percent of the workforce at Potosí, the *mita* system touched a large portion of the indigenous population and influenced settlement patterns throughout the Andean region.

The Global Significance of Silver

The mining industries of Mexico and Peru powered the Spanish economy in the Americas and even stimulated the world economy of early modern times. Silver produced profits for private investors and revenues for the crown. The Spanish government reserved a fifth of the silver production for itself. This share, known as the *quinto,* represented the principal revenue that the crown derived from its American possessions. American silver helped Spanish kings finance a powerful army and bureaucracy, but much of it also went well beyond Spain to lubricate the European and the larger world economies.

Most American silver made its way across the Atlantic to Spain and markets throughout Europe, and from there European merchants traded it for silk, spices, and porcelain in the markets of Asia. Some silver went from Acapulco on the west coast of Mexico across the Pacific in the Manila galleons, and from Manila it also made its way to Asian markets. No matter which direction it went or which oceans it crossed, American silver quickly traveled throughout the world and powerfully stimulated global trade.

The Hacienda

Apart from mining, the principal occupations in Spanish America were farming, stock raising, and craft production. The organization of mining industries created opportunities for cultivators, herders, and artisans to provision mining towns with food, wine, textiles, tools, furniture, and craft items. By the seventeenth century the most prominent site of agricultural and craft production in Spanish America was the estate, or hacienda, which produced foodstuffs for its own use as well as for sale to local markets in nearby mining districts, towns, and cities. The products of the hacienda were mostly of European origin: wheat, grapes, and meat from pigs and cattle were the most prominent agricultural products. Bordering the large estates were smaller properties owned by Spanish migrants or creoles as well as sizable tracts of land held by indigenous peoples who lived in native villages and practiced subsistence agriculture.

Labor Systems

The major source of labor for the haciendas was the indigenous population. Spanish conquerors first organized native workforces under the *encomienda* system. As originally developed in Spain during the era of the *reconquista* (see chapter 20), the *encomienda* system rewarded Spanish conquerors by allowing them to exact both labor and tribute from defeated Moorish populations, while requiring the *encomenderos* to look after the physical and spiritual welfare of their workers. Later, Spanish conquerors transferred the system to the Caribbean, Mexico, and Andean South America. From the 1520s to 1540s, the *encomienda* system led to rampant abuse of indigenous peoples, as Spanish landowners overworked their laborers and skimped on their maintenance. After midcentury, *encomenderos* in agriculturally productive regions increasingly required their subject populations to provide tribute but not labor. Native populations living in native villages under native leadership owned much of the land that they cultivated. In some ways their payments to Spanish colonists resembled the tributes their ancestors had provided to Aztec rulers.

As the *encomienda* system gradually went out of use, Spanish landowners resorted to a system of debt peonage to recruit labor for their haciendas. Under this system, landowners advanced loans to native peoples so that they could buy seeds, tools, and supplies. The debtors then repaid the loans with labor, but wages were so low that they were never able to pay off their debts. Because legal restrictions prevented debtors from fleeing and escaping their obligations, landowners had in effect a captive labor force to work their estates.

Resistance to Spanish Rule

The Spanish regimes in the Americas met considerable resistance from indigenous peoples. Resistance took various forms: rebellion, halfhearted work, and retreat into the mountains and forests where Spanish power did not reach. In 1680, for example, after experiencing nearly a century of forced labor on Spanish estates, several native groups in northern Mexico (the modern-day American state of New Mexico) mounted a large uprising known as the Pueblo revolt. Led by a native shaman named Popé, the rebels attacked missions, killed priests and colonists, and drove Spanish settlers out of the region for twelve years. Spanish forces in Peru faced an even larger rebellion in 1780, when a force of about sixty thousand native peoples revolted in the name of Túpac Amaru, the last of the Inca rulers, whom Spanish conquistadores had beheaded in 1572. This Túpac Amaru rebellion raged for almost two years before Spanish forces suppressed it and executed thousands of its participants.

Felipe Guaman Poma de Ayala depicted himself several times in his letter of complaint. Here, kneeling, he presents a copy of his work to the king of Spain. In fact, Guaman Poma never traveled to Spain, and his letter never reached the king. Nevertheless, Guaman Poma's illustrations offer remarkable images of early colonial Peru.

On some occasions, indigenous peoples turned also to Spanish law and administrators in search of aid against oppressive colonists. In 1615, for example, Felipe Guaman Poma de Ayala, a native of Peru, fired off a 1,200-page letter—accompanied by some four hundred hand-drawn illustrations—to King Philip III of Spain asking for protection for native peoples against rapacious colonists. Guaman Poma's letter went astray: the king never saw it. The missive somehow made its way to Denmark, where it remained unknown in a library until 1908.

Guaman Poma's complaint serves as a record of grievances against Spanish overlords. The author wrote passionately of men ruined by overtaxation and women driven to prostitution, of Spanish colonists who grabbed the lands of native peoples and Spanish priests who seduced the wives of native men. Guaman Poma warned the king that the peoples of Peru were dying fast because of disease and abuse and that if Philip wanted anything to remain of his Andean empire, he should intervene and protect the indigenous peoples of the land.

Sugar and Slavery in Portuguese Brazil

While the Spanish American empire concentrated on the extraction of silver, the Portuguese empire in Brazil depended on the production and export of sugar. The different economic and social foundations of the Spanish and Portuguese empires led to different patterns of labor recruitment. Spanish conquistadores subjugated sedentary peoples with effective administrative systems and compelled them to provide labor in the mines and estates of Mexico and Peru. Portuguese nobles and entrepreneurs established sugar plantations in regions without the administrative machinery to recruit workers and relied instead on imported African slaves as laborers. Indeed, Africans and their descendants became the majority of the population in Brazil, not simply an auxiliary labor force as in Spanish America.

The Engenho

Colonial Brazilian life revolved around the sugar mill, or *engenho*. Strictly speaking, the term *engenho* (related to the English word *engine*) referred only to the mill itself, but it came to represent a complex of land, labor, buildings, animals, capital, and technical skills related to the production of sugar. Unlike other crops, sugarcane required extensive processing to yield molasses or refined sugar as a profitable export. Thus *engenhos* always combined agricultural and industrial enterprises. They depended both on heavy labor for the planting and harvesting of cane and on the specialized skills of individuals who understood the intricacies of the sugar-making process. As a result, *engenhos* were among the most complex business enterprises in the Americas.

In a colonial economy where sugar figured as the most important export, the Portuguese planters and owners of sugar mills were a privileged class, exercising political, social, and economic power. As long as they contributed to the government's revenues, they could usually count on strong royal support. The planters acted like landed nobility, but the nature of their enterprises required them to pay attention to affairs like businessmen. They operated on very small profit margins. Their exalted social position often disguised difficult financial predicaments, and turnover in the business was always high.

The Search for Labor

Like their Spanish counterparts, Portuguese colonists first tried to enlist local populations as laborers. Unlike the inhabitants of Mexico and Peru, however, the peoples of Brazil were not sedentary cultivators. They resisted efforts to commandeer their labor, evaded Portuguese forces by retreating to interior lands, and took every opportunity to escape captors who managed to force them into servitude. From the Portuguese perspective, relying on native peoples as laborers had an additional drawback. In Brazil, as elsewhere in the Americas, epidemic diseases devastated indigenous populations. During the 1560s smallpox and measles ravaged the whole Brazilian coast, making it difficult for Portuguese settlers even to find potential laborers, let alone force them to work.

Slavery

Faced with these difficulties, the colonists turned to another labor source: the African slave. Portuguese plantation managers imported slaves as early as the 1530s, but they began to rely on African labor on a large scale only in the 1580s. The labor demands of cane cultivation and sugar production exacted a heavy toll from slave communities. Arduous working conditions, mistreatment, tropical heat, poor nutrition, and inadequate housing combined to produce high rates of disease and mortality: *engenhos* typically lost 5 to 10 percent of their slaves annually. In Brazil, as in most other plantation societies, the number of deaths in the slave population usually exceeded the number of births, so there was a constant demand for more slaves.

The system had its critics, but government officials mostly left matters of labor management to slave owners. To them the balance sheet of sugar production dictated practices that paid scant heed to the preservation of slaves' lives, as long as the owners realized profits. Indeed, if a slave lived five to six years, the investment of the average owner doubled and permitted him to purchase a new and healthy slave without taking a monetary loss. Hence owners had little economic incentive to improve conditions for slaves or to increase their birthrates. Children required financial outlays for at least twelve years, which from the perspective of the owner represented a financial loss. All told, the business of producing Brazilian sugar was so brutal that every ton of the sweet substance cost one human life.

Fur Traders and Settlers in North America

The Fur Trade

European mariners first frequented North American shores in search of fish. Although fishing was a profitable enterprise, trade in furs became far more lucrative. The North American fur trade began when fishermen bartered for fur with local peoples. After explorers found a convenient entrance to rich fur-producing regions through the Hudson Strait and Hudson Bay, they began the systematic exploitation of the northern lands. Royal agents, adventurers, businessmen, and settlers began to connect large parts of the North American interior by a chain of forts and trading posts. Indigenous peoples trapped animals for Europeans and exchanged the pelts for manufactured goods such as wool blankets, iron pots, firearms, and distilled spirits. The hides went mostly to Europe, where capitalist markets experienced burgeoning demand for beaver skin hats and fur clothing.

Effects of the Fur Trade

The fur trade generated tremendous conflict. American beaver populations, which were the chief targets of the trade, declined so rapidly that trappers constantly had to push farther inland in search of untapped beaver grounds. When hunting grounds became depleted, native peoples poached or invaded others' territories, which frequently led to war.

The fur trade also took place in the context of competition between European states. This competitive atmosphere contributed to further conflict, as indigenous peoples became embroiled in their patrons' rivalries. During the mid-seventeenth century, for example, Iroquois peoples who were allies of Dutch fur traders in New Amsterdam launched a war against Hurons living north of the Great Lakes. Equipped with firearms supplied by their Dutch allies, the Iroquois sought to exterminate the Hurons and extend their trapping to the northern lands. Hurons survived the war, although in greatly diminished numbers, but the Iroquois vastly increased their strength and destroyed Huron power.

Settler Society

European settler-cultivators posed an even more serious challenge to native ways of life than did the fur traders, since they displaced indigenous peoples from the land and turned hunting grounds into plantations. The earliest colonists experienced difficult times, since European crops like wheat did not grow well in their settlements. Indeed, many of the early colonies would have perished except for maize, game, and fish supplied by native peoples. Over time, however, French and especially English migrants stabilized their societies and distinguished them sharply from those of indigenous peoples.

Cash Crops

As colonists' numbers increased, they sought to integrate their American holdings into the larger capitalist economy of the Atlantic Ocean basin by producing cash crops that they could market in Europe. In the English colonies of Virginia and Carolina, settlers concentrated on the cultivation of tobacco. As early as 1616, Virginia colonists exported 2,300 pounds of tobacco. European demand for the addictive weed resulted in skyrocketing exports amounting to two hundred thousand pounds in 1624 and three million pounds in 1638. By the eighteenth century settlers in the southern colonies had established plantation complexes that produced rice and indigo as well as tobacco, and by the nineteenth century cotton also had become a prominent plantation crop.

European moralists often denounced tobacco as a noxious weed, and they associated its use with vices like drunkenness, gambling, and prostitution. Nevertheless, its popularity surged in Europe, and later in Africa and Asia as well, after its introduction from the Americas.

Indentured Labor

The plantations created high demand for cheap labor. Colonists in North America displaced indigenous peoples but could not subjugate them or induce them to labor in their fields. Planters initially met the demand for cheap labor by recruiting indentured servants from Europe. People who had little future in Europe—the chronically unemployed, orphans, political prisoners, and criminals—were often willing to sell a portion of their working lives in exchange for passage across the Atlantic and a new start in life. Throughout the seventeenth and eighteenth centuries, indentured servants streamed into the American colonies in hopes that after they had satisfied their obligation to provide four to seven years of labor they might become independent artisans or planters themselves. (The indentured labor trade in the Americas continued on a smaller scale even into the early twentieth century.) Some indentured servants went on to become prominent figures in colonial society, but many died of disease or overwork before completing their terms of labor, while others found only marginal employment.

Slavery in North America

Most indentured servants eventually gained their freedom, but other suppliers of cheap labor remained in bondage all their lives. Like settlers in the Iberian colonies, English settlers in North America found uses for slave labor from Africa. In 1619 a group of about twenty Africans reached Virginia, where they worked alongside European laborers as indentured servants. Over time, some individual blacks fell into permanent servitude, while others continued to work as indentured laborers, and some gained their freedom. In 1661, however, Virginia law recognized all blacks as slaves, and after 1680 planters increasingly replaced indentured servants with African slaves. By 1750 about 120,000 black slaves tilled Chesapeake tobacco, and another 180,000 cultivated Carolina rice.

Slave labor was not prominent in the northern colonies, principally because the land and climate were not suitable for the cultivation of labor-intensive cash crops. Nevertheless, the economies of these colonies also profited handsomely from slavery. Many New England merchants traded in slaves destined for the West Indies: by the mid-eighteenth century, half the merchant fleet of Newport carried human cargo. The economies of New York and Philadelphia benefited from the building and outfitting of

An eighteenth-century engraving depicts work on a plantation: African slaves prepare flour and bread from manioc (left) while others hang tobacco leaves to dry in a shed (right). A male turkey—a fowl native to the Americas—ignores the bustle and displays his feathers (right foreground).

slave vessels, and the seaports of New England became profitable centers for the distillation of rum. The chief ingredient of this rum was slave-produced sugar from the West Indies, and merchants traded much of the distilled spirits for slaves on the African coast. Thus, although the southern plantation societies became most directly identified with a system that exploited African labor, all the North American colonies participated in and profited from the slave trade.

Christianity and Native Religions in the Americas

Like Buddhists and Muslims in earlier centuries, European explorers, conquerors, merchants, and settlers took their religious traditions with them when they traveled overseas. The desire to spread Christianity was a prominent motive behind European ventures overseas, and missionaries soon made their way to the Americas as well as other lands where Europeans established a presence.

Spanish Missionaries

From the beginning of Spanish colonization in Mexico and Peru, priests served as representatives of the crown and reinforced civil administrators. Franciscan, Dominican, and Jesuit missionaries campaigned to Christianize indigenous peoples. In Mexico, for example, a group of twelve Franciscan missionaries arrived in 1524. They founded a school in Tlatelolco, the bustling market district of the Aztec capital of Tenochtitlan, where they educated the sons of prominent noble families in Latin, Spanish, and Christian doctrine. The missionaries themselves learned native languages and sought to explain Christianity in terms understandable to their audiences. They also compiled a vast amount of information about native societies in hopes of learning how best to communicate their message. The work of the Franciscan Bernardino de Sahagún was especially important. Sahagún preserved volumes of information about the language, customs, beliefs, literature, and history of Mexico before the arrival of Spanish forces there. His work remained largely unstudied until

Contexts & Connections

The Holy Herb Nicotine

When he arrived at the island of San Salvador in 1492, Christopher Columbus observed the native Tainos smoking the leaves of a local plant through a pipe called a *tobago*—the origin of the word *tobacco*. Later, European visitors frequently recorded tobacco consumption among indigenous American peoples, who had used the plant as early as two thousand years ago for ritual, medicinal, and social purposes. Maya worshipers blew tobacco smoke from their mouths as offerings to the gods. Priests of the Aztec empire both smoked tobacco and took it in the form of snuff as an accompaniment to religious sacrifices. Elsewhere, native peoples of the Americas rubbed tobacco into their bodies, chewed it, ate it, or drank tobacco tea.

The widespread popularity of this plant was due to the addictive nature of nicotine, an oily, toxic substance present in tobacco leaves and named after the French diplomat, Jean Nicot, who introduced tobacco to Paris in 1560. In small quantities, nicotine acts as a stimulant, both speeding up the heartbeat and increasing the flow of adrenaline in users' systems, while also inducing a sense of relaxation and suppressing sensations of hunger and thirst. In large doses, it causes users to experience visions, fall into trances, or even lapse into catatonia.

Spanish and English promoters first touted the health benefits of tobacco to European consumers. Many European physicians ascribed miraculous powers to tobacco, which they referred to as "the herb panacea," "divine tobacco," or "the holy herb nicotine." Some maintained that tobacco would cure cancer, sores, and broken limbs, while others even claimed that it would protect users from bubonic plague. The notion that tobacco had health benefits was not a European monopoly: Chinese physicians also heralded tobacco as a medicine for the treatment of skin disease, colds, malaria, and obesity.

In any case, merchants and mariners soon spread the use of tobacco throughout Europe and beyond to all parts of the world that European ships visited. Portuguese mariners were particularly effective emissaries: they introduced tobacco smoking to India, China, Japan, sub-Saharan Africa, and southwest Asia. In 1612 English settlers cultivated the first commercial crop of tobacco in the colony of Virginia, and within a few years tobacco had become the colony's largest export. By the late seventeenth century, most consumers were using tobacco for pleasure and social reasons rather than the alleged health benefits, which never quite lived up to expectations.

Tobacco came under serious scrutiny in the twentieth century when scientists recognized the addictive nature of nicotine and the risk of lung cancer associated with smoking. In the 1930s German physician Fritz Lickint coined the term "passive smoking" and showed that it posed a health threat to nonsmokers. The Nazi regime (1933–1945) subsequently launched an aggressive antismoking campaign involving public education, advertising bans, and restrictions on smoking in public places. Nazi measures had limited effect on German smoking habits, but after the 1950s scientists in other lands amply confirmed the dangers of smoking. although no longer considered holy or healthful, tobacco nevertheless remains a major commercial crop around the globe.

the twentieth century, but in recent times it has shed enormous light both on Aztec society and on the methods of early missionaries in Mexico.

Survival of Native Religions

Christian missionaries encountered considerable resistance in the Americas. In both Mexico and Peru, indigenous peoples continued to observe their inherited faiths into the seventeenth century and beyond, even though Spanish authorities sponsored the Roman Catholic faith and tried to eliminate the worship of pagan deities. Native peoples honored idols in caves and inaccessible mountain sites, and they may have occasionally even continued to sacrifice human victims to their traditional gods.

Yet Christianity won adherents in Spanish America. In the wake of conquest and epidemic disease, many native leaders in Mexico concluded that their gods had abandoned them and looked to the missionaries for spiritual guidance. When native peoples adopted Christianity, however, they blended their own interests and traditions with the faith taught by Spanish missionaries. When they learned about Roman Catholic saints, for example, they revered saints with qualities like those of their inherited gods or those whose feast days coincided with traditional celebrations.

The Virgin of Guadalupe

In Mexico, Christianity became especially popular after the mid-seventeenth century, as an increasingly mestizo society took the Virgin of Guadalupe almost as a national symbol. According to legends, the Virgin Mary appeared before a peasant near Mexico City in 1531. The site of the apparition soon became a popular local shrine visited mostly by Spanish settlers. By the 1640s the shrine attracted pilgrims from all parts of Mexico, and the Virgin of Guadalupe gained a reputation for working miracles on behalf of individuals who visited her shrine. The popularity of the Virgin of Guadalupe helped to ensure that Roman Catholic Christianity would dominate cultural and religious matters in Mexico.

French and English Missions

French and English missionaries did not attract nearly as many converts to Christianity in North America as their Spanish counterparts did in Mexico and Peru, partly because French and English colonists did not rule over conquered populations of sedentary cultivators: it was much more difficult to conduct missions among peoples who frequently moved about the countryside than among those who lived permanently in villages, towns, or cities. In addition, English colonists displayed little interest in converting indigenous peoples to Christianity. The colonists did not discourage converts, but they made little effort to seek them, nor did they welcome native converts into their agricultural and commercial society. By contrast, French missionaries worked actively among native communities in the St. Lawrence, Mississippi, and Ohio River valleys and experienced modest success in spreading Christianity. Even though native peoples did not embrace Christianity, however, the burgeoning settlements of French and especially English colonists guaranteed that European religious traditions would figure prominently in North American society.

Europeans in the Pacific

Though geographically distant from the Americas, Australia and the Pacific islands underwent experiences similar to those that transformed the western hemisphere in early modern times. Like their American counterparts, the peoples of Oceania had no inherited or acquired immunities to diseases that were common to peoples throughout the eastern hemisphere, and their numbers plunged when epidemic disease struck their populations. For the most part, however, Australia and the Pacific islands experienced epidemic disease and the arrival of European migrants later than did the Americas. European mariners thoroughly explored the Pacific basin between the sixteenth and eighteenth centuries, but only in Guam and the Mariana Islands did they establish permanent settlements before the late eighteenth century. Nevertheless, their scouting of the region laid a foundation for much more intense interactions between European, Euro-American, Asian, and Oceanic peoples during the nineteenth and twentieth centuries.

Australia and the Larger World

At least from the second century C.E., European geographers had speculated about *terra australis incognita*—"unknown southern land"—that they thought must exist in the world's southern hemisphere to balance the huge landmasses north of the equator. As European mariners reconnoitered the Atlantic and Pacific Oceans during early modern times, they watched expectantly for a southern continent. Yet their principal interest was trade, and they rarely abandoned the pursuit of profit to sail out of their way in search of an unknown land.

Dutch Exploration

When they visited the islands of southeast Asia in the quest for spices, however, they approached Australia from the west. Portuguese mariners most likely charted much of the western and northern coast of Australia as early as the 1520s, but Dutch sailors made the first recorded European sighting of the southern continent in 1606. The Dutch VOC authorized exploratory voyages, but mariners found little to encourage further efforts. In 1623, after surveying the dry landscapes of western Australia, the Dutch mariner Jan Carstenzs reported that his party had not seen "one fruit-bearing tree, nor anything that man could make use of: there are no mountains or even hills, so that it may be safely concluded that the land contains no metals, nor yields any precious woods," and he described the land as "the most arid and barren region that could be found anywhere on earth."

Nevertheless, Dutch mariners continued to visit Australia. By the mid-seventeenth century they had scouted the continent's northern, western, and southern coasts, and they had ascertained that New Guinea and Tasmania were islands separate from Australia itself. Dutch explorers were so active in the reconnaissance of Australia that Europeans referred to the southern continent as "New Holland" throughout the seventeenth

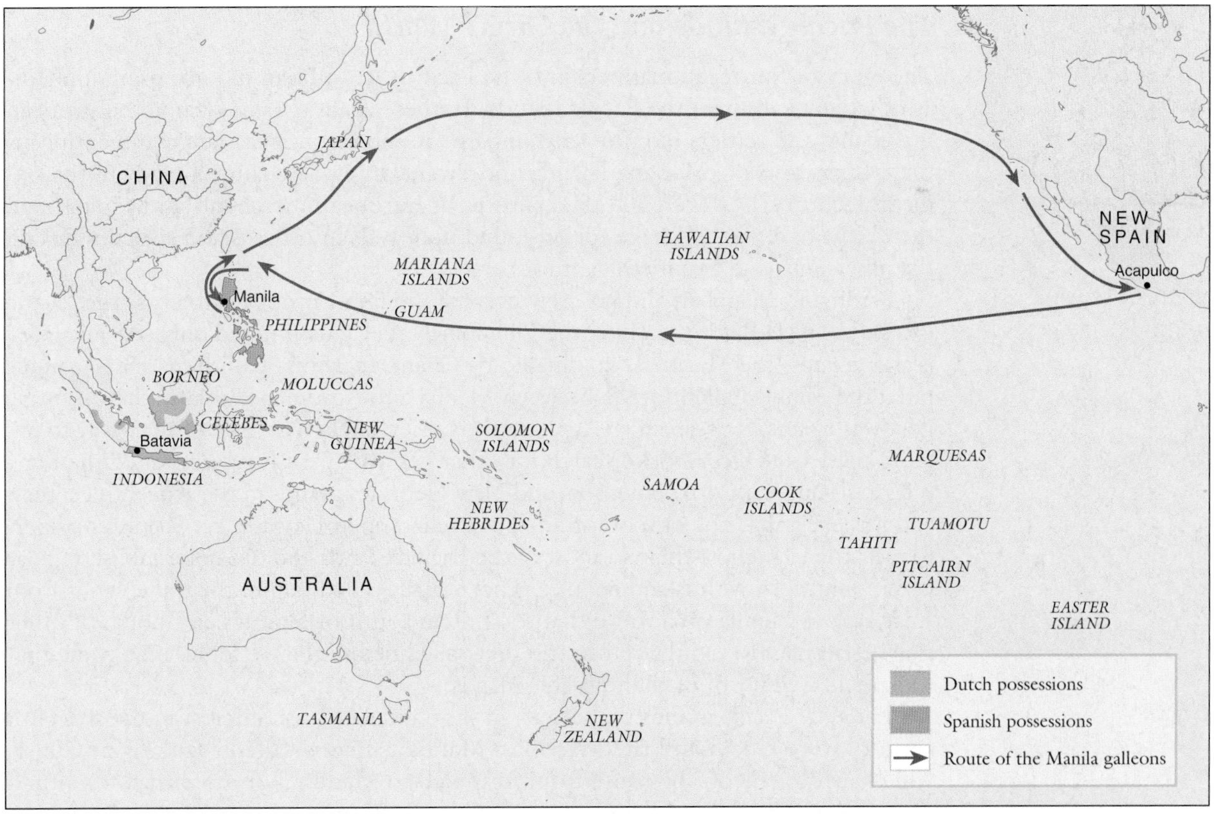

MAP [25.2]
Manila galleon route and the lands of Oceania, 1500–1800.

century. Yet neither Dutch nor any other European seamen visited the eastern coast until James Cook approached Australia from the southeast and charted the region in 1770, barely escaping destruction on the Great Barrier Reef.

Although European mariners explored Australian coastlines in the seventeenth and eighteenth centuries, they made only brief landfalls and had only fleeting encounters with indigenous peoples. The aboriginal peoples of Australia had formed many distinct foraging and fishing societies, but European visitors did not linger long enough to become familiar with either the peoples or their societies. Because they were nomadic foragers rather than sedentary cultivators, Europeans mostly considered them wretched savages. In the absence of tempting opportunities to trade, European mariners made no effort to establish permanent settlements in Australia.

British Colonists

Only after Cook's charting of the eastern coast in 1770 did European peoples become seriously interested in Australia. Cook dropped anchor for a week at Botany Bay (near modern Sydney) and reported that the region was suitable for settlement. In 1788 a British fleet arrived at Sydney carrying about one thousand passengers, eight hundred of them convicts, who established the first European settlement in Australia as a penal colony. For half a century Europeans in Australia numbered only a few thousand, most of them convicts who herded sheep. Free settlers did not outnumber convicted criminal migrants until the 1830s. Thus exploratory voyages of the seventeenth and eighteenth centuries led to fleeting encounters between European and aboriginal Australian peoples, but only in the nineteenth and twentieth centuries did a continuing stream of European migrants and settlers link Australia more directly to the larger world.

The Pacific Islands and the Larger World

The entry of European mariners into the Pacific Ocean basin did not bring immediate change to most of the Pacific islands. In these islands, as in Australia, European merchants and settlers did not arrive in large numbers until the late eighteenth century. Guam and the Mariana Islands underwent dramatic change already in the sixteenth century, however, and the ventures of European merchants and explorers in the Pacific basin set the stage for profound upheavals in other island societies during the nineteenth and twentieth centuries.

Spanish Voyages in the Pacific

Ferdinand Magellan and his crew became the first Europeans to cross the Pacific Ocean in 1521. Before reaching the Philippines, they encountered only one inhabited island group—the Marianas, dominated by Guam. In 1565 Spanish mariners inaugurated the Manila galleon trade between Manila and Acapulco. Because their primary goal was to link New Spain to Asian markets, they rarely went out of their way to explore the Pacific Ocean or to search for other islands. Spanish vessels visited the Marquesas, Tuamotu, Cook, Solomon, and New Hebrides islands in the sixteenth century, and it is likely that one or more stray ships fetched up in Hawai`i. Yet Spanish mariners found little to interest them in most of the Pacific islands and did not establish regular communications with island peoples. They usually sailed before the trade winds from Acapulco to Manila on a route that took them south of Hawai`i and north of other Polynesian islands. On the return trip they sailed before the westerlies on a route that took them well north of all the Pacific islands.

Guam

The only Pacific islands that attracted substantial Spanish interest in the sixteenth century were Guam and the Marianas. Manila galleons called regularly at Guam, which lay directly on the route from Acapulco to Manila. For more than a century, they took on fresh provisions and engaged in mostly peaceful trade with the indigenous Chamorro people. During the 1670s and 1680s, Spanish authorities decided to consolidate their position in Guam and bring the Mariana Islands under the control of the viceroy of New Spain in Mexico. They dispatched military forces to the islands to impose Spanish rule and subject the Chamorro to the spiritual authority of the Roman Catholic church. The Chamorro stoutly opposed these efforts, but a smallpox epidemic in 1688 severely reduced their numbers and crippled their resistance. By 1695 the Chamorro population had declined from about fifty thousand at mid-century to five thousand, partly because of Spanish campaigns but mostly because of smallpox. By the end of the seventeenth century, Spanish forces had established garrisons throughout the Mariana Islands and relocated surviving Chamorro into communities supervised by Spanish authorities.

Visitors and Trade

Like the aboriginal peoples of Australia, the indigenous peoples of the Pacific islands had mostly fleeting encounters with European visitors during early modern times. By the late eighteenth century, however, growing European and Euro-American interest in the Pacific Ocean basin led to sharply increased interactions between islanders and mariners. English and French mariners explored the Pacific basin in search of commercial opportunities and the elusive northwest passage from Europe to Asia. They frequently visited Tahiti after 1767, and they soon began to trade with the islanders: European mariners received provisions and engaged in sexual relations with Tahitian women in exchange for nails, knives, iron tools, and textiles. Although trade was mostly peaceful, misunderstandings often led to minor skirmishes, and European captains occasionally trained their cannons on fleets of war canoes or villages in the Pacific islands.

Captain Cook and Hawai`i

The experiences of Captain James Cook in Hawai`i illustrate a common pattern. In 1778, while sailing north from Tahiti in search of the northwest passage, Cook happened across the Hawaiian Islands. He immediately recognized Hawaiians as a people related to Tahitians and other Polynesians whose lands he had visited during his explorations of the Pacific Ocean since 1768, and he was able to communicate with Hawaiians on the basis of familiarity with Polynesian languages. Apart from some early concerns about thievery, Cook and his crew mostly got along well with Hawaiians, who readily traded pigs and provisions for iron wares. Sailors and island women avidly consorted with one another, resulting in the transmission of venereal diseases to Hawai`i, even though Cook had ordered infected crewmen to remain

As depicted in 1816 by artist Ludwig Choris, the port of Honolulu in the Hawaiian Islands was home to European ships, horses, cattle, and warehouses as well as Hawaiians inhabiting traditional dwellings and keeping native pigs.

Sources from the Past

Captain James Cook on the Hawaiians

Spanish mariners may well have been the first Europeans to visit the Hawaiian Islands, but Captain James Cook made the earliest surviving record of a European visit. His journal entries for the first few days of his visit depict a thriving society closely related to those of Tahiti and other Polynesian islands.

[Monday, 19 January 1778] There were three and four men in each [canoe] and we were agreeably surprised to find them of the same nation as the people of Otahiete [Tahiti] and the other [Polynesian] islands we had lately visited. It required but very little address to get them to come along side, but we could not prevail upon any one to come on board; they exchanged a few fish they had in the Canoes for any thing we offered them, but valued nails, or iron above every other thing; the only weapons they had were a few stones in some of the Canoes and these they threw overboard when they found they were not [needed]. . . . As soon as we made sail the Canoes left us, but others came off from the shore and brought with them roasting pigs and some very fine [sweet] Potatoes, which they exchanged, as the others had done, for whatever was offered them; several small pigs were got for a sixpenny nail or two apiece, so that we again found our selves in the land of plenty. . . .

[Tuesday, 20 January 1778] The next morning we stood in for the land and were met by several Canoes filled with people, some of them took courage and ventured on board. I never saw Indians so much astonished at the entering a ship before, their eyes were continually flying from object to object, the wildness of their looks and actions fully expressed their surprise and astonishment at the several new objects before them and evinced that they never had been on board of a ship before. However the first man that came on board did not with all his surprise forget his own interest, the first moveable thing that came in his way was the lead and line, which he without asking any questions took to put into his Canoe and when we stopped him said "I am only going to put it into my boat" nor would he quit it till some of his countrymen spoke to him. . . .

As there were some venereal complaints on board both the Ships, in order to prevent its being communicated to these people, I gave orders that no Women, on any account whatever were to be admitted on board the Ships, I also forbid all manner of connection with them, and ordered that none who had the venereal upon them should go out of the ships. But whether these regulations had the desired effect or not time can only discover. . . .

[Wednesday, 21 January 1778] As soon as every thing was settled to my satisfaction, I . . . took a walk up the Valley, accompanied by Dr. Anderson and Mr. Webber, conducted by one of the Natives and attended by a tolerable train. Our guide proclaimed our approach and every one whom we met fell on their faces and remained in that position till we passed. This, as I afterwards understood, is done to their great chiefs. Our road lay in among the Plantations, which were chiefly of Taro, and sunk a little below the common level so as to contain the water necessary to nourish the roots. . . .

At the beach I found a great crowd and a brisk trade for pigs, fowls and roots which was carried on with the greatest good order, though I did not see a man that appeared of more consequence than another if there was they did not show themselves to us. . . . No people could trade with more honesty than these people, never once attempting to cheat us, either ashore or along side the ships. Some indeed at first betrayed a thievish disposition, or rather they thought they had a right to any thing they could lay their hand upon but this conduct they soon laid aside.

SOURCE: James Cook. *The Journals of Captain Cook*. Ed. by Philip Edwards. London: Penguin, 1999, pp. 530–34. [Translation slightly modified.]

How does Cook's record of his first meeting with the Hawaiians compare and contrast with Christopher Columbus's account, presented earlier, of his first encounter with indigenous American peoples?

aboard ship. After a few weeks' stay in the islands, Cook resumed his northern course to seek the northwest passage. When he revisited Hawai`i late in 1779, he faced a very different climate, one in which islanders were less accommodating than before. Indeed, he lost his life when disputes over petty thefts escalated into a bitter conflict between his crew and islanders of Hawai`i.

Nevertheless, in the wake of Cook, whose reports soon became known throughout Europe, whalers began to venture into Pacific waters in large numbers, followed by missionaries, merchants, and planters. By the early nineteenth century, European and Euro-American peoples had become prominent figures in all the major Pacific islands groups. During the nineteenth and twentieth centuries, interactions between islanders, visitors, and migrants brought rapid and often unsettling change to Pacific islands societies.

The Americas underwent thorough transformation in early modern times. Smallpox and other diseases sparked ferocious epidemics that devastated indigenous populations and undermined their societies. In the wake of severe depopulation, European peoples toppled imperial states, established mining and agricultural enterprises, imported enslaved African laborers, and founded colonies throughout much of the western hemisphere. Some indigenous peoples disappeared entirely as distinct groups. Others maintained their communities, identities, and cultural traditions but fell increasingly under the influence of European migrants and their Euro-American offspring. In Oceania only Guam and the Mariana Islands felt the full effects of epidemic disease and migration in the early modern era. By the late eighteenth century, however, European and Euro-American peoples with advanced technologies had thoroughly explored the Pacific Ocean basin, and epidemic diseases traveled with them to Australia and the Pacific islands. As a result, during the nineteenth and twentieth centuries, Oceania underwent a social transformation similar to the one experienced earlier by the Americas.

CHRONOLOGY

1492	First voyage of Christopher Columbus to the western hemisphere
1494	Treaty of Tordesillas
1518	Smallpox epidemic in the Caribbean
1519–1521	Spanish conquest of Mexico
1532–1540	Spanish conquest of Peru
1545	Spanish discovery of silver near Potosí
1604	Foundation of Port Royal (Nova Scotia)
1607	Foundation of Jamestown
1608	Foundation of Quebec
1623	Foundation of New Amsterdam
1630	Foundation of the Massachusetts Bay Colony
1688	Smallpox epidemic on Guam
1754–1763	French and Indian war in North America
1763	Transfer of French Canadian possessions to British rule
1768–1779	Captain James Cook's exploration of the Pacific Ocean
1788	Establishment of first European colony in Australia

FOR FURTHER READING

James Axtell. *The Invasion Within: The Contest of Cultures in Colonial North America.* New York, 1985. Insightful study of the interactions between French, English, and indigenous peoples in colonial North America.

Alvar Nuñez Cabeza de Vaca. *Castaways.* Trans. by F. M. López-Morillas. Berkeley, 1993. Translation of Cabeza de Vaca's account of his shipwreck and travels through what is now the southwestern United States to Mexico.

Colin G. Callaway. *New Worlds for All: Indians, Europeans, and the Remaking of Early America.* Baltimore, 1997. Scholarly synthesis examining interactions and cultural exchanges between European and indigenous American peoples.

William Cronon. *Changes in the Land: Indians, Colonists, and the Ecology of New England.* New York, 1983. Brilliant study concentrating on the different ways English colonists and native peoples in colonial New England used the environment.

Philip D. Curtin. *The Rise and Fall of the Plantation Complex: Essays in Atlantic History.* 2nd ed. Cambridge, 1998. Examines plantation societies and slavery as institutions linking lands throughout the Atlantic Ocean basin.

Bernal Díaz del Castillo. *The Conquest of New Spain.* Trans. by J. M. Cohen. Harmondsworth, 1963. A conveniently available translation of Bernal Díaz's account of the conquest of Mexico from the viewpoint of a soldier.

Nancy M. Farriss. *Maya Society under Colonial Rule: The Collective Enterprise of Survival.* Princeton, 1984. A richly detailed analysis of early interactions between Spanish colonists and the Maya of the Yucatan.

K. R. Howe. *Where the Waves Fall: A New South Sea Island History from First Settlement to Colonial Rule.* Honolulu, 1984. A thoughtful survey of Pacific islands history emphasizing interactions between islanders and visitors.

Frances A. Karttunen. *Between Worlds: Interpreters, Guides, and Survivors.* New Brunswick, N.J., 1994. Reflective essays on Doña Marina and others who served as translators or interpreters between their own society and the larger world.

John E. Kicza. *Resilient Cultures: America's Native Peoples Confront European Colonization, 1500–1800.* Upper Saddle River, N.J., 2002. A comprehensive comparative study assessing the impact of colonization on indigenous American peoples as well as native influences on American colonial history.

Karen Ordahl Kupperman. *Indians and English: Facing Off in Early America.* Ithaca, N.Y., 2000. Fascinating reconstruction of the early encounters between English and indigenous American peoples, drawing on sources from all parties to the encounters.

Jacques Lafaye. *Quetzlcóatl and Guadalupe: The Formation of Mexican National Consciousness, 1531–1813.* Trans. by B. Keen. Chicago, 1976. Examines the blending of indigenous beliefs with Spanish beliefs and the role of religion in the formation of a Mexican national consciousness.

Miguel León-Portilla. *The Broken Spears: The Aztec Account of the Conquest of Mexico.* Rev. ed. Boston, 1992. Offers translations of indigenous accounts of the Spanish conquest of the Aztec empire.

James Lockhart. *The Nahuas after the Conquest.* Stanford, 1992. A thorough, scholarly analysis of indigenous society in central Mexico from the sixteenth to the eighteenth century.

James Lockhart and Stuart B. Schwartz. *Early Latin America: A History of Colonial Spanish America and Brazil.* New York, 1982. The best survey of colonial Latin American history.

Sabine MacCormack. *Religion in the Andes: Vision and Imagination in Early Colonial Peru.* Princeton, 1991. Analyzes the encounter between native religious beliefs and Spanish Christianity in Peru.

Gary B. Nash. *Red, White, and Black: The Peoples of Early America.* 3rd ed. Englewood Cliffs, N.J., 1992. Outstanding survey of early American history focusing on the interactions between peoples of European, African, and American ancestry.

Stuart B. Schwartz. *Sugar Plantations and the Formation of Brazilian Society.* Cambridge, 1985. Examines the roles of sugar and slavery in early colonial Brazil.

Steve J. Stern. *Peru's Indian Peoples and the Challenge of Spanish Conquest.* 2nd ed. Madison, 1993. Scholarly analysis concentrating on the social history of indigenous peoples following the Spanish conquest of Peru.

David J. Weber. *The Spanish Frontier in North America.* New Haven, 1992. A comprehensive study of Spanish efforts to explore and colonize lands north of Mexico.

Richard White. *The Middle Ground: Indians, Empires, and Republics in the Great Lakes Region, 1650–1815.* Cambridge, 1991. Insightful study of relations between French, English, and indigenous peoples in the Great Lakes region.

See our **Online Learning Center at www.mhhe.com/bentley3** for additional readings, practice maps, quizzes, and internet activities.

Unfamiliar words? Check out the **Primary Source Investigator CD-ROM** for an interactive glossary, interactive maps, more images, and primary sources.

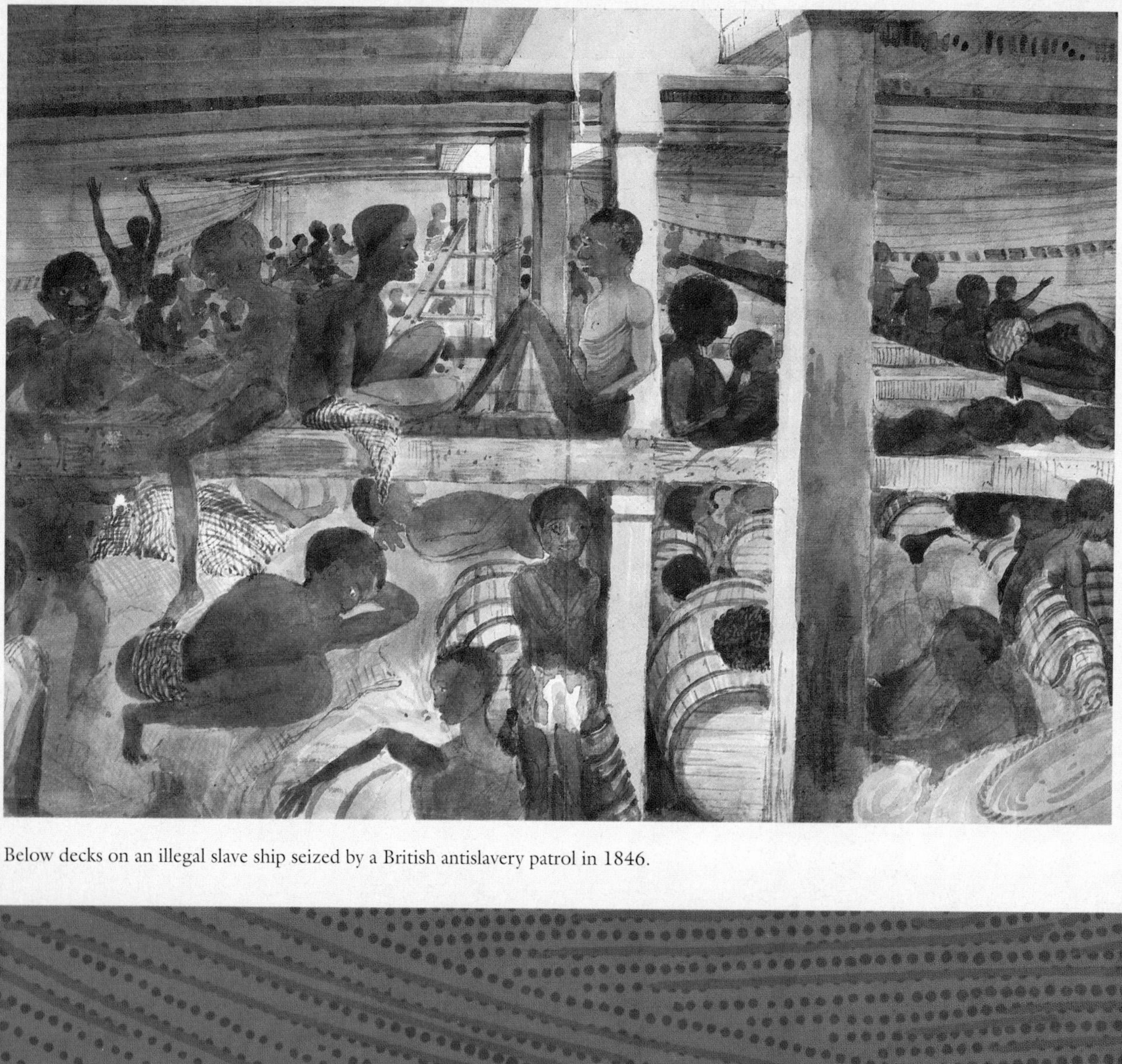

Below decks on an illegal slave ship seized by a British antislavery patrol in 1846.

CHAPTER 26

AFRICA AND THE ATLANTIC WORLD

Between 1760 and 1792, a west African man known to history as Thomas Peters crossed the Atlantic Ocean four times. In 1760 slave raiders captured Peters, whose original African name is unknown, marched him to the coast, and sold him to French slave merchants. He traveled in a slave ship to the French colony of Louisiana, where he probably worked on a sugar plantation. But Peters was not a docile servant. He attempted to escape at least three times, and his master punished him by beating him, branding him with a hot iron, and forcing him to wear shackles around his legs. During the 1760s his French master sold Peters to an English planter, and about 1770 a Scottish landowner in North Carolina bought him.

During the 1770s, as English colonists in North America prepared to rebel against the British government in the interests of "life, liberty, and the pursuit of happiness," slaves of African ancestry considered their own prospects and looked for ways to obtain personal freedom. Peters was among them. When war broke out, he made his way with his wife and daughter to British lines and joined the Black Pioneers, a company of escaped slaves who fought to maintain British rule in the colonies. When the colonists won the war, Peters escaped to Nova Scotia with his family and many other former slaves.

Blacks were legally free in Nova Scotia, but the white ruling elites forced them to till marginal lands and live in segregated villages. In hopes of improving their lot, some two hundred black families designated Peters as their spokesman and sent him to London to petition the government for better treatment or resettlement in a more favorable land. In 1790 Peters sailed to England, where he promoted the establishment of a colony for former slaves in Sierra Leone. His efforts succeeded, and the next year he returned to Nova Scotia to seek recruits for the colony. In 1792 he led 1,196 blacks aboard a convoy of fifteen ships and began his fourth crossing of the Atlantic Ocean. The colonists arrived safely at Freetown, and Peters served as a leader of the black community there. His time was short—he lived for less than four months after arriving in Sierra Leone—but through his own life and experiences Thomas Peters personified the links connecting the lands of the Atlantic Ocean basin.

For the most, part the peoples of sub-Saharan Africa continued to follow established patterns of life in early modern times. They built states and organized societies based on kinship groups as their Bantu-speaking predecessors had done for centuries. In west Africa and coastal east Africa, they also traded regularly with Muslim merchants from north Africa and southwest Asia.

Yet the establishment of global trade networks brought deep change to sub-Saharan Africa. Commercial opportunities drew European vessels to the coasts of west Africa, and maritime trade soon turned west African attention to the Atlantic. Maritime commerce did not put an end to the trans-Saharan caravan trade that linked west Africa to the Mediterranean, but it helped promote the emergence of prosperous port cities and the establishment of powerful coastal kingdoms that traded through the ocean rather than the desert. In central Africa and south Africa, European merchants brought the first substantial opportunities for long-distance trade, since Muslim merchants had not ventured to those regions in large numbers.

Trade through the Atlantic profoundly affected African society because it involved human beings. African peoples had made a place for slavery in their own societies for centuries, and they had also supplied slaves to Muslim merchants who transported them to markets in the Mediterranean and the Indian Ocean basin. The Atlantic slave trade, however, was vastly larger than the African and Islamic slave trades, and it had more serious consequences for African society. Between the fifteenth and nineteenth centuries, it not only siphoned millions of people from their own societies but also provoked turmoil in much of sub-Saharan Africa, as some peoples raided others' communities in search of captives for sale to slave traders.

The vast majority of Africans sold into the Atlantic slave trade went to destinations in the Caribbean or the Americas. Most worked on plantations cultivating cash crops for export, although some worked as domestic servants, miners, or laborers. Together they made up the largest migration in history before the nineteenth century and gave rise to an African diaspora in the western hemisphere. Under the restrictive conditions of slavery, they did not reconstitute African societies, but they also did not join European or Euro-American society. Instead, they preserved some African traditions and blended them with European and American traditions to create hybrid African-American societies.

African Politics and Society in Early Modern Times

For perhaps three millennia (2000 B.C.E. to 1000 C.E.), Bantu-speaking peoples migrated throughout sub-Saharan Africa. Many organized themselves into villages and clans governed by kinship groups rather than formal states. As their numbers grew, they devised political structures and built a series of chiefdoms and regional kingdoms. Muslim merchants, who ventured to sub-Saharan Africa after the eighth century, brought trade that encouraged the formation of large kingdoms and empires in west Africa and thriving city-states in east Africa.

African peoples continued to form states during the early modern era, but under the influence of maritime trade the patterns of state development changed. Regional kingdoms replaced the imperial states of west Africa as peoples organized their societies to take advantage of Atlantic as well as trans-Saharan commerce. The city-states of east Africa fell under the domination of Portuguese merchant-mariners seeking commercial opportunities in the Indian Ocean basin. The extension of trade networks also led to the formation of regional kingdoms in central Africa and south Africa. As the volume of long-distance trade grew, both Islam and Christianity became more prominent in sub-Saharan African societies.

The States of West Africa and East Africa

Between the eighth and sixteenth centuries, powerful kingdoms and imperial states ruled the savannas of west Africa. The earliest was the kingdom of Ghana, which originated perhaps as early as the fourth or fifth century and established its dominance in the region in the eighth century. By controlling and taxing the trans-Saharan trade in gold, the kings of Ghana gained the financial resources they needed to field a large army and influence affairs in much of west Africa. In the thirteenth century the Mali empire replaced Ghana as the preeminent power in west Africa, but the Mali rulers continued the Ghana policy of controlling trans-Saharan trade.

The Songhay Empire

By the fifteenth century the Mali empire had begun to weaken, and the expansive state of Songhay emerged to take its place as the dominant power of the western grasslands. Based in the trading city of Gao, Songhay rulers built a flourishing city-state perhaps as early as the eighth century. In the early fifteenth century, they rejected Mali authority and mounted raids deep into Mali territory. In 1464 the Songhay ruler Sunni Ali (reigned 1464–1493) embarked on a campaign to conquer his neighbors and consolidated the Songhay empire (1464–1591). He brought the important trading cities of Timbuktu and Jenne under his control and used their wealth to dominate the central Niger valley.

Songhay Administration

Sunni Ali built an elaborate administrative and military apparatus to oversee affairs in his realm. He appointed governors to oversee provinces and instituted a hierarchy of command that turned his army into an effective military force. He also created an imperial navy to patrol the Niger River, which was an extremely important commercial highway in the Songhay empire. Songhay military might enabled Sunni Ali's successors to extend their authority north into the Sahara, east toward Lake Chad, and west toward the upper reaches of the Niger River.

Timbuktu, the commercial and cultural center of the Mali and Songhay empires, as sketched by a French traveler in 1828. Though long in decline, the city's mosques, mud-brick dwellings, and crowds of people bespeak a prosperous community.

Map [26.1]
African states, 1500–1650.

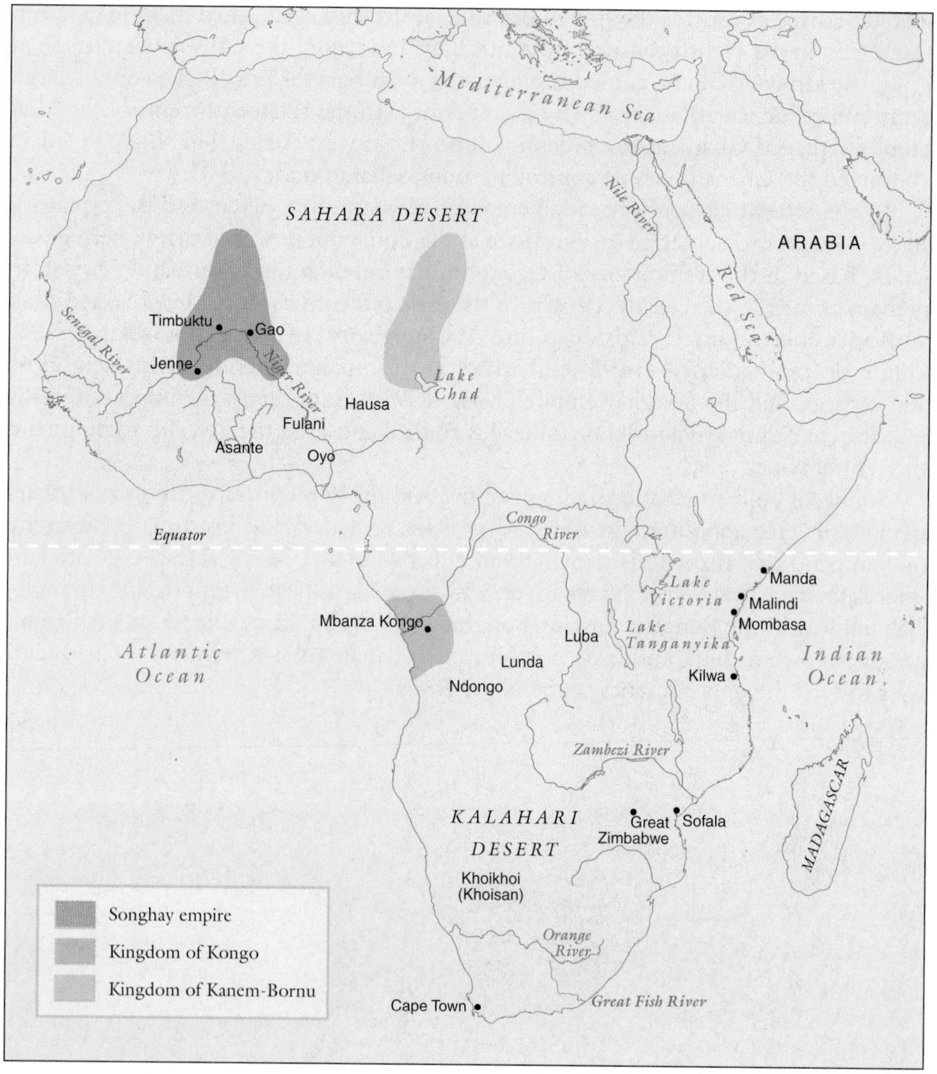

The Songhay emperors presided over a prosperous land. The capital city of Gao had about seventy-five thousand residents, many of whom participated in the lucrative trans-Saharan trade that brought salt, textiles, and metal goods south in exchange for gold and slaves. The emperors were all Muslims: they supported mosques, built schools to teach the Quran, and maintained an Islamic university at Timbuktu. Like the rulers of Ghana and Mali, the Songhay emperors valued Islam as a cultural foundation for cooperation with Muslim merchants and Islamic states in north Africa. Nevertheless, the Songhay emperors did not abandon traditional religious practices: Sunni Ali himself often consulted pagan diviners and magicians.

Fall of Songhay

The Songhay empire dominated west Africa for most of the sixteenth century, but it was the last of the great imperial states of the grasslands. In 1591 a musket-bearing Moroccan army trekked across the Sahara and opened fire on the previously invincible Songhay military machine. Songhay forces withered under the attack, and subject peoples took the opportunity to revolt against Songhay domination.

As the Songhay empire crumbled, a series of small, regional kingdoms and city-states emerged in west Africa. The kingdom of Kanem-Bornu dominated the region around Lake Chad, and the Hausa people established thriving commercial city-states to the west. In the forests south of the grasslands, Oyo and Asante peoples built powerful regional kingdoms. On the coasts Diula, Mande, and other trading peoples established a series of states that entered into commercial relations with European merchant-mariners who called at west African ports after the fifteenth century. The increasing prominence of Atlantic trade in west African society worked against the interests of imperial states like Mali and Songhay, which had relied on control of trans-Saharan trade to finance their empires.

Swahili Decline

While regional states displaced the Songhay empire in west Africa, the Swahili city-states of east Africa fell on hard times. When the Portuguese mariner Vasco da Gama made his way up the east African coast en route to India in 1497 and 1498, he skirmished with local forces at Mozambique and Mombasa. On his second voyage to India in 1502, he forced the ruler of Kilwa to pay tribute, and his followers trained their cannons on Swahili ports all along the east African coast. In 1505 a massive Portuguese naval expedition subdued all the Swahili cities from Sofala to Mombasa. Portuguese forces built administrative centers at Mozambique and Malindi and constructed forts throughout the region in hopes of controlling trade in east Africa. They did not succeed in this effort, but they disrupted trade patterns enough to send the Swahili cities into a decline from which they never fully recovered.

The Kingdoms of Central Africa and South Africa

The Kingdom of Kongo

As trade networks multiplied and linked all regions of sub-Saharan Africa, an increasing volume of commerce encouraged state-building in central Africa and south Africa. In central Africa the principal states were the kingdoms of Kongo, Ndongo, Luba, and Lunda in the basin of the Congo River (also known as the Zaire River). Best known of them was the kingdom of Kongo, since abundant written records throw light on its experience in early modern times. The kingdom emerged in the fourteenth century. Its rulers built a centralized state with officials overseeing military, judicial, and financial affairs, and by the late fifteenth century Kongo embraced much of the modern-day Republic of Congo and Angola.

In 1483 a small Portuguese fleet reconnoitered the estuary of the Congo River and initiated commercial relations with the kingdom of Kongo. Within a few years, Portuguese merchants had established a close political and diplomatic relationship with the kings of Kongo. They supplied the kings with advisors, provided a military garrison to support the kings and protect Portuguese interests, and brought tailors, shoemakers, masons, miners, and priests to Kongo.

The kings of Kongo converted to Christianity as a way to establish closer commercial relations with Portuguese merchants and diplomatic relations with the Portuguese monarchy. The kings appreciated the fact that Christianity offered a strong endorsement of their monarchical rule. The new faith was convenient also because the saints of the Roman Catholic church were similar to spirits long recognized in Kongolese religion. King Nzinga Mbemba of Kongo, also known as King Afonso I (reigned 1506–1542), became a devout Roman Catholic and sought to convert all his subjects to Christianity. Portuguese priests in Kongo reported that he attended religious services daily and studied the Bible so zealously that he sometimes neglected to eat. The Kongo capital of Mbanza—known to Europeans as São Salvador—had so many churches during the sixteenth century that contemporaries referred to it as "Kongo of the Bell."

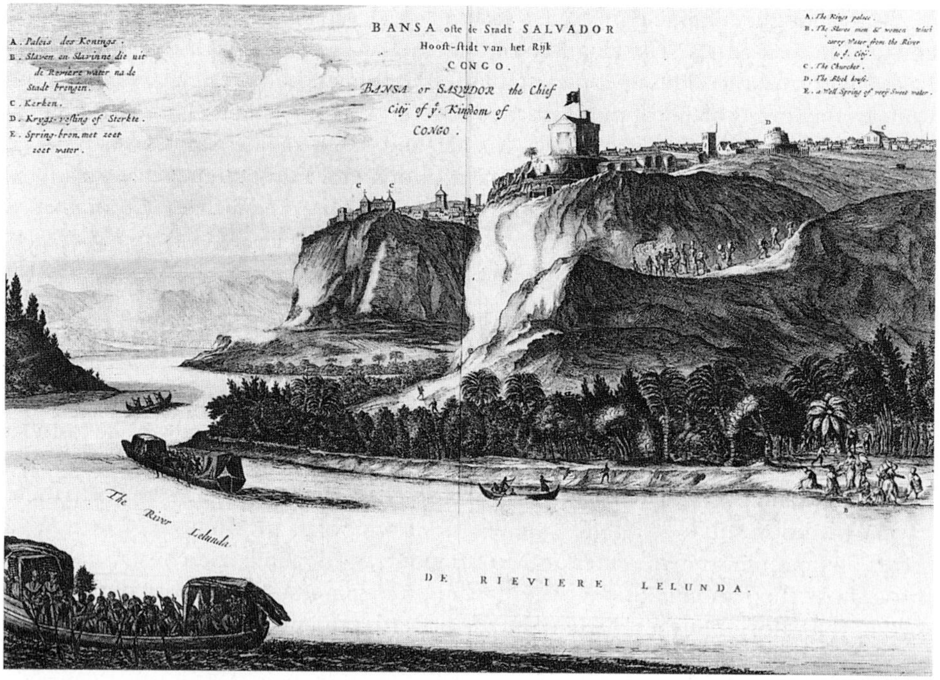

An engraving depicts São Salvador in Angola in the late seventeenth century. A flag flies over the royal palace while the Portuguese citadel (to the right of the palace) guards the city. Churches appear at the center and on the far right side of the engraving.

Slave Raiding in Kongo

Relations with Portugal brought wealth and foreign recognition to Kongo but also led eventually to the destruction of the kingdom and the establishment of a Portuguese colony in Angola. In exchange for the textiles, weapons, advisors, and artisans that they brought to Kongo, Portuguese merchants sought high-value merchandise such as copper, ivory, and most of all, slaves. They sometimes embarked on slaving expeditions themselves, but more often they made alliances with local authorities in interior regions and provided them with weapons in exchange for slaves. Some of their local allies were enemies of the kings of Kongo, while others were royal subordinates. In either case, Portuguese tactics undermined the authority of the kings, who appealed repeatedly but unsuccessfully for the Portuguese to cease or at least to limit their trade in slaves.

In spite of periodic invasions, Kongo remained strong until the mid-seventeenth century. Portuguese forces aided Kongo in expelling invaders, but at the same time they continued to trade in slaves. Some Portuguese merchants even settled in Kongo, took local wives, and henceforth looked more after the interests of their adoptive home than their native land. Over time, though, relations between Kongo and Portugal deteriorated, particularly after Portuguese agents began to pursue opportunities south of Kongo. By 1665 Portuguese colonists to the south even went to war with Kongo. Portuguese forces quickly defeated the Kongolese army and decapitated the king. Soon thereafter, Portuguese merchants began to withdraw from Kongo in search of more profitable business in the kingdom of Ndongo to the south. By the eighteenth century the kingdom of Kongo had largely disintegrated.

The Kingdom of Ndongo

Meanwhile, Portuguese explorers were developing a brisk slave trade to the south in the kingdom of Ndongo, which the Portuguese referred to as Angola from the title of the king, *ngola*. During the sixteenth century, Ndongo had grown from a small chiefdom subject to the kings of Kongo to a powerful regional kingdom, largely on the basis of the wealth it was able to attract by trading directly with Portuguese merchants rather than through Kongolese intermediaries. Portuguese merchants

Sources from the Past

King Afonso I Protests Slave Trading in the Kingdom of Kongo

King Afonso I of Kongo wrote some twenty-four official letters to his fellow monarchs, the kings of Portugal. The letters touch on many themes—relations between Portugal and Kongo, Afonso's devotion to Christianity, and the slave trade. The following excerpts come from two letters of 1526, when Portuguese slave trading was causing serious disruption in Kongo, prompting Afonso to request help in controlling the activities of Portuguese merchants.

And we cannot reckon how great the damage [caused by Portuguese merchants] is, since the mentioned merchants are taking every day our natives, sons of the land and the sons of our noblemen and vassals and our relatives, because the thieves and men of bad conscience grab them wishing to have the things and wares of this Kingdom which they are ambitious of; they grab them and get them to be sold; and so great, Sir, is the corruption and licentiousness that our country is being completely depopulated, and Your Highness should not agree with this nor accept it as in your service. And to avoid it we need from [your] Kingdoms no more than some priests and a few people to teach in schools, and no other goods except wine and flour for the holy sacrament. That is why we beg of Your Highness to help and assist us in this matter, commanding your factors that they should not send here either merchants or wares, because it is *our will that in these Kingdoms there should not be any trade of slaves nor outlet for them.* Concerning what is referred [to] above, again we beg of Your Highness to agree with it, since otherwise we cannot remedy such an obvious damage. . . .

Moreover, Sir, in our Kingdoms there is another great inconvenience which is of little service to God, and this is that many of our people, keenly desirous as they are of the wares and things of your Kingdoms, which are brought here by your people, and in order to satisfy their voracious appetite, seize many of our people, freed and exempt men, and very often it happens that they kidnap even noblemen and the sons of noblemen, and our relatives, and take them to be sold to the white men who are in our Kingdoms. . . .

And as soon as they are taken by the white men they are immediately ironed and branded with fire, and when they are carried to be embarked, if they are caught by our guards' men the whites allege that they have bought them but they cannot say from whom, so that it is our duty to do justice and to restore to the freemen their freedom, but it cannot be done if your subjects feel offended, as they claim to be.

And to avoid such a great evil we passed a law so that any white man living in our Kingdoms and wanting to purchase goods [i.e., slaves] in any way should first inform three of our noblemen and officials of our court whom we rely upon in this matter, . . . who should investigate if the mentioned goods are captives or free men, and if cleared by them there will be no further doubt nor embargo for them to be taken and embarked. But if the white men do not comply with it they will lose the aforementioned goods. And if we do them this favor and concession it is for the part Your Highness has in it, since we know that it is in your service too that these goods are taken from our Kingdom, otherwise we should not consent to this.

SOURCE: Basil Davidson. *The African Past.* Boston: Little, Brown, 1964, pp. 191–93.

On the basis of these letters, does it appear that King Afonso opposed all slave trading or only certain kinds of slave trading?

founded a small coastal colony in Ndongo as early as 1575. After 1611 they steadily increased their influence inland by allying with neighboring peoples who delivered increasing numbers of war captives to feed the growing slave trade. Over the next

Queen Nzinga of Ndongo speaks with the Portuguese governor of Angola at his headquarters. The governor refused to provide Nzinga with a chair, so she seated herself on the back of a servant while her "concubines" looked on at the right.

several decades, Portuguese forces campaigned in Ndongo in an effort to establish a colony that would support large-scale trading in slaves.

Queen Nzinga

The conquest of Angola did not come easily. For forty years Queen Nzinga (reigned 1623–1663) led spirited resistance against Portuguese forces. Nzinga came from a long line of warrior kings. She dressed as a male warrior when leading troops in battle and insisted that her subjects refer to her as king rather than queen. She sometimes went so far in playing male roles as to travel with a group of "concubines"—young men dressed as women companions of the "king." She mobilized central African peoples against her Portuguese adversaries, and she also allied with Dutch mariners, who traded frequently on the African coast during the mid-seventeenth century. Her aim was to drive the Portuguese from her land, then expel the Dutch, and finally create a vast central African empire embracing the entire lower Congo basin.

The Portuguese Colony of Angola

Although she was a cunning strategist and effective military leader, Nzinga was unable to oust Portuguese forces from Ndongo. She stymied Portuguese efforts to extend their influence, but with their powerful arms and considerable wealth, Portuguese forces were able to exploit the political divisions that perennially plagued central Africa. When Nzinga died, Portuguese forces faced less capable resistance, and they both extended and tightened their control over Angola, the first European colony in sub-Saharan Africa.

Regional Kingdoms in South Africa

Historical records do not shed as much light on the political structures of south Africa as they do on Kongo and Angola, but it is clear that in the south, as in central Africa, regional kingdoms dominated political affairs. Kingdoms had begun to emerge as early as the eleventh century, largely under the influence of trade. Merchants from the Swahili city-states of coastal east Africa sought gold, ivory, and slaves from the interior regions of south Africa. By controlling local commerce, chieftains increased their wealth, enhanced their power, and extended their authority. By 1300 rulers of one such kingdom had built a massive, stone-fortified city known as Great Zimbabwe, near the city of Nyanda in modern Zimbabwe, and they dominated the gold-bearing plain between the Zambesi and Limpopo rivers until the late fifteenth century.

European Arrival in South Africa

After the fifteenth century a series of smaller kingdoms displaced the rulers of Great Zimbabwe, and Portuguese and Dutch mariners began to play a role in south African affairs. In search of commercial opportunities, Europeans struck alliances with local peoples and intervened in disputes with the aim of supporting their allies and advancing their own interests. They became especially active after Dutch mariners built a trading post at Cape Town in 1652. There they encountered the hunting and gathering Khoikhoi people, whom they referred to pejoratively as Hottentots. With the aid of firearms, they claimed lands for themselves and commandeered Khoikhoi labor with relative ease. By 1700 large numbers of Dutch colonists had begun to arrive in south Africa, and by midcentury they had established settlements throughout the region bounded by the Orange and the Great Fish rivers. Their conquests laid the foundation for a series of Dutch and British colonies, which eventually became the most prosperous European possessions in sub-Saharan Africa.

Islam and Christianity in Early Modern Africa

Indigenous religions remained influential throughout sub-Saharan Africa in early modern times. Although many African peoples recognized a supreme, remote creator god, they devoted most of their attention to powerful spirits who were thought to intervene directly in human affairs. African peoples associated many of these spirits with prominent geographic features such as mountains, waters, or forests. Others they thought of as the "living dead"—spirits of ancestors who roamed the world, not only distributing rewards to descendants who led worthy lives and who honored the memories of departed kin but also meting out punishments to those who did not.

Islam in Sub-Saharan Africa

Although most Africans continued to observe their inherited religions, both Islam and Christianity attracted increasing interest in sub-Saharan Africa. Islam was most popular in the commercial centers of west Africa and the Swahili city-states of east Africa. In the sixteenth century the trading city of Timbuktu had a prominent Islamic university and 180 schools that taught the Quran. Students flocked to Timbuktu by the thousands from all parts of west Africa.

Most African Muslims blended Islam with indigenous beliefs and customs. The result was a syncretic brand of Islam that not only made a place for African beliefs in spirits and magic but also permitted men and women to associate with one another on much more familiar terms than was common in north Africa, Arabia, and southwest Asia. Although it appealed to Africans, this syncretic Islam struck many devout Muslims as impure and offensive. Muslim merchants and travelers from north Africa and Arabia often commented on their shock at seeing women in tropical Africa who went out in public with bare breasts and socialized freely with men outside their own families.

The Fulani and Islam

Some Muslims in sub-Saharan Africa also shared these concerns about the purity of Islam. Most important of them were the Fulani, originally a pastoral people who for centuries kept herds of cattle in the savannas of west Africa. By the late seventeenth century, many Fulani had settled in cities, where they observed a strict form of Islam like that practiced in north Africa and Arabia. Beginning about 1680 and continuing through the nineteenth century, the Fulani led a series of military campaigns to establish Islamic states and impose their own brand of Islam in west Africa.

The Fulani did not by any means stamp out African religions, nor did they eliminate indigenous elements from the syncretic Islam practiced in west Africa. But they founded powerful states in what is now Guinea, Senegal, Mali, and northern Nigeria, and they promoted the spread of Islam beyond the cities to the countryside. They even established schools in remote towns and villages to teach the Quran and Islamic doctrine. Their campaigns strengthened Islam in sub-Saharan Africa and laid a foundation for new rounds of Islamic state-building and conversion efforts in the nineteenth and twentieth centuries.

Christianity in Sub-Saharan Africa

Like Islam, Christianity made compromises with traditional beliefs and customs when it spread in sub-Saharan Africa. The Portuguese community in Kongo and Angola supported priests and missionaries who introduced Roman Catholic Christianity to central Africa. They found strong interest among rulers like King Afonso I of Kongo and his descendants, who eagerly adopted European-style Christianity as a foundation for commercial and political alliances with Portugal. Beyond the ruling courts, however, Christian teachings blended with African traditions to form syncretic cults. Africans regarded Christian missionaries as magicians and wore crosses and other Christian symbols as amulets to ward off danger from angry spirits.

The Antonian Movement

A particularly influential syncretic cult was the Antonian movement in Kongo, which flourished in the early eighteenth century, when the Kongolese monarchy faced challenges throughout the realm. The Antonian movement began in 1704 when an aristocratic woman named Dona Beatriz proclaimed that St. Anthony of Padua had possessed her and chosen her to communicate his messages. St. Anthony was a thirteenth-century Franciscan missionary and popular preacher. Though born in Italy, St. Anthony died in Lisbon, and he became the patron saint of Portugal. He

The kings of Kongo retained their Christian faith even after their relations with European merchants and missionaries became strained in the seventeenth century. Here King Garcia II—with European-style boots and a cross attached to his left sleeve—receives a Dutch embassy in 1642.

was extremely popular among Portuguese Christians, who introduced his cult to Kongo. Dona Beatriz gained a reputation for working miracles and curing diseases, and she used her prominence to promote an African form of Christianity. She taught that Jesus Christ had been a black African man, that Kongo was the true holy land of Christianity, and that heaven was for Africans. She urged Kongolese to ignore European missionaries and heed her disciples instead, and she sought to harness the widespread popular interest in her teachings and use it to end the wars plaguing Kongo.

Dona Beatriz's movement was a serious challenge to Christian missionaries in Kongo. In 1706 they persuaded King Pedro IV of Kongo to arrest the charismatic prophetess on suspicion of heresy. Upon examining her, the missionaries satisfied themselves that Dona Beatriz was a false prophet and that she knowingly taught false doctrine. On their recommendation the royal government sentenced her to death and burned her at the stake. Yet the Antonian movement did not disappear: Dona Beatriz's disciples continued working to strengthen the monarchy and reconstruct Kongolese society. In 1708 an army of almost twenty thousand Antonians challenged King Pedro, whom they considered an unworthy ruler. Their efforts illustrate clearly the tendency of Kongolese Christians to fashion a faith that reflected their own needs and concerns as well as the interests of European missionaries.

Social Change in Early Modern Africa

Despite increased state-building activity and political turmoil, African society followed long-established patterns during the early modern era. Kinship groups, for example, the most important social units that emerged after the Bantu migrations, continued to serve as the basis of social organization and sometimes political organization as well. Within agricultural villages throughout sub-Saharan Africa, clans under the leadership of prominent individuals organized the affairs of their kinship groups and disciplined those who violated community standards. In regions where kingdoms and empires had not emerged, clan leaders consulted with each other and governed large regions. Indeed, even in lands ruled by formal states, clan leaders usually implemented state policy at the village level.

Yet interaction with European peoples brought change to African society in early modern times. Trade brought access to European textiles and metal goods. Africans had produced textiles and high-quality steel for centuries before the arrival of Portuguese mariners, but European products of different materials and styles became popular as complements to native African wares.

American Food Crops in Sub-Saharan Africa

Trade also brought new food crops to sub-Saharan Africa. In the mid-sixteenth century, American crops such as manioc, maize, and peanuts arrived in Africa aboard Portuguese ships. These crops supplemented bananas, yams, rice, and millet, the principal staple foods of sub-Saharan Africa. The most important American crop was manioc because of its high yield and because it thrived in tropical soils not well suited to cultivation of the other crops.

Population Growth

By the eighteenth century, bread made from manioc flour had become a staple food in much of west Africa and central Africa, where it helped to underwrite steady population growth. In 1500 C.E. the population of sub-Saharan Africa was about thirty-four million. By 1600 it had increased by almost one-third to forty-four million, and it continued climbing to fifty-two million in 1700 and sixty million in 1800. This strong demographic expansion is all the more remarkable because it took place precisely when millions of Africans underwent an involuntary, forced migration to destinations in the Caribbean and the Americas. Despite this migration, American food crops supported expanding populations in all regions of sub-Saharan Africa during early modern times.

THE ATLANTIC SLAVE TRADE

Of all the processes that linked Africa to the larger Atlantic world in early modern times, the most momentous was the Atlantic slave trade. From the fifteenth to the nineteenth century, European peoples looked to Africa as a source of labor for massive plantations that they established in the western hemisphere. In exchange for slaves, African peoples received European manufactured products—most notably firearms, which they sometimes used to strengthen military forces that then sought further recruits for the slave trade. Only in the early nineteenth century did the Atlantic slave trade come to an end. During the course of the century, most states abolished the institution of slavery itself.

Foundations of the Slave Trade

Slavery in Africa

The institution of slavery appeared in remote antiquity, and until the nineteenth century many settled agricultural peoples made some place for slaves in their societies. Slavery was common throughout Africa after the Bantu migrations spread agriculture to all parts of the continent. As in other societies, most slaves in Africa came from the ranks of war captives, although criminals and individuals expelled from their clans also frequently fell into slavery. Once enslaved, an individual had no personal or civil rights. Owners could order slaves to perform any kind of work, punish them at will, and sell them as chattel. African slaves usually worked as cultivators in societies far from their homes, although some worked as administrators, soldiers, or even highly placed advisors. The Songhay emperors, for example, often employed slaves as administrators and soldiers, since the rulers distrusted free nobles, whom they considered excessively ambitious and undependable. Agricultural plantations in the Songhay empire often had hundreds of slave laborers, many of them working under the management of slave administrators.

Law and society made African slavery different from bondage in Europe, Asia, and other lands. African law did not recognize private property, but rather vested ownership of land in communities. Thus wealth and power in Africa came not from the possession of land but, rather, from control over the human labor that made the land productive. Slaves were a form of private investment, a type of heritable property, and a means of measuring wealth. Those who controlled large numbers of individuals were able to harvest more crops and accumulate more wealth than others. Africans routinely purchased slaves to enlarge their families and enhance their power. Often they assimilated slaves into their kinship groups so that within a generation a slave might obtain both freedom and an honorable position in a new family or clan.

The Islamic Slave Trade

After the eighth century, Muslim merchants from north Africa, Arabia, and Persia sought African slaves for sale and distribution to destinations in the Mediterranean basin, southwest Asia, India, and even southeast Asia and China. This organized commerce found ready markets for slaves. When traditional sources proved insufficient to satisfy the demand for slaves, merchants created new supplies by raiding villages, capturing innocent individuals, and forcing them into servitude. State officials sometimes allied with the merchants by providing cavalry forces to mount lightning raids on undefended communities. Merchants then transported the freshly recruited slaves across the Sahara desert by camel caravan for distribution in the Mediterranean basin or boarded them on ships at the Swahili port cities of east Africa for delivery to destinations across the Indian Ocean. During a millennium and more of the Islamic slave trade, which lasted into the twentieth century, as many as ten million Africans may have left their homeland in servitude.

By the time Europeans ventured to sub-Saharan Africa in the fifteenth and sixteenth centuries, traffic in slaves was a well-established feature of African society, and a system for capturing, selling, and distributing slaves had functioned effectively for more than five hundred years. When Europeans began to pursue commercial interests in Africa and the Americas, the slave trade expanded dramatically. After 1450 European peoples tapped existing networks and expanded commerce in African slaves from the Mediterranean and the Indian Ocean to the Atlantic Ocean basin. This Atlantic slave trade brought about an enormous involuntary migration that influenced the development of societies throughout the Atlantic Ocean basin.

Human Cargoes

The Atlantic slave trade began small, but it grew steadily and eventually reached massive proportions. The earliest European slave traders were Portuguese explorers who reconnoitered the west African coast in the mid-fifteenth century. In 1441 a raiding party seized twelve African men and took them to Portugal as slaves. Portuguese mariners encountered stiff resistance when they attempted to capture slaves, as African warriors fired thousands of poison-tipped arrows at gangs of would-be slave raiders. Soon, however, the mariners learned that they could purchase slaves rather than capturing them, and by 1460 they were delivering five hundred slaves per year to Portugal and Spain. In Europe, African slaves usually worked as miners, porters, or domestic servants, since free peasants and serfs cultivated the land.

The Early Slave Trade

Slave traders also delivered their human cargoes to Portuguese island colonies in the Atlantic. There was no supply of labor to work plantations in the Azores, Madeiras, Cape Verde Islands, and São Tomé, all of which were uninhabited when explorers discovered them in the fifteenth century. The Portuguese population was too small to provide large numbers of colonists. Sugar planters on the island of São Tomé in particular called for slaves in increasing quantities. They relied on slave labor, and production soared along with the demand for sugar in Europe. By the 1520s some two thousand slaves per year went to São Tomé. Soon thereafter Portuguese entrepreneurs extended the use of slave labor to South America. During the 1530s Portuguese planters imported slaves directly from Kongo and Angola to Brazil, which eventually became the wealthiest of the sugar-producing lands of the western hemisphere.

Meanwhile, Spanish explorers and conquerors also sought laborers to work lands in the Caribbean and the Americas. As imported diseases ravaged indigenous populations in the western hemisphere, the conquerors found themselves in possession of vast stretches of land but few laborers to work it. The Spanish attempted to harness the labor of those who survived the diseases, but native peoples frequently revolted against their overlords or simply escaped into the hinterlands. Gradually Spanish settlers began to rely on imported African slaves as laborers. In 1518 the first shipment of slaves went directly from west Africa to the Caribbean, where they worked on recently established sugar plantations. During the 1520s Spanish authorities introduced slaves to Mexico, where they worked as cultivators and miners. By the early seventeenth century, English colonists had introduced slaves also to the North American mainland.

Triangular Trade

The demand for labor in the western hemisphere stimulated a profitable commerce known as the triangular trade, since European ships often undertook voyages of three legs. On the first leg they carried horses and European manufactured goods—mostly cloth and metal wares, especially firearms—that they exchanged in Africa for slaves. The second leg took enslaved Africans to Caribbean and American destinations. Upon arrival merchants sold their human cargoes to plantation owners for two to three times what they had cost on the African coast. Sometimes they exchanged

A bronze plaque from Benin offers an early African view of Europeans: it depicts a Portuguese soldier armed with a musket and accompanied by a dog.

slaves for cash, but in sugar-producing regions they often bartered slaves for sugar or molasses. Then they filled their vessels' hulls with American products before embarking on their voyage back to Europe.

At every stage of the process, the slave trade was a brutal and inhumane business. The original capture of slaves in Africa was almost always a violent affair. As European demand for slaves grew, some African chieftains organized raiding parties to seize individuals from neighboring societies. Others launched wars for the purpose of capturing victims for the slave trade. They often snatched individuals right out of their homes, fields, or villages: millions of lives changed instantly, as slave raiders grabbed their quarries and then immediately spirited them away in captivity. Bewilderment and anger was the lot not only of the captives but also of their family members, who would never again see their kin.

The Middle Passage

Following capture, enslaved individuals underwent a forced march to the coast where they lived in holding pens until a ship arrived to transport them to the western hemisphere. Then they embarked on the dreadful "middle passage," the trans-Atlantic journey aboard filthy and crowded slave ships. Enslaved passengers traveled below decks in hideously cramped quarters. Most ships provided slaves with enough room to sit upright, although not to stand, but some forced them to lie in chains on shelves with barely half a meter (twenty inches) of space between them. Conditions were so bad that many slaves attempted to starve themselves to death or mounted revolts. Ship crews attempted to preserve the lives of slaves, intending to sell them for a profit at the end of the voyage, but often treated the unwilling passengers with cruelty and contempt. Crew members used tools to pry open the mouths of those who refused to eat and pitched sick individuals into the ocean rather than have them infect others or waste limited supplies of food.

Barring difficulties, the journey to Caribbean and American destinations took four to six weeks, during which heat, cold, and disease levied a heavy toll on the human cargo. During the early days of the slave trade on particularly cramped ships, mortality sometimes exceeded 50 percent. As the volume of the trade grew, slavers built larger ships, carried more water, and provided better nourishment and facilities for their cargoes, and mortality eventually declined to about 5 percent per voyage. Over the course of the Atlantic slave trade, however, approximately one-quarter of individuals enslaved in Africa did not survive the middle passage.

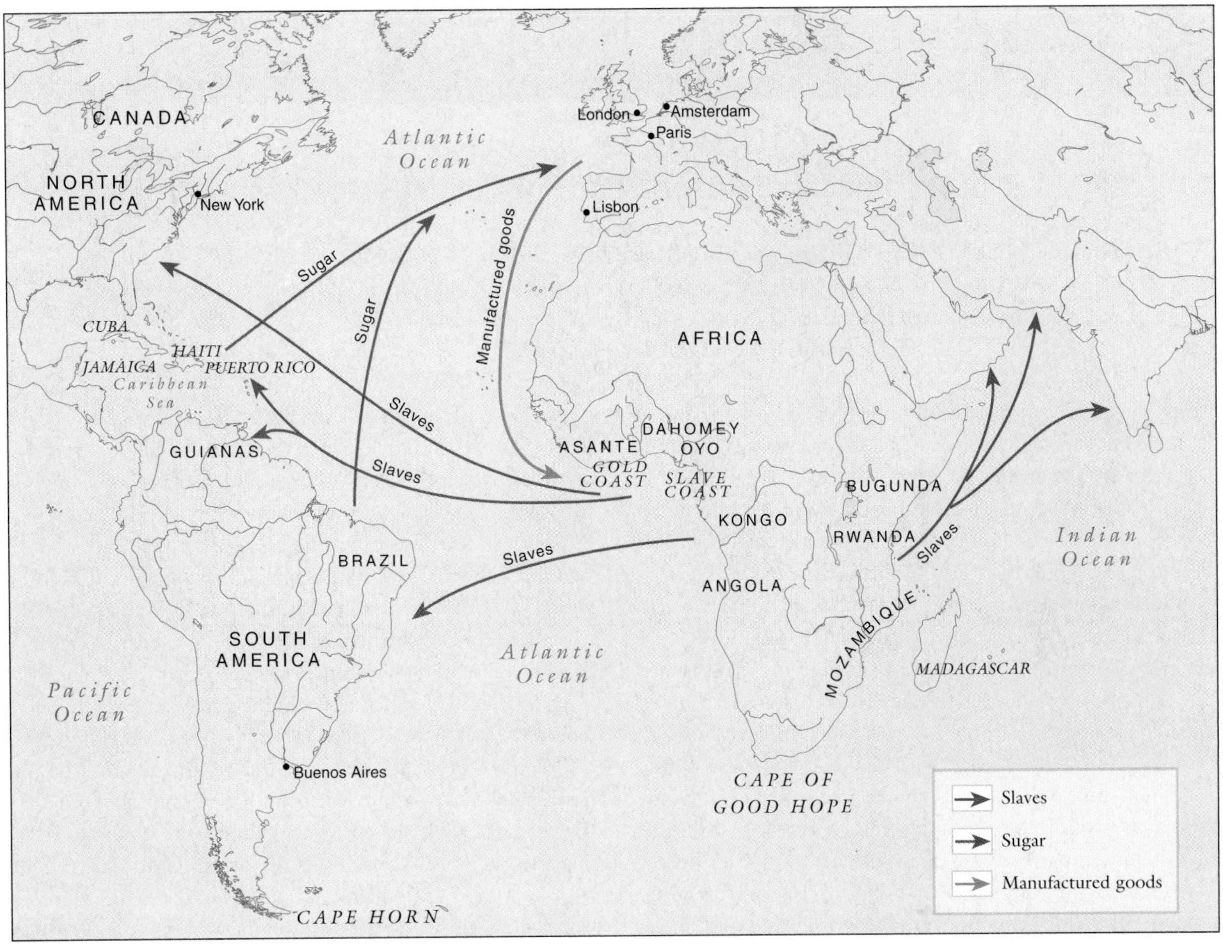

Map [26.2]
The Atlantic slave trade, 1500–1800.

The Impact of the Slave Trade in Africa

Volume of the Slave Trade

Before 1600 the Atlantic slave trade operated on a modest scale. Export figures varied considerably from one year to the next, but on average about two thousand slaves left Africa annually during the late fifteenth and sixteenth centuries. During the seventeenth century, slave exports rose dramatically to twenty thousand per year, as European peoples settled in the western hemisphere and called for African labor to cultivate their lands. The high point of the slave trade came in the eighteenth century, when the number of slaves exported to the Americas averaged fifty-five thousand per year. During the 1780s slave arrivals averaged eighty-eight thousand per year, and in some individual years they exceeded one hundred thousand. From beginning to end the Atlantic slave trade brought about the involuntary migration of about twelve million Africans to the western hemisphere. Another four million or more died resisting seizure or during captivity before arriving at their intended destination.

For an interactive version of this map, go to www.mhhe.com/bentley3ch26maps.

The impact of the slave trade varied over time and from one African society to another. The kingdoms of Rwanda and Bugunda on the great lakes and the herding societies of the Masai and Turkana of east Africa largely escaped the slave trade, partly because they resisted it and partly because their lands were distant from the major slave ports on the west African coast. Other societies flourished during early modern times and benefited economically from the slave trade. Those Africans who raided, took captives, and sold slaves to Europeans profited handsomely from the trade, as

Sources from the Past

Olaudah Equiano on the Middle Passage

Olaudah Equiano (1745–1797) was a native of Benin in west Africa. When he was ten years old, slave raiders seized him and his sister at home while their parents were tending the fields. He spent the next twenty-one years as a slave. Then Equiano purchased his freedom and worked against the slave trade for the rest of his life. In his autobiography of 1789, Equiano described the horrors of the middle passage.

The first object which saluted my eyes when I arrived on the coast was the sea, and a slave ship which was then riding at anchor and waiting for its cargo. These filled me with astonishment, which was soon converted into terror when I was carried on board. I was immediately handled and tossed up to see if I were sound by some of the crew, and I was now persuaded that I had gotten into a world of bad spirits and that they were going to kill me. . . .

I was not long suffered to indulge my grief; I was soon put down under the decks, and there I received such a salutation in my nostrils as I had never experienced in my life: so that with the loathsomeness of the stench and crying together, I became so sick and low that I was not able to eat, nor had I the least desire to taste anything. I now wished for the last friend, death, to relieve me; but soon, to my grief, two of the white men offered me eatables, and on my refusing to eat, one of them held me fast by the hands and laid me across I think the windlass and tied my feet while the other flogged me severely. I had never experienced anything of this kind before, and although not being used to the water I naturally feared that element the first time I saw it, yet nevertheless if I could have gotten over the nettings I would have jumped over the side, but I could not; and besides, the crew used to watch very closely over those of us who were not chained down to the decks, lest we should leap into the water: and I have seen some of these poor African prisoners most severely cut for attempting to do so, and hourly whipped for not eating. This indeed was often the case with myself. . . .

One day when we had a smooth sea and moderate wind, two of my wearied countrymen who were chained together (I was near them at the time), preferring death to such a life of misery, somehow made through the nettings and jumped into the sea: immediately another quite dejected fellow, who on account of his illness was suffered to be out of irons, also followed their example; and I believe many more would very soon have done the same if they had not been prevented by the ship's crew, who were instantly alarmed. Those of us that were the most active were in a moment put down under the deck, and there was such a noise and confusion amongst the people of the ship as I never heard before, to stop her and get the boat to go after the slaves. However, two of the wretches were drowned, but they got the other and afterwards flogged him unmercifully for thus attempting to prefer death to slavery. In this manner we continued to undergo more hardships than I can now relate, hardships which are inseparable from this accursed trade.

SOURCE: Olaudah Equiano. *The Interesting Narrative of the Life of Olaudah Equiano, or Gustavus Vassa, the African, Written by Himself,* 2 vols. London, 1789. (Translation slightly modified.)

On the basis of Equiano's account, what measures did the crews of slave ships take to ensure maximum profits from their business of transporting human cargoes?

did the port cities and the states that coordinated trade with European merchants. Asante, Dahomey, and Oyo peoples, for example, took advantage of the slave trade to obtain firearms from European merchants and build powerful states in west Africa. In the nineteenth century, after the abolition of slavery, some African merchants complained bitterly about losing their livelihood and tried to undermine the efforts of the British navy to patrol Atlantic waters and put an end to slave trading.

Armed escorts march a group of freshly captured Africans to the coast for sale on slave markets.

Social Effects of the Slave Trade

On the whole, however, Africa suffered serious losses from the slave trade. The Atlantic slave trade alone deprived African societies of about sixteen million individuals, in addition to another several million consumed by the continuing Islamic slave trade during the early modern era. Although total African population rose during the early modern era, partly because American food crops enriched diets, several individual societies experienced severe losses because of the slave trade. West African societies between Senegal and Angola were especially vulnerable to slave raiding because of their proximity to the most active slave ports.

While diverting labor from Africa to other lands, the slave trade also distorted African sex ratios, since approximately two-thirds of all exported slaves were males. Slavers preferred young men between fourteen and thirty-five years of age, since they had the best potential to repay their buyers' investments by providing heavy labor over an extended period of time. This preference for male slaves had social implications for lands that provided slaves. By the late eighteenth century, for example, women made up more than two-thirds of the adult population of Angola. This sexual imbalance encouraged Angolans to practice polygamy and forced women to take on duties that in earlier times had been the responsibility of men.

Political Effects of the Slave Trade

Apart from its demographic and social effects, the slave trade also brought turmoil to African societies. During early modern times, African peoples fought many wars for reasons that had little or nothing to do with the slave trade, but it encouraged them to participate also in conflicts that might never have occurred in the absence of the trade.

Violence escalated especially after the late seventeenth century, when African peoples increasingly exchanged slaves for European firearms. When the kingdom of Dahomey obtained effective firearms, for example, its armies were able to capture slaves from unarmed neighboring societies and exchange them for more weapons. During the eighteenth century, Dahomey expanded rapidly and absorbed neighboring societies by increasing its arsenal of firearms and maintaining a constant flow of slaves to the coast. Indeed, the Dahomey army, which included a regiment of women soldiers, became largely a slave-raiding force. By no means did all African states take such advantage of the slave trade, but Dahomey's experience illustrates the potential of the slave trade to alter the patterns of African politics and society.

THE AFRICAN DIASPORA

Some slaves worked as urban laborers or domestic servants, and in Mexico and Peru many worked also as miners. The vast majority, however, provided agricultural labor on plantations in the Caribbean or the Americas. There they cultivated cash crops that made their way into commercial arteries linking lands throughout the Atlantic Ocean basin. Although deprived of their freedom, slaves often resisted their bondage, and they built hybrid cultural traditions compounded of African, European, and American elements. Most European and American states ended the slave trade and abolished slavery during the nineteenth century. By that time the African diaspora—the dispersal of African peoples and their descendants—had left a permanent mark throughout the western hemisphere.

Plantation Societies

Most African slaves went to plantations in the tropical and subtropical regions of the western hemisphere. When European peoples arrived in the Caribbean and the Americas, they found vast stretches of fertile land and soon began to envision huge profits from plantations that would satisfy the growing European demand for sugar and other agricultural commodities. Spanish colonists established the first of these plantations in 1516 on the island of Hispaniola (which embraces modern Haiti and the Dominican Republic) and soon extended them to Mexico as well. Beginning in the 1530s Portuguese entrepreneurs organized plantations in Brazil, and by the early seventeenth century English, Dutch, and French plantations had also appeared in the Caribbean and the Americas.

Cash Crops

Many of these plantations produced sugar, which was one of the most lucrative cash crops of early modern times. But plantations produced other crops as well. During the seventeenth century, tobacco rivaled sugar as a profitable product. Rice also became a major plantation product, as did indigo. By the eighteenth century many plantations concentrated on the cultivation of cotton, and coffee had begun to emerge as a plantation specialty.

Regardless of the crops they produced, Caribbean and American plantations had certain elements in common. All of them specialized in the production of some agricultural crop in high demand: plantations often maintained gardens that produced food for the local community, but their purpose was to profit from the production and export of commercial crops. In efforts to operate efficiently and profitably, plantations relied almost exclusively on slave labor: plantation communities often included a hundred or more slaves, whose uncompensated labor services helped keep their agricultural products competitive. Plantations also featured a sharp, racial division of labor: small numbers of European or Euro-American supervisors governed

In an engraving of 1667, a European supervisor (lower right) directs slaves on a sugar plantation in Barbados as they haul cane, crush it to extract its juice, boil it to produce molasses, and distill the product into rum.

plantation affairs, and large numbers of African or African-American slaves performed most of the community's physical labor.

Regional Differences

In spite of their structural similarities, plantation societies differed considerably from one region to another. In the Caribbean and South America, slave populations usually were unable to sustain their numbers by natural means. Many slaves fell victim to tropical diseases like malaria and yellow fever. On the plantations they faced brutal working conditions and low standards of sanitation and nutrition. Moreover, slaves had low rates of reproduction because plantation owners mostly imported male slaves and allowed only a few to establish families. Thus, in the Caribbean and South America, plantation owners imported continuing streams of slaves from Africa to maintain their workforces. Of all the slaves delivered from Africa to the western hemisphere, about half went to Caribbean destinations, and another third went to Brazil. Smaller numbers went to other destinations in South America and Central America.

Only about 5 percent of enslaved Africans went to North American destinations. Diseases there were less threatening than in the Caribbean and Brazil, and in some ways the conditions of slaves' lives were less harsh than in the more southerly regions. North American planters imported larger numbers of female slaves and encouraged their slaves to form families and bear children. Their support for slave families was especially strong in the eighteenth century, when the prices of fresh slaves from Africa rose dramatically.

Resistance to Slavery

No matter where they lived, slaves did not meekly accept their servile status, but like Thomas Peters resisted it in numerous ways. Some forms of resistance were mild but costly to slave owners: slaves often worked slowly for their masters but diligently in their own gardens, for example. They occasionally sabotaged plantation equipment or work routines. A more serious form of resistance involved running away from the plantation community. Runaways known as maroons gathered in mountainous, forested, or swampy regions and built their own self-governing communities. Maroons often raided nearby plantations for arms, tools, provisions, and even slaves to increase their own numbers or to provide labor for their communities. Many maroons had gained military experience in Africa, and they organized escaped slaves into effective military forces. Maroon communities flourished throughout slave-holding regions of the western hemisphere, and some of them survived for centuries. In present-day Suriname, for example, the Saramaka people maintain an elaborate oral tradition that traces their descent from eighteenth-century maroons.

Slave Revolts

The most dramatic form of resistance to slavery was the slave revolt. Slaves far outnumbered others in most plantation societies, and they had the potential to organize and overwhelm their masters. Slave revolts brought stark fear to plantation owners and supervisors, and they often resulted in widespread death and destruction. Yet slave revolts almost never brought slavery itself to an end, because the European and Euro-American ruling elites had access to arms, horses, and military forces that extinguished most rebellions. Only in the French sugar colony of Saint-Domingue did a slave revolt abolish slavery as an institution (1793). Indeed, the slaves of Saint-Domingue declared independence from France, renamed the land Haiti, and established a self-governing republic (1804). The Haitian revolution terrified slave owners and inspired slaves throughout the western hemisphere, but no other slave rebellion matched its accomplishments.

Slaves were vulnerable to cruel treatment that often provoked them to run away from their plantations or even mount revolts. A French visitor to Brazil in the early nineteenth century depicted a Portuguese overseer administering a brutal whipping to a bound slave on a plantation near Rio de Janeiro.

Slavery and Economic Development

The physical labor of African and African-American slaves made crucial contributions to the building of new societies in the Americas and also to the making of the early modern world as a whole. Slave labor cultivated many of the crops and extracted many of the minerals that made their way around the world in the global trade networks of the early modern era. Slaves themselves did not enjoy the fruits of their labors, which flowed disproportionately to European peoples and their Euro-American descendants. Except for the labor of enslaved African peoples and their African-American descendants, however, it would have been impossible for prosperous new societies to emerge in the Americas during the early modern era.

The Making of African-American Cultural Traditions

Enslaved Africans did not enjoy the luxury of maintaining their inherited cultural traditions in the western hemisphere. They often preserved African traditions, including languages and religions, but had to adapt to societies compounded of various European and American as well as African elements. When packed in slave ships for the middle passage, they found themselves in the company of Africans from societies other than their own. When sold to masters in the Caribbean and the Americas, they joined societies shaped by European and American traditions. In adapting to new circumstances, slaves constructed distinctive African-American cultural traditions.

African and Creole Languages

European languages were the dominant tongues in the slave societies of the western hemisphere, but African languages also influenced communication. Occasionally African slaves from a particular region were numerous enough to speak among themselves in their native tongues. More often they spoke a creole tongue that drew on several African and European languages. In the low country of South Carolina and Georgia, for example, slaves made up about three-quarters of the population in the eighteenth century and regularly communicated in the creole languages Gullah and Geechee, respectively.

African-American Religions

Like their languages, slaves' religions also combined elements from different societies. Some slaves shipped out of Africa were Christians, and many others converted to Christianity after their arrival in the western hemisphere. Most Africans and African-Americans did not practice European Christianity, however, but rather a syncretic faith that made considerable room for African interests and traditions. Because they developed mostly in plantation societies under conditions of slavery, these syncretic religions usually did not create an institutional structure or establish a hierarchy of priests and other church officials. Yet in several cases—most notably Vodou in Haiti, Santeria in Cuba, and Candomblé in Brazil—they became exceedingly popular among slaves.

All the syncretic, African-American religions drew inspiration from Christianity: they met in parish churches, sought personal salvation, and made use of European Christian paraphernalia like holy water, candles, and statues. Yet they also preserved African traditions. They associated African deities with Christian saints and relied heavily on African rituals like drumming, dancing, and sacrificing animals. Indeed, the core of these syncretic faiths was often participation in rituals like those observed in Africa. They also preserved beliefs in spirits and supernatural powers: magic, sorcery, witchcraft, and spirit possession all played prominent roles in African-American religions.

African-American Cultural Traditions

African traditions also made their effects felt throughout much of the western hemisphere. Slaves introduced African foods to Caribbean and American societies and helped give rise to distinctive hybrid cuisines. They combined African okra, for example, with European-style sautéed vegetables and American shellfish to produce magnificent gumbos, which found their way to Euro-American as well as African-American tables. (*Okra* and *gumbo* are both African words.) Slaves introduced rice cultivation to tropical and

Olaudah Equiano as depicted in the first edition of his autobiography (1789).

subtropical regions, including South Carolina, Georgia, and Louisiana, and added variety to American diets. They also built houses, fashioned clay pots, and wove grass baskets in west African styles. In many ways the African diaspora influenced the ways all peoples lived in plantation societies.

The End of the Slave Trade and the Abolition of Slavery

Almost as old as the Atlantic slave trade itself were voices calling for its abolition. The American and French revolutions stimulated the abolitionist cause. The American call for "life, liberty, and the pursuit of happiness" and the French appeal for "liberty, equality, and fraternity" suggested that there was a universal human right to freedom and equality.

Olaudah Equiano

Africans also took up the struggle to abolish commerce in human beings. Frequent slave revolts in the eighteenth and nineteenth centuries made the institution of slavery an expensive and dangerous business. Some freed slaves contributed to the abolitionist cause by writing books that exposed the brutality of institutional slavery. Most notable of them was the west African Olaudah Equiano (1745–1797), who in 1789 published an autobiography detailing his experiences as a slave and a free man. Captured at age ten in his native Benin (in modern Nigeria), Equiano worked as a slave in the West Indies, Virginia, and Pennsylvania. He accompanied one of his masters on several campaigns of the Seven Years' War before purchasing his freedom in 1766. Equiano's book became a best-seller, and the author traveled throughout the British isles giving speeches and denouncing slavery as an evil institution. He lobbied government officials and members of Parliament, and his efforts strengthened the antislavery movement in England.

The Economic Costs of Slavery

Quite apart from moral and political arguments, economic forces also contributed to the end of slavery and the slave trade. Plantations, slavery, and the slave trade continued to flourish as long as they were profitable, notwithstanding the efforts of abolitionists. Yet it gradually became clear that slave labor did not come cheap. The possibility of rebellion forced slave societies to maintain expensive military forces. Even in peaceful times slaves often worked unenthusiastically, but owners had to care for them throughout their lives no matter how hard they worked. Furthermore, in the late eighteenth century a rapid expansion of Caribbean sugar production led to declining prices. About the same time, African slave traders and European merchants sharply increased the prices they charged for fresh slaves.

As the profitability of slavery declined, Europeans began to shift their investments from sugarcane and slaves to newly emerging manufacturing industries. Investors soon found that wage labor in factories was cheaper than slave labor on plantations.

Contexts & Connections

The Globalization of African Music

The Atlantic slave trade forced millions of African captives to toil in strange lands, far distant from the familiar comforts and cultural patterns of their home societies. For many of these involuntary laborers, the playing of African music brought a sense of home and community to mind. It represented precisely what the slaves had lost—a sense of cultural grounding and belonging.

African slaves in the Americas initiated a trend that has continued to the present day and spread well beyond the African-American community. They adapted African musical traditions, including both their rhythmic and their oratorical elements, to their new environments as a means of buffering the shock of transition, as a way to survive and also to resist the horrid conditions of their new lives. In the process, they managed to create musical forms that made their influence felt not only in slave quarters but also in the multicultural societies of the Caribbean and the Americas and ultimately in the larger world.

Slaves fashioned a sense of identity and strength by bending west African instruments and musical traditions to European languages, Christian religion, and the work routines of American plantations. Slave musicians played drums and stringed instruments like banjos that closely resembled traditional African instruments. They adapted west African "call and response" patterns of singing to the rhythms of field work on plantations. The call and response format also found its way into the music of spirituals that blended Christian, European, and African influences.

Many slave owners dismissed drumming and African-influenced music as heathenism, and some sought to ban it altogether out of fears that it harbored subversive potential. Slave owners in South Carolina recalled, for example, that slaves had used drums to signal one another to rise up during the Stono rebellion of 1739. Despite efforts to suppress African influences, the music of slaves and later of their free descendants survived and testified to the continuing relevance of music as a means of shaping community identity and resistance to oppression. From work songs and spirituals to the blues, jazz, and soul, African-American music evolved to mirror the difficult and often chaotic circumstances of black life in the Americas.

As retooled by black musicians in the United States and the Caribbean, African musical traditions profoundly influenced the aural experience of American societies. African-influenced popular music came to dominate entertainment, especially in the twentieth century. Today the popularity of African-influenced music has reached global proportions. The success of displaced Africans in handing down musical traditions that have appealed both to blacks and to larger global audiences is most evident in the remarkable spread of reggae and rap or hip-hop music. Grounded in African traditions, including wordplay and rhyming, reggae and rap artists have not hesitated to address contemporary social issues of poverty, injustice, oppression, and war. Their music enjoys a worldwide audience and marks yet another phase in the globalization of African music that began during the era of the Atlantic slave trade.

As an additional benefit, free workers spent much of their income on manufactured goods. Meanwhile, European investors realized that leaving Africans in Africa where they could secure raw materials and buy manufactured goods in exchange was good business. Thus European entrepreneurs began to look upon Africa as something other than a source of slave labor.

End of the Slave Trade

In 1803 Denmark abolished trade in slaves, and other lands followed the Danish example: Great Britain in 1807, the United States in 1808, France in 1814, the Netherlands in 1817, and Spain in 1845. The end of the legal commerce in slaves did not abolish the institution of slavery itself, however, and as long as plantation slavery continued, a clandestine trade shipped slaves across the Atlantic. British naval squadrons sought to prevent this trade by patrolling the west coast of Africa conducting search and seizure operations, and gradually the illegal slave trade ground to a halt. The last documented ship that carried slaves across the Atlantic arrived in Cuba in 1867.

The Abolition of Slavery

The abolition of the institution of slavery itself was a long and drawn-out process: emancipation of all slaves came in 1833 in British colonies, 1848 in French colonies, 1865 in the United States, 1886 in Cuba, and 1888 in Brazil. Saudi Arabia and Angola abolished slavery in the 1960s. Officially, slavery no longer exists, but millions of people live in various forms of servitude even today. According to the Anti-Slavery Society for the Protection of Human Rights, debt bondage, contract labor, sham adoptions, servile marriages, and other forms of servitude still oppress more than two hundred million people, mostly in Africa, south Asia, and Latin America. Meanwhile, the legacy of the Atlantic slave trade remains visible throughout much of the western hemisphere, where the African diaspora has given rise to distinctive African-American communities.

During the early modern era, the peoples of sub-Saharan Africa organized societies on the basis of kinship groups as they had since the early days of the Bantu migrations. They also built states and traded with Islamic societies as they had since the eighth century C.E. Yet African peoples also experienced dramatic changes as they participated in the formation of an integrated Atlantic Ocean basin. The principal agents of change were European merchant-mariners who sought commercial opportunities in sub-Saharan Africa. They brought European manufactured goods and introduced American food crops that fueled population growth throughout Africa. But they also encouraged vast expansion of existing slave-trading networks as they sought laborers for plantations in the western hemisphere. The Atlantic slave trade violently removed sixteen million or more individuals from their home societies, and it led to political turmoil and social disruption throughout much of sub-Saharan Africa. Enslaved Africans and their descendants were mostly unable to build states or organize societies in the western hemisphere. But they formed an African diaspora that maintained some African traditions and profoundly influenced the development of societies in all slave-holding regions of the Caribbean and the Americas. They also collaborated with others to bring about an end to the slave trade and the abolition of slavery itself.

CHRONOLOGY

1441	Beginning of the Portuguese slave trade
1464–1493	Reign of Sunni Ali
1464–1591	Songhay empire
1506–1542	Reign of King Afonso I of Kongo
1623–1663	Reign of Queen Nzinga of Ndongo
1706	Execution of Doña Beatriz
1745–1797	Life of Olaudah Equiano
1793–1804	Haitian revolution
1807	End of the British slave trade
1865	Abolition of slavery in the United States

FOR FURTHER READING

Paul Bohannan and Philip D. Curtin. *Africa and Africans.* 3rd ed. Prospect Heights, Ill., 1988. General discussion of African society, religion, and history by an anthropologist and a historian.

George E. Brooks. *Landlords and Strangers: Ecology, Society, and Trade in Western Africa, 1000–1630.* Boulder, Colo., 1993. Careful study exploring the political and social development of west Africa in environmental context.

Judith A. Carney. *Black Rice: The African Origin of Rice Cultivation in the Americas.* Cambridge, Mass., 2001. Fascinating study demonstrating how African slaves introduced a sophisticated agricultural technology to the low country of Carolina and Georgia.

Michael L. Conniff and Thomas J. Davis. *Africans in the Americas: A History of the Black Diaspora.* New York, 1994. A comprehensive survey of African-European relations, the slave trade, and the African diaspora.

Philip D. Curtin. *The Rise and Fall of the Plantation Complex: Essays in Atlantic History.* 2nd ed. Cambridge, 1998. Examines plantation societies and slavery as institutions linking lands throughout the Atlantic Ocean basin.

———, ed. *Africa Remembered: Narratives by West Africans from the Era of the Slave Trade.* Madison, 1967. Translations of works in which ten enslaved Africans recounted their memories of early modern Africa.

Basil Davidson. *The African Slave Trade.* Rev. ed. Boston, 1980. A popular history of the slave trade by a prominent student of African history.

David Brion Davis. *Slavery and Human Progress.* New York, 1984. A rich and thoughtful book that places African slavery in a larger historical context.

Christopher Ehret. *The Civilizations of Africa: A History to 1800.* Charlottesville, Va., 2002. An important contribution that views Africa in the context of world history.

David Eltis. *The Rise of African Slavery in the Americas.* Cambridge 1999. Emphasizes both the economic and the cultural foundations of Atlantic slavery.

Olaudah Equiano. *Equiano's Travels.* Ed. by Paul Edwards. Oxford, 1967. An abridged and conveniently available edition of Equiano's autobiography.

Leland Ferguson. *Uncommon Ground: Archaeology and Early African America, 1650–1800.* Washington, 1992. Enriches the understanding of slave society in the southeastern United States on the basis of archaeological discoveries.

Joseph E. Harris, ed. *Global Dimensions of the African Diaspora.* 2nd ed. Washington, 1993. A collection of scholarly essays on Africans in the Americas and the larger world.

Anne Hilton. *The Kingdom of Kongo.* Oxford, 1985. A valuable synthesis.

Patrick Manning. *Slavery and African Life: Occidental, Oriental, and African Slave Trades.* Cambridge, 1990. Concentrates on the impact of the slave trade on Africa.

Sidney Mintz. *Sweetness and Power: The Place of Sugar in Modern History.* New York, 1985. Important study of sugar, slavery, politics, and society by a prominent anthropologist.

Sidney W. Mintz and Richard Price. *The Birth of African-American Culture: An Anthropological Perspective.* Boston, 1992. A provocative study analyzing the forging of African-American cultural traditions under the influence of slavery.

Richard Price. *First-Time: The Historical Vision of an Afro-American People.* Baltimore, 1983. Fascinating reconstruction of the experiences and historical self-understanding of the Saramaka maroons of modern Suriname.

James Rawley. *The Transatlantic Slave Trade: A History.* New York, 1981. A reliable survey concentrating on the roles of European and Euro-American peoples in the slave trade.

Elias N. Saad. *Social History of Timbuktu: The Role of Muslim Scholars and Notables, 1400–1900.* Cambridge, 1983. Emphasizes the role of Muslim scholars in one of west Africa's most important commercial and cultural centers.

Mechal Sobel. *The World They Made Together: Black and White Values in Eighteenth Century Virginia.* Princeton, 1987. Argues persuasively that African-American slaves deeply influenced the development of early American society.

Barbara L. Solow, ed. *Slavery and the Rise of the Atlantic System.* Cambridge, 1991. An important collection of scholarly essays on slavery and its implications for the history of the Atlantic Ocean basin.

Robert Farris Thompson. *Flash of the Spirit: African and African-American Art and Philosophy.* New York, 1983. Fascinating study that documents and analyzes the maintenance and adaptation of African cultural traditions in the Americas.

John Thornton. *Africa and Africans in the Making of the Atlantic World, 1400–1800.* 2nd ed. New York, 1997. A rich analysis of African peoples and their roles in the Atlantic Ocean basin.

———. *The Kongolese Saint Anthony: Doña Beatriz Kimpa Vita and the Antonian Movement, 1684–1706.* Cambridge, 1998. Excellent scholarly study of Doña Beatriz and the Antonian movement in the kingdom of Kongo.

Jan Vansina. *Kingdoms of the Savanna.* Madison, 1966. The best history of central Africa in early modern times.

———. *Paths in the Rainforest: Toward a History of Political Tradition in Equatorial Africa.* Madison, 1990. A thoughtful analysis that considers both native traditions and external influences on African history.

See our **Online Learning Center at www.mhhe.com/bentley3** for additional readings, practice maps, quizzes, and internet activities.

Unfamiliar words? Check out the **Primary Source Investigator CD-ROM** for an interactive glossary, interactive maps, more images, and primary sources.

European-style buildings on the waterfront in eighteenth-century Guangzhou, where foreign merchants conducted their business.

the new arrivals proceeded along narrow lanes to a honeycomb of small, cell-like rooms barely large enough to accommodate one man and his possessions. Aside from a bench, a makeshift bed, and boards that served as a desk, the rooms were empty. For the next three days and two nights, the cramped rooms were home to the candidates, who spent all their time writing "eight-legged essays"—literary compositions with eight distinct sections—on questions posed by the examiners. There were no interruptions, nor was there any communication between candidates. If someone died during the examination period, officials wrapped his body in a straw mat and tossed it over the high walls that ringed the compound.

The Examination System and Chinese Society

The possibility of bureaucratic service—with prospects for rich social and financial rewards—ensured that competition for degrees was ferocious at all levels. As a result, cheating candidates and corrupt examiners occasionally compromised the system. Yet a degree did not ensure government service. During the Qing dynasty the empire's one million degree holders competed for twenty thousand official civil service positions. Those who passed only the district exams had few opportunities for bureaucratic employment and usually spent their careers "plowing with the writing brush" by teaching in local schools or serving as family tutors. Those who passed the metropolitan examinations, however, could look forward to powerful positions in the imperial bureaucracy.

The examination system was a pivotal institution. By opening the door to honor, power, and rewards, the examinations encouraged serious pursuit of a formal education. Furthermore, since the system did not erect social barriers before its recruits, it provided an avenue for upward social mobility. Years of education and travel to examination sites were expensive, so candidates from wealthy families enjoyed advantages over others, but the exams themselves were open to all males regardless of age or social class. Finally, in addition to selecting officials for government service, the education and examination system molded the personal values of those who managed day-to-day affairs in imperial China. By concentrating on Confucian classics and neo-Confucian commentaries, the examinations guaranteed that Confucianism would be at the heart of Chinese education and that Confucians would govern the state.

Economic and Social Changes

By modeling their governmental structure on the centralized imperial states of earlier Chinese dynasties, the Ming and Qing emperors succeeded in their goal of restoring and maintaining traditional ways in China. They also sought to preserve the traditional hierarchical and patriarchal social order. Yet, while the emperors promoted conservative political and social policies, China experienced economic and social changes, partly as a result of influences from abroad. Agricultural production increased dramatically—especially after the introduction of new food crops from the Americas—and fueled rapid population growth. Meanwhile, global trade brought China enormous wealth, which stimulated the domestic economy by encouraging increased trade, manufacturing, and urban growth. These developments deeply influenced Chinese society and partly undermined the stability that the Ming and Qing emperors sought to preserve.

The Patriarchal Family

Filial Piety

Moralists portrayed the Chinese people as one large family, and they extended family values to the larger society. Filial piety, for example, implied not only duties of children toward their fathers but also loyalty of subjects toward the emperor. Like the imperial government, the Chinese family was hierarchical, patriarchal, and authoritarian. The father was head of the household, and he passed leadership of the family to his eldest son. The veneration of ancestors, which the state promoted as a matter of Confucian propriety, strengthened the authority of the patriarchs by honoring the male line of descent in formal family rituals. Filial piety was the cornerstone of family values. Children had the duty to look after their parents' happiness and well-being, and a crucial obligation was to support parents in their old age. Young children heard stories of sons who went so far as to cut off parts of their bodies to ensure that their parents had enough to eat!

The social assumptions of the Chinese family extended into patrilineal descent groups such as the clan. Sometimes numbering into the thousands, clan members came from all social classes, though members of the gentry usually dominated a given clan. Clans assumed responsibilities that exceeded the capacities of the nuclear family, such as the maintenance of local order, organization of local economies, and provision for welfare. Clan-supported education gave poor but promising relatives the opportunity to succeed in the civil service examinations. The principal motives behind this charity were corporate self-interest as well as altruism. A government position brought prestige and prosperity to the entire clan, so educational support was a prudent investment. Finally, clans served as a means for the transmission of Confucian values from the gentry leaders to all social classes within the clan.

Gender Relations

Within the family, Confucian principles subjected women to the authority of men. The subordination of females began at an early age. Chinese parents preferred boys over girls. Whereas a boy might have the opportunity to take the official examinations, become a government official, and thereby bring honor and financial reward to the entire clan, parents regarded a girl as a social and financial liability. After years of expensive upbringing, most girls would marry and become members of other

To encourage widows to remain unmarried, the Ming and Qing governments constructed arches in honor of those who remained chaste. These arches erected during the Qing dynasty still stand in Anhui province in the Yangzi River valley.

households. Under these circumstances it was not surprising that life was precarious for newborn girls, who were the primary victims of infanticide.

During the Ming and Qing dynasties, patriarchal authority over females probably became tighter than ever before in China. Since ancient times, relatives had discouraged widows from remarriage, but social pressures increased during the Ming dynasty. Friends and relatives not only encouraged widows to honor the memory of their departed husbands but also heaped posthumous honors on those who committed suicide and followed their spouses to the grave.

Foot Binding

Moreover, foot binding, a custom that probably originated in the Song dynasty, became exceptionally popular during the late Ming and Qing dynasties. Tightly constrained and even deformed by strips of linen, bound feet could not grow naturally and so would not support the weight of an adult woman. Bound feet were small and dainty, and they sometimes inspired erotic arousal among men. The practice of foot binding became most widespread among the wealthy classes, since it demonstrated an ability to support women who could not perform physical labor, but commoners sometimes bound the feet of especially pretty girls in hopes of arranging favorable marriages that would enhance the family's social standing.

Marriage itself was a contractual affair whose principal purpose was to continue the male line of descent. A bride became a member of the husband's family, and there was no ambiguity about her position in the household. On her wedding day, as soon as she arrived at her husband's home, the bride performed ritual acts demonstrating subservience to her husband and her new family. Women could not divorce their husbands, but men could put aside their wives in cases where there was no offspring or where the wife was guilty of adultery, theft, disobedience to her husband's family, or even being too talkative.

Thus custom and law combined to strengthen patriarchal authority in Chinese families during the Ming and Qing dynasties. Yet, while family life continued to develop along traditional lines, the larger Chinese society underwent considerable change between the sixteenth and eighteenth centuries.

Population Growth and Economic Development

China was a predominantly agricultural society, a fact that meshed agreeably with the Confucian view that land was the source of everything praiseworthy. The emperor himself acknowledged the central importance of agriculture by plowing the first furrow of the season. Yet only a small fraction of China's land is suitable for planting: even today only about 11 percent is in cultivation. To feed the country's large population, China's farmers relied on intensive, garden-style agriculture that was highly productive. On its strong agrarian foundation, China supported a large population and built the most highly commercialized economy of the preindustrial world.

American Food Crops

By intensively cultivating every available parcel of land, Chinese peasants increased their yields of traditional food crops—especially rice, wheat, and millet—until the seventeenth century. Beginning about the mid-seventeenth century, as peasants approached the upper limits of agricultural productivity, Spanish merchants coming by way of the Philippines introduced American food crops to China. American maize, sweet potatoes, and peanuts permitted Chinese farmers to take advantage of soils that previously had gone uncultivated. The introduction of new crops increased the food supply and supported further population growth.

Population Growth

In spite of recurring epidemic diseases such as plague, which claimed the lives of millions, China's population rose rapidly from 100 million in 1500 to 160 million in 1600. Partly because of rebellion and war, it fell to 140 million in the mid-seventeenth century, but returned to 160 million by 1700 and then surged to 225 million by 1750, thus registering more than a 40 percent increase in half a century. This rapid demographic growth set the stage for economic and social problems, since agricultural production could not keep pace with population over a long term. Acute problems did not occur until the nineteenth century, but per capita income in China began to decline as early as the reign of Qianlong.

While an increasing population placed pressure on Chinese resources, the growing commercial market offered opportunities for entrepreneurs. Because of demographic expansion, entrepreneurs had access to a large labor force that was both occupationally and geographically mobile, so they were able to recruit workers readily at low cost. After the mid-sixteenth century the Chinese economy benefited also from the influx of Japanese and American silver, which stimulated trade and financed further commercial expansion.

Foreign Trade

Global trade brought tremendous prosperity to China, especially during the early Qing dynasty. Chinese workers produced vast quantities of silk, porcelain, lacquerware, and tea for consumers in the Indian Ocean basin, central Asia, and Europe. The silk industry was especially well organized: weavers worked in workshops for regular wages producing fine satins and brocades for export. Chinese imports were relatively few: they included spices from Maluku, exotic products like birds and animal skins from tropical regions, and small quantities of woolen textiles from Europe. Compensation for exports came most importantly in the form of silver bullion, which supported the silver-based Chinese economy and fueled manufacturing.

A Ming-era vase painting depicts a woman weaving silk as an attendant pours tea.

Economic growth and commercial expansion took place mostly in an atmosphere of tight government regulation. During the early fifteenth century, the Ming emperor Yongle sought to establish a Chinese presence in the Indian Ocean basin, and he sponsored a series of seven massive maritime expeditions (1405–1433) led by the eunuch admiral Zheng He. The Chinese fleets included as many as 317 vessels and 28,000 men. Zheng He called at ports from Java to Malindi, suppressed pirates in southeast Asian waters, intervened in local conflicts in Sumatra and Ceylon, intimidated local authorities with shows of force in southern Arabia and Mogadishu, and made China's presence felt throughout the Indian Ocean basin.

After the reign of Yongle, however, the Ming government withdrew its support for expensive maritime expeditions and even tried to prevent Chinese subjects from dealing with foreign peoples. In its effort to pacify southern China during the later seventeenth century, the Qing government tried to end maritime activity altogether. An imperial edict of

1656 forbade "even a plank from drifting to the sea," and in 1661 the emperor Kangxi ordered evacuation of the southern coastal regions. These policies had only a limited effect—small Chinese vessels continued to trade actively in Japan and southeast Asian ports—and when Qing forces pacified southern China in the 1680s, government authorities rescinded the strictest measures. Thereafter, however, Qing authorities closely supervised the activities of foreign merchants in China. They permitted Portuguese merchants to operate only at the port of Macau, while British agents had to deal exclusively with the official merchant guild in Guangzhou.

While limiting the activities of foreign merchants, government policies also discouraged the organization of large-scale commercial ventures by Chinese merchants. In the absence of government approval, it was impossible, for example, to maintain shipyards that could construct large sailing ships like the mammoth, nine-masted "treasure ships" that Zheng He had led throughout the Indian Ocean. Similarly, it was impossible to organize large trading firms like the English East India Company or the Dutch VOC.

Trade and Migration to Southeast Asia

Nevertheless, thousands of Chinese merchants worked either individually or in partnerships, plying the waters of the China seas to link China with global trade networks. Chinese merchants were especially prominent in Manila, where they exchanged silk and porcelain for American silver that came across the Pacific Ocean with the Manila galleons. They were also frequent visitors at the Dutch colonial capital of Batavia, where they supplied the VOC with silk and porcelain in exchange for silver and Indonesian spices. Entrepreneurial Chinese merchants ventured also to lands throughout southeast Asia—the Philippines, Borneo, Sumatra, Malaya, Thailand, and elsewhere—in search of exotic tropical products for Chinese consumers. Indeed, the early modern era was an age when merchants established a prominent Chinese presence throughout southeast Asia.

Government and Technology

China's economic expansion took place largely in the absence of technological innovation. During the Tang and Song dynasties, Chinese engineers had produced a veritable flood of inventions, and China was the world's leader in technology. Yet by early Ming times, technological innovation had slowed. Imperial armed forces adopted European cannons and advanced firearms for their own uses—thus borrowing forms of gunpowder technology that had originated in China and that Europeans had refined and improved—but little innovation in agricultural and industrial technologies occurred during the Ming and Qing dynasties.

Part of the explanation for the slowdown has to do with role of the government. During the Tang and Song dynasties, the imperial government had encouraged technological innovation as a foundation of military and economic strength. In contrast, the Ming and Qing regimes favored political and social stability over technological innovation, which they feared would lead to unsettling change. Alongside government policy, the abundance and ready availability of skilled workers also discouraged technological innovation. When employers wanted to increase production, they found that hiring additional workers was less costly than making large investments in new technologies. In the short run this tactic maintained relative prosperity in China while keeping most of the population gainfully employed. Over the longer term, however, it ensured that China lost technological ground to European peoples, who embarked on a round of stunning technological innovation beginning about the mid-eighteenth century.

Gentry, Commoners, Soldiers, and Mean People

Privileged Classes

Except for the emperor and his family, scholar-bureaucrats and gentry occupied the most exalted positions in Chinese society. Because of their official positions, the scholar-bureaucrats ranked slightly above gentry. Nevertheless, scholar-bureaucrats

Sources from the Past

Qianlong on Chinese Trade with England

Qing administrators tightly restricted foreign trade. Foreign merchants had to deal with government-approved agents outside the city walls of Guangzhou and had to depart as soon as they had completed their business. In 1793 a British diplomat representing King George III of England bestowed gifts on the emperor Qianlong and petitioned for the right to trade at ports other than Guangzhou. In a letter to King George, Qianlong outlined his views on Chinese trade with England. His letter also bespeaks clearly the importance of government policy for commerce and economic affairs in China.

You, O king, from afar have yearned after the blessings of our civilization, and in your eagerness to come into touch with our influence have sent an embassy across the sea bearing a memorandum. I have already taken note of your respectful spirit of submission, have treated your mission with extreme favor and loaded it with gifts, besides issuing a mandate to you, O king, and honoring you with the bestowal of valuable presents. . . .

Yesterday your ambassador petitioned my ministers to memorialize me regarding your trade with China, but his proposal is not consistent with our dynastic usage and cannot be entertained. Hitherto, all European nations, including your own country's barbarian merchants, have carried on their trade with our Celestial Empire at Guangzhou. Such has been the procedure for many years, although our Celestial Empire possesses all things in prolific abundance and lacks no product within its own borders. There was therefore no need to import the manufactures of outside barbarians in exchange for our own produce. But as the tea, silk, and porcelain which the Celestial Empire produces are absolute necessities to European nations and to yourselves, we have permitted, as a signal mark of favor, that trading agents should be established at Guangzhou, so that your wants might be supplied and your country thus participate in our beneficence. But your ambassador has now put forward new requests which completely fail to recognize our throne's principle to "treat strangers from afar with indulgence," and to exercise a pacifying control over barbarian tribes the world over. . . . Your England is not the only nation trading at Guangzhou. If other nations, following your bad example, wrongfully importune my ear with further impossible requests, how will it be possible for me to treat them with easy indulgence? Nevertheless, I do not forget the lonely remoteness of your island, cut off from the world by intervening wastes of sea, nor do I overlook your excusable ignorance of the usages of our Celestial Empire. I have consequently commanded my ministers to enlighten your ambassador on the subject, and have ordered the departure of the mission. . . .

If, after the receipt of this explicit decree, you lightly give ear to the representations of your subordinates and allow your barbarian merchants to proceed to Zhejiang and Tianjin, with the object of landing and trading there, the ordinances of my Celestial Empire are strict in the extreme, and the local officials, both civil and military, are bound reverently to obey the law of the land. Should your vessels touch the shore, your merchants will assuredly never be permitted to land or to reside there, but will be subject to instant expulsion. In that event your barbarian merchants will have had a long journey for nothing. Do not say that you were not warned in due time! Tremblingly obey and show no negligence! A special mandate!

SOURCE: J. O. P. Bland. *Annals and Memoirs of the Court of Peking*. Boston: Houghton Mifflin, 1914, pp. 325–31. (Translation slightly modified.)

What considerations might have prompted the Chinese government to take such a restrictive approach to foreign trade?

had much in common with the gentry: they came largely from gentry ranks, and after leaving government service they usually rejoined gentry society. The scholar-bureaucrats and gentry functioned as intermediaries between the imperial government and local society. By organizing water control projects and public security measures, they played a crucial role in the management of local society.

Scholar-bureaucrats and gentry were easy to identify. They wore distinctive clothing—black gowns with blue borders adorned with various rank insignia—and commoners addressed them with honorific terms. They received favorable legal treatment that reflected their privileged status. As a rule, commoners could not call members of privileged classes to appear as witnesses in legal proceedings. They also enjoyed immunity from corporal punishment and exemption from labor service and taxes.

Most of the gentry owned land, which was their major source of income. As long as they did not have to perform physical labor, some gentry also supplemented their income by operating pawn and rice shops. Many of them were also silent business partners of merchants and entrepreneurs. Their principal source of income, however, came from the government service to which only they had access by virtue of their academic degrees. In contrast to landed elites elsewhere, who often lived on rural estates, China's gentry resided largely in cities and towns, where they tended to political, social, and financial affairs.

Working Classes

Confucian tradition ranked three broad classes of commoners below the gentry: peasants, artisans or workers, and merchants. By far the biggest class consisted of peasants, a designation that covered everyone from day laborers to tenant farmers to petty landlords. Confucian principles regarded peasants as the most honorable of the three classes, since they performed honest labor and provided the food that supported the entire population.

The category of artisans and workers encompassed a wide spectrum of occupations. Despite their lower status, crafts workers, tailors, barbers, physicians, and workers in manufacturing plants generally enjoyed higher income than peasants did. Artisans and workers were usually employees of the state or of gentry and merchant families, but they also pursued their occupations as self-employed persons.

Merchants

Merchants, from street peddlers to individuals of enormous wealth and influence, ranked at the bottom level of the Confucian social hierarchy. Because moralists looked upon them as unscrupulous social parasites, merchants enjoyed little legal protection, and government policy was always critically important to their pursuits. Yet Chinese merchants often garnered official support for their enterprises, either through bribery of government bureaucrats or through profit-sharing arrangements with gentry families. Indeed, the participation of gentry families in commercial ventures such as warehousing, money lending, and pawnbroking blurred the distinction between gentry and merchants. In addition, merchants blurred the distinction further by providing their sons with an education that prepared them for government examinations, which in turn could result in promotion to gentry status and appointment to civil service positions.

This engraving depicts a peasant couple in harness pulling a plow. Note that the man wears the braided queue that Manchus required their male Chinese subjects to wear.

The prominence of artisans and merchants pointed up the social and economic development of China since the time of Confucius. Although China was still a basically agricultural land, manufacturing and commerce had become much more economically important than in ancient times. As a result, those who could recognize and exploit opportunities had the potential to lead comfortable lives and even to climb into the ranks of the privileged gentry class. Yet Chinese merchants and artisans did not forge cooperative relationships with government authorities like the political-commercial alliances formed in the English and Dutch states in early modern times. Late Ming and Qing authorities permitted Chinese merchants to engage in small-scale commerce, and they allowed foreigners to trade through the official merchant guild in Guangzhou. Their principal concern, however, was to preserve the stability of a large agrarian society, not to promote rapid economic development through trade. Thus, unlike some of their European counterparts, Chinese authorities did not adopt policies designed to strengthen both merchants and the state by authorizing merchants to pursue their efforts aggressively in the larger world.

Lower Classes

Beyond the Confucian social hierarchy were members of the military forces and the so-called mean people. Confucian moralists regarded armed forces as a wretched but necessary evil and attempted to avoid military dominance of society by placing civilian bureaucrats in the highest command positions, even at the expense of military effectiveness. The mean people included slaves, indentured servants, entertainers, prostitutes, and other marginal groups like the "beggars of Jiangsu" and the "boat people of Guangdong."

The Confucian Tradition and New Cultural Influences

The Ming and Qing emperors looked to Chinese traditions for guidance in framing their cultural as well as their political and social policies. They provided generous support for Confucianism, particularly in the form of neo-Confucianism articulated by the twelfth-century scholar Zhu Xi, and they ensured that formal education in China revolved around Confucian thought and values. Yet the Confucian tradition was not the only cultural alternative in Ming and Qing China. Demographic and urban growth encouraged the emergence of a vibrant popular culture in Chinese cities, and European missionaries reintroduced Roman Catholic Christianity to China and acquainted Chinese intellectuals with European science and technology as well.

Neo-Confucianism and Pulp Fiction

Imperial sponsorship of Chinese cultural traditions meant primarily support for the Confucian tradition, especially as systematized by the Song dynasty scholar Zhu Xi, the most prominent architect of neo-Confucianism. Zhu Xi combined the moral, ethical, and political values of Confucius with the logical rigor and speculative power of Buddhist philosophy. He emphasized the values of self-discipline, filial piety, and obedience to established rulers, all of which appealed to Ming and Qing emperors seeking to maintain stability in their vast realm. Cultural policies of the Ming and Qing dynasties made the neo-Confucian tradition the reigning imperial ideology from the fourteenth to the early twentieth century.

Confucian Education

In order to promote Confucian values, the Ming and Qing emperors supported educational programs at several levels. They funded the Hanlin Academy, a research institute for Confucian scholars in Beijing, and maintained provincial schools throughout China where promising students could study for the civil service examinations. The exams themselves encouraged the cultivation of Confucian values, since they focused largely on Confucian texts and neo-Confucian commentaries.

Ming and Qing courts also provided generous funding for other projects emphasizing Chinese cultural traditions. The Ming emperor Yongle sponsored the compilation of the *Yongle Encyclopedia,* a vast collection of Chinese philosophical, literary, and historical texts that filled almost twenty-three thousand scrolls. During the Qing dynasty both Kangxi and Qianlong organized similar projects. Kangxi's *Collection of Books* was smaller than the *Yongle Encyclopedia,* but it was more influential because the emperor had it printed and distributed, whereas Yongle's compilation was available only in three manuscript copies. Qianlong's *Complete Library of the Four Treasuries* was too large to publish—it ran to 93,556 pamphlet-size volumes—but the emperor deposited manuscript copies in seven libraries throughout China.

Popular Culture

While the imperial courts promoted Confucianism, a lively popular culture took shape in the cities of China. Most urban residents did not have an advanced education and knew little about Confucius, Zhu Xi, or other intellectual luminaries. Many of them were literate merchants, however, and they preferred entertainment and diversion more intellectually engaging than that found in local teahouses and wine shops. Popular novels met their needs.

Popular Novels

Confucian scholars looked down on popular novels as crude fiction that had little to do with the realities of the world. Printing made it possible to produce books cheaply and in mass quantities, however, and urban residents eagerly consumed the fast-paced novels that flooded Chinese cities during the Ming and Qing eras. Many of the novels had little literary merit, but their tales of conflict, horror, wonder, excitement, and sometimes unconcealed pornography appealed to readers.

Yet many popular novels also offered thoughtful reflections on the world and human affairs. The historical novel *The Romance of the Three Kingdoms,* for example, explored the political intrigue that followed the collapse of the Han dynasty. *The Dream of the Red Chamber* told the story of cousins deeply in love who could not marry because of their families' wishes. Through the prism of a sentimental love story, the novel shed fascinating light on the dynamics of wealthy scholar-gentry families. In a different vein, *Journey to the West* dealt with the seventh-century journey to India of the famous Buddhist monk Xuanzang. In the popular novel, Xuanzang's traveling companion was a monkey with magical powers who among other things could jump 10,000 kilometers (6,215 miles) in a single bound. While promoting Buddhist values, *Journey to the West* also made the trickster monkey a wildly popular and celebrated character in Chinese literature. As recently as 1987, Chinese-American novelist Maxine Hong Kingston adapted this character to modern times in her novel *Tripmaster Monkey.*

The Return of Christianity to China

Nestorian Christians had established churches and monasteries in China as early as the seventh century C.E., and Roman Catholic communities were prominent in Chinese commercial centers during the Yuan dynasty. After the outbreak of epidemic plague and the collapse of the Yuan dynasty in the fourteenth century, however, Christianity disappeared from China. When Roman Catholic missionaries returned in the sixteenth century, they had to start from scratch in their efforts to win converts and establish a Christian community.

Matteo Ricci

The most prominent of the missionaries were the Jesuits, who worked to strengthen Roman Catholic Christianity in Europe and also to spread their faith abroad. Founder of the mission to China was the Italian Jesuit Matteo Ricci (1552–1610), who had the ambitious goal of converting China to Christianity, beginning with the Ming emperor Wanli. Ricci was a brilliant and learned man as well as a polished diplomat, and he became a popular figure at the Ming court. Upon arrival at Macau in 1582, Ricci immersed himself in the study of the Chinese language and the Confucian classics. He had a talent for languages, and his phenomenal memory enabled him to master the thousands of characters used in literary Chinese writing. By the time he first traveled to Beijing and visited the imperial court in 1601, Ricci was able to write learned Chinese and converse fluently with Confucian scholars.

Ricci's mastery of Chinese language and literature opened doors for the Jesuits, who then dazzled their hosts with European science, technology, and mechanical gadgetry. Ricci and his colleagues had an advanced education in mathematics and astronomy, and they were able to correct Chinese calendars that consistently miscalculated solar eclipses. The Jesuits also prepared maps of the world—with China placed diplomatically at the center—on the basis of geographic knowledge that Europeans had gained during their voyages through the world's seas. The Jesuits even supervised the casting of high-quality bronze cannons for Ming and early Qing armies.

The Jesuits piqued Chinese curiosity also with mechanical devices. Finely ground glass prisms became popular because of their refraction of sunlight into its component parts. Harpsichords also drew attention, and Jesuits with musical talents often composed songs for their hosts. Most popular of all, however, were the devices that Chinese called "self-ringing bells"—spring-driven mechanical clocks that kept tolerably accurate time, chimed the hours, and sometimes even struck the quarter hours as well.

Confucianism and Christianity

The Jesuits sought to capture Chinese interest with European science and technology, but their ultimate goal was always to win converts. They portrayed Christianity as a faith very similar to Chinese cultural traditions. Ricci, for example, wrote a treatise entitled *The True Meaning of the Lord of Heaven* in which he argued that the doctrines of Confucius and Jesus were very similar, if not identical. Over the years, according to Ricci, neo-Confucian scholars had altered Confucius's own teachings, so adoption of Christianity by Chinese would represent a return to a more pure and original Confucianism. The Jesuits also held religious services in the Chinese language and allowed converts to continue the time-honored practice of venerating their ancestors.

Matteo Ricci (left) with Xu Quangqi, his most famous Chinese disciple. Both men wear the distinctive gowns of educated, refined scholar-gentry. A distinguished scholar who held an appointment at the Hanlin Academy, Xu helped Ricci translate Euclid's geometrical works into Chinese.

In spite of their tolerance, flexibility, and genuine respect for their hosts, the Jesuits attracted few converts in China. By the mid-eighteenth century, Chinese Christians numbered about 200,000—a tiny proportion of the Chinese population of 225 million. Chinese hesitated to adopt Christianity partly because of its exclusivity: for centuries, Chinese had honored Confucianism, Daoism, and Buddhism at the same time. Like Islam, though, Christianity claimed to be the only true religion, so conversion implied that Confucianism, Daoism, and Buddhism were inferior or even fallacious creeds—a proposition most Chinese were unwilling to accept.

End of the Jesuit Mission

Ultimately, the Roman Catholic mission in China came to an end because of squabbles between the Jesuits and members of the Franciscan and Dominican orders, who also sought converts in China. Jealous of the Jesuits' presence at the imperial court, the Franciscans and Dominicans complained to the pope about their rivals' tolerance of ancestor veneration and willingness to conduct Chinese-language services. The pope sided with the critics and in the early eighteenth century issued several proclamations ordering missionaries in China to suppress ancestor veneration and conduct services according to European standards. In response to this demand, the emperor Kangxi ordered an end to the preaching of Christianity in China. Although he did not strictly enforce the ban, the mission weakened, and by the mid-eighteenth century it had effectively come to an end.

The Roman Catholic mission to China did not attract large numbers of Chinese converts, but it nonetheless had important cultural effects. Besides making European science and technology known in China, the Jesuits also made China known in Europe. In letters, reports, and other writings distributed widely throughout Europe, the Jesuits described China as an orderly and rational society. The Confucian civil service system attracted the attention of European rulers, who began to design their own civil service bureaucracies in the eighteenth century. The rational morality of Confucianism also appealed to the Enlightenment philosophes, who sought alternatives to Christianity as the foundation for ethics and morality. For the first time since Marco Polo, the Jesuits made firsthand observations of China available to Europeans and stimulated strong European interest in east Asian societies.

THE UNIFICATION OF JAPAN

During the late sixteenth and early seventeenth centuries, the political unification of Japan ended an extended period of civil disorder. Like the Ming and Qing emperors in China, the Tokugawa shoguns sought to lay a foundation for long-term political and social stability, and they provided generous support for neo-Confucian studies in an effort to promote traditional values. Indeed, the shoguns went even further than their Chinese counterparts by promoting conservative values and tightly restricting foreign influence in Japan. As in China, however, demographic expansion and economic growth fostered social and cultural change in Japan, and merchants introduced Chinese and European influences into Japan.

The Tokugawa Shogunate

From the twelfth through the sixteenth century, a *shogun* ("military governor") ruled Japan through retainers who received political rights and large estates in exchange for military services. Theoretically, the shogun ruled as a temporary stand-in for the Japanese emperor, the ultimate source of political authority. In fact, however, the emperor was nothing more than a figurehead, and the shogun sought to monopolize power. After the fourteenth century the conflicting ambitions of shoguns and retainers led to constant turmoil, and by the sixteenth century Japan was in a state of civil war. Japanese historians often refer to the sixteenth century as the era of *sengoku*—"the country at war."

Tokugawa Ieyasu

Toward the end of the sixteenth century, powerful states emerged in several regions of Japan, and a series of military leaders brought about the unification of the land. In 1600 the last of these chieftains, Tokugawa Ieyasu (reigned 1600–1616), established a military government known as the Tokugawa *bakufu* ("tent government," since it theoretically was only a temporary replacement for the emperor's rule). Ieyasu and his descendants ruled the bakufu as shoguns from 1600 until the end of the Tokugawa dynasty in 1867.

MAP [27.3]
Tokugawa Japan, 1600–1867.

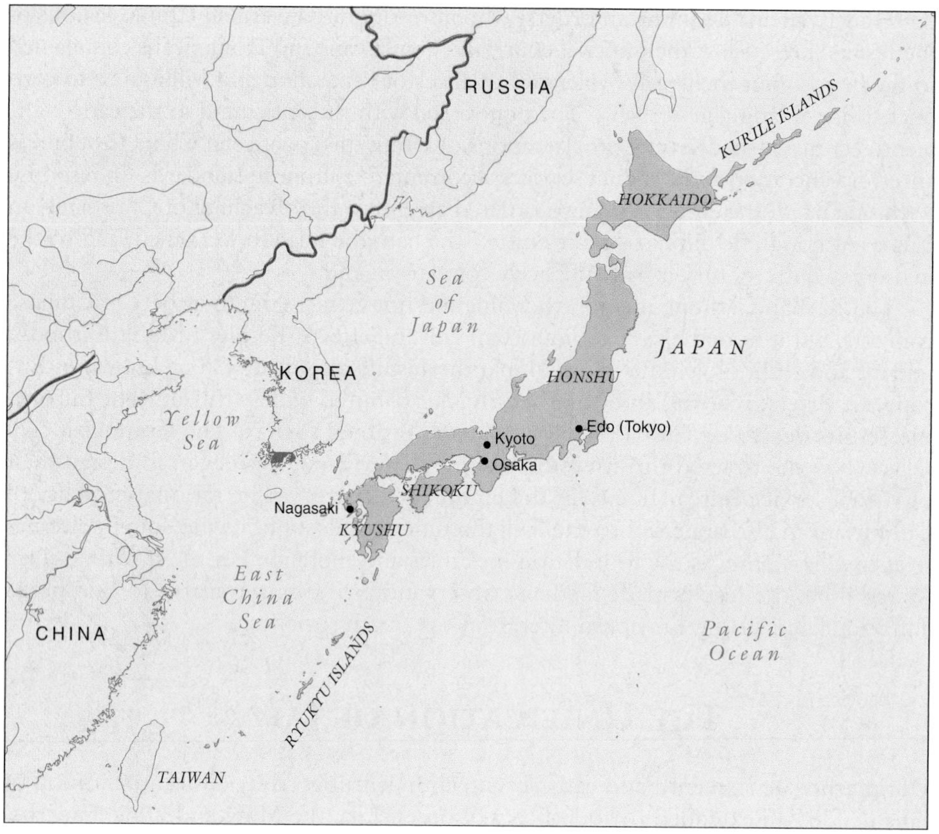

The principal aim of the Tokugawa shoguns was to stabilize their realm and prevent the return of civil war. Consequently, the shoguns needed to control the *daimyo* ("great names"), powerful territorial lords who ruled most of Japan from their vast, hereditary landholdings. The 260 or so daimyo functioned as near-absolute rulers within their domains. Each maintained a government staffed by military subordinates, supported an independent judiciary, established schools, and circulated paper money. Moreover, after the mid-sixteenth century, many daimyo established relationships with European mariners, from whom they learned how to manufacture and use gunpowder weapons. During the last decades of the *sengoku* era, cannons and personal firearms had played prominent roles in Japanese conflicts.

Control of the Daimyo

From the castle town of Edo (modern Tokyo), the shogun governed his own personal domain and sought to extend his control to the daimyo. The shoguns instituted the policy of "alternate attendance," which required daimyo to maintain their families at Edo and spend every other year at the Tokugawa court. This policy enabled the shoguns to keep an eye on the daimyo, and as a side effect it encouraged daimyo to spend their money on lavish residences and comfortable lives in Edo rather than investing it in military forces that could challenge the bakufu. The shoguns also subjected marriage alliances between daimyo families to bakufu approval, discouraged the daimyo from visiting one another, and required daimyo to obtain permits for construction work on their castles. Even meetings between the daimyo and the emperor required the shogun's permission.

In an effort to prevent European influences from destabilizing the land, the Tokugawa shoguns closely controlled relations between Japan and the outside world. They knew that Spanish forces had conquered the Philippine Islands in the sixteenth century, and they feared that Europeans might jeopardize the security of the bakufu itself. Even if Europeans did not conquer Japan, they could cause serious problems by making alliances with daimyo and supplying them with weapons.

Control of Foreign Relations

Thus during the 1630s the shoguns issued a series of edicts sharply restricting Japanese relations with other lands that remained in effect for more than two centuries. The policy forbade Japanese from going abroad on pain of death and prohibited the construction of large ships. It expelled Europeans from Japan, prohibited foreign merchants from trading in Japanese ports, and even forbade the import of foreign books. The policy allowed carefully controlled trade with Asian lands, and it also permitted small numbers of Chinese and Dutch merchants to trade under tight restrictions at the southern port city of Nagasaki.

During the seventeenth century, Japanese authorities strictly enforced this policy. In 1640 a Portuguese merchant ship arrived at Nagasaki in hopes of engaging in trade in spite of the ban. Officials beheaded sixty-one of the party and spared thirteen others so that they could relate the experience to their compatriots. Yet authorities gradually loosened the restrictions, and the policy never led to the complete isolation of Japan from the outside world. Throughout the Tokugawa period, Japan carried on a flourishing trade with China, Korea, Taiwan, and the Ryukyu Islands, and Dutch merchants regularly brought news of European and larger world affairs.

Economic and Social Change

By ending civil conflict and maintaining political stability, the Tokugawa shoguns set the stage for economic growth in Japan. Ironically, peace and a booming economy encouraged social change that undermined the order that the bakufu sought to preserve.

Economic growth had its roots in increased agricultural production. New crop strains, new methods of water control and irrigation, and the use of fertilizer brought increased yields of rice. Production of cotton, silk, indigo, and sake also increased dramatically. In many parts of Japan, villages moved away from subsistence farming in favor of production for the market. Between 1600 and 1700, agricultural production doubled.

Population Growth

Increased agricultural production brought about rapid demographic growth: during the seventeenth century the Japanese population rose by almost one-third, from twenty-two million to twenty-nine million. Thereafter, however, Japan underwent a demographic transition, as many families practiced population control in order to maintain or raise their standard of living. Between 1700 and 1850 the Japanese population grew moderately, from twenty-nine million to thirty-two million. Contraception, late marriage, and abortion all played roles in limiting population growth, but the principal control measure was infanticide, euphemistically referred to as "thinning out the rice shoots." Japanese families resorted to these measures primarily because Japan was land poor. During the seventeenth century, populations in some areas strained resources, causing financial difficulties for local governments and distress for rural communities.

The Tokugawa era was an age of social as well as demographic change in Japan. Because of Chinese cultural influence, the Japanese social hierarchy followed Confucian precepts in ranking the ruling elites—including the shogun, daimyo, and samurai warriors—as the most prominent and privileged class of society. Beneath them were peasants and artisans. Merchants ranked at the bottom, as they did in China.

Social Change

The extended period of peace ushered in by Tokugawa rule undermined the social position of the ruling elites. Since the twelfth century the administration of local affairs had fallen mostly to daimyo and samurai warriors. Once Japan was stable, however, the

Dutch sailing ships and smaller Japanese vessels mingle in Nagasaki harbor. Dutch merchants conducted their business on the artificial island of Deshima, at left.

interest of Tokugawa authorities was to reduce the numbers of armed professional warriors, so they pushed daimyo and samurai to become bureaucrats and government functionaries. They even encouraged daimyo and samurai to turn their talents to scholarship, a pursuit that their martial ancestors would have utterly despised. As they lost their accustomed place in society, many of the ruling elite also fell into financial difficulty. Their principal income came in the form of rice collected from peasant cultivators of their lands. They readily converted rice into money through brokers, but the price of rice did not keep pace with other costs. Moreover, daimyo and samurai lived in expensive and sometimes ostentatious style—particularly daimyo who sought to impress others with their wealth while residing at Edo in alternate years. Many of them became indebted to rice brokers and gradually declined into genteel poverty.

Meanwhile, as in China, merchants in Japan became increasingly wealthy and prominent. Japanese cities flourished throughout the Tokugawa era—the population of Edo approached one million by 1700—and merchants prospered handsomely in the vibrant urban environment. Rice dealers, pawnbrokers, and sake merchants soon controlled more wealth than the ruling elites did. Those who became especially wealthy sometimes purchased elite ranks or contracted marriages with elite families in efforts to improve their social standing. Others did not go to such lengths but won respect anyway, in spite of occupations that ranked low in the ideal Confucian social order.

Neo-Confucianism and Floating Worlds

Japan had gone to school in China, and the influence of China continued throughout the Tokugawa era. Formal education began with study of Chinese language and literature. As late as the nineteenth century, many Japanese scholars wrote their philosophical, legal, and religious works in Chinese. The common people embraced Buddhism, which had come to Japan from China, and Confucianism was the most influential philosophical system.

Neo-Confucianism in Japan

Like the Ming and Qing emperors in China, the Tokugawa shoguns promoted the neo-Confucianism of Zhu Xi. With its emphasis on filial piety and loyalty to superiors, neo-Confucianism provided a respectable ideological underpinning for the bakufu. The shoguns patronized scholars who advocated neo-Confucian views, which figured prominently in the educational curriculum. All those who had a formal education—including the sons of merchants as well as offspring of government officials—received constant exposure to neo-Confucian values. By the early eighteenth century, neo-Confucianism had become the official ideology of the Tokugawa bakufu.

Native Learning

Yet even with Tokugawa sponsorship, neo-Confucianism did not dominate intellectual life in Japan. Although most scholars recognized Japan's debt to Chinese intellectual traditions, some sought to establish a sense of Japanese identity that did not depend on cultural kinship with China. Particularly during the eighteenth century, scholars of "native learning" scorned neo-Confucianism and even Buddhism as alien cultural imports and emphasized instead the importance of folk traditions and the indigenous Shinto religion for Japanese identity. Many scholars of native learning viewed Japanese people as superior to all others and xenophobically regarded foreign influence as perverse. They urged the study of Japanese classics and glorified the supposed purity of Japanese society before its adulteration by Chinese and other foreign influences.

While scholars of neo-Confucianism and native learning debated issues of philosophy and Japanese identity, the emergence of a prosperous merchant class encouraged the development of a vibrant popular culture. During the seventeenth and eighteenth centuries, an exuberant middle-class culture flourished in cities like Kyoto, the imperial capital; Edo, Japan's largest city and home to bureaucrats and daimyo; and Osaka, the commercial hub of the islands. In these and other cities, Japan's finest creative talents catered to middle-class appetites.

Floating Worlds

The centers of Tokugawa urban culture were the "floating worlds" *(ukiyo),* entertainment and pleasure quarters where teahouses, theaters, brothels, and public baths offered escape from social responsibilities and the rigid rules of conduct that governed public behavior in Tokugawa society. In contrast to the solemn, serious proceedings of the imperial court and the bakufu, the popular culture of urban residents was secular, satirical, and even scatological. The main expressions of this lively culture were prose fiction and new forms of theater.

Ihara Saikaku (1642–1693), one of Japan's most prolific poets, helped create a new genre of prose literature, the "books of the floating world." Much of his fiction revolved around the theme of love. In *The Life of a Man Who Lived for Love,* for example, Ihara chronicled the experiences of a townsman who devoted his life, beginning at the tender age of eight, to a quest for sexual pleasure. Ihara's treatment of love stressed the erotic rather than the aesthetic, and the brief, episodic stories that

The courtesan district of Kyoto hummed with activity in the mid-seventeenth century. In this woodblock print, courtesans await clients behind the wooden grill while urban residents fill the streets.

A colored woodcut by Okumura Masanobu depicts the audience at a seventeenth-century kabuki theater. Enthusiastic actors often ran down wooden ramps and played their roles among the audience.

made up his work appealed to literate urban residents who were not inclined to pore over dense neo-Confucian treatises.

Beginning in the early seventeenth century, two new forms of drama became popular in Japanese cities. One was *kabuki* theater, which usually featured several acts consisting of lively and sometimes bawdy skits where stylized acting combined with lyric singing, dancing, and spectacular staging. A crucial component of kabuki was the actor's ability to improvise and embellish the dialogue, for the text of plays served only as guides for the dramatic performance. The other new dramatic form was *bunraku,* the puppet theater. In bunraku, chanters accompanied by music told a story acted out by puppets. Manipulated by a team of three, each puppet could execute the subtlest and most intricate movements, such as brushing a tear from the eye with the sleeve of a kimono. Both kabuki and bunraku attracted enthusiastic audiences in search of entertainment and diversion.

Christianity and Dutch Learning

Christian Missions

Alongside neo-Confucianism, native learning, and middle-class popular culture, Christian missionaries and European merchants contributed their own distinctive threads to the cultural fabric of Tokugawa Japan. The Jesuit Francis Xavier traveled to Japan in 1549 and opened a mission to seek converts to Christianity. In the early decades of their mission, Jesuits experienced remarkable success in Japan. Several powerful daimyo adopted Christianity and ordered their subjects to do likewise. The principal interest of the daimyo was to establish trade and military alliances with Europeans, but many Japanese converts became enthusiastic Christians and worked to convert their compatriots to the new faith. By the 1580s about 150,000 Japanese had converted to Christianity, and by 1615 Japanese Christians numbered about 300,000.

Although Christians were only a tiny minority of the Japanese population, the popularity of Christianity generated a backlash among government officials and moralists seeking to preserve Japanese religious and cultural traditions. The Tokugawa shoguns restricted European access to Japan largely because of concerns that Christianity might serve as a cultural bridge for alliances between daimyo and European adventurers, which in turn could lead to destabilization of Japanese society and even threats to the bakufu. Meanwhile, Buddhist and Confucian scholars resented the Christian conviction that their faith was the only true doctrine. Some Japanese converts to Christianity themselves eventually rejected their adopted faith out of frustration because European missionaries refused to allow them to become priests or play leadership roles in the mission.

Anti-Christian Campaign

Between 1587 and 1639, shoguns promulgated several decrees ordering a halt to Christian missions and commanding Japanese Christians to renounce their faith. In 1612 the shoguns began rigorous enforcement of these decrees. They tortured and executed European missionaries who refused to leave the islands as well as Japanese Christians who refused to abandon their faith. They often executed victims by crucifixion or burning at the stake, which Tokugawa authorities regarded as especially appropriate punishments for Christians. The campaign was so effective that even some European missionaries abandoned Christianity. Most notable of them was the Portuguese Jesuit Christovão Ferreira, head of the Jesuit mission in Japan, who gave up Christianity under torture, adopted Buddhism, and interrogated many Europeans who fell into Japanese hands in the mid-seventeenth century. By the late seventeenth century, the anti-Christian campaign had claimed tens of thousands of lives, and Christianity survived as a secret, underground religion observed only in rural regions of southern Japan.

Dutch Learning

Tokugawa policies ensured that Christianity would not soon reappear in Japan, but they did not entirely prevent contacts between Europeans and Japanese. After 1639 Dutch merchants trading at Nagasaki became Japan's principal source of information about Europe and the world beyond east Asia. A small number of Japanese scholars learned Dutch in order to communicate with the foreigners. Their studies, which they called "Dutch learning," brought considerable knowledge of the outside world to Japan. After 1720 Tokugawa authorities lifted the ban on foreign books, and Dutch learning began to play a significant role in Japanese intellectual life.

European art influenced Japanese scholars interested in anatomy and botany because of its accurate representations of objects. Scholars translated Dutch medical and scientific treatises into Japanese and learned to draw according to the principles of linear perspective, which enabled them to prepare textbooks that were more accurate than the Chinese works they had previously used. European astronomy was also popular in Japan, since it enabled scholars to improve calendars and issue accurate predictions of eclipses and other celestial events. By the mid-eighteenth century the Tokugawa shoguns themselves had become enthusiastic proponents of Dutch learning, and schools of European medicine and Dutch studies flourished in several Japanese cities.

Sources from the Past

Fabian Fucan Rejects Christianity

Fabian Fucan was a Japanese Buddhist who converted to Christianity and entered the Jesuit order as a novice in 1586. In the early seventeenth century, however, his relations with the Jesuits soured, and he eventually left the order. In 1620 he composed a treatise entitled Deus Destroyed *that leveled a spirited attack at Christianity and its God ("Deus" in Latin). His work reveals deep concerns about European imperial expansion as well as Christian doctrine.*

I joined this creed at an early age; diligently, I studied its teachings and pursued its practices. Due to my stupidity, however, I was long unable to realize that this was a perverse and cursed faith. Thus fruitlessly I spent twenty years and more! Then one day I clearly perceived that the words of the adherents of Deus were very clever and appeared very near reason—but in their teaching there was little truth. So I left their company. Some fifteen years have passed since: every morning I have lamented my desertion of the Great Holy True Law [of Buddhism]; every evening I have grieved over my adherence to the crooked path of the barbarians. All that effort to no effect! But I had a friend who remonstrated with me, saying: "'If you have made a mistake, do not be afraid of admitting the fact and amending your ways' [a Confucian precept]. Here, this is the Confucians' golden rule of life—act on it! Before, you learned all about the cursed faith of Deus; take pen in hand now, commit your knowledge to writing, and counter their teachings. Not only will you thereby gain the merit of destroying wickedness and demonstrating truth; you will also supply a guide toward new knowledge."

All right. Though I am not a clever man, I shall by all means try to act on this advice. I shall gather the important points about the teachings of the Deus sect and shall skip what is not essential; my aim is to write concisely. Thus shall I mount my attack; and I shall call my volume DEUS DESTROYED. . . .

Japan is the Land of the Gods. The generations of our rulers have received the Imperial Dignity from [the gods] Amaterasu Omikami, through U-gaya-fuki-awsezu no Mikoto and his August Child Jimmu Tenno, who became the progenitor of our Hundred Kings. The Three Divine Regalia [symbols of rule received from the gods] became the protectors of the Empire, so that among all the customs of our land there is not one which depends not on the Way of the Gods. . . .

And this, the adherents of Deus plan to subvert! They bide their time with the intent to make all of Japan into their own sectarians, to destroy the Law of Buddha and the Way of the Gods. Because the Law of Buddha and the Way of the Gods are planted here, the Royal Sway also flourishes; and since the Royal Sway is established here the glory of the Buddhas and the gods does grow. And therefore the adherents of Deus have no recourse but to subvert the Royal Sway, overthrow the Buddhas and the gods, eliminate the customs of Japan, and then to import the customs of their own countries; thus only will advance the plot they have concocted to usurp the country themselves.

They have dispatched troops and usurped such countries as Luzon [the Philippines] and Nova Hispania [Mexico], lands of barbarians with nature close to animal. But our land by far surpasses others in fierce bravery; and therefore the ambition to diffuse their faith in every quarter and thus to usurp the country, even if it take a thousand years, has penetrated down to the very marrow of their bones. Ah!—but what a gloomy prospect awaits them! For the sake of their faith they value their lives less than trash, than garbage. *Martyr,* they call this. When a wise sovereign rules the Empire good is promoted and evil is chastised. Rewards promote good and punishments chastise evil. There is no greater punishment than to take away life; but the adherents of Deus, without even fearing that their lives be cut, will not change their religion. How horrible, how awful it is!

SOURCE: George Elison. *Deus Destroyed: The Image of Christianity in Early Modern Japan.* Cambridge, Mass.: Harvard University Press, 1973, pp. 259–60, 283–84.

Discuss the various religious, cultural, historical, political, and social aspects of Fabian Fucan's attack on Christianity.

Both China and Japan controlled their own affairs throughout the early modern era and avoided the turmoil that afflicted societies in the Americas and much of sub-Saharan Africa. After driving the Mongols to the steppe lands of central Asia, rulers of the Ming dynasty built a powerful centralized state in China. They worked diligently to eradicate all vestiges of Mongol rule and restore traditional ways by reviving Chinese political institutions and providing state sponsorship for neo-Confucianism. In the interest of stability, authorities also restricted foreign merchants' access to China and limited the activities of Christian missionaries. The succeeding Qing dynasty pursued similar policies. The Ming and Qing dynasties both brought political stability, but China experienced considerable social and economic change in early modern times. American food crops helped increase agricultural production, which fueled rapid population growth, and global trade stimulated the Chinese economy, which improved the position of merchants and artisans in society. The experience of the Tokugawa era in Japan was much like that of the Ming and Qing eras in China. The Tokugawa bakufu brought political order to the Japanese islands and closely controlled foreign relations, but a vibrant economy promoted social change that enhanced the status of merchants and artisans.

CHRONOLOGY

1368–1644	Ming dynasty (China)
1368–1398	Reign of Hongwu
1403–1424	Reign of Yongle
1552–1610	Life of Matteo Ricci
1572–1620	Reign of Emperor Wanli
1600–1867	Tokugawa shogunate (Japan)
1616–1626	Reign of Nurhaci
1642–1693	Life of Ihara Saikaku
1644–1911	Qing dynasty (China)
1661–1722	Reign of Kangxi
1736–1795	Reign of Qianlong
1793	British trade mission to China

FOR FURTHER READING

Timothy Brook. *The Confusions of Pleasure: Commerce and Culture in Ming China.* Berkeley, 1998. Fascinating social and cultural analysis of Ming China focusing on the role of commerce as an agent of social change.

George Elison. *Deus Destroyed: The Image of Christianity in Early Modern Japan.* Cambridge, Mass., 1973. Scholarly study of the Jesuit mission in Japan and its end during the early Tokugawa era.

Mark C. Elliott. *The Manchu Way: The Eight Banners and Ethnic Identity in Late Imperial China.* Stanford, 2001. Important scholarly study focusing on relations between Manchus and Chinese during the Qing dynasty.

Mark Elvin. *The Pattern of the Chinese Past: A Social and Economic Interpretation.* Stanford, 1973. A brilliant analysis of Chinese history concentrating on economic, social, and technological themes.

Jacques Gernet. *China and the Christian Impact.* Trans. by J. Lloyd. Cambridge, 1985. A careful study of the Jesuit mission in China, concentrating on the cultural differences between Chinese and Europeans.

Susan B. Hanley. *Economic and Demographic Change in Pre-Industrial Japan, 1600–1868.* Princeton, 1977. Argues that the Tokugawa period was crucial for the development of modern Japanese history.

Harry D. Harootunian. *Things Seen and Unseen: Discourse and Ideology in Tokugawa Nativism.* Chicago, 1988. A challenging scholarly analysis of the efforts by Tokugawa thinkers to construct a distinctive Japanese identity.

Ray Huang. *1587: A Year of No Significance.* New Haven, 1981. A very good history of the late Ming, with insights into daily life.

Donald Keene. *The Japanese Discovery of Europe, 1720–1830.* Rev. ed. Stanford, 1969. A highly readable account of Japanese encounters with Europe by way of Dutch merchants.

Ichisada Miyazaki. *China's Examination Hell: The Civil Service Examinations in Imperial China.* Trans. by Conrad Schirokauer. New Haven, 1981. Explores all aspects of the labyrinthine civil service examination system.

Susan Naquin and Evelyn S. Rawski. *Chinese Society in the Eighteenth Century.* New Haven, 1987. A lucid and well-organized discussion of Chinese social history.

Kenneth Pomeranz. *The Great Divergence: China, Europe, and the Making of the Modern World Economy.* Princeton, 2000. Pathbreaking scholarly study that illuminates the economic history of the early modern world through comparison of economic development in Asian and European lands.

Anthony Reid, ed. *Sojourners and Settlers: Histories of Southeast Asia and the Chinese.* Honolulu, 2001. Important collection of scholarly essays on Chinese migration to southeast Asian lands.

Jonathan D. Spence. *The Death of Woman Wang.* New York, 1978. Engaging reconstruction of life in rural China during the early Qing dynasty.

———. *Emperor of China: Self-Portrait of K'ang-Hsi.* New York, 1974. Outstanding introduction to the reign of Kangxi based partly on numerous documents, some written by the emperor himself.

Ronald P. Toby. *State and Diplomacy in Early Modern Japan: Asia in the Development of the Tokugawa Bakufu.* Princeton, 1984. An important study dealing with Japanese trade and relations with other lands under Tokugawa rule.

Conrad Totman. *Early Modern Japan.* Berkeley, 1993. An outstanding survey of Tokugawa ecological, political, social, economic, and cultural history.

H. Paul Varley. *Japanese Culture.* 4th ed. Honolulu, 2000. Places the cultural history of the Tokugawa era in its larger historical context.

Frederic Wakeman Jr. *The Great Enterprise: The Manchu Reconstruction of the Imperial Order in Seventeenth-Century China.* 2 vols. Berkeley, 1985. Important scholarly analysis of early Qing history.

Arthur Waldron. *The Great Wall of China: From History to Myth.* Cambridge, 1990. Fascinating work that places the Great Wall of Ming China in the context of earlier efforts to build defensive walls.

OLC

See our **Online Learning Center at www.mhhe.com/bentley3** for additional readings, practice maps, quizzes, and internet activities.

PSI

Unfamiliar words? Check out the **Primary Source Investigator CD-ROM** for an interactive glossary, interactive maps, more images, and primary sources.

The Taj Mahal, a sumptuous mosque and tomb built between 1632 and 1649 by Shah Jahan in memory of his wife, Mumtaz Mahal.

CHAPTER 28

The Islamic Empires

In 1635 Shah Jahan, the emperor of Mughal India, took his seat on the Peacock Throne. Seven years in the making, the Peacock Throne is probably the most spectacular seat on which any mortal human being has rested. Shah Jahan ordered the throne encrusted with ten million rupees' worth of diamonds, rubies, emeralds, and pearls. Atop the throne itself stood a magnificent, golden-bodied peacock with a huge ruby and a fifty-carat, pear-shaped pearl on its breast and a brilliant elevated tail fashioned of blue sapphires and other colored gems.

Yet, for all its splendor, the Peacock Throne ranks a distant second among Shah Jahan's artistic projects: pride of place goes to the incomparable Taj Mahal. Built over a period of eighteen years as a tomb for Shah Jahan's beloved wife, Mumtaz Mahal, who died during childbirth in 1631, the Taj Mahal is a graceful and elegant monument both to the departed empress and to Shah Jahan's Islamic faith.

The emperor and his architects conceived the Taj Mahal as a vast allegory in stone symbolizing the day when Allah would cause the dead to rise and undergo judgment before his heavenly throne. Its gardens represented the gardens of paradise, and the four water channels running through them symbolized the four rivers of the heavenly kingdom. The domed marble tomb of Mumtaz Mahal represented the throne of Allah, and the four minarets surrounding the structure served as legs supporting the divine throne. Craftsmen carved verses from the Quran throughout the Taj Mahal. The main gateway to the structure features the entire text of the chapter promising that on the day of judgment, Allah will punish the wicked and gather the faithful into his celestial paradise.

The Peacock Throne and the Taj Mahal testify to the wealth of the Mughal empire, and the tomb of Mumtaz Mahal bespeaks also the fundamentally Islamic character of the ruling dynasty. But the Mughal realm was not the only well-organized Islamic empire of early modern times. The Ottoman dynasty ruled a powerful empire that expanded from its base in Anatolia to embrace much of eastern Europe, Egypt, and north Africa. The Safavid dynasty never expanded far beyond Persia, but its rulers challenged the Ottomans for dominance in southwest Asia, and the Safavid realm prospered from its role in trade networks linking China, India, Russia, southwest Asia, and the Mediterranean basin.

All three Islamic empires of early modern times had Turkish ruling dynasties. The Ottomans, Safavids, and Mughals came from nomadic, Turkish-speaking peoples of central Asia who conquered the settled agricultural lands of Anatolia, Persia, and India, respectively. All three dynasties retained political and cultural traditions that their ancestors had adopted while leading nomadic lives on the steppes, but they also adapted readily to the city-based agricultural societies that they conquered. The Ottoman dynasty made especially effective use of the gunpowder weapons that transformed early modern warfare, and the Safavids and Mughals also incorporated gunpowder weapons into their arsenals. All three dynasties officially embraced Islam and drew cultural guidance from Islamic values.

During the sixteenth and early seventeenth centuries, the three Islamic empires presided over expansive and prosperous societies. About the mid-seventeenth century, however, they all began to weaken. Their waning fortunes reflected the fact that they had ceased to expand territorially and gain access to new sources of wealth. Instead, each empire waged long, costly wars that drained resources without bringing compensating benefits. The empires also faced domestic difficulties. Each of them was an ethnically and religiously diverse realm, and each experienced tensions when conservative Muslim leaders lobbied for strict observance of Islam while members of other communities sought greater freedom for themselves. Furthermore, the Islamic empires made little investment in economic and technological development. By the mid-eighteenth century the Safavid empire had collapsed, and the Ottoman and Mughal realms were rapidly falling under European influence.

Formation of the Islamic Empires

The Islamic empires began as small warrior principalities in frontier areas. They expanded at varying rates and with varying degrees of success at the expense of neighboring states. As they grew, they devised elaborate administrative and military institutions. Under the guidance of talented and energetic rulers, each empire organized an effective governmental apparatus and presided over a prosperous society.

The Ottoman Empire

Osman

The Ottoman empire was an unusually successful frontier state. The term *Ottoman* derived from Osman Bey, founder of the dynasty that continued in unbroken succession from 1289 until the dissolution of the empire in 1923. Osman was chief *(bey)* of a band of seminomadic Turks who migrated to northwestern Anatolia in the thirteenth century. Osman and his followers sought above all to become *ghazi,* Muslim religious warriors. In his encomium of the Ottomans, the poet Ahmadi described their ethos: "The Ghazi is the instrument of the religion of Allah, a servant of God who purifies the earth from the filth of polytheism; the Ghazi is the sword of God, he is the protector and the refuge of the believers. If he becomes a martyr in the ways of God, do not believe that he has died—he lives in beatitude with Allah, he has eternal life."

Ottoman Expansion

The Ottomans' location on the borders of the Byzantine empire afforded them ample opportunity to wage holy war. Their first great success came in 1326 with the capture of the Anatolian city of Bursa, which became the capital of the Ottoman principality. Around 1352 they established a foothold in Europe when they seized the fortress of Gallipoli while aiding a claimant to the Byzantine throne. Numerous *ghazi,* many of them recent converts, soon flocked to join the Ottomans. The city of Edirne (Adrianople) became a second Ottoman capital and served as a base for further expansion into the Balkans. As warriors settled in frontier districts and pushed their boundaries forward, they took spoils and gathered revenues that enriched both the *ghazi* and the central government. Bursa developed into a major commercial and intellectual center with inns, shops, schools, libraries, and mosques.

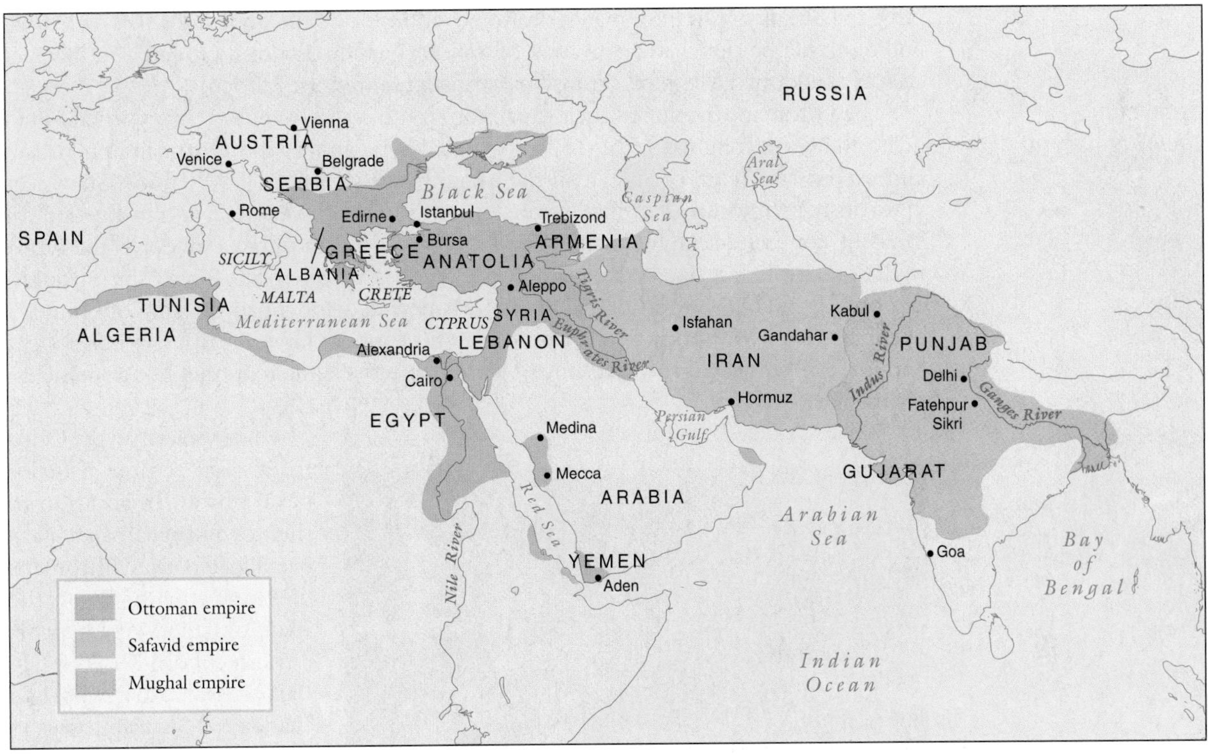

Map [28.1]
The Islamic empires, 1500–1800.

For an interactive version of this map, go to www.mhhe.com/bentley3ch28maps.

A formidable military machine drove Ottoman expansion. Ottoman military leaders initially organized *ghazi* recruits into two forces: a light cavalry and a volunteer infantry. As the Ottoman state became more firmly established, it added a professional cavalry force equipped with heavy armor and financed by land grants. After expanding into the Balkans, the Ottomans created a supremely important force composed of slave troops. Through an institution known as the *devshirme,* the Ottomans required the Christian population of the Balkans to contribute young boys to become slaves of the sultan. The boys received special training, learned Turkish, and converted to Islam. According to individual ability, they entered either the Ottoman civilian administration or the military. Those who became soldiers were known as Janissaries, from the Turkish *yeni cheri* ("new troops"). The Janissaries quickly gained a reputation for esprit de corps, loyalty to the sultan, and readiness to employ new military technology. Besides building powerful military forces, the Ottomans outfitted their forces with gunpowder weapons and used them effectively in battles and sieges.

Mehmed the Conqueror

The capture of Constantinople in 1453 by Mehmed II (reigned 1451–1481)—known as Mehmed the Conqueror—opened a new chapter in Ottoman expansion. With its superb location and illustrious heritage, Constantinople became the new Ottoman capital, subsequently known as Istanbul, and Mehmed worked energetically to stimulate its role as a commercial center. With the capture of the great city behind him, Mehmed presented himself not just as a warrior sultan but as a true emperor, ruler of the "two lands" (Europe and Asia) and the "two seas" (the Black Sea and the Mediterranean). He laid the foundations for a tightly centralized, absolute monarchy, and his army faced no serious rival. He completed the conquest of Serbia, moved into southern Greece and Albania, eliminated the last Byzantine outpost at Trebizond, captured Genoese ports in the Crimea, initiated a naval war with Venice in the Mediterranean, and reportedly hoped to cross the Straits of Otranto, march on Rome, and capture the pope himself. Toward the end of his life he launched an invasion of Italy and briefly occupied Otranto, but his successors abandoned Mehmed's plans for expansion in western Europe.

Süleyman the Magnificent

The Ottomans continued their expansion in the early sixteenth century when sultan Selim the Grim (reigned 1512–1520) occupied Syria and Egypt. Ottoman imperialism climaxed in the reign of Süleyman the Magnificent (reigned 1520–1566). Süleyman vigorously promoted Ottoman expansion both in southwest Asia and in Europe. In 1534 he conquered Baghdad and added the Tigris and Euphrates valleys to the Ottoman domain. In Europe he kept the rival Habsburg empire on the defensive throughout his reign. He captured Belgrade in 1521, defeated and killed the king of Hungary at the battle of Mohács in 1526, consolidated Ottoman power north of the Danube, and in 1529 subjected the Habsburgs' prized city of Vienna to a brief but nonetheless terrifying siege.

Sultan Süleyman (center, on horse) leads Ottoman forces as they march on Europe.

Under Süleyman the Ottomans also became a major naval power. In addition to their own Aegean and Black Sea fleets, the Ottomans inherited the navy of the Mamluk rulers of Egypt. A Turkish corsair, Khayr al-Din Barbarossa Pasha, who had challenged Spanish forces in Tunisia and Algeria, placed his pirate fleet under the Ottoman flag and became Süleyman's leading admiral. Thus Süleyman was able to challenge Christian vessels throughout the Mediterranean as well as Portuguese fleets in the Red Sea and Indian Ocean. The Ottomans seized the island of Rhodes from the Knights of St. John, besieged Malta, secured Yemen and Aden, and even dispatched a squadron to attack the Portuguese fleet at Diu in India.

The Safavid Empire

In 1499 a twelve-year-old boy named Ismail left the swamps of Gilan near the Caspian Sea, where he had hidden from the enemies of his family for five years, to seek his revenge. Two years later he entered

Sources from the Past

Ghislain de Busbecq's Concerns about the Ottoman Empire

Ogier Ghislain de Busbecq was a diplomat who traveled to Istanbul in 1555 as a representative of Habsburg King Ferdinand of Hungary and Bohemia to negotiate a border dispute between Ferdinand and Sultan Süleyman the Magnificent. In a series of four letters to a friend, Ghislain commented on Ottoman state, society, customs, and military forces. His observations left him deeply concerned about the prospects of Christian Europe in the event of conflict with the Ottoman realm.

The Sultan, when he sets out on a campaign, takes as many as 40,000 camels with him, and almost as many baggage-mules, most of whom, if his destination is Persia, are loaded with cereals of every kind, especially rice. Mules and camels are also employed to carry tents and arms and warlike machines and implements of every kind. . . . They are careful, however, to avoid touching the supplies which they carry with them as long as they are marching against their foes, but reserve them, as far as possible, for their return journey, when the moment for retirement comes and they are forced to retrace their steps through regions which the enemy has laid waste, or which the immense multitude of men and baggage animals has, as it were, scraped bare, like a swarm of locusts. It is only then that the Sultan's store of provisions is opened, and just enough food to sustain life is weighed out each day to the Janissaries and the other troops in attendance upon him. The other soldiers are badly off, if they have not provided food for their own use; most of them, having often experienced such difficulties during their campaigns—and this is particularly true of the cavalry—take a horse on a leading-rein loaded with many of the necessities of life. These include a small piece of canvas to use as a tent, which may protect them from the sun or a shower of rain, also some clothing and bedding and a private store of provisions, consisting of a leather sack or two of the finest flour, a small jar of butter, and some spices and salt; on these they support life when they are reduced to the extremes of hunger. They take a few spoonfuls of flour and place them in water, adding a little butter, and then flavour the mixture with salt and spices. This, when it is put on the fire, boils and swells up so as to fill a large bowl. They eat of it once or twice a day, according to the quantity, without any bread, unless they have with them some toasted bread or biscuit. They thus contrive to live on short rations for a month or even longer, if necessary. . . .

All this will show you with what patience, sobriety, and economy the Turks struggle against the difficulties which beset them, and wait for better times. How different are our soldiers, who on campaign despise ordinary food and expect dainty dishes (such as thrushes and beccaficoes) and elaborate meals. If these are not supplied, they mutiny and cause their own ruin; and even if they are supplied, they ruin themselves just the same. . . . I tremble when I think of what the future must bring when I compare the Turkish system with our own; one army must prevail and the other be destroyed, for certainly both cannot remain unscathed. On their side are the resources of a mighty empire, strength unimpaired, experience and practice in fighting, a veteran soldiery, habituation to victory, endurance of toil, unity, order, discipline, frugality, and watchfulness. On our side is public poverty, private luxury, impaired strength, spirit, lack of endurance and training; the soldiers are insubordinate, the officers avaricious; there is contempt for discipline; licence, recklessness, drunkenness, and debauchery are rife; and worst of all, the enemy is accustomed to victory, and we to defeat. Can we doubt what the result will be?

SOURCE: Ghislain de Busbecq. *The Turkish Letters of Ogier Ghislain de Busbecq.* Trans. by E. S. Foster. Oxford: Clarendon Press, 1927, pp. 209–14.

Why might Ghislain de Busbecq have assumed that conflict between Turkish and Habsburg forces was inevitable?

Shah Ismail and the *qizilbash*. This miniature painting from a Safavid manuscript depicts the shah and his *qizilbash* warriors wearing the distinctive red pleated cap that was their emblem of identity.

Tabriz at the head of an army and laid claim to the ancient Persian imperial title of shah. The young Shah Ismail (reigned 1501–1524) also proclaimed that the official religion of his realm would be Twelver Shiism, and he proceeded to impose it, by force when necessary, on the formerly Sunni population. Over the next decade he seized control of the Iranian plateau and launched expeditions into the Caucasus, Anatolia, Mesopotamia, and central Asia.

The Safavids

For propaganda purposes Shah Ismail and his successors carefully controlled accounts of their rise to power—and expediently changed the story when circumstances warranted. They traced their ancestry back to Safi al-Din (1252–1334), leader of a Sufi religious order in northwestern Persia. The famous tomb and shrine of Safi al-Din at Ardabil became the home of Shah Ismail's family (named "Safavids" after the holy man himself), the headquarters of his religious movement, and the center of a determined, deliberate conspiracy to win political power for his descendants. The Safavids changed their religious preferences several times in the hope of gaining popular support before settling on a form of Shiism that appealed to the nomadic Turkish tribes moving into the area in the post-Mongol era.

Twelver Shiism

Twelver Shiism held that there had been twelve infallible imams (or religious leaders) after Muhammad, beginning with the prophet's cousin and son-in-law Ali. The twelfth or "hidden" imam had gone into hiding around 874 to escape persecution, but the Twelver Shiites believed he was still alive and would one day return to take power and spread his true religion. Ismail's father had instructed his Turkish followers to wear a distinctive red hat with twelve pleats in memory of the twelve Shiite imams, and they subsequently became known as the *qizilbash* ("red heads"). Safavid propaganda also suggested that Ismail was himself the hidden imam, or even an incarnation of Allah. Although most Muslims, including most Shiites, would have regarded these pretensions as utterly blasphemous, the *qizilbash* enthusiastically accepted them, since they resembled traditional Turkish conceptions of leadership that associated military leaders with divinity. The *qizilbash* believed that Ismail would make them invincible in battle, and they became fanatically loyal to the Safavid cause.

Battle of Chaldiran

Shah Ismail's curious blend of Shiism and Turkish militancy gave his regime a distinctive identity, but it also created some powerful enemies. Foremost among them were the staunchly Sunni Ottomans who detested the Shiite Safavids and feared the spread of Safavid propaganda among the nomadic Turks in their own territory. As soon as Selim the Grim became sultan, he launched a persecution of Shiites in the Ottoman empire and prepared for a full-scale invasion of Safavid territory.

At the critical battle on the plain of Chaldiran (1514), the Ottomans deployed heavy artillery and thousands of Janissaries equipped with firearms behind a barrier of carts. Although the Safavids knew about gunpowder technology and had access to firearms, they declined to use devices that they saw as unreliable and unmanly. Trusting in the protective charisma of Shah Ismail, the *qizilbash* cavalry fearlessly attacked the Ottoman line and suffered devastating casualties. Ismail had to slip away, and the Ottomans temporarily occupied his capital at Tabriz. The Ottomans badly damaged the Safavid state but lacked the resources to destroy it completely, and the two empires remained locked in intermittent conflict for the next two centuries.

Later Safavid rulers recovered from the disaster at Chaldiran. They relied more heavily than Ismail had on the Persian bureaucracy and its administrative talents. Ismail's successors abandoned the extreme Safavid ideology that associated the emperor with Allah in favor of more conventional Twelver Shiism, from which they still derived legitimacy as descendants and representatives of the imams. They also assigned land grants to the *qizilbash* officers to retain their loyalty and give them a stake in the survival of the regime.

Shah Abbas the Great

Shah Abbas the Great (reigned 1588–1629) fully revitalized the Safavid empire. He moved the capital to the more central location of Isfahan, encouraged trade with other lands, and reformed the administrative and military institutions of the empire. He incorporated "slaves of the royal household" into the army, increased the use of gunpowder weapons, and sought European assistance against the Ottomans and the Portuguese in the Persian Gulf. With newly strengthened military forces, Shah Abbas led the Safavids to numerous victories. He attacked and defeated the nomadic Uzbeks in central Asia, expelled the Portuguese from Hormuz, and harassed the Ottomans mercilessly in a series of wars from 1603 to the end of his reign. His campaigns brought most of northwestern Iran, the Caucasus, and Mesopotamia under Safavid rule.

The Mughal Empire

Babur

In 1523 Zahir al-Din Muhammad, known as Babur ("the Tiger"), a Chagatai Turk who claimed descent from both Chinggis Khan and Tamerlane, suddenly appeared in northern India. Unlike the Ottomans, who sought to be renowned *ghazis*, or the Safavids, who acted as champions of Shiism, Babur made little pretense to be anything more than an adventurer and soldier of fortune in the manner of his illustrious ancestors. His father had been the prince of Farghana, and Babur's great ambition was to transform his inheritance into a glorious central Asian empire. Yet envious relatives and Uzbek enemies frustrated his ambitions.

Never able to extend his authority much beyond Kabul and Qandahar and reduced at times to hardship and a handful of followers, Babur turned his attention to India. With the aid of gunpowder weapons, including both artillery and firearms, Babur mounted invasions in 1523 and 1525, and he took Delhi in 1526. Ironically, Babur cared little for the land he had conquered. Many in his entourage wanted to

Sources from the Past

A Conqueror and His Conquests: Babur on India

Babur was a talented writer as well as a successful warrior. His memoirs make fascinating reading and provide a unique perspective on early Mughal India. His writings include his reflections on the territories he conquered in India, which he compared unfavorably to his central Asian homeland, and on his decision to stay in India and found an empire.

Most of the inhabitants of India are infidels, called Hindus, believing mainly in the transmigration of souls; all artisans, wage-earners and officials are Hindus. In our countries the desert dwellers get tribal names; here people settled in the cultivated villages also get tribal names. Again, every artisan follows the trade handed down to him from his forefathers.

India is a country of few charms. The people lack good looks and good manners. They have no social life or exchange of visits. They have no genius or intelligence, no polite learning, no generosity of magnanimity, no harmony or proportion in their arts and crafts, no lead-wire or carpenter's square. They lack good horses and good dogs; grapes, melons, and any good fruit; ice and cold water; good food or good bread in the markets. They have no baths and no advanced educational institutions. . . . There are no running streams in their gardens or residences, no waters at all except the large rivers and the swamps in the ravines and hollows. Their residences have no pleasant and salubrious breezes, and in their construction [there is] no form or symmetry. . . .

Among the charms that India does possess is that it is a large country, with large quantities of gold and silver. Its air in the rainy season is very fine. Sometimes it rains ten or fifteen or even twenty times a day, and in such torrents that rivers flow where no water was previously. While it rains, and throughout the rainy season, the air is remarkably fine, not to be surpassed for mildness and pleasantness. Its only fault is its great humidity, which spoils bows. . . .

It was the hot season when we came to Agra. All the inhabitants had run away in terror. We could find neither grain for ourselves nor corn for our horses. The villages, out of hostility and hatred for us, had taken to thieving and highway-robbery, and it was impossible to travel on the roads. We had not yet the opportunity to distribute the treasure and to assign men in strength to each district. Moreover, the year was a very hot one, pestilential simooms [sandstorms] were striking people down in heaps, and masses were beginning to die off.

For all these reasons, most of the best warriors were unwilling to stay in India; in fact, they determined to leave. . . .

When I discovered this unsteadiness among my people, I summoned all the leaders and took counsel. I said, "Without means and resources there is no empire and conquest, and without lands and followers there is no sovereignty and rule. By the effort of long years, through much tribulation and the crossing of distant lands, by flinging ourselves into battle and danger, we have through God's favor overcome so many enemies and conquered such vast lands. And now, what force compels us, what necessity has arisen, that we should, without cause, abandon a country taken at such risk of life? And if we returned to Kabul, we would again be left in poverty and weakness. Henceforth, let no well-wisher of mine speak of such things! But let not those turn back from going who cannot bear the hardship and have determined to leave." With such words I reasoned with them and made them, willy-nilly, quit their fears.

SOURCE: Babur. *The Babur-nama in English (Memoirs of Babur)*. Trans. by Annette Susannah Beveridge. London: Luzac, 1922. (Translation slightly modified.)

What does Babur's reaction to India suggest about his views of his own central Asian homeland?

take their spoils of war and leave the hot and humid Indian climate, which ruined their finely crafted compound bows, but Babur elected to stay. He probably hoped to use the enormous wealth of India to build a vast central Asian empire like that of Tamerlane—an elusive dream that his successors would nonetheless continue to cherish. By the time of his death in 1530, Babur had built a loosely knit empire that stretched from Kabul through the Punjab to the borders of Bengal. He founded a dynasty called the *Mughal* (a Persian term for "Mongol"), which expanded to embrace almost all the Indian subcontinent.

This manuscript illustration from about 1590 depicts Akbar (at top, shaded by attendants) inspecting construction of a new imperial capital at Fatehpur Sikri.

Akbar

The real architect of the Mughal empire was Babur's grandson Akbar (reigned 1556–1605), a brilliant and charismatic ruler. Akbar gathered the reins of power in his own hands in 1561 following an argument with Adham Khan, a powerful figure at the imperial court and commander of the Mughal army. Akbar threw Adham Khan out a window, then dragged him back from the palace courtyard, and tossed him out again to make sure he was dead. Thereafter Akbar took personal control of the Mughal government and did not tolerate challenges to his rule. He created a centralized administrative structure with ministries regulating the various provinces of the empire. His military campaigns consolidated Mughal power in Gujarat and Bengal. He destroyed the Hindu kingdom of Vijayanagar, thus laying the foundation for later Mughal expansion in southern India.

Although he was a no-nonsense ruler, Akbar was also a thoughtful, reflective man deeply interested in religion and philosophy. He pursued a policy of religious toleration that he hoped would reduce tensions between Hindu and Muslim communities in India. Although illiterate (probably due to dyslexia), he was extremely intelligent and had books read to him daily. Instead of imposing Islam on his subjects, he encouraged the elaboration of a syncretic religion called the "divine faith" that focused attention on the emperor as a ruler common to all the religious, ethnic, and social groups of India.

Aurangzeb

The Mughal empire reached its greatest extent under Aurangzeb (reigned 1659–1707). During his long reign, Aurangzeb waged a relentless campaign to push Mughal authority deep into southern India. By the early eighteenth century, Mughals ruled the entire subcontinent except for a small region at the southern tip.

Although he greatly expanded Mughal boundaries, Aurangzeb presided over a troubled empire. He faced rebellions throughout his reign, and religious tensions generated conflicts between Hindus and Muslims. Aurangzeb was a devout Muslim, and he broke with Akbar's policy of religious toleration. He demolished several famous Hindu temples and replaced them with mosques. He also imposed a tax on Hindus in an effort to encourage conversion to Islam. His promotion of Islam appealed strongly to the Mughals themselves and other Indian Muslims as well, but it provoked deep hostility among Hindus and enabled local leaders to organize movements to resist or even rebel against Mughal authority.

Imperial Islamic Society

Despite many differences, there were striking similarities in the development of Ottoman, Safavid, and Mughal societies. All relied on bureaucracies that drew inspiration from the steppe traditions of Turkish and Mongol peoples as well as from the heritage of Islam. They adopted similar economic policies and sought ways to maintain harmony in societies that embraced many different religious and ethnic groups. Rulers of all the empires also sought to enhance the legitimacy of their regimes by providing for public welfare and associating themselves with literary and artistic talent.

The Dynastic State

The Ottoman, Safavid, and Mughal empires were all military creations, regarded by their rulers as their personal possessions by right of conquest. The rulers exercised personal command of the armies, appointed and dismissed officials at will, and adopted whatever policies they wished. In theory, the emperors owned all land and granted use of it to peasant families on a hereditary basis in return for the payment of fixed taxes. The emperors and their families derived revenues from crown lands, and revenues from other lands supported military and administrative officials.

The Emperors and Islam

In the Ottoman, Safavid, and Mughal empires, the prestige and authority of the dynasty derived from the personal piety and the military prowess of the ruler and his ancestors. The Safavids were prominent leaders of a Sufi religious order, and the Ottomans and Mughals associated closely with famous Sufis. Devotion to Islam encouraged rulers to extend their faith to new lands. The *ghazi* ideal of spreading Islam by fighting infidels or heretics resonated with the traditions of Turkish and Mongolian peoples: on the steppes fighting was routine, and successful warriors became charismatic leaders.

Steppe Traditions

The autocratic authority wielded by the rulers of the Islamic empires also reflected steppe traditions. The early emperors largely did as they pleased, irrespective of religious and social norms. The Ottoman sultans, for example, unilaterally issued numerous legal edicts. The greatest of these were the many *kanun* ("laws") issued by Süleyman—Europeans called him "Süleyman the Magnificent," but the Ottomans referred to him as Süleyman Kanuni, "the Lawgiver." Safavid and Mughal rulers went even further than the Ottomans in asserting their spiritual authority. Shah Ismail did not hesitate to force his Shiite religion on his subjects. Akbar issued a decree in 1579 claiming broad authority in religious matters, and he promoted his own eclectic religion, which glorified the emperor as much as Islam.

Steppe practices also brought succession problems. In the steppe empires the ruler's relatives often managed components of the states, and succession to the throne became a hot contest between competing members of the family. The Mughal empire in particular became tied up in family controversies: conflicts among Mughal princes and rebellions of sons against fathers were recurrent features throughout the history of the empire. The Safavids also engaged in murderous struggles for the throne. Shah Abbas himself lived in fear that another member of the family would challenge him. He kept his sons confined to the palace and killed or blinded relatives he suspected, almost wiping out his family in the process.

The early Ottomans assigned provinces for the sultan's sons to administer but kept the empire as a whole tightly unified. After the fifteenth century, however, the sultans moved to protect their position by eliminating family rivals. Mehmed the Conqueror decreed that a ruler could legally kill off his brothers after taking the throne. His successors observed this tradition in Turko-Mongol style—by strangling victims with a silk bow string so as not to shed royal blood—until 1595, when the new sultan executed nineteen brothers, many of them infants, as well as fifteen expectant mothers. After that episode, sultans confined their sons in special quarters of the imperial harem and forbade them to go outside except to take the throne.

Women and Politics

Even though Muslim theorists universally agreed that women should have no role in public affairs and decried the involvement of women in politics as a sure sign of decadence, women played important roles in managing the Islamic empires. Many Ottoman, Safavid, and Mughal emperors followed the example of Chinggis Khan, who revered his mother and his first wife. In the Islamic empires the ruler's mother and his chief wife or favorite concubine enjoyed special privileges and authority. Ottoman courtiers often complained loudly about the "rule of women," thus offering eloquent testimony to the power that women could wield. Süleyman the Magnificent, for example, became infatuated with Hürrem Sultana (also known as Roxelana), a concubine of Ukrainian origin. Süleyman elevated her to the status of a legal wife, consulted her on state policies, and deferred to her judgment even to the point of executing his eldest son for treason when Hürrem wanted him eliminated to secure the succession of her own child. After Hürrem's death, Süleyman constructed a mausoleum for her next to his own in the courtyard of the great mosque in Istanbul.

Women also played prominent political roles in the Safavid and Mughal empires. In Safavid Persia, Mahd-e Olya, the wife of one shah, was the de facto ruler. Her efforts to limit the power of the *qizilbash* so enraged them that they murdered her. The aunt of another shah scolded the ruler for neglecting his duties and used her own money to raise an army to put down a revolt. The Mughal emperor Jahangir was content to let his wife Nur Jahan run the government, and even the conscientious Muslim Aurangzeb listened to his daughter's political advice. Shah Jahan's devotion to his wife, Mumtaz Mahal, has become world famous because of the Taj Mahal.

Agriculture and Trade

Food Crops

Productive agricultural economies were the foundations of all the Islamic empires. Each empire extracted surplus agricultural production and used it to finance armies and bureaucracies. Mostly the Islamic empires relied on crops of wheat and rice that had flourished for centuries in the lands they ruled. The Columbian exchange brought American crops to all the Islamic empires but without the same dramatic effects as in Europe, east Asia, and Africa. European merchants introduced maize, potatoes, tomatoes, and other crops to the Islamic empires, and the new arrivals soon found a place in regional cuisines. Potatoes appeared in the curries of southern India, and tomatoes enlivened dishes in the Ottoman empire as well as other Mediterranean lands. Maize did not appeal to human palates in the Islamic empires, but it became popular as feed for animal stocks, especially in the Ottoman empire.

The Columbian exchange strongly encouraged consumption of coffee and tobacco, especially in the Ottoman and Safavid empires. Although native to Ethiopia and cultivated in southern Arabia, coffee did not become popular in Islamic lands until the sixteenth century. Like sugar, it traveled to Europe and from there to the Americas, where plantations specialized in the production of tropical crops for the world market. By the eighteenth century, American producers and European merchants supplied Muslim markets with both coffee and sugar.

A bustling bazaar in Mughal India. At the center of this painting, a soothsayer attracts a crowd as he consults a manual while telling fortunes. Sacks of coins at his side suggest that he has done good business. Elsewhere in the market consumers buy watermelons, cloth, and peanuts.

Tobacco

According to the Ottoman historian Ibrahim Pechevi, English merchants introduced tobacco around 1600, claiming it was useful for medicinal purposes. Within a few decades it had spread throughout the Ottoman empire. The increasing popularity of coffee drinking and pipe smoking encouraged entrepreneurs to establish coffeehouses where customers could indulge their appetites for caffeine and nicotine at the same time. The popularity of coffeehouses provoked protest from moralists who worried that these popular attractions were dens of iniquity that distracted habitués from their religious duties and attracted crowds of idlers and riffraff. Pechevi complained about the hideous odor of tobacco, the messy ashes, and the danger that smoking could cause fires, while religious leaders claimed that coffee was an illegal beverage and that it was worse to frequent a coffeehouse than a tavern. Sultan Murad IV went so far as to outlaw coffee and tobacco and to execute those who continued to partake. This effort, however, was a losing battle.

Both pastimes eventually won widespread acceptance, and the coffeehouse became a prominent social institution in the Islamic empires.

Population Growth

American food crops had less demographic effect in the Islamic empires than in other parts of the world. The population of India surged during early modern times, growing from 105 million in 1500 to 135 million in 1600, 165 million in 1700, and 190 million in 1800. But population growth in India resulted more from intensive agriculture along traditional lines than from the influence of new crops. The Safavid population grew less rapidly, from 5 million in 1500 to 6 million in 1600, and to 8 million in 1800. Ottoman numbers grew from 9 million in 1500 to 28 million in 1600, as the empire enlarged its boundaries to include populous regions in the Balkans, Egypt, and southwest Asia. After 1600, however, the Ottoman population declined to about 24 million, where it remained until the late nineteenth century. The decline reflected loss of territory more than a shrinking population, but even in the heartland of Anatolia, Ottoman numbers did not expand nearly as dramatically as those of other lands in early modern times. From 6 million in 1500, the population of Anatolia rose to 7.5 million in 1600, 8 million in 1700, and 9 million in 1800.

Trade

The Islamic empires ruled lands that had figured prominently in long-distance trade for centuries and participated actively in global trade networks in early modern times. In the Ottoman empire, for example, the early capital at Bursa was also the terminus of a caravan route that brought raw silk from Persia to supply the Italian market. The Ottomans also granted special trading concessions to merchants from England and France to cement alliances against common enemies in Spain and central Europe. Aleppo became an emporium for foreign merchants engaged primarily in the spice trade and served as local headquarters for the operations of the English Levant Company.

In this anonymous painting produced about 1670, Dutch and English ships lie at anchor in the harbor of the busy port of Surat in northwestern India.

Shah Abbas promoted Isfahan as a commercial center, extending trading privileges to foreign merchants and even allowing Christian monastic orders to set up missions there to help create a favorable environment for trade. European merchants sought Safavid raw silk, carpets, ceramics, and high-quality craft items. The English East India Company, the French East India Company, and the Dutch VOC all traded actively with the Safavids. To curry favor with them, the English company sent military advisors to help introduce gunpowder weapons to Safavid armed forces and provided a navy to help them retake Hormuz in the Persian Gulf from the Portuguese.

The Mughals did not pay as much attention to foreign trade as the Ottomans and Safavids did, partly because of the enormous size and productivity of the domestic Indian economy and partly because the Mughal rulers concentrated on their land empire and had little interest in maritime affairs. Nevertheless, the Mughal treasury derived significant income from foreign trade. The Mughals allowed the creation of trading stations and merchant colonies by Portuguese, English, French, and Dutch merchants. Meanwhile, Indian merchants formed trading companies of their own, ventured overland as far as Russia, and sailed the waters of the Indian Ocean to port cities from Persia to Indonesia.

Religious Affairs in the Islamic Empires

Religious Diversity

All the Islamic empires had populations that were religiously and ethnically diverse, and imperial rulers had the daunting challenge of maintaining harmony between different religious communities. The Ottoman empire included large numbers of Christians and Jews in the Balkans, Armenia, Lebanon, and Egypt. The Safavid empire embraced sizable Zoroastrian and Jewish communities as well as many Christian subjects in the Caucasus. The Mughal empire was especially diverse. Most Mughal subjects were Hindus, but large numbers of Muslims lived alongside smaller communities of Jains, Zoroastrians, Christians, and devotees of syncretic faiths such as Sikhism.

Christian Mission in India

Portuguese Goa became the center of a Christian mission in India. Priests at Goa sought to attract converts to Christianity and established schools that provided religious instruction for Indian children. In 1580 several Portuguese Jesuits traveled to the Mughal court at Akbar's invitation. They had visions of converting the emperor to Christianity and then spreading their faith throughout India, but their hopes went unfulfilled. Akbar received the Jesuits cordially and welcomed their participation in religious and philosophical discussions at his court, but he declined to commit to an exclusive faith that he thought would alienate many of his subjects.

Akbar's Divine Faith

Indeed, Akbar was cool even to his own Islamic faith. In his efforts to find a religious synthesis that would serve as a cultural foundation for unity in his diverse empire, he supported the efforts of the early Sikhs, who combined elements of both Hinduism and Islam in a new syncretic faith. He also attempted to elaborate his own "divine faith" that emphasized loyalty to the emperor while borrowing eclectically from different religious traditions. Akbar never explained his ideas systematically, but it is clear that they drew most heavily on Islam. The divine faith was strictly monotheistic, and it reflected the influence of Shiite and Sufi teachings. But it also glorified the emperor: Akbar even referred to himself as the "lord of wisdom," who would guide his subjects to understanding of the world's creator god. The divine faith was tolerant of Hinduism, and it even drew inspiration from Zoroastrianism in its effort to bridge the gaps between Mughal India's many cultural and religious communities.

Status of Religious Minorities

The Islamic empires relied on a long-established model to deal with subjects who were not Muslims. They did not require conquered peoples to convert to Islam but extended to them the status of a protected people *(dhimmi)*. In return for their loyalty and payment of a special tax known as *jizya, dhimmi* communities retained their personal freedom, kept their property, practiced their religion, and handled their own legal affairs. In the Ottoman empire, for example, autonomous religious communities known as *millet* retained their own civil laws, traditions, and languages. *Millet* communities usually also assumed social and administrative functions in matters concerning birth, marriage, death, health, and education.

In a seventeenth-century painting the emperor Akbar presides over discussions between representatives of various religious groups. Two Jesuits dressed in black robes kneel at the left.

The situation in the Mughal empire was different, since its large number of religious communities made a *millet* system impractical. Mughal rulers reserved the most powerful military and administrative positions for Muslims, but in the day-to-day management of affairs, Muslims and Hindus cooperated closely. Some Mughal emperors sought to forge links between religious communities. Akbar in particular worked to integrate Muslim and Hindu elites. In an effort to foster communication and understanding among the different religious communities of his realm, he abolished the *jizya,* tolerated all faiths, and sponsored discussions and debates between Muslims, Hindus, Jains, Zoroastrians, and Christians.

Promotion of Islam

Policies of religious tolerance were not popular with many Muslims, who worried that they would lose their religious identity and that toleration might lead to their absorption into Hindu society as another caste. They therefore insisted that Mughal rulers create and maintain an Islamic state based on Islamic law. When Aurangzeb reached the Mughal throne in 1659, this policy gained strength. Aurangzeb reinstated the *jizya* and promoted Islam as the official faith of Mughal India. His policy satisfied zealous Muslims but at the cost of deep bitterness among his Hindu subjects. Tension between Hindu and Muslim communities in India persisted throughout the Mughal dynasty and beyond.

The massive Süleymaniye mosque built for Sultan Süleyman the Magnificent by the Ottoman architect Sinan Pasha in 1556.

Cultural Patronage of the Islamic Emperors

As the empires matured, the Islamic rulers sought to enhance their prestige through public works projects and patronage of scholars. They competed to attract outstanding religious scholars, poets, artists, and architects to their courts. They lavished resources on mosques, palaces, government buildings, bridges, fountains, schools, hospitals, and soup kitchens for the poor.

Istanbul

Capital cities and royal palaces were the most visible expressions of imperial majesty. The Ottomans beautified both Bursa and Edirne, but they took particular pride in Istanbul. Dilapidated and deserted after the conquest, it quickly revived and became a bustling, prosperous city of more than a million people. At its heart was the great Topkapi palace, which housed government offices, such as the mint, and meeting places for imperial councils. At its core was the sultan's residence with its harem, gardens, pleasure pavilions, and a repository for the most sacred possessions of the empire, including the mantle of the prophet Muhammad. Sultan Süleyman the Magnificent was fortunate to be able to draw on the talents of the architectural genius Sinan Pasha (1489–1588) to create the most celebrated of all the monuments of Istanbul. Sinan built a vast religious complex called the Süleymaniye, which blended Islamic and Byzantine architectural elements. It combined tall, slender minarets with large domed buildings supported by half domes in the style of the Byzantine church Hagia Sofia (which the Ottomans converted into the mosque of Aya Sofya).

Isfahan

Shah Abbas made his capital, Isfahan, into the queen of Persian cities and one of the most precious jewels of urban architectural development anywhere in the world: its inhabitants still boast that "Isfahan is half the world." Abbas concentrated markets, the palace, and the royal mosque around a vast polo field and public square. Broad, shaded avenues and magnificent bridges linked the central city to its suburbs. Safavid architects made use of monumental entryways, vast arcades, spacious courtyards, and intricate, colorful decoration. Unlike the sprawling Ottoman and Mughal palaces, the Safavid palaces in Isfahan were relatively small and emphasized natural settings with gardens and pools. They were also much more open than Topkapi, with its series of inner courts and gates. Ali Qapu, the palace on the square in Isfahan, had a striking balcony, and most of the palaces had large, open verandas. The point was not only to enable the shah to observe outside activities but also to emphasize his visibility and accessibility, qualities long esteemed in the Persian tradition of kingship.

To some extent, in accordance with steppe traditions, the early Mughals regarded the capital as wherever the ruler happened to camp. Yet they too came to sponsor urban development. Their work skillfully blended central Asian traditions with elements of Hindu architecture, and they built on a scale that left no doubt about their wealth and resources. They constructed scores of mosques, fortresses, and palaces and sometimes created entire cities.

The Royal Mosque of Isfahan, centerpiece of the city as rebuilt by Shah Abbas at the end of the sixteenth century. With its combination of an open space flanked by markets, the palace, and religious structures, Isfahan stands as a unique example of urban planning in Islamic lands.

Fatehpur Sikri

The best example was Fatehpur Sikri, a city planned and constructed by Akbar that served as his capital from 1569 to 1585. It commemorated his conquest of the prosperous commercial province of Gujarat in a campaign that enabled Akbar to head off both Portuguese attacks and Ottoman intervention there. With its mint, records office, treasury, and audience hall, the new city demonstrated Akbar's strength and imperial ambitions. Fatehpur Sikri was also a private residence and retreat for the ruler, reproducing in stone a royal encampment with exquisite pleasure palaces where Akbar indulged his passions for music and conversation with scholars and poets. At yet another level, it was a dramatic display of Mughal piety and devotion, centered on the cathedral mosque and the mausoleum of Akbar's Sufi guru, Shaykh Salim Chisti. Despite their intensely Islamic character, many of the buildings consciously incorporated Indian elements such as verandas supported by columns and decorations of stone elephants. Even the tomb of Shaykh Chisti bore some resemblance to a Hindu shrine. Unfortunately, Akbar selected a poor site for the city and soon abandoned it because of its bad water supply.

The Taj Mahal

The most famous of the Mughal monuments—and one of the most prominent of all Islamic edifices—was the Taj Mahal. Shah Jahan had twenty thousand workers toil for eighteen years to erect the exquisite white marble mosque and tomb. He originally planned to build a similar mausoleum out of black marble for himself, but his son Aurangzeb deposed him before he could carry out the project. Shah Jahan spent his last years confined to a small cell with a tiny window, and only with the aid of a mirror was he able to catch the sight of his beloved wife's final resting place.

Fatehpur Sikri, built by Akbar in the 1570s, commemorated the emperor's military conquests and housed the tomb of his religious guide. It included a palace, an audience hall where Akbar attended religious and philosophical debates, and a great mosque.

THE EMPIRES IN TRANSITION

The Islamic empires underwent dramatic change between the sixteenth and eighteenth centuries. The Safavid empire disappeared entirely. In 1722 a band of Afghan tribesmen marched all the way to Isfahan, blockaded the city until its starving inhabitants resorted to cannibalism, forced the shah to abdicate, and executed thousands of Safavid officials as well as many members of the royal family. After the death of Aurangzeb in 1707, Mughal India experienced provincial rebellions and foreign invasions. By midcentury the subcontinent was falling under British imperial rule. By 1700 the Ottomans, too, were on the defensive: the sultans lost control over remote provinces such as Lebanon and Egypt, and throughout the eighteenth and nineteenth centuries European and Russian states placed political, military, and economic pressure on the shrinking Ottoman realm.

The Deterioration of Imperial Leadership

Strong and effective central authority was essential to the Islamic empires, and Muslim political theorists never tired of emphasizing the importance of rulers who were diligent, virtuous, and just. Weak, negligent, and corrupt rulers would allow institutions to become dysfunctional and social order to break down. The Ottomans were fortunate in having a series of talented sultans for three centuries, and the Safavids and Mughals produced their share of effective rulers as well.

Dynastic Decline

Eventually, however, all three dynasties had rulers who were incompetent or more interested in spending vast sums of money on personal pleasures than in tending to affairs of state. Moreover, all three dynasties faced difficulties because of suspicion and fighting among competing members of their ruling houses. The Ottomans sought to limit problems by confining princes in the palace, but this measure had several negative consequences. The princes had no opportunity to gain experience in government, but they were exposed to plots and intrigues of the various factions maneuvering to bring a favorable candidate to the throne. Notorious examples of problem rulers included Süleyman's successor Selim the Sot (reigned 1566–1574) and Ibrahim the Crazy (reigned 1640–1648), who taxed and spent to such excess that government officials deposed and murdered him. Several energetic rulers and talented ministers attempted to keep the government on track. Nonetheless, after the late seventeenth century, weak rule increasingly provoked mutinies in the army, provincial revolts, political corruption, economic oppression, and insecurity throughout the Ottoman realm.

Religious Tensions

Political troubles often arose from religious tensions. Conservative Muslim clerics strongly objected to policies and practices that they considered affronts to Islam. Muslim leaders had considerable influence in the Islamic empires because of their monopoly of education and their deep involvement in the everyday lives and legal affairs of ordinary subjects. The clerics mistrusted the emperors' interests in unconventional forms of Islam such as Sufism, complained bitterly when women or subjects who were not Muslims played influential political roles, and protested any exercise of royal authority that contradicted Islamic law.

In the Ottoman empire, disaffected religious students often joined the Janissaries in revolt. A particularly serious threat came from the Wahhabi movement in Arabia, which denounced the Ottomans as dangerous religious innovators who were unfit to rule. Conservative Muslims fiercely protested the construction of an astronomical observatory in Istanbul and forced the sultan to demolish it in 1580. In 1742 they also forced the closure of the Ottoman printing press, which they regarded as an impious technology.

The Safavids, who began their reign by crushing Sunni religious authorities, fell under the domination of the very Shiites they had supported. Shiite leaders pressured the shahs to persecute Sunnis, non-Muslims, and even the Sufis who had helped establish the dynasty. Religious tensions also afflicted Mughal India. Already in the seventeenth century, the conservative Shaykh Ahmad Sirhindi (1564–1624) fearlessly rebuked Akbar for his policy of religious tolerance and his interest in other faiths. In the mid-eighteenth century, as he struggled to claim the Mughal throne, Aurangzeb drew on Sirhindi's ideas when he required non-Muslims to pay the poll tax and ordered the destruction of Hindu temples. These measures inflamed tensions between the various Sunni, Shiite, and Sufi branches of Islam and also fueled animosity among Hindus and other Mughal subjects who were not Muslims.

Economic and Military Decline

In the sixteenth century, all the Islamic empires had strong domestic economies and played prominent roles in global trade networks. By the eighteenth century, however, domestic economies were under great stress, and foreign trade had declined dramatically or had fallen under the control of European powers. The Islamic empires were well on their way to becoming marginal lands that depended on goods produced elsewhere.

Economic Difficulties

The high cost of maintaining an expensive military and administrative apparatus helped to bring about economic decline in the Islamic empires. As long as the empires were expanding, they were able to finance their armies and bureaucracies with fresh resources extracted from newly conquered lands. When expansion slowed, ceased, or reversed, however, they faced the problem of supporting their institutions with limited resources. The long, costly, and unproductive wars fought by the Ottomans with the Habsburgs in central Europe, by the Safavids and Ottomans in Mesopotamia, and by Aurangzeb in southern India exhausted the treasuries of the Islamic empires without making fresh resources available to them. As early as 1589 the Ottomans tried to pay the Janissaries in debased coinage and immediately provoked a mutiny. The next 150 years witnessed at least six additional military revolts.

As expansion slowed and the empires lost control over remote provinces, officials reacted to the loss of revenue by raising taxes, selling public offices, accepting bribes, or resorting to simple extortion. All these measures were counterproductive. Although they might provide immediate cash, they did long-term economic damage. To make matters worse, the governments viewed foreign trade as just another opportunity to bring in revenue. The Ottomans expanded the privileges enjoyed by foreign merchants, and the Mughals encouraged the establishment of Dutch and English trading outposts and welcomed the expansion of their business in India. Imperial authorities were content to have foreign traders come to them. None made serious efforts to establish commercial stations abroad, although Indian merchants organized their own private trading companies.

Military Decline

As they lost initiative to western European peoples in economic and commercial affairs, the Islamic empires also experienced military decline because they did not seek actively to improve their military technologies. As early as the fifteenth century, the Ottomans had relied heavily on European technology in gunnery; indeed, the cannon that Mehmed the Conqueror used in 1453 to breach the defensive wall of Constantinople was the product of a Hungarian gun-founder. During the sixteenth and early seventeenth centuries, the Islamic empires were able to purchase European weapons in large numbers and attract European expertise that kept their armies supplied with powerful gunpowder weapons. In 1605, for example, the cargo of an English ship bound for Anatolia included seven hundred barrels of gunpowder, one thousand musket barrels, five hundred fully assembled muskets, and two thousand sword blades, alongside wool textiles and bullion.

By about the mid-seventeenth century, European military technology was advancing so rapidly that the Islamic empires could not keep pace. None of the empires had a large armaments industry, so they had to rely on foreign suppliers. They still were able to purchase European weapons and expertise, but their arsenals became increasingly dated, since they depended on technologies that European peoples had already replaced. By the late eighteenth century, the Ottoman navy, which had long influenced maritime affairs in the Mediterranean, Red Sea, Persian Gulf, and Arabian Sea, was closing its shipbuilding operations and ordering new military vessels from foreign shipyards.

All the Islamic empires fought numerous wars, many of which exhausted resources without adding to the productive capacities of the empires. This illustration depicts Ottoman forces (right) clashing with heavily armored Austrian cavalry near Budapest in 1540.

Cultural Conservatism

While experiencing economic and military decline, the Islamic empires also neglected cultural developments in the larger world. Europeans who visited the Islamic empires attempted to learn as much as possible about the language, religion, social customs, and history of the host countries. They published accounts of their travels that became extremely popular in their homelands, and they advocated serious study of Islamic lands. In the early seventeenth century, for example, the English scholar William Bedwell described Arabic as the only important language of trade, diplomacy, and religion from Morocco to the China seas.

Piri Reis

To some extent, information also flowed in the other direction. During the sixteenth century, just as European mariners were scouting Atlantic waters, Ottoman mariners reconnoitered the Indian Ocean basin from east Africa to Indonesia—a project that reflected military concerns about European and other naval forces in the region. Ottoman geographers also manifested great interest in European knowledge of geography, some of which had considerable military value. The Ottoman admiral and cartographer Piri Reis produced several large-scale maps and a major navigational text, the *Book of Seafaring*, which drew on reports and maps from European mariners and explorers. Piri Reis even managed to consult a copy of a chart drawn by Christopher Columbus during his first voyage to the western hemisphere. Some of Piri Reis's maps included the Atlantic coast of North America and the lands visited by Columbus, which the cartographer probably learned about from Spanish sailors captured in naval conflicts with Ottoman forces.

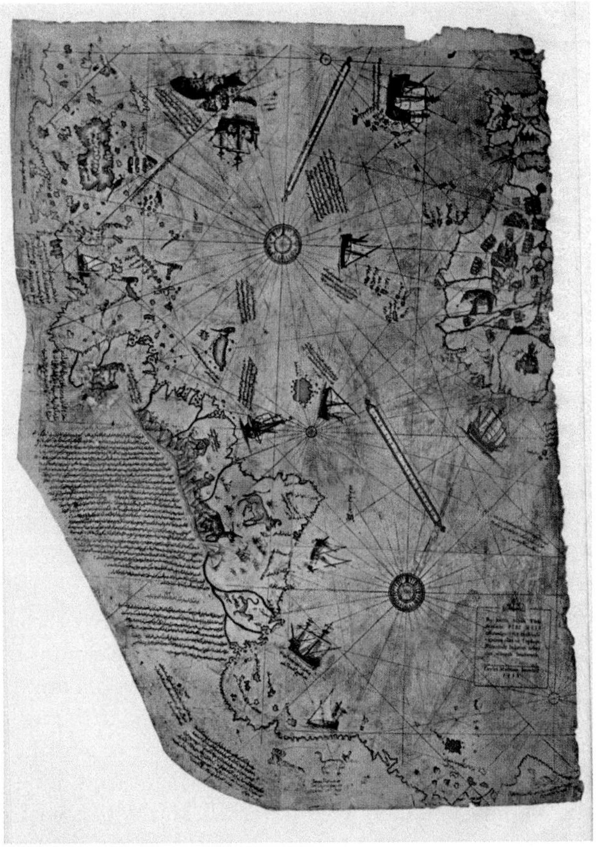

Ottoman cartographer Piri Reis drew on European charts when preparing this map of the Atlantic Ocean basin in 1513. Caribbean and South American coastlines are visible at left, while Iberian and west African coastlines appear in the upper right corner.

Cultural Conservatism

Yet few Muslims traveled willingly to the infidel lands of "the Franks." Muslim rulers and their Muslim subjects were confident of their superiority and believed that they had nothing to learn from Europeans. As a result, most Muslims remained largely oblivious to European cultural and technological developments. Not until 1703 was there an attempt to introduce European scientific instruments such as the telescope into astronomical observatories. Then conservative Muslim clerics soon forced the removal of the foreign implements, which they considered impious and unnecessary.

The Printing Press

The early experience of the printing press in the Islamic empires illustrates especially well the resistance of conservative religious leaders to cultural imports from western Europe. Jewish refugees from Spain introduced the first printing presses to Anatolia in the late fifteenth century. Ottoman authorities allowed them to operate presses in Istanbul and other major cities as long as they did not print books in the Turkish or Arabic language. Armenian and Greek printers soon established presses in the Ottoman realm and published books in their own languages. Not until 1729 did government authorities lift the ban on the printing of books in the Turkish and Arabic languages.

During the next thirteen years, a Turkish press published seventeen books dealing mostly with history, geography, and language before conservative Muslims forced its closure in 1742. Only in 1784 did a new Turkish press open, and printing spread throughout the Ottoman empire soon thereafter.

Printing also caught on slowly in Mughal India. Jesuit missionaries in Goa published books, including translations of the Bible into Indian and Arabic languages, as early as the 1550s. Yet Mughal rulers displayed little interest in the press, and printing did not become prominent in Indian society until the establishment of British colonial rule in Bengal in the eighteenth century.

To some extent, aesthetic considerations stood in the way of the printing press: particularly in the Ottoman and Safavid empires, as in many other Muslim lands, scholars and general readers alike simply preferred elegant handwritten books to cheaply produced printed works, especially when the book in question was the Quran. Yet resistance to printing also reflected the concerns of conservative religious leaders that readily available printed books would introduce all manner of new and dangerous ideas to the public—indeed, that an active publishing industry might spread inconvenient questions about the organization of Muslim societies or even about the Islamic faith itself.

Thus like imperial China and Tokugawa Japan, the Islamic empires resisted the introduction of cultural influences from western European societies. Rulers of the Islamic empires readily accepted gunpowder weapons as enhancements to their military and political power, but they and their subjects drew little inspiration from European religion, science, or ideas. Moreover, under the influence of conservative religious leaders, Islamic authorities actively discouraged the circulation of ideas that might pose unsettling challenges to the social and cultural order of the Islamic empires. Like the Ming, Qing, and Tokugawa rulers, the Ottoman, Safavid, and Mughal emperors preferred political and social stability to the risks that foreign cultural innovations might bring.

Like China and Japan, the Islamic empires largely retained control of their own affairs throughout the early modern era. Ruling elites of the Ottoman, Safavid, and Mughal empires came from nomadic Turkish stock, and they all drew on steppe traditions in organizing their governments. But the rulers also adapted steppe traditions to the needs of settled agricultural societies and devised institutions that maintained order over a long term. During the sixteenth and seventeenth centuries, all the Islamic empires enjoyed productive economies that enabled merchants to participate actively in the global trade networks of early modern times. By the early eighteenth century, however, these same empires were experiencing economic difficulties that led to political and military decline. Like the Ming, Qing, and Tokugawa rulers in east Asia, the Islamic emperors mostly sought to limit foreign and especially European influences in their realms. The Islamic emperors ruled lands that were religiously and ethnically diverse, and most of them worried that the expansion of foreign religious and cultural traditions would threaten political and social stability. They allowed their subjects to practice faiths other than Islam, and the Mughal emperor Akbar even promoted a syncretic religion in hopes that it would defuse tensions between Hindus and Muslims. For the most part, however, rulers of the Islamic empires followed the advice of conservative Muslim clerics, who promoted Islamic values and fought the introduction of foreign cultural imports, such as the printing press and European science, that might undermine their authority. By the late eighteenth century, the Safavid empire had collapsed, while economic difficulties and cultural insularity had severely weakened the Ottoman and Mughal empires.

CHRONOLOGY

1289–1923	Ottoman dynasty
1451–1481	Reign of Mehmed the Conqueror
1453	Ottoman conquest of Constantinople
1501–1524	Reign of Shah Ismail
1501–1722	Safavid dynasty
1514	Battle of Chaldiran
1520–1566	Reign of Süleyman the Magnificent
1526–1858	Mughal dynasty
1556–1605	Reign of Akbar
1588–1629	Reign of Shah Abbas the Great
1659–1707	Reign of Aurangzeb

FOR FURTHER READING

Esin Atil. *The Age of Sultan Süleyman the Magnificent.* Washington, 1987. Richly illustrated volume that emphasizes Süleyman's role as a patron of the arts.

Franz Babinger. *Mehmed the Conqueror and His Time.* Trans. by R. Manheim. Princeton, 1978. A magisterial biography of the sultan who conquered Constantinople.

Palmira Brummett. *Ottoman Seapower and Levantine Diplomacy in the Age of Discovery.* Albany, 1994. A scholarly study of Ottoman military strategy and diplomacy in the Mediterranean during the sixteenth century.

Stephen Frederic Dale. *Indian Merchants and Eurasian Trade, 1600–1750.* Cambridge, 1994. Examines the workings of an Indian trading community that conducted business in Persia, central Asia, and Russia.

Suraiya Faroghi. *Towns and Townsmen of Ottoman Anatolia.* Cambridge, 1989. A valuable contribution to an understanding of the Ottoman domestic economy.

Naimur Rahman Farooqi. *Mughal-Ottoman Relations.* Delhi, 1989. Illustrates the tensions between the two empires and uses them to shed new light on the motivations behind Akbar's policies.

Irfan Habib. *The Agrarian System of Mughal India, 1556–1707.* Bombay, 1963. A penetrating and influential assessment of the role of agriculture in the Mughal economy and the development of the empire.

Halil Inalçik. *The Ottoman Empire: The Classical Age, 1300–1600.* New York, 1973. A reliable survey by the foremost historian of the early Ottoman empire.

Halil Inalçik and Donald Quataert, eds. *An Economic and Social History of the Ottoman Empire, 1300–1914.* Cambridge, 1994. An exhaustive survey of Ottoman economic history.

Norman Itzkowitz. *Ottoman Empire and Islamic Tradition.* Chicago, 1972. A brief but insightful survey of Ottoman history.

Çemal Kafadar. *Between Two Worlds: The Construction of the Ottoman State.* Berkeley, 1995. Studies the origins and early development of the Ottoman empire.

Bernard Lewis. *The Muslim Discovery of Europe.* New York, 1982. An important study that charts Muslim interest in European affairs.

Bruce Masters. *The Origins of Western Economic Dominance in the Middle East: Mercantilism and the Islamic Economy in Aleppo, 1600–1750.* New York, 1988. A stimulating case study of an important trading city caught between a central government in chaos and European mercantile pressure.

David Morgan. *Medieval Persia, 1040–1797.* London, 1988. A brief and insightful survey that examines Persian history through the Safavid dynasty.

Leslie Pierce. *The Imperial Harem: Women and Sovereignty in the Ottoman Empire.* Oxford, 1993. Challenges many stereotypes about the role of women in the imperial Ottoman elite.

John F. Richards. *The Mughal Empire.* Cambridge, 1993. A concise and reliable overview of Mughal history, concentrating on political affairs.

Roger Savory. *Iran under the Safavids.* Cambridge, 1980. A rich and authoritative survey of Safavid history, especially interesting for its views on Safavid origins, culture, and commercial relations.

Stanford J. Shaw. *History of the Ottoman Empire and Modern Turkey.* 2 vols. Cambridge, 1976–77. A comprehensive survey of Ottoman history.

Douglas E. Streusand. *The Formation of the Mughal Empire.* Delhi, 1989. A new interpretation of the establishment and development of Mughal rule.

Paul Wittek. *The Rise of the Ottoman Empire.* London, 1938. Still the most insightful and stimulating interpretation of the *ghazi* role in the making of the Ottoman empire.

Madeline Zilfi. *The Politics of Piety: The Ottoman Ulema in the Postclassical Age, 1600–1800.* Minneapolis, 1988. Examines the influence and changing role of the Ottoman religious leadership.

See our **Online Learning Center at www.mhhe.com/bentley3** for additional readings, practice maps, quizzes, and internet activities.

Unfamiliar words? Check out the **Primary Source Investigator CD-ROM** for an interactive glossary, interactive maps, more images, and primary sources.

Glossary and Pronunciation Key

AH *a* sound, as in *car, father*
IH short *i* sound, as in *fit, his, mirror*
OO long *o* sound, as in *ooze, tool, crew*
UH short *u* sound, as in *up, cut, color*
A short *a* sound, as in *asp, fat, parrot*
EE long *e* sound, as in *even, meet, money*
OH long *o* sound, as in *open, go, tone*
EH short *e* sound, as in *ten, elf, berry*
AY long *a* sound, as in *ape, date, play*
EYE long *i* sound, as in *ice, high, bite*
OW dipthong *o* sound, as in *cow, how, bow*
AW dipthong *a* sound, as in *awful, paw, law*

Note on emphasis: Syllables in capital letters receive the accent. If there is no syllable in capitals, then all syllables get equal accent.

Abbasid (ah-BAH-sihd) Cosmopolitan Arabic dynasty (750–1258) that replaced the Umayyads; founded by Abu al-Abbas and reached its peak under Harun al-Rashid.

Abolitionism Antislavery movement.

Absolutism Political philosophy that stressed the divine right theory of kingship: the French king Louis XIV was the classic example.

Abu Bakr (ah-BOO BAHK-uhr) First caliph after the death of Muhammad.

Achaemenid empire (ah-KEE-muh-nid) First great Persian empire (558–330 B.C.E.), which began under Cyrus and reached its peak under Darius.

Aeshylus (ES-kuh-luhs) Greek tragedian, author of the *Oresteia*.

Age grades Bantu institution in which individuals of roughly the same age carried out communal tasks appropriate for that age.

Ahimsa (uh-HIM-suh) Jain term for the principle of nonviolence to other living things or their souls.

Ahmosis (AH-moh-sis) Egyptian pharaoh (c. 1500 B.C.E.), founder of the New Kingdom.

Ahura Mazda (uh-HOORE-uh MAHZ-duh) Main god of Zoroastrianism who represented truth and goodness and was perceived to be in an eternal struggle with the malign spirit Angra Mainyu.

Al-Andalus (al-ANN-duh-luhs) Islamic Spain.

Allah (AH-lah) God of the monotheistic religion of Islam.

Ali'i nui Hawaiian class of high chiefs.

Amon-Re (AH-muhn RAY) Egyptian god, combination of the sun god Re and the air god Amon.

Angkor (AHN-kohr) Southeast Asian Khmer kingdom (889–1432) that was centered around the temple cities of Angkor Thom and Angkor Wat.

Anti-Semitism Term coined in late nineteenth century that was associated with a prejudice against Jews and the political, social, and economic actions taken against them.

Antonianism African syncretic religion, founded by Dona Beatriz, that taught that Jesus Christ was a black African man and that heaven was for Africans.

Apartheid (ah-PAHR-teyed) South African system of "separateness" that was implemented in 1948 and that maintained the black majority in a position of political, social, and economic subordination.

Appeasement British and French policy in the 1930s that tried to maintain peace in Europe in the face of German aggression by making concessions.

Arianism Early Christian heresy that centered around teaching of Arius (250–336 C.E.) and contained the belief that Jesus was a mortal human being and not coeternal with God; Arianism was the focus of Council of Nicaea.

Artha Hindu concept for the pursuit of economic well-being and honest prosperity.

Arthashastra (AR-thah-sha-strah) Ancient Indian political treatise from the time of Chandragupta Maurya; its authorship was traditionally ascribed to Kautalya, and it stressed that war was inevitable.

Aryans (AIR-ee-anns) Indo-European tribes who settled in India after 1500 B.C.E.; their union with indigenous Dravidians formed the basis of Hinduism.

Association of Southeast Asian Nations (ASEAN.) Regional organization established in 1967 by Thailand, Malaysia, Singapore, Indonesia, and the Philippines; the organization was designed to promote economic progress and political stability; it later became a free-trade zone.

Assyrians (uh-SEAR-ee-uhns) Southwest Asian people who built an empire that reached its height during the eighth and seventh centuries B.C.E.; it was known for a powerful army and a well-structured state.

Astrolabe Navigational instrument for determining latitude.

Aten Monotheistic god of Egyptian pharaoh Akhenaten (r. 1353–1335 B.C.E.) and a very early example of monotheism.

Audiencias Spanish courts in Latin America.

Australopithecus (ah-strah-loh-PITH-uh-kuhs) "Southern ape," oldest known ancestor of humans; it lived from around four million down to around one million years ago, and it could walk on hind legs, freeing up hands for use of simple tools.

Austronesians People who as early as 2000 B.C.E. began to explore and settle islands of the Pacific Ocean basin.

Avesta Book that contains the holy writings of Zoroastrianism.

Aztec empire Central American empire constructed by the Mexica and expanded greatly during the fifteenth century during the reigns of Itzcoatl and Motecuzoma I.

Axum African kingdom centered in Ethiopia that became an early and lasting center of Coptic Christianity.

Balfour Declaration British declaration from 1917 that supported the creation of a Jewish homeland in Palestine.

Bantu (BAN-too) African peoples who originally lived in the area of present-day Nigeria; around 2000 B.C.E. they began a centuries-long migration that took them to most of sub-Saharan Africa; the Bantu were very influential, especially linguistically.

Bedouins (BEHD-oh-ihnz) Nomadic Arabic tribespeople.

Benefice Grant from a lord to a vassal, usually consisting of land, which supported the vassal and signified the relationship between the two.

Berlin Conference Meeting organized by German chancellor Otto von Bismarck in 1884–1885 that provided the justification for European colonization of Africa.

Bhagavad Gita (BUH-guh-vahd GEE-tuh) "Song of the Lord," an Indian short poetic work drawn from the lengthy *Mahabharata* that was finished around 400 C.E. and that expressed basic Hindu concepts such as karma and dharma.

Bhakti (BAHK-tee) Indian movement that attempted to transcend the differences between Hinduism and Islam.

Black Hand Pre–World War I secret Serbian society; one of its members, Gavrilo Princip, assassinated Austrian archduke Francis Ferdinand and provided the spark for the outbreak of the Great War.

Blitzkrieg German style of rapid attack through the use of armor and air power that was used in Poland, Norway, Denmark, Belgium, the Netherlands, and France in 1939–1940.

Boddhisatvas (BOH-dih-SAT-vuhs) Buddhist concept regarding individuals who had reached enlightenment but who stayed in this world to help people.

Bolshevik (BOHL-shih-vehk) Russian communist party headed by Lenin.

Bourgeoisie Middle class in modern industrial society.

Boyars (BOY-ahrs) Russian nobles.

Brahmins (BRAH-minz) Hindu caste of priests.

Brezhnev Doctrine Policy developed by Leonid Brezhnev (1906–1982) that claimed for the Soviet Union the right to invade any socialist country faced with internal or external enemies; the doctrine was best expressed in Soviet invasion of Czechoslovakia.

Buddha (BOO-duh) The "enlightened one," the term applied to Siddhartha Gautama after his discoveries that would form the foundation of Buddhism.

Buddhism (BOO-diz'm) Religion, based on Four Noble Truths, associated with Siddhartha Gautama (563–483 B.C.E.), or the Buddha; its adherents desired to eliminate all distracting passion and reach nirvana.

Bunraku (boon-RAH-koo) Japanese puppet theater.

Bushido (BOH-shee-DOH) The "way of the warrior," the code of conduct of the Japanese samurai that was based on loyalty and honor.

Byzantine Empire (BIHZ-ann-teen) Long-lasting empire centered at Constantinople; it grew out of the end of the Roman empire and carried legacy of Roman greatness and was the only classical society to survive into the early modern age; it reached its early peak during the reign of Justinian (483–565).

Caesaropapism Concept relating to the mixing of political and religious authority, as with the Roman emperors, that was central to the church versus state controversy in medieval Europe.

Cahokia (kuh-HOH-kee-uh) Large structure in modern Illinois that was constructed by the mound-building peoples; it was the third largest structure in the Americas before the arrival of the Europeans.

Caliph (KAL-ihf) "deputy," Islamic leader after the death of Muhammad.

Capetian (cah-PEE-shuhn) Early French dynasty that started with Hugh Capet.

Capitalism An economic system with origins in early modern Europe in which private parties make their goods and services available on a free market.

Capitulation Highly unfavorable trading agreements that the Ottoman Turks signed with the Europeans in the nineteenth century that symbolized the decline of the Ottomans.

Carolingians Germanic dynasty that was named after its most famous member, Charlemagne.

Carthage Northern African kingdom, main rival to early Roman expansion, that was defeated by Rome in the Punic Wars.

Çatal Hüyük Important Neolithic settlement in Anatolia (7250–6150 B.C.E.).

Cathars Medieval heretics, also known as the Albigensians, who considered the material world evil; their followers renounced wealth and marriage and promoted an ascetic existence.

Catholic Reformation Sixteenth-century Catholic attempt to cure internal ills and confront Protestantism; it was inspired by the reforms of the Council of Trent and the actions of the Jesuits.

Caudillos (KAW-dee-ohs) Latin American term for nineteenth-century local military leaders.

Central Powers World War I term for the alliance of Germany, Austria-Hungary, and the Ottoman empire.

Chaghatai One of Chinggis Khan's sons, whose descendants ruled central Asia through the Chaghatai khanate.

Chan Buddhism (CHAHN BOO-diz'm) Most popular branch of Buddhism in China, with an emphasis on intuition and sudden flashes of insight instead of textual study.

Chanchan (chahn-chahn) Capital of the pre-Incan, South American Chimu society that supported a large population of fifty thousand.

Chavín cult Mysterious but very popular South American religion (1000–300 B.C.E.).

Chimu Pre-Incan South American society that fell to Incas in the fifteenth century.

Chinampas Agricultural gardens used by Mexica (Aztecs) in which fertile muck from lake bottoms was dredged and built up into small plots.

Chivalry European medieval code of conduct for knights based on loyalty and honor.

Chola Southern Indian Hindu kingdom (850–1267), a tightly centralized state that dominated sea trade.

Chucuito Pre-Incan South American society that rose in the twelfth century and fell to the Incas in the fifteenth century.

City-state Urban areas that controlled surrounding agricultural regions and that were often loosely connected in a broader political structure with other city-states.

Cohong Specially licensed Chinese firms that were under strict government regulation.

Collectivization Process beginning in the late 1920s by which Stalin forced the Russian peasants off their own land and onto huge collective farms run by the state; millions died in the process.

COMECON The Council for Mutual Economic Assistance, which offered increased trade within the Soviet Union and eastern Europe; it was the Soviet alternative to the United States's Marshall Plan.

Communalism A term, usually associated with India, that placed an emphasis on religious rather than national identity.

Communism Philosophy and movement that began in middle of the nineteenth century with the work of Karl Marx; it has the same general goals as socialism, but it includes the belief that violent revolution is necessary to destroy the bourgeois world and institute a new world run by and for the proletariat.

Confucianism (kuhn-FYOO-shuhn-iz'm) Philosophy, based on the teachings of the Chinese philosopher Kong Fuzi (551–479 B.C.E.), or Confucius, that emphasizes order, the role of the gentleman, obligation to society, and reciprocity.

Congress of Vienna Meeting in 1815 of the victorious powers (England, Russia, Prussia, and Austria) in order to determine the settlement of Europe after the defeat of Napoleon; the congress established a system of international diplomacy for the nineteenth century and beyond.

Conquistadores (kohn-KEE-stah-dohr-ayz) Spanish adventurers like Cortés and Pizarro who conquered Central and South America in the sixteenth century.

Constitutionalism Movement in England in the seventeenth century that placed power in Parliament's hands as part of a constitutional monarchy and that increasingly limited the power of the monarch; the movement was highlighted by the English Civil War and the Glorious Revolution.

Containment Concept associated with the United States and specifically with the Truman Doctrine during the cold war that revolved around the notion that the United States would contain the spread of communism.

Corporation A concept that reached mature form in 1860s in England and France; it entailed private business owned by thousands of individual and institutional investors who financed the business through the purchase of stocks.

Corpus iuris civilis (KOR-puhs yoor-uhs sih-VEE-lihs) *Body of the Civil Law,* the Byzantine emperor Justinian's attempt to codify all Roman law.

Criollos (kree-OH-lohs) Creoles, people born in the Americas of Spanish or Portuguese ancestry.

Cro-Magnon (CROW MAG-nuhn) *Homo sapiens sapiens,* who appeared forty thousand years ago during the Paleolithic age and were the first human beings of the modern type.

Cross staff Device that sailors used to determine latitude by measuring the angle of the sun or pole star above the horizon.

Cuneiform Written language of the Sumerians, probably the first written script in the world.

Daimyo (DEYEM-yoh) Powerful territorial lords in early modern Japan.

Dao Key element in Chinese philosophy that means the "way of nature" or the "way of the cosmos."

Daodejing (DOW-DAY-JIHNG) Book that is the fundamental work of Daoism.

Daoism (DOW-i'zm) Chinese philosophy with origins in the Zhou dynasty; it is associated with legendary philosopher Laozi, and it called for a policy of non-competition.

Dar al-Islam The "house of Islam," a term for the Islamic world.

Declaration of Independence Written by Thomas Jefferson in 1776; the document expressed the ideas of John Locke and the Enlightenment, represented the idealism of the American rebels, and influenced other revolutions.

Declaration of the Rights of Man and the Citizen Document from the French Revolution (1789) that was influenced by the American Declaration of Independence and in turn influenced other revolutionary movements.

Decolonization Process by which former colonies achieved their independence, as with the newly emerging African nations in the 1950s and 1960s.

Deism (DEE-iz'm) An Enlightenment view that accepted the existence of a god but denied the supernatural aspects of Christianity; in deism, the universe was an orderly realm maintained by rational and natural laws.

Descamisados "Shirtless ones," Argentine poor who supported Juan and Eva Peron.

Détente A reduction in cold war tension between the United States and the Soviet Union from 1969 to 1973.

Devshirme Ottoman requirement that the Christians in the Balkans provide young boys to be slaves of the sultan.

Dharma (DAHR-muh) Hindu concept of obedience to religious and moral laws and order.

Dhimmi (dihm-mee) Islamic concept of a protected people that was symbolic of Islamic toleration during the Mughal and Ottoman empires.

Dhow Indian, Persian, and Arab ships, one hundred to four hundred tons, that sailed and traded throughout the Indian Ocean basin.

Diaspora People who have settled far from their original homeland but who still share some measure of ethnic identity.

Dionysus Greek god of wine, also known as Bacchus; Greek plays were performed in his honor.

Dravidians Peoples who produced the brilliant Harappan society in India, 3000–1500 B.C.E.

Dreadnoughts A class of British battleships whose heavy armaments made all other battleships obsolete overnight.

Duma Russian parliament, established after the Revolution of 1905.

Dutch learning European knowledge that reached Tokugawa Japan.

East India Company British joint-stock company that grew to be a state within a state in India; it possessed its own armed forces.

Eight-legged essay Eight-part essays that an aspiring Chinese civil servant had to compose, mainly based on a knowledge of Confucius and the Zhou classics.

Encomienda (ehn-KOH-mee-ehn-dah) System that gave the Spanish settlers *(encomenderos)* the right to compel the indigenous peoples of the Americas to work in the mines or fields.

Engenho Brazilian sugar mill; the term also came to symbolize the entire complex world relating to the production of sugar.

Enlightenment Eighteenth-century philosophical movement that began in France; its emphasis was on the preeminence of reason rather than faith or tradition; it spread concepts from the Scientific Revolution.

Epicureans (ehp-ih-kyoo-REE-uhns) Hellenistic philosophers who taught that pleasure—as in quiet satisfaction—was the greatest good.

Equal-field system Chinese system during the Han dynasty in which the goal was to ensure an equitable distribution of land.

Essenes Jewish sect that looked for the arrival of a savior; they were similar in some of their core beliefs to the early Christians.

Etruscans (ih-TRUHS-kuhns) Northern Italian society that initially dominated the Romans; the Etruscans helped convey Greek concepts to the expanding Romans.

Eunuchs (YOO-nihks) Castrated males, originally in charge of the harem, who grew to play major roles in government; eunuchs were common in China and other societies.

European Community (EC) Organization of European states established in 1957; it was originally called the European Economic Community and was renamed the EC in 1967; it promoted economic growth and integration as the basis for a politically united Europe.

European Union Established by the Maastricht Treaty in 1993, a supranational organization for even greater European economic and political integration.

Fascism Political ideology and mass movement that was prominent in many parts of Europe between 1919 and 1945; it sought to regenerate the social, political, and cultural life of societies, especially in contrast to liberal democracy and socialism; fascism began with Mussolini in Italy, and it reached its peak with Hitler in Germany.

Five Pillars The foundation of Islam; (1) profession of faith, (2) prayer, (3) fasting during Ramadan, (4) alms, and (5) pilgrimage, or hajj.

Five-year plans First implemented by Stalin in the Soviet Union in 1928; five-year plans were a staple of communist regimes in which every aspect of production was determined in advance for a five-year period; five-year plans were opposite of the free market concept.

Four Noble Truths The foundation of Buddhist thought: (1) life is pain, (2) pain is caused by desire, (3) elimination of desire will bring an end to pain, (4) living a life based on the Noble Eightfold Path will eliminate desire.

Front de Libération Nationale (FLN) The Algerian organization that fought a bloody guerilla war for freedom against France.

Fulani (foo-LAH-nee) Sub-Saharan African people who, beginning in the seventeenth century, began a series of wars designed to impose their own strict interpretation of Islam.

Gathas (GATH-uhs) Zoroastrian works believed to be compositions by Zarathustra.

Gauchos (GOW-chohz) Argentine cowboys, highly romanticized figures.

General Agreement on Tariffs and Trade (GATT) Free trade agreement first signed in 1947; by 1994 it had grown to 123 members and formed the World Trade Organization (WTO).

Ghana (GAH-nuh) Kingdom in west Africa during the fifth through the thirteenth centuries whose rulers eventually converted to Islam; its power and wealth was based on dominating trans-Saharan trade.

Ghaznavids Turkish tribe under Mahmud of Ghazni who moved into northern India in the eleventh century and began a period of greater Islamic influence in India.

Ghazi (GAH-zee) Islamic religious warrior.

Gilgamesh Legendary king of the Mesopotamian city-state of Uruk (ca. 3000 B.C.E.), subject of the *Epic of Gilgamesh,* world's oldest complete epic literary masterpiece.

Glasnost (GLAHS-nohst) Russian term meaning "openness" introduced by Mikhail Gorbachev in 1985 to describe the process of opening Soviet society to dissidents and public criticism.

Globalization The breaking down of traditional boundaries in the face of increasingly global financial and cultural trends.

Global warming The emission of greenhouse gases, which prevents solar heat from escaping the earth's atmosphere and leads to the gradual heating of the earth's environment.

Golden Horde Mongol tribe that controlled Russia from the thirteenth to the fifteenth centuries.

Greater East Asia Co-Prosperity Sphere Japanese plan for consolidating east and southeast Asia under their control during World War II.

Great Game Nineteenth-century competition between Great Britain and Russia for the control of central Asia.

Great Zimbabwe Large sub-Saharan African kingdom in the fifteenth century.

Greenpeace An environmental organization founded in 1970 and dedicated to the preservation of earth's natural resources.

Guomindang (GWOH-mihn-dahng) Chinese nationalist party founded by Sun Yatsen (1866–1925) and later led by Jiang Jieshi; it has been centered in Taiwan since the end of the Chinese civil war.

Gupta (GOOP-tah) Indian dynasty (320–550 C.E.) that briefly reunited India after the collapse of the earlier Mauryan dynasty.

Hacienda (HAH-see-ehn-dah) Large Latin American estates.

Hagia Sophia (HAH-yah SOH-fee-uh) Greek orthodox temple constructed by the Byzantine emperor Justinian and later converted into a mosque.

Hajj (HAHJ) Pilgrimage to Mecca.

Hammurabi's Code (hahm-uh-RAH-beez) Sophisticated law code associated with the Babylonian king Hammurabi (r. 1792–1750 B.C.E.).

Harappan (hah-RAP-puhn) Early brilliant Indian society centered around Harappa and Mohenjo-Daro.

Harijans "Children of God," Gandhi's term for the Untouchables.

Hebrews Semitic-speaking nomadic tribe influential for monotheistic belief in Yahweh.

Heian (HAY-ahn) Japanese period (794–1185), a brilliant cultural era notable for the world's first novel, Murasaki Shikibu's *The Tale of Genji.*

Hellenic Era Phase in Greek history (ca. 800–328 B.C.E.), which was highlighted by the Golden Age of Athens in the fifth century B.C.E.

Hellenistic Era Phase in Greek history (328–146 B.C.E.), from the conquest of Greece by Philip of Macedon until Greece's fall to the Romans; this era was a more cosmopolitan age facilitated by the conquests of Alexander the Great.

Hieroglyphics (heye-ruh-GLIPH-iks) Ancient Egyptian written language.

Hijra Muhammad's migration from Mecca to Medina in 622, which is the beginning point of the Islamic calendar and is considered to mark the beginning of the Islamic faith.

Hinayana (HEE-nah-yah-nuh) Branch of Buddhism known as the "lesser vehicle," also known as Theravada Buddhism; its beliefs include strict, individual path to enlightenment, and it is popular in south and southeast Asia.

Hinduism Main religion of India, a combination of Dravidian and Aryan concepts; Hinduism's goal is to reach spiritual purity and union with the great world spirit; its important concepts include dharma, karma, and samsara.

Holocaust German attempt in World War II to exterminate the Jews of Europe.

Home front Term made popular in World War I and World War II for the civilian "front" that was symbolic of the greater demands of total war.

Hominid (HAWM-ih-nihd) A creature belonging to the family Hominidae, which includes human and humanlike species.

Homo erectus (HOH-MOH ee-REHK-ruhs) "Upright-walking human," which existed from two million to two hundred thousand years ago; *Homo erectus* used cleavers and hand axes and learned how to control fire.

Homo sapiens (HOH-MOH SAY-pee-uhns) "Consciously thinking human," which first appeared around two hundred fifty thousand years ago and used sophisticated tools.

Homo sapiens sapiens (HOH-MOH SAY-pee-uhns SAY-pee-uhns) First human being of the modern type, which appeared roughly one hundred thousand years ago; Cro-Magnon falls into this category.

Hundred Days of Reform Chinese reforms of 1898 led by Kang Youwei and Liang Qichao in their desire to turn China into a modern industrial power.

Huitzilopochtli (wee-tsee-loh-pockt-lee) Sun god and patron deity of the Aztecs.

Hyksos (HICK-sohs) Invaders who seized the Nile delta and helped bring an end to the Egyptian Middle Kingdom.

Iconoclasts (eye-KAHN-oh-klasts) Supporters of the movement, begun by the Byzantine Emperor Leo III (r. 717–741), to destroy religious icons because their veneration was considered sinful.

Ilkhanate (EEL-kahn-ate) Mongol state that ruled Persia after abolition of the Abbasid empire in the thirteenth century.

Imperialism Term associated with the expansion of European powers and their conquest and colonization of African and Asian societies, mainly from the sixteenth through the nineteenth centuries.

Inca empire Powerful South American empire that would reach its peak in the fifteenth century during the reigns of Pachacuti Inca and Topa Inca.

Indentured labor Labor source for plantations; wealthy planters would pay the European poor to sell a portion of their working lives, usually seven years, in exchange for passage.

Indo-Europeans Series of tribes from southern Russia who, over a period of millennia, embarked on a series of migrations from India through western Europe; their greatest legacy was the broad distribution of Indo-European languages throughout Eurasia.

Indra Early Indian god associated with the Aryans; Indra was the king of the gods and was associated with warfare and thunderbolts.

Investiture (ihn-VEHST-tih-tyoor) One aspect of the medieval European church-versus-state controversy, the granting of church offices by a lay leader.

Iroquois (EAR-uh-kwoi) Eastern American Indian confederation made up of the Mohawk, Oneida, Onondaga, Cayuga, and Seneca tribes.

Islam Monotheistic religion announced by the prophet Muhammad (570–632); influenced by Judaism and Christianity, Muhammad was considered the final prophet because the earlier religions had not seen the entire picture; the Quran is the holy book of Islam.

Jainism (JEYEN-iz'm) Indian religion associated with the teacher Vardhamana Mahavira (ca. 540–468 B.C.E.) in which every physical object possessed a soul; Jains believe in complete nonviolence to all living beings.

Jati Indian word for a Hindu subcaste.

Jizya (JIHZ-yuh) Tax in Islamic empires that was imposed on non-Muslims.

Joint-stock companies Early forerunner of the modern corporation; individuals who invested in a trading or exploring venture could make huge profits while limiting their risk.

Ka'ba (KAH-buh) Main shrine in Mecca, goal of Muslims embarking on the hajj.

Kabuki (kah-BOO-kee) Japanese theater in which actors were free to improvise and embellish the words.

Kama Hindu concept of the enjoyment of physical and sexual pleasure.

Kamikaze (KAH-mih-kah-zee) A Japanese term meaning "divine wind" that is related to the storms that destroyed Mongol invasion fleets; the term is symbolic of Japanese isolation and was later taken by suicide pilots in World War II.

Kanun (KAH-noon) Laws issued by the Ottoman Süleyman the Magnificent, also known as Süleyman Kanuni, "the Lawgiver."

Kapu Hawaiian concept of something being taboo.

Karma (KAHR-mah) Hindu concept that the sum of good and bad in a person's life will determine his or her status in the next life.

Khoikhoi South African people referred to pejoratively as the Hottentots by Europeans.

Kongo Central African state that began trading with the Portuguese around 1500; although their kings, such as King Affonso I (r. 1506–1543), converted to Christianity, they nevertheless suffered from the slave trade.

Koumbi-Saleh Important trading city along the trans-Saharan trade route from the eleventh to the thirteenth centuries.

Kshatriayas (KSHAHT-ree-uhs) Hindu caste of warriors and aristocrats.

Kulaks Land-owning Russian peasants who benefited under Lenin's New Economic Policy and suffered under Stalin's forced collectivization.

Kush Nubian African kingdom that conquered and controlled Egypt from 750 to 664 B.C.E.

Lamaist Buddhism (LAH-muh-ihst BOO-diz'm) Branch of Buddhism that was similar to shamanism in its acceptance of magic and supernatural powers.

La Reforma Political reform movement of Mexican president Benito Juárez (1806–1872) that called for limiting the power of the military and the Catholic church in Mexican society.

Latifundia (LAT-ih-FOON-dee-uh) Huge state-run and slave-worked farms in ancient Rome.

League of Nations Forerunner of the United Nations, the dream of American president Woodrow Wilson, although its potential was severely limited by the refusal of the United States to join.

Lebensraum (LAY-behnz-rowm) German term meaning "living space"; the term is associated with Hitler and his goal of carving out territory in the east for an expanding Germany.

Legalism Chinese philosophy from the Zhou dynasty that called for harsh suppression of the common people.

Levée en Masse (leh-VAY on MASS) A term signifying universal conscription during the radical phase of the French revolution.

Lex talionis (lehks tah-lee-oh-nihs) "Law of retaliation," laws in which offenders suffered punishments similar to their crimes; the most famous example is Hammurabi's Laws.

Li (LEE) Confucian concept, a sense of propriety.

Linear A Minoan written script.

Linear B Early Mycenaean written script, adapted from the Minoan Linear A.

Luddites Early-nineteenth-century artisans who were opposed to new machinery and industrialization.

Machismo (mah-CHEEZ-moh) Latin American social ethic that honored male strength, courage, aggressiveness, assertiveness, and cunning.

Madrasas (MAH-drahs-uhs) Islamic institutions of higher education that originated in the tenth century.

Magyars (MAH-jahrs) Hungarian invaders who raided towns in Germany, Italy, and France in the ninth and tenth centuries.

Mahabharata (mah-hah-BAH-rah-tah) Massive ancient Indian epic that was developed orally for centuries; it tells of an epic civil war between two family branches.

Mahayana (mah-huh-YAH-nah) The "greater vehicle," a more metaphysical and more popular northern branch of Buddhism.

Majapahit Southeast Asian kingdom (1293–1520) centered on the island of Java.

Mali (MAH-lee) West African kingdom founded in the thirteenth century by Sundiata; it reached its peak during the reign of Mansa Musa.

Manchus Manchurians who conquered China, putting an end to the Ming dynasty and founding the Qing dynasty (1644–1911).

Mandate of Heaven Chinese belief that the emperors ruled through the mandate, or approval, of heaven contingent on their ability to look after the welfare of the population.

Mandate system System that developed in the wake of World War I when the former colonies ended up mandates under European control, a thinly veiled attempt at continuing imperialism.

Manichaeism (man-ih-KEE-iz'm) Religion founded by the prophet Mani in the third century C.E., a syncretic version of Zoroastrian, Christian, and Buddhist elements.

Manor Large estates of the nobles during the European middle ages, home for the majority of the peasants.

Maori (MAY-oh-ree) Indigenous people of New Zealand.

Marathon Battlefield scene of the Athenian victory over the Persians in 490 B.C.E.

Marae Polynesian temple structure.

Maroons Runaway African slaves.

Marshall Plan U.S. plan, officially called the European Recovery Program, that offered financial and other economic aid to all European states that had suffered from World War II, including Soviet bloc states.

Mauryan empire Indian dynasty (321–185 B.C.E.) founded by Chandragupta Maurya and reaching its peak under Ashoka.

Maya (Mye-uh) Brilliant Central American society (300–1100) known for math, astronomy, and a sophisticated written language.

May Fourth Movement Chinese movement that began 4 May 1919 with a desire to eliminate imperialist influences and promote national unity.

Medes (meeds) Indo-European branch that settled in northern Persia and eventually fell to another branch, the Persians, in the sixth century B.C.E.

Meiji Restoration (MAY-jee) Restoration of imperial rule under Emperor Meiji in 1868 by a coalition led by Fukuzawa Yukichi and Ito Hirobumi; the restoration enacted western reforms to strengthen Japan.

Melaka (may-LAH-kah) Southeast Asian kingdom that was predominantly Islamic.

Mesopotamia Term meaning "between the rivers," in this case the Tigris and Euphrates; Sumer and Akkad are two of the earliest societies.

Mestizo (mehs-TEE-zoh) Latin American term for children of Spanish and native parentage.

Métis (may-TEE) Canadian term for individuals of mixed European and indigenous ancestry.

Millet An autonomous, self-governing community in the Ottoman empire.

Ming Chinese dynasty (1368–1644) founded by Hongwu and known for its cultural brilliance.

Minoan (mih-NOH-uhn) Society located on the island of Crete (ca. 2000–1100 B.C.E.) that influenced the early Mycenaeans.

Missi dominici (mihs-see doh-mee-nee-chee) "Envoys of the lord ruler," the noble and church emissaries sent out by Charlemagne.

Mithraism (MITH-rah-iz'm) Mystery religion based on worship of the sun god Mithras; it became popular among the Romans because of its promise of salvation.

Mochica (moh-CHEE-kuh) Pre-Incan South American society (300–700) known for their brilliant ceramics.

Moksha Hindu concept of the salvation of the soul.

Monotheism (MAW-noh-thee-iz'm) Belief in only one god, a rare concept in the ancient world.

Monroe Doctrine American doctrine issued in 1823 during the presidency of James Monroe that warned Europeans to keep their hands off Latin America and that expressed growing American imperialistic views regarding Latin America.

Mughals (MOO-guhls) Islamic dynasty that ruled India from the sixteenth through the eighteenth centuries; the construction of the Taj Mahal is representative of their splendor; with the exception of the enlightened reign of Akbar, the increasing conflict between Hindus and Muslims was another of their legacies.

Muhammad (muh-HAH-mehd) Prophet of Islam (570–632).

Muslim A follower of Islam.

Mycenaean (meye-seh-NEE-uhn) Early Greek society on the Peloponese (1600–1100 B.C.E.) that was influenced by the Minoans; the Mycenaeans' conflict with Troy is immortalized in Homer's *Odyssey.*

Nara era Japanese period (710–794), centered around city of Nara, that was the highest point of Chinese influence.

National Policy Nineteenth-century Canadian policy designed to attract migrants, protect industries through tariffs, and build national transportation systems.

NATO The North Atlantic Treaty Organization, which was established by the United States in 1949 as a regional military alliance against Soviet expansionism.

Ndongo (n'DAWN-goh) Angolan kingdom that reached its peak during the reign of Queen Nzinga (r. 1623–1663).

Neandertal (nee-ANN-duhr-tawl) Early humans (100,000 to 35,000 years ago) who were prevalent during the Paleolithic period.

Negritude (NEH-grih-tood) "Blackness," a term coined by early African nationalists as a means of celebrating the heritage of black peoples around the world.

Neo-Confucianism (nee-oh-kuhn-FYOO-shuhn-iz'm) Philosophy that attempted to merge certain basic elements of Confucian and Buddhist thought; most important of the early Neo-Confucianists was the Chinese thinker Zhu Xi (1130–1200).

Neolithic New Stone Age (10,000–4000 B.C.E.), which was marked by the discovery and mastery of agriculture.

Nestorian (neh-STOHR-ee-uhn) Early branch of Christianity, named after the fifth-century Greek theologian Nestorius, that emphasized the human nature of Jesus Christ.

New Economic Policy (NEP) Plan implemented by Lenin that called for minor free market reforms.

Nirvana (nuhr-VAH-nuh) Buddhist concept of a state of spiritual perfection and enlightenment in which distracting passions are eliminated.

Noble Eightfold Path Final truth of the Buddhist Four Noble Truths that called for leading a life of balance and constant contemplation.

North American Free Trade Agreement (NAFTA) Regional accord established in 1993 between the United States, Canada, and Mexico; it formed world's second largest free-trade zone.

Nubia (NOO-bee-uh) Area south of Egypt; the kingdom of Kush in Nubia invaded and dominated Egypt from 750 to 664 B.C.E.

Oceania Term referring to the Pacific Ocean basin and its lands.

Olmecs Early Mesoamerican society (1200–100 B.C.E.) that centered around sites at San Lorenzo, La Venta, and Tres Zapotes and that influenced later Maya.

Oprichnina (oh-PREEK-nee-nah) A Russian term meaning the "land apart," Muscovite territory that the Russian Tsar Ivan IV (r. 1533–1584) demanded to control; the tsar created a new class of nobles called the *oprichniki* for this territory.

Oracle bones Chinese Shang dynasty (1766–1122 B.C.E.) means of foretelling the future.

Organization of African Unity (OAU) An organization started in 1963 by thirty-two newly independent African states and designed to prevent conflict that would lead to intervention by former colonial powers.

Organization of Petroleum Exporting Countries (OPEC) An organization begun in 1960 by oil-producing states originally for purely economic reasons but that later had more political influence.

Osiris Ancient Egyptian god that represented the forces of nature.

Ottoman empire Powerful Turkish empire that lasted from the conquest of Constantinople (Istanbul) in 1453 until 1918 and reached its peak during the reign of Süleyman the Magnificent (r. 1520–1566).

Paleolithic Old Stone Age, a long period of human development before the development of agriculture.

Palestinian Liberation Organization (PLO) Organization created in 1964 under the leadership of Yasser Arafat to champion Palestinian rights.

Paris Peace Accords Agreement reached in 1973 that marked the end of the United States's role in the Vietnam War.

Parsis (pahr-SEES) Indian Zoroastrians.

Parthians Persian dynasty (247 B.C.E.–224 C.E.) that reached its peak under Mithradates I.

Pater familias (PAH-tur fuh_MEE-lee-ahs) Roman term for the "father of the family," a theoretical implication that gave the male head of the family almost unlimited authority.

Patriarch (PAY-tree-ahrk) Leader of the Greek Orthodox church, which in 1054 officially split with the Pope and the Roman Catholic church.

Patricians Roman aristocrats and wealthy classes.

Pax Americana "American Peace," a term that compares American domination in the years after World War II with the power of Rome at its peak.

Pax Romana (Pahks roh-MAH-nah) "Roman Peace," a term that relates to the period of political stability, cultural brilliance, and economic prosperity beginning with unification under Augustus and lasting through the first two centuries C.E.

Peninsulares (pehn-IHN-soo-LAH-rayz) Latin American officials from Spain or Portugal.

Perestroika (PAYR-eh-stroy-kuh) "Restructuring," a Russian term associated with Gorbachev's effort to reorganize the Soviet state.

Pharaohs (FARE-ohs) Egyptian kings considered to be gods on earth.

Plebians (plih-BEE-uhns) Roman common people.

Polis (POH-lihs) Greek term for the city-state.

Popol Vuh (paw-pawl vuh) Mayan creation epic.

Prehistory The period before the invention of writing.

Proletariat Urban working class in a modern industrial society.

Protestant Reformation Sixteenth-century European movement during which Luther, Calvin, Zwingli, and others broke away from the Catholic church.

Putting-out system Method of getting around guild control by delivering unfinished materials to rural households for completion.

Ptolemaic (TAWL-oh-may-ihk) Term used to signify both the Egyptian kingdom founded by Alexander the Great's general Ptolemy and the thought of the philosopher Ptolemy of Alexandria (second century C.E.), who used mathematical formulas in an attempt to prove Aristotle's geocentric theory of the universe.

Qadi Islamic judges.

Qanat (kah-NAHT) Persian underground canal.

Qi (chee) Chinese concept of the basic material that makes up the body and the universe.

Qin (chihn) Chinese dynasty (221–207 B.C.E.) that was founded by Qin Shihuangdi and was marked by the first unification of China and the early construction of defensive walls.

Qing (chihng) Chinese dynasty (1644–1911) that reached its peak during the reigns of Kangxi and Qianlong.

Quetzalcoatl (keht-zahl-koh-AHT'l) Aztec god, the "feathered serpent," who was borrowed originally from the Toltecs; Quetzalcoatl was believed to have been defeated by another god and exiled, and he promised to return.

Quinto (KEEN-toh) The one-fifth of Mexican and Peruvian silver production that was reserved for the Spanish monarchy.

Quipu (KEE-poo) Incan mnemonic aid comprised of different colored strings and knots that served to record events in the absence of a written text.

Qizilbash (gih-ZIHL-bahsh) Term meaning "red heads," Turkish tribes that were important allies of Shah Ismail in the formation of the Safavid empire.

Quran (koo-RAHN) Islamic holy book that is believed to contain the divine revelations of Allah as presented to Muhammad.

Ramayana (rah-mah-yah-nah) Ancient Indian masterpiece about the hero Rama that symbolized the victory of *dharma* (order) over *adharma* (chaos).

Rape of Nanjing Japanese conquest and destruction of the Chinese city of Nanjing in the 1930s.

Realpolitik (ray-AHL-poh-lih-teek) The Prussian Otto von Bismarck's "politics of reality," the belief that only the willingness to use force would actually bring about change.

Reconquista (ray-kohn-KEE-stah) Crusade, ending in 1492, to drive the Islamic forces out of Spain.

Reconstruction System implemented in the American South (1867–1877) that was designed to bring the Confederate states back into the union and also extend civil rights to freed slaves.

Repartimiento (reh-PAHR-tih-mehn-toh) Spanish labor system in Latin America, supposed to replace the *encomienda* system, in which native communities were compelled to provide laborers for the farms or mines and the Spanish employers were expected to pay fair wages.

Romanov (ROH-mah-nahv) Russian dynasty (1610–1917) founded by Mikhail Romanov and ending with Nicholas II.

Rubaiyat (ROO-bee-aht) "Quatrains," famous poetry of Omar Khayyam that was later translated by Edward Fitzgerald.

Safavid (SAH-fah-vihd) Later Persian empire (1501–1722) that was founded by Shah Ismail and that became a center for Shiism; the empire reached its peak under Shah Abbas the Great and was centered around the capital of Isfahan.

Sakk Letters of credit that were common in the medieval Islamic banking world.

Saljuqs (sahl-JYOOKS) Turkish tribe that gained control over the Abbasid empire and fought with the Byzantine empire.

Samsara (sahm-SAH-ruh) Hindu term for the concept of transmigration, that is, the soul passing into a new incarnation.

Samurai (SAM-uhr-eye) A Japanese warrior who lived by the code of *bushido.*

Sasanids (suh-SAH-nids) Later powerful Persian dynasty (224–651) that would reach its peak under Shapur I and later fall to Arabic expansion.

Sati (SOO-TEE) Also known as *suttee,* Indian practice of a widow throwing herself on the funeral pyre of her husband.

Satraps (SAY-traps) Persian administrators, usually members of the royal family, who governed a satrapy.

Satyagraha (SAH-tyah-GRAH-hah) "Truth and firmness," a term associated with Gandhi's policy of passive resistance.

Scholasticism Medieval attempt of thinkers like St. Thomas Aquinas to merge the beliefs of Christianity with the logical rigor of Greek philosophy.

Scientific racism Nineteenth-century attempt to justify racism by scientific means; an example would be Gobineau's *Essay on the Inequality of the Human Races.*

Self-determinism Belief popular in World War I and after that every people should have the right to determine their own political destiny; the belief was often cited but ignored by the Great Powers.

Self-strengthening movement Chinese attempt (1860–1895) to blend Chinese cultural traditions with European industrial technology.

Seleucids (sih-LOO-sihds) Persian empire (323–83 B.C.E.) founded by Seleucus after the death of Alexander the Great.

Semitic (suh-miht-ihk) A term that relates to the Semites, ancient nomadic herders who spoke Semitic languages; examples of Semites were the Akkadians, Hebrews, Aramaics, and Phoenicians, who often interacted with the more settled societies of Mesopotamia and Egypt.

Sepoys Indian troops who served the British.

Seppuku A Japanese term for ritual suicide committed by the samurai when he had been dishonored.

Serfs Peasants who, while not chattel slaves, were tied to the land and who owed obligation to the lords on whose land they worked.

Shamanism (SHAH-mah-niz'm) Belief in shamans or religious specialists who possessed supernatural powers and who communicated with the gods and the spirits of nature.

Shari'a (shah-REE-ah) The Islamic holy law, drawn up by theologians from the Quran and accounts of Muhammad's life.

Shia (SHEE-ah) Islamic minority in opposition to the Sunni majority; their belief is that leadership should reside in the line descended from Ali.

Shintoism (SHIHN-toh-iz'm) Indigenous Japanese religion that emphasizes purity, clan loyalty, and the divinity of the emperor.

Shiva (SHEE-vuh) Hindu god associated with both fertility and destruction.

Shogun (SHOH-gun) Japanese military leader who ruled in place of the emperor.

Shudras (SHOO-druhs) Hindu caste of landless peasants and serfs.

Siddhartha Gautama (sih-DHAR-tuh GOW-tau-mah) Indian *kshatriya* who achieved enlightenment and became known as the Buddha, the founder of Buddhism.

Sikhs (SIHKS) Indian syncretic faith that contains elements of Hinduism and Islam.

Silk roads Ancient trade routes that extended from the Roman empire in the west to China in the east.

Social Darwinism Nineteenth-century philosophy, championed by thinkers such as Herbert Spencer, that attempted to apply Darwinian "survival of the fittest" to the social and political realm; adherents saw the the elimination of weaker nations as part of a natural process and used the philosophy to justify war.

Socialism Political and economic theory of social organization based on the collective ownership of the means of production; its origins were in the early nineteenth century, and it differs from communism by a desire for slow or moderate change compared to the communist call for revolution.

Solidarity Polish trade union and nationalist movement in the 1980s that was headed by Lech Walesa.

Song (SOHNG) Chinese dynasty (960–1279) that was marked by an increasingly urbanized and cosmopolitan society.

Soviets Russian elected councils that originated as strike committees during the 1905 St. Petersburg disorders; they represented a form of local self-government that went on to become the primary unit of government in the Union of Soviet Socialist Republics. The term was also used during the cold war to designate the Soviet Union.

Spanish Inquisition Institution organized in 1478 by Fernando and Isabel of Spain to hunt out heretical or contrary opinions; subjects of persecution included Protestants, Jews, Muslims, and witches.

Srivijaya (sree-VIH-juh-yuh) Southeast Asian kingdom (670–1025), based on the island of Sumatra, that used a powerful navy to dominate trade.

Stateless societies Term relating to societies such as those of sub-Saharan Africa after the Bantu migrations that featured decentralized rule through family and kinship groups instead of strongly centralized hierarchies.

Stoics (STOH-ihks) Hellenistic philosophers who encouraged their followers to lead active, virtuous lives and to aid others.

Strabo (STRAH-boh) Greek geographer (first century C.E.).

Strategic Arms Limitations Talk (SALT) Agreement in 1972 between the United States and the Soviet Union.

Stupas (STOO-pahs) Buddhist shrines.

Sufis (SOO-fees) Islamic mystics who placed more emphasis on emotion and devotion than on strict adherence to rules.

Sui (SWAY) Chinese dynasty (589–618) that constructed Grand Canal, reunified China, and allowed for the splendor of the Tang dynasty that followed.

Süleyman (SOO-lee-mahn) Ottoman Turkish ruler Süleyman the Magnificent (r. 1520–1566), who was the most powerful and wealthy ruler of the sixteenth century.

Sumerians (soo-MEHR-ee-uhns) Earliest Mesopotamian society.

Sundiata (soon-JAH-tuh) Founder of the Mali empire (r. 1230–1255), also the inspiration for the *Sundiata,* an African literary and mythological work.

Sunni (SOON-nee) "Traditionalists," the most popular branch of Islam; Sunnis believe in the legitimacy of the early caliphs, compared to the Shiite belief that only a descendent of Ali can lead.

Suu Kyi, Aung San (SOO KEY, AWNG SAHN) Opposition leader (1945–) in Myanmar; she was elected leader in 1990 but she was not allowed to come to power; she was a Nobel Peace Prize recipient in 1991.

Swahili (swah-HEE-lee) East African city-state society that dominated the coast from Mogadishu to Kilwa and was active in trade.

Taino (TEYE-noh) A Caribbean tribe who were the first indigenous peoples from the Americas to come into contact with Christopher Columbus.

Taiping rebellion (TEYE-pihng) Rebellion (1850–1864) in Qing China led by Hong Xiuquan, during which twenty to thirty million were killed; the rebellion was symbolic of the decline of China during the nineteenth century.

Taliban Strict Islamic organization that ruled Afghanistan from 1996 to 2002.

Tang Taizong (TAHNG TEYE-zohng) Chinese emperor (r. 627–649) who founded the Tang dynasty (618–907).

Tanzimat "Reorganization" era (1839–1876), an attempt to reorganize the Ottoman empire on Enlightenment and constitutional forms.

Temüjin (TEM-oo-chin) Mongol conqueror (ca. 1167–1227) who later took the name Chinggis Khan, "universal ruler."

Tenochtitlan (the-NOCH-tee-tlahn) Capital of the Aztec empire, later Mexico City.

Teotihuacan (tay-uh-tee-wah-KAHN) Central American society (200 B.C.E.–750 C.E.); its Pyramid of the Sun was the largest structure in Mesoamerica.

Teutonic Knights Crusading European order that was active in the Baltic region.

Third Rome Concept that a new power would rise up to carry the legacy of Roman greatness after the decline of the Second Rome, Constantinople; Moscow was referred to as the Third Rome during the fifteenth century.

Three Principles of the People Philosophy of Chinese Guomindang leader Sun Yatsen (1866–1925) that emphasized nationalism, democracy, and people's livelihood.

Tian (TEE-ehn) Chinese term for heaven.

Tikal (tee-KAHL) Maya political center from the fourth through the ninth centuries.

Timur-i lang (tee-MOOR-yee LAHNG) "Timur the Lame," known in English as Tamerlane (ca. 1336–1405), who conquered an empire ranging from the Black Sea to Samarkand.

Tokugawa (TOH-koo-GAH-wah) Last shogunate in Japanese history (1600–1867); it was founded by Tokugawa Ieyasu who was notable for unifying Japan.

Toltecs Central American society (950–1150) that was centered around the city of Tula.

Trail of Tears Forced relocation of the Cherokee from the eastern woodlands to Oklahoma (1837–1838); it was symbolic of U.S. expansion and destruction of indigenous Indian societies.

Triangular trade Trade between Europe, Africa, and the Americas that featured finished products from Europe, slaves from Africa, and American products bound for Europe.

Triple Alliance Pre–World War I alliance of Germany, Austria-Hungary, and Italy.

Triple Entente (ahn-TAHNT) Pre–World War I alliance of England, France, and Russia.

Truman Doctrine U.S. policy instituted in 1947 by President Harry Truman in which the United States would follow an interventionist foreign policy to contain communism.

Tsar (ZAHR) Old Russian term for king that is derived from the term *caesar.*

Twelver Shiism (SHEE'i'zm) Branch of Islam that stressed that there were twelve perfect religious leaders after Muhammad and that the twelfth went into hiding and would return someday; Shah Ismail spread this variety through the Safavid empire.

Uighurs (WEE-goors) Turkish tribe.

Ukiyo Japanese word for the "floating worlds," a Buddhist term for the insignificance of the world that came to represent the urban centers in Tokugawa Japan.

Ulama Islamic officials, scholars who shaped public policy in accordance with the Quran and the *sharia.*

Ulaanbaatar (OO-lahn-bah-tahr) Mongolian city.

Umayyad (oo-MEYE-ahd) Arabic dynasty (661–750), with its capital at Damascus, that was marked by a tremendous period of expansion to Spain in the west and India in the east.

Umma (UM-mah) Islamic term for the "community of the faithful."

United Nations (UN) Successor to the League of Nations, an association of sovereign nations that attempts to find solutions to global problems.

Upanishads (oo-PAHN-ee-shahds) Indian reflections and dialogues (800–400 B.C.E.) that reflected basic Hindu concepts.

Urdu (OOR-doo) A language that is predominant in Pakistan.

Uruk (OO-rook) Ancient Mesopotamian city from the fourth millennium B.C.E. that was allegedly the home of the fabled Gilgamesh.

Vaishyas (VEYES-yuhs) Hindu caste of cultivators, artisans, and merchants.

Vaqueros (vah-KEHR-ohs) Latin American cowboys, similar to the Argentine gaucho.

Varna (VAHR-nuh) Hindu word for caste.

Varuna (vuh-ROO-nuh) Early Aryan god who watched over the behavior of mortals and preserved the cosmic order.

Vedas (VAY-duhs) "Wisdom," early collections of prayers and hymns that provide information about the Indo-European Aryans who migrated into India around 1500 B.C.E.; *Rig Veda* is most important collection.

Velvet revolution A term that describes the nonviolent transfer of power in Czechoslovakia during the collapse of Soviet rule.

Venta, La (VEHN-tuh, lah) Early Olmec center (800–400 B.C.E.).

Venus figurines Small Paleolithic statues of women with exaggerated sexual features.

Vernacular (ver-NA-kyoo-lar) The language of the people; Martin Luther translated the Bible from the Latin of the Catholic church into the vernacular German.

Versailles (vehr-SEYE) Palace of French King Louis XIV.

Viet Minh North Vietnamese nationalist communists under Ho Chi Minh.

Vijayanagar (vee-juh-yah-NAH-gahr) Southern Indian kingdom (1336–1565) that later fell to the Mughals.

Vishnu (VIHSH-noo) Hindu god, preserver of the world, who was often incarnated as Krishna.

Vodou (voh-DOW) Syncretic religion practiced by African slaves in Haiti.

Volksgeist (FOHLKS-geyest) "People's spirit," a term that was coined by the

German philosopher Herder; a nation's volksgeist would not come to maturity unless people studied their own unique culture and traditions.

Volta do mar (VOHL-tah doh MAHR) "Return through the sea," a fifteenth-century Portuguese sea route that took advantage of the prevailing winds and currents.

Voltaire (vohl-TAIR) Pen name of French philosophe Francois-Marie Arouet (1694–1778), author of *Candide.*

Walesa, Lech (WAH-lehn-sah, LEHK) Leader of the Polish Solidarity movement.

Waldensians Twelfth-century religious reformers who criticized the Roman Catholic church and who proposed that the laity had the right to preach and administer sacraments; they were declared heretics.

Wanli (wahn-LEE) Chinese Ming emperor (r. 1572–1620) whose refusal to meet with officials hurried the decline of Ming dynasty.

War Communism The Bolshevik policy of nationalizing industry and seizing private land during the civil war.

Warsaw Pact Warsaw Treaty Organization, a military alliance formed by Soviet bloc nations in 1955 in response to rearmament of West Germany and its inclusion in NATO.

Wind wheels Prevailing wind patterns in the Atlantic and Pacific Oceans north and south of the equator; their discovery made sailing much safer and quicker.

Witte, Sergei (VIHT-tee, SAYR-gay) Late-nineteenth-century Russian minister of finance who pushed for industrialization.

World Health Organization (WHO) United Nation organization designed to deal with global health issues.

World Trade Organization (WTO) An organization that was established in 1995 with more than 120 nations and whose goal is to loosen barriers to free trade.

Wuwei (woo-WAY) Daoist concept of a disengagement from the affairs of the world.

Xia (shyah) Early Chinese dynasty (2200–1766 B.C.E.) that is known mainly from legend.

Xianyang (SHYAHN-YAHNG) Capital city of Qin empire.

Xiao (SHAYOH) Confucian concept of respect for one's parents and ancestors.

Xinjiang (shin-jyahng) Western Chinese province.

Xuanzang (SHWEN-ZAHNG) Seventh-century Chinese monk who made a famous trip to India to collect Buddhist texts.

Yahweh (YAH-way) God of the monotheistic religion of Judaism that influenced later Christianity and Islam.

Yangshao (YAHNG-show) Early Chinese society (2500–2200 B.C.E.).

Yangzi (YAHNG-zuh) River in central China.

Yongle (YAWNG-leh) Chinese Ming emperor (r. 1403–1424) who pushed for foreign exploration and promoted cultural achievements such as the *Yongle Encyclopedia.*

Young Turks Nineteenth-century Turkish reformers who pushed for changes within the Ottoman empire, such as universal suffrage and freedom of religion.

Yu (yoo) Legendary founder of the Xia dynasty (ca. 2200 B.C.E.).

Yuan (yoo-AHN) Chinese dynasty (1279–1368) that was founded by the Mongol ruler Khubilai Khan.

Yucatan (yoo-kuh-TAN) Peninsula in Central America, home of the Maya.

Yurts (yuhrts) Tents used by nomadic Turkish and Mongol tribes.

Zaibatsu (zeye-BAHT-soo) Japanese term for "wealthy cliques," which are similar to American trusts and cartels but usually organized around one family.

Zambos (ZAHM-bohs) Latin American term for individuals born of indigenous and African parents.

Zamudio, Adela (ZAH-moo-dee-oh, ah-DEH-lah) Nineteenth-century Bolivian poet, author of "To Be Born a Man."

Zarathustra (zar-uh-THOO-struh) Persian prophet (ca. 628–551 B.C.E.) who founded Zoroastrianism.

Zen Buddhism Japanese version of Chinese Chan Buddhism, with an emphasis on intuition and sudden flashes of insight instead of textual study.

Zhou (JOH) Chinese dynasty (1122–256 B.C.E.) that was the foundation of Chinese thought formed during this period: Confucianism, Daoism, Zhou Classics.

Zhu Xi (ZHOO-SHEE) Neo-Confucian Chinese philosopher (1130–1200).

Ziggurats (ZIG-uh-rahts) Mesopotamian temples.

Zimbabwe (zihm-BAHB-way) Former colony of Southern Rhodesia that gained independence in 1980.

Zemstvos (ZEHMST-voh) District assemblies elected by Russians in the nineteenth century.

Zoroastrianism (zohr-oh-ASS-tree-ahn-iz'm) Persian religion based on the teaching of the sixth-century-B.C.E. prophet Zarathustra; its emphasis on the duality of good and evil and on the role of individuals in determining their own fate would influence later religions.

Credits

CHAPTER 13

Text Credits From *The Alexiad of Anna Comnenea,* E. R. A. Sewter, trans. (Penguin Classics, 1969). Copyright © E. R. A. Sewter, 1969. **Photo Credits p. 316, 320,** © Erich Lessing/Art Resource, NY; **p. 322,** © Scala/Art Resource, NY; **p. 323,** © Robert Frerck/Odyssey; **p. 324,** © The Granger Collection, New York; **p. 326,** © Giraudon/Art Resource, NY; **p. 327,** © Bibliotheque Nationale de France, Paris (RCA12523); **p. 328,** © Bibliotheque Nationale de France (GREC 923 Fol 206v, RCC 10078); **p. 332,** Historical Museum, Moscow; **p. 338,** © Erich Lessing/Art Resource, NY; **p. 339,** © Biblioteca Apostolica, Vatican Library/Index S.A.S.

CHAPTER 14

Photo Credits p. 344, By permission of the British Library (Ms. add. 27261, f. 363a); **p. 347,** © Robert Harding Picture Library; **p. 349,** Reproduced by kind permission of the Trustees of the Chester Beatty Library, Dublin; **p. 352,** © The Granger Collection, New York; **p. 355,** © Archivo Iconografico S.A./Corbis; **p. 360,** © Bibliotheque Nationale de France, Paris (Ms Arabe 5847 fol 138); **p. 361,** © Bibliotheque Nationale de France, Paris (Ms Arabe 5847 fol 89); **p. 362,** © Bodleian Library, University of Oxford, MS. Pococke 275 folios 3v-4r; **p. 363,** © Bibliotheque Nationale de France, Paris (Ms Arabe 5847 fol 105); **p. 364,** © Benjamin Rondel/Corbis; **p. 366,** © Bibliotheque Nationale de France, Paris (Ms Arabe 5847 fol 5v); **p. 367,** Courtesy of the Arthur M. Sackler Museum, Harvard University Art Museums. Promise gift of Mr. and Mrs. Stuart Cary Welch, Jr. Partially owned by the Metropolitan Museum of Art and the Arthur M. Sackler Museum, Harvard University, 1988. In honor of the students of Harvard University and Radcliffe College (1988.460.3).

CHAPTER 15

Text Credits From "A Song of War Chariots," *Anthology of Chinese Literature,* Cyril Birch, ed. Copyright © 1965 by Grove Press, Inc. Used by permission of Grove/Atlantic, Inc. **Photo Credits p. 374,** The Metropolitan Museum of Art, Gift of Mrs. Edward S. Harkness, 1947 (47.81.1). Photograph © 1995 The Metropolitan Museum of Art; **p. 378,** © Réunion des Musées Nationaux/Art Resource, NY; **p. 380, 384,** Cultural Relics Publishing House, Beijing; **p. 385,** British Museum/© Carousel/Laurie Platt Winfrey, Inc.; **p. 387,** By permission of the British Library (OR. 8210 fol. 2); **p. 391, 393,** Cultural Relics Publishing House, Beijing; **p. 394,** © Fujita Museum of Art; **p. 396,** © Victoria & Albert Picture Library; **p. 398,** Scroll with Depictions of the Night Attack on the Sanjo Palace. Japan, Kamakura period, second half of the 13th century. Fenollosa-Weld Collection. (11.4000). Courtesy Museum of Fine Arts, Boston. All rights reserved.

CHAPTER 16

Text Credits From *Sources of Indian Tradition,* Vol. 1, pp. 325–26, 328, Ainslie T. Embree and Stephen Hay, eds. © 1988 Columbia University Press. Reprinted with the permission of the publisher; Muhammad Ali Jinnah, from *Sources of Indian Tradition,* 2nd ed., Vol. 2, Stephen Hay, ed. (New York: Columbia University Press, 1988). Reprinted by permission of Columbia University Press. **Photo Credits p. 404,** © The British Museum; **p. 409,** Edinburgh University Library (Or. ms. 20, fol. 121); **p. 410,** © DPA/NMK/The Image Works; **p. 413,** © Adam Woolfit/Robert Harding Picture Library; **p. 414,** © George Holton/Photo Researchers, Inc.; **p. 416,** Courtesy The British Library (AS10 5809); **p. 419,** © Giraudon/Art Resource, NY; **p. 420,** © The New York Public Library/Art Resource, NY; **p. 422,** By permission of the British Library (J-55[3]); **p. 426,** © Rapho; **p. 427,** © Alain Evrard/Photo Researchers, Inc.

CHAPTER 17

Photo Credits p. 432, © Erich Lessing/Art Resource, NY; **p. 436,** © Bibliotheque Nationale de France, Paris (RCA39570); **p. 437,** © Erich Lessing/Art Resource, NY; **p. 441T,** © The Pierpont Morgan Library/Art Resource, NY; **p. 441B,** © Werner Foreman Archive/Art Resource, NY; **p. 444,** © The British Museum (Roy.20.D.XI fol. 134v.Min.); **p. 447,** © Biblioteca Medicia Lorenziana, Florence/Index S.A.S; **p. 451,** © Giraudon/Art Resource, NY; **p. 452,** © Biblioteca Seminario Vescovile, Florence/Index S.A.S.; **p. 453,** © The Pierpont Morgan Library/Art Resource, NY.

CHAPTER 18

Photo Credits p. 460, © National Palace Museum, Taipei, Taiwan, Republic of China; **p. 464,** Cultural Relics Publishing House, Beijing; **p. 465,** © The Nasser D. Khalili Collection of Islamic Art (POT 1310); **p. 467,** © National Palace Museum, Taipei, Taiwan, Republic of China; **p. 468,** © Bibliotheque Nationale de France, Paris (Ms. Persian Suppl. 1113 f.49); **p. 471,** © National Palace Museum, Taipei, Taiwan, Republic of China; **p. 473,** © Bibliotheque Nationale de France, Paris (Ms. Persian Suppl. 1113 f.180v); **p. 476,** © Art Resource, NY; **p. 479,** © Bibliotheque Nationale de France, Paris (Ms. fr. 9087, v. 207 Rcc 286).

CHAPTER 19

Text Credits From D. T. Niane, Sundiata: *An Epic of Old Mali,* pp. 80–82. © Longman Group Limited, 1965, reprinted by permission of Pearson Education Limited; from Said Hamdun and Noel King, *Ibn Battuta in Black Africa* (Princeton: Markus Wiener Publishers, 1994), pp. 15–19. Reprinted by permission. **Photo Credits p. 482,** The Metropolitan Museum of Art, Gift of Mr. and Mrs. Klaus G. Perls, 1990 (1990.332). Photograph © 1991 The

Metropolitan Museum of Art; **p. 486,** © Dirk Bakker; **p. 487,** From Travels in North and Central America by Heinrich Barth, 1857–58, vol. 4, plate facing pg. 404; **p. 491,** © Werner Forman Archive/Art Resource, NY; **p. 492,** © Bibliotheque Nationale de France, Paris; **p. 493, 494,** © Werner Foreman Archive/Art Resource, NY; **p. 497,** © The British Museum; **p. 498,** © Georg Gerster/Photo Researchers, Inc.; **p. 500,** © Marc and Evelyne Bernheim/Woodfin Camp and Associates; **p. 501,** © Chester Higgins, Jr./Photo Researchers, Inc.; **p. 502,** © C. J. Lenars/Photo Researchers, Inc.

CHAPTER 20

Text Credits *St. Francis of Assisi: Writings and Early Biographies,* Marion A. Habig, ed. English Omnibus of Sources for the Life of St. Francis. Quincy, IL: Franciscan Press, 2000, pp. 229–31, 288–92. Reprinted by permission. **Photo Credits p. 508,** © Bibliotheque Nationale de France, Paris (Rcc 677); **p. 513,** Bibliotheque Nationale, Paris, France/© The Bridgeman Art Library; **p. 514,** © Erich Lessing/Art Resource, NY; **p. 515,** © Scala/Art Resource; **p. 517,** © Bodleian Library, University of Oxford (MS Bodl. 264, fol. 218r); **p. 518,** By permission of the British Library (Add. Ms 27, 695, f. 8); **p. 522,** © Bibliotheque Nationale de France, Paris (RCB 4189); **p. 523,** © Bildarchiv Preussischer Kulturbesitz/Art Resource, NY; **p. 526, 527,** © Scala/Art Resource, NY; **p. 532L,** Bibliotheque Nationale, Paris, France/© The Bridgeman Art Library; **p. 532R,** © Erich Lessing/Art Resource, NY.

CHAPTER 21

Text Credits Bernardino de Sahagun, *Florentine Codex: General History of the Things of New Spain,* 13 vols, Arthur J. O. Anderson and Charles E. Dibble, trans. Salt Lake City: University of Utah Press, 1950–82, 13:19–20. Santa Fe, NM and Salt Lake City: The School of American Research and The University of Utah Press. Reprinted by permission; Teuira Henry and others, *Voyaging Chiefs of Havai'I,* Dennis Kawaharada, ed. Copyright 1995. pp. 138–39, 144–46. Kalamaku Press. Reprinted by permission of Kalamaku Press. **Photo Credits p. 538,** Neg. #5004(2) Cat. No. B/1619, Courtesy Department of Library Services, American Museum of Natural History. Photo by John Bigelow Taylor; **p. 542,** © Robert Frerck/Woodfin Camp and Associates; **p. 544,** Bodleian Library, University of Oxford (MS Arch. Selden, A.1, fol. 31r); **p. 546,** © Biblioteca Apostolica Vaticana/Index S.A.S.; **p. 547,** © Biblioteca Nazionale Centrale, Florence/Index S.A.S.; **p. 549,** © Georg Gerster/Photo Researchers, Inc.; **p. 553,** Neg. #3614(2). Courtesy Department of Library Services, American Museum of Natural History. Photo by Perkins/Becket; **p. 554, 555,** Det Kongelige Bibliotek, Copenhagen; **p. 558,** Honolulu Academy of Arts, Gift of George R. Carter, 1927 (5945); **p. 559,** © Douglas Peebles/Corbis.

CHAPTER 22

Text Credits From Said Hamdun and Noel King, *Ibn Battuta in Black Africa* (Princeton: Markus Wiener Publishers, 1994), pp. 49–50, 58–59. Reprinted by permission. **Photo Credits p. 564,** © National Palace Museum, Taipei, Taiwan, Republic of China; **p. 567,** © Josephine Powell Photograph, Courtesy of Historic Photographs, Fine Arts Library, Harvard College Library; **p. 570,** © Bibliotheque Nationale de France, Paris (Ms Fr. 2810 fol 84); **p. 576,** © Escorial Monastery, Madrid/Oroñoz; **p. 577,** By permission of the British Library (MS 14 E IV f. 23); **p. 578,** © Bibliotheque Nationale de France, Paris (RCC9816); **p. 580,** White porcelain with under glaze blue decoration. China Ming dynasty, early 15th century. With permission of the Royal Ontario Museum © ROM (925.25.15a–b); **p. 582,** © Scala/Art Resource, NY; **p. 583,** © Sylvain Grandadam/Photo Researchers, Inc.; **p. 584,** © Scala/Art Resource, NY; **p. 590,** World map engraving, 1532, Typus Comsmographicus Universalis by Münster, Sebastian. With permission of the Royal Ontario Museum © ROM (956.186.2).

CHAPTER 23

Text Credits From *Diario of Christopher Columbus's First Voyage to America, 1492–1493,* Oliver C. Dunn and James E. Kelley, Jr., trans. and eds. Published by the University of Oklahoma Press, 1989. Reprinted by permission of the publisher. All rights reserved. **Photo Credits p. 596,** © Rijksmuseum Amsterdam; **p. 600,** © Bibliotheque Nationale de France, Paris (MS. EDP 30 f3v); **p. 606,** Germanisches National Museum, Nürenberg; **p. 608,** Osterreichische National Bibliothek, Vienna. Photo © Bildarchiv, ONB, Wien; **p. 609,** © National Maritime Museum, Greenwich, London; **p. 617,** © Maritiem Museum, Rotterdam. P-2161-31; **p. 619,** © Oregon Historical Society (OrHi 97421); **p. 622,** Peabody Museum, Harvard University (N29636); **p. 623,** Courtesy of the James Ford Bell Library, University of Minnesota; **p. 625,** © The New York Public Library, Rare Book Division, Astor, Lenox and Tilden Foundations/Art Resource, NY.

CHAPTER 24

Photo Credits p. 630, 634, © Scala/Art Resource, NY; **p. 636,** Anne S. K. Brown Military Collection, Brown University Library; **p. 640,** © Bibliotheque National de France, Paris; **p. 642,** © The Granger Collection, New York; **p. 643,** © Giraudon/Art Resource, NY; **p. 646,** © AKG London; **p. 650,** Amsterdam Historisch Museum (INV.NR.SA3025); **p. 651,** © The Granger Collection, New York; **p. 656, 657,** © Corbis; **p. 659,** © Erich Lessing/Art Resource, NY.

CHAPTER 25

Text Credits Bernardino de Sahagun, *Florentine Codex: General History of the Things of New Spain,* 13 vols. Arthur J. O. Anderson and Charles E. Dibble, trans. Salt Lake City: University of Utah Press, 1950–82, 13:19–20. Santa Fe, NM and Salt Lake City: The School of American Research and The University of Utah Press. Reprinted by permission. **Photo Credits p. 664,** Benson Latin American Collection, General Libraries, University of Texas at Austin; **p. 667,** © The New York Public Library, Spencer Collection, Astor, Lenox and Tilden Foundations/Art Resource, NY; **p. 670,** Det Kongeliage Bibliothek, Copenhagen; **p. 674,** Courtesy of Whitehall-Robins Company, Photograph by Don Eiler; **p. 677,** Museo Nacional de Historia, Mexico City; **p. 678,** Courtesy of the Hispanic Society of America, New York; **p. 680,** Det Kongelige Bibliothek, Copenhagen; **p. 683,** © The New York Public Library, Arents Collection, Astor, Lenox and Tilden Foundations/Art Resource, NY; **p. 684,** © The New York Public Library, Arents Collection, Astor, Lenox and Tilden Foundations/Art Resource, NY; **p. 689,** Honolulu Academy of Arts, Gift of the Honolulu Art Society, 1944 (12,161).

CHAPTER 26

Text Credits Copyright © 1964 by Basil Davidson. Reprinted by permission of Curtis Brown, Ltd. **Photo Credits p. 694,**

National Maritime Museum, London/Bridgeman Art Library; **p. 697,** © Bibliotheque National de France, Paris (RC C 1619); **p. 700,** © The New York Public Library, Rare Books Division, Astor, Lenox and Tilden Foundations/Art Resource, NY; **p. 702,** From Description de l'Afrique by Olifert Dapper, 1686; **p. 704,** © The New York Public Library, Rare Books Division, Astor, Lenox and Tilden Foundations/Art Resource, NY; **p. 708,** © The British Museum; **p. 711,** © North Wind Picture Archives; **p. 713,** © The New York Public Library, Arents Collection, Astor, Lenox and Tilden Foundations/Art Resource, NY; **p. 714,** From Debret, Voyages Pittoresque et Historiques au Bresil, 1816–1831; **p. 716,** © The New York Public Library, Manuscripts, Archives and Rare Books Division, Schomberg Center for Research in Black Culture, Astor, Lenox and Tilden Foundations/Art Resource, NY.

CHAPTER 27

Text Credits George Elison, *Deus Destroyed: The Image of Christianity in Early Modern Japan.* Cambridge, Mass. Harvard University, Council on East Asian Studies, 1973, pp. 259–60, 283–84. © The President and Fellows of Harvard College, 1973. Reprinted by permission of the Harvard University Asia Center. **Photo Credits p. 722,** Peabody Essex Museum. Photo by Mark Sexton; **p. 726,** © Harvey Lloyd/Corbis; **p. 728,** The Metropolitan Museum of Art, Rogers Fund, 1942. (42.141.2). Photograph © 1980 The Metropolitan Museum of Art; **p. 730,** National Palace Museum, Taipei, Taiwan, Republic of China; **p. 732,** © Dennis Cox/ChinaStock; **p. 734,** Golestan Palace, Tehran, Iran/© Giraudon/Bridgeman Art Library; **p. 737,** © The New York Public Library, Rare Books Division, Astor, Lenox and Tilden Foundations/Art Resource, NY; **p. 740,** © The New York Public Library, Rare Books Division, Astor, Lenox and Tilden Foundations/Art Resource, NY; **p. 744,** © Carousel/Laurie Platt Winfrey, Inc.; **p. 745,** Scenes from the Pleasure Quarters of Kyoto,
17th Century, Edo Period. One of a pair of 6-panel folding screens. Denman Waldo Ross Collection. Courtesy Museum of Fine Arts, Boston. Photograph © 2001 Museum of Fine Arts, Boston. All rights reserved.; **p. 746,** © British Museum.

CHAPTER 28

Text Credits Ghislain de Busbeceq, *The Turkish Letters of Ogier Ghislain de Busbecq.* E. S. Foster, trans. Oxford: Clarendon Press, 1927. Reprinted by permission of Oxford University Press. **Photo Credits p. 752,** © Andrea Pistolesi/The Image Bank/Getty Images; **p. 756,** © Giraudon/Art Resource, NY; **p. 758,** By permission of the British Library (OR.3248, f. 55v); **p. 761,** © Victoria & Albert Museum, London/Art Resource, NY; **p. 764,** Museum Reitberg, Zurich (Ms. 39 fol. 102v). Photo by Wettstein & Kauf; **p. 765,** © Rijksmuseum Amsterdam; **p. 767,** Reproduced by kind permission of the Trustees of the Chester Beatty Library; **p. 768,** © Harvey Lloyd/Corbis; **p. 769,** © William Hubbell/Woodfin Camp and Associates; **p. 770,** © Byron Crader/Ric Ergenbright Photography; **p. 772,** Topkapi Palace Museum (no. H.1517, fol. 422a). Photo: Ergun Company; **p. 773,** Topkapi Palace Museum.

INDEX

Page numbers in italics and followed by the letter *f* refer to figures, photographs, and illustrations; followed by the letter *m* refer to maps; and followed by the letter *t* refer to tables.